The Progressives' Century

The Institution for Social and Policy Studies at Yale University

THE YALE ISPS SERIES

THE PROGRESSIVES' CENTURY

POLITICAL REFORM, CONSTITUTIONAL GOVERNMENT, AND THE MODERN AMERICAN STATE

EDITED BY

Stephen Skowronek

Stephen M. Engel

Bruce Ackerman

Yale UNIVERSITY PRESS   *New Haven and London*

Published with assistance from the foundation established
in memory of Philip Hamilton McMillan of the Class of
1894, Yale College.

Yale University Press books may be purchased in quantity
for educational, business, or promotional use. For
information, please e-mail sales.press@yale.edu (U.S. office)
or sales@yaleup.co.uk (U.K. office).

Set in Scala type by IDS Infotech, Ltd. Printed in the United
States of America.

ISBN 978-0-300-20484-1
Library of Congress Control Number: 2016935627
A catalogue record for this book is available from the British
Library.

This paper meets the requirements of ANSI/NISO
Z39.48-1992 (Permanence of Paper).

10 9 8 7 6 5 4 3 2 1

CONTENTS

PART IV | AN UNSETTLED LEGACY

ACKNOWLEDGMENTS

The Progressives' Century has been a collaborative effort. The editors were supported by a cooperative initiative of Yale University's Institute for Social and Policy Studies and the Yale Law School. Resources from the law school's Oscar M. Ruebhausen Fund and the director of ISPS allowed us to convene a multidisciplinary conference at Yale to assess the Progressive legacy in November 2013, and they have supported publication of this volume. We are grateful to Robert Post, dean of the Yale Law School, and to Jacob Hacker, director of ISPS, for their interest in cooperative ventures of this sort and, in particular, for their ready promotion of this one.

Most of the chapters that appear in this volume were first vetted at the conference. We are grateful to the faculty members across Yale University who commented on the original papers. They included Akhil Amar, Jack Balkin, Seyla Benhabib, Samuel DeCanio, Jacob Hacker, Jennifer Klein, Jerry Mashaw, David Mayhew, Judith Resnik, Susan Rose-Ackerman, and Vesla Mae Weaver. These commentaries instigated a series of revisions to not only the individual papers but also the conception of the project itself. Thanks also to Blake Emerson, a joint-degree student in law and political theory, who participated as an astute critic and a skilled organizer, and to Pamela Green, conference coordinator for ISPS, for administrative support in pulling together the event and the volume.

Finally, we owe a great debt to William Frucht, executive editor of Yale University Press, for his interest in this project; to the Press's two anonymous reviewers for their evaluation of our efforts; and to Phillip King, Kip Keller, and Jaya Chatterjee for their assistance with the production of the book. All helped stimulate our thinking about the differences between a conference and a book and to steer us clear of a simple transposition of the former into the latter. Any shortfall on that score lies with us.

THE PROGRESSIVES' CENTURY

Introduction • The Progressives' Century

Stephen Skowronek and Stephen M. Engel

A hundred years ago, Progressivism was an insurgent political movement poised to dislodge an allegedly outmoded, unjust, and unworkable system of government. The insurgents pressed a comprehensive critique of the old order, indicting its social, political, and constitutional foundations. Behind that critique was an alternative template, a guide to reconstruction. The reformers envisioned a new kind of national government, one released from time-bound institutional constraints and reorganized for programmatic action. They agitated for a new kind of democracy, with citizens attuned to the positive uses of national power and engaged with government in wide-ranging exchanges. Over the ensuing decades, these ideas were adapted and redeployed by others. The Progressives' approach to governing informed successive waves of political innovation and embedded itself in the operations, assumptions, and expectations of the modern American state.

Today, the tables have turned. Progressivism is on the defensive. Once the inspiration for a reconstruction of the American state, the movement now bears the heavy weight of its many shortfalls. These vulnerabilities have fed a counterinsurgency. Contemporary conservatives have laid siege to the Progressives' handiwork, indicting their programs, their priorities, and their basic precepts. Progressives stand accused of abandoning values bequeathed to the nation at its founding, of distorting relations of power and authority, and of setting government on an unsustainable course. Even those determined to protect and extend Progressivism's historic achievements struggle with uncertainties about reform's legacy and future. The Progressives' promise of a new democracy strains under a rising tide of popular cynicism and political manipulation; its promise of nimble and responsive government is mocked by interest cartels and institutional gridlock.

I

The Progressives' Century returns to the original thrust of reform, in search of fresh insight into the current juncture. It directs attention back to the ideas, aspirations, and practices that took the offensive in the development of modern American government. In taking advantage of the uniquely holistic character of these diagnoses and prescriptions, it seeks to open up the current conversation about government and politics, to push beyond controversies over the fate of particular policies. Our focus is on the nation-state and its legitimating norms. Arguably, Progressivism had a more immediate impact on government at the local level—on the delivery of services by towns and cities and on the reorganization of municipal government. But these reformers wrestled with the fundamentals of the American regime, and we are interested here in the unsettled legacy of their efforts to rework them.

Benchmarks for a retrospective assessment of this sort are ready at hand: 1912, the presidential campaign that first put Progressivism on the national agenda; 2012, the reelection to the presidency of a resolute contemporary progressive determined to keep it there. These two dates hold in view a seminal reform impulse repeatedly reaffirmed in its political appeal but governmentally at its wit's end. By adopting such a tidy temporal frame, we do not mean to suggest that Progressive ideas burst on the scene all at once; the essays in this volume attest to their long gestation and varied sources. Nor do we mean to suggest that the story has come full circle and is racing to a close, that the travails of the Obama administration have sealed the fate of progressivism. But we do mean to use this embattled centenary as an occasion for critical reflection on what has happened to the essential elements of the reconstructive vision. We want to take stock of issues unresolved in the project as it was first conceived, to consider difficulties encountered in the follow-through, and to sort through what might be reclaimed.

Many will find the notion of the "progressives' century" jarring. For most Americans today, progressivism is just a label for programs and priorities staked out by the Democratic Party; that is to say, we have come to think of it as a policy agenda that jockeys for support with an equally robust Republican alternative. From time to time, Democrats succeed in enacting proposals for business regulation, social provision, redistributive taxation, and the like; from time to time, their initiatives are defeated and their advances rolled back. Our everyday view of the matter marks progressivism's advances and retreats policy by policy on a closely contested field of partisan combat.

But that everyday view obscures the significance of Progressivism in modern American political development and underestimates the historic character of the challenges that currently beset it. At issue in this volume is the field of play on which contemporary policy disputes are contested, a field that progressive reformers redefined. Progressives committed the nation to a particular conception of government and a new way of governing. They did not just install policies here and there, now and again; they reorganized the policy-making machinery and prepared the polity for programmatic government. Conservative opponents have begun to respond in kind, with a root-and-branch rejection of this regime's premises. American politics is now polarized around the governing mores of the progressives' century. One result of this widening divide is that today neither progressivism nor conservatism offers a reliable source of shared understandings about how to proceed in governing the nation. The semblance of mutual engagement in a common enterprise has all but collapsed. Moving forward is no longer just a matter of enacting this program or that, for programmatic government itself has become the issue of the day.

Many scholars may find the notion of the "progressives' century" strange as well. Much of the energy in studying the great reform waves of the past hundred years has gone into distinguishing them one from another. Historians have traditionally demarcated the Progressive era as a period lasting from 1890 to 1920, and they have identified it with a political movement of the white Protestant middle class. The reformers of that time tended to be moralistic, suspicious of class conflict, uneasy about the nation's growing ethnic diversity, and indulgent, sometimes positively supportive of the consolidation of Jim Crow laws. In contrast, New Deal reform was driven by the labor movement. It had a decidedly working-class and ethnic bias. The reform wave of the 1960s and '70s was different again. Spearheaded by a movement to overthrow Jim Crow, it opened on to a more wide-ranging "minority-rights revolution."

There is no gainsaying the fact that Progressivism began with a limited social purview. More important for the future, however, was its assault on limits, for that left the movement open to recurrent reformulations of its social constituency and political agenda. As James Kloppenberg's essay in this volume reminds us, pragmatism has been the guiding light of progressive reform; adaptation and overcoming are encoded in the template and a key to its success. Late in 2011, President Obama traveled to Osawatomie, Kansas, to commemorate the launch of Teddy Roosevelt's "New Nationalism" campaign and to identify the commitments and priorities of his own bid for reelection with the venerable spirit of middle-class reform. He appealed to the common sense of progressivism, to the expectation that government would respond to the nation's problems with constructive solutions. He let the visual reality of

the first African American president convey the staggering changes to the social presuppositions of that idea.

We do not propose here to pass so lightly over the different incarnations of
twentieth-century reform. Adaptation is seldom seamless. Many elements of
the original reform impulse were carried forward by later generations, but
other elements were jettisoned, and new ones were added to the mix. The
emergent amalgam was an unsteady brew, straddling different sides of what
were once some of the most basic questions at issue. One of the reasons to
entertain a discussion of the "progressives' century" is to open to examination
the tensions and trade-offs that have accumulated within the reform vision, to
put initial assumptions and expectations up against latter-day adjustments,
extensions, accommodations, and compromises. By projecting progressive
ideas forward through time, we want to call attention to issues submerged in
their adaptation and to consider what has been lost and gained in progressivism's metamorphosis.

Least likely to be taken aback by the thought of the "progressives' century"
are those sympathetic to today's conservative insurgency. They need no convincing that the Progressives altered the template of American government
and politics and built a new regime. As the conservative critique of the modern American state has grown more radical, the reappraisal of its motivating
ideas and aspirations has become more polemical. As the essays by Ken Kersh
and Steven Teles detail, conservative intellectuals have been scouring the diagnoses and prescriptions of reformers at the turn of the twentieth century to
document the brazen novelty of Progressive designs and to arraign their legacy for pushing the nation decisively down the wrong path. Piece by piece,
they are knitting together an alternative history of reform, one in which Woodrow Wilson appears un-American and the *Lochner* Court is the authentic voice
of social justice. Whatever else might be said about this scholarship, it testifies
to the impact the Progressive movement continues to have on our politics.
Conservative revisionism all but compels a broad reconsideration of the rise of
Progressivism as the pivot point in the development of modern American
government.

The Progressives' Century is neither a broadside against this reform tradition
nor a polemic in defense. There is no denying that progressive ideas stand
open to serious and critical scrutiny, but to dismiss the project as a colossal
mistake and an abject failure strains reason. Progressive solutions to the problems of governing carried the United States through the great crises of the
twentieth century—the "American century," as it is now commonly called. It

is an open question whether conservative insurgents in our day will ultimately have the same impact on the progressives' legacy as progressives did on their own inheritance. But sweeping aside the state fashioned over the course of the past century will not be easy, and at present the wholesale repudiation of its intellectual foundations appears little more than a formula for gridlock.

The disposition toward public affairs so roundly renounced today by conservatives should be familiar to most Americans. It puts an abiding faith in the government's problem-solving capacities. It is impatient with traditions and practices that thwart timely responses to new challenges as they arise. The assumptions are that government is responsible for social amelioration and economic improvement and that, to meet these responsibilities, it must continually adjust to changes in its environment. The common sense of progressivism is that the shape and boundaries of government are not fixed, that they can and should be altered to demands expressed democratically. The approach to law is instrumental, and the approach to governmental forms and procedures is pragmatic. Confidence runs high in the active management of interest conflicts, in the consensus-inducing capacities of science, expertise, and professionalism, and in the enlightened leadership of an informed public.

This template can accommodate wide variations in specific policy prescriptions, and until recently, it has found adherents on both sides of the party divide. It is not at all clear that the American people are prepared to jettison these assumptions and expectations, and for all the resistance they are currently engendering, it is not at all clear what the rejectionists have in mind as a replacement. *The Progressives' Century* takes stock of an outlook on government. It is a retrospective assessment of its enduring attractions and accumulated burdens.

An Unresolved Critique, a Battered Faith

The original reform impulse linked a multifront assault on the ties binding American government to the politics of the past with faith in an equally comprehensive alternative. The two elements drew strength from each other, the former emboldened by belief in the latter. The opposite holds as well: irresolution in the break with the old order would eventually take its toll on the operational and intellectual coherence of the new. The essays in this volume examine the progressive disposition from this perspective, ranging widely across the critique and its attendant aspirations in order to assess the achievement and its controversial legacy. To guide what follows, we identify in this section six reform themes, three critical and three aspirational, that together filled out an overarching reconception of the nation-state. These are the tenets on which a new regime was constructed, and from which our authors draw their particular assessments. Each theme captures an essential aspect of progressivism; in equal measure, they sustained the forward thrust of reform. More important for today, each in its own way now seems bereft, wavering and uncertain as a guide for the future.

First was the Progressives' critique of the Constitution. The Progressive movement was born of discontent with the division and dispersion of power in the American system. Reformers railed against timeless, mechanical conceptions of a balance of powers, against institutional checks that blocked concerted action. They assailed the limited social foundations of the Framers' handiwork, and its failure to grapple with the evolving interests of the polity as a whole. To create a genuinely national democracy and to render governmental action more cooperative, purposive, and positive, they called for "a new Declaration of Independence" and an overthrow of "the monarchy of the Constitution."

Save perhaps for the writings of the most radical abolitionists, the Progressives' critique of the Constitution stands unrivaled in the annals of reform for its directness and thoroughness. It dispelled the notion that the Constitution was a work of timeless truth and that later generations were compelled to defer to the Framers' ideas. By historicizing the document and exposing the social assumptions behind it, the critics opened a general assault on the limits of received ways of governing. Their alternative, what we today call the "living Constitution," was open-ended with regard to the possibilities of government and more amenable to programmatic action aimed at changing social circumstances.

By spurring a sea change in thinking about what government might do and how it might do it, the Progressives' critique of the Constitution facilitated the construction of the modern American state. But a survey of the scene today prompts questions about whether this critique went too far, or perhaps not far enough. The erosion of the Constitution's division of institutional labor, the expansion of executive and administrative power, the blurring of the structural boundaries that once delimited the exercise of power—these are among Progressivism's most profound legacies. But the Constitution was not discarded, and as Aziz Rana points out, the onset of the Cold War dampened enthusiasm for the Progressives' brand of candid, critical reassessment at the very time when institutional adjustments began to accelerate. As a result, new operating principles were left to compete with the old, and the basic institutions, radically transformed in their practical working relationship to one another, appeared by turns to be either abdicating their constitutional responsibilities or defying the commonsense demands of the day. Several contributors to this volume—Eldon Eisenach, Aziz Rana, Brian Tamanaha, Ken Kersh—reflect on the lingering tensions between the old legal frame and the reformers' aspirations for a new state, a tension that has never been fully resolved.

Closely related to the Progressives' critique of the Constitution's institutional encumbrances was a critique of rights. Received ideas about individual rights, like old thinking about institutional structure, constrained the field of governmental action, and Progressives sought to overhaul both. Just as their "living Constitution" subordinated structural concerns to the public's interests in the positive uses of power, their "legal realism" focused questions of justice on power relationships within society and rendered rights less formal, abstract, and absolute.

The reformers assaulted the old regime for turning rights, particularly individuals' claims to property rights and state claims to rights against federal action, into impediments to the development of democracy. As they saw it, the old regime's preoccupation with rights was creating an ever more formidable bulwark of legal protections for historically privileged interests. Their new democracy was to be less constrained by the protection of rights and more concerned with their creation and wider distribution. Rights would be trimmed for some, extended to others, balanced across an expanding array of claimants, and rendered more negotiable.

In the middle of the twentieth century, reformers submerged this critique of rights and embraced a "rights revolution." But the return to a discourse of rights bears the mark of progressive realism, and as Karen Orren points out, the preoccupation with rights in our day obscures just how thoroughly rights have changed. The proliferation of rights has loosened the system of rights overall, opening it to more active governmental intervention in the interest of reconciling competing claims. With rights more widely shared, new rights holders have been left none too secure in what exactly they possess. Sonu Bedi follows up, registering skepticism about progressives' renewed deference to rights in the wake of the minority-rights revolution. He would revive the critique of the early Progressives, candidly acknowledge the altered status of rights, and reinsert considerations of political power more directly into jurisprudential thinking about social justice. That, however, might well compound what Brian Tamanaha identifies as an already-engrained rhetorical disadvantage for the progressive approach in court.

Along with their critique of rights and the Constitution, Progressives assaulted political parties. Creations of an earlier day, American parties, like
separated powers and individual rights, had come over time to thwart the development of new forms of government and the expression of new democratic
ideals. Reinforcing localism and elevating narrow interests, these relics of the
old democracy appeared ill adapted for national actions aimed at the great governing challenges of the day. They served instead as structural reinforcement
for what were seen to be the most problematic tendencies of the old order.

American political parties embodied everything that Progressives wanted
to avoid in their new democracy. They had fostered bossism, corruption, and
incompetent administration. They thrived on voter ignorance of the great issues; they stirred up ethnic animosities; their operations seemed hopelessly
parochial. But just as surely as the reform movement gained traction by setting itself against the old machine style of rule, its critique left only the haziest
notions of what role parties might play in a democracy reconstructed on progressive principles. Progressives sought instead to link government and citizens together in new ways. They experimented with "direct democracy,"
thinking that they might eliminate intermediaries and put power in the hands
of the people themselves. They looked to federated associations of social and
economic interests to build new kinds of political influence. They tapped the
churches and the mobilizing energy generated by the social gospel. In 1912,
they tried to create a new kind of party, one that might serve as a magnet for
various reform movements and newly organized interests and supersede machine politics in the promotion of direct democracy. The Progressive Party
presented itself as the face of this new politics; its purpose was to displace the
old. As Sidney Milkis puts it, it was a party to end the reign of parties. But as
with its assault on rights and the Constitution, reform did not displace partisanship or party conflict, nor did it clarify the role of parties in the new order.

Progressive democracy was to be built on consensual ground, on a shared
understanding of the "promise of American life" and on impartial interventions by experts dedicated to its realization. The energy that these reformers
put into creating a common sense of national purpose was not misplaced, for
programmatic government requires a modicum of consensus. The irony of
the Progressive Party, as John Milton Cooper points out, was that it fought for
principles that were, by 1912, already widely endorsed. The success of the
movement in that regard shortened its life as a party. But in a nation as large
and diverse as the United States, consensus is fleeting, and the Progressive
movement proved far more effective in displacing the old machines than in

providing a secure democratic foundation for programmatic government. With the conservative assault on programmatic government resurgent today and party divisions deepening, that shortfall has never been more apparent.

The Progressives' assault on the ties binding American government to the politics of the past moved forward on these three fronts simultaneously. The critique of the Constitution, of rights, and of parties took aim at the principal constraints on concerted national action. It leveraged legitimacy for new ways of governing and more direct responses to the governmental challenges of the day. But Progressives did not ask Americans to take a leap in the dark. Three other themes explored in this volume revisit the foundations of the reformers' faith in a new order, the assumptions and expectations they hoped to instill in the new regime.

First among these was the Progressives' faith in expertise. In proposing to reorganize government to solve social and economic problems as they arose, progressives put a premium on know-how. In particular, they looked to science and knowledge-based communities to build consensus behind policy solutions, and they elevated the position of policy adviser and program administrator to great authority in the affairs of state. A new governing class—highly educated, thoroughly professional, and technically savvy—would over time come to occupy a vastly expanded executive branch, and an extensive "parastate" of think tanks, universities, foundations, professional societies, and lobbying organizations would come to surround it.

Not unlike the Framers they so roundly criticized, the Progressives bolstered confidence in their plans to empower government with assurances that this new power would be exercised responsibly. The difference was that the Progressives thought that the Framers' formula for making power safe— divide it, check it, riddle it with conflicting interests—had rendered government incompetent. Their alternative was to concentrate power while anchoring its exercise in science and objectivity. Progressives believed that the authority of experts could, at once, unshackle the government and lend it a new discipline; that it could ease political conflict, spur constructive action, and guide the nation safely through the problems of the new age.

From the start, this faith was sorely tested. Paul Frymer's essay recovers the frustration of a few intrepid African Americans who pressed the facts of their case in progressive style as researchers for the newly created Department of Labor, only to find their work submerged in the prejudices of the wider political culture. Progressives were attuned to the knowledge basis of power in the modern state, but their prescription was oversold, most especially for its consensus-inducing capacities. The vastly expanded parastate has itself grown more internally conflicted over time, and its value as an antidote to divisions within the polity at large has been correspondingly compromised. This is not to say that faith in expertise has diminished. As John Skrentny and Natalie Novick point out, it is now a part of the civil religion, and its invocation as a cure-all for whatever ails America has reached absurd proportions. Perhaps more troubling is the detachment of faith in expertise from the larger progressive project, a development that Sheila Jasanoff describes as a weakened resolve to embed knowledge-based authority in broader commitments to enlightened citizenship, to make it an extension of, rather than a substitute for, self-governance. The empowerment of experts is easily perverted, and progressive faith on this score tempts practices that undermine its democratic pretentions.

Closely related to Progressives' faith in expertise was their faith in a managed economy. Economic regulation was the programmatic centerpiece of Progressive reform, and the managed economy is arguably its most enduring legacy. Reformers believed in what Herbert Croly called "constructive discrimination," governmental intervention to correct market malfunctions and to regulate economic relationships in the public interest. Progressives built an extensive regulatory apparatus on this promise, confident that they could realize both greater equity and improved performance.

Faith in the managed economy pressed state and society into new working relationships and transformed the operations of government itself. As the essays in this volume indicate, however, the significance of this change is hotly contested. Was it, as Daniel Carpenter argues, largely a matter of scale, an expanded application of practices operating in several states and of purposes implicit in Article I of the Constitution? Or did the Progressive model of economic management alter basic governing principles, a point argued in different ways by Richard Epstein and Joanna Grisinger? Progressives like Croly cast their aspirations for a new political economy as the resurrection of an old American idea, a reworking of Hamiltonian strategies. Still, it is hard to ignore the categorical nature of the change associated with the extension of economic management to labor relations, or the strain in basic constitutional relationships entailed by the concentration of executive, legislative, and judicial power in administrative agencies.

Although the early Progressives were in the forefront of advocacy for a managed economy, their heirs were among the first to express qualms about the way in which that idea had been operationalized. They decried regulatory capture, interest-group liberalism, and the eclipse of the public interest. Those criticisms have now been generalized and radicalized by progressivisms' fiercest opponents, and as confidence in government's ability to manage the economy effectively has been undermined, so too has the case for using government to secure greater equity in economic relationships. John Milton Cooper traces this change through presidential and partisan rhetoric; Michael McGerr finds it particularly pronounced in tax policy. Contemporary progressives mount convincing evidence of growing inequality, but confidence in their remedy has worn thin.

Underlying all of the above was the Progressives' faith in a national community. Progressives wanted the national government to speak and act in the "public interest," but they recognized that a public robust and self-conscious enough to express its interests nationally did not exist. Americans had long been organized into local communities, and the nationalization of the economy and the society had proved more disorientating than liberating. The people appeared to lack the resources necessary for full participation in a more proactive national government. At the nexus of the Progressive vision of a new state and a new democracy lay what John Dewey called the problem of creating the "Great Community."

Progressivism has never drawn sharp distinctions between nation building and state building; reformers worked on both sides of the compound "nation-state," often simultaneously. But in a country as diverse as the United States, nation building has been more difficult than state building. As the essays in this volume indicate, Progressives pursued all sorts of ideas for rearticulating the nation and bringing it into a more constructive alignment with the new state. In her discussion of eugenics, Nicole Mellow reminds us that some of the ideas they entertained were quite alarming; in her discussion of the community-building work of the settlement houses, Carol Nackenoff points to others that were more promising. Michael McGerr finds Progressives expressing their idea of the national community most effectively in the negative, in potent assaults on economic royalists and the specter of an American aristocracy. Rogers Smith traces forward the once robust idea of consumerism to show that Progressive ideas of a national community were easily hollowed out and turned toward antithetical ends.

The diversity and apparent incompatibility of Progressive ideas about the character of their prospective national community lend credence to the charge that there was at bottom little coherence to the reform movement overall. The disparate and ultimately fragile ideas it put forward seem to suggest nothing so much as the limits of middle-class radicalism. In another sense, however, the Progressives' preoccupation with this problem and the range of their solutions is both impressive and portentous. These reformers would not be surprised by the rise of political alienation, distrust, and polarization in our day. They knew that a strong central state not moored by an engaged public with a credible sense of common purpose would be vulnerable to a host of maladies. As Bruce Ackerman details in the concluding essay of this volume, many of these darker possibilities now loom large over American scene. Contemporary progressives will have to do better, and Ackerman, fully attuned to the reformers' original aspirations, offers an agenda with which they might start.

Different Voices, Common Concerns

The interplay among these six themes should be obvious. They were not separate strands of reform but integral parts of a new way of governing. Progressives were emboldened to challenge the structural constraints of the Constitution because they were confident in the new discipline to be provided by science and the objectivity of experts. They were emboldened to challenge the Supreme Court and its stalwart defense of rights because they were confident that enlightened administration and hands-on management could produce more equitable outcomes for interests in conflict. They were emboldened to assault the party-based democracy that had grown up over the nineteenth century because they were confident that a coherent national community was in the offing. The critique would never have advanced as far as it did if it was not bolstered by a firm sense of alternatives.

As the essays in this volume demonstrate, however, these interdependencies proved rather precarious in practice, and the uneven follow-through has left the new regime vulnerable on all counts. The authors do not speak to this situation in a single voice, but they do advance a common concern with the historical unraveling of the Progressive synthesis and the implications of that breakdown for government and politics today. Eldon Eisenach follows up this introduction with an overarching assessment of the apparent contradiction between the fierce criticisms that early Progressives launched against the cornerstones of the old order and their evident willingness to work with them in practice, to proceed through a Constitution they decried as outmoded and even to build a political party of their own. He resolves these disparities by emphasizing the reform movement's overriding sense of national identity. Progressives originally dealt with political and institutional divisions by denying their authenticity and assuming the higher ground of common purpose. By implication, division became an imposing obstacle to reformers' objectives when this higher ground was ceded, when state and nation were shorn of their presumptive unity and national policy became a grab bag of interest services.

To draw out interrelationships such as these and to examine shortfalls holistically, we have pulled together commentaries on the six themes of Progressive reform into three broad groupings. Our table of contents presents them in what seems to us the most straightforward configuration, one that follows directly from Eisenach's focus on the Constitution, the nation, and the state. We begin with Progressive responses to the traditional preoccupation of American liberalism with constraints on government—that is, with rights and the Constitution. We proceed then to nation building and the Progressive turn from party-based democracy to the knottier challenges of building consensus and activating a national community. Next we turn to their new state, their authorization of expertise and national economic management.

We do not, however, want this threefold categorization to limit attention to the issues raised among these essays, and readers will quickly discover resonances and dissonances that stretch beyond these groupings. Reading across sections illustrates not only the comprehensiveness of the Progressive diagnosis but also the depth of the tensions that ran through their particular prescriptions for reordering state and nation. We close out these introductory remarks by flagging a few of these issues. They are the sorts of concerns one might expect to figure in any effort to make the nation-state at once more democratic and more effective in pursuit of its objectives. Nevertheless, the ambiguities in the Progressive stance on these issues have grown more pronounced over time, so much so that they appear today inescapable, the central aspects of an unsettled legacy.

One nexus of concern arises in the tension between inclusion and exclusion in twentieth-century reform. The essays collected here pose the issue in different ways. For some, the problem arises within Progressivism itself and exposes the conceptual limitations of the reform framework. Nicole Mellow, for instance, relates resolute faith in a coherent national interest to concerns expressed by early Progressives about who would be fit to engage the new state and to dubious efforts to cultivate just the right kind of citizen. Reform became more inclusive later on, but, as Mellow notes, greater inclusion left the original Progressive concern with common interests submerged in the vagaries of pluralism and interest-group liberalism. Richard Epstein's examination of the political economy of Progressivism suggests an equally disturbing trade-off. In their determination to incorporate the interests of organized labor into industrial decision making and to replace class warfare with conflict management, Progressives implicated the government in dubious forms of economic discrimination and in the creation of new and inefficient forms of interest privilege.

Other essays pose the issue differently, pointing to tensions in the relationship between Progressivism and the larger political culture of which it was a part. For Paul Frymer, Progressivism has been too quickly tarred with charges of exclusion and racism. He notes that Progressives offered those excluded from full participation in the American polity strong tools for advocating their cause, and he suggests that the frustration of their efforts to employ those tools in behalf of more inclusive policies says more about prejudices in the American polity at large than about Progressivism in particular. Similarly, James Kloppenberg hears the distinctive voice of Progressivism in President Obama's call for transcending political divisions in a higher unity, and in his insistence that "we are all in this together," and he relates the fierce resistance to these overtures to darker currents of long standing in American culture. These perspectives suggest that Progressivism, whatever its limitations, might remain part of the solution.

Another crosscutting nexus of issues arises out of tensions between the top-down and bottom-up aspects of Progressive reform. Retrieving the latter and affirming its value as a source of creativity and legitimacy is a central concern of the essays by Daniel Carpenter, Sheila Jasanoff, and Bruce Ackerman. Carpenter and Jasanoff both express skepticism on this ground about recent experiments in public policy that employ top-down tactics to "nudge," to manipulate citizen preferences and forgo more direct forms of input and involvement. While recognizing that progressivism has always relied on a strong, active, and purposeful national government, they find this tilt toward top-down management a subtle betrayal of Progressivism's historical commitment to democratic exchange. Looking at the matter from the other end, Ackerman finds that the bottom-up tools developed by Progressives to generate and register the interests of the public have not kept up with the times and that the continued vitality of the project hinges on thinking about new ways to keep them current.

As others see it, however, these problems appear to go deeper than the tactics employed. They point to the difficulties inherent in a project that seeks at once to improve the efficiency of, and participation in, government. For Carol Nackenoff, cities were the incubators of the most vibrant and promising currents of Progressive reform, and alternative modalities of reform from above threatened from the beginning to squeeze them out. For Sidney Milkis, the Progressives' enthusiasm for democratic exchanges—top-down and bottom-up—was genuine but never well anchored institutionally. Milkis shares Ackerman's concern for the degeneration of progressivism into presidentialism, but whereas Ackerman calls for updates to revive the progressive vision of democracy, Milkis wonders if the vision was well thought out in the first place.

A third nexus of issues speaks to the character of American political development and, in particular, the character of the modern American state. At the heart of the matter is the question whether, or to what extent, reform constructed a regime different in kind from that which preceded it. How exactly did the new ideas that the reformers put on the table relate to the original ideal with which the nation began, and how did the new arrangements negotiated pragmatically in the course of solving problems relate to the reform ideals that inspired them? As Ken Kersh and Steven Teles show, those who take the Progressives' frontal assault on the cornerstones of the old order most seriously today are contemporary conservatives out to hoist the reformers on their own petard. These conservatives stress the sharp break with the past in order to question the authenticity of the progressives' principles and to submerge their problem-solving ethos in charges of cultural betrayal. But there is nothing so stark in the actual results. The essays by Eldon Eisenach and Karen Orren suggest that the question of continuity or change is multidimensional, productive of odd combinations and uneasy syntheses. Others downplay the break and emphasize the continuities. Dan Carpenter reaches back to nineteenth-century practices to smooth the course of development and give pride of place to pragmatic problem solving in the American political tradition.

Change or continuity is the central axis on which American political development turns, and although there is ample material in progressive reform to spin a narrative one way or the other, the essays in this volume, considered collectively, suggest that problems of development are not easily resolved. Progressive reform unleashed a principled assault on fundamentals, and the problem-solving impulse of reform led reformers to seek accommodations pragmatically. Uneasy resolutions—in the progressive approach to the Constitution (Rana), to rights (Orren), to law (Tamanaha), to parties (Milkis), to citizenship (Mellow), to race (Frymer), to administration (Grisinger)—frame the contemporary predicament. The temptation is strong to choose sides on the legacy of progressivism, but that seems unlikely to clear a compelling path forward. Better to begin by confronting dilemmas that reform has bequeathed to us, for they are all too real.

1 • A Progressive Conundrum

Federal Constitution, National State, and Popular Sovereignty

Eldon Eisenach

Progressives fiercely criticized a number of institutions and practices that they were unwilling to jettison altogether. As a result, a persistent series of conundrums pervaded their political ideas, and without closer attention to the issues behind these puzzles, it is hard for us today to reconstruct and reinvigorate their reform vision. Take first the Progressives' stance toward the U.S. Constitution. Herbert Croly's broadside against the "monarchy of the Constitution" was echoed by the economic and class analysis of Charles Beard. But coupled with that critique was a defense: the Constitution was the essential framework for the development of American power and nationality. Against populists and other radicals writing at the beginning of the twentieth century, both Croly and Beard defended John Marshall's view of judicial review.

A second conundrum appeared in Progressive understandings of the historical relationship between constitutional development in America and American nationality. They used the terms "nation," "union," "people," and "society" both to critique and to support the changing Constitution. Lincoln, the hero of the Progressive story of American nationality, was understood by them in dialectical and historicist ways. After decades of delusional and irresponsible ways of thinking about authority and freedom, Lincoln both subverted and saved the Constitution. By shifting the grounds of authority to union, an organic society, and nationality, the Progressives sought to emancipate America from ways of political thinking that had begun to subvert both authority and freedom. Depending on how it was understood, the Constitution both hindered and aided this national, Hegelian, Hebraic project.

A third conundrum in Progressive thinking was the relationship of political parties to democratic governance. We properly understand the movement as having been founded in a critique that viewed the prevailing party system as the key causal element in the perceived injustices, corruptions, and distortions of American political ideas and practices of the time. Progressives viewed the existing parties as barriers to authentic citizenship and the achievement of public good. Yet their *historical* understanding of party—like their historical understanding of the Constitution—presented a different perspective. Given the many types and purposes of parties, party movements, and party factions in American historical experience (not least the sudden formation of the Republican Party and the election of Lincoln), the Progressives were familiar with many examples of party as central both to the American founding and to national development, most notably America's redemption from slavery. The Progressives' ambivalent judgments of party reflected their understanding of and commitment to "popular sovereignty" as the authentic ground of national authority. This commitment and vision were at once "constitutional," "national," and "partisan."

The three conundrums are linked. All come to bear on Progressives' struggles with the relationship of nationality to institutions and to issues of political authority and legitimacy. Confronted by an inherently ambiguous field of choices, Progressives were compelled to combine ideas and practices of long historical pedigree with the intellectual and moral resources provided by new ways of thinking in philosophy, religion, and the social sciences. It was from these new resources that the Progressives constructed a compelling narrative of reform. And it was within this reform narrative that one sees an implicit idea of the *state*—an idea that incorporates not only the Constitution and the major political parties but also all the durable national institutions of our economic, intellectual, cultural, and ethical-religious life. It was clear to the Progressive reformers that the Constitution, governments, and political majorities—separately or combined—could not stand in for or fully represent the American people in their collective capacity. Their narrative of progress was grounded in a sense of nationality at once more coherent and encompassing than the elements that might at times promote it.[1]

A comprehensive and many-sided idea of the state was complemented by an equally comprehensive and many-sided idea of *citizenship*. Just as political authority was found in many places, so too were the rights and responsibilities of citizenship. Wherever located, however, citizenship—like authority—was held together by nationality and service to a larger public good. Both a "statist" and a "citizenship" assumption are much less evident among those today who might hope for a new progressive moment within the Democratic Party. The lack of such a grounding confounds and confuses the political appeal and the intellectual coherence of today's progressives. And by abandoning a formative role for nationality within a larger reform narrative, today's progressives cede to the more ideologically coherent Republican Party intellectual, moral, and political advantage.

Constitution

In *Progressive Democracy* (1914), Herbert Croly called for a "revolution" in our political thinking before we can begin serious projects of political, economic, and social reform. A first step in this revolution was emancipation of our political thinking from the Constitution. Fealty to the "monarchy of the Constitution" was the expression of the "conservative spirit to which progressivism finds itself opposed. . . . [This conservative spirit] is based on an unqualified affirmation of the necessity of the traditional constitutional system to . . . American democracy." Democracy and the monarchy of the Constitution were in conflict, and the monarchy had to give way. "Doctrinaire and dogmatic" constitutional ideals of political authority and political legitimacy had produced a rights-dominated individualism that inhibited social progress.[2] But the tide was changing: "The ideal of individual justice is being supplemented by the ideal of social justice. . . . Now the tendency is to conceive the social welfare, not as an end which can be left to the happy harmonizing of individual interests, but as an end which must be consciously willed by society and efficiently realized. Society, that is, has become a moral ideal."[3]

By framing the issue historically, Croly both critiques and affirms the constitutional founding. The critique ("The Constitution was really king. Once the kingdom of the Word had been ordained, it was almost as seditious to question the Word as it was to plot against the kingdom.") is quickly followed by an affirmation ("Its government was at once authoritative, national and educational. It instructed the American people during their collective childhood. It trained them during their collective youth. With its assistance the American people have become a nation").[4]

At a time when America was being inundated by partisan political attacks on the judiciary that were buttressed by historical argument undermining the very legitimacy of judicial review,[5] Charles Beard wrote a ringing defense, "The Supreme Court—Usurper or Grantee?" After a painstaking historical analysis of the Constitutional Convention, he concludes that the critics failed to show that "the American federal system was not designed primarily to commit the established rights of property to the guardianship of a judiciary removed from direct contact with popular electorates." Further, those arguing for modifying or eliminating judicial review could not look to the Framers for support: "Whether this system is outworn, whether it has unduly exalted property rights, is a legitimate matter for debate; but those who hold the affirmative cannot rest their case on the intent of the eighteenth-century statesmen who framed the Constitution."[6]

In partisan political terms, both Croly and Beard were retrospective "Federalists" who carried that constitutional nationalism into their historical analyses and into the present era.[7] The main threat to national political integrity had its roots in Anti-Federalism, its branches in the formation of the Jeffersonian Republican Party (with its hints of nullification), and its bitter fruits in Southern secession.

The issue for Beard and Croly was not the constitutional text itself but how it was understood—whether as a buttress and guarantor of national political authority or as an excuse to evade political responsibility. Beard condemned Jeffersonian-Jacksonian agrarianism on two levels: first, it was a way of life that was unique to American political geography, condemned to extinction by every progressive advance in American national development; second, when organized by a political party into a governing majority, it yielded destructive results.[8] Indeed, in Beard's popular and long-lived textbook on American government, he assures his students that the battle over the Constitution has largely been won on national and progressive terms: "No longer do statesmen spend weary days over finely spun theories about strict and liberal interpretations of the Constitution, about the sovereignty and reserved rights of states. . . . One has only to compare the social and economic legislation of the last decade with that of the closing years of the nineteenth century, for instance, to understand how deep is the change in the minds of those who have occasion to examine and interpret the Constitution bequeathed to them by the Fathers."[9]

The nullification crisis was seen by both Croly and Beard as the occasion for reinstating the nationalist views of John Marshall, especially through the legal writings of Joseph Story and the Senate oratory of Daniel Webster. And the more these neonationalist views took hold, the more the expansion of slavery became the ultimate constitutional test. Here was the heart of the Progressive critique of the Constitution: although the Constitution, in their view, clearly granted the national government the power to outlaw slavery in the territories (even the Articles of Confederation, through the Northwest Ordinance, allowed that), it sanctioned slavery through states' rights.[10] With slavery, Americans

could not become one people. America was saved as a nation not by the Constitution but by the Republican Party and the Union victory in the Civil War.

Paradoxically, then, Lincoln both destroyed the old regime (like a Cromwell
or a Bismarck) and (like John Winthrop and the Founders) rebuilt its original
foundations. The Progressives believed, with Lincoln, that "the Union is much
older than the Constitution,"[11] or as Lincoln put it in a letter addressing concerns of the constitutionality of the Emancipation Proclamation, "Was it possible to lose the nation, and yet preserve the Constitution?"[12] The Constitution
was endorsed as part of American national history and destiny. Without that
narrative grounding, it was suspect, a sterile text locked into the virtues and
vices of prevailing power.

Nation and Constitution

A letter to the *New Yorker* in 2008, responding to an article on the decline
of newspapers and the rise of the "blogosphere," asserts the following: "The
United States is in the unusual position of never having been a nation in the
sense of sharing a common culture or language. Our monumental faults notwithstanding, this country exists as an idea—an attempt to better organize
society. The Constitution came first, not 'the people.'" The writer concludes by
voicing the cosmopolitan hope that America will become "the first nation
forged through the community of the World Wide Web."[13] Even discounting
the parochial demographic of *New Yorker* readers, this letter raises an issue,
expressed in contemporary political theory today as "constitutional patriotism," that was central to the Progressive critique of the Constitution. Here are
two historical examples of what the Progressives were up against:

> John C. Calhoun, 1831: "The truth is that the very idea of an American
> people, as constituting a single community, is a mere chimera. Such a
> community never, for a moment, existed, neither before, nor since the
> dec[laration] of Independence."[14]

> Woodrow Wilson, 1908: "Constitutional government can exist only
> where there is actual community of interest and of purpose, and cannot,
> if it be also self-government, express the life of any body of people that
> does not constitute a veritable community. Are the United States a com-
> munity? In some things, yes; in most things, no."[15]

Little wonder that Progressives eyed Wilson skeptically. The stream of an
encompassing Progressive nationalism runs from Hamilton, Jay, and Marshall

through the legal writings of James Wilson and Joseph Story to the Whig Party, and culminates in Lincoln and the Republican Party.

> John Jay, 1787: "Providence has been pleased to give this one connected country to one united people—a people descended from the same ancestors, speaking the same language, professing the same religion, attached to the same principles of government."[16]

> Whig Party, 1844: "We wish, fully and entirely, to nationalize the institutions of our land and to identify ourselves with our country; to become a single great people, separate and distinct in national character, political interest, social and civil affinities from any and all other nations, kindred and people on the earth."[17]

> Justice Bradley, 1871: "The United States is not only a government, but it is a National Government, and the only government in this country that has the character of nationality . . . invested with all those inherent and implied powers which, at the time of adopting the Constitution, were generally considered to belong to every government as such."[18]

If the support of the Constitution for a strong national government rests on the historical coherence of American nationality, and if that coherence has existed to varying degrees over time, are there *permanent* principles behind nationality that might anchor a *permanent* authority of the national government? One answer, quite familiar in Progressive political culture, is that we are the new Hebraic nation: John Winthrop was our nation's founder, our Nehemiah Americanus, and the Constitution is but one of a series of national covenants—covenants that Americans as often betrayed as fulfilled.[19]

This Hebraic-biblical-Hegelian understanding of America, so eloquently expressed in Lincoln's Second Inaugural Address, finds its way into the Republican platform of 1876: "When, in the economy of Providence, this land was to be purged of human slavery, and when the strength of government of the people . . . was to be demonstrated, the Republican Party came into power."[20] While these ideas might be viewed as mere rhetoric to appeal to the Whig and Republican base of northern and midwestern evangelical Protestants, recourse to its historicist-nationalist structure has often been a felt necessity at particular moments to preserve or extend the authority of the national government. In this sense, American nationality can be seen as anchoring constitutional legitimacy. How else can one explain Woodrow Wilson's very different language in a speech to the Senate in 1919 on the meaning of

U.S. entry into the world war? "Our participation in the war established our position among the nations. . . . The whole world saw at last . . . a Nation they had deemed material and now found to be compact of the spiritual forces that must free men of every nation of every unworthy bondage. . . . The stage is set, the destiny is disclosed. It has come about by no plan of our conceiving, but by the hand of God who led us into this way. We cannot turn back. We can only go forward . . . to follow the vision. It was of this that we dreamed at our birth. America shall in truth show the way."[21]

We can forgive Wilson's late learning curve because he was a trained southern lawyer before he became a Ph.D. student at Johns Hopkins, the first "German" graduate university in America. Translated into history, philosophy, theology, and the social sciences, German scholarship was explicitly nation centered; its historicist methodologies had their roots both in Hegel and in a Bible-centric Protestantism. American Progressive intellectuals were raised in this latter tradition and saw in its new historicist articulation a way of grappling with the wrenching social, economic, and political transformations they witnessed in post–Civil War America.[22]

For our purposes, three elements of this German influence stand out. The first was its stress on historical periodicity as part of a social-evolutionary understanding of man and society, a periodicity marked by transformative "moments." The second was that historically meaningful moments in the modern era were always and everywhere *national* ones, whatever the particular governmental forms. The third element—and this was like honey to American bees—was that these national moments were always revelatory of higher human ends and ideals. The American nation was the site where the freedom and justice "dreamed at our birth" were achieved in history. Combined, these three elements constituted the ligaments of a compelling narrative that enlisted the resources of higher learning and a higher spirit in philosophy, religion, and the social sciences in a common cause of national renewal.

Party, Nationality, and Constitution

Since the Progressive movement's ideological beginnings in the 1880s, one of its leitmotifs was its attack on political parties. The appeal of this critique was nicely captured by Samuel Batten, a Social Gospel clergyman from Iowa. Party "stands between the people and the government and makes a fully democratic government impossible." The "subtle and silent . . . tyranny" of party mirrors the hidden despotism of the unredeemed American individualist.

Even at its best, party government rests on appeal to prevailing interests and appetites, resulting in "stagnation" mired in "commonplace ideas and past issues." At its worst, it "spells compromise and not principles . . . mediocrity and inferiority where it does not mean cowardice and corruption." The inescapable result: "A good partisan cannot be a good citizen."[23]

The Progressives, however, condemned only standing parties, or "Old Parties," in their 1912 platform. *Their* party, "unhampered by tradition [and] uncorrupted by power," would become the "instrument of the people . . . to build a new and nobler commonwealth."[24] Only if a political party was formed on national principles and projects, and only if those principles and projects gained authority, could it be viewed as an authoritative expression of the whole people. Using a religious analogy, the Progressive Party was to be a nonsectarian, "broad church."

Even though Progressives outpolled the Republican Party, from which they bolted in 1912, they did not think that their quick demise as a party was to be mourned. They thought that their primary purpose, to alter public opinion and to shift the ground for appealing to America's most informed and morally serious citizens, had largely been achieved. Indeed, they knew that this educative process had begun long before their formation as a party and would continue through the many flourishing organizations and institutions permeated with national and progressive values.

In another way, then, the appeal of "antiparty" national parties has an affinity with appeals to judicial review and constitutionalism, which are also "above politics." For example, Beard's college textbook quotes John Burgess's defense of judicial supremacy as the bedrock of "the permanent existence of republican government," necessitated because "elective government must be party government—majority government." Without protection of property by a source independent of party, "such government degenerates into party absolutism and then to Caesarism."[25] Political majorities are creatures of party, and parties thrive on patronage, logrolling, and service to special interests.[26] Good citizens active in reform organizations, journalism, and social movements engaged in this same form of antiparty, or higher, politics.

For Beard and Croly, antiparty parties had arisen in America at particular times and occasions and made "constitutive" choices that furthered the cause of equality and justice. "Patriots" founded the nation against "loyalists," and "Unionists" sustained it against "Confederates." Notions of party above mere majoritarian politics drew upon a civic republican tradition that periodically migrated into national party politics; these parties or party factions were best understood as "movement" parties charged with common purposes. In ordinary times, civic virtue and the common good were furthered by citizens living responsible lives within America's "free institutions"—families, churches, businesses, voluntary associations, and local and state governments—a virtue that went "all the way down" into the minutiae of everyday life. In extraordinary times, however, a higher duty became obligatory. Ordinary justice, ordinary laws, ordinary constitutional understandings, and even ordinary morality had to give way.[27]

Setting aside the difficulty and risk entailed in identifying such transformative moments, hegemonic success, both political and military, then presented its own difficulties. The new institutions and practices that marked success, like charisma itself, were soon moderated and routinized. "Mere justice" and mere party-political majorities again came to rule, and the comforting illusion of "constitutional" permanence soon followed. Consider the Whig politician and lawyer Rufus Choate. In an 1845 oration at Harvard's law school, he urged an unqualified political affirmation: "This is what we need,—personal, moral, mental reform,—not civil—not political! No, no! Government, substantially as it is; jurisprudence, substantially as it is; the general arrangements of liberty, substantially as they are; the Constitution and the Union, exactly as they are,—this is to be wise, according to the wisdom of America."[28]

Lincoln and the Republican Party rejected affirmation of this sort. Like them, the Progressives challenged the "constitutional" routinization of parties and politics in post–Civil War America, launching a nationwide crusade against the prevailing political and party institutions and the prevailing political culture. At the heart of this crusade was a call to reconceive an idea of American nationality, one that would transcend prevailing ideas of constitutional and political boundaries. As in past "reconstitutions," a party of transformation would become the necessary engine of history, driving the nation to a higher destiny.

Popular Sovereignty, Citizenship, and the State

The Progressives faced difficulties at every point at which they sought to anchor their claims to authority and legitimacy. The constitutional text created rather fixed boundaries, not only between governmental branches, but also between federal and state authority, and the Bill of Rights honored Anti-Federalist and states' rights values. The authority of union, nation, and nationality seemed anchored in extraordinary times and events, controlled less by human purpose than miracle and fate. And the parties that rode to power in those times were equally extraordinary, soon to become established and entrenched.

In response to these conundrums, the concept of a larger sovereignty suggested itself. While it is tempting to see the Progressives answering the siren call of authoritarian (that is, Germanic) state theory,[29] the Progressive response was both more original and more anchored in American tradition. It was more original because, in contrast with European thinking, its theory of sovereignty was never located in governing institutions, starting with kings and aristocrats and ending with mass political parties and popularly elected parliaments. It was more American because it presumed from the start a non-institutional theory of popular sovereignty.

Progressive understandings of citizenship and popular sovereignty bore only a tangential relationship to Jeffersonian-Jacksonian understandings. They were Jeffersonian only in that the Progressives assumed that *all* government, starting with self-government and the family and working its way up through local, state, and, finally, the federal government, came from the people. They broke with Jefferson categorically in denying that the states had any particular or special claims to sovereignty[30] and in insisting that many other voluntary organizations and institutions also derived their authority from the people. Local organizations such as families, churches, schools, libraries, and small business, and emerging national institutions such as business, trade, and professional associations, research universities, and national industrial and financial corporations were all institutions governing our conduct and receive their authority from the people.[31] Francis Lieber, the founding father of American political science, explained in his *Encyclopedia Americana* of 1830 that "all the American governments are corporations created by charters, viz. their constitutions." Indeed, "the whole political system is made up of a concatenation of various corporations, political, civil, religious, social and economical," with the "nation itself . . . the great corporation, comprehending all others."[32]

The Progressive understanding of citizenship was more republican than liberal-Lockean because it denied any strict separation of public and private, a separation founded in natural-rights theory and social contracts. Popular sovereignty, as Tocqueville recognized so well, is at once informal, voluntary, and atmospheric, penetrating into all areas of American life, with equal citizenship as its foundation:

There are countries where a power in a way external to the social body acts on it and forces it to march on a certain track. There are others where force is divided, placed at once in society and outside it. Nothing like this is seen in the United States; there society acts *by itself and on itself.* Power exists only within its bosom; almost no one is encountered who dares to conceive and above all to express the idea of seeking it elsewhere. . . . One can say that they govern themselves, so weak and restricted is the part left to the administration, so much does the latter feel its popular origin and obey the power from which it emanates. The people reign over the American political world as God over the universe. They are the cause and the end of things; everything comes out of them and everything is absorbed into them.[33]

By maintaining this same principle of plenary popular sovereignty—but seeing it through the lens of periodized history and making it an aspirational final goal or project—Progressives sought to ground both long-standing and newly emergent institutions of governance, from family through business and professional organizations to the national government, in a shared legitimacy. An early expression of this ideal is found in an 1888 essay by John Dewey: "If, then, society and the individual are really organic to each other, then the individual is society concentrated. . . . The organism must have its spiritual organs; having a common will, it must express it. . . . In democracy . . . the governors and the governed are not two classes, but two aspects of the same fact—the fact of the possession by society of a unified and articulate will. It means that government is the organ of society, and is as comprehensive as society."[34]

A later formulation is that of Mary Follett: "The old idea of natural rights postulated the particularist individual; we know now that no such person exists. . . . We see that to obey the group which we have helped to make and of which we are an integral part is to be free because we are then obeying ourself. Ideally the state is such a group, actually it is not, but it depends upon us to make it more and more so. The state must be no external authority which restrains and regulates me, but it must be myself acting as the state in every smallest detail of life."[35]

This ideal of comprehensive citizenship is restated in the writings of the sociologists Charles Cooley, Franklin Giddings, and Albion Small, all writers of definitive college texts in their field. Democratic citizenship is a fusion of the increasing facts of social interdependence, a growing consciousness of these facts, and the political expression of this consciousness in a higher and authoritative "public opinion." In the words of Cooley, "The general or public phase of larger consciousness is what we call Democracy. . . . Public opinion is . . . an organization, a cooperative product of communication and reciprocal influence."[36]

In *The Public and Its Problems* (1927), Dewey extends and deepens this analysis. Without an uncoerced shared consciousness, no democratic citizens and no "public" can be created, and without a "public," democracy cannot be achieved. The final expression of this connection is the state: "A public articulated and operating through representative officers is the state; there is no state without a government, but also there is none without the public."[37] The "eclipse" of past publics occurred when new and distant interdependencies overawed and subordinated local self-determination by expanding, multiplying, and intensifying "the scope of indirect consequences." Under these circumstances, "the new public which is generated remains long inchoate, unorganized, because it cannot use inherited political agencies," which, "if elaborate and well institutionalized, obstruct the organization of the new Public." In short, "the State must always be rediscovered."[38] The issue "is, in the first instance, an *intellectual* problem."

> Human associations may be ever so organic in origin and firm in operation, but they develop into societies in a human sense only as their consequences, being known, are esteemed and sought for. Even if "society" were as much an organism as some writers have held, it would not on that account be society. Interactions, transactions, occur *de facto* and the results of interdependence follow. But participation in activities and sharing in results are additive concerns. They demand *communication* as a prerequisite.[39]

Creating a new public required the creation of new citizens. Working through settlement houses, social work, reform journalism, and sociology, economics, and ethics textbooks, Progressives were committed to creating democratic citizens appropriate to a new democratic state and society.[40]

Insofar as constitutional understandings, laws, and prevailing values were obstacles to the achievement of an integrated and democratic society, they had to be reformed by the "state," understood as "society" or "public" in this organic sense. What might sound harsh and authoritarian coming from Follett sounded soft and voluntarist in the language of social and educational psychology. But make no mistake: a clear conception of an authoritative will was required in both iterations, a national and democratic will that embraced but transcended constitutions, parties, and the whole complex of nongovernmental economic and social organizations. Put starkly, whether the term used was "state," "public," or "society," all governing institutions had to become as integrated and interdependent as national and local economies had become,[41] directed and infused by a shared set of beliefs and values. This was what the Progressives (and their Whig and Republican forebears) meant by nationalization and democratization and what Social Gospelers (and their "theocratic" forebears) called "Christianization."[42] Parties, federal and state constitutions, the courts, business corporations, churches, and families had to be reformed—"democratized"—by shaping their values and purposes to serve a civic, republican ideal of common ends.

Progressive social scientists imported this Americanist form of citizenship and state theory into the very marrow of their theories of society, theories that ran all the way from individual psychology through political economy to state and federal governments. Social science, grounded in this common narrative, was to serve as an authoritative master science, providing not only empirical maps of how society functions but also common programs of social reform. Even more, these common purposes and programs would serve as a "common faith," fusing individual meaning and social purpose.[43]

Left, Right, and American

We know that the Progressives, organized briefly as a political party contending for political majorities, failed.[44] We also know that their ideas—their way of thinking about American institutions and practices and about how American society worked—dominated American political and academic culture in the early twentieth century.

Two features of their success stand out. Progressivism had a core constituency, one attuned to its methods of deriving political authority and responsive to its nationalist message. A shared northern and midwestern liberal-evangelical Protestantism created the Republican Party as well as almost all national reform associations, the faculties and leaders of the leading colleges and universities, both public and private, and almost all realms of higher journalism. If ever a clearly identifiable subculture became hegemonic, this was it.[45] This somewhat narrow base came to appeal to an ever-wider array of groups in America, not only through its dominance of national organizations but also through its ability to restate its particular values across the board, to lodge them in the universal terms of family values, ecumenical and moral religion, and, not least, the prestige of science and economic progress. Together, these appeals constituted an attractive ideal of American citizenship. More specifically, they gave explanations and reasons for current discontents, explanations and reasons that ran from personal and family conduct through national economic and political organizations.[46]

A second feature, suggested at many points above and accounting for the general power of Progressive ideas to penetrate deeply into other sectors of society, was their capacity to shape their specific explanations and reform programs within a larger patriotic narrative, a national narrative of reform that included all the major and dynamic segments of society. At every point in their search for authority, they created historical narratives that both critiqued and justified the leadership, institutions, and practices of the past in a way that could be resolved only through commitment to progressive reform values. This narrative was also an invitation to participate in "achieving our country" by engaging in undertakings that enlarged the self as it democratized society.[47] Put differently, they (like contemporary pragmatists such as Richard Rorty and Stanley Fish) were usually against "principles," whether found in the iron laws of classical economics, the frozen doctrines of Bible-centric Protestantism, the authoritarian rigidities of child rearing, or the fixities of the law of contracts. While Croly's *Promise of American Life* is exemplary, history marked by critical "moments" pervaded almost all expressions of the Progressive mind, giving to their reform proposals a kind of dynamic-pragmatic pedigree that would partially vindicate and partially redeem the past.[48]

Does contemporary liberalism have anything approaching such a national narrative? A pessimist would say no.[49] Many liberal hopes for political transformation are entrapped in "rights talk,"[50] a form of discourse appropriate for courts, some administrative agencies, and law schools, but ill suited for participatory politics. Indeed, rights talk spoken in these venues is the counterpart of the transformation of expertise, a transformation traced later in this volume by Sheila Jasanoff from the role of shaping public opinion to that of creating a distinct discourse among policy elites. A parallel is found in the erosion of a shared public or national component in justifications for the management of the economy. Without this component, economic policies and economic redistributions are seen as serving particular interests and groups— as forms of patronage—rather than as parts of a shared enterprise. Both scientific expertise and economic management have become disconnected from a national narrative of shared purpose.

The absence of shared purpose is ratified in the larger sphere of liberal-progressive public philosophy. The field of play on which public policy is contested has been radically altered in American academic culture. What was once a commonsense pragmatism informed by social science has merged with the postmodernism of the cultural left, and the combination has served to subvert the very idea of a national community.[51] Beginning with the assumption of American exceptionalism as a reactionary myth, even the celebration of past democratic achievements is viewed as hiding and devaluing the victims these achievements submerged or sacrificed. And when contemporary rights talk is tailored to redress these hidden victims, the very idea of American nationality becomes suspect.[52] Under the sign of "antifoundationalism," ethnic pluralism and multiculturalism has often moved from demographic description to fixed policy principles, deepening felt differences in the process.

The implicit and explicit hostility to "We the People" is compounded by attempts by the cultural left to purge religious discourse from contemporary politics. While it is difficult to find nineteenth- and twentieth-century Americans who were opposed to the separation of church and state, it is even more difficult to find Progressive political and intellectual leaders who did not see religious discourse as an integral part of democratic discourse and democratic reform. More broadly, they could not conceive of American democracy without this sacred dimension. Even the least obviously "religious," John Dewey and Herbert Croly, rested their democratic hopes on a shared national faith.[53]

Without the shaping of a new national narrative and, with it, a shared conception of equal citizenship, transformational politics in the progressive tradition will be hard to re-create. Liberals and progressives will continue to win political majorities, but they will also continue to fail the critical test: to convert those majorities into government by "We the People"—a common civic will with a clear set of national priorities.[54] As we have seen in the recent past, liberal politics will largely be a holding action that entrenches past interests and past victories. Much like Choate in the 1840s, liberals today are hunkered down in a politics of affirmation. In part, this defensive posture results from the tendency to equate big government, represented by welfare programs, with a strong and authoritative national state. As stated somewhat differently in the introduction to this volume and demonstrated repeatedly in the essays that follow, "nation building has been more difficult than state building." And without a self-conscious national community, state building becomes reduced to "big government." The knee-jerk charge against today's conservatives as launching "attacks against the state" driven by an "anti-government" political philosophy disguises this distinction.[55]

For today's conservatives, the most serious issue is "the new politics of public policy":[56] a combination of executive orders, new administrative bodies, and federal rule expansion through litigation in the federal courts by self-appointed but court-recognized public interest groups and nongovernmental organizations (NGOs)—all together promoting the persistent growth of permanent and largely autonomous state institutions. Here (at last), one might say, America has finally grown up and created both administrative institutions and a political class whose lives are wholly dedicated to serving the state by addressing extant social problems through dispassionate social and legal analysis, free from the demands of parochial and selfish interests and the myths and delusions of popular opinion.[57] This ideal—rule by judicial and administrative mandarins distributing rights and resources in accord with an egalitarian public reason—is a tempting prospect.[58] But it is a mere shadow of the ideal that inspired it, and it remains vulnerable to the charge that these new statesmen might have their own group interests and might tailor their rules to advantage particular groups and subcultures in the larger society. Just as an earlier "interest-group liberalism" was attacked from both the left and the right from the late 1960s onward, so this rapidly expanding administrative state and its clients might be more closely scrutinized by its friends, lest it be discredited *tout court* by the populist attacks from its enemies.[59]

To equate the new system of regulation, reflexively and automatically, with the "objective" progress of democracy—even in the face of electoral reversals—is to invite electoral and judicial backlash in the name of participatory democracy and equal treatment under the law. Both big government per se and the growth of administrative patronage and autonomy are difficult to justify under any convincing national and civic narrative. No expansion of policy studies and expert testimony, no philosophical refinements of rights talk, no ephemeral and media-centric "demonstrations"—not even appeals to temporary electoral or "polled" majorities—can take the place of political reforms demanded by durable, coherent, and organized publics willing to subordinate their particular ends, identities, and interests to higher forms of citizenship. Transformational politics require transformational narratives and genuinely national ideas. Too much of today's liberalism is merely principled, and these principles, expressed in the new "policy state,"[60] seem better designed for voting blocs, clients, patients, and victims than for citizens. In such a state, there are no invitations to join "We the People," just the promise (or threat) that material benefits and symbolic respect will continue only so long as this particular state is electorally sustained. The civic ideals achieved are the aggregate products of the system, not the conscious achievement of democratic citizens.

Progressives held that freedom was an earned achievement and, once earned, required one to treat one's fellow citizens as equals, no more and no less. Today, one is more likely to hear this appeal (and this invitation) from the

Republican than from the Democratic Party. Despite gleeful predictions of the Republicans being defeated by ideology and demography, its appeal to core constitutional values is a proxy both for American exceptionalism and for ideals of equal citizenship and shared civic and social responsibilities. This appeal will continue to remain a powerful force even against temporary electoral defeats and an entrenched bureaucracy because it is capable of forging durable political wills in a way that a politics of patronage and favor can never achieve.[61]

On this reading, Republican attacks on big government are often part of attempts to create a more durable and authoritative national state and a more public-regarding citizenry. On this reading, "big government" stands for the patronage distribution of rights in exchange for electoral support. Each victory on these terms only further divides the public. This is especially the case when the distribution of these rights is not the act of laws enacted by elected legislatures but the result of court decisions that sanction executive orders or administrative regulation.

The paradox for progressives today is most evident in American universities, the most loyal and articulate bastions of progressive ideals in the Democratic Party. For the past thirty years, the most enduring legacies of the New Left critique of interest group liberalism are the institutional flourishing of public policy schools, public interest groups, and policy-oriented law schools: they have spawned a whole universe of NGOs and other nonprofit organizations that have, in turn, gentrified our nation's capital and staffed much of the national media, Congress, the bureaucracy, and the courts. The paradoxical result is that academia has and continues to produce tens of thousands of would-be democratic "statesmen" without, at the same time, providing the intellectual and moral foundations for an authoritative democratic state.

Notes

1. As if retroactively anticipating the disintegration of a coherent national liberal-progressive establishment from the late 1960s onward, two major articles maintained that Progressivism was never a coherent ideological and political force: Peter Filene, "An Obituary for the 'Progressive Movement,'" *American Quarterly* 22 (1970): 20–34; and Daniel T. Rodgers, "In Search of Progressivism," *Reviews in American History* 10 (1982): 113–32.

2. Herbert Croly, *Progressive Democracy* (New York: Macmillan, 1914), 20–21.

3. Ibid., 148–49. John Dewey speaks of "the unchanged persistence of a legal institution inherited from the preindustrial age" (*The Public and Its Problems: An Essay in*

Political Inquiry, ed. Melvin L. Rogers [University Park: Pennsylvania State University Press, 2012], 100).

4. Croly, *Progressive Democracy*, 131, 145–46.

5. William G. Ross, *A Muted Fury: Populists, Progressives, and Labor Unions Confront the Courts, 1890–1937* (Princeton, N.J.: Princeton University Press, 1994), chaps. 1–4; Larry D. Kramer, *The People Themselves: Popular Constitutionalism and Judicial Review* (New York: Oxford University Press, 2004), chaps. 7–8.

6. Charles Beard, "The Supreme Court—Usurper or Grantee?," *Political Science Quarterly* 27 (1912): 1–35, 31. Pope McCorkle, "The Historian as Intellectual: Charles Beard and the Constitution Reconsidered," *American Journal of Legal History* 28 (1984): 314–63, is the best discussion of this feature of Beard's thought.

7. See Herbert Croly, *The Promise of American Life* (New York: Macmillan, 1909), chap. 2; Charles Beard, *Economic Origins of Jeffersonian Democracy* (New York: Macmillan, 1915), 130–31, compares Hamilton and Jefferson.

8. In his American government textbook, Beard called this political economy "a type of economic society such as had never before appeared in the history of the world and can never exist again" (Beard, *American Government and Politics* [New York: Macmillan, 1928], 132). On how both Croly and Beard drew on the earlier writings of German-trained political economists who contrasted industrial profits with agricultural rents, see Eldon Eisenach, *The Lost Promise of Progressivism* (Lawrence: University Press of Kansas, 1994), 171–81.

9. Beard, *American Government*, 100–101.

10. Jean M. Yarbrough maintains that Theodore Roosevelt put the Northwest Ordinance "on a par with the Declaration of Independence, the Constitution, Washington's Farewell Address, the Emancipation Proclamation, and Lincoln's Second Inaugural" because "the states that were eventually carved out of the Northwest Territory were 'creatures of the nation' acquired through conquest" (*Theodore Roosevelt and the American Political Tradition* [Lawrence: University Press of Kansas, 2012], 73).

11. Abraham Lincoln, First Inaugural Address, 1861. John Quincy Adams anticipated Lincoln in identifying the Declaration of Independence with America's founding as a nation: "The Declaration of Independence was a social compact, by which the whole people covenanted with each citizen of the United Colonies, and each citizen with the whole people" (*Works* [Boston: Little, Brown, 1851], 4:193).

12. Lincoln to A. G. Hodges, April 4, 1864, quoted in Ronald C. White Jr., *Lincoln's Greatest Speech: The Second Inaugural* (New York: Simon and Schuster, 2002), app. 2, 207.

13. *New Yorker*, "The Mail," April 26, 2008, 5.

14. Quoted in Keith Whittington, *Constitutional Construction: Divided Powers and Constitutional Meaning* (Cambridge, Mass.: Harvard University Press, 1999), 82.

15. Woodrow Wilson, *Constitutional Government in the United States* (New York: Columbia University Press, 1908), 51.

16. *Federalist* 2.

17. *American Republican* [Whig], November 7, 1844, quoted in Eldon Eisenach, *Sacred Discourse and American Nationality* (Lanham, Md.: Rowman & Littlefield, 2012), 7.

18. *Knox v. Lee*, 1871, quoted in Bruce Ackerman, *We the People: Transformations* (Cambridge, Mass.: Harvard University Press, 1998), 240.

19. Sacvan Bercovitch, *The Puritan Origins of the American Self* (New Haven, Conn.: Yale University Press, 1975); White, *Lincoln's Greatest Speech;* Daniel Walter Howe, *The Political Culture of the American Whigs* (Chicago: University of Chicago Press, 1979); Eisenach, *Lost Promise*. A late-nineteenth-century college text on English literature by Vida Dutton Scudder incorporates this same Hebraic-covenantal understanding; see Eldon Eisenach, ed., *The Social and Political Thought of American Progressivism* (Indianapolis: Hackett, 2006), 232–36.

20. Donald Bruce Johnson and Kirk H. Porter, eds., *National Party Platforms, 1840–1975* (Urbana: University of Illinois Press, 1975), 53.

21. Wilson, speech to the Senate, July 10, 1919. This speech was a direct repudiation of everything the Democratic Party had stood for since its founding. Every party platform, starting with the first in 1840 and repeated as a litany in every succeeding platform (often verbatim, as in 1848, 1852, 1856) into the twentieth century, rested on the principle that the Constitution is a contract among sovereign states and, therefore, a denial of any shared religious or ethnocentric understanding of American political identity. To the Democratic Party, nationalism on Federalist, Whig, and, later, Republican Party terms was the parent of centralism, and centralism was the seedbed of aristocracy. Gerald Leonard portrays the national Democratic Party as having been founded on this constitutionalist understanding; see Leonard, *The Invention of Party Politics: Federalism, Popular Sovereignty, and Constitutional Development in Jacksonian Illinois* (Chapel Hill: University of North Carolina Press, 2002).

22. This is discussed in Eisenach, *Sacred Discourse,* chap. 4. George Bancroft (1800–1891) was the first German-trained U.S. Hegelian. He and other "Young America" spokesmen translated earlier Puritan ideas of American exceptionalism into America's "manifest destiny." For Democrats, however, this ideal became enmeshed in the expansion of slavery. For a discussion of Bancroft, see James W. Ceaser, "The Origins and Character of American Exceptionalism," *American Political Thought* 1 (Spring 2012): 3–28.

23. Quoted in Eisenach, *Lost Promise,* 113.

24. In Eisenach, *Social and Political Thought,* 274.

25. Beard, *American Government,* 117, quoting Burgess.

26. In the index to Beard's *American Government,* the entry "Politics" reads, "*See* Parties." Dewey sees parties as among "the extra-legal agencies which have grown up" to "fill the void between government and the public" (*Public and Its Problems,* 106).

Only when an authentic, conscious, and purposeful "public" comes into being will parties fade away.

27. See "Jumping Out of Ordinary Time: Sacred Rhetoric in American Political Discourse," in Eisenach, *Sacred Discourse*, 3–19.

28. Rufus Choate, "The Position and Functions of the American Bar, as an Element of Conservatism in the State," in *The Legal Mind in America*, ed. Perry Miller (Garden City, N.Y.: Anchor, 1962), 264.

29. Yarbrough, *Theodore Roosevelt*, 37–49. This connection is often tied to unbridled executive power.

30. Periodically, Democrats declared that their *party* was sovereign because it was the people—or at least a majority of them—who were committed to states' rights; see Leonard, *Invention of Party Politics*, 267.

31. Part 1 of a high school textbook by Charles and Mary Beard, *American Citizenship* (New York: Macmillan, 1914/1927), includes a chapter (3) on the family and a concluding one (18) on public opinion, which includes schools, private societies, libraries, and churches.

32. Francis Lieber, ed., *Encyclopedia Americana* (Philadelphia: Carey and Lee, 1830), 3:547.

33. Alexis de Tocqueville, *Democracy in America*, trans. Harvey C. Mansfield and Delba Winthrop (Chicago: University of Chicago Press, 2000), 1:55.

34. John Dewey, "The Ethics of Democracy," in *Early Works* (Carbondale: Southern Illinois University Press, 1969), 1:227–49. Much later, in *Public and Its Problems*, Dewey uses the terms "Great Community" and "public" to express this ideal (chap. 5). Dewey dismisses the European ideal of the state by calling it "pure myth" (37): "The moment we utter the words 'The State' a score of intellectual ghosts rise to obscure our vision" (44).

35. Mary Parker Follett, *The New American State: Group Organization in the Solution of Popular Government* (New York: Longmans, Green, 1918), 137–38. Follett's idea of good citizenship does not involve voting or running for office, but in seeing "that all the visions of their highest moments, all the aspirations of their spiritual nature can be satisfied through their common life, that only thus do we get 'practical politics'" (372).

36. Charles Cooley, *Social Organization: A Study of the Larger Mind* (New York: Scribner, 1909), quoted in Eisenach, *Social and Political Thought*, 95, and see 72–111. Croly seconded this argument; Americans feared "administration" he said, because it represented "an essentially coercive conception of sovereignty." The American administrator had to be "wholly different from . . . a continental bureaucrat" by deriving his authority "from the consent of public opinion" (*Progressive Democracy*, 353).

37. Dewey, *Public and Its Problems*, 76. Dewey integrates common education into this larger project of citizenship creation in *Democracy and Education* (New York: Macmillan, 1916).

38. Dewey, *Public and Its Problems*, 110, 56–57.

39. Ibid., 121, 124.

40. See David Paul Thelen, *The New Citizenship: Origins of Progressivism in Wisconsin, 1885–1890* (Columbia: University of Missouri Press, 1972).

41. This is a meaning Dewey gives to a "great society," requiring a public or "great community" in order to be democratic (*Public and Its Problems*, 94, 110–11).

42. Walter Rauschenbusch, *Christianizing the Social Order* (New York: Macmillan, 1912); Samuel Zane Batten, *The New Citizenship; Christian Character in its Biblical Ideals, Sources, and Relations* (Philadelphia: Union Press, 1898).

43. This is discussed more fully in Eldon Eisenach, "Social Science, Social Reform, and Social Religion: American Progressive Sociologists and Political Economists, 1890–1915" (unpublished paper, 2013).

44. Benjamin Park De Witt, *The Progressive Movement: A Non-Partisan, Comprehensive Discussion of Current Tendencies in American Politics* (Seattle: University of Washington Press, 1915/1968).

45. The strengths and limitations of this shared nationalist vision are discussed by Rogers Smith later in this volume.

46. Michael McGerr, *A Fierce Discontent: The Rise and Fall of the Progressive Movement, 1870–1920* (New York: Free Press, 2003); Marc Stears, *Demanding Democracy: American Radicals in Search of a New Kind of Democracy* (Princeton, N.J.: Princeton University Press, 2010).

47. Jane Addams, "The Subjective Necessity of Social Settlements," in *Philanthropy and Social Progress,* ed. Henry Carter Adams (New York: Crowell, 1893).

48. In more grandiose terms, the Progressives might have agreed with Walt Whitman, who proclaimed in his notebook: "Only Hegel is fit for America—is large enough and free enough" (quoted in Richard Rorty, *Achieving Our Country: Leftist Thought in Twentieth-Century America* [Cambridge, Mass.: Harvard University Press, 1999], 20).

49. David Ricci, *Why Conservatives Tell Stories and Liberals Don't: Rhetoric, Faith, and Vision on the American Right* (Boulder, Colo.: Paradigm, 2012).

50. Mary Ann Glendon, *Rights Talk: The Impoverishment of American Political Discourse* (New York: Free Press, 1991).

51. A more hopeful view of the relationship between Progressive-era pragmatism and contemporary antifoundationalism in the public philosophy of President Obama is found in James Kloppenberg's essay in this volume. For a critique of the cultural left on these terms, see Rorty, *Achieving Our Country.*

52. In this volume, Rogers Smith traces the rise of ethnic and racial pluralism and transnationalism in Progressive thought to the post–World War I writings of Randolph Bourne, Horace Kallen, and W. E. B. Du Bois, with some indirect support from John Dewey.

53. Dewey is central here. See Jared Hickman, "The Theology of Democracy," *New England Quarterly* 81 (2008): 204–10; Melvin L. Rogers, *The Undiscovered Dewey: Religion, Morality, and the Ethos of Democracy* (New York: Columbia University Press,

2008); and essays by William Dean, Richard J. Bernstein, Carl G. Vaught, and Robert Westbrook in Stuart Rosenbaum, ed., *Pragmatism and Religion* (Urbana: University of Illinois Press, 2003).

54. As Sidney Milkis maintains in this volume, however, a more populist-charismatic presidency is also embedded in the Progressives' transparty and consensual ideal and is found in both Democratic and Republican Party electoral appeals.

55. From Paul Pierson and Theda Skocpol, eds., *The Transformation of American Politics: Activist Government and the Rise of Conservatism* (Princeton, N.J.: Princeton University Press, 2007), 113, 218.

56. James Q. Wilson, "New Politics, New Elites, Old Publics," in *The New Politics of Public Policy*, ed. Marc K. Landy and Martin A. Levin (Baltimore: Johns Hopkins University Press, 1995); Stephen Skowronek, "Taking Stock," in *The Unsustainable American State*, ed. Lawrence Jacobs and Desmond King (New York: Oxford University Press, 2009).

57. This ideal is powerfully defended in Cass Sunstein, *Why Nudge? The Politics of Libertarian Paternalism* (New Haven, Conn.: Yale University Press, 2014).

58. See Ken Kersch, "Justice Breyer's Mandarin Liberty," *University of Chicago Law Review* 73 (2006): 759–822.

59. Theodore Lowi, *The End of Liberalism* (New York: Norton, 1969).

60. See Karen Orren and Stephen Skowronek, "Pathways to the Present: Political Development in America," in *Oxford Handbook of American Political Development*, ed. Robert Lieberman, Suzanne Mettler, and Richard Valelly (New York: Oxford University Press, 2016).

61. This conclusion parallels the form but not the content of the essay by Nicole Mellow in this volume.

PART I
ALTERED FOUNDATIONS: RIGHTS AND THE CONSTITUTION

2 • Progressivism and the Disenchanted Constitution

Aziz Rana

The Problem of American Exceptionalism

The U.S. Constitution is deeply interwoven in American life with the notion that the country enjoys a special destiny. As Alexis de Tocqueville famously claimed nearly two centuries ago, Americans are placed in an "exceptional situation," one that stands outside Europe's contested histories of feudalism and class oppression.[1] The Constitution embodies this distinctive character, generating a political order grounded in democratic consent, pluralism, and equal rights for all. In Cass Sunstein's words, "exceptionalism is real," and "it began in 1787, with the Constitution's effort to establish a large, self-governing republic, in which diverse views serve as both a safeguard and a creative force."[2] Quoting Alexander Hamilton's language in *Federalist* 1, Sunstein declares that whereas European history, marked by monarchical despotism and class conflict, has been the product of "accident and force," the defining feature of the American experiment—expressed most profoundly by that initial act of constitutional construction—has instead been the effort to base politics on "reflection and choice."[3]

Above all, this means that the Constitution must not be jettisoned or rejected. Indeed, for Laurence Tribe, the very idea of being "American" makes sense only against the backdrop of the Constitution. According to Tribe, the document cannot "simply be replaced by a temporary upgrade or substitute when the fire bells sound in the darkest night. Its text and invisible structure are part of the nation's beating heart—the solar plexus at which the vast diversity of American narratives inevitably converges, and the conversation through which we remain tied to past and future generations. 'We the People' cannot simply bracket our Constitution . . . for that very notion presupposes a 'we' that exists outside the Constitution's frame."[4] In effect, national identity and the Constitution are locked together precisely because the text's writing and ratification are the constituent acts of American exceptionalism, embodying in the moment of founding both the collective break from absolutist Europe and the specifically American ideal of self-making.

If this romance of American exceptionalism continues to have a powerful hold on the collective imagination, it comes with significant costs. To begin with, to the extent that one finds a historical record riddled with inegalitarian and illiberal features, the exceptionalist tendency is to view these features as aberrational. Gunnar Myrdal declared in the 1940s that the country had only partially achieved its ideals, but posited that "the main trend" in American "history" was "the gradual realization of the American creed."[5] But the problem with reading the collective past in these terms is that it seeks to keep the American promise distinct from and uncontaminated by practices of subordination. For many citizens, systems of exclusion did not compromise basic values but were, in fact, the very method by which one expressed and lived national principles. If anything, instead of separate and competing currents, beliefs that the United States was a special site of possibility often gained strength and meaning precisely through hierarchical frameworks. And such rhetoric, perhaps above all, worked to occlude from view persistent structures of unfreedom, which—although real—failed to resonate with collective self-perception. As the theorist George Shulman writes, "by abstracting an ideal or dream nation from actual life in an unequal, divided society,"[6] these exceptionalist frames have long participated in sustaining "regressive forms of self-denial or willful blindness."[7]

The deep psychic linkage between the Constitution and ideas of special destiny raises a real question for reformers suspicious of exceptionalism's cultural and political function. How should one orient oneself to the text without unwittingly falling into the dark side of nationalist discourse? This is a question that—despite all the ink spilled over the document—appears with little frequency in American constitutional debate today. In large part this is because of an unspoken but powerful sentiment, standing in the background of the arguments above from Sunstein and Tribe. Regardless of historical accuracy or potential downsides, so the argument goes, left-liberal reformers have no choice but to embrace the romance of national destiny, given its discursive hold on American consciousness. As Richard Rorty proclaimed fifteen years ago, the only way "to mobiliz[e] Americans as political agents" is to "share in a national hope" of exceptionalism.[8] To deny such national pride is to court marginality and to veer between "self-disgust" and "self-mockery."[9] Thus, one can either embrace reformist politics, by accepting exceptionalism along with the symbolic function of the Constitution, or retreat into defeatism and irrelevancy.

And yet a hundred years ago, these same worries about exceptionalist rhetoric lay at the heart of many of the debates about constitutional interpretation and even the text's basic legitimacy. Key reformers during the Progressive period, the very figures Rorty imagines as exemplars of a "good" left, focused especially on breaking collective assumptions about unique national destiny. In particular, a crucial strain of Progressive constitutional critique, especially from a social democratic perspective, worried about how the Constitution and the initial act of framing were commonly invoked to create a false political image of class harmony and to press against efforts by democratic majorities to confront oppressive economic relations. They saw the Constitution's primary cultural purpose as preserving a Tocquevillian narrative of individualism and boundless social mobility, one that represented social reality less and less and served instead as a counterproductive political myth.

In response, these critics presented two distinct views of how Americans should relate to the Constitution and, through it, to exceptionalist narratives. On one hand, external critics such as American socialists maintained that at the end of the day, the Constitution was inherently ill equipped to serve as the basis of a just society. The document had to be systematically rewritten—and if need be formally replaced through a second convention—to the extent that it would no longer be textually recognizable as the 1787 Constitution. For these critics, the existing text was too overlaid with particular cultural meanings and structural democratic limitations. Even if judicially reinterpreted to take account of prevailing conditions, or marginally improved through isolated amendments, the Constitution nonetheless sustained a prophetic vision of American politics in which the country was on an ineluctable path to fulfilling its classless essence. As a consequence, socialists worried that finding the 1787 document to be consistent with small-scale ameliorative reforms would only reinforce driving national narratives and in the long run constrain more meaningful shifts.

On the other hand, internal critics—like the seminal historian Charles Beard—believed that even revolutionary transformation could take place without formal changes to the Constitution. These critics argued that the written text need not be thought of as a constraint and that in fact extensive reform could be pursued by simply reimagining existing constitutional interpretations and traditions. For those like Beard, the Constitution in practice was fundamentally open-ended and therefore could be reconstructed to mean whatever social movements wanted the text to mean. By rereading the document to serve popular ends, citizens could empty it of any troubling symbolic power. In effect, the problem of the Constitution's linkage with claims about exceptionalism was therefore not a problem of the Constitution per se, but instead of what Beard called the "cult of certitude" that surrounded it. As a result, these internal critics saw no basic reason to call for extensive formal revisions, since the document had little fixed content. As long as one maintained an emotional distance from the text, and did not invest it with inherent value, the Constitution in practice could be a malleable tool of social change without reinforcing nationalist fantasies.

What returning to both views highlights is the falseness of the choice offered by Rorty. Each mode of critique—internal and external—held firm to a political vision of equal and effective freedom, especially in the context of structural class hierarchies. And each mode saw this vision, although not distinctively "American," as a powerful discursive basis for organizing ordinary citizens to improve their collective lot. Moreover, such critics remained optimistic about the possibility of social change without accepting notions of national fulfillment or destiny. In other words, these voices of the Left charted a path between narratives of exceptionalism and of fatalism and thereby provided both a politics of reform and a critical method for interrogating the legitimacy of existing practices. Thus, returning to their arguments offers a useful tool in the present for thinking politically about the role of the Constitution in public life.

In section two, I begin by recovering the basic social democratic critique of the Constitution during the Progressive era, especially in the context of worries about the incompatibility between Tocquevillian myths and industrial realities. In sections three and four, I work through the political disagreement among Progressives over whether citizens needed to engage in a formal act of wholesale textual revision and even refounding. Both sides agreed that the 1787 framework had to be fundamentally altered, but internal and external critics reached different conclusions about whether change could be achieved without explicit rupture and whether surface constitutional fidelity would necessarily reproduce exceptionalist tropes. Finally, by way of a conclusion, I focus on lessons for the present—especially on how Progressive-era critics press Americans to disenthrall themselves and to conceive of the Constitution instrumentally, to judge questions of constitutional support not by expectations of national fulfillment or on aspirational desires for the text, but instead by debates over political utility and effective freedom.

The Progressive Attack on the Constitution

In the early twentieth century, Americans confronted a dramatic new economic landscape, one marked by heightened bureaucracy, corporate concentration, and wild cycles of booms and busts.[10] These developments produced a highly inegalitarian society: by 1890, 51 percent of all property was held by the top 1 percent, and 88 percent of the population controlled just 14 percent of the wealth.[11] Making matters worse, the industrialization of the economy went hand in hand with the increasing interpenetration of political decision making by corporate interests. At virtually every level of government during what came to be called the Gilded Age, giant corporations wielded influence over politicians from both major parties; railroad companies and industrial magnates enjoyed particular access and privilege.[12]

For reformers and intellectuals, these features of collective life made apparent an undeniable fact: industrialization had generated social problems of wage labor and destitution in the United States fundamentally analogous to those in Europe. These hard truths cut against a deeply embedded element of American self-conception, namely, the idea that the country was free and equal, at least in class terms, to a degree yet unknown in human history. As Herbert Croly, cofounder of the *New Republic* and a key intellectual figure behind Theodore Roosevelt's 1912 presidential campaign, wrote of the classic national script, "The American pioneer or territorial democrats were, according to their own lights, freemen in both the economic and political sense."[13] But the closing of the frontier and, above all, the power of corporate capital had "converted" Americans from "freehold[ers]" into increasingly regimented and impoverished industrial employees.[14] In Croly's view, the nation's basic predicament was, "How can the wage-earners obtain an amount or a degree of economic independence analogous to that upon which the pioneer democrat could count?"[15]

Croly was hardly alone in highlighting the decline of exceptionalism as a plausible account of collective life. The pages of the *American Journal of Sociology* took as axiomatic that European-style class divisions were growing in America, and debated whether a deepening class war had become "inevitable."[16] Progressive historians such as Charles and Mary Beard went further and challenged whether exceptionalist premises, and especially the idea of a special American destiny, had ever made sense as an account of the collective past. Rather than embodying an advance for the Enlightenment or a genuinely new phenomenon based on Hamiltonian "reflection and choice," the national experience, they argued, formed "merely one phase in the long and restless movement of mankind on the surface of the earth."[17]

Fostering such views was a "transatlantic moment" of political and scholarly exchange, one that led reformers on both sides of the ocean to understand themselves as bound by similar conditions, challenges, and political goals.[18] This sense of a shared project highlighted the importance to American activists of adapting European innovations—including labor laws, social welfare measures, proportional representation, and parliamentary structures—in order to confront industrial strife and thus make governing institutions both more democratic and less anachronistic. According to reformers, if European social democrats had begun imagining ways to combine modern industrial realities with economic and political freedom, it was incumbent on Americans as well to experiment with institutional forms and existing structures.

Standing in the way, however, was the constitutional order. The text, and the discursive traditions that had emerged in the century since its ratification, systematically thwarted Progressive ambitions by dividing legislative authority and empowering a business-run federal judiciary. Even worse, the Constitution embodied the preeminent symbol of American exceptionalism, promoting a public discourse that often depicted necessary reform as disloyal for violating a unique national heritage of individualism and market self-regulation. At the center of this discourse were what the Progressive journalist Norman Hapgood derisively called the "Professional Patriots," groups—like the American Bar Association, chambers of commerce, and Rotary and Kiwanis clubs—committed to "defending the existing property and political system without change."[19] These legal and corporate bodies poured money and political energy into vigorous educational campaigns that proclaimed the supposed perfection of the text and the genius of the Founders, all with the aim of deploying the Constitution's full symbolic power to check popular discontent and to preserve the status quo.[20]

Thus, for many Progressives, industrial realities underscored not only the need for basic structural reform but also the importance of systematically disabusing Americans of their emotional bonds with the Framers and the 1787 text. As Croly concluded, the greatest inhibition to change was not the judiciary or a specific institutional structure, but Americans' lingering loyalty to the Constitution as it was. In his view, such loyalty had to be repudiated because by "consecrat[ing] one particular machinery of possible righteous expression," the ideology of constitutional perfection had transformed "reverence for order" into a destructive "reverence for an established order."[21]

This desire to disenthrall Americans and thereby open discursive space for wide-ranging reform generated countless muckraking exposés and historical works highlighting the democratic weaknesses of the existing constitutional system.[22] It also helps explain why so much of the writing assessed present-day constitutional failures by revisiting the text's framing and ratification. By dramatizing the problematic genesis of the Constitution and by depicting the Framers as flawed and self-interested, critics emphasized the unavoidable similarities between the American experience and feudal Europe. In effect, just as social democrats on the Continent sought to break free from class binds, Americans too needed to recognize the class-based nature of their own politics and thus the critical importance of democratic experimentation and legal change.

For Beard, whose approach became the "generally accepted view of the founding"[23] among Progressive intellectuals, the hidden key to unlocking the real nature of the Constitution lay with James Madison's *Federalists* 10 and 51.[24] Reading these documents together spoke to the Framers' very particular account of the problem of arbitrary power. According to the Framers, the major causes of potential despotism came from two principal sources: governmental officials and "an interested and overbearing majority"[25] (those ordinary citizens with little or no property). What Madison and others very consciously ignored was a third source: the destructive role that socioeconomic elites could play in political life.

According to *Federalist* 51, a key purpose of constitutional construction was to constrain the ability of officeholders to claim absolutist authority, as in monarchical Europe, by dividing and limiting governmental power itself. For Madison, the most dangerous potential branch was the legislative. Thus, ensuring that officeholders did not wield power unjustly above all meant avoiding legislative supremacy: "The remedy . . . is to divide the legislature into different branches; and to render them, by different modes of election and different principles of action, as little connected with each other as the nature of their common functions and their common dependence on the society will admit."[26]

Beard argued that one could fully understand why Madison believed that legislatures were the most dangerous branch only by reading these structural suggestions against the backdrop of arguments in *Federalist* 10 about factionalism.

Beard noted that when the Framers focused on the sources within society that promoted the rise of despotism, they overwhelmingly emphasized worries about self-interested majorities—especially how poorer citizens could use strong legislatures to undermine property rights. As a consequence, the Constitution was most directly designed to address dangers to republican order by public officials exercising power on behalf of the less affluent. And the Framers pursued these ends by insulating political decision making, to the greatest extent possible, from common citizens.

The deeper implication was that the 1787 structure—precisely because it viewed poor majorities as the root cause of instability and tyranny—did very little institutionally to restrain the capacity of wealthy citizens to use their economic power to overrun the political process. In the words of the English Fabians Sidney and Beatrice Webb, "The framers of the United States Constitution . . . saw no resemblance or analogy between the personal power which they drove from the castle, the altar and the throne, and that which they left unchecked in the farm, the factory and the mine."[27] Indeed, the very effect of the Framers' structure of divided government was that it allowed socioeconomic elites to dominate quietly the instruments of statecraft while making it very difficult for poor citizens—whose only meaningful resource was sheer numbers—to use elections and mass pressure to overcome the variety of veto points embedded in political decision making. The result was that despite the text's invocation of a democratic "We the People," the constitutional system facilitated rule by what Charles Edward Russell, journalist and cofounder of the National Association for the Advancement of Colored People (NAACP), called the "Invisible Government"[28] of class elites.

For this strain of Progressivism, it was not simply an oversight that explained why the Framers' Constitution constrained the political power of governmental officials and poor majorities while providing no vigorous controls for dominant socioeconomic groups. The Framers themselves came from elite class backgrounds and therefore associated tyranny primarily with those forces that threatened their positions. As Beard wrote, "The wealth, the influence, and a major portion of the educated men of the country were drawn together in a compact group, 'informed by a conscious solidarity of interests,' as President Wilson has so tersely put it."[29] This shared socioeconomic sensibility spoke to why the Framers were so deeply committed to entrenching within the new federal structure classically aristocratic institutions such as the Senate. As Madison and others well knew, from ancient Rome to Renaissance Florence, senatorial frameworks and upper houses provided a key space for wealthy citizens to shape political life. This meant that, as William Allen White concluded, the failure of the Constitution in practice to constrain socio-economic elites was no failure at all, but the basic impulse animating the Framers' text:

> It seems necessary to inquire if this capture of the Constitution by our only aristocracy—that of wealth—was not in truth merely a recapture of what was intended in the beginning by the Fathers to belong to the minority. The checks and balances put in that Constitution to guard against the rule of the majority protected slavery for fifty years, and perhaps they bound the nation to the rule of the privileged classes in the Nineties. Perhaps these same checks and balances were put into the Constitution deliberately—the judiciary which annuls statutes and remakes laws, the rigidity of the fundamental law to amendment, the remoteness of the Senators from popular election and control.[30]

These Progressives hoped that making evident this hidden history would help citizens appreciate how, despite the constitutional panegyrics of legal and business elites, no country including the United States had been—let alone remained—free of class hierarchy and elite control. In the process, ordinary Americans would see through those myths of exceptionalism and constitutional perfection that sustained prevailing arrangements; they would recognize the basic incompatibility between the 1787 text and their own collective hopes for a democratic industrial order. Above all, by creating emotional distance between Americans and the great symbols of nationhood—the Constitution chief among them—citizens would develop a much more instrumental relationship to prevailing institutions. Rather than gifts from mythic Founders, highlighting a national destiny, these institutions would be viewed as just one among many possibilities whose necessity and legitimacy were hardly given.

Class Deference and Socialist Constitutional Opposition

This mode of Progressive criticism essentially took for granted that the prevailing constitutional order had to be fundamentally reconstructed for a new political age. Thus, critics disagreed among themselves not about whether but rather how to change the Constitution. Over time, internal critics came to argue that one could simply reinterpret the text to mean whatever democratically mobilized social movements commanded. In other words, constitutional actors, through a process of revolutionary reformism, could improvise and entrench a new governing order without formally and systematically rewriting the text. As this section explores, external critics, especially in the Socialist Party, remained suspicious of whether such transformative change was possible without a conscious break in the public's identification with the Constitution, embodied through a new convention or large-scale amendment revisions. They argued that the combination of the text's hardwired features and its preservationist symbolic role in public culture would in the final analysis inhibit revolutionary reform.

It is worthwhile to appreciate the sheer intensity of calls to formally alter the language of the Constitution at the beginning of the twentieth century. As the sociologist Amy Myrick notes, between 1899 and 1925 a remarkable 1,004 separate amendment proposals were introduced in Congress.[31] Just as telling, for a text notoriously difficult to change through the Article V process, four amendments were implemented in a seven-year period, affecting some of the most contentious issues of the day—taxation, the direct election of senators, Prohibition, and women's suffrage. Much to the chagrin of conservative business and judicial elites, institutional experimentalism and "Constitution tinkering"[32] were the order of the day.

In fact, calls for change were so widespread that real political pressure existed to convene a convention to write a new document—something that today would be nearly unimaginable. Walter Clark, the Populist chief justice of the North Carolina Supreme Court and one of the state's most well respected politicians, wrote repeatedly about his hopes and suggestions for "The Next Constitutional Convention."[33] Between 1893 and 1911, thirty-one states passed seventy-three petitions demanding a convention to propose an amendment for the direct election of senators. And depending on how one counted the petitions, this number was either one short or exactly the two-thirds necessary under Article V to trigger one. Even more telling, over a dozen of these applications were part of general convention requests issuing from the states to revise root and branch the existing text.[34] In fact, only after the successful passage of the Sixteenth and Seventeenth Amendments, providing for a national income tax and direct senatorial election, did momentum for a new convention begin to stall.

It was against this backdrop of significant amendment and convention activism that the Socialist Party of America, more than any other group, came to stand for the call for explicit constitutional rupture. For the first three decades of the century—the entire life of the Socialist Party as a serious electoral power[35]—its national platform included proposals for dramatic formal changes to the Constitution aimed at producing a system more in line with the mass democracies and parliamentary modes emerging in Europe. The 1912 platform included "political demands" for "proportional representation, nationally as well as locally," "the abolition of the Senate and of the veto power of the President," "the election of the President and Vice-President by direct vote," "the abolition of the power usurped by the Supreme Court of the United States to pass upon the constitutionality of . . . legislation enacted by Congress," "national laws to be repealed only by act of Congress or by a referendum vote of the whole people," "abolition of the present restrictions upon the amendment of the constitution, so that instrument may be amenable by a majority of the votes in a majority of the States," "the granting of the right to suffrage in the District of Columbia with representation in Congress and a democratic form of municipal government," "unrestricted and equal suffrage for men and women," "the election of all judges for short terms," and, finally, "the calling of a convention for the revision of the constitution of the United States."[36]

To underscore the seriousness of these commitments, when the Wisconsin Socialist Victor Berger was first elected to Congress in 1910, he focused especially on constitutional reforms, introducing a resolution calling for the abolition of the Senate despite threats of censure from conservative representatives. Berger described the upper house as an "obstructive and useless body, a menace to the liberties of the people"; he declared that "the Senate has run its course" and like "the British House of Lords" must "yield" to principles of democratic self-government.[37] As a further indication of constitutional seriousness, the party's presidential nominee in 1916 was Allan Benson, who before then was principally known to the public as the muckraking author of *Our Dishonest Constitution* (1914).

These Socialists took as given that for the United States to become a cooperative commonwealth, the Constitution would have to be systematically rewritten. At a basic level, this required eliminating certain hardwired features of the 1787 text, such as the Senate, which they saw as inherently undemocratic and standing in theory and practice for rule by the few. But perhaps more critically, Socialist opposition to the Framers' document was not solely a matter of particular institutions. In their view, not only did the text need to be overhauled, but the *way* that Americans imagined what defined a constitution also had to shift. Whereas the Framers had conceived of a relatively short document, one that laid out universal principles and was institutionally insulated from ordinary political contestation, Socialists embraced a very different theory of design. For them, the key constitutional mechanism was a much easier amendment process, something that became a persistent party platform demand between 1908 and 1936.[38] This change was meant to bridge the chasm between higher and ordinary lawmaking, making constitutional and legislative practice far more equivalent. Armed with a flexible amendment structure, the text could be negotiated and renegotiated easily in response to immediate popular needs; in addition, it would include detailed policy goals and extensive provisions for positive rights.

This basic vision meant that Progressive-era Socialists were deeply concerned about the long-term implications of one-off amendment success in a context divorced from any systematic textual overhaul. Berger, Benson, and others were not necessarily opposed to amendments, and generally supported individual reform initiatives such as women's suffrage or a graduated income tax. But they viewed amendments as an alternative method to an actual convention for packaging demands together in a way that reconceived constitutional design and in practice generated an explicit rupture with the Framers' Constitution. In other words, rather than perfecting the existing legal order, they approached the amendment process as a path toward writing a wholly different Constitution, one that no longer would be recognizable as the 1787 text. Because of this, Socialists worried that occasional changes would only deepen veneration for the prevailing constitutional regime. As underscored by the decline of interest in a new convention following the passage of the Sixteenth and Seventeenth Amendments, such reforms would convince citizens that no truly significant alterations to institutional structure or design were necessary. One-off successes would operate to transform social critique into what the theorist Sacvan Bercovitch decades later called cultural "rites of assent,"[39] in which the successful achievement of even minor reform helps preserve the national self-image of a country truly defined by free and equal conditions. Without uprooting prevailing socioeconomic hierarchies, the Constitution's seeming adaptability would nonetheless reinforce the thought that whatever the problems in the present, conditions in the future inevitably would be better.

For this reason, Socialists believed that it was essential to maintain a posture of frontal opposition to the existing constitutional system, irrespective of shifts in judicial interpretation or new amendments. In their view, opposition was part of a general strategy of heightening class consciousness and of creating a laboring community suspicious of all status hierarchies. Socialists maintained that the best method for controlling, in the here and now, socioeconomic elites came from robust and healthy class contestation. Above all, this meant that poorer citizens had to resist the temptation to fall prey to the belief that powerful co-nationals shared their interests, an error that too often resulted in the related tendency to defer to elite authority. As Charles Edward Russell stated, "So long as it [the laboring community] deludes itself into the belief that it can trust anybody outside of its own class it will thus be tricked fooled and defeated."[40] The Constitution, especially its invocation in public discourse as proof of basic American social equality, stood out for Socialists as a key source of the persistence of such deference. The idea of the Constitution embodying both the will of the people and thus a special and shared national destiny was routinely employed by business groups and legal elites to inhibit class consciousness and to promote nationalist attachments.

For Socialists, this spoke to why even poor wage earners were often willing to accept governmental actions that in fact contradicted their specific interests—like brutal crackdowns on striking workers or military adventurism abroad. Trying to make sense of the continuing "attitude of unquestioned admiration for the state and society,"[41] the editors of the *International Socialist Review* republished translations of large portions of the German sociologist Werner Sombart's work on class consciousness in America. According to Sombart, the idea embedded in the Constitution and "drilled into the American worker from childhood" that "the sovereign people alone decide what shall be legal in the realm of the American union"[42] had a profound popular effect. It meant that the citizen "look[ed] upon the government of his country as a sort of divine institution, . . . which he honors with faithful respect."[43] Moreover, ordinary Americans intuitively took for granted that governmental policy was his or her own, even when it actually derived from dominant socioeconomic interests; "however . . . imaginary it may really be," the assumption that in the United States the sovereign people ruled instilled "in each individual a boundless feeling of power."[44]

Thus, Socialists saw their arguments against the Constitution as having more at stake than simply matters of ideal institutional design. Although recognizing that actual refounding or wholesale textual revision might not occur in the short or medium term, they nonetheless hoped that their positions would foster within citizens an oppositional relationship toward government and corporate power. Such a relationship would sustain a climate of reformist energy by stripping away class deference and presenting laborers with the fighting ideal of another political order. As a consequence, these Socialists were especially skeptical of reformers who deemphasized textual rupture and rejectionism, due to the worry that Americans would read adaptation as proof of the basic legitimacy of the existing institutions. In their view, the belief that revolutionary reform was possible with only minor textual shifts—or even without any formal revision—would have the long-run effect of protecting exceptionalist premises and undermining class contestation.

Beard's Living Constitution and Separating Symbol from Reality

Internal critics, by contrast, maintained that the type of oppositional identity that Socialists sought did not require formally repudiating the Constitution, through either actual refounding or wholesale structural revision. In practice, one could achieve nearly all desired policy reforms and democratic changes while superficially holding on to the 1787 text. This was because, for the most radical internal critics, the document had minimal intrinsic meaning other than that imposed by popular constituencies at particular historical moments. Therefore, as long as Americans recognized the text's open-endedness and drained the Constitution of substantive value, they could both pursue revolutionary reform and avoid reinscribing mythic narratives of founding and exceptionalism. In this way, citizens could transform the Constitution from a deified embodiment of national promise into one among many pliable instruments for social improvement. The result would combine surface fidelity to the text with a disenthralled relationship to it. This section explores such Progressive views by focusing especially on Charles Beard's notion of the "living Constitution."

To begin with, Beard—himself a fellow traveler within socialist circles—read the Constitution far less formalistically than Berger and Benson did. According to him, their focus on the seemingly hardwired elements of the text ignored the extent to which everything in the Constitution, including its basic theory of design, was at the end of the day implemented by popular and collective action. As Beard reminded Americans, there was nothing talismanic about the text: "The words and phrases cannot rise out of the Constitution and interpret themselves. Some human being, with all the parts and passions of such a creature, must undertake the task of giving them meaning in subsidiary laws and practices."[45] In other words, no matter what the Constitution says, even the most textually strict language required interpretation by citizens—citizens who therefore held within them the power to reread the meaning of the text to suit their purposes.

Moreover, the Constitution invited just such interpretation because so much of the text's language was unavoidably indeterminate, a collection of "vague words" and "ambiguous expressions."[46] Beard wrote that this ambiguity cloaked constitutional meaning in "huge shadow[s] in which the good and wise can wander indefinitely without ever coming to any agreement respecting the command made by the 'law.' "[47] The ultimate implication was that the Constitution was a "living thing"[48] with little definite content; it was the product primarily of what workable democratic majorities on the ground could impose through political action: "The Constitution . . . is what living men and women think it is, recognize as such, carry into action, and obey. It is just that."[49]

Given this view of the text, Beard's larger concern with external criticism was that it inadvertently undermined precisely those reformist ends that the Socialist Party sought to champion. First, it demeaned rather than heightened the self-assertiveness of mobilized constituencies by viewing workers as the passive subjects of the Constitution. In Beard's view, external criticism tended to regard the text as an animate entity, wielding power over ordinary citizens (as in Werner Sombart's explanation of class deference), when instead the Constitution was a creation of active and ongoing agency and so was open to limitless change. Most telling, precisely because of the small likelihood of wholesale revision, let alone a second convention, the practical consequence of viewing the text as having strong hardwired effects was to reinforce the conservative status quo. Since extensive formal change was largely off the table, the Socialists' focus on fixity in effect reaffirmed the legal formalism, and preservationist politics, of their corporate enemies. As the Progressive magazine *Outlook* remarked, Socialist arguments unwittingly helped cement discursively the regressive notion that the Constitution entailed "a series of cast-iron rules"[50] derived from mythic Founders. Socialists may have coded the text and the 1787 Framers in negative terms, but they too read the existing document as having only one true meaning for most issues of public import and as essentially lying outside the bounds of popular contestation. According to *Outlook*'s editors, "The reactionary and the Socialist agree in their interpretation of the Constitution. Extremes meet."[51] And to further highlight that apparent agreement, Socialist formalism—like its conservative counterpart—deemphasized the most popularly accessible method of change in the here and now: ongoing textual reinterpretation by social movements, politicians, and lawyers.

Crucially, for Beard, it was not only pragmatic concerns that led him to embrace internal criticism and its antiformalist posture. No fan of exceptionalism, Beard believed that one could reject counterproductive myths of social mobility and class harmony while superficially accepting the 1787 text. In particular, reading the Constitution as essentially indeterminate allowed one to strip the document of its dominant cultural valences. Unlike the professional patriots in the ABA, with their "cult of constitutional certitude,"[52] understanding the Constitution as no less and no more than what Americans accepted entailed denying the text any privileged status. Rather than "a 'sheet anchor,' a 'lighthouse,' an 'ark of the covenant,' a 'beacon,' and a 'fundamental law,'"[53] the Constitution was simply a collection of good and bad legal and political practices. Beard wrote, "These symbols are supposed to represent some reality, something tangible, a substance which all good and wise men can see and agree upon. Yet in truth they are mere poetic images that correspond to no reality at all, and the employment of them is sheer animism."[54]

By regarding the Constitution as devoid of telos or inherent goodness, Beard believed that he could sever whatever destructive function the text played in nationalist mythmaking: "If the Constitution is a sheet anchor, then it may be 'lost.' If it is a lighthouse, then a storm may bring destruction. If it is an ark of the covenant, the wicked may steal it away. A beacon can be 'extinguished.'"[55] But if, on the other hand, the Constitution was understood as none of these things—simply as a practice fungible for countless innocent or wicked purposes—then the document could move wherever popular social movements took it. Even without the formal changes demanded by the Socialist Party, the Constitution in practice could still be a site of ongoing democratic energy and participatory involvement. In this way, Beard hoped to combine two seemingly contradictory impulses: citizens would participate in superficial practices of fidelity while nonetheless denying the Constitution any idealized or meaningful psychic loyalty. In effect, such an approach would foster within Americans a productive ambivalence toward the text, creating the type of affective distance that focused political energy on democratic experimentation without collapsing back into preservationism or prideful nationalist fantasies.

Conclusion: Progressive Lessons for an Enchanted Age

In recent years, especially in the wake of the financial crisis, much has been made of the parallelism between the early twenty-first century and the early twentieth; as Lawrence Lessig writes, "We were here at least once before."[56] Just as a hundred years ago the country struggled through the Gilded Age of corporate power, corruption, and striking economic inequality, so too do many Americans worry that we are now living through a second Gilded Age marked by dysfunctional political institutions and deepening class divides. Given such concerns, what can Progressive critiques offer current reformers thinking about the Constitution?

A striking feature of the contemporary climate is the extent to which this strain of Progressive thought, with its disenchanted relationship both to the Constitution and to intertwined myths of exceptionalism, has receded from public conversation. For instance, although there are a few notable constitutional opponents in the academy,[57] there exist no mobilized political blocs frontally rejecting the document or calling for systematic revision, as was the case a century ago. Precisely why such Progressive-era critiques declined so dramatically is of course a complicated matter.[58] They began to collapse with the New Deal's victory over Supreme Court intransigence, and especially with U.S. entry into World War II. In justifying American involvement in the war effort, New Dealers focused on the perceived cultural and political differences between the United States and the country's collectivist or totalitarian foes. In particular, policy makers rallied around the claim that the United States had been defined from the founding by neither race nor religion, but rather by a creedal faith in fundamental rights, the rule of law, and basic equality— Enlightenment principles that, they argued, made the country the first truly universal nation. As concrete proof of these inherent commitments, and thus of the war effort's moral rectitude, these New Dealers turned to the specific language of the Constitution, rediscovering the document's Bill of Rights and to a lesser extent the Fourteenth Amendment's Equal Protection Clause. In the process, such voices very consciously deemphasized their doubts about the legitimacy of the Constitution's governance structures and instead embraced an account of American identity that placed constitutional reverence at the forefront.

And in the years after World War II, this liberal identification with the Constitution became ever more widespread. The decision in *Brown v. Board of Education,* combined with political aversion to the excesses of McCarthyism, led many Cold War–era liberals to see the document as doing more than simply facilitating much-needed racial and economic reform. According to growing numbers of commentators, academics, and politicians, it promoted a civic culture that valued moderation and reasoned debate and thus charted a path between fascist and communist extremism. The result was a remarkable shift in the politics of American constitutionalism. In the matter of just over a generation, the Constitution, which had faced extensive center-left skepticism well into the 1930s, became an affirmative site of patriotic attachment for most mainstream liberal constituencies—constituencies that were key inheritors of the New Deal.

This means that today's constitutional imagination is far more resonant with the country's Cold War frameworks than it is with earlier Progressive arguments. Not unlike the 1950s consensus attitude, present-day liberals and conservatives both overwhelmingly embrace visions of constitutional meaning and interpretation that inscribe within the text aspirational narratives of fulfillment. Indeed, we essentially have an enchanted version of the old debate between formalists and antiformalists. On the one hand, conservative formalists imagine a relatively fixed text, but like their ABA predecessors during the Gilded Age and unlike Socialists, they code this text in highly salutary terms as expressing a special national character, akin to that "sheet anchor" always in danger of being "lost" through destructive change.[59] On the other hand, liberal antiformalists follow Beard in imagining a living Constitution of infinite flexibility, but unlike him, they mostly see such change as proof of the country's capacity to achieve a historic promise—one present since the founding.[60] But whether liberal or conservative, all sides seem to repeat Gunnar Myrdal's midcentury contention that the Constitution and the American creed are one and the same, and that through the text "the nation early laid down as the moral basis for its existence the principles of liberty and equality."[61]

Therefore, more than anything else, returning to Progressive claims helps us recognize the real limitations of this prevailing sensibility. To begin with, it highlights the remarkably constrained vision that marks so much of contemporary American constitutional discourse, one that takes for granted that any constitutional order must carry with it the Framers' emphasis on a marked divide between higher and ordinary law. In contrast with the Madisonian focus on insulation from popular politics, key Progressive-era reformers experimented with antithetical design principles aimed at facilitating easy and continual political renegotiation. And as the legal scholars Mila Versteeg and Emily Zackin demonstrate, a Progressive approach—emphasizing participatory involvement and democratic responsiveness—in fact has won the day as a matter of general global practice. Not only is the idea of a flexible, participatory, and elaborate constitutional document by and large how American state constitutions operate, world constitutions today also tend to be far less "entrench[ed]" than our 1787 model and to embrace relatively simple amendment processes as well as detailed rights and policy provisions.[62]

But even beyond matters of constitutional design, revisiting Progressive-era arguments underscores how radical critiques of both exceptionalism and constitutional legitimacy played a central role in fostering a political climate open in fundamental ways to revolutionary reform. At present, commentators— whether liberal or conservative—overwhelmingly share a specific vision of politics in which reformers must maintain unconditional attachment to the Constitution and to the key symbols of American nationhood; in the process, they must also operate in line with politically realizable, though narrow, reform agendas. What this perspective misses is the deeply interconnected relationship in American history—as highlighted by the Progressive period—between even limited reformist achievements and the threat of more revolutionary politics.

One need look only at the amendment victories between 1913 and 1920 to appreciate this fact. On the one hand, these victories can be read negatively, as Socialists often did: changes that promoted the overall commitment to "Constitution tinkering." Indeed, essential as Progressive-era amendments have been—the right of women to vote, most obviously—one may well wonder whether the amendments nonetheless played a not insignificant role in sustaining constitutional faith and thus helping foster today's preservationist and reverential climate. On the other hand, one could conclude that even these reforms—not to mention later New Deal–era shifts in judicial interpretation— were possible only because of a radical political climate of constitutional critique. The direct election of senators offers but one clear example. Whether or not moderate politicians at the time wanted to admit it, the real and growing threat of a second constitutional convention affected how elected officials viewed the practical consequences of continuing to block such amendment proposals.

In other words, key reforms during the Progressive period, however constrained, were able to gain widespread institutional support precisely because these goals appeared moderate against the backdrop of politically relevant and more transformative alternatives. Although this may not have been the conscious desire of internal and external critics of the Constitution, the existence of a vibrant radical discourse gave strength generally to reformers' ambitions. Indeed, the very absence today of either internal or external modes of critique has come at a profound cost to reformist politics. It is not a coincidence that our current climate of constitutional reverence goes hand in hand with conservative legal and political ascendancy. There are of course many reasons for the steady decline of left-liberal constitutional projects, but I would argue that the disappearance of a politically robust and radically disenthralled approach to the Constitution has removed—perhaps counterintuitively—a critical pillar of support for even limited and constitutionally respectful changes.

All this suggests that whatever the disagreements between Progressive-era internal and external critics over how formalistically to read the Constitution, there is a clear space and need for full-throated accounts of both in today's public square. These critics remind us that the politics of generating dissent often rests just as much on practices of ambivalence, disavowal, or even outright rejection as it does on those of aspiration and fulfillment. Especially in contexts marked by systematic and structural oppression, the very possibility of meaningful change may require being willing to sever one's ties with the great symbols of nationhood. In such circumstances, to embrace an account of national self-becoming may well embody a powerful psychic means of accommodating oneself to existing conditions. For both Beard and those in the Socialist Party, revolutionary reform was thus sustained—above all—by an oppositional political identity. But if *all* the relevant reform and constitutional discourses today persist in viewing the country as defined more by what it will be than by what it is in the present, one can well ask what becomes of this necessary defiance and opposition.

Notes

1. Alexis de Tocqueville, *Democracy in America*, ed. J. P. Mayer, trans. George Lawrence (New York: Doubleday, 1969), 455.

2. Cass Sunstein, "The Real Meaning of American Exceptionalism," *Bloomberg*, September 23, 2013, www.bloomberg.com/news/2013–09–23/the-real-meaning-of-american-exceptionalism.html.

3. Ibid.

4. Laurence Tribe, "America's Constitutional Narrative," *Daedalus* 141 (2012): 18–42, quotation on 23.

5. Gunner Myrdal, *An American Dilemma: The Negro Problem and Modern Democracy* (New York: Harper & Row, 1944), 2:1021.

6. George Shulman, "Hope and American Politics," *Raritan* 21 (2002): 1–19, quotation on 17.

7. Ibid., 18.

8. Richard Rorty, *Achieving Our Country: Leftist Thought in Twentieth-Century America* (Cambridge, Mass.: Harvard University Press, 1998), 8.

9. Ibid., 6.

10. See Walter Licht, *Industrializing America: The Nineteenth Century* (Baltimore: Johns Hopkins University Press, 1995), 183.

11. Ibid.

12. See Aziz Rana, *The Two Faces of American Freedom* (Cambridge, Mass.: Harvard University Press, 2010), 185. See generally Alan Trachtenberg, *The Incorporation of*

America: Culture and Society in the Gilded Age (New York: Hill and Wang, 2007); Jack Beatty, *Age of Betrayal: The Triumph of Money in America* (New York: Vintage, 2008).

13. Herbert Croly, *Progressive Democracy* (New York: Macmillan, 1914), 379.

14. Ibid., 380.

15. Ibid. For more on Croly's concerns about the impact of industrialization on class equality, see Rana, *Two Faces*, 242–43.

16. See, for example, the roundtable discussion "Is Class Conflict in America Growing and Is It Inevitable?," *American Journal of Sociology* 13 (1908): 756–83. It includes an introductory piece by John Commons; responses from Graham Taylor, Jane Addams, Alvin Johnson, Henry Raymond Mussey, Robert Hoxie, and C. P. Gilman; and a final reply from Commons.

17. Charles Beard and Mary Beard, *The Rise of American Civilization*, rev. ed. (New York: Macmillan Co., 1964), 3; also quoted in Daniel Rodgers, "Exceptionalism," in *Imagined Histories: American Historians Interpret the Past*, ed. Anthony Molho and Gordon S. Wood (Princeton, N.J.: Princeton University Press, 1998), 21–40, 26.

18. See especially Daniel Rodgers, *Atlantic Crossings: Social Politics in a Progressive Age* (Cambridge, Mass.: Belknap, 1998), and James Kloppenberg, *Uncertain Victory: Social Democracy and Progressivism in European and American Thought, 1870–1920* (New York: Oxford University Press, 1986).

19. See Norman Hapgood, *Professional Patriots* (New York: Boni, 1927), 8.

20. For a very helpful account of the politics of constitutional veneration in the early twentieth century, see Michael Kammen, *A Machine That Would Go of Itself: The Constitution in American Culture* (New York: Knopf, 1986), 219–35.

21. Croly, *Progressive Democracy*, 45.

22. See especially Sydney George Fisher, *True History of the American Revolution* (Philadelphia: Lippincott, 1902); J. Allen Smith, *The Spirit of American Government* (New York: Macmillan, 1907) and *The Growth and Decadence of Constitutional Government* (New York: Holt, 1930); Allen Benson, *Our Dishonest Constitution* (New York: Huebsch, 1914); Gustavus Myers, *History of the Supreme Court of the United States* (Chicago: Kerr, 1912); Gilbert Roe, *Our Judicial Oligarchy* (New York: Huebsch, 1912); Louis Boudin, *Government by Judiciary* (New York: Godwin, 1932); and most prominently, Charles Beard, *An Economic Interpretation of the Constitution of the United States* (New York: Macmillan, 1913).

23. See Forrest McDonald, "A New Introduction," in Beard, *An Economic Interpretation of the Constitution of the United States* (New York: Free Press, 1986), xxi.

24. According to Forrest McDonald, Charles Beard was central to the scholarly "discover[y]" of *Federalist* 10 as an important account of Madisonian political thought: "[Beard] had doubtless read *The Federalist* as a graduate student and perhaps earlier, but the emphasis in those days was upon the later essays, which are concerned with the structure of government and the formal distribution of powers; number 10 had been generally neglected by scholars" (McDonald, "New Introduction," xii). By contrast with

existing approaches, Beard read the structural discussion in *Federalist* 51 through *Federalist* 10 and placed both at the center of his theory of the Constitution.

25. James Madison, *The Federalist Papers: No. 10*, http://avalon.law.yale.edu/18th_century/fed10.asp.

26. James Madison, *The Federalist Papers: No. 51*, http://avalon.law.yale.edu/18th_century/fed51.asp.

27. Quoted in William Noyes, "The Implications of Democracy," *International Socialist Review* 1 (1900): 199.

28. Charles Edward Russell, "The Invisible Government," *International Socialist Review* 14 (August 1913): 71.

29. Charles Beard, *An Economic Interpretation of the Constitution of the United States*, 2nd ed. (New York: Macmillan, 1935), 61.

30. William Allen White, *The Old Order Changeth: A View of American Democracy* (New York: Macmillan, 1910), 22. For more on muckraking and the Constitution, see Jason Maloy's excellent analysis of Progressive-era journalism, "The Muck of Politics and the Rake of Realism" (manuscript on file with the author).

31. Amy Myrick, "Constitutional Amendment Activism in the Progressive Era, c. 1900–1925: The Emergent Problem of Broad Substance and Narrow Text" (manuscript on file with author).

32. For more on conservatives' anxieties in the Progressive era over what they labeled "Constitution tinkering," see Kammen, *Machine That Would Go*, 204–8, 226–31.

33. See Walter Clark, "The Next Constitutional Convention of the United States," *Yale Law Journal* 16 (1906): 65–83; see also Walter Clark, "The Revision of the Constitution of the United States," *American Law Review* 32 (1898): 1–13. As with other Progressive-era critics, Clark viewed the electoral college, the indirect election of senators, and lifetime appointed tenure for federal judges as antiquated holdovers from a feudal and monarchical age. These veto points were "anachronism[s] . . . a survival from times when the people's representatives could not legislate without the assent of the monarch expressly given to each act" (7).

34. See Cyril Brickfield, *Problems Relating to a Federal Constitutional Convention* (Washington, D.C.: Government Printing Office, 1957), app., table 2, 89–91.

35. Socialists during the era forged a significant and broad-based social movement. As a presidential candidate, Eugene V. Debs twice received nearly a million votes, Victor Berger and Meyer London were each elected to Congress, and socialist candidates filled hundreds of state and local offices throughout the country; see James Weinstein, *The Decline of Socialism in America* (New York: Monthly Review Press, 1967), 116–18. For more on the regional diversity and national dimensions of the Socialist Party of America at the beginning of the century, see especially David Shannon's excellent and still essential volume *The Socialist Party of America: A History* (New York: Macmillan, 1955), 1–42.

36. "Socialist Platform of 1912," *National Party Platforms, 1840–1956*, vol. 1, ed. Donald Bruce Johnson (Chicago: University of Illinois Press, 1978), 188, 190–91.

37. Quoted in "Wants House Abolished: Berger of the House May Be Disciplined for Criticism in Resolution," *New York Times*, April 28, 1911.

38. See *National Party Platforms, 1840–1956*, 1:166, 190, 210, 241, 353, 371.

39. See Sacvan Bercovitch, *The Rites of Assent: Transformations in the Symbolic Construction of America* (New York: Routledge, 1993).

40. Russell, "Invisible Government," 75.

41. Werner Sombart, "Studies in the History of the Development of the North American Proletariat," *International Socialist Review* 6 (December 1905): 364.

42. Ibid., 365.

43. Ibid.

44. Ibid.

45. Charles Beard, "The Living Constitution," *Annals of the American Academy of Political and Social Science* 185 (1936): 30.

46. Ibid.

47. Ibid.

48. Ibid., 31.

49. Ibid., 34.

50. "Extremes Meet," *Outlook*, May 1913, 54.

51. Ibid.

52. Beard, "Living Constitution," 30.

53. Ibid., 29.

54. Ibid.

55. Ibid.

56. Lawrence Lessig, *Republic, Lost: How Money Corrupts Congress—and a Plan to Stop It* (New York: Twelve, 2011), 3.

57. See especially Robert Dahl, *How Democratic Is the American Constitution?* (New Haven, Conn.: Yale University Press, 2001); Sanford Levinson, *Our Undemocratic Constitution: Where the Constitution Goes Wrong (and How We the People Can Correct It)* (New York: Oxford University Press, 2006); Louis Michael Seidman, *On Constitutional Disobedience* (New York: Oxford University Press, 2012).

58. The arguments in the following two paragraphs on the decline of the Progressive critique are drawn from Aziz Rana, "Making American Constitutional Consensus" (book manuscript on file with author).

59. In Steven Calabresi's words, "Americans are a special people, in a special land, on a special mission." This means that "American constitutional law is exceptional because America is exceptional" (Calabresi, " 'A Shining City on a Hill': American Exceptionalism and the Supreme Court's Practice of Relying on Foreign Law," *Boston University Law Review* 86 [2006]: 1365, 1407).

60. As Jack Balkin and Reva Siegel write of the egalitarian achievements in American history, "All these changes came about because people believed in their Constitution and in the importance of continually examining our practices in the light of our principles" ("Introduction: The Constitution in 2020," in *The Constitution in 2020*, ed. Jack Balkin and Reva Siegel [New York: Oxford University Press, 2009], 3).

61. Myrdal, *An American Dilemma*, 2:1021.

62. For more on how the Framers' design is an outlier both within the United States and globally, see Mila Versteeg and Emily Zackin's excellent article "American Constitutional Exceptionalism Revisited," *University of Chicago Law Review* 81 (2014): 1641–1707, esp. 1679–81.

3 • The Progressive Struggle with the Courts

A Problematic Asymmetry

Brian Z. Tamanaha

Progressives in the early twentieth century castigated court-imposed restrictions on organized labor and limitations on social welfare legislation. They launched an all-fronts assault on the obstacles to their social ambitions. Efforts to break through the primary institutional defenses of vested rights included the recall of judges, the recall of judicial decisions, the election of federal judges, judicial term limits, restrictions on court jurisdiction, the elimination of judicial review, a supermajority vote of justices to strike legislation, and a lower threshold for constitutional amendments to enable repeals of conservative judicial decisions.[1]

A century later, progressives are again proposing initiatives to curb court power. In a history of the Supreme Court, James MacGregor Burns argues that progressives are foolish to put their faith in judicial power:

> The idea of the court as friend to the weak and powerful lingers. Yet, as we have seen, for much of its history, the Supreme Court has more often been indifferent to the wants and needs of the great majority of Americans. It has wielded its supremacy over the Constitution to deny them economic and political power. . . .
>
> Indeed, over the course of the Supreme Court's long history, the leadership of a Marshall or a Warren has been a luminous exception to the rule. In retrospect, the court has far more often been a tool for reaction, not progress. Whether in the Gilded Age of the late nineteenth century or the Gilded Age at the turn of the twenty-first, the justices have most fiercely protected the rights and liberties of the minority of the powerful and the propertied.[2]

Burns urges progressive presidents flatly to refuse the validity of court decisions that invalidate legislation.[3] In a similar vein, Mark Tushnet proposed a
constitutional amendment to abolish judicial review.[4] Other progressives have
suggested a grab bag of ways to discipline the judiciary: impeaching judges,
restricting jurisdiction, packing the court with new members, starving its budget, and setting term limits.[5]

Conservatives have also criticized courts throughout this period, particularly the Warren Court. But there is a crucial difference in the thrust of the two
sides' critiques. Progressives have criticized conservative judges for serving
the rich and failing to do justice. John Gibbons issued this complaint in 1897:
"Security under the law is vouchsafed in unstinted measures to property
rights, but niggardly doled out when personal rights seek redress and recognition at the bar of justice. The plea of the powerful is potent, but the plaint of
the poor is too often unheard."[6] Conservatives, in contrast, criticize liberal
judges for failing to apply the law. In 1956, nineteen senators and seventy-
seven members of the House raised this objection to the Warren Court: "The
Supreme Court of the United States, with no legal basis for such action, un-
dertook to exercise their naked judicial power and substituted their personal
political and social ideas for the established law of the land."[7]

In a century-long battle over the courts, conservatives are defenders of the
rule of law, while progressives are the champions of justice. This difference
has created an asymmetry: conservatives occupy the rhetorical high ground,
and progressives struggle to square their position with the judicial duty to apply the law.

The current divide between conservative and progressive judicial philosophies reflects this asymmetry. Justice Scalia's textualism-originalism, Justice
Thomas's originalism, and Justice Roberts's claim that judges call balls and
strikes—all emphasize fidelity to the law. Compare that with Justice Breyer's
pragmatic view of judging as a means to social ends,[8] or with Justice Sotomayor's statement (when still a circuit judge), "I would hope that a wise Latina
woman with the richness of her experiences would more often than not reach
a better [judicial] conclusion than a white male who hasn't lived that life."[9]

The advantage of the conservative stance is apparent when progressives are
forced to repudiate their previous positions. In her confirmation hearings for
appointment to the Supreme Court, Sotomayor denied that personal views
have an impact on judicial decisions: "It's not the heart that compels conclusions in cases, it's the law."[10] Judges must make "a decision that is limited to
what the law says on the facts before the judge," she insisted. Republican sena-

tor Lindsey Graham dryly commented, "I listen to you today, I think I'm listening to [Chief Justice John] Roberts."[11] When writing as an academic, Elena Kagan observed that differences in constitutional interpretation derive from "divergent understandings of the values embodied in the Constitution and the proper role of judges in giving effect to those values";[12] she criticized confirmation hearings as "a vapid and hollow charade," filled with a "repetition of platitudes," because candidates would not discuss their substantive values.[13] In her confirmation hearings, however, "Like Sonia Sotomayor before her, Kagan would not embrace an openly 'liberal' or 'progressive' constitutional vision. . . . 'We are all originalists,' she explained, adding later in the day that 'it's law all the way down' when judges make decisions."[14] That progressives feel compelled to mimic the language and disposition of conservatives speaks to their predicament. This essay explores why progressives find themselves hooked on this asymmetry and what they might do to extricate themselves from it.

Progressives Challenge the Courts

Early in the twentieth century, the Progressive standard-bearer Senator Robert La Follette issued a scorching critique of courts:

Evidence abounds that, as constituted to-day, the courts pervert justice almost as often as they administer it. Precedent and procedure have combined to make one law for the rich and another for the poor. The regard of the courts for fossilized precedent, their absorption in technicalities, their detachment from the vital living facts of the present day, their constant thinking on the side of the rich and powerful and privileged classes have brought our courts into conflict with the democratic spirit and purposes of this generation. Moreover, by usurping the power to declare laws unconstitutional and by presuming to read their own views into statutes without regard to the plain intention of the legislators, they have become in reality the supreme law-making and law-giving institution of our government. They have taken to themselves a power it was never intended they should exercise; a power greater than that entrusted to the courts of any other enlightened nation. And because this tremendous power has been so generally exercised on the side of the wealthy and powerful few, the courts have become at last the strongest bulwark of privilege.[15]

Most legal Progressives struck a more measured tone, one critical of judicial decisions but stopping short of directly impugning the personal integrity of judges. Walter Clark, chief judge of the North Carolina Supreme Court, pointed to subconscious views:

> But the passage of a judge from the bar to the bench does not necessarily destroy his prejudices or his predilections. . . . And usually with a natural and perhaps unconscious bias from having spent their lives at the bar in advocacy of corporate claims, this will unconsciously, but effectively, be reflected in the decisions they make. Having attempted as lawyers to persuade courts to view debated questions from the standpoint of aggregated wealth, they often end by believing sincerely in the correctness of such views, and not unnaturally put them in force when in turn they themselves ascend the bench.[16]

The Due Process and Equal Protection Clauses, Clark said, "are very elastic and mean whatever the court passing upon the statute thinks most effective for its destruction. This, of course, makes of vital importance the inquiry, 'What are the beliefs of the majority of the court on economic questions, and what happens to be their opinion of sound public policy?' A power so great and so irreviewable and therefore so irresponsible, has become the mainstay of the anti-progressive element."[17]

Other prominent legal Progressives placed the bulk of the blame on conservative tendencies within law itself. Stability is an aspect of legality. Adherence to precedent is built into the common law, allowing for slow, piecemeal changes. New legislation is not easy to enact. Prohibitively high hurdles inhibit amendments to the Constitution. "In this sense, law is often in very truth a government of the living by the dead,"[18] wrote Roscoe Pound. The inherent conservatism of law is conducive to certainty and predictability, which are beneficial qualities, but a system slow to change can become dysfunctional in times of rapid social transformation. Louis Brandeis highlighted this clash: "Since the adoption of the federal constitution, and notably within the last fifty years, we have passed through an economic and social revolution which affected the life of the people more fundamentally than any political revolution known to history. . . . But legal science—the unwritten or judge-made laws as distinguished from legislation—was largely deaf and blind to [these revolutionary changes]."[19]

In a widely publicized speech, "The Causes of Popular Dissatisfaction with the Administration of Justice," Pound identified "the individualist spirit of our common law, which agrees ill with a collectivist age."[20] Making matters worse, "law is in the hands of a highly cautious and conservative profession whose

thought on such matters lags behind."[21] Like other Progressives, Pound situated individuals within society: "But to-day the isolated individual is no longer
taken for the center of the universe. We see now that he is an abstraction, and
has never had a concrete existence. . . . We recognize that society is in some
wise a co-worker with each in what he is and in what he does, and that what he
does is quite as much wrought through him by society as wrought by him
alone."[22] Individualist-oriented property rights and freedom of contract did
not match modern circumstances and had to give way, he argued: "Sooner or
later what public opinion demands will be recognized and enforced by the
courts."[23]

Progressive complaints about the unwillingness of judges to adjust law to
meet the needs of the times applied to all forms of law. "The Flexibility of Law"
(1911), an editorial in the *Outlook,* a progressive journal for which Theodore
Roosevelt was a contributing editor, asserted that law was "the expressed and
formulated will of the community."[24] In this frame, "The common law is a
creation of the courts, and the modern judges are to carry on that process of
creation by adapting to modern conditions the principles of social justice, as
their predecessors on the bench adapted to previous conditions the principles
of social justice."[25] Likewise with the Constitution:

> To turn back to the written Constitution, formulated over one hundred
> and twenty years ago, and attempt to limit the National life within the
> letter of that document, is to misread alike the object of the written Con-
> stitution and the function of the court. The fundamental principles in
> that written Constitution cannot be changed except by a vote of the
> people. But there is room for an almost unlimited growth of National
> development in the free reading and free interpretation of the principles
> embodied in that document to the real life of the nation, grown from
> thirteen States to forty-six, from a strip along the Atlantic coast to a terri-
> tory extending from ocean to ocean, and from a population of three or
> four million to one approximating one hundred million.[26]

The notion of a living Constitution moving with the times was a credo of Progressivism, the cutting edge of its commitment to progress.

Progressives insisted that it was not radical for judges to update the law
through interpretation. "As a historic fact it cannot be denied that the vast body
of constitutional law has been made by our courts in accordance with their
sense of justice or public policy,"[27] declared Morris Cohen, a legal philosopher.
Indeed, Progressive critics argued, laissez-faire doctrines had become part of

contemporary constitutional law through this very process. An 1890 article in the *Harvard Law Review* demonstrated the novelty of recent judicial analysis that struck down legislation, contending that "liberty" had always narrowly meant freedom from physical restraint: "As regards the tendency to give the [Due Process] clause a broad interpretation, and at least to include within the term 'liberty' the right to follow any lawful calling, natural and reasonable as such a construction may at first glance appear, it seems, upon examination, to have little real foundation either in history or principle."[28] Another critic asserted, "In the discussion of the possibility by judicial interpretation of adapting the constitution to changing economic and social needs we must then remember . . . that our constitution has been made by past judicial interpretation to take on a meaning which is not necessarily the only meaning which may be given to it."[29]

Conservative Defense of the Rule of Law

In "A Government of Law or a Government of Men?," U.S. Supreme Court associate justice Horace Lurton responded that judges were merely carrying out their judicial duty.[30] Judicial review was consistent with democracy: "If the exercise of that duty require him to declare that an enactment in the form of law is no law, because repugnant to the law of primary obligation, he is obviously obeying the supreme expression of the popular will as found in a law directly enacted by the sovereign authority of the people."[31] A judge had to enforce the plain meaning of the law; when meaning was doubtful, judges had to interpret legislation and the Constitution in accordance with the intent and purposes of those who enacted it.[32] Lurton conceded that sometimes judges see fit to "shape and mould a statute, or even a constitutional provision, as to minimize the effect of a law deemed unwise, as to render it harmless or capable of subserving some genuine public good."[33] But this was a "dangerous notion of judicial power," inconsistent with the rule of law:[34] "Neither a Constitution nor a statute is to be treated by either the executive or the judiciary as if it were a 'nose of wax,' to be twisted and moulded according to the fancy of the occasion."[35]

Lurton hurled a challenge back at critics: "If our Constitution is too rigid and the restraints upon our legislative power too great, let us amend the Constitution."[36] This was extremely difficult, of course. Progressives floated several proposals to make the Constitution easier to amend,[37] though it was a hopeless exercise in the face of existing hurdles to amendment and American veneration of the Constitution.[38]

Defenders of courts against Progressive criticisms routinely invoked "rule of law" arguments. The Supreme Court correctly followed the "theory of strict construction," argued one southern supporter: "It refuses, as we have ever refused, to admit the argument from convenience to overthrow the plain letter of the constitution."[39] Before he achieved national prominence, federal circuit judge William Howard Taft mixed Progressive political leanings with a strong commitment to the law to defend the judiciary: "When charges made against Federal courts of favoritism toward corporations are stripped of their rhetoric and epithet, and the specific instances upon which the charges are founded are reviewed, it appears that the action of the courts complained of was not only reasonable but rested on precedents established, decades ago, and fully acquiesced in since."[40] Court defenders worried that the independence of the judiciary was at stake: "The feeling of distrust of, and opposition to, all courts and particularly the Federal courts, resulting from the hasty conclusions that they have in these matters arbitrarily assumed an authority which does not belong to them, and through sheer love of power and desire to favor the rich have conspired to oppress the people, is widespread enough to constitute a grave danger to our institutions."[41]

The Asymmetry in Place

Progressive criticisms of courts ranged from radical to moderate. La Follette's blast was at the harsh end of the spectrum, though he had company. Another prominent legal Progressive, Judge Seymour Thompson, said of the Supreme Court's invalidation of the income tax, "Our judicial annals do not afford an instance of a more unpatriotic subserviency to the demands of the rich and powerful classes."[42] An author spewed forth in the *Yale Law Journal*, "So long as our judicial opinions are formed by the mental processes of the intellectual bankrupts these will only be crude justifications of predispositions acquired through personal or class interests and sympathy, 'moral' superstitions, or whim and caprice."[43] Less extreme though still sharp were critics like Judge Clark, who suggested that judges' subconscious class bias was to blame. The decidedly more moderate line taken by Pound, Cohen, Brandeis, and other legal Progressives was that although judges were acting in good faith, they were trapped in old legal thought, held back by the conservative tendencies of law. "I do not criticize these decisions," Pound wrote. "As the law stands, I do not doubt that they were rightly decided."[44] In another essay, he elaborated: "We should not, then, hold the judges or the courts primarily responsible for the want of sympathy with social legislation which has been so much in evidence in the immediate past. . . . It is rather our legal thinking and legal teaching which are to be blamed."[45] After legal doctrines were brought in sync with social needs, these tensions would be resolved and judicial fidelity to the law could carry on for the benefit of society.

Progressive critics agreed that judges were subject to influence—whether consciously or subconsciously—by social views of justice in their legal decisions, and they agreed that judges should update law to meet the times. Moreover, they advocated that jurists consult newly developing social sciences to discern the legal regimes that best serve social welfare. By insisting that judicial decisions were not strictly a matter of law, Progressives embarked on a path toward skepticism about judging, which they avoided on the assumption that desired decisions could be grounded in science or some other objective factor.

On the opposing side, the conservative position was avowedly law-centric. Judges who allowed social views of justice or policy to determine their legal decisions violated their oath to apply the law. Conservative jurists were well aware that social influences could seep into judging in various ways,[46] but this occurred at the margins and was not central to the judicial task.

The asymmetry was set, rooted in contrasting descriptive and prescriptive claims about judging. The Progressive position was that law had to respond to changing social conditions and views of justice; judicial decisions remained objective insofar as judges applied the community's sense of justice and drew on social science to determine how to advance social welfare. In the conservative view, Progressives undermined legality by inviting judges to apply subjective views of justice and policy that had no place in judicial decision making.

Instrumental View of Rights and Law

Prominent critics of classical liberalism at the close of the nineteenth century, responding to social harms caused by industrialization, argued that rights were instrumental, not absolute. They supported limits on child labor, working hours for women, safety conditions, compensation for injuries at work, mandatory primary education, and other legislative efforts to ameliorate the abysmal conditions of the working poor. Rights are "valuable only as a means to an end," to enhance the lives of individuals and the collective, wrote the English philosopher T. H. Green.[47] Legislatures, accordingly, had the power to enact legislation that limited contractual freedom and property rights. "To uphold the sanctity of contracts is doubtless a prime business of government," Green wrote, "but it is no less its business to provide against contracts being made, which, from the helplessness of one of the parties to them, instead of being a security for freedom, become an instrument of disguised oppression."[48] Another English theorist, L. T. Hobhouse, who reoriented classical liberalism by placing individuals within society, argued that all legal rights were socially created ("property is social") and could be limited as necessary for the general benefit.[49] The American Henry Carter Adams argued in economic terms that the "doctrine of *laissez faire* cannot lay claim to scientific pretensions";[50] it was, rather, an economic policy that should be followed only when "the best possible results may be expected for society, as a whole."[51]

Progressives would likewise adopt an instrumental view of law and rights while critiquing judicial invocations of absolutist rights to obstruct social legislation. John Dewey was skeptical of natural law and justice (including laissez-faire notions of liberty), charging that "one of the chief offices of the idea of nature in political and judicial practice has been to consecrate the existing state of affairs, whatever its distribution of advantages and disadvantages, of benefits and losses; and to idealize, rationalize, moralize, the physically given."[52] He later stated the contrary, pragmatic case: "The question of the limits of individual powers, or liberties, or rights, is finally a question of the most efficient use of means for ends."[53] Another Progressive pragmatist, George Herbert Mead, argued that "natural rights" did not have inherent meaning.[54] Rights were abstract and empty of content, filled in only through social battles.[55] And since "we never fight the same battles over again," new questions emerge with new situations, and the content of rights thus continually changes.[56] Dewey cast skepticism regarding rights as a function of power, and Mead emptied rights of inherent content. A worrisome implication of their instrumentalism was that law and rights might be up for grabs.

The failure of legislatures and courts to properly determine the public good when establishing rights and obligations was a major problem, the Progressive Herbert Croly contended: "Throughout the nineteenth century economic conditions in the United States encouraged the confusion of public and private interest. . . . The public interest, to be promoted by economic expansion, was conceived merely as a collection of individual and class interests. The dominant object of state legislation as the expression of the public interest was the satisfaction of these eager individual and class interests."[57] The public was rebelling against this, Croly said, seeking "a public interest, which was something more than and different from a mere collection of private and special interests."[58]

There remained the problem of determining the public good in the face of sharp disagreement. The public-spirited reformism of many Progressives was fueled by their Protestant beliefs,[59] which supplied their values and informed their visions of the public good, but that limited grounding would not suffice in the public arena. Social science was supposed to deliver the solution. Leading Progressive intellectuals, trained in economics and political science, and having faith in expertise,[60] believed that public deliberation informed by social science could identify the public good and the best ways to achieve it.[61] Since judges relied on their sense of justice, particularly when deciding constitutional issues, Morris Cohen argued, it was necessary to develop a sound theory of justice,[62] which the social sciences could facilitate through an empirical inquiry into universal values.[63]

A Failed Progressive Search for Values

Not all Progressives shared this optimism. Explaining his eventual disenchantment with fellow Progressives, Randolph Bourne wrote, "We were instrumentalists, but we had our private utopias so clearly before our minds that the means fell always into its place as contributory. And Dewey, of course, always meant his philosophy, when taken as a philosophy of life, to start with values. But there was always that unhappy ambiguity in his doctrine as to just how values were created, and it became easier and easier to assume that just any growth was justified and almost any activity valuable so long as it achieved ends."[64] The president of the University of Chicago, Robert Hutchins, attacked Dewey's instrumentalism and scientism for their inability to identify ultimate values.[65] "We know that there is a natural moral law, and we can understand what it is because we know that man has a nature and we can understand it,"[66] Hutchins wrote. "The difference between us and Mr. Dewey is that we can defend Mr. Dewey's goals, we can argue for democracy and human ends, and Mr. Dewey cannot. All he can do is say he is for them. He cannot say why, because he can appeal only to science."[67]

Roscoe Pound grappled with this issue throughout his long career. He argued, "Law is a means, not an end. The end is justice between living beings here and now, and as social conditions change, the law must keep pace."[68] To help achieve this, he advocated sociological jurisprudence as a new, empirically informed approach to law. Two factors made justice especially problematic. It was a skeptical age: "Absolute theories of morals and supernatural sanctions have lost their hold."[69] Complicating matters, it was a transitional period during which "the community is divided and diversified, and groups and classes and interests, understanding each other none too well, have conflicting ideas of justice."[70]

A "purely individualist" view focused on ensuring maximum freedom had, Pound argued, become entrenched: "It seeks by means of law to prevent all interference with individual self-development and self-assertion so far as this may be done consistently with a like self-development and self-assertion on the part of others."[71] Courts had enforced this understanding. But a new sense of justice developed in the current generation was not focused on freedom but on the "satisfaction of human wants":[72] "The new justice must consider how it can secure for each individual a standard of living and such a share in the fruits of civilization as shall make possible a full moral life."[73] Finding an "ideal compromise" among these wants was the task of justice.[74] For Pound, social convention determined values: "The judge must apply the ethics of the community, not his own."[75] When a community was divided, courts had to proceed cautiously: "They must go with the main body, not with the advance guard, and with the main body only when it has attained reasonably fixed and settled conceptions."[76]

Like those who critiqued Dewey's instrumentalism, critics charged that Pound's view deprived law of inherent values and principles.[77] It was fallacious to think that conflicting wants could be balanced through some ideal compromise, they argued, particularly since certain wants were unworthy. According to Walter B. Kennedy, "It does not suffice to shuffle the mass of wants and claims of the litigants into a confused pile and then give effect to as many of them as we can in so far as harmony will permit."[78] Draining law of values would turn it into an instrument of power used by whichever social groups prevailed in battles to control law.[79]

Progressives who struggled with this problem came full circle. Herbert Croly late in life showed a strong renewed interest in religion, which an intellectual biographer speculated was motivated by his struggle to find secure moral foundations for reconfigured liberalism.[80] In the aftermath of World War II, another prominent early Progressive, Walter Lippmann, urged the West to reaffirm its traditional faith in objective, natural law principles in order to help stave off totalitarianism.[81] The Progressive legal critic Jerome Frank asserted in the preface of a subsequent edition of his irreverent classic *Law and the Modern Mind*, "I do not understand how any decent man today can refuse to adopt, as the basis of modern civilization, the fundamental principles of Natural Law, relative to human conduct, as stated by Thomas Aquinas."[82] Roscoe Pound later in his career called for a revival of natural law in order to set constraints on legal instrumentalism: "Today the role of the ideal element in law and the need of a canon of values and techniques of applying it are recognized by all"[83]—though he never specified the content of this revived natural law.

Progressive critics of courts thus arrived at a quandary. They excoriated conservative judges for rendering decisions contrary to social justice, but were unable to specify how social justice was to be identified. Their faith that social science would fill this in had been disappointed. Though science could help identify efficient means and document consequences, it had little to say about how to decide among social ends that turned on value choices. In effect, telling judges to achieve social justice when applying the common law, legislation, and the Constitution exhorts them to make value choices not determined by the law and not discernible by any objective means. By comparison, the conservative legal position embodied self-effacing humility. It denied that judges had the qualifications or authority to make lofty decisions about social justice or public policy, and instructed them to stick to the law.

A Conservative Society and Law

Another factor has contributed to the asymmetry: present-day progressives are pushing their agenda uphill, trying to reconcile it with antithetical ends. They are committed to liberal capitalism while striving to temper its excesses. They seek to counter wealth disparities through greater redistribution, to provide protection for those at the bottom, and to secure genuine equality of opportunity. They promote individual rights in conjunction with a sense of shared social responsibility. They are concerned about the corrupting influence wealth exerts on all institutions of government. But the deep individualism of American culture, coexisting alongside strains of social conservatism from religiosity to racism, within an economic ethos of freewheeling capitalism, overlaid by a political system infused by moneyed interests, all combine to tilt the entire system (polity, economy, law) against progressive aims. Law is structurally and substantively conservative because, in the main, American society is like that.

Charles Beard disagreed with other Progressives who argued that judicial review was an unauthorized power grab by courts. The "framers and enactors of the federal Constitution represented the solid, conservative, commercial and financial interests of the country,"[84] he wrote. "No historical fact is more clearly established than the fact that the framers of the Constitution distrusted democracy and feared the rule of mere numbers."[85] Consequently, the system committed "the established rights of property to the guardianship of a judiciary removed from direct contact with popular electorates."[86] His point was that the system was conservative by design, so we should not be surprised when judicial decisions protected the interests of the wealthy. Judge Clark likewise argued that the Constitution in its origin was a "reactionary document," "admirably adapted for what has come to pass—the absolute domination of the Government by the business interests."[87]

Working within a system with a conservative bent—aside from occasional major victories wrought in times of crisis or generational or electoral shifts— progressives will less often get their desired legislation through, will less often get executive backing and administrative regulations to their liking, and will less often enjoy a judiciary that interprets law in a manner that advances progressive causes. Progressives thus regularly find themselves at odds with law. Whatever gains they achieve must continually be defended from conservative forces seeking retrenchment (witness the steady assault on *Roe v. Wade* and affirmative action). Defensive maneuvering by progressives has given rise to novel contentions. Bruce Ackerman, for example, has argued at length that the New Deal settlement and civil rights revolution constitute genuine constitutional amendments;[88] others have argued that certain entrenched "super precedents" merit special protected status.[89]

Read the Constitution!—a conservative legalist would harrumph exasperatedly in response—amendments can be made *only* through Article V. A realistic observer reading these progressive arguments would scoff that all it takes to erase a seemingly entrenched progressive precedent or statute is five votes on the Supreme Court, as the conservative majority recently demonstrated anew by invalidating section 4 of the venerable Voting Rights Act.[90]

Progressives have long been in the position of minority opposition, fighting for advancements within a culture and system that lean against them. Significant progress has been made in achieving their agenda, but haltingly and partially, and subject to frustrating setbacks. They clamor for social justice because laws regularly do not comport with progressive visions of justice. Meanwhile, conservatives enjoy the luxury of promoting legality because law and judges in the main enforce their preferred order.

Originalism and *Brown*

The stunning ascendance of originalism provides the latest manifestation of this asymmetry. The assertion that when discerning the meaning of constitutional provisions, judges should follow original understandings at the time of their enactment, at first blush seems intuitively correct—and yet absurd. What is correct is that the Constitution is authoritative because the Framers and ratifiers voted for it as the supreme foundational document, and it helps to know what people thought they were approving. What is absurd is the proposition that understandings surrounding constitutional provisions enacted more than two centuries ago, under wholly different circumstances, can provide determinate answers to legal issues arising today.

Originalist theory was born in the conservative backlash against the Warren Court.[91] Its intellectual roots lay in charges by Raoul Berger and Robert Bork that justices on the Warren and Burger Courts read their own subjective values into the Constitution, inventing rights not in the document.[92] The only way to constrain judges, they argued, was to bind them to original understandings.[93] "What does it mean to say that a judge is bound by law?" Bork asked. "It means that he is bound by the only thing that can be called law, the principles of the text, whether Constitution or Statute, as generally understood at enactment."[94] The argument was couched in terms of fidelity to law, though it also served the conservative desire to constrain liberal judges, for it would be hard to square liberal decisions with original understandings. Former attorney general Edwin Meese, who served under President Reagan, announced, "It has been and will continue to be the policy of this administration to press for a *jurisprudence of original intention*."[95]

As with the clash early in the twentieth century, battle lines were drawn between progressives, who advocated that judges bring law into conformity with justice, versus conservatives, who wanted judges to hew to the law. Once again, the former argued that the Constitution had to be updated to reflect current values and times, and the latter countered that the proper way to change the Constitution was through the Article V amending clause.

Progressives might argue that conservatives' eventual widespread support for *Brown v. Board of Education* shows that they too believe justice must prevail in constitutional interpretation. *Brown* has always been legally shaky.[96] "A lawyer reading *Brown* was sure to ask, 'where's the law?'" wrote Lucas Powe, describing the reaction to the opinion.[97] Despite this, few conservative legal intellectuals today question the propriety of the decision (though it was excoriated in the South at the time); indeed, now they enlist *Brown* to advance their vision of a color-blind Constitution.[98] But their acceptance of *Brown* is not an endorsement of the proposition that justice takes primacy. Legally imposed segregation was a terrible blight on law that had to end; conservatives recognize this, and also that the country has come to embrace the decision, so nothing would be gained by challenging it.[99] To reconcile the decision with his theory, Bork contended that *Brown* was consistent with originalism, in that while ratifiers did not understand the Fourteenth Amendment to prohibit legally imposed segregation, the principle of equality they meant to enact entailed this result, even if they did not recognize it at the time.[100] The general original principle they knowingly adopted trumped their specific expectations.

Raising the level of analysis to general standards and principles (as Bork did with *Brown*), in combination with shifting away from original expected application to original meaning, makes it possible to switch the political valence of originalism from conservative to progressive. Jack Balkin carries this move off in a masterly way in *Living Originalism*.[101] His theory smacks of an oxymoron: originalism (attention to the Framers and ratifiers) heretofore has stood in opposition to living constitutionalism (injecting contemporary values).

And yet Balkin's embrace of originalism to serve progressive aspirations exemplifies the conservative-progressive asymmetry, with a twist. Rather than remain hooked on the disadvantageous side of the opposition, where living constitutionalists stand, Balkin crossed over to seize the rhetorical high ground of originalist fidelity to law, much as progressive judges do when they mimic conservatives in confirmation hearings. As quoted earlier, Justice Kagan declared, "We are all originalists," and "It's law all the way down." Whether progressives can construct persuasive originalist arguments to support matters like abortion rights and gay marriage remains to be seen.[102] What matters here is the fact that, once again, progressives increasingly drape themselves in conservative positions to comport with the strictures of legality.

Two Ways to Dissolve the Asymmetry

A progressive might say that the ultimate reason for the asymmetry is fear of candor. Legal conservatives are willing to perpetuate the myth that judicial decisions on high courts are determined exclusively by the law. Morris Cohen addressed this a century ago:

> When I pointed this out in a recent essay, the deans of some of our largest law schools wrote me that while the contention that judges do have a share in making the law is unanswerable, it is still advisable to keep the fiction [that they do not]. . . . If, however, we recognize that courts are constantly remaking the law then it becomes of the utmost social

importance that the law should be made in accordance with the best available information which it is the object of science to supply. Law deals with human affairs, and it is impossible to legislate or make any judgment with regard to them without involving all sorts of assumptions or theories.[103]

The insistence that the law provides the answer for every legal question is a "noble lie" that maintains public respect for judges. Cohen countered that the legal system would function better by dropping this pretense, acknowledging that external factors come into play in legal decisions, and explicitly applying expertise and science to improve law.

The real difference, then, is that progressives frankly acknowledge law does not provide all the answers, while conservatives know this but stay mum about it to secure the rhetorical high ground. The asymmetry would dissolve if progressives and conservatives alike candidly admitted that there is flex and uncertainty in law and that judges are influenced in certain ways by their background views. Progressives and conservatives would still differ on how judges should proceed when faced with legal uncertainty or laws contrary to social values, but no longer would conservatives insist (falsely) that judging is law all the way down.

This solution contains an element of truth. But though it will appeal to progressives, it lets them off the hook too easily, absolving them of responsibility for the asymmetry. Setting aside the dim prospect that conservatives will unilaterally relinquish their rhetorically superior position for no benefit, their "noble lie" admits of another interpretation. Viewed from a different angle, it is not a myth at all but a regulative ideal essential to the maintenance of legality, worth aspiring to even if judges cannot fully achieve it.

Progressives for the past century have aggressively pushed to inscribe their values in the law via judges. But a crucial difference must be noted between early Progressives and their more recent successors. In the first wave of Progressivism, conservative judges obstructed democratically enacted legislation. Though Progressives were unable to provide an objective grounding for their views of social justice, the gap was filled by favorable popular opinion. Progressives since the 1960s, in contrast, have often implored judges to implement their views of justice even when they are ahead of public opinion and contrary to legislation. Contemporary progressives thus lack an important form of legitimation that backed early Progressives, and conservatives can credibly attack this effort as liberal intellectual elites imposing their preferred values on everyone else.

It also bears remembering that two influential critics of the Warren Court, Herbert Wechsler and Raoul Berger, were on the moderate-to-left side of the political spectrum. Their concerns were to maintain legality and the proper role of judges in a democracy. They issued a warning: if liberal judges were free to write their values into the law, there was nothing to stop conservative judges from doing the same. To continue in this direction would result in increasing judicial impositions on politics as well as a politicization of the judiciary, ultimately corroding law.[104]

Another way to dissolve the asymmetry would be for progressives to renounce their campaign for social justice via judging and to move closer to the conservative emphasis on fidelity to law. If progressives want the law to comport with justice, they might focus more directly on winning social and political battles to enact progressive legislation than on encouraging judges to implement desired changes. Progressives would then be on side of legality because law would more often reflect their vision of a just society. The hope for legal progressives lies in a more progressive society.

Notes

1. For a terrific account of progressive initiatives, see J. Patrick White, "Progressivism and the Judiciary: A Study of the Movement for Judicial Reform, 1901–1917" (Ph.D. diss., Univ. of Michigan, 1957).

2. James MacGregor Burns, *Packing the Court* (New York: Penguin, 2009), 251–52.

3. Ibid., 253.

4. Mark Tushnet, "Democracy Versus Judicial Review: Is It Time to Amend the Constitution?," *Dissent* 52, no. 2 (2005): 59–63. Some conservatives have called for abolishing judicial review; see Lino A. Graglia, "Constitutional Law Without the Constitution: The Supreme Court's Remaking of America," in *A Country I Do Not Recognize: The Legal Assault on American Values*, ed. Robert H. Bork (Palo Alto, Calif.: Hoover Institute Press, 2005).

5. See Larry D. Kramer, *The People Themselves: Popular Constitutionalism and Judicial Review* (Oxford: Oxford University Press, 2004), 249–53. For a review of changes in court-curbing tactics over time, see Stephen M. Engel, *American Politicians Confront the Court: Opposition Politics and Changing Responses to Judicial Power* (New York: Cambridge University Press, 2011). The idea of term limits has been endorsed by both conservatives and liberals; see Jamal Greene, "Revisiting the Constitution: Term Limits for Federal Judges," *New York Times*, July 8, 2012, www.nytimes.com/roomfordebate/2012/07/08/another-stab-at-the-us-constitution/revisiting-the-constitution-we-need-term-limits-for-federal-judges.

6. John Gibbons, "Security Under the Law Is the Staff and Shield of the Republic," *American Lawyer* 5 (1897): 439.

7. *Congressional Record* 102 (March 12, 1956): 4460, 4515–16, quoted in Charles Hyneman, *The Supreme Court on Trial* (Westport, Conn.: Greenwood, 1974), 19.

8. See Stephen Breyer, *Active Liberty* (New York: Vintage, 2006). Paul Gewirtz summarizes Breyer's approach: "Judging is a pragmatic and purposeful activity in which interpretation and decision must always be attentive to the purposes of legal provisions, the multiplicity of factors involved in specific cases, and the practical consequences of judicial decisions, and should not focus exclusively on textual exegesis and uncovering original understandings" (Gewirtz, "The Pragmatic Passion of Stephen Breyer," *Yale Law Journal* 115 [2006]: 1676).

9. Quoted in Charlie Savage, "A Judge's View of Judging Is on the Record," *New York Times*, May 14, 2009, www.nytimes.com/2009/05/15/us/15judge.html?_r=0.

10. Quoted in Ari Shapiro, "Sotomayor Differs with Obama on 'Empathy' Issue," *NPR*, July 14, 2009, www.npr.org/templates/story/story.php?storyId=106569335&refresh=true.

11. Ibid.

12. Elena Kagan, "Confirmation Messes, Old and New," *Chicago Law Review* 62 (1995): 935.

13. Ibid., 941.

14. Jonathan H. Adler, "The Judiciary Committee Grills Elena Kagan," *Washington Post*, June 29, 2010, www.washingtonpost.com/wp-dyn/content/article/2010/06/29/AR2010062902652.html.

15. Robert M. La Follette, "Introduction," in Gilbert E. Roe, *Our Judicial Oligarchy* (New York: Huebsch, 1912), vi–vii.

16. Walter Clark, "Some Defects of the Constitution of the United States," April 27, 1906, in *The Papers of Walter Clark*, ed. Aubrey Lee Brooks and Hugh Talmage Lefler (Chapel Hill: University of North Carolina Press, 1950), 2:570.

17. Ibid., 2:578.

18. Roscoe Pound, "The Causes of Popular Dissatisfaction with the Administration of Justice," *American Lawyer* 14 (1906): 445.

19. Louis D. Brandeis, "The Living Law," *Illinois Law Review* 10 (1916): 463–64.

20. Pound, "Causes of Popular Dissatisfaction," 447.

21. Roscoe Pound, "The Need of a Sociological Jurisprudence," *Annual Reports of the American Bar Association* 31 (1907): 990–91; see also Pound, "Common Law and Legislation," *Harvard Law Review* 6 (1908): 383–407; Pound, "Mechanical Jurisprudence," *Columbia Law Review* 8 (1908): 605–23; Pound, "Spurious Interpretation," *Columbia Law Review* 6 (1907): 379–86.

22. Roscoe Pound, "Do We Need a Philosophy of Law?" *Columbia Law Review* 5 (1905): 346.

23. Pound, "Sociological Jurisprudence," 925.

24. Editors, "The Flexibility of Law," *Outlook,* December 17, 1910, 849. The editor in chief was Lyman Abbott, and the associate editor was Hamilton W. Mabie.

25. Ibid.

26. Ibid., 851.

27. Morris R. Cohen, "Legal Theories and Social Science," *International Journal of Ethics* 25 (1915): 484.

28. Charles E. Shattuck, "The True Meaning of the Term 'Liberty' in Those Clauses in the Federal and State Constitutions Which Protect 'Life, Liberty, and Property,'" *Harvard Law Review* 4 (1890): 392; see also "The Right to Freedom of Contract," *Harvard Law Review* 11 (1897): 56–58 (unsigned article).

29. Frank J. Goodnow, "Judicial Interpretation of Constitutional Provisions," *Proceedings of the Academy of Political Science in the City of New York* 3 (1913): 9.

30. Horace H. Lurton, "A Government of Law or a Government of Men?," *North American Review* 193 (1911): 9.

31. Ibid., 19.

32. Ibid., 23.

33. Ibid.

34. Ibid., 24.

35. Ibid.

36. Ibid.

37. See Munroe Smith, "Shall We Make Our Constitution Flexible?," *North American Review* 194 (1911): 657.

38. See Seymour D. Thompson, "Government by Lawyers," *American Law Review* 30 (1896): 672–89.

39. F. Charles Hume, "The Supreme Court of the United States," *American Law Review* 33 (1899): 649.

40. William H. Taft, "Criticisms of the Federal Judiciary," *American Law Review* 29 (1895): 667.

41. William G. Peterkin, "Government by Injunction," *American Lawyer* 6 (1898): 5.

42. Thompson, "Government by Lawyers," 685.

43. Theodore Schroeder, "Social Justice and the Courts," *Yale Law Journal* 22 (1912): 26–27.

44. Pound, "Do We Need a Philosophy of Law?," 345.

45. Roscoe Pound, "Social Justice and Legal Justice," *Central Law Journal* 75 (1912): 455, 462.

46. See Brian Z. Tamanaha, *Beyond the Formalist-Realist Divide: The Role of Politics in Judging* (Princeton, N.J.: Princeton University Press 2010), which shows that early-twentieth-century jurists had realistic perceptions of judging; Tamanaha, "The Mounting Evidence Against the 'Formalist Age,'" *Texas Law Review* 92 (2014): 1667–84, which shows that turn-of-the century jurists had very realistic perceptions of judging.

47. Thomas Hill Green, "Lecture on Liberal Legislation and Freedom of Contract," in *Works of Thomas Hill Green,* edited by R. L. Nettleship (London: Longmans, Green, 1888), 1:372.

48. Ibid., 1:382.

49. See L. T. Hobhouse, *Liberalism* (Oxford: Oxford University Press, 1964; orig. pub. 1911), 98, 99.

50. Henry Carter Adams, "Relation of the State to Industrial Action," *Publications of the American Economic Association* 1 (1887): 27; a more concise statement of his views can be found in Henry Carter Adams, "Economics and Jurisprudence," *Science* 8 (1886): 15.

51. Adams, "Relations of the State to Industrial Action," 31.

52. John Dewey, "Nature and Reason in Law," *International Journal of Ethics* 25 (1914): 30–31.

53. John Dewey, "Force and Coercion," *International Journal of Ethics* 26 (1916): 366.

54. George Herbert Mead, "Natural Rights and the Theory of the Political Institution," *Journal of Philosophy, Psychology, and Scientific Methods* 12 (1915): 147.

55. Ibid., 151.

56. Ibid., 147.

57. Herbert Croly, "State Political Reorganization," *American Political Science Review* 6 (1912): 127.

58. Ibid., 128.

59. See Jeffery C. Isaac, *The Poverty of Progressivism* (Lanham, Md.: Rowman & Littlefield, 2003), 79–84.

60. Ibid., 84–88.

61. On the connections between pragmatism and the progressive faith in science and administration, see R. Jeffrey Lustig, *Corporate Liberalism: The Origins of Modern Political Theory, 1890–1920* (Berkeley: University of California Press, 1982), chap. 6.

62. For a summary of Cohen's presentation, see G. A. Tawney, "Proceedings of the Conference on Legal and Social Philosophy," *International Journal of Ethics* 25 (1914): 95–96.

63. Morris R. Cohen, "Jus Naturale Redivivum," *Philosophical Review* 6 (1916): 761–77.

64. Randolph S. Bourne, *War and Intellectuals: Collected Essays, 1915–1919,* ed. Carl Resek (New York: Harper, 1964), 60–61.

65. For an informative account of their exchange, see James Scott Johnston, "The Dewey-Hutchins Debate: A Dispute over Moral Teleology," *Educational Theory* 61 (2011): 1–16.

66. Robert Hutchins, "Toward a Durable Society," *Fortune,* June 1943, quoted in Johnston, "Dewey-Hutchins Debate," 12.

67. Robert Hutchins, "Education for Freedom," *Christian Century,* November 15, 1944, 1315, quoted in Johnston, "Dewey-Hutchins Debate," 13. Morris Cohen also

criticized Dewey for this failure, though without offering a solution himself; see Gabriel Kolko, "Morris R. Cohen: The Scholar and/or Society," *American Quarterly* 9 (1957): 325–26.

68. Morris R. Cohen characterizes Pound's views in "New Leadership in the Law," *New Republic,* March 11, 1916, 138–39.

69. Pound, "Causes of Popular Dissatisfaction," 450.

70. Ibid., 448.

71. Pound, "Social Justice and Legal Justice," 458.

72. Ibid., 459.

73. Ibid.

74. Pound, "Causes of Popular Dissatisfaction," 446.

75. Ibid., 461.

76. Ibid., 462.

77. See Walter B. Kennedy, "Pragmatism as a Philosophy of Law," *Marquette Law Review* 9 (1924): 63.

78. Ibid.

79. See Brian Z. Tamanaha, *Law as a Means to an End: Threat to the Rule of Law* (New York: Cambridge University Press, 2006), 71–74; Edward A. Purcell Jr., *The Crisis of Democratic Theory: Scientific Naturalism and the Problem of Value* (Lexington: University of Kentucky Press, 1973), 172–74.

80. See Edward A. Stettner, *Shaping Modern Liberalism: Herbert Croly and Progressive Thought* (Lawrence: University Press of Kansas, 1993), 144–53, 167–69.

81. See Walter Lippmann, *The Public Philosophy* (New York: Mentor, 1955), 132–38; John Patrick Diggins, "From Pragmatism to Natural Law: Walter Lippmann's Quest for the Foundations of Legitimacy," *Political Theory* 19 (1991): 519–38.

82. Jerome Frank, "Preface to the Sixth Printing," *Law and the Modern Mind* (New York: Anchor, 1963 [1948]), quoted in Purcell, *Crisis of Democratic Theory,* 173.

83. Roscoe Pound, *The Formative Era of American Law* (Boston: Little, Brown, 1938), 28–29.

84. Charles Beard, "The Supreme Court—Usurper or Grantee?," *Political Science Quarterly* 27 (1912): 1–29.

85. Ibid., 30.

86. Ibid., 31.

87. Clark, "Some Defects of the Constitution," 559.

88. See the three volumes of Bruce Ackerman's *We the People* series, published by Harvard University Press: *Foundations* (1993), *Transformations* (2000), and *The Civil Rights Revolution* (2014).

89. See Michael Gerhardt, "Super Precedent," *Minnesota Law Review* 90 (2006): 1204–31.

90. See *Shelby County v. Holder,* 570 U.S. ___ (2013).

91. For a historical account of the rise of originalism, see Johnathan O'Neill, *Originalism in American Law and Politics: A Constitutional History* (Baltimore: Johns Hopkins University Press, 2005); see also Jamal Greene, "On the Origins of Originalism," *Texas Law Review* 88 (2009): 1–80.

92. See Raul Berger, *Government by Judiciary: The Transformation of the Fourteenth Amendment* (Cambridge, Mass.: Harvard University Press, 1977); Robert H. Bork, "Neutral Principles and Some First Amendment Problems," *Indiana Law Journal* 47 (1971): 1–35. Berger's objections were not politically motivated, but based on his positivist view of law.

93. See Jack M. Balkin, *Living Originalism* (Cambridge, Mass.: Harvard University Press, 2011), 100–104.

94. Robert Bork, *The Tempting of America: The Political Seduction of the Law* (New York: Macmillan, 1990), 5.

95. Edwin Meese, "The Supreme Court of the United States: Bulwark of a Limited Constitution," *South Texas Law Review* 27 (1986): 465.

96. See Herbert Wechsler, "Toward Neutral Principles of Constitutional Law," *Harvard Law Review* 73 (1959): 1–35. Even shakier is the companion case, *Bolling v. Sharpe*, 347 U.S. 487 (1954), which used the Due Process Clause to reach the same outcome.

97. Lucas A. Powe, *The Warren Court in American Politics* (Cambridge, Mass.: Harvard University Press, 2000), 40.

98. See *Parents Involved in Community Schools v. Seattle School District No. 1.*, 551 U.S. 701 (2007).

99. Pragmatic concession to reality also explains why few originalists would press for undoing the New Deal settlement, and why they accept long-standing precedents even when inconsistent with originalism; see Antonin Scalia, "Originalism: The Lesser Evil," *University of Cincinnati Law Review* 57 (1981): 849–65.

100. Bork, *Tempting of America*, 82. A stronger originalist defense of *Brown* is Michael W. McConnell, "Originalism and the Desegregation Decisions," *Virginia Law Review* 81 (1995): 947–1140.

101. Balkin, *Living Originalism.*

102. For one example of an originalist defense of a right to abortion, see Jack M. Balkin, "Abortion and Original Meaning," *Constitutional Commentary* 24 (2007): 291–352.

103. Cohen, "Legal Theories and Social Science," 485.

104. Additional grounds for this worry are provided in Tamanaha, *Law as a Means to an End.*

4 • Rights as Process

A View from the Progressives' Century

Karen Orren

The major upheavals in the history of American rights do not include the Progressive era. They occur with the Revolution and constitutional framing, the Civil War, the New Deal, and the rolling "rights revolution" of the last half of the twentieth century. Rights in the Progressive era were not static; they changed with the vote for women, the income tax, and the new method of electing U.S. senators. But these developments do not compare with the effective destruction of the ancient common law hierarchies and their associated rights ordering religion, monarchy, slavery, the workplace, and gender, or with the overthrow of the hierarchy of whites over African Americans that was Jim Crow. Arraying the great transformations of rights in their proper historical sequence would, in fact, place the Progressive era near dead center, a period in which reformist lawmakers took stock and built upon prior changes before resuming fully in the 1930s.

It was in the Progressive era, on the other hand, that the most provocative critique of rights since independence, known collectively as "legal realism," came to be written.[1] Oliver Wendell Holmes led the way. Holmes declared in his 1887 speech "The Path of the Law" that rights were "but prophesies," expectations about what judges would do, based not on logic but on experience.[2] Wesley Newcomb Hohfeld split the atom. In "Some Fundamental Legal Conceptions as Applied to Judicial Reasoning," he separates "rights" from "liberties," with inherent obedience attributed only to the former.[3] Felix Frankfurter and Nathan Green pushed forward, writing at the threshold of the New Deal in 1931: "The creation of rights is the business of legislatures; so also is the task of defining with particularity the area within which they may be exercised."[4]

These realists were also normativists. Each proposed a new definition of what rights "are," one that would depart from traditional and rigid rules to more generously endow with rights the many participants in their own society. In particular, they sought to level the positions of those parties privileged by "liberty of contract" and similar concepts. Both Holmes and Frankfurter and Green opened up the category of rights, and Hohfeld refined it; but each sought consistency. To allow for variation in the core conception would have blunted the Progressive project in its entirety. Modern commentators today follow their example, with much less excuse. A full century later, it is still the case that, as another Progressive might have put it, "a right-is-a-right-is-a-right."[5] In the wake of all that has unfolded historically since the realist critique, few have asked directly what rights have become in reality. Consider the most prominent definition today: Ronald Dworkin's "rights are trumps."[6] Really? With Dworkin as our guide, a search of the legal scene for what is real, rather than what ought to be, will turn up relatively few of the species.

This chapter builds on a different realist insight, which is the demonstrable distance between rights as claims and rights in practice. To survey rights in the Progressive century, I propose to define rights less as a thing and more as a process, to wit: "A right is a claim, made against a person or action of another, either a citizen or governmental officer, enforceable in a court of law." Like other processes, a "right" has a beginning and an end. The beginning is the claim itself; the end, its anticipated enforcement. A rights claim may rest on pure assertion, ipse dixit, or it may be grounded in established rules or precedent; enforcement may be entirely at the will of the judge or other authority in charge, or it may be mandatory, following as a matter of routine. A particular right that in practice consistently falls near the rule-bound end on both dimensions is a "trump." If it falls in practice at the discretionary end on either dimension, it is a "chip." Rights as trumps secure privileged treatment in law, overcoming contending claims and purposes; chips provide a ticket to ride, a place at the table, a day in court, with the outcome uncertain.

The advantages of this definition are several. First, the concept offers the flexibility required for analysis in separate social areas and time periods. This is something that attention to neither the "language" of rights nor to the role rights play in different historical periods can provide.[7] Second, the definition stays close enough to its popular understanding that the political baby is not drowned in conceptual bathwater. Third, the definition does not distinguish qualitatively between the rights of citizens and the rights of officers. By this strategy, it is able to register rights claims along the entire process and on either side of the society-state divide.[8]

One objection that may be anticipated immediately is that the definition privileges courts and judicial decisions, not legislators, say, or demands voiced by social movements. Agreed. A premise of the survey is that courts, short of constitutional amendment, finally decide rights, even though they may originate elsewhere. Implied also is a reasonable span of time within which a claim must be given legal recognition to be counted as a right. To that extent, the definition excludes generalized or aspirational "human rights," although these may be selectively transformed into rights in the meaning proposed. Finally, it is also the case that the scheme is lopsided in favor of chips; I believe this accurately reflects historical developments and the essentially contingent field of rights today.

This chapter begins by briefly situating the Progressive era in a broader story of rights as defined above. Then a handful of rights disputes in state and federal courts from the Progressive era forward are discussed, and the definition proposed is briefly applied to particular cases. The cases were not selected on any special basis; others would have served as well. They are discussed only to give the approach a trial run. The point is not to put things in boxes but to consider rights in a fresh way, both over this historical span and in general.

Before Progressivism

Writing about the legal-rights debate in the Progressive era, Joseph Singer states that "Hohfeld effectively annihilated the views" of previous analysts, who argued from the individualist premises of classical analysis.[9] So it will be useful to state at the outset that my definition of rights, minus the specified dimensions, bears a close resemblance to those of Hohfeld's annihilatees. Here, for one, is Jeremy Bentham:

> When the law exempts a man from punishment in case of his dealing with your person in a manner that either stands a chance or is certain of being disagreeable to you, it thereby confers on him a power: it gives him a power over you; a power over your person. Now this is what it may find necessary to do for various purposes: for the sake of providing for the discharge of the several functions of the husband, the parent, the guardian, the master, the judge, the military officer, and the sovereign. ... These powers form so many exceptions to the general rule that no man has the right to meddle with another person.[10]

Within Bentham's formulation, the variable that makes it suitable to historical analysis is contained in the phrase "what [the law] may find necessary to do for various purposes." This is a different way of getting to the second dimension I propose, that is, how predictably a given claim will be enforced in court. What Bentham calls "powers," I describe as "rights."

Like the Progressives, Bentham also did not write in a historical vacuum. He had a keen appreciation of the larger institutional events changing rights as he understood them. In particular, he was a great critic of common law judges and what he considered their pervasive bad influence, and his categories attest to the continuing vitality of the common law in the society of his time. Each of the persons authorized to meddle with others without punishment were, under existing common law rules, superiors in prescribed relations with specifically designated inferiors: wife, child, ward, servant, litigant, subaltern, citizen. Note that Bentham includes the sovereign and the judge, but not the legislator. Had he written three centuries earlier, he would have included as superiors bishops and royal officers. Their rights and restrictions within legally defined jurisdictions, as well as those of the others listed, constituted the governance of England.

Note also that Bentham says nothing about businessmen. By the time he wrote, at the end of the eighteenth century, the affairs of commerce—along with those of religion and governmental organization—had passed into the authority of Parliament; common law in these fields had become changeable by Parliament and, provisionally, by the judiciary on its own.[11] This meant that when the common law was brought to the United States, the part of it still intact, outside courtroom procedures proper, primarily regulated the hierarchies that Bentham's great enemy Blackstone called the "private relations": husband and wife, parent and child, master and servant, guardian and ward.[12] (James Kent, in his treatise on American law, added master and slave.)[13] Referred to as "domestic relations" in American law, these were by and large the jurisdiction of the separate states, alongside their other authority under the new Constitution.

A few observations about this transplantation across the Atlantic are in order. In the United States, superiors' rights did not enjoy the status of "property," as they had in England, being, from an early date, subject to modification for reasons of public safety or morality. Still, they continued to exert usually unquestioned, trumplike effects within their designated spheres. Judges continued to make the final call in disputes, but their opinions were constrained by centuries of common law precedent. Second, these hierarchies were characterized by self-help: all superiors enjoyed rights of chastisement and protection from outside interference, whether by public or private parties. These circumstances greatly narrowed the chasm that exists today between rights claims and rights enforcement. Third, it should be underscored that the rights associated with commerce, which included property ownership, were chips, subject to change by legislation. The Constitution anticipates commercial regulation by both the state and the federal governments—thus, the protections provided. The rights of commerce would be joined later under legislative authority by the rights of the newly freed ex-slaves, with their rights too, eminently, chips.

The chronology is important if for no other reason than so much emphasis in historical scholarship is put on the rights of businessmen.[14] In America, with no kings or archbishops to cut down to size, rights attached to commercial transactions, including the buying and selling of land, were the prototype chip. No major piece of commercial legislation passed by Congress during the Gilded Age or before was reversed by the Supreme Court based on property rights; a similar pattern was found in the states, under the police power. As policy, the programs of Progressive lawmakers to regulate businesses were impressively innovative. As for rights, while considerable internal shuffling occurred among governmental officers, little changed qualitatively.

As we begin our discussion of the Progressive era, then, this division of authority, both among and, in an authoritative sense, over rights, was well established, and the projects of the legal realists and their activist allies were in part on solid ground. Rights of commerce, of "property," satisfied the requirement for rights of action—standing—in court. But they enjoyed no trump position, no a priori legal advantage over the rights of others, including over the rights of governmental officers. Masters, husbands, fathers, and whites (vis-à-vis African Americans) still held trumps. Those are the patterns to which we now turn.

Trumps and Chips in the Progressive Era

Illustrative of the arrangement described are two decisions in the New York courts at a time when that system was dominated by Progressive judges.[15] The first, in 1908, *Colby v. Equitable Trust Co.*, concerned commercial or property rights in the form of shareholding. Plaintiffs were minority shareholders in one of two insurance trusts whose assets were about to be absorbed in a merger with the defendant, a third insurance trust. The directorships among the three were thickly intermingled, and the plaintiffs alleged that their assets had been considerably undervalued. Supported by a long line of common law precedent, minority shareholders of corporations had the right to petition the court for injunctions against impending corporate decisions, even decisions supported by the shareholder majority, when they could show reasonable suspicion of fraud or obvious disregard for their interests or the interests of the corporation as a whole. A lower court granted the injunction, but the appeals court reversed the order, a decision affirmed without opinion by the New York high court.

The merger had proceeded under an 1892 banking law granting companies organized under its auspices the permission to enter mergers without unanimous shareholder consent. The plaintiffs pointed out that neither their company nor the one with which it was being merged had been organized under the 1892 law, whose rules in any case did not bind corporations such as theirs, organized in 1871. The court overcame these technicalities: it found another law on the books under which "at least one company was organized," and that law could be read "in conjunction" with the one challenged.[16] Moreover, "the Legislature has the right at any time it sees fit to alter, suspend, or repeal the charters of corporations."[17] The legislature, "of course, cannot confiscate property, but it is under its fiat that the corporation comes into existence and the power which creates may thereafter change or destroy."[18]

The opinion concedes that a "superficial examination of the proposed merger would seem to indicate it was unfair to the [merged corporation's] stockholders."[19] But it confronts the evidence of intermingling by "a large number of directors and officers," the uncontested valuation of plaintiffs' stock at a third lower than its historical performance, the fact that the stock would be exchanged for fewer shares than shares in the second merged company, that no compensation was provided for goodwill ("unquestionably an asset")—all to conclude that none of these seeming disabilities caused the transaction to be "so unfair" as to justify intervention.[20] Weighing the earnings projected and "the great advantage that will accrue to the [new] company" against "the injustice which the stockholders of [the company merged] will suffer," the opinion concludes that a court of equity "should not interfere and prevent [the merger's] consummation."[21] If the shareholders remained unhappy, they could, under the banking law, petition the court for a new appraisal of their assets.

Colby was a milestone in the coming of the "entity theory" of the corporation.[22] Of interest to us here is the flexible, pragmatic, future-looking process by which the court went about determining the shareholders' rights. Neither bound by rules nor overly impressed by evidence, the court's proceedings typify the adjudication of rights as chips. Notice that they are chips not because of how the verdict turned out, but because of the reasoning by which it was reached. The Progressives did not invent this style—it had regularly been applied to commercial cases earlier on both sides of the Atlantic—but they eventually championed it across the board.[23]

That said, it would be incorrect to conclude that rights were characteristically chips in the Progressive era. Consider a second case in the same New York courts, a bit later, concerning the law of master and servant, with a group of judges decidedly more "progressive" in composition than in the shareholders' case. *Auburn Draying v. Wardell* (227 N.Y. 1) was a suit for injunction brought by a trucking company whose name had been placed on an "unfair list" by a central council of twenty-two labor unions and distributed to the company's customers and suppliers, notifying them that union members across the city would withdraw their patronage if their business with the company was not curtailed. The reason for this list was the trucking company's stated neutrality regarding its employees' membership in the Teamsters union. The company sued the central council and the union that passed on its name, asking the court to order the unions to discontinue their action, and to award the company damages for injuries to its business.

Auburn Draying is not one of the fire-breathing antilabor opinions that were prominent in some courtrooms at the time; it is not even strident. It foresees no violence threatened or likely to erupt. The decision centers on the rule that "the right of property embraces the right to make contracts for the purchase of the labor of others and equally the right to make contracts for the sale of one's own labor and the employment of one's individual and industrial resources."[24] It affirms the rights of workmen to associate; to bring all laborers into unions; and through "coherent and solidified power and influence flowing from association," even by coercive methods, to secure their collective interests; it says these rights are "beyond question."[25] It then invokes another rule: "The individual cannot injure the property rights of another by the means of causing or controlling through duress, coercion, oppression or fraud, the acts of third persons which produce the injury."[26] The decision of the lower court, that the plaintiff was entitled to injunctions and to recover damages, was affirmed, with costs.

This is a classic "formalist" opinion; in that respect, it typifies the great majority of the labor opinions that were issued in state and federal courts until the time of the New Deal. It has all the earmarks: it employs spatial metaphors; the defendants isolated the plaintiff's business, pressuring present and future customers "to ignore its existence."[27] It bears the famous hairsplitting of the formalist style, between ultimate purposes and immediate efforts, between coercion in intent and coercion in effect. It makes no mention of the applicable penal statutes relied on by the two lower courts, or of any other positive law. The court says that based on the evidence in the record, the plaintiff is "entitled" to the decree.

One does not endorse the logic of either opinion in observing that the rights asserted in both cases refer to clear-enough rules. But in *Colby*, the rule, namely, that vested property rights cannot be confiscated, leads to the court immediately finding a way around it, through an interpretation of confiscation that does not encompass forced sale. In *Auburn Draying*, one rule leads to another, supporting rule of no pressure permitted on third parties. The next step in the shareholders' suit was for the judge to make the discretionary call, based on what today's Securities and Exchange Commission calls "forward looking statements," concluding that the prospects of the merger outweighed any demonstrated disadvantages to the plaintiffs. "If I am right in this conclusion," he remarks, then there was no reason for the court to intervene.[28] In *Auburn Draying*, the judge goes from rule to evidence to decree as if he has no discretion in the matter. The shareholders' right was a chip; the employers' right was a trump.

The New Deal and Labor

In developments over the course of the Progressive century, chips proliferated and trumps receded. The next decision considered comes after the Progressive era proper, in the New Deal. This is the labor case *Republic Aviation Corp. v. National Labor Relations Board* (324 U.S. 793). *Republic Aviation* may stand for the post-common-law regime of labor relations. It reflects the conscious decision made by the authors of the National Labor Relations Act, at the urging of Progressive intellectuals led by Felix Frankfurter, to rest the new regime of labor governance entirely on statutes, without seeking support in the Thirteenth Amendment or some newly crafted constitutional provision.[29] I pick it because it is a decision often held up by scholars sympathetic to unions as illustrating the style in which labor rights should be adjudicated.[30]

Issued in 1945, a decade after the National Labor Relations Act's original passage, *Republic Aviation* flies high the Progressive flag, and no wonder. Felix Frankfurter was by then a justice. All the justices except one, Owen Roberts, were either self-proclaimed progressives or FDR appointees or both, and

Roberts was the sole dissenter. The question concerned under what circumstances the Court should defer to orders of the NLRB, whose members, according to the statute, were appointed for their reputations as experts in labor relations. In this case, the board, citing section 8 of the NLRA, had labeled as "unfair practices" the company's dismissal of employees for soliciting union membership on company property during lunch time and wearing "steward" buttons before union certification and after they were asked to remove them. It ordered the company to cease and desist and to reinstate the employees with back pay. It made no finding that the company had acted with malice toward unions.[31] The company sought review by the court of appeals as provided by statute, arguing that the board's orders were in violation of its rights to manage the plant and to be afforded "due administrative process." The court of appeals upheld the board, and the Supreme Court affirmed.

The Supreme Court focused its opinion on whether there was sufficient evidence to support the board's rulings. Section 9 of the National Labor Relations Act provides that in petitions for enforcement appeals, the board's findings of fact, "if supported by evidence," were to be treated as conclusive.[32] With regard to soliciting members, the Court averred that it could not "properly be said that there was evidence or a finding that the plant's physical location made solicitation away from company property ineffective to reach prospective union members."[33] In regard to the buttons, the opinion comments: "No evidence was offered that any unusual conditions existed" in the plant. The record did contain, it said, "evidentiary facts" outlining the dispute; the "theory" that moved the board to its conclusions; and the board's "reasons" for ordering as it did.[34] Moreover, the board "succinctly expressed the requirements of proof which it considered appropriate" to overcome its "presumption as to rules concerning solicitation."[35] One of the purposes of labor relation boards was to allow decisions to be "made by experienced officials with an adequate appreciation of the complexities of the subject which is entrusted to their administration."[36] The company offered no evidence that labor conditions at its plant differed from those in any other large establishment.

Since the topic under consideration here is the manner by which rights are determined, and not the results per se, the opinion of the circuit court is equally instructive. Authored by the famous Progressive Learned Hand, it reads section 8 as "too indefinite to allow the tribunal which enforces it to avoid" deciding the question of law, that is, where the balance of benefits and prejudices to and on the parties falls.[37] But "on this record"—consisting only of case citations and a "general conclusion" of membership discussions on company premises but not during working hours being "reasonable"—such balancing could not be justified. This, the court adds, was "particularly true because even if by specific findings the legal question was brought out clear and definite, we should still have to give presumptive validity to the Board's decision."[38] In other words, the statute placed the burden on the company to overcome the presumption in favor of the board; but in the absence of the presentation of evidence, that possibility had to be forgone.

For the parties in dispute and their counterparts in later years, *Republic Aviation* signaled the redistribution of workplace rights under the supervision of the New Deal. But by assessing rights for their quality and not just their array, the Supreme Court's decision, while favorable, places labor's rights in the chip position of the shareholders in *Colby v. Equitable Trust* rather than in the trump position enjoyed by the trucking company in *Auburn Draying*. Rights in *Republic Aviation* derive from the broad language of the NLRA, and from there they are dependent on the judges' deference to the board. To be sure, the act anticipated judicial deference to the board's expertise, but this was qualified by the provision that orders would proceed from facts elicited at hearings. The Court did not read this as a rule impairing its discretion in the absence of evidence, and given the circumstances, it proved not to be.[39]

The chip status of all concerned was confirmed by the passage of the Taft-Hartley amendments two years later in 1947, which for the first time wrote into the NLRA protection against unfair practices by employees. The issue of organizing on company property was on a doctrinal seesaw for the next half century, not because of explicit changes to rules, but because of the detailed facts offered in successive cases. The advantage shifted from employees to employers roughly every decade. By the close of the 1980s, relations between the board and the unions had chilled.[40] If the objection is made that this last is an effect of politics, that elections and changing political alignments changed the membership of the board and the courts, that is true; but multiple levels of deference and a judicial system not itself dependably removed from pressures by long-established rules found union "rights" undefended when surroundings turned less hospitable.

Trumps to Chips in Civil Rights

Purely statutory rights could be appealing to labor unions and their allies, whose experience under the Constitution had been less than satisfactory. But for a civil rights movement, well acquainted with statutes standing alone, the renewed constitutionalism after World War II was a better match. *Brown v. Board of Education of Topeka* (347 U.S. 483), decided squarely on the Fourteenth Amendment in 1954, comes as close to an instance of rights as trumps as any in recent history. To be sure, *Brown* is, in some ways, characteristically Progressive: forward looking; not bound by precedent; drawing on experience and social science; avoiding formalist reasoning and technical points generally. Yet it lays down a clear rule: "Separate facilities are inherently unequal. Therefore, we hold that the plaintiffs and others similarly situated for whom the actions have been brought are, by reason of the segregation complained of, deprived of the equal protection of the laws guaranteed by the Fourteenth Amendment."[41]

Brown II, on the remedy, issued after consultation with attorneys general in the affected states, was likewise unequivocal: "It should go without saying that the vitality of these constitutional principles cannot be allowed to yield simply because of disagreement with them."[42] Though criticized for its illusive requirement of "all deliberate speed," *Brown II* was followed in quick succession by Court opinions, all issued per curiam, both upholding and reversing lower courts, desegregating golf courses, parks, beaches, and public buses, generalizing the repudiation of "separate but equal" outside education.[43] Over a two-decade advance, antidiscrimination was strenuously resisted but not on that account wavering or deferential. Segregation, both de facto and intentional, was largely eliminated in public accommodations, voting, employment, and higher education.[44] De facto segregation, or "disparate impact," was paradigmatic of the movement's trump position: absent exacting proof by the defendant party or institution of an acceptable nonracial explanation, civil rights plaintiffs' claims prevailed. Intentions had no role in the equation.[45]

Disparate-impact analysis parallels the burden of proof placed on the company in *Republic Aviation*. Progressive to the core, that decision, identifying unions' rights as chips despite the immediate victory, anticipated other elements in the ongoing legal saga of African American rights. In this regard, I briefly comment on the 1978 decision of *Regents of the University of California v. Bakke* (438 U.S. 265), which may stand for the change of the right to equal education from a trump to a chip. *Bakke* was a suit for racial discrimination by an unsuccessful white applicant to the University of California Davis School of Medicine who claimed he was denied the "equal protection of the laws" in the Fourteenth Amendment by the school's racial classification plan for admitting a greater-than-otherwise number of minority students. The Court agreed and ordered his admission. The plan had its impetus in section 6 of the Civil Rights Act of 1964, which provides for the withdrawal of federal financial assistance from any institution whose programs or activities "excluded from participation . . . [or] denied the benefits of . . . [or] subjected to discrimination" any person on the basis of "race, color or national origin." Like the NLRA, worded in similarly sweeping terms that made no mention of workers' predictable intrusions on the rights of employers, section 6 made no allowance for applicants who, like Alan Bakke, might find themselves newly disadvantaged as a result of the admissions plan.

The NLRB in *Republic Aviation* finds its counterpart in *Bakke* in the medical school admissions committee that designed and administered the plan. Justice Powell's opinion does not finally defer to its expertise, but he comments at length on the importance of the university's autonomy in selecting its students and on the "good faith" presumed to characterize its decisions. These passages set up the reasoning behind the next major affirmative action case, *Grutter v. Bollinger* (539 U.S. 306), decided in 2003.[46] The parallel also points to the indirect nature of the African American rights involved, since minority interests were not represented on either side of the counsel table; this was often the position of unions in NLRA litigation. The scathing criticism of *Bakke*'s management leveled by African American lawyers associated with the case was not unlike the falling-out, after decades, between the NLRB and the union movement, only greatly compressed in time.[47]

The resonance between the two decisions is found most importantly in the adjudication itself. The Court in *Republic Aviation*, lacking evidence other than the board's embodiment of industrial relations know-how, made its ruling based finally on the failure of the company to bear its burden of proving why it should not defer to the board. In *Bakke*, the standard of strict scrutiny applied to the admissions program stands as a proxy for a rule delimiting impermissible discrimination, and the result rides on the university's inability to prove that its program was narrowly tailored. Both opinions confess the Court's incompetence to decide pressing issues on the table. The *Republic Aviation* Court was comfortable ceding judgment to "experienced officials with an adequate appreciation of the complexities."[48] Justice Powell regretted that "the difficulties entailed in varying the level of judicial review according to a perceived 'preferred' status of a particular racial or ethnic group are intractable."[49] In the event, questions left open by *Republic Aviation* were answered by the Taft-Hartley amendments. In *Bakke*, instability going forward was mitigated by the rule of "diversity."

Diversity is a rule only a progressive could love. Justice Powell elaborates: "An otherwise qualified medical student with a particular background— whether it be ethnic, geographic, culturally advantaged or disadvantaged— may bring to a professional school of medicine experiences, outlooks, and ideas that enrich the training of its student body and better equip its graduates to render with understanding their vital service to humanity."[50] Justice Marshall, in his solo opinion, registers the devaluation from trumps to chips under way: "The experience of Negroes in America has been different in kind, not just in degree, from that of other ethnic groups. Now, when a State acts to remedy the effects of that legacy of discrimination, I cannot believe that this same Constitution stands as a barrier."[51] Metaphorically, the justice had it exactly wrong. African American rights in these circumstances were adversely affected by the Constitution not by its impermeability but by its porousness.

A Woman's Due Process

A reading of *Town of Castle Rock v. Gonzales,* decided in 2005 and still good law after a decade, both completes our survey and permits some general conclusions. The case concerned a woman in Colorado, Jessica Gonzales, who, over several hours, telephoned local police repeatedly, pleading with them to enforce a court restraining order and arrest her estranged husband, who, contrary to an agreed-upon schedule, had taken their three daughters away from home. In the early morning hours, the husband arrived at the police station, began shooting a handgun, and was shot dead in the return fire, after which police found the daughters in the cab of his truck, murdered. Gonzales sued the Town of Castle Rock and members of its police force, based on section 1983 of the U.S. Code, which, pursuant to the Fourteenth Amendment, allows suits for damages in federal court against state officers who violate plaintiffs' rights guaranteed by the Constitution or the laws of the United States.

The fact that Gonzales was able to obtain the restraining order (first temporary, then made permanent) by itself distinguishes her from her predecessors who lived during the period when Bentham described "the powers of . . . the husband, the parent," and long afterward as well. As late as 1970, most American states prevented women, by the common law rule of "interstitial torts," from bringing any legal action against their husband except in the setting of divorce proceedings. Rather than continue on the theme of women gaining "chips," however, I will directly engage the idea that rights are a process and speak briefly to some of the implications of that idea. We have glimpsed them already: in the rights of labor, vitiated by the politics on which the unions staked their claim, and in the civil rights movement, snagged in the capacious net of the Fourteenth Amendment.

In neither of these movements, however, does it seem to have been a prominent question whether rights were "real," that is, once acknowledged or provided they would actually materialize in the form of enforcement. On the Court itself, that concern was the motive for a major bolstering of civil rights through an expansion of section 1983's applicability in 1961.[52] Subsequently, to bring a greater diversity of constitutional injuries under federal protection, judges in the 1970s crafted new meanings for the word "property" in the Fourteenth Amendment. Property was no longer only the tangible things of common law, but more akin to the abstract rights of commerce like stocks and bonds and promises in contracts.[53] This portmanteau was valuable, especially to persons and situations not referred to directly in the Constitution but dependent for aspects of their well-being on governmental officers.

Among this last group are women, including, prominently, wives and mothers like Gonzales in *Castle Rock*.[54] Several years earlier, Colorado, like other American states exercising primary jurisdiction over both family relations and the policing of local crime, passed a statute intended to address the slippage between women's reports of violent husbands or fathers and the responses by police. The legislation provided that police officers "shall arrest" by "all reasonable means" persons reported to be in disobedience of a restraining order. The back page of all Colorado restraining orders contained these words:

"*NOTICE TO LAW ENFORCEMENT OFFICIALS*," "YOU SHALL USE EVERY REASONABLE MEANS TO ENFORCE THIS RESTRAINING ORDER. YOU SHALL ARREST, OR, IF AN ARREST WOULD BE IMPRACTICAL UNDER THE CIRCUMSTANCES, SEEK A WARRANT FOR THE ARREST OF THE RESTRAINED PERSON WHEN YOU HAVE INFORMATION AMOUNTING TO PROBABLE CAUSE THAT THE RESTRAINED PERSON HAS VIOLATED OR ATTEMPTED TO VIOLATE ANY PROVISION OF THIS ORDER AND THE RESTRAINED PERSON HAS BEEN PROPERLY SERVED WITH A COPY OF THIS ORDER OR HAS RECEIVED ACTUAL NOTICE OF THE EXISTENCE OF THIS ORDER."[55] (emphasis in the original)

Justice Scalia, writing for the majority in *Castle Rock*, denied that Gonzales stated a valid constitutional claim. This was not a complete surprise. A similar ruling had been made in a recent case concerning serious harm inflicted on a child as a result of custody decisions made by state social workers. That decision held there was no "substantive" right to state protection against violence that was actionable under the Due Process Clause of the Fourteenth Amendment.[56] But Gonzales's suit was different, resting on a state statute, one specifically passed to protect persons in her particular position. On its face, this would seem the kind of lapse between a right and its enforcement that section 1983 was designed to remedy. Moreover, in the complicated climb-down by the Court from what many jurists by then agreed had been its overly expansive definition of constitutional "property," one landing place arrived at was this: property is not created by the Constitution but instead is "defined by existing rules or understandings that stem from an independent source such as state law."[57] The Colorado statute would seem to amply fill that bill.

The *Castle Rock* opinion is multifaceted, not to say scattershot. For the discussion at hand, however, it does three important things. First, it concludes that the Colorado statute, despite its use of the word "shall," was too imprecisely worded to overcome the discretion that policemen have traditionally enjoyed in performing duties like the enforcement of restraining orders; neither did the Court find in the legislation any intention to provide "third parties" like Gonzales with any legal action in the event of officers' disobedience of the statutory requirements. Therefore, she could not show the injury to "property" required to make a claim under section 1983: "A benefit is not a protected entitlement if government officials may grant or deny it in their discretion."[58] Second, the opinion suggests that even if it is agreed that the Colorado statute was intended to be truly mandatory, or if the legislature were able to fashion such unambiguous law in the future, the discretion that "inheres"[59] in the police might still remain. Third, the opinion calls a halt, for federal constitutional purposes, to definitions of property that rest on failures of state legal processes and instead advocates "traditional" understandings of property that normally can be expressed in monetary value.[60]

Each aspect promotes thought. With regard to the first, Gonzales's section 1983 claim was defeated because her alleged right to enforcement was, manifestly, "denied" by officers "in their discretion."[61] In this holding, Justice Scalia endorses rights as process, with a vengeance. Note that the second phase of the process, endorsement of the right, does not weaken the right to a chip, as was the case with decisions discussed before this one. It cancels the claim altogether, in a tail-wags-dog motion reminiscent of Hohfeld's division a century earlier between "rights" and "liberties." The Court might have let the suit proceed and the evidence show the actual reasons for the police nonaction. What it did here instead was by no means an unusual event. Indeed, it can be described as typical of section 1983 suits in which claims that must be seen as close calls are shut down at the starting gate, decided on officers' qualified immunity, foreclosed from receiving a hearing on the merits.

Second, the above, when added to the possibility that *no* legislation could succeed in eliminating sufficient discretion for a due process claim, raises, in the context of *Castle Rock* and analogous cases, the question whether the police officer replaces "the husband, the father" as the holder of rights as trumps. The view that some necessary quantum of police discretion would prevent any Colorado statute from clearing the bar for U.S. constitutional purposes would seem to hamper Congress in a similar attempt as well. When litigants in some dozen states asked late-nineteenth-century courts to abandon the ban on interspousal torts, all rejected the invitation. When Congress passed an act for the District of Columbia in 1901 that stated, "Married women shall have the power . . . to sue for torts committed against them, as fully and freely as if they were unmarried," the U.S. Supreme Court held that it changed nothing: the legislation had not expressly mentioned "one's spouse."[62] Are Scalia and other justices attempting to turn back the clock?

It is tempting to answer in the affirmative. The *Castle Rock* opinion calls up a style of judging typical of a time when rights as trumps over women and others was common: distinctions between direct and indirect; hairsplitting definitions of words; the repeated invocation of tradition; the deployment of worst-case consequentialism. Going further, can the unremovable discretion attributed to policemen be extended to analogous operatives and circumstances, yielding the prospect of American constitutional rights being enclosed within a great elastic cage,[63] in which the only certain rights are those enjoyed by discretionary officers, including, foremost among them, justices on the Supreme Court? Any serious answer to this question would require a far more searching inventory of constitutional and tort law remedies than is possible here. More importantly, any positive conclusion would assume more staying power on the Court of the *Castle Rock* doctrine and several others than recent history causes us to expect.

This brings us to *Castle Rock*'s call for a return to a former, tangible definition of property. In its broadest sense, taken to refer to the source of rights more widely understood, this concern is not confined to "conservatives" on or off the Court. In the same decision, Justices Souter and Breyer wrote a concurring opinion, adding their view that no due process property right could adhere to something that itself constituted due process, like the enforcement of a court order.[64] In the meantime, as we have seen, the grounding and ungrounding of rights, whether based on statutes or on provisions such as the

Fourteenth Amendment, both trumps and chips, hangs ultimately on the Supreme Court's "right to say what the law is."[65] When the words just quoted were penned, however, a great many rights were still regarded by judges as unchangeable, including rights that legal realists targeted with their critique. After a full Progressive century of experience, all the aforementioned might see matters with added nuance. In particular, they might be expected to have a more circumspect understanding of what the "law" of rights "is."

Notes

Thanks to Jack Balkin for comments on an earlier draft. Ideas in this essay are further explored in a forthcoming book, *The Policy State,* coauthored with Stephen Skowronek.

1. For a general overview, see Karl N. Llewellyn, "Some Realism About Realism— Responding to Dean Pound," *Harvard Law Review* 44, no. 8 (1930–31): 1222.

2. Oliver Wendell Holmes Jr., "The Path of the Law," *Harvard Law Review* 10, no. 8 (1897): 457–58. Holmes anticipated this argument in his book *The Common Law* (Boston: Little, Brown, 1881).

3. Wesley Newcomb Hohfeld, "Some Fundamental Legal Conceptions as Applied to Judicial Reasoning," *Yale Law Journal* 27, no. 1 (1917–18): 66–103.

4. Felix Frankfurter and Nathan Green, "Congressional Power over the Labor Injunction," *Columbia Law Review* 31, no. 3 (1931): 405.

5. Gertrude Stein, *Geography and Plays* (Madison: University of Wisconsin Press, 1922), 90.

6. Ronald Dworkin, "Is There a Right to Pornography?," *Oxford Journal of Legal Studies* 1, no. 2 (Summer 1981): 200.

7. For example, within the rights-as-trumps perspective, see Richard Primus, "Equal Protection and Disparate Impact: Round Three," *Harvard Law Review* 117, no. 2 (2003–4): 493–587; see also Bruce A. Ackerman, *We the People*, vol. 1, *Foundations* (Cambridge, Mass.: Harvard University Press, 1991).

8. Karen Orren, "Officers' Rights: Toward a Unified Field Theory of American Constitutional Development," *Law and Society Review* 34, no. 4 (2001): 873–909.

9. Joseph William Singer, "The Legal Rights Debate in Analytic Jurisprudence from Bentham to Hohfeld," *Wisconsin Law Review* 1982, no. 6: 979.

10. Quoted in Singer, "Legal Rights Debate," 1002.

11. This accounts for the towering significance of Lord Mansfield in the eighteenth century.

12. See William Blackstone, *Commentaries on the Laws of England* (Oxford: Clarendon Press, 1765–69), vol. 1, sections 14–17.

13. See James Kent, *Commentaries on American Law* (New York: Halsted, 1826), vol. 2, sections 24–32.

14. A good deal of the discussion centers on the Supreme Court's decision in *Lochner v. New York,* 198 U.S. 45 (1905), striking down a New York statute limiting the working hours of bakery employees on the grounds of "liberty of contract" in the Fourteenth Amendment. The standard reading of this decision is of a reactionary judiciary, drawing its perspective from classical economics and social Darwinism, fearful of labor unions and protective of business corporations. For two influential examples, see Benjamin R. Twiss, *Lawyers and the Constitution: How Laissez-Faire Came to the Supreme Court* (Princeton, N.J.: Princeton University Press, 1942), and Arnold M. Paul, *Conservative Crisis and the Rule of Law: Attitudes of the Bench and Bar, 1887–1895* (Ithaca, N.Y.: Cornell University Press, 1960). More recently, a range of *Lochner* "revisionism" has appeared, the newest of which interprets *Lochner* as the Court's attempt to protect citizens' liberties against growing governmental encroachment. For overviews, see Gary D. Rowe, "*Lochner* Revisionism Revisited," *Law and Social Inquiry* 24, no. 1 (1991): 221–52; Barry Cushman, "Some Varieties and Vicissitudes of Lochnerism," *Boston University Law Review* 85, no. 3 (2005): 881–1000. For a different version, consistent with this essay, see Karen Orren, "The Laws of Industrial Organization, 1870–1920," in *Cambridge History of Law in America,* vol. 2, ed. Michael Grossberg and Christopher Tomlins (New York: Cambridge University Press, 2008).

15. That is, by judges appointed by Governor Theodore Roosevelt or his allies, or else originally appointed by Democrats but during this period supported for reelection by both parties.

16. *Colby v. Equitable Trust Co.,* 124 App. Div. 262, 262 (N.Y. 1908).

17. *Id.* at 265.

18. *Id.*

19. *Id.* at 269.

20. *Id.* at 262, 272.

21. *Id.* at 270, 272.

22. See Dierdre A. Burgman and Paul N. Cox, "Reappraising the Role of the Shareholder in the Modern Public Corporation: *Weinberger's* Procedural Approach to Fairness in Freezeouts," *Wisconsin Law Review* 1984, no. 3: 596–97.

23. Orren, "Laws of Industrial Organization."

24. *Auburn Draying Co. v. Wardell,* 227 N.Y. 1, 8 (1919).

25. *Id.* at 10.

26. *Id.*

27. *Id.* In *Colby,* the plaintiff pointed to the right of the company's "existence," which was about to be no more with the merger. The court brushed this plaint aside with the comment that "the State has absolute control under its reserve power" (*Colby,* 124 App. Div. at 266).

28. *Colby,* 124 App. Div. at 265.

29. James Gray Pope, "The Thirteenth Amendment Versus the Commerce Clause: Labor and the Shaping of American Constitutional Law, 1921–1957," *Columbia Law Review* 102, no. 1 (2002): 1–122.

30. See, for example, Craig Becker, "Democracy in the Workplace: Union Representation Elections and Federal Labor Law," *Minnesota Law Review* 77, no. 3 (Feb. 1993): 561. See also Archibald Cox, "The Right to Engage in Concerted Activities," *Indiana Law Journal* 26, no. 3 (1950–51): 320 and n. 4.

31. This case was considered at the same time as another with comparable facts: *Le Tourneau Co. v. N.L.R.B.*, 143 F.2d 67 (5th Cir. 1944).

32. National Labor Relations Act, 29 U.S.C. §§ 151–69 (1935), cited in *Republic Aviation Corporation v. N.L.R.B.*, 324 U.S. 793, 799 (1945).

33. *Republic Aviation*, 324 U.S. at 798.

34. *Id.* at 803.

35. *Id.*

36. *Id.* at 800.

37. *Republic Aviation Corporation v. N.L.R.B.*, 142 F.2d. 193, 196 (2d Cir. 1944). Section 7 of the National Labor Relations Act (NLRA) provides that employees shall have the right to self-organization; to form, join, or assist labor organizations; to bargain collectively through representatives of their own choosing; and to engage in concerted activities for the purpose of collective bargaining or other mutual aid or protection. Section 8 of the act provides that it shall be an unfair labor practice for an employer to interfere with, restrain, or coerce employees in the exercise of the rights guaranteed in section 7 by discrimination in regard to hire or tenure of employment or any term or condition of employment in order to encourage or discourage membership in any labor organization (National Labor Relations Act, 29 U.S.C. §§ 151–69).

38. *Republic Aviation*, 142 F.2d. at 196.

39. Cox, "Right to Engage"; Theodore R. Iserman, "The Labor-Management Act: New Law as to Evidence and the Scope of Review," *American Bar Association Journal* 33, no. 8 (1947): 760–64.

40. For background, see Terry M. Moe, "Interests, Institutions, and Positive Theory: The Politics of the NLRB," *Studies in American Political Development* 2 (Spring 1987): 236–99; see also Cynthia L. Estlund, "The Ossification of American Labor Law," *Columbia Law Review* 102, no. 6 (2002): 1527–612.

41. *Brown v. Board of Education of Topeka*, 347 U.S. 483, 495 (1954). For a good overview, see Reva B. Siegel, "From Colorblindness to Antibalkanization: An Emerging Ground of Decision in Race Equality Cases," *Yale Law Journal* 120, no. 6 (2010–11): 1278–367.

42. *Brown v. Board of Education of Topeka*, 349 U.S. 294, 298–99 (1954).

43. See, for instance, *Baltimore v. Dawson*, 350 U.S. 877 (1955); *Holmes v. Atlanta*, 350 U.S. 879 (1955); *Gayle v. Browder*, 352 U.S. 903 (1956); and *New Orleans City Park Improvement Association v. Detiege*, 358 U.S. 54 (1958).

44. The end point is usually marked by *Milliken v. Bradley*, 418 U.S. 717 (1974), in which the Court held that planned desegregation busing was impermissible unless there was actual evidence that multiple school districts had intentionally engaged in policies of segregation. De facto segregation in the school context was no longer a sufficient reason to undertake remedial desegregation efforts.

45. See, for example, *Griggs et al. v. Duke Power Co.*, 401 U.S. 424 (1970). *Griggs* was later reversed by *Washington v. Davis*, 426 U.S. 229 (1976).

46. *Regents of the University of California v. Bakke*, 438 U.S. 265, 312, 318–19 (1978); *Grutter v. Bollinger*, 539 U.S. 306, 329 (2003).

47. See Derek Bell, "*Bakke*, Minority Admissions, and the Usual Price of Racial Remedies," *California Law Review* 67, no. 1 (1979): 3–20; see also Ralph R. Smith, "Reflections on a Landmark: Some Preliminary Observations on the Development and Significance of *Regents of the University of California v. Allan Bakke*," *Howard Law Journal* 21, no. 1 (1978): 72–127.

48. *Republic Aviation*, 324 U.S. at 800.

49. *Bakke*, 438 U.S. at 295.

50. *Id.* at 314.

51. *Id.* at 400.

52. *Brown v. Board of Education of Topeka* was a section 1983 action. First provided in 1871, these became available to non-civil-rights plaintiffs in *Monroe v. Pape* (365 U.S. 167) in 1961. Today chapter 42 of the U.S. Code, section 1983, reads:

> Every person who, under color of any statute, ordinance, regulation, custom, or usage, of any State or Territory or the District of Columbia, subjects, or causes to be subjected, any citizen of the United States or other person within the jurisdiction thereof to the deprivation of any rights, privileges, or immunities secured by the Constitution and laws, shall be liable to the party injured in an action at law, suit in equity, or other proper proceeding for redress, except that in any action brought against a judicial officer for an act or omission taken in such officer's judicial capacity, injunctive relief shall not be granted unless a declaratory decree was violated or declaratory relief was unavailable. For the purposes of this section, any Act of Congress applicable exclusively to the District of Columbia shall be considered to be a statute of the District of Columbia.

In 1978, in *Monell v. Department of Social Services of New York City* (456 U.S. 658), these suits were extended to municipalities.

53. See the discussion in Thomas W. Merrill, "The Landscape of Constitutional Property," *Virginia Law Review* 86, no. 5 (2000): 885–999. Justice Scalia relied on this article in his opinion in *Castle Rock v. Gonzales*, 545 U.S. 748, 766–67 (2005).

54. Again, there is the inevitable comparison with husbands and fathers of an earlier day. Should a wife, perhaps taking children with her, abscond, the husband enjoyed the right of forcible "recaption," qualified only by the proviso that he accomplish it

without trespass or disturbance of the peace. This was the law in the United States in the Gilded Age. See Rollin C. Hurd, *A Treatise on the Right of Personal Liberty and on the Right of Habeas Corpus* (Albany, N.Y.: Little, 1876), 30–31.

55. *Castle Rock,* 545 U.S. at 752.

56. *DeShaney v. Winnebago County Department of Social Services,* 489 U.S. 189 (1989).

57. *Board of Regents of State Colleges v. Roth,* 408 U.S. 564, 577 (1972).

58. *Castle Rock,* 545 U.S. at 756.

59. In *Castle Rock,* the Court quotes approvingly *Natale v. Ridgefield,* 170 F.3d 258, 263 (2d Cir. 1999): "There is no reason . . . to restrict the 'uncertainty' that will preclude existence of a federally protectable property interest to the uncertainty that inheres in the exercise of discretion" (545 U.S. at 764).

60. *Castle Rock,* 545 U.S. at 765.

61. *Id.* at 784.

62. *Thompson v. Thompson,* 218 U.S. 611, 618 (1910).

63. Reference, and apologies, to Max Weber.

64. *Castle Rock,* 545 U.S. at 770.

65. *Marbury v. Madison,* 5 U.S. 137 (1803).

5 • Reclaiming the Conceptual Legacy of the Progressives' Critique of Rights

Equal Protection Without Higher Scrutiny

Sonu Bedi

The Progressives mounted a serious critique of constitutional rights, arguing that such rights thwart the democratic powers of government. According to the conventional view, the U.S. Supreme Court has affirmed only half this critique. That is, the modern Court has "disavowed precedents that protected economic rights, but elaborated upon, reinterpreted, and most importantly preserved and expanded its list of civil rights and civil liberties precedents."[1] Or as Richard Epstein puts it: "The Progressives' claim, cast in modern terms, was that a rational-basis approach should apply to all conflicts between government power and individual rights to property and contract."[2] And although constitutional liberals have endorsed this approach for economic legislation, "a different attitude took hold on matters of speech, religion, and race."[3] This places modern constitutional liberals in a bind: they reject economic rights but then seem to insist on affirming social ones.

This chapter challenges the conventional view, arguing that contemporary liberals can avoid this bind by adhering to the Progressives' rejection of rights and their simultaneous endorsement of democratic power. Doing so not only resolves the inconsistency of liberals embracing some rights but not others, but also holds liberals as being truer than conservatives to the Progressives' historical advocacy of limited judicial authority in a democracy.[4] Contemporary rights jurisprudence, particularly in the area of equal protection, treats certain groups or categories as suspect, so laws that affect that group or invoke that category receive a searching level of scrutiny. The more the Court scrutinizes a law, the more likely it is to strike the law down. This doctrine of suspect classes and tiers of scrutiny easily invites judicial ideological discretion. For once the Court applies higher scrutiny, its argumentative hurdle to strike down the law is low. This, in turn, makes it easier for a justice to thwart democratic majorities by invalidating the relevant law or policy.

To avoid this problem, contemporary liberals must shift their focus from *rights* to those *reasons* that are constitutionally inadmissible. In other words, rather than asserting that an individual has a certain right at stake, the Court should determine whether the law rests on an inadmissible reason or purpose. Focusing in particular on the Court's equal protection jurisprudence,[5] this chapter shows how this turn to reasons permits the Court to uphold laws establishing a minimum wage and maximum hours, for example, as well as to strike down racist and homophobic laws without resort to rights. This approach is not just a conceptual or theoretical one. It is both explicitly grounded in the Progressives' aspiration to move beyond rights claims and also maintains the policy aims and aspirations that contemporary liberals hold dear and that are emblematic of the mid- to late-twentieth-century "minority rights revolution."[6] This approach is neo-progressive insofar as it emphasizes democratic institutions and decision making while de-emphasizing the countermajoritarian potential of judicial authority.

One theme of this volume is to assess the impact of Progressive thought on the contemporary Constitution, and this impact is not always straightforward. As Aziz Rana contends, Progressive ideology may point toward systematic constitutional revision or even rejection. And as Brian Tamanaha writes, by championing progressive aims, contemporary liberals often invite the charge of judicial subjectivity in a way that their legal conservative counterparts do not. Or as Karen Orren argues, critiques of rights suggest a rethinking of rights, not as "trumps," but as "chips," as a kind of modality in legal reasoning.

This chapter contributes to that theme; it assesses the legal implication of the Progressive agenda by drawing attention to the distinction between rights and state or governmental powers. Although the Progressives may not have envisioned it in these terms (hence the "neo" in "neo-progressive"), their emphasis on democratic powers instead of rights provides an undertheorized way to *limit* what government may do, one that in fact motivates extant constitutional jurisprudence. By focusing on such powers, this chapter reclaims the conceptual legacy of the Progressives' critique of rights and ultimately resolves the paradox of how the Progressive critique gave way to their liberal descendants' seemingly antithetical embrace of rights. It informs the Progressives' skepticism of courts and individual rights and their faith in building the capacities of democratic institutions.

The chapter proceeds in three parts. First, I present the Progressive critique of rights and its view of the Constitution as a document centrally about the powers of government and not about rights. In doing so, I argue that repudiating *Lochner v. New York* (1905) means that although the state may act on reasons relating to health or safety, other reasons may be constitutionally off-limits. Second, I illuminate this argument by analyzing the Court's jurisprudence on certain laws that discriminate against gays and lesbians. These cases point to a doctrinal framework that is not so much about vindicating rights as about ensuring that the state does not act on a bare desire to harm. Third, I consider this framework in light of the Court's jurisprudence on race. If laws based on animus are unconstitutional, the Court can strike down racist laws like bans on interracial marriage without invoking strict scrutiny, the high level of scrutiny the Court currently imposes on laws that discriminate on the basis of race. A turn from strict scrutiny stands as one way to rehabilitate the Progressive legacy on racial equality. In short, while contemporary rights jurisprudence relies on an elaborate yet increasingly convoluted doctrine of scrutiny and protected-class analysis,[7] a progressive focus on state powers, and on whether laws are based on animus or a bare desire to harm, provides a clearer way to maintain individual liberty while limiting judicial discretion, in line with democratic aims.

The Progressives' Critique of Rights: The Turn to Powers

The Progressives mounted a strident critique of constitutional rights, arguing that such rights thwart the powers of government.[8] Herbert Croly, for instance, explained that the Framers "knew that no government could be efficient unless its powers equaled its responsibilities."[9] After all, as Croly went on to say, the Constitution

> was wrought both as the organ of the national interest and as the bulwark of certain individual and local rights. . . . The security of private property and personal liberty, and a proper distribution of activity between the local and the central governments, demanded at that time, and within limits still demand, adequate legal guarantees. It remains none the less true, however, that every popular government should in the end, and after a necessarily prolonged deliberation, possess the power of taking any action, which, in the opinion of a decisive majority of the people, is demanded by the public welfare.[10]

By emphasizing the powers of government, Croly argued against a "stringent bill of individual and state rights."[11] Rights, in this critique, stand to limit what government may do.

Lochner v. New York (1905)[12] is the flash point for this critique. In *Lochner,* the State of New York passed a law prohibiting bakers from working more than sixty hours a week. The Court struck down the law, reasoning, in part: "The statute necessarily interferes with the right of contract between the employer and employees concerning the number of hours in which the latter may labor in the bakery of the employer. The general right to make a contract in relation to his business is part of the liberty of the individual protected by the Fourteenth Amendment of the Federal Constitution."[13] *Lochner* represents a commitment to the substantive due process rights to property or contract, unenumerated constitutional rights that thwart the powers of government. In repudiating the underlying rationale of *Lochner,* Progressives rejected these constitutional rights.

During the New Deal, the Court abandoned these rights, in line with the Progressives' critique. In a series of cases, including *Nebbia v. New York* (1934),[14] *West Coast Hotel Co. v. Parrish* (1937),[15] and *United States v. Carolene Products Co.* (1938),[16] the Court upheld laws and policies concerning commercial or economic transactions, including minimum wages, maximum hours, and the like. In *Nebbia,* for instance, the Court upheld a New York law that regulated minimum and maximum retail prices. Contra *Lochner,* the *Nebbia* Court reasoned: "Neither property rights nor contract rights are absolute; for government cannot exist if the citizen may at will use his property to the detriment of his fellows, or exercise his freedom of contract to work them harm."[17] Similarly, in *West Coast Hotel,* the Court upheld the constitutionality of Washington's minimum wage law: "In dealing with the relation of employer and employed, the Legislature has necessarily a wide field of discretion in order that there may be suitable protection of health and safety."[18]

Carolene Products seemingly consummated the Progressives' critique of rights. Here the Court upheld a congressional prohibition on the shipment of certain skim-milk compounds. In the Court's reasoning: "The existence of facts supporting the legislative judgment is to be presumed, for regulatory legislation affecting ordinary commercial transactions is not to be pronounced unconstitutional unless, in the light of the facts made known or generally assumed, it is of such a character as to preclude the assumption that it rests upon some rational basis within the knowledge and experience of the legislators."[19] This standard of review, one the Court imposed on the federal prohibition, requires that laws have some rational basis. After outlining this standard, in its famous footnote 4, *Carolene Products* reasons that "there may be narrower scope for operation of the presumption of constitutionality when legislation appears on its face to be within a specific prohibition of the Constitution, such as those of the first ten amendments ... or when legislation appears on its face" to discriminate against "discrete and insular minorities."[20]

This bifurcation is a core feature of modern constitutional jurisprudence. Laws that infringe a fundamental right or discriminate against a "discrete and insular" group (invoking a suspect classification) receive higher scrutiny. Laws and policies that do not infringe a fundamental right or invoke a suspect classification receive rational review. The higher the level of scrutiny, the more likely the law will be struck down. By implication, then, the rights to property and contract are *not fundamental*. In subjecting federal law to this lower level of scrutiny, the Court held that Congress had passed such a prohibition because "the use of filled milk as a substitute for pure milk is generally injurious to health and facilitates fraud on the public."[21]

The conventional view of these cases, juxtaposed against *Lochner*, is that government has unlimited power to pass economic legislation, precisely because the Court repudiated the rights to property and contract. This is often seen as the conceptual legacy of the Progressives' critique of rights. The motivating impulse of this chapter is that the legacy of this critique is more nuanced than this account suggests. A turn to powers does not automatically mean government may do whatever it likes. For once we turn our attention away from rights and toward the underlying reason or rationale for a law, these cases reveal limits on governmental power. *Nebbia, West Coast Hotel,* and *Carolene Products* held that government has the power to regulate retail prices, set minimum wages, and prohibit shipment of certain goods. These cases certainly rejected the rights to property and contract.

But in doing so, they discussed the reason or rationale that underlay such laws. The Court in *Nebbia* reasoned that government may "regulate" property or contract interests "in the common interest."[22] In *West Coast Hotel,* it noted that the state may take into account the unequal bargaining position of the parties in an employment contract. Although conceding that the parties were competent to contract, the Court held that in such relationships the "parties do not stand upon an equal footing."[23] Here, as the Court made clear, the law sought to protect the "health and safety" of the citizens of Washington. This reasoning emphasized that these laws and policies were based on "common interest" or the "protection of health and safety." In fact, in *Carolene Products,* the Court conceded that a law may be "of such a character as to preclude the assumption that it rests upon some rational basis."[24] This implied that laws and policies may violate rational review, precisely because they rest on some inadmissible rationale or purpose.

This concern with purpose is a central feature of the analysis in *Lochner.* Justice Rufus W. Peckham's majority opinion directly engages it: "We are justified in saying so when, from the character of the law and the subject upon which it legislates, it is apparent that the public health or welfare bears but the most remote relation to the law."[25] In fact, extant scholarly work reinterprets *Lochner* and other cases as not really being about rights but about limits on the state's police powers.[26] Howard Gillman, who makes the most forceful argument in this regard, argues that *Lochner* stands for the principle that the state does not have the power to enact " 'class' or 'partial' legislation; that is, laws that (from [the justices'] point of view) promoted only the narrow interests of particular groups or classes rather than the general welfare."[27] In the case of *Lochner,* the law singled out bakeries but not other trades in limiting the number of hours worked. This emphasis away from rights and toward powers is noteworthy. But this line of interpretation seems to proffer too broad a limit on government power. If government could not act in the interests of some group over another, it would be unable to do almost anything. States routinely pass laws and policies that favor one class over another: criminal laws favor law followers over lawbreakers, property protections favor property owners over those who do not own property.

The emphasis should not be on whether the law invokes or discriminates against some in favor of others, but, as I elucidate below, whether the law is based on nothing more than a bare desire to harm. In other words, does the law's purpose rest on animus? The law in *Lochner* is inapposite. Peckham concedes that there may be some health issues related to the hours a baker works. The opinion does not go so far as to claim that the maximum-hours law is patently irrational or that it rests on a bare desire to harm those who employ bakers. Nowhere does Peckham use the language of "animus" or "hostility." Rather, according to him, these concerns are too inconsequential to justify regulating the employer-employee contract: "There must be more than the mere fact of the possible existence of some small amount of unhealthiness to warrant legislative interference with liberty."[28] Otherwise, it would mean that the state would be able to regulate the hours of almost any employee, because "no trade, no occupation, no mode of earning one's living could escape this all-pervading power."[29] This analysis wrestles with the fact that the concern with health and safety was small compared with the infringement of the employer's right to contract. By ultimately invoking the language of rights, *Lochner* refuses to leave this trade-off between health or safety and contractual liberty to the democratic polity. A "small amount of unhealthiness" is just not sufficient to warrant a violation of rights.

But it is precisely this cost-benefit analysis that Justice Holmes's dissent reasons ought to be left to the democratic polity. Holmes, in Progressive fashion, does not emphasize the language of rights but rather the reasonableness of the law: "A reasonable man might think it a proper measure on the score of health."[30] Individuals may disagree about whether limits on a baker's working hours are a good way to ensure health or safety. Perhaps there are other, better ways of doing so. This does not mean, however, that the maximum-hours law was based on a bare desire to harm bakers or those who employ them. It is true that deferring to the democratic polity in this way means that government may have the power to "regulate the hours of almost any employee." But it does not mean that such power is unlimited.

Rejecting *Lochner* not only entails a rejection of the rights to property and contract. This is the conventional view of the legacy of the Progressives' critique. Properly understood, a rejection of *Lochner* also means that there may be inherent limits to governmental power, limits that are about the underlying reason or rationale of a law. Without the language of rights, government indeed has the power to pass laws and policies that are, at least in some way, based on the "common interest" or on securing the health or safety of its citizens. When government does not act on the basis of this kind of rationale or purpose, it exceeds its power under the Constitution. This is what the rejection of *Lochner* and the holdings in cases such as *Nebbia, West Coast Hotel,* and *Carolene Products* seem to imply.

Beyond the Rights of Gays and Lesbians: Animus and Equal Protection "Class of One" Cases

The Court's recent cases striking down antigay laws and policies make clear that the state does not have the power to enact legislation based on animus or a bare desire to harm. Once we appreciate this constitutional limit on governmental power, we do not need to invoke the rights of gays and lesbians. This points to an undertheorized legacy of the Progressives' critique of rights, and one that suggests at least some reasons that are constitutionally inadmissible in justifying legislation. The motivating impulse of this chapter is to focus not on what government may do but on what it may *not* do, and in particular on the reasons or rationales upon which it may not act. This focus on constitutionally inadmissible reasons provides an alternative way for the Court to strike down laws and policies without invoking rights.

Footnote 4 of *Carolene Products* articulates the conventional rights-based approach by reasoning that laws "within a specific prohibition of the Constitution, such as those of the first ten amendments," and legislation that "appears on its face" to discriminate against "discrete and insular minorities" should receive higher-level review. The focus of this essay is on the second branch of the footnote 4 analysis, in which laws that discriminate against the equal rights of certain groups or classes such as racial minorities or women receive a higher form of scrutiny.[31] This class-based interpretation of the Equal Protection Clause means that it is presumptively unconstitutional to discriminate against certain classifications but not others.

Under current constitutional doctrine, laws discriminating on the basis of race,[32] alienage,[33] and national origin[34] get strict scrutiny, in which the Court asks whether the law is narrowly tailored to serve a compelling state purpose. Laws discriminating against sex get intermediate scrutiny: the Court asks whether the law is substantially related to serving an important governmental purpose.[35] Those laws that do not invoke a suspect classification merely receive rational review, the most deferential standard. Legislation, like the one at issue in *Lochner*, that discriminates between employers and employees or bakers and nonbakers would receive only rational review. Under rational review, legislation need only have a legitimate purpose, and the means must be rationally related to that purpose. The more the Court strictly scrutinizes a law, the more likely it is to be struck down. According to Adam Winkler, for instance, between 1990 and 2003, 73 percent of all race-conscious laws subjected to strict scrutiny in federal courts were struck down.[36]

Currently, gays and lesbians do not count as a suspect class, so laws discriminating on the basis of sexual orientation do not receive higher scrutiny. Scholarly work has argued that gays and lesbians ought to count as a suspect class, thereby rendering sexual orientation a suspect classification.[37] This is the conventional identity-rights, class-based approach to equal protection jurisprudence. Insofar as constitutional liberals affirm it, they seem to endorse the very language of rights that Progressives criticized. On one hand, the Progressives' critique of rights and turn to powers stands in opposition to affirming the equal rights of gays and lesbians, or any group for that matter. On the other hand, these identity-rights claims seem central to a liberal idea of equality under the law.

We can avoid this predicament by focusing on the constitutional principle that government does not have the power to act on animus.[38] For instance, if government can act on reasons relating to health or safety—as New York sought to do in *Lochner*—this entails that other, less benign reasons may be constitutionally inadmissible. If there are such inadmissible reasons or rationales, we do not need to invoke the language of rights or the higher scrutiny that often accompanies it. This approach is evident in *Romer v. Evans* (1996)[39] and *United States v. Windsor* (2013),[40] two cases in which the Court invalidated antigay legislation without invoking the language of rights and the higher scrutiny that accompanies it. Both cases point to the idea that a bare desire to harm is a constitutionally inadmissible rationale or purpose. Laws based on such an inadmissible purpose are therefore unconstitutional.

In *Romer*, the Court struck down an amendment to the Colorado Constitution prohibiting all local and state legislative, executive, and judicial action from protecting gays, lesbians, and bisexuals on the basis of this kind of review. This amendment stripped gays and lesbians of legal rights of nondiscrimination that existed under local ordinances in Colorado. Discrimination against gays and lesbians does not trigger higher scrutiny under the Court's current doctrinal framework. This did not stop the Court from invalidating the Colorado amendment under a rational review analysis. The Court reasoned that this standard of review requires that at the very least there be "a sufficient factual context"[41] to justify the legislation. This is sometimes interpreted as a kind of rational review "with bite."[42] Here the discrimination against the group was "born of animosity."[43] If "equal protection of the laws means anything, it must at the very least mean that a bare . . . desire to harm a politically unpopular group cannot constitute a legitimate governmental interest."[44]

More recently, in *Windsor*, the Court invalidated the Defense of Marriage Act (DOMA), a federal law that did not recognize valid state marriages between same-sex couples. The Court did not subject the law to higher scrutiny. It did not deem gays and lesbians a suspect class. The Court reasoned, as it did in *Romer*, that DOMA's purpose was based on nothing but animus: "DOMA's principal effect is to identify a subset of state-sanctioned marriages and make them unequal. The principal purpose is to impose inequality, not for other reasons like governmental efficiency."[45] The Court concluded, drawing on the Fifth Amendment's Due Process Clause, that "the federal statute is invalid, for no legitimate purpose overcomes the purpose and effect to disparage and to injure those whom the State, by its marriage laws, sought to protect in personhood and dignity."[46] The language of "legitimate purpose" is the language of rational review. Nowhere does *Windsor* hold that gays and lesbians are a suspect class, and it thereby does not trigger some kind of higher-level scrutiny. Rather, Justice Kennedy's majority opinion reasoned that the law was motivated substantially by animus: "[The] history of DOMA's enactment and its own text demonstrate that interference with the equal dignity of same-sex marriages . . . was more than an incidental effect of the federal statute. It was its essence."[47] *Windsor* concludes that DOMA rested on a "bare congressional desire to harm a politically unpopular group."[48]

Romer and *Windsor* reveal that the Court was able to conclude that these laws did not rest on a benign purpose but rather on animus against a particular group—here, gays and lesbians—without invoking higher scrutiny. Drawing in part on *Windsor*, the Court invalidated bans on same-sex marriage in *Obergefell v. Hodges* (2015) without imposing the doctrinal requirement of higher scrutiny.[49] In fact, although *Windsor* did not decide whether state bans on same-sex marriage were constitutional, it is worth noting that federal district courts in at least five states that struck down their states' bans on same-sex marriage before the decision in *Obergefell* explicitly did so under a rational review analysis.[50] These rulings indicate that strict scrutiny is not necessary to invalidate laws and policies that are based on animus or that impose inequality for its own sake. As a result, liberals do not need to invoke a discourse of fundamental rights for gays and lesbians in order to strike down certain kinds of antigay legislation. Government, including states and Congress, simply do not have the power to act on animus.

This limitation on power is perhaps clearest in *Village of Willowbrook v. Olech* (2000),[51] a case that is often neglected in scholarly work on equal protection. Here the Court considered what it described as an equal protection "class of one" case.[52] Grace Olech, the claimant, asked the Village of Willowbrook, Illinois, to connect her to the local municipal water supply. The village conditioned the connection on Olech granting the municipality a thirty-three-foot easement instead of the standard fifteen-foot easement required of other residents who sought a similar connection. Olech contended that the village treated her differently because she had filed an unrelated lawsuit against the city. She sued, claiming that the village violated the Equal Protection Clause in asking for an additional eighteen feet. Olech did not claim that the city discriminated against her on the basis of an identity classification such as sex, race, or sexual orientation.

The district court dismissed the suit precisely for this reason, holding that an equal protection claim had to be based on identity rights in order to succeed. The federal appeals court reversed. The appeals court made clear that a claimant "can allege an equal protection violation by asserting that state action was motivated solely by a 'spiteful effort to "get" him for reasons wholly unrelated to any legitimate state objective.'"[53] The Court unanimously upheld the appellate decision, reasoning that even without such spite, the village's decision to ask for fifteen more feet was "irrational and wholly arbitrary," thereby violating the Equal Protection Clause.[54] And there was no language of higher scrutiny—after all, there was no allegation of discrimination on the basis of a suspect classification.

Justice Breyer's concurrence suggests that it was the addition of animus in the municipality's action that triggered the equal protection violation.[55] Scholarly work on *Olech* wrestles with the issue of whether animus or hostility is necessary in order to make a successful "class of one" claim.[56] That is, should Justice Breyer's concurrence be the controlling principle in these cases? While I do not seek to answer this question definitively here, consider that many kinds of line drawing are arbitrary: highway speed limits, having to drive on the right side of the road, or the amount of a speeding fine. These acts do not violate equal protection. To suggest that they do would unduly burden governmental power, resulting in a definition of animus that would invalidate too many laws and policies. As in the case of the maximum-hours law in *Lochner*, there is no sense in which hostility underlies the decision to set the speed limit at sixty-five or to require individuals to drive on the right side of the road. This is why animus, "a bare desire to harm"—directed at a group or an individual—may seem necessary in holding that state action is unconstitutional.

The scholarly work that considers the underlying theory of *Olech* is generally critical or skeptical of it, arguing that the decision does not sit well with traditional, *Carolene Products* footnote 4, equal protection jurisprudence and its focus on groups or identity rights.[57] *Olech* points to an equal protection framework that focuses only on whether the reason or rationale underlying a law or policy is constitutionally inadmissible, not whether the law discriminates against a suspect class and thereby triggers higher scrutiny.

Reconsidering the Need for Strict Scrutiny: Racial Equality Without Rights

If claims of equal rights for gays and lesbians are not necessary to strike down antigay laws and policies, the Court can do the same for racist legislation. Here, too, liberals do not need higher scrutiny in order to secure equality.

If the Equal Protection Clause bans the state from acting on a bare desire to harm, this is sufficient to ensure racial equality without the language of rights while simultaneously permitting democratic majorities to pass remedial race-conscious legislation more easily.

There are two primary justifications for deploying strict scrutiny. First, since racial minorities are obviously minorities in the democratic process, they are susceptible to majority tyranny. Thus, the Court must be particularly wary of laws that invoke race. John Ely's classic defense of judicial review provides this justification for strict scrutiny, one in which the Court's role is to remedy defects in the democratic process.[58] Second, strict scrutiny is how the Court determines whether a policy is remedial (one of inclusion) or racist (one of exclusion). In *City of Richmond v. Croson* (1989),[59] analyzing a city's policy of giving preference to minority-owned businesses in municipal contracts, the Court suggested that without "searching judicial inquiry into the justification for such race-based measures, there is simply no way of determining . . . what classifications are in fact motivated by illegitimate notions of racial inferiority or simple racial politics."[60]

But if these are the justifications for strict scrutiny, the doctrine turns out to be unnecessary, since the Court has invalidated antigay laws like Colorado's Amendment 2 and DOMA without invoking it. Gays and lesbians are certainly a political minority requiring protection from the democratic process.[61] Their interests may not be properly represented. But *Romer* and *Windsor* reveal that the Court is able to strike down laws that contain such democratic defects without invoking strict scrutiny. Simultaneously, the Court was able to conclude that these laws did not rest on a benign purpose, but rather on animus against a particular group. The Court can fulfill the alleged justifications for imposing strict scrutiny without actually invoking it.

Consider in particular, then, the similarity between bans on same-sex marriage and bans on interracial marriage. One of the first cases in which the Court invalidated an anti-racial-minority law explicitly on the basis of strict scrutiny was *McLaughlin v. State of Florida* (1964),[62] followed by *Loving v. Virginia* (1967).[63] *McLaughlin* entailed a challenge to a law that punished only interracial unmarried couples living together. The Court invalidated the law under the Equal Protection Clause, and its reasoning is instructive. The Court began by noting that the law required some "overriding statutory purpose"[64]— the conventional appeal to higher, or strict, scrutiny.

The state proffered the reduction of promiscuity as the purpose for the law. The Court reasoned: "There is no suggestion that a white person and a Negro are any more likely habitually to occupy the same room together than the white or the Negro couple or to engage in illicit intercourse if they do."[65] Even assuming that curtailing promiscuity was the actual purpose of the law, the distinction between same- and opposite-race cohabitation was irrelevant to accomplishing it. There is "no suggestion" that the means were related to the law's alleged purpose. If that is the case, there is no need to subject the law to exacting scrutiny. The Court could have simply concluded that singling out interracial cohabitation was based on animus against interracial couples—that was the law's essence, just as DOMA was based on animus against same-sex couples.

In fact, up until the early 1970s, the American Psychiatric Association listed homosexuality as a clinical disorder.[66] With the passage of time, many of us (though perhaps not all) have come to consider antigay legislation to be arbitrary, in line with the holdings in *Romer* and *Windsor*. Under this logic, perhaps strict scrutiny was useful in the mid–twentieth century as a kind of "judicial training" in order to ensure that judges would take a second look at legislation that discriminated on the basis of race.[67] It was worth noting that the Progressives' emphasis on social science often endorsed the kind of scientific racism that we now dismiss as bogus.[68]

But even if this training argument is accurate, it hardly seems necessary to continue to deploy strict scrutiny. After all, *Romer* was decided in 1996. No higher scrutiny was needed in order to combat homophobic legislation that may have seemed legitimate only twenty years before. For example, in 1972 the Court dismissed an appeal of the Minnesota Supreme Court's decision denying a marriage license to same-sex couples "for want of a substantial federal question."[69] Just forty-one years later, the Court in *Windsor* made an about-face, deciding not only that there was a justiciable issue but also that DOMA was unconstitutional. This doctrinal turn occurred without the explicit language of higher scrutiny, representing what Stephen Engel argues is the "erosion of the doctrine as an empirical matter."[70]

Why then is strict scrutiny necessary for racist laws and policies?[71] Put differently, even if strict scrutiny is a kind of training or learning curve for judges, that training should now be over. Just as strict scrutiny is not necessary to strike down antigay laws, it is not necessary to invalidate ones based on "notions of racial inferiority." And if rational review is sufficient to invalidate antigay policies, it ought to be sufficient to invalidate racist ones, policies based on "notions of racial inferiority." Just as the law at issue in *Romer* was based on hostility to or animus against "being gay," Jim Crow laws were based on hostility to or animus against "being black." The logic is the same.[72]

The Court currently imposes higher scrutiny when a law explicitly discriminates against certain groups or classes. Mere disparate impact on a suspect class is not sufficient on its own to trigger this kind of scrutiny.[73] Rather, the Court requires that "the decisionmaker . . . selected or reaffirmed a particular course of action at least in part 'because of,' not merely 'in spite of,' its adverse effects upon an identifiable group."[74] This means that the Court imposes strict scrutiny only on precisely those laws that intentionally discriminate on the basis of race. But those are the very kinds of laws whose invalidation does not require such scrutiny.[75] It is relatively easy to realize that laws like the ones in *Romer* or *Loving* were based on animus.

We need not look just to the Court's recent cases concerning antigay or racist legislation. In one of the first equal protection cases concerning racial discrimination, the Court invalidated a racist policy without invoking higher scrutiny, strict or otherwise. In *Yick Wo v. Hopkins* (1886),[76] a unanimous Court held that San Francisco authorities did not have the power under the Equal Protection Clause to grant laundry licenses to whites but to deny such licenses to those of Chinese descent. The Court reasoned that executing a law in this manner was an instance of "arbitrary power."[77] The Court made clear that "no reason for [such discrimination] exists except hostility to the race and nationality to which the petitioners belong, and which, in the eye of the law, is not justified."[78] The Court did not resort to any kind of higher scrutiny in realizing that this action by government was based on animus.

This framework provides one way to explain why both *Lochner* and *Plessy v. Ferguson* (1896) (upholding Louisiana's public segregation law)[79] were wrongly decided. Constitutional liberals often focus on the fact that both decisions validated the unjust status quo.[80] Although this may be true, it misses the more important focus on the state's power to act on certain reasons rather than others, which was, of course, what Progressives sought to emphasize in their rejection of rights in the first place. The law in *Plessy* was based on a bare desire to harm blacks. It singled them out for no other reason than to single them out. This was the same kind of constitutionally inadmissible rationale that underlay Amendment 2, DOMA, or the Village of Willowbrook's decision to condition Grace Olech's water supply on a thirty-three-foot easement. In contrast, the maximum-hours law for bakers was not based on a bare desire to harm. Tellingly, although Justice Peckham cited *Yick Wo*, he refrained from holding that no reason existed for the bakery law "except hostility" to bakers or those who employed them.

Recasting the Equal Protection Clause as a ban on the state's power to act on animus leads to a reevaluation of the constitutionality of affirmative action. Without strict scrutiny—it was unnecessary to invalidate laws like the ones in *Plessy* and *Loving*—the state may more freely enact remedial race-conscious legislation without judicial interference. In *Grutter v. Bollinger* (2003),[81] in a 5–4 decision, the Court upheld the University of Michigan Law School's "plus" system, in which certain racial minorities receive a plus in the admission's process in order to ensure racial diversity in the incoming class.

Although *Grutter* upheld affirmative action, Justice O'Connor was part of the majority. She has been replaced by Justice Alito, who is likely to side with the more ideologically conservative members of the Court in striking down affirmative action. And the doctrinal tool that will permit the Court to do so will be strict scrutiny. In fact, the Court has recently made clear that this level of scrutiny is indeed stringent.[82] Again, between 1990 and 2003, 73 percent of all race-conscious laws subjected to strict scrutiny in federal courts were struck down. Adding insult to injury, invariably the laws struck down in that period were ones, such as affirmative action policies, that sought to ameliorate the status of racial minorities.

But all members of the *Grutter* Court agreed that a law that discriminates on the basis of race (irrespective of whether it discriminates against a racial majority or minority) ought to receive strict scrutiny.[83] The only difference among them was whether this standard was applied correctly. While the five-person majority in *Grutter* concluded that law school's policy did pass strict scrutiny, the dissent argued otherwise.

Writing for the Court, Justice O'Connor reasoned that a diverse student body in the context of higher education promotes "cross-racial understanding," which "helps to break down racial stereotypes, and enables [students] to better understand persons of different races."[84] Moreover, the Court concluded that a policy of giving individuals of racial groups a plus in the admissions process was indeed narrowly tailored, because race was just one factor among many in this process.

The dissent argued that strict scrutiny had not been appropriately applied. For instance, Justice Thomas stridently argued that the majority "purports to apply"[85] strict scrutiny but in fact does not. He argued that previous cases held that "national security" or "a government's effort to remedy past [racial] discrimination for which it is responsible" constituted a compelling purpose.[86] Neither rationale, he reasoned, was applicable here. Thomas made a good point. If laws discriminating on the basis of race must pass such a high and stringent test, did Michigan's policy really pass it? After all, as Thomas stated, the University of Michigan Law School could simply lower admission standards in order to achieve racial diversity. For him, it strained the strict scrutiny standard to suggest that Michigan's need to maintain its "elite" status constituted a compelling purpose.[87]

We can avoid this debate by simply rejecting strict scrutiny. It was unnecessary for striking down laws such as those in *Loving, Yick Wo, Romer,* and *Windsor.* Those laws were based on a bare desire to harm a particular group. But laws like the one at issue in *Grutter* are not based on animus. Even Justice Thomas does not suggest that Michigan's policy is based on hostility to whites—or any racial group, for that matter. In fact, none of the dissenting justices in *Grutter* claimed that affirmative action was based on a kind of animus similar to Jim Crow. Laws that provide preferential treatment for such minority groups do not seek to "stick it" to whites. Such laws do not rest on the kind of hostility that underlay Amendment 2, DOMA, or the village's decision in *Olech.* Rather, such laws seek to increase racial diversity or to remedy disadvantage, rationales that have nothing to do with animus.

Justice Thomas's objection is only that such rationales are "inconsistent with the very concept of 'strict scrutiny.'"[88] This points to the fundamental difficulty with higher-level scrutiny, not with the actual justification or reason underlying affirmative action. His dissent in *Grutter* points to the fact that reasonable people may very well disagree about the merits of adopting such policies, just as reasonable people may disagree about the merits of maximum-hours legislation. But once the relevant democratic body has passed such legislation—either an affirmative action program for racial minorities or a minimum-wage or maximum-hour law—the Court ought not to invalidate it. These kinds of laws do not rest on a constitutionally inadmissible rationale. They are not based on animus or a bare desire to harm.

Conclusion

At stake is not merely achieving, via an alternative pathway, judicial outcomes that liberals desire. The focus on state powers rather than on claims of individual rights as the linchpin for securing liberal aims is doctrinally simpler (and indeed well rooted in Supreme Court jurisprudence) and more in line with Progressive goals. This approach more clearly links contemporary liberals with their Progressive ancestors instead of positioning contemporary liberals in the bind of advocating rights in the service of their own aims. It is worth remembering that Progressives did the exact opposite.

Furthermore, the shift advocated here is consistent with the Progressive critique of excessive judicial power, which seems institutionally anomalous in a democracy. The higher-scrutiny approach, with its suspect classes and tiers, more easily invites judicial ideological discretion in striking down laws and policies. After all, the argumentative hurdle for striking down a law is higher under what might be referred to as the neo-progressive approach outlined in this chapter. To strike down an affirmative action measure, judges would have to argue that the policy was based on animus. They could not hide behind the morass of higher-scrutiny justifications and say that the purpose was not important or compelling enough. Indeed, the scrutiny doctrine invites the very kind of policy and ideological decision making by judges that the Progressives would have decried. Ultimately, focusing analysis on state power and the reasons for state action may serve to temper the so-called countermajoritarian difficulty.

Finally, by turning away from rights and the identity or higher-scrutiny framework that accompanies them, we can confront and rebut the Progressives' troubled legacy on racial equality. The Court may enforce equality under the law without the need for higher scrutiny. If we insist on the language of equal rights, it becomes hard to square that insistence with the Progressives' focus on powers. The Progressives generally did not care about the predicament of racial minorities.[89] They seemed hostile to undoing Jim Crow. But by appreciating the conceptual legacy of their distinction between rights and powers, we gain the resources to ensure racial equality without rights—something the Progressives themselves did not envision. If animus is a constitutionally inadmissible purpose, the state does not have the power to enact laws like the ones at issue in *Loving* and *Romer*. The Court does not need strict scrutiny in order to strike down such laws. Simultaneously, this scrutiny does not stand in the way of upholding remedial race-conscious legislation.

The Court's more recent equal protection cases—*Romer, Olech,* and *Windsor*—and one of its earliest, *Yick Wo,* point to a framework for invalidating laws and policies because they are based on animus, not because they violate rights. When constitutional liberals invoke the rights of racial minorities or gays and lesbians but reject the rights to property and contract, they seem to endorse only part of the Progressives' critique of rights. We can reclaim the conceptual legacy of this critique by taking seriously the Court's extant constitutional principle that government does not have the power to act on animus or a bare desire to harm.

Notes

I thank the editors of this volume for their helpful and incisive comments and edits on an earlier draft.

1. David Bernstein, *Rehabilitating "Lochner": Defending Individual Rights Against Progressive Reform* (Chicago: University of Chicago Press, 2011), 5.

2. Richard A. Epstein, *How Progressives Rewrote the Constitution* (Washington, D.C.: Cato Press, 2006), 12.

3. Ibid., 112.

4. See William G. Ross, *A Muted Fury: Populists, Progressives, and Labor Unions Confront the Courts, 1890–1937* (Princeton, N.J.: Princeton University Press, 1994).

5. Fourteenth Amendment: No state shall "deny to any person . . . the equal protection of the laws."

6. John D. Skrentny, *The Minority Rights Revolution* (Cambridge, Mass.: Belknap Press, 2004).

7. See Stephen Engel, "How the Collapse of Progressive Jurisprudence and the Erosion of Scrutiny Doctrine Ironically Secured *Some* Gay Rights" (2014, draft available from the author).

8. Martha Derthick and John J. Dinan, "Progressivism and Federalism," in *Progressivism and the New Democracy,* ed. Sidney M. Milkis and Jerome M. Mileur (Amherst: University of Massachusetts Press, 1999), 81–102; E. J. Dionne, *They Only Look Dead: Why Progressives Will Dominate the Next Political Era* (New York: Simon and Schuster, 1996); James W. Ely Jr., "The Progressive Era Assault on Individualism and Property Rights," *Social Philosophy and Policy* 29, no. 2 (2012): 255–82; Otis L. Graham Jr., *An Encore for Reform: The Old Progressives and the New Deal* (New York: Oxford University Press, 1967); Arthur Mann, ed., *The Progressive Era: Liberal Renaissance or Liberal Failure* (New York: Holt, Rinehart and Winston, 1963); Daniel T. Rodgers, "Rights Consciousness in American History," in *The Bill of Rights in Modern America*, rev. ed., ed. David J. Bodenhamer and James W. Ely Jr. (Bloomington: Indiana University Press, 2008); see generally Eldon J. Eisenach, "Some Second Thoughts on Progressivism and Rights," *Social Philosophy and Policy* 29, no. 2 (2008): 196–219.

9. Herbert Croly, *The Promise of American Life* (Cambridge, Mass.: Belknap Press, 1909), 34.

10. Ibid., 35.

11. Ibid.

12. *Lochner v. New York,* 198 U.S. 45 (1905).

13. *Id.* at 53.

14. *Nebbia v. New York,* 291 U.S. 502 (1934).

15. *West Coast Hotel Co. v. Parrish,* 300 U.S. 379 (1937).

16. *United States v. Carolene Products Co.,* 304 U.S. 144 (1938).

17. *Nebbia,* 291 U.S. at 510.

18. *West Coast Hotel*, 300 U.S. at 393.

19. *Carolene Products*, 304 U.S. at 152.

20. *Id.* at 153n4.

21. *Id.* at 149.

22. *Nebbia*, 291 U.S. at 510.

23. *West Coast Hotel*, 300 U.S. at 394.

24. *Carolene Products*, 304 U.S. at 152.

25. *Lochner*, 198 U.S. at 64.

26. See, for example, Bernstein, *Rehabilitating "Lochner"*; Howard Gillman, *The Constitution Besieged: The Rise and Demise of "Lochner" Era Police Powers Jurisprudence* (Durham, N.C.: Duke University Press, 1933); Michael Les Benedict, "Laissez-Faire and Liberty: A Re-Evaluation of the Meaning and Origins of Laissez-Faire Constitutionalism," *Law and History Review* 3, no. 2 (1985): 293–331; Michael J. Phillips, *The "Lochner" Court, Myth and Reality: Substantive Due Process from the 1890s to the 1930s* (Westport, Conn.: Praeger, 2000).

27. Gillman, *Constitution Besieged*, 7.

28. *Lochner*, 198 U.S. at 59.

29. *Id.*

30. *Id.* at 76, dissenting.

31. My previous work focuses on the fundamental rights branch of this analysis; see Sonu Bedi, *Rejecting Rights* (Cambridge: Cambridge University Press, 2009).

32. See, for example, *Bolling v. Sharpe*, 347 U.S. 497 (1954); *Loving v. Virginia*, 388 U.S. 1 (1967); and *Grutter v. Bollinger*, 539 U.S. 306 (2003).

33. See *Graham v. Richardson*, 403 U.S. 365 (1971).

34. See, for example, *Oyama v. California*, 332 U.S. 633 (1948); *Korematsu v. United States*, 323 U.S. 214 (1944).

35. See, for example, *Craig v. Boren*, 429 U.S. 190 (1976).

36. Adam Winkler, "Fatal in Theory and Strict in Fact: An Empirical Analysis of Strict Scrutiny in the Federal Courts," *Vanderbilt Law Review* 59 (2006): 839.

37. Bruce Ackerman, "Beyond Carolene Products," *Harvard Law Review* 98 (1985): 713; John Ely, *Democracy and Distrust: A Theory of Judicial Review* (Cambridge, Mass.: Harvard University Press, 1980); Chai R. Feldblum, "Sexual Orientation, Morality, and the Law: Devlin Revisited," *University of Pittsburgh Law Review* 57 (1996): 237; Cass R. Sunstein, "Sexual Orientation and the Constitution: A Note on the Relationship between Due Process and Equal Protection," *University of Chicago Law Review* 55 (1988): 1161; Carol Steiker, "The Constitutional Status of Sexual Orientation: Homosexuality as a Suspect Classification," *Harvard Law Review* 98 (1985): 1285; Kenji Yoshino, "The Literary Argument for Heightened Scrutiny for Gays," *Columbia Law Review* 96 (1996): 1753.

38. I argue elsewhere that appeal to mere considerations of morality is also constitutionally inadmissible; see Sonu Bedi, "Repudiating Morals Legislation: Rendering the Constitutional Right to Privacy Obsolete," *Cleveland State Law Review* 53 (2005):

447; Bedi, *Beyond Race, Sex, and Sexual Orientation: Legal Equality Without Identity* (New York: Cambridge University Press, 2013).

39. *Romer v. Evans*, 517 U.S. 620 (1996).

40. *United States v. Windsor*, 570 U.S. 12 (2013).

41. *Romer*, 517 U.S. at 632.

42. Gayle Lynn Pettinga, "Rational Basis with Bite: Intermediate Scrutiny by Any Other Name," *Indiana Law Journal* 62 (1987): 779.

43. *Romer*, 517 U.S. at 634.

44. *Id.*

45. *Windsor*, 570 U.S. at 22.

46. *Id.* at 25–26.

47. *Id.* at 21.

48. *Id.* at 20.

49. *Obergefell v. Hodges*, 576 U.S. __ (2015).

50. See *Bostic, et al. v. Rainey*, E.D. Va. 2014, 34–37; *Leon, et al. v. Perry*, W.D. Tex. 2014, 24–31; *Bishop, et al. v. BLAG*, N.D. Okla. 2014, 51–67; *Kitchen, et al. v. Herbert*, D. Utah 2013, 41–50; *Perry v. Schwarzenegger*, N.D. Cal. 2010, 995–1003; see also *Bourke, et al. v. Beshear*, W.D. Ky. 2014, 10–18; *Obergefell, et al. v. Wymyslo*, S.D. Ohio 2013, 37–43.

51. *Village of Willowbrook v. Olech*, 528 U.S. 562 (2000).

52. *Id.* at 564.

53. *Id.*

54. *Id.* at 565.

55. *Id.* at 566, concurring.

56. See, for example, William D. Araiza, "Irrationality and Animus in Class-of-One Equal Protection Cases," *Ecology Law Quarterly* 34 (2007): 493; Matthew M. Morrison, comment, "Class Dismissed: Equal Protection, the 'Class-of-One,' and Employment Discrimination after *Engquist v. Oregon Department of Agriculture*," *University of Colorado Law Review* 80 (2009): 839; Jefferson Powell, "Reasoning About the Irrational: The Roberts Court and the Future of Constitutional Law," *Washington Law Review* 86 (2011): 217.

57. See, for example, Robert C. Farrell, "The Equal Protection Class-of-One Claim: *Olech, Engquist,* and the Supreme Court's Misadventure," *South Carolina Law Review* 61 (2009): 1; Nicole Richter, "A Standard for 'Class of One' Claims Under the Equal Protection Clause of the Fourteenth Amendment: Protecting Victims of Non-Class Based Discrimination from Vindictive State Action," *Valparaiso University Law Review* 35 (2000): 197; Timothy Zick, "Angry White Males: The Equal Protection Clause and 'Classes of One,'" *Kentucky Law Journal* 89 (2001): 69.

58. Ely, *Democracy and Distrust*.

59. *City of Richmond v. Croson*, 488 U.S. 469 (1989).

60. *Id.* at 493.

61. Ely, *Democracy and Distrust*, 162–65.

62. *McLaughlin v. State of Florida*, 379 U.S. 184 (1964).

63. *Loving v. Virginia*, 388 U.S. 1 (1967).

64. *McLaughlin*, 379 U.S. at 192.

65. *Id.* at 193–94 (citations omitted).

66. See generally Ronald Bayer, *Homosexuality and American Psychiatry: The Politics of Diagnosis* (Princeton, N.J.: Princeton University Press, 1981).

67. Suzanne B. Goldberg, "Equality Without Tiers," *Southern California Law Review* 77 (2004): 481; see also Yoshino, *Heightened Scrutiny for Gays*.

68. See, for example, Thomas Gossett, *Race: The History of an Idea in America* (Dallas: Southern Methodist University Press, 1963), 154–74; Dewey W. Grantham Jr., "The Progressive Movement and the Negro," *South Atlantic Quarterly* 54 (1955): 472; Randall Kennedy, "Race Relations Law and the Tradition of Celebration: The Case of Professor Schmidt," *Columbia Law Review* 86 (1986): 1632.

69. *Baker v. Nelson*, 291 Minn. 310 (1971).

70. Engel, "Collapse of Progressive Jurisprudence," 8.

71. See generally Sonu Bedi, "How Constitutional Law Rationalizes Racism," *Polity* 42, no. 4 (2010): 542–67.

72. See Akhil Reed Amar, "Attainder and Amendment 2: *Romer*'s Rightness," *Michigan Law Review* 95 (1996): 208.

73. *Washington v. Davis*, 426 U.S. 229 (1976).

74. *Personnel Administrator of Mass. v. Feeney*, 442 U.S. 256, 279 (1979).

75. Strict scrutiny may be useful for laws that currently do not receive it; see generally Sonu Bedi, "Collapsing Suspect Class with Suspect Classification: Why Strict Scrutiny Is Too Strict and Maybe Not Strict Enough," *Georgia Law Review* 47 (2013): 301.

76. *Yick Wo v. Hopkins*, 118 U.S. 356 (1886).

77. *Id.* at 370.

78. *Id.* at 374.

79. *Plessy v. Ferguson*, 163 U.S. 537 (1896).

80. See, for example, Bruce Ackerman, *We the People*, vol. 1, *Foundations* (Cambridge, Mass.: Belknap Press, 1993), 147; Derrick A. Bell, *Silent Covenants: "Brown v. Board of Education" and the Unfulfilled Hopes for Racial Reform* (New York: Oxford University Press, 2005), 84; Cass R. Sunstein, *The Partial Constitution* (Cambridge, Mass.: Harvard University Press, 1993), 45.

81. *Grutter v. Bollinger*, 539 U.S. 306 (2003).

82. *Fisher v. Texas*, 570 U.S. __ (2013).

83. *Grutter*, 539 U.S. at 326 (citations omitted).

84. *Id.* at 330.

85. *Id.* at 351, dissenting.

86. *Id.*

87. *Id.* at 356, dissenting.

88. *Id.* at 350, dissenting.

89. See, for example, Bernstein, *Rehabilitating "Lochner,"* 78; Elvin Lim, *The Lovers' Quarrel: The Two Foundings and American Political Development* (New York: Oxford University Press, 2014), 124–25; Michael E. McGerr, *A Fierce Discontent: The Rise and Fall of the Progressive Movement in America, 1870–1920* (New York: Oxford University Press, 2003), 182–218.

6 · Constitutional Conservatives Remember the Progressive Era

Ken I. Kersch

Since the 1980s, conservative legalists have successfully advanced originalism—the conviction that the Constitution should be understood as it was at
the time of its adoption—as their consensus theory of constitutional interpretation. Less noticed is a related project taking place on the intellectual and
popular right, which tells the story of how the Founders' "original" Constitution was abandoned. The Progressives are at the heart of this story.

This is a shift. For conservatives, legalist and nonlegalist alike, the conventional focus has long been on the constitutional betrayals of FDR and the New
Deal. Although attacked for abandoning constitutional rules and restraints for
ever-shifting policy imperatives, the New Deal was famously pragmatic and
untheorized. Progressivism, by contrast, was affirmatively and elaborately
theorized. Its deeper and more extensive conceptualization has enabled contemporary conservatives to trace later liberal policies back to their (purported)
origins in a political theory that was at once substantive and systematic. Doing
so moves the contemporary conservative critique well beyond the relatively
one-dimensional (legalist) charge that "law" was abandoned for "politics."
Rather, it characterizes Progressivism, and the long line of reforms it spawned,
as a wholesale abandonment of the Constitution and founding principles.[1]
This holistic focus on Progressivism's fertile corpus offers new possibilities
on the right for forging common ground within a movement characterized by
long-standing philosophical tensions and for emboldening a conservative federal judiciary to wield its ("new") originalism aggressively in the service of
substantive conservative ends.[2]

Later in this volume, Steve Teles examines the contemporary political
and intellectual networks that streamlined and broadly disseminated this

conservative critique. This essay, by contrast, maps the contemporary right's nascent obsession with the Progressive era as a developmental phenomenon—as a stage in the trajectory of a political-intellectual movement advancing through time. To that end, I venture three main claims. First, the recent conservative focus on Progressivism represents a shift on the right of understandings of the historical location or source of contemporary constitutional problems, an understanding informed by the sequence of constitutional conservatism's development through time: whereas (old) "originalist" legal conservatives adopted Progressive thinking in focusing their attention on countermajoritarian "activist judges" and criticized the New Deal for its weightless, substance-free pragmatism, recent conservatives have forged a more global critique of contemporary constitutional practice that moves beyond judges to the entire modern structure and theory of American government, finding its weighty and substantive blueprint in the Progressive era, and its extension and institutionalization in the New Deal. Second, this more foundational and comprehensive constitutional critique was forged outside legal academia in political science, particularly by Straussian political theorists. And third, the overarching character of this critique centered on the Progressive era serves a movement-building function by offering a set of understandings that can win the assent of the movement's diverse factions, including (it is said, the theoretically opposed and irreconcilable) social conservatives and religious traditionalists, on the one hand, and economic conservatives and libertarians on the other. This chapter considers the potential of this new, Progressive era–centered narrative to motivate, integrate, and expand the size of the modern conservative movement, and offers a brief (critical) assessment.

Straussians Against the Progressives

The disposition of conservatives toward Progressivism has changed over time. Late-nineteenth- and early-twentieth-century conservatives confronted and resisted Progressives directly, defending long-standing common law categories and rules, the authority of a traditionalist bench and bar, and the aggressive judicial policing of constitutional limitations.[3] After that, the most important critical assessments of Progressive constitutionalism migrated from the realm of law to political theory, where they were undertaken by students of the émigré University of Chicago political philosopher Leo Strauss. Drawing upon close readings of ancient political thought (mostly Greek) and of the moderns who had (problematically, in his view) set out in new directions,

Strauss challenged the historicism, nihilism, relativism, and faith in progress rampant in the West, and called for a return to the study of the timeless truths of nature and natural right.[4]

Strauss said nothing about the Constitution (and reportedly voted for Adlai Stevenson). But his writings became a foundation for new departures in conservative constitutional theory. Before Strauss, Charles Kesler recently opined, liberals and conservatives alike "had lost touch, like Antaeus, with the ground of the Constitution in natural right. . . . They could never take the ideas of the . . . Constitution seriously." But "thanks to this intellectual rebirth, the case against Progressivism and in favor of the Constitution is stronger and deeper than . . . ever."[5]

Many conservatives credit Martin Diamond, the first of Strauss's students to focus on American political thought, with the revival of the Founders' Constitution. The theorist Diamond joined a small cohort of early Cold War historians in striving to unseat the then dominant Progressive critique of the Founders' (allegedly) disfiguring elitism and mistrust of democracy.[6] Diamond insisted that the Founders had conveyed a "useable past . . . available to us for the study of modern problems"—that they remained "necessary," carrying "both the authority of the founding and a wisdom . . . [un]surpassed within the American tradition." Catherine and Michael Zuckert—who called Diamond's achievement the "rough equivalent to Strauss's rediscovery of the ancients"—praised Diamond's insistence that the founding was "a beginning that must be re-won in the face of progressivist prejudices that steadfastly reject the beginning as superseded."[7]

Diamond devoted his career to explaining both why Americans needed the Founders now and how to get them right. He sympathized with Henry Cabot Lodge Sr.'s 1911 lament of the decline in the once "universally held . . . conviction . . . by Americans of the original and continuing excellence of their Constitution." Like Lodge, Diamond held the Progressives responsible. "The conventional wisdom of those who give academic and intellectual opinion to the nation" had been formed by Charles Beard's contention that the Constitution was "the handiwork of a reactionary oligarchy," and by Populist and Progressive demands that the Constitution be democratized.[8] This fostered a fundamental misunderstanding of the relationship the Founders had struck between democracy and liberty, and fomented a succession of misguided attempts at reform in democracy's name. Since the Progressive view of the founding was "false in both history and political philosophy," Diamond called for a "renewed appreciation of our fundamental institutions and rededication to their perpetuation."[9]

The Progressives held that the Revolution's democratic spirit—as affirmed in the Declaration of Independence—had been snuffed out by the Founders in the Constitution and in the rationalizations of *The Federalist*. Diamond, in contrast, treated the Declaration as a statement of Lockean contractualism, "neutral with regard to the democratic form," holding only that the people had the right to choose their own form of government. The Constitution was designed to form a popular government that would sagely correct for democracy's well-known deficiencies (like the tyranny of the majority) by protecting the legitimate (low, modern) ends of government—security, "the pursuit of happiness," and the protection of rights. It was in this specific sense that the Founders were friends of democracy, an argument Diamond dilated on in a career-long exegesis of *The Federalist*.[10]

Diamond venerated the Founders but, notably, did not insist that we were strictly obliged to abide by their understandings. "With us the Founding Fathers have great authority," he explained in 1963.

> The Constitution they framed is our fundamental legal document. The worthiness of their work has rightly earned from us a profound respect for their political wisdom. [They thus] have for us the combined authority of law and wisdom. . . . But to pay our respect to that authority—*to know how to obey intelligently or, sometimes, when and how to differ intelligently*—we must know precisely what their Constitution meant and the political thought of which it is the legal expression. "What you have inherited from your fathers / You must first learn to make your own." Ours is such a patrimony that its possession requires constant recovery by careful study.[11]

Also, unlike later Straussian constitutionalists (to say nothing of contemporary law school originalists), Diamond (who published in neoconservative outlets and was generally supportive of the New Deal and the modern welfare state) threw a spotlight on founding-era disagreements. He cheerfully noted that "the framers were not themselves unanimous regarding the actual character of the document they framed," and that "the Constitution was ratified on the basis of many understandings." While steadfastly declaring the 1787 Constitution "still the fundamental document of the American polity . . . still the source of its basic institutions and principles" (and *The Federalist* "the brilliant and authoritative exposition of [its] meaning and intention"), Diamond frankly conceded the need for an evolving constitutional analysis: "There have been two centuries of amendment, interpretation, and the sheer working of great events and massive changes in our way of life. All these things must be taken into account in an understanding of what the Constitution was and is."[12]

Diamond lectured liberals and conservatives alike for, while professing Madisonianism, "fundamentally misconstrue[ing]" the Constitution's nature by misreading a crucial portion of *Federalist* 51: "A *dependence on the people* is . . . the primary control on the government; but experience has taught mankind the necessity of *auxiliary precautions*." Liberals favored the people over the precautions, and conservatives "ambiguously accept[ed] the 'dependence' but . . . vastly esteem[ed] the 'auxiliary precautions.'"[13] Diamond argued that Madison had conceived of these two elements as constituting a coherent whole entailing "the fundamental compatibility of the Constitution's restraining devices with a system of majority rule." While Progressives were "understandably outraged by late-nineteenth-century scholarship and statesmanship that tended to convert the Constitution into a fixed and immutable code enshrining liberty of contract," they were mistaken in holding the Constitution fundamentally undemocratic—an error repeated by later liberals and conservatives alike. This was political gamesmanship. What liberals really objected to, Diamond said, was "the character of the majorities that result from the constitutionally generated process of majority coalition." "The real complaint is that majorities simply do not act as Liberals want them to act"—in a way that would transform the human condition.[14] Liberals thus saw programmatic parties as their great hope. Conservatives answered by anathematizing parties as constitutional corruptions. This led to an ironic result: "The Liberal dislikes the Constitution for what . . . are correct reasons. The Conservative likes the Constitution for what . . . are wrong reasons. . . . [This makes] the Liberal . . . the intelligent foe of the Constitution and the Conservative its foolish partisan." The views were equally dangerous: "Given the dominance of either the Constitution would perish."[15]

For the Founders, Diamond argued, it was liberty that was "the comprehensive good, the end against which political things had to be measured." The particular guarantor of liberty was less important: "Democracy was only a form of government which, like any other form of government, had to prove itself adequately instrumental to the securing of liberty."[16] Progressives and liberals were right to say that the Framers were sharp critics of democracy, but these criticisms had to be contextualized: "The American Founders, like all sensible men before them, regarded *every* form of government as problematic, in the sense of having a peculiar liability to corruption, and they accepted the necessity to cope with the problematics peculiar to their *own* form of government."

"*Of course,* the Founders criticized the defects and dangers of democracy," Diamond riposted, "and did not waste much breath on the defects and dangers of the other forms of government. For . . . they were not founding any other kind of government; they were establishing a democratic form, and it was the dangers peculiar to it against which all their efforts had to be bent."[17]

The Progressives (and their liberal successors) had demanded "imprudent democratizing reforms" occasioning potentially serious threats to liberty. Making matters worse, in the 1960s and 1970s liberals launched yet another assault on the Founders' Constitution—"a vast inflation of the idea of equality, a conversion of the [Declaration's] idea of equal political liberty into an ideology." This "demand for equality in every aspect of human life . . . [amounting to] a kind of absolutization of a single principle," when conjoined with the "absolutization of the democratic form of government understood as the vehicle for that complete equality," amounted to a systematic critique of the Founders' entire regime.[18]

This "originalism" was different from the legalist originalism being forged at about the same time by Raoul Berger and Robert Bork. Preoccupied with matters of design, structure, and principle, Straussians said relatively little about judicial review and how it should be exercised. The law professors, by contrast, were focused primarily on remedying the "problem" of (Warren Court) judicial activism. Far from repudiating Progressivism, their strategy was to appropriate its majoritarianism—its conceptualization of judicial review as "counter-majoritarian," its suspicion of a politicized judiciary, its call for judicial restraint, and its attack on "Lochnerism"—to indict Warren-era liberals for hypocrisy.[19] On today's right, remnants of this "old" legalist originalism—genealogically Progressive—are conjoined in complex ways with the more comprehensive and structuralist Straussian constitutional theory. Add to that a classically liberal, rights-celebrating, judge-focused, *Lochner*-celebrating libertarianism, along with a fledgling revival of the Gilded Age conservative legalism of the likes of Lodge's, and the vibrant, contested lifeworld of the contemporary constitutional right begins to come into view.[20]

From Theory to History

In the 1950s, Straussians discussed history but didn't write it. Diamond, Harry Jaffa, Herbert Storing, and others looked to American history to recover a few great texts: *The Federalist* (Diamond), the Declaration of Independence and the speeches and writings of Abraham Lincoln (Jaffa), and the Anti-Federalist writings and Frederick Douglass (Storing). Their point was that these texts (like those of Plato or Aristotle) had distilled timeless truths, which were at hand now as then as unsurpassed founts of political wisdom.

Today's Straussians have reversed their teachers' emphasis, writing history assessed by the yardstick of political-philosophical truth. Rewriting the history of Progressivism is their overriding preoccupation. Contemporary conservatives tell many stories about the Progressive era and its constitutionalism. They write in a variety of arenas, including serious scholarship from R. J. Pestritto (on Woodrow Wilson) and Jean Yarbrough (on Theodore Roosevelt), quasi-scholarly polemics (such as by Fox News's Andrew Napolitano and *National Review*'s Jonah Goldberg), and innumerable magazine articles, policy papers, and blog posts. I use a wide lens here to capture and present a culture, a frame of mind that seems informed and coherent to initiates, and incomprehensible, even absurd, to outsiders—most especially to liberals.[21]

At the core of the new conservative histories of the Progressive era is a story of faithlessness, betrayal, and treachery: Progressives impiously, proudly, and purposefully spurned the Constitution and the Founders, and substituted a heretical, antinomian political theory destructive of foundational political principles (like liberty).[22] While Diamond had criticized the Progressives' abandonment of the Framers as a prelude to adjudicating the very real constitutional dilemmas they confronted, the newer accounts prosecute the Progressives as quislings. Pestritto repeatedly refers to Woodrow Wilson's "self-conscious rejection of the theory that had animated the founding era." Hillsdale College offers an online course titled "Constitution 201: The Progressive Rejection of the Founding and the Rise of Bureaucratic Despotism."[23] Many note that Wilson was the first president to mock the nation's "Fourth of July sentiments," "to speak disparagingly of the Constitution," and to call it "obsolete."[24] Yarbrough's study is structured around the contrast between Theodore Roosevelt's professed admiration for the Constitution, the Founders, and *The Federalist,* and the lion's share of his statements and actions stabbing them in the back. For TR, "the blind, unconscious movement of a whole people supplanted the founders' emphasis on deliberation and choice, and history, rather than natural right" supplied "the moral ground on which political actions were to be judged." Whereas the Founders looked to (timeless) human nature (including self-interest) in fashioning the Constitution's architecture, TR believed in pure, disinterested public-spiritedness and the imperatives of growth and expansion.[25]

Kesler prefers the Populists to the Progressives, not only because of the former's suspicion of elites and (especially centralized, executive) governmental power, but also because Populists rooted their politics in the Declaration and the Constitution and "insist[ed] that the Constitution had been betrayed," while the Progressives retorted that it had "become outmoded."[26] Today's conservatives now trace the theory of "living constitutionalism" to this Progressive abandonment, holding "living" to be a contemporary euphemism for (this once frank) rejection. "From the beginning," conservatives say, that history shows that modern liberalism has repudiated "traditional American political principles," including the timeless truths of human nature and natural right. It has "sought to sap and undermine constitutional morality, the habits of mind and heart appropriate to republican government under the Constitution, and to supplant it with a new morality appropriate to a living constitution."[27] A call has gone out to the conservative movement to learn this history and to rally—despite their differences—in defense of the Founders' Constitution.[28]

Themes

Beyond denouncing the Progressives for betraying the founding, contemporary conservative histories level five substantive charges against them: statism; democratism; elitism; hostility to free markets, business, and accumulated wealth; and racism.

While the Progressive rejection of an inherent human nature and of natural right might be characterized as skepticism, if not nihilism, most of these histories describe the Progressives as seized by an outsized faith—alas in the state itself, which they looked to with a "messianic" zeal redolent of the French Revolution, charged with realizing heaven on earth. Progressives, they say, believed "the day of the organic redeemer state was dawning . . . [and] the Constitution must evolve or be thrown into the dustbin of history." This fanatical faith—alien to the Founders—is seen as the real threat, far more dangerous than today's "obscene moral panic over the role of Christians in public life."[29]

The Progressive faith, they charge, was that all was possible through the application of man's (scientific) mind wielding the instrumentalities of the state, unrestrained by any natural or God-given laws. This faith, they claim, adumbrated a fundamental error that reached its apotheosis in the twentieth century's totalitarian and fascist dictatorships.[30] Liberals may "remember the progressives as do-gooders who cleaned up the food supply and agitated for a more generous social welfare state and better working conditions." But the Nazis and the Italian Fascists did the same thing "for the same reasons and in loyalty to roughly the same principles." Unregenerate statism has the theoretical potential to do good, but unrestrained by a Constitution, it has the potential to do *anything*, including the most radical evil.[31]

When the state is all, natural rights and civil liberties are nothing. Anticonstitutionalism and suppression went hand-in-hand for Woodrow Wilson, who "was prepared to bend any rule, avoid any constitutional principle, and crush any individual liberty for what he believed was the common good." As Goldberg teaches, "nothing that happened under the mad reign of Joe McCarthy remotely compares with what Wilson and his fellow progressives foisted on America." Besides "silencing dissent" through criminal prosecutions, Wilson (through George Creel's Committee on Public Information) created "the West's first modern ministry for propaganda."[32]

Progressives supplemented Creel's work with compulsory education, "brainwashing" impressionable children in Progressive nostrums and credos. (Napolitano's education chapter is titled "Reeducation Camps.") While the Constitution made education a reserved power of the states, Wilson expressed high hopes that through national leadership, the public schools would make America's children (especially Catholics) "as unlike their fathers as we can."[33]

Progressives invented our separation-of-powers and federalism-flouting national administrative and regulatory bureaucracies. Wilson argued that the Founders' design of checked and diffused powers no longer made sense when the American people were coming to understand themselves as an organic whole possessed of a single will. Rather than perpetuate those outdated structures through "blind worship" of the Constitution, we should forge new understandings better suited to the realization of the nation's emerging general will.[34]

Drawing on Hegel's *Philosophy of Right,* Wilson argued that salaried, lifetime civil service appointments would insulate bureaucrats from politics and the pursuit of self-interest, freeing them to dispassionately implement society's objective will. Large swaths of Wilson's essay on this were "dedicated to the argument that the age of constitutionalism was over and an age of administration was upon us."[35] Where the Founders were foundationalists rooted in the laws of nature and nature's God, Hegel was an antifoundationalist taking history as his guide. The Founders' teacher, Locke, held that rights belonged to the individual; Hegelian historicists held them to be gifts of a purposive state stocked with elite bureaucrats doling out rights they discerned as unfolding history required. This created an endless need for more government, stocked with ever more bureaucrats and administrators, fed by ever-larger federal budgets.[36] To launch this dynamic, Progressives allegedly adopted Bismarck's "Machiavellian masterstroke" of making the middle class dependent on the state, and undermining its members' status as self-determining authors of enlightened government.[37]

Some polemical accounts describe these developments as no less than the arrival, during World War I, of an American fascism. Progressives hoped that the wartime statist breakthrough would become the peacetime status quo (which happened in the New Deal).[38] Goldberg therefore situates Progressivism within an early-twentieth-century transnational "fascist moment" in the West in which "a coalition of intellectuals going by various labels—Progressive, communist, socialist, and so forth—believed the liberal moment was drawing to a close. It was time for man to lay aside the anachronisms of natural law, traditional religion, constitutional liberty, capitalism . . . and rise to the responsibility of remaking the world in his own image." In this way, Mussolini's motto—"Everything in the State, nothing outside the State, nothing against the State"—became an American credo.[39]

It is alleged that Progressives eased the path to statism with their leveling brand of democratism. Conservative accounts of Progressive constitutionalism emphasize its rejection of the Founders' commitment to fragmented and opposing powers—rooted in man's self-interested (or, for Christians, "fallen") nature—in favor of a direct, plebiscitary democracy premised on individuals' and society's perfectability, and on government's purpose to serve their will.[40] Since Progressives didn't distinguish between government and will, formal and permanent limits on the state were unnecessary, if not harmful—hence, their invention of "living" constitutionalism.

The Madisonian framework for limiting government, Wilson and others believed, had met the needs of a time when Americans were most concerned with limiting power and protecting rights. But the time had come to concentrate power, and for Wilson that meant that democracy was imperative.[41] Wilson's position gave short shrift to the Framers' view that democracy had problems, that it was susceptible to popular passions and elite manipulations. Napolitano described this Progressive embrace of democracy as a coup installing a revolutionary new "constitutional" rule of pure majoritarianism, setting us on the road to fascism, where will is law and might makes right. (Kesler concluded, less alarmingly, that leading Progressives and the American people were too genuinely democratic to travel these more dangerous [European] paths.)[42]

Progressive democratism informed, in turn, the movement's views on executive power. When Wilson and TR touched on the vices of democracy, they insisted that they could be transcended through visionary leadership ("the perfect confusion of the triumph of justice with the triumph of the will"). While Wilson had begun his career calling for a parliamentary system to replace the Founders' system of dispersed powers, he changed his mind after watching TR effectively wield executive power, determining instead that presidential leadership was the way to go.[43]

The modern president's authority would be derived not from the Constitution but directly from the people, whose will—as their leader (a term Wilson celebrated, but the Founders deprecated)—he would intuit and interpret. This meant that the president would regularly appeal to and guide the will of a mass public. Today's conservative critics point out that while the Founders would have feared this as a recipe for demagoguery, Wilson seemed to believe the public-spiritedness of modern men rendered that fear obsolete.[44] Indeed, Wilson's "unintentionally chilling" essay "Leaders of Men" (1890) for the first time put "vision" and "compassion" at the core of the presidency. In *Constitutional Government in the United States* (1908), Wilson allegedly flirted with fascist dictatorship by exhorting the president to be "as big a man as he can be."[45]

Yarbrough explains that for the Founders, the military was leadership's native soil. She traces TR's novel "stewardship" and "inherent powers" theory of the executive, along with his passion to lead, to his wartime exploits and adventures. Yarbrough says that TR took Oliver Cromwell (and not, as some say, the constitutionalists Andrew Jackson and Abraham Lincoln) as his model for executive leadership in a republic.[46] For TR, "the whole point of the stewardship [and inherent powers] theory was precisely that the president did not have to cite a specific constitutional provision or statute for his actions so long as the needs of the people required it, and it was not explicitly forbidden."[47]

Democratism fueled Progressive understandings of judicial power as well. TR's hostility to the judiciary famously grew over time as the judges insisted on enforcing constitutional limits (he eventually called for direct democratic checks on judicial review). While, unlike TR, Wilson recognized the important role that courts played in preserving constitutional liberty, his understanding of how they should interpret the Constitution to protect that liberty was historicist: judges should read it in light of the needs of the time—a different route to the same (anticonstitutional) end.[48]

The new conservatives tell us that Progressives were not only misguided democrats but also unregenerate elitists. They sought to turn the nation's new (Germanic) post–Civil War research universities into "the fourth branch of government." Under the "Wisconsin Model, the university could be trusted to define the state's social problems, prescribe cures, and then evaluate the success of the very programs it had recommended." "Nothing separated Progressivism from Populism, or for that matter from all previous American democracy more sharply," Kesler avers, "than this faith in the presumptive expertise, integrity, and political authority of the academic mandarins," entailing "rule by sociologists," with modern problems "forever managed by science."[49] These "priestly experts" saw themselves as empirical and apolitical, but they were armed with "a new religion of the divinized state and the nation as an organic community." The Constitution was an obstacle for them to overcome: whatever the purported limits on government, they would "plan, exhort, badger, and scold" the populace into submission.[50]

Conservative accounts of Progressive elitism are often scathingly populist. Napolitano calls Wilson "an old, stiff, cold academic who really believed he was smarter than anyone else" and "a power-hungry authoritarian academic who wanted to bend the country and the Constitution to his will." TR was "the bellicose Nanny Stater from Oyster Bay" who mocked the constitutionalist William Howard Taft as a "puzzlewit." Napolitano finds TR's dismissal of Taft as stupid "similar to the tactic used by the modern Left to describe Republican candidates such as George W. Bush, Sarah Palin, and Michele Bachmann."[51]

Students force-fed "popular legend[s]" about noble muckrakers, as opposed to the Founders' more sober understandings of human nature, might believe these bureaucrats were working to advance society's collective interests. But, many of these histories argue, recent scholarship has shown that modern administration was instituted by large, established national corporations to stave off competition from smaller local (and more entrepreneurial) businesses. This suggests the folly of governmental agencies "picking [market] winners and losers."[52]

Progressives hated free markets, businessmen, and accumulated wealth. Conservatives have been rewriting the history of the Gilded Age and the Progressive era to transform those whom liberals dub "robber barons" into fully realized, public-spirited, Christian American heroes whose beneficent projects were nearly thwarted by reformers who subjected them to constant opprobrium and harassment. These histories give businessmen equal billing with politicians and reformers as significant public actors and present them, in contrast with reformers (whose weaknesses and foibles are underlined), as the nation's true leaders, innovators, and builders.[53]

Burton Folsom's *The Myth of the Robber Barons* (1987)—providing a series of engaging didactic profiles in entrepreneurship (of Cornelius Vanderbilt, James J. Hill, the Scrantons, Charles Schwab, John D. Rockefeller, and Andrew W. Mellon)—is a touchstone. It distinguishes between "market entrepreneurs," who innovate to create and market a superior product at low cost, benefiting consumers and society alike, and "political entrepreneurs," who feed on federal subsidies and favors, collusion, and speculation, without incentives to reduce cost or price. Folsom describes a historical trajectory, beginning in the Gilded Age, in which, first, government (futilely) sought to promote economic development by servicing political entrepreneurs. This only rewarded incompetence and indifference to public wants and needs. The result was economic dysfunction—shoddy products at high prices—and angry consumers, who called for aggressive regulation. Reformist politicians responded to these complaints by passing laws, again with (bad) unintended consequences. This made things worse, generating cries for even more regulation, and the cycle continued, leading—tragically—to our own heavily regulated, dysfunctional economy. By these lights, Progressive-era regulation was the byproduct of government efforts to resolve problems that government had created in the first place—and the first step in an insalubrious cycle leading to the counterproductive, ever more intrusive, ever-expanding government of the present.[54]

Although critical of political entrepreneurs, Folsom defends the accumulation of vast wealth by market entrepreneurs, who "created something out of nothing," generating wealth and income for numberless others.[55] Far from exemplifying a rapacious social Darwinist ethic, many of these heroes preached Christian stewardship. New conservative histories emphasize the philanthropic munificence of Carnegie, Rockefeller, and Mellon, which liberal historians (allegedly) either downplayed or ignored in perversely celebrating the era's bitter, carping muckrakers.[56] Polemics accuse the Progressives of wielding "class-warfare politics—where successful businessmen and women are treated as the enemies of working folks . . . [as] greedy and corrupt." TR's celebrated trust-busting was more about a voracious power-seeking executive "hell-bent on tak[ing] down the wealthy" than about economics.[57]

The taxes needed to fund the ever expanding state menaced this entrepreneurial and philanthropic good work. Many of these histories recount Andrew Mellon's valiant antitax philosophy and activism.[58] Since most people aren't rich, there is a natural (selfish) inclination (in a democracy especially) to soak those who are. Mellon, however, taught that high taxes "were the chief parasites draining the lifeblood of the American economy." The redistribution of tax revenue from market to political entrepreneurs—growing the government perpetually larger—was even more galling.[59]

Napolitano calls the income tax "slavery" and "grand larceny," insisting (falsely) "the original Constitution never contemplated that the federal government would have a financial relationship with individual persons." While there were long-standing trends in that direction, in *Pollock v. Farmers' Loan & Trust* (1895), which found income taxes collected under an 1894 law to be unconstitutional, "the Supreme Court finally rallied to defend the integrity of the Constitution." The Sixteenth and Seventeenth Amendments, authorizing the income tax and providing for the direct election of senators, were unconstitutional amendments because they "profoundly upset the structural framework of the federal government," empowering it to blow past the Constitution's enumerated limits on national power and violate the Fifth Amendment's Takings and Due Process Clauses. By denying Americans the natural right to the fruits of their labor and provoking them to tax evasion, moreover, the income tax corrupted their morals.[60]

The much-maligned *Lochner* Court attempted to hold the line for the protection of "individual freedom of choice and fundamental rights," including natural rights like liberty of contract (violated by minimum-wage statutes and other labor laws).[61] Only "the twisted rhetoric of the Progressives and their progeny," Napolitano insists, "inject[ed] into the national psyche that the economic rights of business owners and workers, their natural rights to trade goods and services and money, and the natural economic laws of supply and demand did not exist or deserve protection."[62]

By contrast, Yarbrough shares TR's condemnation of "the vulgar excesses of the Gilded Age." But she admonishes him, especially as "one who professed to admire *The Federalist*," for "fail[ing] to appreciate the ways ... America's commercial spirit might contribute to a distinctive form of democratic greatness and encourage 'the capable, masterful, and efficient' qualities he most admired." It got worse as he began cultivating a "hostility to capitalism." While TR called Lincoln a hero, he "did not share Lincoln's faith that individual talent and effort when protected by law were generally sufficient to produce just rewards and to give hope to those who had not yet prospered." Instead, TR insisted that government supervise great wealth, tolerating it only when it was "honorably obtained and well-used." Traditionally, Yarbrough explains, government's role was to supply the conditions of justice (such as the protection of property rights), and "each individual received according to his merit."

TR newly held it government's job to secure a "just balance," a "Square Deal," between diverse classes and competing economic interests, to achieve (redistributionist) social justice. On these grounds, Yarbrough (no libertarian) defends *Lochner*—a decision that TR, like all Progressives, anathematized.[63]

Finally, stories about Progressive racism have convinced many conservatives that they themselves are the country's most reliable antiracists, since only foundationalists are anchored in the timeless principle (here, the equality of natural rights) that makes antiracism possible. Historicists, evolutionists, pragmatists, and secularists are dangerously unmoored, with consequences these histories describe.[64]

Contemporary conservatives frolic in the many Progressive allusions to Anglo-Saxon superiority (see TR) and Darwinism (see Wilson), observing that they "bear a striking resemblance to the arguments advanced by the supporters of slavery." Links to Nazism are even more direct.[65] Progressives—whom Yarbrough calls morally bankrupt—opened the space for this virulent racism by repudiating the Founders' natural rights philosophy as enshrined in the Declaration of Independence. In *On the Origin of Species,* Darwin "quietly unseated God as the author of creation, substituting chance and relentless random mutations that favored one species over another in the unceasing struggle for food and place," making it "no longer possible to speak intelligibly of natural rights," of "a fixed human nature." The nation's centennial set the stage for an apocalyptic encounter between "the emerging [Darwinian] progressive worldview" and "the Declaration's insistence that every human being was created equal and endowed with certain inalienable rights."[66]

The terrible moral consequences of this framework were evident in the Progressive enthusiasm for eugenics. "Today," Napolitano reports, "it is generally known that the Nazis in Germany committed awful atrocities . . . because of a racial belief that the descendants of the Aryans . . . were destined to rule the world. . . . Less known is that much of the same ideology was shared by . . . Wilson and Roosevelt." The Supreme Court's infamous *Buck v. Bell* (1927) decision upholding compulsory sterilization for the mentally retarded (authored by the TR appointee Oliver Wendell Holmes Jr.) "could have been written by Adolf Hitler." The lone dissent was from the Court's only Catholic.[67] After describing *Buck,* Napolitano immediately segues into a discussion of *Roe v. Wade,* described as "the judicial culmination of Rooseveltian and Wilsonian eugenics."[68]

Margaret Sanger's eugenics advocacy is spotlighted by many, citing her genius for "hitching the racist-eugenic campaign to sexual pleasure and female liberation," or her campaign for birth control (to reduce the number of black babies). Goldberg contrasts Sanger's views with those of the Founders anchored in natural law (prefigured, he says, by Saint Thomas Aquinas), "which holds that rights are derived not from government but by our very humanity and ultimately from the Creator of humanity, God." He then rallies his readers, insisting that "conservative religious and political dogma—under relentless attack from the left—may be the single greatest bulwark against eugenic schemes" and their cousins: genetic engineering, euthanasia, and abortion. "Good dogma," he concludes, "is the most profound inhibiting influence against bad ideas and the only guarantor that men will act on good ones."[69]

Few were as racist as the elite university professors so central to Progressivism. Goldberg takes E. A. Ross as illustrative. Ross "helped Roscoe Pound formulate the new 'sociological jurisprudence'—the foundation for 'living constitutionalism.'" He also advocated minimum-wage laws to prevent white workers from being undercut by blacks and "Coolies."[70] Napolitano champions *Lochner* for countering the Progressive racism that inspired the state maximum-hours law for bakers, which targeted the "small immigrant bakery owners whose habits the white Anglo-Saxon government elite wanted to change."[71]

Skeins of Meaning

Individually, these themes are familiar to students (and critics) of Progressivism. Conservatives, however, have woven them together creatively to form a dense ideological matrix that bids to displace the dominant (liberal) matrix as the new common sense.[72] This "recombinative cultural politics," in which "political identifications and social cleavages are made," also works to reinforce long-standing (conservative) political identities, forge new ones, and knit together diverse elements of an otherwise philosophically fractious political movement.[73]

Recombinative cultural politics pervades these stories. By noting that only in God are legislative, executive, and judicial power united, for example, Kesler roots separation-of-powers formalism in religious foundationalism.[74] Pestritto associates a professionalized civil service with racism (because Wilson argued that bureaucrats could best intuit and implement the public's objective will in a racially homogeneous society).[75] Appeals to "good science" by academics are relentlessly undercut by stories about how those appeals issue from the same unmoored intellectual and moral space that underwrote Progressive advocacy of racism, eugenics, and assaults on contract and property rights.[76] Eugenics and abortion are presented as essentially the same issue—with dog-whistle implications for the establishment of a national health care system in which amoral, science-wielding bureaucrats would govern matters of life and death (including euthanasia for the old and sick).[77] Goldberg presents affirmative action as the spawn of Progressive racism in which "the state . . . pick[s] winners and losers based on accidents of birth" (the Founders' natural rights philosophy, they teach, was color-blind). The same obsession with "organiz[ing] society on racial lines" that informed Wilson's commitment to "self-determination" underwrites today's "identity politics," in which people "organize themselves into . . . spiritual and biological units."[78]

Within this matrix, economic and social conservatism are conjoined. The growth-killing income tax involves a repudiation of God's laws that personally corrupts.[79] Before the Seventeenth Amendment, when senators answered only to state legislatures and not national interest groups, parties, or the press, senators didn't need to cultivate interested power centers and demagogically appeal to mass publics. These are the dynamics, Napolitano explains, that have brought us runaway federal spending, the Patriot Act, Obamacare, and the Troubled Asset Relief Program, as well as the (racially biased) assaults on rights and liberties associated with the wars on drugs and terror.[80]

These discursive links, associations, and recombinations transform a list of Progressive themes into a devil's brew, setting the stage for the conservative movement's comprehensive rejection of the long-dominant liberal Democratic political coalition.

Conclusion

Today's conservatives read contemporary politics and modern liberalism through the scrim of a constructed memory of the Progressive era. The Progressives, they teach, were united by a foundational commitment to the "destruction of the political and moral authority of the U.S. Constitution," a malign achievement carried forward by liberals, which, by "denying permanent principles of right derived from nature and reason," has corrupted modern America.[81] We cannot understand conservative reaction to, for example, Michelle Obama's recommendations on healthy eating, or President Obama's leadership on financial and health care reform, or calls for an active compassionate federal government, or Republican intransigence on the budget, or the defunding of social science grants, or skepticism about climate science without taking into account the stories conservatives tell about Progressivism's wholesale assault on the Constitution.

The mid-twentieth-century successors of the pre–New Deal Old Right—especially legal academics—were so immersed in the New Deal's Progressive-liberal regime that they adopted Progressive yardsticks themselves, stumping for democratic majorities and decrying *Lochner*-ite judicial activism. This implied either accepting the New Deal or arguing that judges had no business stopping it. Many conservatives rejected rigid interpretive theories premised on the possibility of discovering and applying fixed constitutional dictates to present controversies.[82] Straussians, however, started constitutional conservatism on a different path by all but ignoring—and implicitly denying—the alleged countermajoritarian problem. They insisted on the centrality of the founding, as a matter of structure and design, to contemporary constitutional questions. Beard had sought to discredit the broader political theory of the founding as mere rationalization and subterfuge. Diamond called for its redemption. Notwithstanding Diamond's circumspection in this regard, we can see in retrospect that his demur from the Progressive critique laid the groundwork for a "new originalism" in which conservatives would seek the restoration of the Founders' Constitution, understood literally and substantively. Outright repudiation of the Progressives' handiwork makes aggressive use of (originalist) judicial review an unproblematic part of the process. The Straussian critique of Progressives has liberated conservatism from (Borkian, Progressive-conservative) hand-wringing about the antidemocratic nature of this practice and bolstered the reclamation project.[83]

The charges lodged by contemporary conservatives against early-twentieth-century Progressives are familiar, and broadly accurate. They nevertheless present themselves in these histories as if through a fun-house mirror. Diamond and Storing (and a few of their more moderate contemporary successors) emphasized that Progressives faced genuine problems about how to live under the Constitution in a radically altered context where wrenching new problems troubled prevailing understandings. Whereas Diamond was open to intelligent criticism of—and even divergence from—the Founders, contemporary conservative histories of the Progressive era present the matter as a stark, Manichean—indeed, world-historical—choice. Like the Cold War framing of Whittaker Chambers's *Witness* (1952) or Jaffa's *Crisis of the House Divided* (1959), the choice between the Progressives and the Founders is transmogrified—literally—into a choice between God and man.[84] When joined with the spirit of legalist originalists like Bork and Berger, who alleged an abandonment of law for politics, they transform (familiar) critiques of Progressivism into apocalyptic stories of faith and heresy, salvation and damnation, friends and enemies, loyalty and treason. This, at the far reaches, is constitutionalism as McCarthyism.

These histories present Progressives as a monolithic army on the march. In fact, as this volume's other essays demonstrate, the movement was diverse and often self-contradicting, and many of its participants challenged the same extreme formulations that agitate contemporary conservatives. Drawn to the role of truth tellers ministering to the hoodwinked masses, these conservatives—whether from calculation or ignorance—say next to nothing about the extensive academic literature (and political critique) from the modern liberal Left challenging Progressivism's statism, elitism, scientism, ethnocentrism, and racism. Conservatives never explain that modern American liberalism and the postwar Left were forged both as an outgrowth of, and in reaction against, Progressivism.

Whatever its virtues, contemporary conservative insistence on an oathlike allegiance to a natural law–natural rights foundationalism as our only stay against tyranny and barbarism is astonishingly naive about history. Time and again, foundationalist appeals to natural law have been used to justify the most tyrannical and barbaric oppression—including slavery and segregation.[85] The contemporary conservative compulsion to showcase the Progressives' smoking-gun philosophical-theological error and, having exposed them as "moral relativists," to denounce them as heretics amounts to a dogmatic refusal of history's teachings about the dangers of righteous pride. Thus, what began as a critique of man's sinfulness and pride ends up replicating it, reenacting the very egoism they hold damnable in their enemies.

These conservative stories about Progressivism, which are both accurate and distorted, provide an increasingly powerful template for a fundamental assault on the modern, post–New Deal American state, one that cuts much deeper than the standard legalist-originalist critique of judicial activism ever did or could. Efforts to sustain that state must aggressively challenge these histories, where meanings—and perhaps worlds—are made.

Notes

1. Thomas West and William A. Schambra, "The Progressive Movement and the Transformation of American Politics," Heritage Foundation First Principles Series Report 12 (July 18, 2007), 1.

2. See Robert Post and Reva Siegel, "Democratic Constitutionalism," in *The Constitution in 2020,* ed. Jack Balkin and Reva Siegel (Oxford, 2009), 26; Keith E. Whittington, "The New Originalism," *Georgetown Journal of Law and Public Policy* 2 (2004): 599–613.

3. See Johnathan O'Neill and Joseph Postell, "Introduction: The Conservative Response to Progressivism: Myth and Reality"; O'Neill, "Constitutional Conservatism During the Progressive Era: The National Association for Constitutional Government and *The Constitutional Review*"; and William Schambra, "The Election of 1912 and the Origins of Constitutional Conservatism," all in *Toward an American Conservatism: Constitutional Conservatism During the Progressive Era,* ed. Joseph W. Postell and Johnathan O'Neill (Palgrave Macmillan, 2013).

4. Leo Strauss, *Natural Right and History* (Chicago, 1953). See also John Marini, "Progressivism, Modern Political Science, and the Transformation of American Constitutionalism," in *The Progressive Revolution in Politics and Political Science: Transforming the American Regime,* ed. John Marini and Ken Masugi (Rowman and Littlefield, 2005), 235–43.

5. Kesler, *I Am the Change: Barack Obama and the Crisis of Liberalism* (Broadside, 2012), 230–31.

6. Douglass Adair, *Fame and the Founding Fathers,* ed. Trevor Colbourn (Norton, 1974), a collection of essays from the 1940s and 1950s; Robert E. Brown, *Charles Beard and the Constitution: A Critical Analysis of "An Economic Interpretation of the Constitution"* (Princeton, 1956); Forrest MacDonald, *We the People: The Economic Origins of the Constitution* (Chicago, 1958). See Charles A. Beard, *An Economic Interpretation of the Constitution of the United States* (Macmillan, 1913).

7. Catherine Zuckert and Michael Zuckert, *The Truth About Leo Strauss: Political Philosophy and American Democracy* (Chicago, 2006), 209–21.

8. Diamond, "The Declaration and the Constitution: Liberty, Democracy, and the Founders," *Public Interest* 41 (Fall 1975): 39–55, quotations on 39, 40, 42–45.

9. Ibid., 45.

10. Zuckert and Zuckert, *Leo Strauss,* 211–12.

11. Martin Diamond, "What the Framers Meant by Federalism," in *A Nation of States,* ed. Robert Goldwin (Rand McNally, 1963), 25 (emphasis added).

12. Martin Diamond, "Liberals, Conservatives, and the Constitution," *Public Interest* 1 (Fall 1965): 96–97; Diamond, "What the Framers Meant," 25–26, 42.

13. Diamond, "Liberals, Conservatives," 96–97 (emphasis in the original).

14. Ibid., 97–98, 106–8.

15. Ibid., 109.

16. Diamond, "What the Framers Meant," 47–49.

17. Ibid., 51–52 (emphasis in the original).

18. Ibid., 55.

19. Robert H. Bork, "Neutral Principles and Some First Amendment Problems," *Indiana Law Journal* 47 (Fall 1971): 1–35; Raoul Berger, *Government by Judiciary: The Transformation of the Fourteenth Amendment* (Harvard, 1977). See David E. Bernstein, "The Progressive Origins of Conservative Hostility to *Lochner v. New York*," in Postell and O'Neill, *American Conservatism.*

20. See David E. Bernstein, *Rehabilitating "Lochner": Defending Individual Rights Against Progressive Reform* (Chicago, 2011); Randy E. Barnett, *Restoring the Lost Constitution: The Presumption of Liberty* (Princeton, 2004); Postell and O'Neill, *American Conservatism.*

21. The polemicists draw from scholarly sources, but their presentation is cruder and more provocative; see Victoria Hattam and Joseph Lowdes, "The Ground Beneath Our Feet: Language, Culture, and Political Change," in *Formative Acts: American Politics in the Making,* ed. Stephen Skowronek and Matthew Glassman (Pennsylvania, 2007), 199–219, 214, 217.

22. See, for example, Thomas West, *The Progressive Revolution in Politics and Political Science* (Rowman and Littlefield, 2005); Postell and O'Neill, "The Conservative Response to Progressivism," 3; O'Neill, "Constitutional Conservatism During the Progressive Era," 24–25; Schambra, "Election of 1912," 95–96, 116; West, "The Progressive Movement"; John Marini, "Abandoning the Constitution," *Claremont Review of Books,* Spring 2012, 27.

23. See http://kirbycenter.hillsdale.edu.

24. Ronald J. Pestritto, *Woodrow Wilson and the Roots of Modern Liberalism* (Rowman and Littlefield, 2005); Ronald J. Pestritto, "Woodrow Wilson: Godfather of Liberalism," Heritage Foundation, Makers of American Political Thought Series #1 on Political Thought (July 31, 2012). See Glenn Beck, "Progressivism Is the Poison That Is Killing Us," http://mediamatters.org/video/2010/01/21/beck-progressivism-is-the-poison-thats-killing/159366; R. J. Dennis Brady, "Woodrow Wilson, the Cancer of Progressivism, and the Dismantling of the Constitution: The History Lessons That the Progressives Don't Want You to Know," BradyReports.com (March 30, 2011); Steven Hayward, "Liberals and the Constitution," powerlineblog.com (February 7, 2012); Mark Levin, "We're Living in a Post-Constitutional America," www.realclearpolitics.com (January 19, 2012).

25. Pestritto, *Woodrow Wilson,* 2; Jean M. Yarbrough, *Theodore Roosevelt and the American Political Tradition* (Kansas, 2012), 6–7, 64, 83, 159, 220; Jonah Goldberg, *Liberal Fascism: The Secret History of the American Left from Mussolini to the Politics of Meaning* (Doubleday, 2008), 86, 88; Kesler, *Change,* 45–47, 49, 69, 75, 123–24.

26. Goldberg, *Liberal Fascism,* 86, 88; Kesler, *Change,* 33–34, 40–43, 73, 231–32; Yarbrough, *Theodore Roosevelt,* 43, 79, 106, 212, 230–31.

27. Kesler, *Change,* 75–76, 123–24, 187; Yarbrough, *Theodore Roosevelt,* 222–23.

28. See, for example, Peter Berkowitz, *Constitutional Conservatism: Liberty, Self-Government, and Political Moderation* (Hoover Institution, 2013), viii, 43–44, 90;

O'Neill, "Constitutional Conservatism During the Progressive Era," 13–15; Ken I. Kersch, "Ecumenicalism Through Constitutionalism: The Discursive Development of Constitutional Conservatism in *National Review*, 1955–1980," *Studies in American Political Development* 25 (Spring 2011): 86–116.

29. As described in Kesler, *Change*, 158; Goldberg, *Liberal Fascism*, 8, 12–13, 15, 21, 87–88, 216–19; Marini and Masugi, introduction to Marini and Masugi, *Progressive Revolution*, 1–2. See also Richard M. Weaver, *Ideas Have Consequences* (Chicago, 1948); Eric Voegelin, *The New Science of Politics: An Introduction* (Chicago, 1952).

30. Andrew P. Napolitano, *Theodore and Woodrow: How Two American Presidents Destroyed Constitutional Freedom* (Thomas Nelson, 2012), 24.

31. Goldberg, *Liberal Fascism*, 12, 79, 81.

32. Napolitano, *Theodore and Woodrow*, 227–32, 234; Kesler, *Change*, 188; Goldberg, *Liberal Fascism*, 109, 112–13.

33. Napolitano, *Theodore and Woodrow*, xii, 7, 19–26. The final quotation is from Wilson.

34. Pestritto, *Wilson*, 112–27.

35. Kesler, *Change*, 170–71; Yarbrough, *Theodore Roosevelt*, 102; Napolitano, *Theodore and Woodrow*, 37; Pestritto, *Wilson*, 221–46; 227–28. See also Pestritto, *Wilson*, 72–73, 83–85, 100–103, 133–39.

36. Kesler, *Change*, 58–59, 62; Yarbrough, *Theodore Roosevelt*, 13, 19–24, 204–5, 208; Goldberg, *Liberal Fascism*, 52. See also Marini and Masugi, *Progressive Revolution*, 1, 3, 17, 222–33; Bradley C. S. Watson, *Living Constitution, Dying Faith: Progressivism and the New Science of Jurisprudence* (ISI, 2009), 95; James W. Ceaser, *Nature and History in American Political Development* (Harvard, 2006).

37. Goldberg, *Liberal Fascism*, 95–96; Yarbrough, *Theodore Roosevelt*, 220, 225. Yarbrough links American Progressives with Otto von Bismarck, but Kesler observes that World War I made ongoing associations with Germany more difficult, and that many drew also from socially conscious English liberalism, which made it easier for FDR to tie America's liberal future to the Founders and the nation's liberal past; see Kesler, *Change*, 111–13, 119–20.

38. Napolitano, *Theodore and Woodrow*, 137; Goldberg, *Liberal Fascism*, 11–17, 78–120, 132, 221.

39. Goldberg, *Liberal Fascism*, 31.

40. Yarbrough, *Theodore Roosevelt*, 61, 106, 233; Pestritto, *Wilson*, 71–75, 77–78, 104–7; Schambra, "Election of 1912," 96; Marini, "Abandoning the Constitution," 29–30.

41. Kesler, *Change*, 99–102.

42. Napolitano, *Theodore and Woodrow*, 5, 8; but see Kesler, *Change*, 96, 99.

43. Kesler, *Change*, 99–102; Goldberg, *Liberal Fascism*.

44. Pestritto, *Wilson*, 167–72, 206–16; see Jeffrey Tulis, *The Rhetorical Presidency* (Princeton, 1987).

45. Goldberg, *Liberal Fascism*, 80, 85–86, 89; Kesler, *Change*, 91–94, 121, 180–85; Pestritto, *Wilson*, 200–216; see Tulis, *Rhetorical Presidency*.

46. Yarbrough, *Theodore Roosevelt*, 102, 124, 133–37, 139–40, 149, 172.

47. Ibid., 147–50.

48. Pestritto, *Wilson*, 188–201; see also Paul Carrese, "Montesquieu, the Founders, and Woodrow Wilson: The Evolution of Rights and the Eclipse of Constitutionalism," in Marini and Masugi, *Progressive Revolution*, 149–57.

49. Kesler, *Change*, 52–55, 89; Pestritto, *Wilson*, 89–93.

50. Goldberg, *Liberal Fascism*, 6–8, 14; Pestritto, *Wilson*, 89.

51. Napolitano, *Theodore and Woodrow*, xii, 5, 8, 76–77; Goldberg, *Liberal Fascism*, 82.

52. See Napolitano, *Theodore and Woodrow*, 38–43 (on FDR); Richard Epstein, *How Progressives Rewrote the Constitution* (Cato, 2007); James Buchanan and Gordon Tullock, *The Calculus of Consent: Logical Foundations of Constitutional Democracy* (Liberty Fund, 1999 [1962]); Bernstein, *Rehabilitating "Lochner."*

53. See, for example, John G. West, "Darwin's Public Policy: Nineteenth-Century Science and the Rise of the American Welfare State," in Marini and Masugi, *Progressive Revolution*, 253–86; Amity Shlaes, *The Forgotten Man: A New History of the Great Depression* (HarperCollins, 2007); Joseph W. Postell, "'Roaring' Against Progressivism: Calvin Coolidge's Principled Conservatism," in Postell and O'Neill, *Toward an American Conservatism*, 181–208, quotation on 192–93. See also Milton Friedman and Rose Friedman, *Free to Choose: A Personal Statement* (Harcourt Brace, 1980); Thomas E. Woods Jr., *The Politically Incorrect Guide to American History* (Washington, D.C., 2004), 93–98.

54. Burton W. Folsom Jr., *The Myth of the Robber Barons: A New Look at the Rise of Big Business in America*, 6th ed. (Young America's Foundation, 2010 [1987]), x, 1–2, 32, 39, 127.

55. Ibid., 52, 54, 56. On rent seeking and governmental sponsorship of cartels, see Goldberg, *Liberal Fascism*, 291, 293, 303; Napolitano, *Theodore and Woodrow*, 9, 46–48, 64, 54–74; Epstein, *How Progressives Rewrote the Constitution;* see also William Graham Sumner, *What the Social Classes Owe to Each Other* (1883).

56. Folsom, *Robber Barons*, 87, 94–95; Kesler, *Change*, 64–65; Goldberg, *Liberal Fascism*, 258; Yarbrough, *Theodore Roosevelt*, 89; Friedman and Friedman, *Free to Choose;* see also Gertrude Himmelfarb, "Varieties of Social Darwinism," in *Darwin and the Darwinian Revolution* (Ivan R. Dee, 1996 [1959]).

57. Napolitano, *Theodore and Woodrow*, 140–42, 144–46, 155; see also Folsom, *Robber Barons*, 35–39; Yarbrough, *Theodore Roosevelt*, 150–55; Woods, *Politically Incorrect Guide*, 103–8 (section entitled "Antitrust Idiocy" discussing "the absurd and arbitrary character of antitrust law"). Like Yarbrough (and Folsom), Napolitano adds: "Some businessmen of the time were genuinely crooks."

58. See, for example, Folsom, *Robber Barons*, chap. 6; Amity Shlaes, *The Forgotten Man: A New History of the Great Depression* (HarperCollins, 2007), chap. 10, "Mellon's

Gift"; Amity Shlaes, *Coolidge* (HarperCollins, 2013); Postell, "'Roaring' against Conservatism," 197–200.

59. Folsom, *Robber Barons*, 108, 112–14, 120.

60. Napolitano, *Theodore and Woodrow*, 235–37, 240, 242–43, 245, 247.

61. Ibid., 126.

62. Ibid., 130, 131, 133–35, 139; Yarbrough, *Theodore Roosevelt*, 169; see also Epstein, *How Progressives Rewrote the Constitution*.

63. Yarbrough, *Theodore Roosevelt*, 88–90, 127, 129, 187, 192, 214–16, 218.

64. Ken I. Kersch, "Beyond Originalism: Conservative Declarationism and Constitutional Redemption," *Maryland Law Review* 71 (2011): 229–82. See also, for example, Peter C. Myers, "Frederick Douglass's Natural Rights Constitutionalism: The Postwar Pre-Progressive Period," in Marini and Masugi, *Progressive Revolution*, 74–75 ("Douglass's postwar constitutionalism remains grounded in his continuing agreement with . . . the Founders' fundamental principles. . . . Douglass was never a forerunner of Progressivism."); Justin Buckley Dyer, *Slavery, Abortion, and the Politics of Constitutional Meaning* (Cambridge, 2013).

65. Yarbrough, *Theodore Roosevelt*, 60, 74–84, 197; Goldberg, *Liberal Fascism*, 115–16; Napolitano, *Theodore and Woodrow*, 107–8; West and Schambra, "Progressive Movement," 7.

66. Kesler, *Change*, 78–81; Yarbrough, *Theodore Roosevelt*, 10–12, 79–81; Pestritto, *Wilson*, 104, 109; Watson, *Living Constitutionalism*, 38–48. Yarbrough, *Theodore Roosevelt*, 13–14; West and Schambra, "The Progressive Movement," 3, 5. Kersch, "Beyond Originalism." See, for example, Harry V. Jaffa, *Crisis of the House Divided: An Interpretation of the Issues in the Lincoln-Douglas Debates* (Doubleday, 1959).

67. Napolitano, *Theodore and Woodrow*, 106, 107, 109; see also Goldberg, *Liberal Fascism*, 257.

68. Napolitano, *Theodore and Woodrow*, 93–100, 104–7, 109–10, 132; Goldberg, *Liberal Fascism*, 15–16, 254, 272–73.

69. Goldberg, *Liberal Fascism*, 254.

70. Ibid., 260–65.

71. Napolitano, *Theodore and Woodrow*, 93–100, 104–7, 110, 132; Goldberg, *Liberal Fascism*, 15–16, 254, 272–73.

72. Hattam and Lowndes, "Ground Beneath Our Feet," 214, 217–18.

73. Ibid., 201–4, 211; Adam Sheingate, "The Terrain of the Political Entrepreneur," in Skowronek and Glassman, *Formative Acts*, 15, 18–19, 19–20. See also Anthony Grafton and Lisa Jardine, "'Studied for Action': How Gabriel Harvey Read His Livy," *Past and Present* 129 (1990): 30–78; Bruce Miroff, "Leadership and American Political Development," in Skowronek and Glassman, *Formative Acts*, 39.

74. Charles R. Kesler, "What Separation of Powers Means for Constitutional Government," Heritage Foundation, First Principles Series Report #17 (December 17, 2007): "This precaution would not be necessary if reason and passion were utterly

harmonious. . . . These conditions, however, are unique to God, who alone justly unites the legislative, judicial, and executive powers in the same hands."

75. Pestritto, *Wilson*, 73.

76. Goldberg, for example, joins these issues seamlessly across a few short pages; see Goldberg, *Liberal Fascism*, 260–61, 264–65.

77. Napolitano, *Theodore and Woodrow*, 104–7; Goldberg, *Liberal Fascism*, 15–16, 100, 272–73. See C. Everett Koop and Francis Schaeffer, *Whatever Happened to the Human Race?* (Crossway, 1979).

78. Goldberg, *Liberal Fascism*, 254–55.

79. See Napolitano, *Theodore and Woodrow*, 242–43.

80. Ibid., 75–78, 84–85, 87, 89, 172–83.

81. Marini, "Abandoning the Constitution," 27.

82. See, for example, L. Brent Bozell, *The Warren Revolution: Reflections on the Consensus Society* (Arlington House, 1966); Diamond, "What the Framers Meant," 25.

83. Whittington, "The New Originalism."

84. Whittaker Chambers, *Witness* (Random House, 1952); Jaffa, *Crisis of the House Divided*. As Jaffa saw it, Lincoln = God (natural law/natural rights); Stephen Douglas = Man (legal positivism). This is in Strauss from the outset.

85. See Mark Graber, "The Declaration of Independence as Canon Fodder," *Tulsa Law Review* 49 (2013): 469–84.

PART II
NATION BUILDING: PARTY POLITICS AND THE SEARCH FOR A NEW CONSENSUS

7 • From Promoting to Ending Big Government

1912 and the Progressives' Century

John Milton Cooper

The year 2012 featured not only its own memorable presidential election but also the centennial of another especially pivotal contest. In 2012, few people needed to be reminded that one side, the Republicans, were running against strong, activist government—at least as far as the economy and social welfare were concerned. Their iconic hero, Ronald Reagan, had proclaimed three decades earlier, "Government is the problem, not the solution." Their Democratic opponents touted their own specific programs, but shied away from mounting any full-throated defense of activist government. Their one previous president since Reagan, Bill Clinton, had proclaimed sixteen years earlier, "The era of big government is over." In the talk about government, small was beautiful—always for one side and most of the time, rhetorically at least, for the other.

Anyone attuned to the centennial of the 1912 election could not fail to notice a total transformation in the political rhetoric surrounding the size and scope of government. None of the candidates in that contest opposed a bigger and more active government, and three of the four contenders sketched sweeping new conceptions of what a more robust government might achieve. Theodore Roosevelt and Woodrow Wilson, the two leading candidates, squared off in a great debate about how a more active government might best enhance democracy. Their rivalry reminds us that America's political leaders are not culturally constrained to run away from government, and that American electoral politics need not be confined to a simple dichotomous choice between two varieties, big and small.

A Shared Ambition

The 1912 election was an unusually high-minded and well-fought contest. The four contenders were men of great ability and substance. There were three presidents, past, present, and future—Theodore Roosevelt, William Howard Taft, and Woodrow Wilson—and the fourth candidate was the most important radical leader in the nation's history, the Socialist Party's nominee, Eugene Debs. For sheer drama, the 1912 contest offered a party rupture acted out in public at the Republican convention; the birth of a new party, Roosevelt's Progressives; and an assassination attempt on one of the major contenders, Roosevelt. More important still, the campaign operated at an intellectual depth unmatched and rarely approached before or since. As a revelation of how much the political atmosphere has subsequently changed, this election aired differences among candidates each vying to prove that he felt the greatest devotion to big government and that he was the most determined to make this kind of government bigger and stronger still.

This was a fiercely partisan contest. The emerging consensus on the shift to big government was the point of departure for a full airing of differences of approach and style. By dividing the voices of reform, the election underscored the ambivalence that Progressives felt about political parties generally, their sense that the instrument was insufficient to convey the general thrust and unifying power of their reform vision. In an election postmortem, TR complained that the biggest problem he encountered in trying build a Progressive party lay in trying to "shake loose from the old parties many men who profess adherence to our principles." His opponents had "fervidly announced themselves as Progressives, and as regards most of our principles, they [made] believe to be for them, and simply disagree[d] with us as to the methods of putting them into effect."[1] Over the decades, individual Progressives would continue to place themselves on different sides of the party divide, depending on their perception of which organization promised to advance the work of government most effectively. Only lately have progressives found themselves limited to one corner of one party, pushing against the grain.

On strictly intellectual grounds, the winner of the contest for the biggest supporter of government was the Socialist, Debs. Despite his folksiness and sincere fidelity to democratic practices, Debs was no revisionist open to rapprochement with capitalism. He ran on a platform that called for government ownership of the principal means of transportation (railroads) and communication (the telegraph) as well as all "large-scale industries": somewhat contradictorily, income and estate taxes would finance those nationalized industries and level inequalities of wealth.² The Socialists' platform also called for abolishing the Senate and barring the Supreme Court from overturning acts of Congress. Debs's showing in this election was the only real surprise in the outcome. He doubled his vote from his run four years before, polling over 900,000 votes; this was 6 percent of the total and the biggest share ever achieved by a Socialist. Some of that showing reflected Debs's strength as a campaigner, but much of it testified to the attractiveness of visions of big government.

On political grounds, the truly significant contest about government came between the two men whom everyone at the time recognized as the main contenders—Theodore Roosevelt and Woodrow Wilson. Contrary to many views of this campaign, the treatment of big business, "the trusts," was not the central issue between them. Antitrust policy did gain traction during the campaign, but it did not furnish the first major point of contention between Roosevelt and Wilson. Rather, the size and scope of government touched off the first firefight in the battle between them, and it opened the way to their de facto debate over the precise purposes of big government.

Drawing Out Different Conceptions of Big Government

It began with an attack by Roosevelt. His new Progressive Party had started off with a bang at a stirring convention that featured hymn singing and adopted a platform calling for stricter measures of economic regulation, income and inheritance taxes, and women's suffrage. The convention also witnessed the first appearance by a candidate in person to accept the nomination. Roosevelt's acceptance speech afforded him an opportunity to repeat his earlier outcry upon bolting from the Republican convention: "We stand at Armageddon and we battle for the Lord!" Such theatrics were all well and good, but as a politician, Roosevelt recognized that all he had done thus far was to split the Republicans. He knew that wresting away the bigger half of the party's electorate—as he ultimately did—would not be enough to carry him back to the White House. To win, he needed to attract new constituencies, particularly among potentially disaffected Democrats. The way to woo their votes lay, he believed, in appealing to the widespread sentiment in favor of big government, which transcended established party lines and lay at the heart of Progressivism. Roosevelt was out to show that he was not just the capital-*P* Progressive candidate but also the only true small-*p* progressive in the race.

He was convinced that the best way to do that was to impugn the governmental views of his Democratic rival, Wilson.

Roosevelt did not think this would be a hard row to hoe. His opponent was a political neophyte whom Roosevelt once called "pretty thin material for a President."[3] Despite an impressive reformist performance as governor of New Jersey, Wilson did not have much of a record as a Progressive. Better yet from Roosevelt's standpoint, he appeared to have a recent conservative past. New Jersey's bosses had foisted Wilson's gubernatorial nomination on a reluctant party and over the opposition of the state's Progressives. Before that, while still president of Princeton University, Wilson had consorted with the Grover Cleveland wing of the party and attacked Roosevelt's presidential policies from a limited-government, states'-rights stance. Fortuitously for Roosevelt, Wilson furnished an opening for an attack on his governmental views at the outset of the campaign. Newspapers quoted a speech in which Wilson asserted, "The history of liberty is a history of the limitation of governmental power, not the increase of it." In the context of the speech, Wilson was arguing for keeping government in touch with the people. Out of context, as reported in the press, the remark presented Roosevelt with precisely the target he was seeking.[4]

The Progressive nominee seized upon that sentence as "the key to Mr. Wilson's position," which he denounced as "a bit of outworn academic doctrine which was kept in the schoolroom and the professorial study for a generation after it had been abandoned by all who had experience of actual life." Denouncing this "laissez-faire doctrine" of the previous century, Roosevelt affirmed, "In the present day the limitation of governmental action means the enslavement of the people by the great corporations who can only be held in check through the extension of governmental power." For himself and his Progressives, Roosevelt promised "to use government as the most efficient means to uplift our people as a whole, who under Mr. Wilson's *laissez-faire* system, are trodden down in the scrambling rush of an unregulated and purely individualistic industrialism."[5] Later, speaking after being shot during an attempted assassination in Milwaukee, Roosevelt denounced Wilson and the Democrats for clinging to "the old flintlock, muzzle-loaded doctrine of States' rights," whereas he and the Progressives were "for the rights of the people, and if they can be obtained best through the National Government, then we are for national rights."[6]

Roosevelt was aiming to draw blood in an especially sensitive quarter. Oddly for someone who wanted to attract Democrats, he was invoking well-worn Republican appeals. The reference to states' rights evoked memories of the Civil

War, which was then less than fifty years in the past and whose veterans were still serving in Congress and on the Supreme Court. This reminder of many Democrats' secessionist backgrounds ran counter to Progressives' efforts to launch their party in the South, where they organized on a lily-white basis.

But Roosevelt's rhetorical tactic was not as misguided as it might initially seem. When the Democrats nominated William Jennings Bryan for president in 1896, a large majority of them repudiated Cleveland's states'-rights, limited-government persuasion in favor of not just a new face but also a daring platform that called for monetary inflation, stronger antitrust laws, strict regulation of railroads, and an income tax—all to be achieved through expansion of governmental powers at the national level. Since then, despite sporadic efforts by Cleveland's followers, the party had stayed true to Bryan, nominating him for president twice more and sticking to and expanding his agenda, even to the extent in 1908 of calling for governmental ownership of railroads. In Congress, southern and western Democrats faithful to Bryan had supplied the bulk of the votes for Progressive measures during the presidencies of Roosevelt and Taft, whose own party supplied far less support. Some historians have argued the Democrats deserve to be called the true Progressive party of this era.[7]

When Roosevelt cast aspersions on his opponent's lack of devotion to big government, he was drawing on his own deepest convictions. He had been a fervent nationalist since his youth, both venerating Alexander Hamilton and likewise despising Thomas Jefferson for what he perceived as the Virginian's pernicious legacies of states' rights, limited government, and low, self-interested political aims. More recently, with some assistance from Herbert Croly, Roosevelt had proclaimed a "New Nationalism," which he further expounded in this campaign.

Fierce and heartfelt though it was, the attack fell flat. Wilson had no trouble defending himself and turning the tables on his opponent. Speaking in Pennsylvania, he conceded that "there is one principle of Jefferson's which can no longer obtain in the practical politics of America," namely, the dictum "that the best government is that which does as little governing as possible, which exercises its power as little as possible." Wilson avowed that he had no fear of "the utmost exercise of the powers of the government of Pennsylvania, or of the Union, provided they are exercised . . . in the interest of the people who are living under them." Nonetheless, there were limits: "But when it is proposed to set up guardians over those people and to take care of them by a process of tutelage and supervision, in which they have no active part, I utter my absolute objection."[8] Later in the campaign, Wilson returned to that last point. "We do not want a big-brother government," he declared. "I do not want a government that will take care of me. I want a government that will make other men take their hands off so I can take care of myself."[9]

Even though statements such as Wilson's could sound like affirmations of limited government, they were not. Roosevelt's attack on him failed because the charges were not true. Despite his southern birth and upbringing, Wilson had become a nationalist almost as early in life as his rival. Starting in his undergraduate days, he criticized the separation of powers and favored drawing the executive and legislative branches together. As a law student at the University of Virginia, he criticized Jefferson's agrarianism and celebrated the defeat of the Confederacy. As a young professor, he confessed to a fellow academic, "Ever since I have had independent judgments of my own I have been a Federalist (!)"—meaning that he believed in strong central government.[10] Unsurprisingly, he admired Hamilton above all the other Founders, and he was initially cool to Jefferson. He continued to esteem Hamilton highest even after he later reached a political and intellectual reconciliation with Jefferson. Finally, he quickly forsook his fling with Grover Cleveland's vision of democracy, not only because it seemed a losing proposition politically but also, before that, because he could not square limited-government views with his own convictions. Thereafter, he made a rapid and total shift to his own full-fledged Progressivism, which he came to call the "New Freedom."

Trying to judge which man believed more strongly in big government would be fruitless. Worse, it would distract from an appreciation of how each embodied the broader Progressive consensus. Trying to gauge their degree of devotion also risks sidetracking a more important inquiry into what kind of big government each one favored. For several generations, a view has prevailed that there was no significant difference between where Roosevelt and Wilson stood in 1912. William Allen White, the journalist and friend and admirer of Roosevelt, gave the classic expression of this view when he wrote in 1924, "Between the New Nationalism and the New Freedom was that fantastic imaginary gulf that always has existed between tweedle-dum and tweedle-dee."[11] That view could have sprung from the two men's mutual devotion to big government, but it stems more from the similarity in the policies that they advocated in 1912, and that Wilson later enacted, and from their handling of the antitrust issue during the campaign.

Roosevelt entered the contest having bared two long-cloaked convictions. One was that breaking up big businesses was futile because they would only grow and combine again; the other was that such efforts were retrograde, since most big businesses had achieved their size and power by outperforming their competitors. Therefore, the main task of government was to be bigger and stronger so that it could regulate and discipline those businesses. That view did not find a wide following, even among Roosevelt's Progressive cohorts, and it offered Wilson a tempting target. With assistance from his newfound friend and adviser Louis Brandeis, the Democratic nominee charged his opponent with seeking to legalize monopoly and thereby, albeit unwittingly, opening the way for big business to dominate government.

Wilson and Brandeis countered with a vision of an activist government that fostered competition and leveled the playing field for new entries into the marketplace. They favored breaking up many big businesses, believing that those businesses had usually grown by stifling competition, and they wanted to combat the malign influence of financial magnates, whom they dubbed the "Money Trust." Put on the defensive, Roosevelt made a distinction between "good trusts," which could be left alone as long as they behaved themselves, and "bad trusts," which should be broken up or otherwise reined in. Wilson, who did not share Brandeis's visceral aversion to all bigness, distinguished between "big business" and "trusts," by which he meant the same thing and prescribed the same remedies as Roosevelt did. This apparent convergence on the trust issue would become the principal prop supporting the Tweedledum-Tweedledee view.

Despite underlining the Progressive consensus on a larger role for government, this view has had the unfortunate effect of obscuring the profound differences between the two men's thinking both on the trust issue and more deeply on the proper role of government. On the trust issue, they diverged over whether good or bad trusts dominated and, therefore, how much trust-busting needed to be done. Also on that issue, they diverged over the value and purpose of competition. For Roosevelt, competition, where possible, offered a limited and sometimes useful discipline; for Wilson, competition furnished the essential means to maintain not only a vibrant marketplace but also social mobility and national renewal.

This last clash of views got close to the heart of their conflict. In his aspersions on Wilson's supposed governmental views, Roosevelt expanded his quarrel with Jefferson, whose fundamental sin in his eyes had lain less in taking a small-government stance than in promoting low political aspirations, encouraging selfish individual and group interests, and undermining national strength, unity, and ideals. On the campaign trail and even earlier, Roosevelt excoriated, as he did after being shot in Milwaukee, "two recognized creeds fighting one another; . . . the creed of the 'Havenots' arraigned [sic] against the creed of the 'Haves.'" He believed that if people adhered to his New National-ism and harked to his preaching, they could elevate the standard of politics and strive for national unity and greatness. He compared his political vision to his military service, when he and his men had forsaken selfishness and safety for the good of all. He also avowed in Milwaukee, "I never in my life was in any movement in which I was able to serve with such wholehearted devotion as in this; in which I was able to feel as I do in this that common weal. I have fought for the good of our common country."[12]

Notwithstanding his background as the son, grandson, nephew, and son-in-law of Presbyterian ministers, Wilson did not liken his brand of political persuasion to preaching. Instead, and not surprisingly in view of his pre-political career, he saw his task as one of educating. He delighted in parrying jabs by Roosevelt and others at his having been a "professor" and a "school-master." He noted that education was a two-way process of at once teaching to and learning from students and, now, the electorate. He went further and turned this view of leadership into an attack on Roosevelt. He expanded on his rejection of "big-brother government" and one that did not help people take care of themselves to declare, "I do not wish to be your master, I wish to be your spokesman."[13] At bottom for Wilson, leadership consisted of enabling people to get what they wanted, facilitating individuals and groups in Jeffer-son's "pursuit of happiness." Wilson enjoyed tarring Roosevelt with the brush of "paternalism" and contrasting such notions with his own vision of never-ending social revitalization through enterprise and upward mobility. He closed his campaign with the assertion, "If out of the average man we can't get our great men, then we have destroyed the very springs of renewal in this America which we have built in order to show that every man born of every class had the right and the privilege to make the most of himself."[14]

Both men invoked the memory and example of Abraham Lincoln, but each appealed to a different Lincoln. Neither invoked or even mentioned the Great Emancipator; racial concerns remained almost totally and, by later lights, shockingly ignored in white mainstream politics in this era. Roosevelt exalted Lincoln as the savior of the Union, and he portrayed himself as likewise calling upon Americans to set aside and rise above selfish, parochial loyalties in order to serve the greater good and promote national strength and unity. Wilson lauded Lincoln as the apotheosis of the common man, and he pre-sented himself as preserving the economy and society that allowed all persons, no matter how humbly born, to realize the full flowering of their abilities. Those invocations of Lincoln bared the fundamental differences between Roosevelt and Wilson. Roosevelt wanted above all to serve the nation's good, to defend it against those who would disrupt its unity and lower its values and goals. Wilson wanted above all to promote the individual's good, to defend her or him against those who would take away opportunity and bar fulfillment of one's gifts.

What Roosevelt and Wilson offered in 1912, albeit imperfectly and often with malice, was something unique in presidential contests and largely unknown in most campaigns: exposition of political philosophies. The irreducible core of their differences lay in their conceptions of human nature. Belying his public image as a dynamic lover of the common folk, Roosevelt held a pessimistic view of people's capacity for social good: he believed they needed to be guided, in this case through evangelical persuasion and regulatory oversight, in order to overcome their base, narrow bents. Belying his public image as a stern puritanical moralizer, Wilson held an optimistic view of people's capacity for social good: he believed they needed to be freed, through active, persistent governmental intervention, to pursue their dreams and desires. The New Nationalism and the New Freedom offered more than just campaign slogans: they encapsulated the two men's basic political means and ends. Roosevelt was a conservative; oxymoronic though it may sound to post-Reagan, post-Clinton ears, he was a big-government conservative.[15] Wilson was a liberal; uncelebrated as he has been on the leftward side, he was a big-government liberal.

The Republican Party and the Rearticulation of Doubt About Big Government

Clearly, Debs, Roosevelt, and Wilson made enlarging the size and scope of government the overriding thrust of the 1912 campaign. But there was one other candidate in the race, who raised a dissenting voice: William Howard Taft. Up to this time, Taft had been a moderate Progressive, with a decent reform record as president. He had fallen short, however, in the eyes of his party's reformers by not pushing further and by trying to maintain unity by sometimes appeasing probusiness conservative elements. Taft had followed faithfully in Roosevelt's presidential footsteps, but under more trying political conditions than his predecessor had faced. The break between the two men stemmed in part from Roosevelt's unquenched thirst for presidential power and, even more, from conflicting notions about how to meet the challenge posed by progressive Republican insurgents. Each man regarded many of those insurgents as dangerous radicals, but whereas Taft sided with conservatives in fighting them, Roosevelt chose to join and lead them in hopes of restraining them and making them more responsible. With the insurgents, Roosevelt was trying to, in a later generation's word, co-opt them.

What deterred Taft from standing aside in 1912—in addition to the deep hurt caused by his erstwhile friend and patron's personal attacks—were two beliefs. First, he feared that Roosevelt had succumbed to radicalism, particularly in his attacks on the courts and judicial review. Second, he was convinced that the critical concern was to retain control of the party. The conservative bosses felt the same way, and they stuck by Taft even though they harbored little affection for him personally and wrote him off as a sure loser in November. The president summed up his and their thinking when he told a friend, "If I win [the nomination] and Roosevelt bolts, it means a long hard fight with probable defeat. But I can stand defeat if we retain the regular Republican party as a nucleus for future conservative action."[16] At the convention, the regulars turned back Roosevelt's challenge, although their high-handed and probably unnecessary actions gave the ex-president a perfect pretext for making the bolt that he had already planned. Taft stayed in the race, as he privately admitted, to block Roosevelt's chances to win, and he was relieved when Wilson prevailed. Taft finished third, 600,000 votes behind Roosevelt, with two states with eight electoral votes, to Roosevelt's six states and eighty-eight electoral votes. This remains the only time an outside candidate has outpolled a major-party nominee.

Yet Taft's course was not so futile as it may have seemed at the time. The rest of the Progressive ticket ran behind regular Republicans nearly everywhere except in California, where Governor Hiram Johnson, Roosevelt's Progressive vice presidential running mate, elbowed the regulars off the ticket. In the next presidential contest, the Progressives imploded, mainly because Roosevelt yearned to get back into his old party's fold and defeat Wilson. In that election, conservatives remained in charge and dictated the nominee, the platform, and the terms on which prodigal Progressives were allowed to return. By then, an ideological shift had begun among Republicans. In 1912, Taft had done more than remain on the ballot. While hitting the campaign trail, the first sitting president to do so, he delivered a consistent message during a brief foray in the Northeast. "A National Government cannot create good times," he maintained in one speech. "It cannot make the rain to fall, the sun to shine, or the crops to grow, but it can, by pursuing a meddlesome policy, attempting to change economic conditions, and frightening the investment of capital, prevent a prosperity and a revival of business which might otherwise have taken place."[17]

Part of Taft's message sounded a new note among Republicans. Dire warnings about wrongheaded policies that would scare business had been conservative standbys in the party ever since William McKinley beat Bryan in 1896. But Taft's denigration of governmental action marked a departure and flirted with the small-government views that Roosevelt was trying to pin on Wilson. Such views had previously found their home among Democrats who identified with Cleveland, who were often derisively called "Bourbons"—less for their taste in whiskey than for their alleged ignorance and resistance to change. As members of the party of Lincoln and the Union in the Civil War, Republicans of all stripes had always embraced strong central government, rendering such views even broader than the Progressive consensus. Republican conservatives had hitherto opposed the extension of governmental powers in economic affairs as unwise and unnecessary but not as politically or constitutionally impermissible. Taft's declarations in 1912 marked an early step in the long march of Republicans toward opposition to big government in and of itself.

Aftermath

The 1912 election had profound and long-running consequences, but not all of them were immediate or readily predictable. The results belied the campaign's excitement and intellectual depth. Electorally, the outcome confirmed the alignment seemingly set in stone in 1896. Wilson won by holding on to the normal Democratic minority, with 41.9 percent of the vote and about two hundred thousand fewer votes than Bryan picked up in his third-time run in 1908. Roosevelt and Taft split the normal Republican majority, but their combined totals fell about one hundred thousand short of Taft's showing in 1908. The total vote increased only slightly from four years earlier; strictly as a matter of statistics, the shortfalls in the three main contenders' outcomes could be accounted for by the doubling of Debs's vote from 1908. A real break in electoral patterns would not come until 1916, when Wilson won reelection in the face of a reunited though still bruised Republican Party. He amassed three million more votes than he had gotten in 1912, and he ran six hundred thousand votes ahead of his opponent, Charles Evans Hughes. Wilson was the first

Democrat to win a second consecutive term since Andrew Jackson—although he fell short of a popular majority, as did every winning Democrat between Jackson and Franklin Roosevelt. During the 1916 campaign, Wilson expressed regret that, unlike four years earlier, this was not "an intellectual contest . . . [in which] upon both sides, men would draw upon some fundamental questions of politics."[18]

The longer-term significance of Wilson's reelection remains open to question. On one hand, the electoral alignment of 1896 held firm, with the crucial exceptions of Ohio and California, and that alignment had already begun to reassert itself in the 1914 contests. The Republicans' tide gained momentum in 1918, allowing them to recapture both houses of Congress, and it turned into a tidal wave in 1920 that ushered in their undivided control of the White House and Congress for the next twelve years, marred only by loss of the House in 1930. On the other hand, the 1896 alignment had eroded in 1916 in the Midwest and on the West Coast.[19] Two years later, despite the ongoing Republican resurgence, Democrats cracked the Northeast by electing Al Smith governor of New York and David I. Walsh senator from Massachusetts. Both those winners were Irish Americans, and they spearheaded the emergence of a growing, aroused white ethnic constituency for the Democrats. Of the mainstays of the Democrats' future majority, which would include those ethnics, organized labor, farmers, and the South, only African Americans remained outside the expanding party tent. Moreover, Wilson's spectacular success in enacting reform legislation before 1917 had amply fulfilled his promises of big-government liberalism and won over many of Roosevelt's 1912 followers, who had always warmed more to him personally and his specific programs than to his essentially conservative vision.

The Democrats' success in appropriating to themselves one brand of governmental activism did not necessarily mean that Republicans would turn against such activism. "Normalcy," the slogan of their winning candidate in 1920, Warren Harding, signaled an attempt to return to the days not only before Wilson but also before Roosevelt. That entailed visions and policies updated but fundamentally unchanged from the days of McKinley, not a conversion to the small-government persuasion of Cleveland and his ilk. The Republican administrations of the 1920s were blatantly probusiness, but they were not antigovernment. Instead, as it had been under McKinley, so it was under Harding, Calvin Coolidge, and Herbert Hoover. They restored a happy, mutually beneficial partnership between business and government, both of which could be as big as they pleased.

Though weakened since 1912, Republican Progressivism did not fade away in the 1920s, and its support for robust government persisted as well. Party insurgents, augmented by dissident movements such as the Farmer-Laborites in the Upper Midwest and the Nonpartisan League on the Great Plains, joined with slowly resurgent Democrats to deny conservatives effective control of Congress most of the time. And in 1924, Robert M. La Follette bolted the Republicans to run for president as a Progressive, although he did not form a third party as Roosevelt had done in 1912. The final Republican president of this era, Herbert Hoover, had been a Roosevelt Progressive in 1912; he had served under Wilson during World War I; and he pursued a somewhat chastened form of big-government conservatism in the Cabinets of Harding and Coolidge and during half his term in the White House.

Substantial change in the acceptance of progovernment views across most of the political spectrum really began in the 1930s. The two critical figures in making big government itself the issue were Hoover and his Democratic successor, Franklin Roosevelt. When Hoover's efforts to combat the Depression through his own actions and partnership with business leaders bore scant fruit, he began to speak out against further intervention in the economy and to preach about what government could not do. Some conservatives at the time faulted him for intervening too much as president, but they would have a hard time disagreeing with his later rhetoric, which he kept up for the three decades he lived after leaving the White House.

Franklin Roosevelt felt no compunctions about governmental action, and he enjoyed a unique status as the political heir to both Theodore Roosevelt, his distant cousin and uncle of his wife, and Wilson, under whom he had also served. The perpetual crisis atmosphere surrounding the New Deal and FDR's eclectic, nonintellectual temperament allowed him to draw upon, switch back and forth between, and thoroughly mix up both his forebears' approaches to big government. Many Republicans strove valiantly during the next three decades to resist the siren song of antigovernment arguments, but the Democrats' preemption of big-government ideas opened moderates and Progressives in the GOP to charges of "me-tooism" and of being, as a later generation would put it, "RINOs," Republicans in name only.

It is tempting to view antigovernment rhetoric as a gravitational force inexorably pulling at conservatives and Republicans, but other influences came into play. From later perspectives, two areas were strangely absent from the political mainstream in 1912—race and foreign affairs. Over the following quarter century, African Americans began to change the political context of

race through legal, constitutional, and protest campaigns by civil rights organizations and through the Great Migration, the massive exodus of black people
out of the South to cities in electorally rich northern states. The shift of African
Americans to the Democrats, which started in the 1930s despite the party's
previously abysmal record on race, gave them true political leverage. Ironically, in view of Wilson's weakness on race, they were the perfect example of
people who wanted a government that would make other people take their
hands off and let them live free and equal lives. Conversely, white southerners
began to renounce their earlier allegiance to big-government liberalism based
on economic issues. They came to fear "a big-brother government"—that is, a
federal government—that would not let them conduct their race relations as
they pleased. The irony lost on them was that they themselves wanted to run
big-brother governments at the state and local level over people who were
struggling desperately to get out from under their racial despotism. States'-
rights Bourbon democracy emerged fairly quickly from the shadows to dominate southern politics. This was evidenced by the Dixiecrat candidacy of Strom
Thurmond in 1948 and by his later switch to the Republicans, who in 1964
carried four Deep South states for the first time since Reconstruction. Lyndon
Johnson's definitive commitment of the Democrats to racial justice through
strong civil rights legislation speeded southern white flight to the other party,
bringing with them the baggage of states' rights and limited government.

Even though the 1912 election came less than two years before the outbreak
of World War I, only one of the four candidates, Roosevelt, made any mention
of foreign affairs, and that was a fleeting aside. America's entry into that war
changed facts and attitudes about big government. The Wilson administration
expanded the reach and scope of public authority through a military draft,
sharply increased taxation, a takeover of the railroads and telegraphs, and ra-
tioning and allocation of resources. At the same time, the administration
worked hand in glove with business and financial leaders. As a war president,
Wilson added big-government conservatism to his liberalism, and his policies
offered models for probusiness Republicans in the 1920s and New Deal Democrats in the 1930s.

This governmental activism during World War I also had an ugly side. The
control and censorship of information, stifling of dissent, and repression of
civil liberties gave a taste of a different aspect of big-brother government—the
kind that George Orwell would characterize with the same two words three
decades later in *1984*. One of the 1912 presidential candidates, Eugene Debs,
went to prison for violating a wartime law regulating speech. In 1920, Debs

ran for president one last time, from his cell in a federal penitentiary. He won a few thousand more votes than he had in 1912, but that amounted to half his previous percentage, thanks to the doubling of the electorate through nation-wide women's suffrage. More broadly, wartime repression drove many erst-while Progressives and even radicals to recoil from the concentration of government power. One of them, Randolph Bourne, coined the haunting watchwords "War is the health of the state."[20]

Today's Polarized (Non) Debate About Big Government

The road from the New Nationalism and the New Freedom to "the era of big government is over" was long and tortuous. It led through the New Deal, World War II, the Cold War, the Second Reconstruction, Vietnam, Watergate, economic readjustments, and myriad byways. In all this, there was nothing inevitable about polarization over big government. Theodore Roosevelt's spirit lived on, particularly among such Republicans as his fellow New Yorkers Thomas E. Dewey and Nelson Rockefeller, and in Hiram Johnson's California with Earl Warren and Thomas Kuchel. Many of his followers, however, moved over to the Democrats, men such as Harold Ickes and Edward P. Costigan, and the heirs to La Follette's Progressives and the Farmer-Laborites and Nonparti-san Leaguers injected fresh life into the Democrats in their regions. Despite the divisiveness of race, some white southern Democrats clung to Progressiv-ism and liberalism long enough to produce two presidents in Jimmy Carter and Bill Clinton and a vice president and near president in Al Gore. By and large, however, those Republicans and white southern Democrats were fight-ing for lost causes and pointing to roads not taken.[21]

For all the country's accomplishments of the last century, especially in in-ternational leadership and social and racial betterment, the rhetorical story of American politics has not been a happy one. Antagonists of big government have largely succeeded in identifying it with wasteful meddling, bungling bu-reaucracy, and supercilious, know-it-all paternalism, whereas its would-be de-fenders have made too little of its role as a guard against predatory interests and a champion of social and economic mobility. It is as if a caricature of the less attractive potential of Theodore Roosevelt's big-government conservatism has eclipsed the more attractive promises of Woodrow Wilson's big-government liberalism. This has left Democrats to play on the rhetorical turf defined by the small-government advocates ascendant within the Republican Party. Al Gore's boast as a presidential candidate was that he led the project to shrink government during the Clinton administration. Only Barack Obama has ventured to revive the activist posture, and as James Kloppenberg details later in this volume, that effort has met with a fierce reaction.

The tectonic shift in attitudes toward government points to what may be a fundamental flaw in seeking to advance or resist those attitudes through the mechanism of parties. Despite their frequent railing against machines and their demands for more plebiscitary processes, few Progressives really forsook parties. Not only Roosevelt and Wilson but also others such as Robert La Follette and Hiram Johnson strove to replace "bad" parties (like Roosevelt's "bad trusts") with "good" parties. The long experience of the mid and late twentieth century, when both parties narrowed their differences in search of electoral majorities, suggests that parties do not serve well as vehicles for attitudes toward government, either for or against. On the left, disgruntled Democrats demand a more "populist" approach, by which they mean old-style Progressivism of the Wilson–La Follette variety. On the right, dissatisfied Republicans demand ever stricter fealty to antigovernment views and punish those suspected of insufficient fervor. To paraphrase Lincoln, the prayers of both will not be answered, and the prayers of neither will be answered fully, for such is the nature of parties.

Still, for contemporary progressives who yearn for a revival of big-government liberalism, these reflections need not be a counsel of despair. Imperfect though they were, the Progressives of the first Roosevelt and the Democrats of Wilson, the second Roosevelt, and Johnson wrought great things. Questions remain: If the era of big government is indeed over, why has that come to pass? One hundred years of progressivism, rooted in the big-government consensus of 1912, cannot be swept aside as somehow un-American. Our political culture offers ample support for a robust defense of the democratic purposes of governmental activism. More than half a century ago, Isaiah Berlin responded to proclamations in the first half of the twentieth century that liberalism was dead: "It shouldn't have died." By the same token, for this new century's progressives, the era of big government shouldn't be given up so easily.

Notes

1. Theodore Roosevelt to Benjamin Ide Wheeler, Dec. 21, 1911, in *The Letters of Theodore Roosevelt*, ed. Elting E. Morison (Cambridge, Mass., 1954), 7:641.

2. Socialist Party platform, quoted in Lewis L. Gould, *Four Hats in the Ring: The 1912 Election and the Birth of Modern American Politics* (Lawrence, Kan., 2008), 116. This is by far the best book on the election.

3. Roosevelt to Wheeler, Dec. 21, 1911, *Letters of Theodore Roosevelt*, 7:462.

4. Woodrow Wilson, speech, Sept. 9, 1912, in *The Papers of Woodrow Wilson*, ed. Arthur S. Link (Princeton, N.J., 1978), 25:124.

5. Roosevelt, speech, Sept. 14, 1912, in *The Works of Theodore Roosevelt*, ed. Hermann Hagedorn (New York, 1926), 17:306, 307, 313, 314.

6. Roosevelt, speech, Oct. 14, 1912, in ibid., 17:328–29.

7. This case is made strongly in David Sarasohn, *The Party of Reform: Democrats in the Progressive Era* (Jackson, Miss., 1989), and Elizabeth Sanders, *Roots of Reform: Farmers, Workers, and the American State, 1877–1917* (Chicago, 1999).

8. Wilson, speech, Sept 23, 1912, in *Papers of Wilson*, 25:224–25.

9. Wilson, speech, Oct. 28, 1912, in *The Crossroads of Freedom: The 1912 Campaign Speeches of Woodrow Wilson*, ed. John Wells Davidson (New Haven, Conn., 1956), 491.

10. Wilson to Albert Bushnell Hart, June 3, 1889, in *Papers of Wilson*, 6:243.

11. William Allen White, *Woodrow Wilson* (Boston, 1924), 264. For a contrary view, which informs the following paragraphs, see Cooper, *The Warrior and the Priest: Woodrow Wilson and Theodore Roosevelt* (Cambridge, Mass., 1983), 206–21.

12. Roosevelt, speech, Oct. 14, 1912, in *Works of Roosevelt*, 17:322, 323.

13. Wilson, speech, Oct. 19, 1912, in *Papers of Wilson*, 25:447.

14. Wilson, speech, Nov. 2, 1912, in ibid., 25:505.

15. For a contrary view of Roosevelt's conservatism, by an avowed conservative, see Jean Yarbrough, *Theodore Roosevelt and the American Political Tradition* (Lawrence, Kan., 2012).

16. William Howard Taft to Myron Herrick, June 20, 1912, quoted in Henry F. Pringle, *The Life and Times of William Howard Taft* (New York, 1939), 2:898.

17. Taft, speech, Sept. 28, 1912, *New York Times*, Sept. 29, 1912.

18. Wilson, speech, Sept. 30, 1916, in *Papers of Wilson*, 38:302.

19. For contrasting views of the 1916 result, see Arthur Link, *Wilson: Campaigns for Progressivism and Peace* (Princeton, N.J., 1965), 124; Cooper, *Warrior and Priest*, 256–57; and Cooper, *Woodrow Wilson: A Biography* (New York, 2009), 359–61.

20. See Randolph Bourne, "The State," in Bourne, *War and the Intellectuals: Collected Essays, 1915–1919*, ed. Carl Resek (New York, 1964), 71.

21. On the decline of the Republican left and center, see Geoffrey Kabaservice, *Rule and Ruin: The Downfall of Moderation and the Destruction of the Republican Party, from Eisenhower to the Tea Party* (New York, 2012).

8 • The Progressive Party and the Rise of Executive-Centered Partisanship

Sidney M. Milkis

In December 2011, President Barack Obama traveled to Osawatomie, Kansas, to deliver an important political message. Preparing the rhetorical ground for his reelection campaign, he channeled Theodore Roosevelt's New Nationalism address. TR had journeyed to Osawatomie in 1910, and his speech at the memorial park commemorating John Brown and "Bloody" Kansas launched a campaign that would secure his leadership of a cresting Progressive movement. As the presidential candidate of an insurgent Progressive Party in 1912, TR spearheaded a three-decade-long advance against the bulwarks of industrial capitalism, a breakthrough that would culminate in his cousin Franklin D. Roosevelt's triumphant reelection in 1936.

Obama went to Osawatomie to claim the mantle of the Old Rough Rider. The challenge, a century later, was to reinvigorate—and, to a point, reinvent—Progressivism, to reassert its appeal in the wake of the Reagan revolution and a conservative insurgency still flexing its muscles through the Tea Party movement. Obama also hoped to renew the Progressives' political methods. Like TR, he sought to rally a loose constellation of advocacy groups around his unique personal appeal and to forge them into a new coalition for programmatic action.

The tumultuous early years of the Obama presidency produced unmistakable evidence of a programmatic debt to the Progressive tradition. The Obama administration's dogged pursuit of national health care reform—the holy grail of Progressive reformers since the early part of the twentieth century—was a lineal descendant of the Progressive Party's dedication, as its platform stated, to "the protection of the home life against the hazards of sickness, irregular employment, and old age through a system of social insurance adopted to

American use."[1] In his Osawatomie speech, Obama joined his programmatic ambitions more explicitly to the overarching vision of the polity that TR's Progressive Party campaign championed in 1912. Echoing the Progressive antipathy to political parties, he presented himself as a leader who transcended political divisions. Obama at Osawatomie resembled TR's "steward of the public welfare," a leader who could rise above the polarizing economic and social conflicts of his time to serve the interests of the "whole people."[2] Invoking Roosevelt's admonition that "We are all Americans," Obama sought to defy the recrudescence of partisan polarization by reinvesting faith in the Progressive hope that "our common interests are as broad as the continent."[3]

In the service of this transcendent ideal, the original Progressive reformers had engaged in impressive democratic experimentation. The construction of a national state, Roosevelt and his reform allies argued, had to go hand in hand with "more direct action by the people in their own affairs." The direct primary, TR said at Osawatomie, was a step in this direction. In 1912, Roosevelt engaged the incumbent president, William Howard Taft, in the first presidential primary campaign; then, after being denied the Republican nomination, he formed a new party that gave a full-throated defense of "pure democracy," including popular referenda on court decisions, an easier method of amending the Constitution, and the opportunity for the people to recall all public officials. Strengthening ties between the White House and the people was especially important, for as Thomas Jefferson once argued, only the president could "command a view of the whole ground." Jefferson had used that commanding position to foster an encompassing party of national consensus, albeit one that served a radically decentralized republic. The Progressives, too, sought an encompassing party of national consensus, one that would capture the spirit of the age and break free from the gravitational pull of special interests and petty ambitions. But in fashioning themselves as "neo-Hamiltonians" rather than "neo-Jeffersonians," the Progressives argued that public opinion could realize its unifying potential only when empowered by a centralized state under a strong executive.[4]

Heir to this encompassing vision, Obama gave new life to TR's effort to join charismatic leadership, collective action, and programmatic reform. His remarkable ascendance to the White House involved an experiment in top-down, bottom-up mobilization, a strategy carried out by a personal organization. He tied himself directly to scattered but potentially overwhelming support: minorities, youth, and educated white voters, especially single women. He and his allies built an information-age grassroots network that was critical not only to his two presidential campaigns but also to the enactment and implementation of his signature legislative achievement, the Patient Protection and Affordable Care Act of 2010. Born during the 2008 campaign as Obama for America, this mass-mobilization effort was inserted into the Democratic National Committee as Organizing for America during Obama's first term in the White House; after 2012, it was spun off as a nonprofit social-welfare entity called Organizing for Action. Through all these phases, OFA has sought to merge Obama's magnetic personality with a movement base and to provide a springboard for his leadership of the nation.[5]

The resonance of Osawatomie then and now indicates that the principles and practices championed by Roosevelt and his Progressive Party allies have become enduring features of our political life. Yet the hope that Progressive leaders could rise above factions to articulate public opinion, synthesize the public's interests, and anchor programmatic reform in a unified sense of national purpose has proved an elusive dream. Seeking to navigate a path between conservatives and socialists, Roosevelt claimed to stand against both the "selfish greed of the haves" and the "selfish greed of the have-nots."[6] But this seemingly selfless ambition immediately aroused debate over the essential character and function of parties, indeed about the very meaning of representation. The Democratic candidate, Woodrow Wilson, and the Republican standard bearer, President Taft, actively resisted the displacement of party by a pretentious popular tribune. More enduringly, Roosevelt's battle with Taft drove a wedge between Progressivism and conservatism that would grow wider over time. Although not always expressed through formal party channels, this ideological struggle has confounded the progressive aspiration to transcend partisanship and represent the "whole people."

This chapter examines the wayward path of progressivism from Roosevelt's Bull Moose campaign to the Obama presidency. Committed to "pure democracy," many early-twentieth-century reformers hoped to sweep away intermediary organizations like political parties. In their disdain for partisan politics and their enthusiasm for good government, they sought to fashion the Progressive Party as a party to end parties. The Progressive campaign of 1912, Barry Karl observed, "was as much an attack on the whole concept of political parties as it was an effort to create a single party whose doctrinal clarity and moral purity would represent the true interest of the nation as a whole."[7] The Progressives failed in that ambition, and their shortfall has had profound effects on contemporary government and politics. By transforming rather than transcending parties, they fostered a kindred, though bastardized, alternative: executive-centered partisanship.

The transformation of parties set in motion by the Progressives has subjected both progressivism and conservatism to an executive-centered democracy that subordinates "collective responsibility" to the needs of presidential candidates and incumbents. We can trace this dynamic development through the Democratic Party, in the progressive leadership of Woodrow Wilson, Franklin Roosevelt, and Lyndon Johnson, and we can follow it through the Republican Party, in the conservative leadership of Calvin Coolidge, Richard Nixon, and Ronald Reagan. The new executive-centered party system extended beyond the Progressive campaign of 1912 and proceeded on both sides of the ideological divide, causing Obama's efforts to transcend divisions with a new progressive program to be caught in a maelstrom. Contemporary progressivism remains torn by the contradictions that marked its birth in the Progressive Party, still unable to reconcile its aspirations for national leadership with partisanship, or programmatic reform with national unity.

Roosevelt, the Progressive Party, and the Critique of Party

The Progressive Party was not, as many historians and political scientists have alleged, merely an extension of TR's enormous ambition; rather, it represented a collective effort that included many reformers who were at the vanguard of the surging Progressive movement. For example, Jane Addams, the famous suffragette and settlement house reformer; William Allen White, the prominent Progressive journalist; and Herbert Croly, the founder of the *New Republic* and, arguably, the intellectual godfather of Progressive democracy, all participated in the writing of the platform. Roosevelt and the Progressive Party were able to recruit candidates for most major state and federal offices and to outpoll the Republican Party in the national campaign because they were building on "decades-long organizational entrepreneurship." They connected "the ecumenical social Christianity of liberal Protestant churches, the emerging social science disciplines in the universities, the rapid expansion of popular monthly and weekly magazines, and, most tellingly, the rise of locally based but nationally organized advocacy groups."[8] Indeed, rather than dominating the movements and civic organizations that came together at the 1912 Progressive Party convention, Roosevelt's quest to return to power required a good deal of effort to catch up with a parade that might have left him behind. Though a long-standing supporter of direct primaries and the "stewardship" theory of the presidency, Roosevelt was a late convert to most of the ideas and proposals that mobilized the third party's early supporters. In the course of his

renewed quest for the presidency, however, direct democracy, vigorous regulation of industry, and social justice became the leitmotifs of the campaign, and
the Progressive Party platform that championed these causes sealed the critical but uneasy alliance that Roosevelt formed with Progressive activists.

To Addams and others who had long been in the trenches, the Progressive
Party platform—a compendium of almost every reform the movement had
pushed for during the past decade—brought together social and political insurgents in an unprecedented display of collective ambition. "We all realized,"
Addams wrote, "how inadequate we were in small groups." But the foremost
social reformer in the country recognized something more: the "unique
power" and "magnetic personality" of Roosevelt himself. The attainment of
reforms longed for by a diverse array of political and social activists, Addams
thought, required the leadership of someone with Roosevelt's stature and energy. Thus Addams did not see TR as a threat to the collective responsibility of
the Progressive Party and the reforms it championed; rather, he was an aegis
essential to social reformers' political and programmatic aspirations.[9]

The attempt to break the grip of parties on politics and remake American
democracy was not cut from whole cloth; rather, the Progressive Party's campaign of 1912 marked a critical way station along a long hard road. Since the
late 1880s, reforms in the states had resulted in the advance of the secret or
official ballot; the adoption of registration requirements; the growth of civil
service reforms; and the introduction of the direct primary in state, local, and
congressional elections. Moreover, the enactment of the Pendleton Act in 1883
laid a solid foundation on which to build a federal civil service in succeeding
decades.[10] Significantly, Roosevelt's presidency (1901–9) marked the dividing
line between the old commitment to party patronage in public affairs and the
modern recognition that nonpartisan administration was a principal tool of
governance. These measures, combined with the emergence of mass-
circulation newspapers and magazines, which operated independently of the
traditional party press, had begun to weaken the grip of party organizations on
candidates, government institutions, and the loyalties of voters.[11]

Not until the 1912 election, however, did the ingredients transforming
American politics from a party-centered decentralized republic to a presidency-
centered mass democracy come into full view.[12] Indeed, many characteristics
of contemporary politics, conventionally understood as new (or of very recent
vintage), were born of the Progressive Party's campaign of 1912. TR's crusade
made universal use of the direct primary the cornerstone of a transformative
campaign. He and his insurgent political allies assaulted traditional partisan

loyalties, took advantage of the centrality of the newly emergent mass media, and convened an energetic but uneasy coalition of self-styled public advocacy groups. All these features of Roosevelt's leadership make the election of 1912 look more like that of 2012 than that of 1908.[13] In addition, the campaign of 1912 anticipated an important shift in the conception of the presidency. Previously, the president ran for office and governed as head of a party. The Progressives saw the party system, grounded in local perspectives, as an obstacle to the expansion of national administrative power essential to economic and social justice. They called for the federal government to assume expansive domestic and international responsibilities that presupposed a strong and independent executive.

Roosevelt's very presence at the Progressive Party convention symbolized a new relationship between leaders and those they led. In the past, party nominees had stayed away from the convention, waiting to be officially notified of their nomination; a presidential candidate was expected to demur as a sign of respect for the party's collective purpose. TR's personal appearance at the Progressive convention gave dramatic testimony to his dominance of the proceedings.[14] More significantly, it gave evidence of an important historical change, namely, of presidential campaigns being conducted less by parties than by individual candidates, who appealed directly for the support of the electorate.

In his New Nationalism speech at Osawatomie, Roosevelt argued that the Progressive movement's purpose was to strive for social and industrial justice: "genuine rule of the people" was the means to that end. Yet once he "threw his hat in the ring" and started setting the terms for a Progressive Party campaign, "pure democracy" began to take on a life of its own.[15] National leadership, as he announced in a speech at New York City's Carnegie Hall, should reside in public servants who "answer[ed] and obey[ed], not the commands of the special interests but those of the whole people."[16]

Determined to become the steward of the people at large, TR traded the responsibilities of party leadership for the vagaries of public opinion. Ostensibly, the "cause" of Progressivism—the allegiance that reformers pledged to direct democracy and social and industrial justice—gave reform leadership its dignity, indeed its heroic quality. But the celebration of public opinion risked leaving leaders at the beck and call of the people. The "right of the people to rule" thus demanded more than writing into laws measures such as the direct primary, recall, and referendum. It required rooting firmly in custom the unwritten law that representatives derived their authority "directly" from the people.

The Progressives' attack on political parties resonated in the United States, where the celebration of the democratic individual had always made political parties suspect, but the new politics celebrated by TR and his Progressive allies made it hard for outsiders to distinguish collective purpose from personal ambition. Interested observers abroad viewed the awakening of a "new style" of politics in the United States with great skepticism. The notion that a leader might embody the aspirations of the people seemed an especially mischievous formula for reform. In Great Britain, the reformist *Manchester Guardian* was more critical of TR's insurgency than was the conservative *Times*. Both newspapers noted with disapproval, however, that Roosevelt's campaign was a "combination of restless, emotional and ephemeral elements." To foreign observers, it seemed, Old Guard Republicans celebrated property, regular Democrats touted local issues, and Progressives built their campaign around their "psychological candidate." In the end, the nomination contest between Taft and Roosevelt was less a principled contest than a quarrel full of "personal invective."[17]

Nonetheless Roosevelt's embrace of Progressive principles joined his burning desire to regain the White House to a collective effort, and that effort ultimately rested on the hope of remaking American democracy. Only by freeing the citizenry from the decentralizing associations and institutions that dominated the nineteenth-century polity could individual men and women participate in a national movement of public opinion. Some Progressives, such as Woodrow Wilson and Louis Brandeis, expressed a belief in the possibility of a reformed party politics, one that would abet the creation of a national community. But most reformers viewed parties as "the worst obstacle to the advance of practical democratic participation."[18] Reformers indulged in the hope that once emancipated from the provincialism of partisanship, the people would display their potential for broad-mindedness. "Truly the voice of the people is the voice of God," wrote a Progressive journalist, echoing Andrew Jackson; but, he continued, the celebration of Progressive measures like the direct primary summons "the voice of the *whole* people."[19]

The tension between candidate-centered politics and party politics became palpable during the Republican Party primary campaign. These primary contests were a landmark in the development of presidential elections. Political reforms had established the popular selection of candidates as a fixture of local, state, and congressional elections during the first decade of the twentieth century; however, the 1912 campaign was the first time that direct primaries played a significant role in a presidential election. Before TR's campaign, the direct primary was used to select delegates in only six states: North Dakota, California, New Jersey, Wisconsin, Minnesota, and Nebraska. All of these states, except New Jersey, which enacted a direct primary law as part of Governor Woodrow Wilson's reform program, were in the Midwest and West, where Progressive reforms had to this point made the greatest impact. As a consequence of Roosevelt making the direct primary a cause célèbre, many northern state legislatures fought fiercely over electoral reform. In the end, Massachusetts, Pennsylvania, Illinois, Maryland, Ohio, and South Dakota adopted the device. "With the six states in which the system was already in operation," George Mowry wrote, "this made a sizable block of normal Republican states from which a popular referendum could be obtained."[20]

The Republican primaries resulted in a spirited debate on the merits of Progressive democracy and the fundamental challenge it posed not only to the existing political order but also to foundational principles and institutions as well. The Progressive Party was born of this debate. It was a party with a constitutional understanding of its own, one that challenged the traditional two-party system and substituted popular presidential leadership for party-based democracy.

Progressive Democracy, the Two-Party System, and the Constitution

The Progressive Party's opposition to partisanship was joined to a larger critique of representative government in which parties marked a threat to "constitutionalism." Defenders of parties, viewing them as a bulwark of the federal democracy, saw the threat the other way around. The ensuing battle over the appropriate relationship between parties—indeed, all intermediary organizations—and the Constitution became the fault line of the 1912 campaign. Sensing that "pure democracy" was the glue that held together the movement he sought to lead, Roosevelt made the cause of popular rule the centerpiece of his insurgent presidential campaign. This program was highly controversial, especially its plank calling for popular referenda on court decisions. But TR's campaign was even more controversial than the Progressive platform; it championed an unvarnished majoritarianism. Toward the end of September, he announced in a speech in Phoenix, Arizona, that "he would go even further than the Progressive party platform [in promoting the recall of public officials]; he would apply the recall to everybody, including the President." Roosevelt "stands upon the bald doctrine of unrestricted majority rule," the *Nation* warned.[21] Even the Great Commoner blushed; plebiscitary measures such as the recall and referendum, William Jennings Bryan insisted, should be confined to the states.[22]

The burden of defending representative government and constitutional sobriety fell most heavily on Taft; indeed, there is a real sense in which the most important exchange in the constitutional debate of 1912 was the one between TR and Taft, a struggle that flared in the battle for the Republican nomination. Taft did not take easily to this contest. In 1908, he had been Roosevelt's heir apparent; and as president, he supported and extended the pragmatic Progressive program that was Roosevelt's presidential legacy, working for moderate industrial reforms with the cooperation of Republican Party regulars. And yet Taft now found his own efforts to carry on that pragmatic tradition of reform the object of scorn, the rhetorical counterpoise to TR's "pure democracy." "The initiative, the referendum, and the recall, together with a complete adoption of the direct primary as a means of selecting nominees and an entire destruction of the convention system are now all made the *sine qua non* of a real reformer," Taft lamented. "Everyone who hesitates to follow all of these or any of them is regarded with suspicion and is denounced as an enemy of popular government and of the people."[23] Taft's profound misgivings about this vision propelled him into battle. With Roosevelt's early success in the primary campaigns, Taft believed that he had no recourse but to wage an open fight against him, a reluctant decision encouraged by the importunities of Republican newspapers and party leaders that he had to stand like Horatius at the bridge in the face of TR's popular insurgency. It was his "duty," the GOP newspaper *New York World* lectured in a typical editorial. "The primary contest was not a personal one" between former allies now recast as foes, as the incumbent president at first appeared to believe. Rather, according to the *World,* Roosevelt fought for a "new system of government": "This [was] no ordinary political rivalry for the presidency, but a rivalry that [involved] the conflict of fundamental principles."[24]

Taft's reluctant but ultimately resolute decision to enter the primary contests confirmed the significance of Roosevelt's challenge to received partisan wisdom. In part, the incumbent president's active participation accentuated the candidate-centered nature of the contest, heightening the personal acrimony that the primary fights engendered. At the same time, by breaking precedent—no president had ever actively campaigned for renomination—and going on the stump, Taft testified to the constitutional significance of the presidential campaign. Even as TR's defense of direct democracy found great favor throughout the country, Taft resisted the attempt "to tear down all the checks and balances of a well adjusted, democratic, constitutional, representative government."[25]

Against TR's Progressive assault on partisanship, Taft considered political parties a vital part of a "well adjusted" form of American democracy—"the sheet anchor of popular government." Competition between two parties refined checks and balances in American constitutional government, transforming narrow factionalism into contests of principle.[26] The integrity of party organizations, Taft insisted, warranted his nomination, regardless of the results of the historic primary contests. Taft admitted that many local party leaders were corrupt; indeed, he had no objection to establishing direct primaries in local elections "with certain limitations," calling it "a practical step to oust the boss and destroy the machine built on patronage and corruption." But he defended the state party—the "unit of the national party"—as part and parcel of the collective responsibility that buttressed constitutional government. Taft insisted that the great majority of party leaders at the state and national level were "honest and anxious for the party to succeed by serving the people well in the government with which the party may be entrusted." The convocation of such leaders in state caucuses and the national convention added a critical measure of deliberation to the selection of candidates for office and the statement of party policies. "Conference and discussion lead to wise results," Taft averred, "and conference and discussion and deliberation with reference to party politics was not possible at the polls." Such responsible deliberation would be especially impracticable at the national level "when the electors numbered into the millions."[27]

Even as he defended the two-party system, Taft argued that the Progressive Party's attack on the very idea of representation called for a new understanding of Republican conservatism: he sought to hitch, or elevate, the Republican Party's commitment to industrial capitalism, the cause of William McKinley and Mark Hanna, to a Whiggish defense of constitutional forms, of ordered liberty. The most sacred duty of true conservatives, who would protect constitutional government, was to uphold the courts. This preservation of the Constitution, and not the promotion of unfettered business interests, should be the principal cause of the Republican Party, according to Taft. "It was unthinkable," he told an audience in Boston during the Massachusetts primary, "that Roosevelt should seriously propose to have a plebiscite on questions involving the construction of the Constitution."[28]

To his great disappointment, Taft's defense of constitutional sobriety fell on deaf ears. "I felt," Taft wrote a friend after the election, "like a man crying in the wilderness."[29] Despite Taft's charge that the Progressives threatened to trash the Constitution, despite the hope of TR's political enemies that such a bold campaign would kill him politically, it was not Roosevelt but Taft who suffered a humiliating defeat. TR thrashed him in the primary campaign; of the twelve contests, Roosevelt won nine, including the celebrated and carefully watched battle in Taft's home state of Ohio. In the general election, Taft won only two states—Utah and Vermont—and 23.2 percent of the popular vote. In contrast, although his most radical proposals would never be implemented, TR's strong second-place showing, and his dominant presence in that campaign, signaled the birth of a modern mass democracy in the United States, one that placed the president, whose authority rested on national public opinion—rather than Congress, the states, or political parties—at the center of American democracy. Communicating directly to voters through a newly emergent mass media—the independent newspapers, popular magazines, audio recordings, and movies that Progressives used so skillfully—the Bull Moose campaign resonated especially well in the fastest-growing areas of the country, which best represented America's future.[30]

Reformers argued with considerable political effect that the Progressive idea of democracy was not a radical rejection of the American constitutional tradition but an attempt to restore it. State and local party machines, they argued, had perverted the original design of the Constitution, which was dedicated to emancipating the American people from the kind of provincial and special interests embodied in the Articles of Confederation. Whereas the Articles read, "We the undersigned delegates of the States," the Preamble of the Constitution was declared by "We the People." The change to "We the People," claimed Theodore Gillman at a Progressive rally in Yonkers, New York—in a speech that the third party widely distributed as a campaign pamphlet—"was made at the Federal Convention with the full understanding of the meaning and effect of the new form of words," signifying that the new Constitution represented the aspirations of one sovereign people to create a "more perfect union." Political parties had preempted this original design, shifting power to states and localities in the service of "local self-government." Progressives acknowledged that the creation of a localized party system was necessary to thwart the "aristocratic" pretensions of the Federalists, but the problems thrown up by the Industrial Revolution demanded that reformers revisit the potential for national democracy in the original Constitution. Just as the original theory of the electoral college had been abandoned after the "Revolution of 1800," closing the gap between presidential politics and popular choice, so

Gilman argued that another such change was at hand: "The people now propose to come into closer touch with their representatives by the abolition of the machine, and the substitution thereafter of the direct primary, the initiative, referendum, and recall. This is all one logical and irresistible movement in one direction, having as its object the restoration of our form of government to its original purity and ideal perfection, as a government under the control of 'We, the people,' who formed it."[31]

As a party to end parties, the Progressives did not envisage becoming the sort of social democratic organization that was then emerging in Germany, France, and Great Britain. Taft argued that the Progressive Party's challenge to constitutional principles cried out for a principled conservative party; some of Roosevelt's allies who hoped that TR's campaign might flower into a European-type social democratic party argued that the Progressives' political program would deflect attention from party building on the left. "I am weary to death of the Rule of the People and a millennium created by constant elections and never-ending suspicion of authority," the distinguished jurist Learned Hand wrote in the wake of the storm created by TR's democratic platform. "When will the day come that some courageous men will stand sponsors for a real programme of 'social justice' in the words of our leader?" Gazing enviously across the Atlantic at the progress of social democrats in England, Hand asked Felix Frankfurter plaintively, "Can you see a single man who would really dare to commit himself to any plan like the Fabians? Why have we nowhere any Fabians? Why aren't all of us Fabians?"[32]

And yet the Progressive Party's celebration of public opinion short-circuited the development of a social democratic party in America. As Herbert Croly explained in *Progressive Democracy,* a paean to Roosevelt's insurgency, many well-meaning social democrats in Germany, England, or France, as well as in the United States, favored the formation of a national programmatic party as a vanguard of social and economic reform. Such devotees of a permanent social democratic party disdained direct popular government, Croly pointed out, because they expected that at least in the near future, direct popular government, dependent on the vagaries of public opinion, would increase the difficulty of securing the adoption of many items in a desirable social program. Herein they were right, Croly acknowledged. But reformers of this sort attached too much importance to the accomplishment and maintenance of specific results and not enough to the permanent social welfare of democracy: "An authoritative representative government, particularly one which is associated with inherited leadership and a strong party system, carries with it enormous prestige.

It is frequently in a position either to ignore, to circumvent or to wear down popular opposition. But a social program purchased at such a price is not worth what it costs."[33]

The popularity of the direct primary in the United States, Croly noted, revealed how centralized and disciplined parties went against the looser genius of American politics. To the extent that government became committed to a democratic program that was essentially social in character, the American people would find intolerable a two-party system standing between popular will and governmental machinery. As Jane Addams noted at a Progressive gathering to honor Lincoln, a fundamental principle of the Progressive Party was that a welfare state could not be created in the United States "'unless the power of direct legislation is placed in the hands of the people,' in order that these changes may come not as the centralized government [has] given them, from above down, but may come from the people up; that the people should be the directing and controlling force of legislation."[34]

The Progressive Party's Legacy: Partisanship Without Parties

The Progressive Party's lasting importance does not derive from its brief existence as a political organization, but from its efforts to translate a movement of public opinion into a practical political agenda. It sought to discredit institutions that thwarted direct democracy, to establish the presidency as the center of a new form of popular politics, and, against the hard challenges posed by Taft, to reconcile these innovations with constitutional principles. Inspired by Roosevelt's dynamic leadership, Progressives were the driving force of the 1912 campaign, and while they failed in the end to dislodge party politics, they championed ideas that Republicans and Democrats had to respond to in some way. The third party framed the discourse and marked the terrain of a new political order. It therefore affected the future of both parties and the fortunes of political leaders to come. Since the 1912 election, the Progressive Party's vision of reform leadership has been an enduring feature of the American political landscape.

Woodrow Wilson won the election by championing a more practical version of Progressive reform—the "New Freedom," which was far more sympathetic than TR's New Nationalism to parties and courts. But his reform message moved in Roosevelt's direction over the course of the campaign. The Democratic candidate stopped short of calling for referenda on court decisions and the recall of all public officials, but he championed mass opinion almost as fervently as did Roosevelt. "I would rather be the voice of a nation than the voice of a class," he announced in one of his final campaign speeches. "I would rather interpret the common feeling; I would rather know the common impulse of America than to originate. I would rather be the spokesman of the men who have confidence in me in any crisis, than to pride myself in the belief that I alone could devise a plan to redeem and restore the strength of the human race." Like Roosevelt, Wilson styled himself as an interpreter of public opinion who could transcend particular interests and parties. "America was coming out of the leading strings of parties and was beginning to transact the great business of humanity. Men and measures are the only things worthy of the thought of a great people who are not going to school to politicians, but going to school to their own consciences, following their own visions, realizing their own dreams of what American manhood means and must achieve."[35]

Once in office, Wilson continued moving in his competitor's direction. Indeed, in the wake of the excitement the Progressive Party aroused, Wilson felt compelled, or saw the opportunity, to advance some important features of the New Nationalism. Most famously, he revived the practice, abandoned by Thomas Jefferson, of appearing before Congress to deliver important messages, including the State of the Union address.[36] Wilson's innovation subtly differentiated him from TR and the Progressive insurgents. Rather than arouse public opinion directly, the new president seemed intent on strengthening, rather than denigrating, partisanship, by remodeling the presidency somewhat after the pattern of a prime minister. Still, Wilson appreciated the position of New Nationalists, put most forcefully by Croly, that the executive depended on public opinion "for his weapons."[37] With the rise of the mass media, Wilson believed, such occasions as the State of the Union address would help concentrate public attention on the actions of the president and Congress.[38] Overcoming the resistance of Democrats who still revered Jefferson as the patron saint of their party, Wilson addressed Congress frequently, beginning with an important address on tariff reform, a central issue of his presidential campaign. Well received by most members of Congress and the press, the president's precedent-shattering speech, delivered on April 8, 1913, launched the first successful campaign for serious tariff reform since before the Civil War.

Wilson recalibrated the Progressive Party's vision of democracy by joining direct appeals to the public to a new form of partisanship in which the president, rather than Congress, would "stand at the intersection of party organization and national popular opinion"—where he might "harness each to great national effect."[39] He then joined this partisan version of Roosevelt's concept of the executive as steward of the people to support for bolstering national administrative power, a prospect he had proscribed as paternalistic during the 1912 election.[40] Poaching from the Progressives' platform, he reversed the emblematic stand of his own party on business regulation and pressed for the creation of the Federal Trade Commission, which would have broad discretion in moving against unfair practices. Similarly, Wilson persuaded the Democratic Congress to accept the Federal Reserve Act, which established a board to oversee the national banking and currency system. In each case, Wilson overcame the Democratic Party's traditional antipathy to national administrative power, suggesting that with the advance of Progressive democracy, party leaders in Congress were induced to sacrifice programmatic principles to win the White House.[41] As Croly wrote appreciatively of Wilson's Progressive leadership, "At the final test, the responsibility is his rather than that of his party. The party which submits to such a dictatorship, however benevolent, cannot play its own proper part in a system of partisan government."[42]

In the end, it seemed, the Progressive Party had bequeathed a state of partisanship without parties, replacing the collective partisanship of the nineteenth century with a new executive-centered partisanship that subordinated collective responsibility to the political and programmatic ambitions of presidents. Of course, as the "return to normalcy" of the 1920s—heralded by Warren Harding's landslide election—showed, Wilson's "benign despotism" did not signal the final triumph of Progressive democracy. And yet the changes wrought by the Progressive Party's campaign ensured that localized parties were no longer the principal agents of democracy and that the alliance between decentralization and democracy was gradually weakened in favor of a relationship between the individual and the "state."

With the celebration of public opinion spawned by the Progressive Party's campaign of 1912, even conservatives like Coolidge felt compelled to go directly to the public to ensure support for themselves and their programs. Coolidge, in fact, bestowed bipartisan legitimacy on the executive-centered party, which had begun to take form during Wilson's Democratic administration. He was the first president to make use of a new medium, radio, deploying the device strategically to enhance his image and programmatically to enlist popular support to compel congressional backing of his tax reform plan. "It is because in their hours of timidity the Congress becomes subservient to the importunities of organized minorities that the President comes more and more to stand as the champion of the rights of the whole country," Coolidge wrote in his autobiography.[43] Although Coolidge showed more respect than Progressives had for the critical role of parties in American democracy, his overwhelming first-ballot nomination in 1924 and the landslide he won over his Democratic opponent, James W. Davis, marked an important advance, as Coolidge himself observed, in the emergence of the president as "the sole repository of party responsibility."[44] Taft had deplored the Progressive celebration of "pure democracy" in the 1912 presidential campaign; the future chief justice of the Supreme Court considered judges the Constitution's final authority—and went down to political defeat. In contrast, Coolidge's political effectiveness followed in no small measure from his embrace of public opinion: individual men and women, not judges, he argued, were "the court of last resort and their decisions are final."[45]

It fell to Franklin Roosevelt, whose "purge" campaign and court-packing plan were inspired by TR's 1912 campaign, to make presidency-centered partisanship an enduring feature of the living Constitution. The system of party responsibility, FDR argued, "required that one of its parties be the liberal party and the other be the conservative party."[46] Ultimately, however, Roosevelt and his New Deal allies, many of whom were former Bull Moosers, took action and pursued procedural reforms that would establish candidate-centered elections and executive-centered party organizations. Like the Progressive Party, the New Deal Democratic Party was formed to advance the personal and nonpartisan responsibility of the executive at the expense of collective and partisan responsibility. The New Deal, like its successor in the 1960s, the Great Society, which extended the new liberalism to the cause of civil rights, was less a partisan program than an exercise in extending the president's responsibility to fulfill popular aspirations for social and economic welfare. In calling themselves liberals rather than progressives, these reformers meant to signify that their devotion to individual rights was greater than that of their Progressive forebears. Nevertheless, New Deal and Great Society liberals beheld a transformed liberal tradition. Their efforts redefined in important respects the social contract, leading to rights becoming associated with programmatic endeavors such as social security, consumer and environmental protection, affirmative action, and education. Understood in the context of the Progressive tradition, the New Deal is appropriately viewed as the completion of a political program dedicated to the proposition, to quote the important Brownlow Committee report, that "our national will must be expressed not merely in a brief exultant moment of electoral decision, but in persistent, determined, competent day-by-day administration of what the nation has decided to do."[47]

Just as FDR gave constitutional form to the New Nationalism, so Richard Nixon and Ronald Reagan gave form to what might be called "progressive conservatism." Both sought to remake the Supreme Court in line with popular demands, and both used their positions to speak directly to the people, frequently promoting their programmatic aims over the heads of their party and Congress.[48] Reagan, in particular, who led the "silent majority" more purposefully than had Nixon, saw merit in deploying progressive means for conservative ends. Many present-day champions of the Reagan revolution proclaim, as the Progressives did, that they are fighting for rule by the people and against entrenched elites, who scorn ordinary men and women. Indeed, the contemporary conservative movement has relied heavily on institutions advanced by Progressives; for example, ballot initiatives first became a favorite tactic of conservative activists in California to challenge its progressive establishment. Beginning with Proposition 13, an anti-property-tax measure passed in 1978, conservative activists enacted a number of initiatives constraining government revenues, reducing welfare benefits for illegal aliens, and prohibiting public universities and state agencies from using affirmative action programs in admissions and hiring practices. The popular enthusiasm generated by these measures soon spread beyond California, helping propel Reagan to the White House in 1980 and pushing taxes to the forefront of the national political agenda.

Conservatives' embrace of Progressive-era ideals and institutions is not merely instrumental. Many applaud TR's call for greatness and his vigorous use of executive power, especially in foreign affairs. Moreover, a large number of contemporary conservatives have concluded that the government—even the federal government—has the responsibility to shape proper habits and behavior. Such a view permeates proposals to restrict abortion and same-sex marriage, require work for welfare, and impose performance standards on secondary and elementary schools.[49] Most significantly, conservatives have embraced Progressive aspirations for a modern executive who draws authority directly from public opinion. With the rise of Reagan and the "new" right, conservatives have invested their hope in the idea that the modern presidency, joined to social movements and public opinion, can be cast as a double-edged sword that can cut in a conservative as well as a liberal direction. For all the important differences between contemporary Republicans and Democrats— conservatives and liberals—both are committed to presidential leadership in the Progressive mold: both defend policies that presuppose the deployment of national administrative power, and both claim to use that power in the name of the whole people. Together they divide the nation.

Conclusion: Osawatomie Then and Now

In his Osawatomie speech, Barack Obama sought to rise above the presidential partisanship that had sharply divided American politics and government since the Reagan revolution. Standing where TR had stood, he found himself in circumstances that TR thought the Progressive Party was superseding. Obama wanted to restore the transcendent leadership that seemed, as the centennial of TR's formative insurgency approached, greatly diminished by the executive-centered partisanship that had remade and intractably divided the nation.

These audacious hopes are still elusive. President Obama's efforts to extend and elaborate the progressive tradition in the wake of the Reagan insurgency, now newly invigorated by the Tea Party, have neither transcended parties nor forged more secure footings for reform; they have, on the contrary, fueled the most polarized debate over progressive ambitions since 1912. That the intensification of the battle between contemporary progressives and conservatives has centered on a program that both camps call "Obamacare" makes clear just how executive-centered the partisan conflict has become. The personal nature of the struggle helps explain why the attacks from the left have hardly been less condemnatory than those from the right. Obama's dogged leadership in the fight over national health reform failed to win a single Republican vote in Congress; at the same time, the compromises he was willing to accept—especially his willingness to jettison the most ambitious feature of his plan, the "public option"—incited some of his most ardent supporters to dismiss him as a trimmer. Bereft of this linchpin, Obamacare became a jerry-rigged "marketplace," which, once "rolled out," caused all sorts of problems for the White House.

Obama's most sympathetic critics, such as Andy Stern, the former president of the Service Employees International Union, fault him for "trying to reason with unreasonable people."[50] I would suggest a deeper malady—that the president's travails stem in no small measure from his attempt to resuscitate a flawed ideal. The voice of "reason" in this case was OFA, the president's personal organization. With it, the leader sought to anchor programmatic reforms in the bedrock of popular will. That futile effort confirms once again that an individualized appeal to the whole people cannot transcend fundamental political differences, certainly not with great programmatic ambitions hanging in the balance. The Progressives' old conundrum—how to reconcile the ideals of transcendent leadership with the fundamental conflicts aroused by the promise of progressive democracy—is all the more complex now that conservatives have embraced progressive methods. Once conservatives abandoned the constitutional scruples that animated Taft's debate with TR, the country became embroiled in a battle for the services of the national state, a battle that has rendered progressive stewardship a seemingly impracticable proposition.

Faced with fierce opposition to his right and disappointed expectations to his left, Obama resorted to deploying the original Progressive antiparty trope as a partisan tactic. In the wake of the Obamacare debacle, the White House and OFA urged Democrats to distinguish themselves from Republicans in the 2014 elections by proclaiming their determination to repair rather than repeal the president's signature program. But with the "steward of the public welfare" embroiled in a pitched battle over fundamental principles, this technocratic, commonsense approach to programmatic improvement came across as insipid. TR summed up the stakes of his time in apocalyptic terms: "We stand at Armageddon," he told his followers who bolted from the 1912 Republican convention, "and we battle for the Lord." Today, in a political climate infected with massive distrust of government, it is conservatives, not progressives, who stand at Armageddon, and the progressive president, called upon to defend a century of programmatic reform, appears to have little more to offer than a pragmatist's faith in problem solving.

The "fundamental rule of our national life," Obama proclaimed at Osawatomie, is that "on the whole, and in the long run, we shall go up or down together." Not surprisingly, many Democrats have been reluctant to embrace the president's appeal to a shared fate. But in an age of executive-centered partisanship, they were hard-pressed to refute the president's refrain during the 2014 campaign: even though he was not on the ballot, the campaign, in effect, was a referendum on his policies. Indeed, his fellow partisans were quick to blame Obama for their poor showing in the midterm election, which increased the Republicans' majority in the House and gave them control of the Senate.[51]

Nor did the endorsement of market exchanges work to assuage discontent on the right. For conservatives increasingly hostile to the progressive vision of social and industrial justice, the suggestion that Obamacare is a pragmatic response to a problem that transcends partisanship merely rubs salt in the wound. What Obama demonstrated at Osawatomie was not the vitality of progressive ideals in the face of rising partisan rancor; it was that Progressivism's vision of the president as a unifying national figure spearheading programmatic action in the public interest is illusory. The reality is presidential partisanship, a divisive force that sharpens political conflict and rattles national resolve.

Notes

The author is deeply grateful to Stephen Skowronek and Stephen Engel for their insightful and extensive comments on an earlier version of this chapter.

1. Roosevelt added these words to the platform to clarify the party's commitment to social and industrial justice (draft platform with handwritten changes by TR, in the Progressive Party Archives, Theodore Roosevelt Collection, Houghton Library, Harvard University).

2. "The New Nationalism," in Theodore Roosevelt, *The Works of Theodore Roosevelt*, 26 vols. (New York: Charles Scribner's, 1926), 17:10–20.

3. "Remarks by the President on the Economy in Osawatomie, Kansas, December 6, 2011," www.whitehouse.gov.

4. "I think," the Progressive jurist Leonard Hand wrote Roosevelt, in praising Herbert Croly's influential book *The Promise of American Life*, "that [he] has succeeded in stating more adequately than anyone else,—certainly of those writers whom I know,—the bases and prospective growth of the set of political ideas which can be fairly described as Neo-Hamiltonian, and whose promise is due more to you, as I believe, than anyone else" (Hand to Roosevelt, April 8, 1910, Learned Hand Papers, Harvard University Law School, Cambridge, Massachusetts).

5. For a detailed discussion of OFA's campaign activity and policy advocacy, see Sidney M. Milkis, Jesse H. Rhodes, and Emily J. Charnock, "What Happened to Post-Partisanship? Barack Obama and the New American Party System," *Perspectives on Politics* 10, no. 1: 57–76; and Sidney M. Milkis and John W. York, "Managing Alone: Barack Obama, Organizing for Action, and Policy Advocacy in the Digital Era," paper presented at the 2014 American Political Science Association Meeting, August 28–31, 2014, Washington, D.C.

6. Roosevelt, *Works*, 17:335.

7. Barry Karl, *The Uneasy State: The United States from 1915 to 1945* (Chicago: University of Chicago Press, 1983), 234–35.

8. Eldon Eisenach, review of Sidney M. Milkis, *Theodore Roosevelt, the Progressive Party, and the Transformation of American Democracy* (Lawrence: University Press of Kansas, 2009), *Perspectives on Politics* 8, no. 1 (March 2010): 368–69.

9. Jane Addams, "The New Party," *American Magazine*, November 1912, 14.

10. In addition to the foothold it established for merit hiring and the bar it erected against on-the-job solicitations of campaign funds from federal employees, the Pendleton Act established a bipartisan three-member Civil Service Commission, to be appointed by the president and confirmed by the Senate.

11. For example, see John F. Reynolds, *The Demise of the American Convention System* (New York: Cambridge University Press, 2006).

12. Stephen Skowronek has described the decentralized polity as a "state of courts and parties"; but it might better be described as a state of parties and courts, for party politicians, empowered by a "highly mobilized, highly competitive, and locally oriented democracy," had the commanding voice in late-nineteenth-century American politics and government. The federal judiciary molded the political character of the nineteenth-century state into a formal legal tradition. See Stephen Skowronek, *Building a New American State: The Expansion of National Administrative Capacities, 1877–1920* (New York: Cambridge University Press, 1982), 41; see also Morton Keller, *America's Three Regimes: A New Political History* (New York: Oxford University Press, 2007), chap. 8.

13. In coming to this conclusion, I am elaborating on an observation that Arthur Link and Richard McCormick made in 1983: "The use of the direct primaries, the challenge to traditional party loyalties, the candidates' issue orientation, and the prevalence of interest-group political activities all make the election of 1912 look more like 1980 than that of 1896" (Link and McCormick, *Progressivism* [Wheeling, Ill.: Harland Davidson, 1983], 43).

14. In accepting the Progressive Party's nomination in person, Roosevelt followed the example of previous third-party candidates, such as James B. Weaver of the Populist Party in 1892 and Eugene Debs of the Socialist Party in 1904, who scorned the two-party system. But TR's popularity and the significant support of his newly formed party highlighted his acceptance of the nomination at the Progressive Party convention as a pathbreaking event. "Marking a new departure in the proceedings of national conventions," reported the *San Francisco Examiner*, "the two candidates were notified of their nominations, and in the midst of deafening cheers they appeared before the delegates to voice their acceptance and to pledge their best efforts in the coming campaign" (August 8, 1912). See also John Allen Gable, *The Bull Moose Years: Theodore Roosevelt and the Progressive Party* (Port Washington, N.Y.: Kennikat, 1978), 108.

15. Roosevelt first announced his commitment to a program of "pure democracy"— and officially launched his 1912 campaign—at the Ohio Constitutional Convention, in Columbus, where he delivered an address titled "A Charter for Democracy" (February 21, 1912, Roosevelt Collection).

16. Roosevelt, *Works*, 17:152, 170.

17. "Mr. Taft and Mr. Roosevelt," *Manchester Guardian*, May 16, 1912; "After the Conventions: Mr. Roosevelt and the Old Parties," July 4, 1912, "The Struggle for the Presidency," November 4, 1912, and "The Progressives in the United States," November 22, 1912, *Times* (London).

18. Edward J. Ward, *The Social Center* (New York: Allenton, 1913), 87.

19. William Hemstreet, "Theory and Practice of the New Primary Law," *Arena* 28 (December 1902): 592 (emphasis in the original).

20. George Mowry, *Theodore Roosevelt and the Progressive Movement* (Madison: University of Wisconsin Press, 1946), 228.

21. "Roosevelt Favors Recall of President," *New York Times*, September 30, 1912; "Let the People Rule," *Nation*, September 26, 1912.

22. "Roosevelt Favors Recall of the President."

23. William Howard Taft, "The Sign of the Times," address given before the Electrical Manufacturers Club, Hot Springs, Virginia, November 6, 1913, Taft Papers, Manuscript Division, Library of Congress, Washington, D.C.

24. Editorial, "Taft's Duty," *New York World*, April 23, 1912.

25. Taft, statement dictated to Harry Dunlop for publication in the *New York World*, November 14, 1912, Taft Papers.

26. Ibid.

27. William Howard Taft, *Popular Government* (New Haven, Conn.: Yale University Press, 1913), 117–21.

28. Taft, address at the banquet of the Republican Club, Boston, February 12, 1912, Taft Papers.

29. Taft to Thomas W. Loyless, June 5, 1913, Taft Papers.

30. For a detailed discussion of the Progressive Party vote, see Milkis, *Roosevelt, the Progressive Party, and the Transformation of American Democracy*, 252–60; and Gable, *Bull Moose Years*, 131–56.

31. Theodore Gilman, "The Progressive Party Comes Not to Destroy, But to Fulfill the Constitution," address delivered at a public rally in Yonkers, New York, September 27, 1912, Progressive Party Publications, 1912–16.

32. Learned Hand to Felix Frankfurter, April 4, 1912, Learned Hand Papers. Hand's yearning was not fanciful. Under Eugene Debs's leadership, the Socialist Party reached its peak of popularity, so much so that by 1912, when Debs received 6 percent of the popular vote, a growing number of reformers had come to view it as a reasonable alternative to the two major parties. On how Roosevelt and the Progressives stole much of the Socialist Party's thunder, see Milkis, *Roosevelt, the Progressive Party, and the Transformation of American Democracy*, chaps. 5 and 6.

33. Herbert Croly, *Progressive Democracy* (New York: Macmillan, 1914), 281–82.

34. Addams, "Social Justice Through National Action," in Progressive National Committee, *Nationalism: Its Need in Our Social, Industrial and Political Growth* (New York: Progressive National Committee, 1914), 7.

35. Woodrow Wilson, "A Campaign Address in Burlington, New Jersey," in *The Papers of Woodrow Wilson*, ed. Arthur Link (Princeton, N.J.: Princeton University Press, 1974), 25:490–91, 492.

36. Jeffrey Tulis, *The Rhetorical Presidency* (Princeton, N.J.: Princeton University Press, 1987); James Ceaser, *Presidential Selection: Theory and Development* (Princeton, N.J.: Princeton University Press, 1979), esp. chap. 4.

37. Croly, *Progressive Democracy*, 348.

38. Elmer Cornwell, *Presidential Leadership of Public Opinion* (Bloomington: Indiana University Press, 1965), 46. For a careful analysis of Wilson's effective, albeit short-lived, joining of party leadership and Progressive hostility to party, see Peri Arnold, *Remaking the Presidency: Roosevelt, Taft, and Wilson, 1901–1916* (Lawrence: University Press of Kansas, 2009), chaps. 6 and 7.

39. Scott James, "The Evolution of the Presidency: Between the Promise and the Fear," in *The Executive Branch*, ed. Joel Auberbach and Mark Peterson (New York: Oxford University Press, 2005), 19.

40. John Milton Cooper, *The Warrior and the Priest: Woodrow Wilson and Theodore Roosevelt* (Cambridge, Mass.: Harvard University Press, 1983), 195.

41. Scott James, *Presidents, Parties, and the State: A Party System Perspective on Democratic Regulatory Choice, 1884–1936* (New York: Cambridge University Press, 2000).

42. Croly, *Progressive Democracy*, 346.

43. Calvin Coolidge, *The Autobiography of Calvin Coolidge* (Honolulu: University Press of the Pacific, 2004; reprinted from the 1929 ed.), 229.

44. Ibid., 231.

45. Ibid., 228.

46. Franklin D. Roosevelt, *Public Papers and Addresses*, ed. Samuel I. Rosenman (New York: Random House, 1938–50), 7: xxviii–xxxii.

47. *Report of the President's Committee on Administrative Management* (Washington, D.C.: Government Printing Office, 1937), 53. The President's Committee on Administrative Management, headed by Louis Brownlow, played a central role in the planning and policies of New Deal institutions. Charles Merriam, an influential adviser to TR in 1912, was an important member of this committee. On the link between Progressivism and the New Deal, see Sidney M. Milkis, *The President and the Parties: The Transformation of the American Party System Since the New Deal* (New York: Oxford University Press, 1993).

48. I am grateful to Taeku Lee for suggesting how contemporary partisanship operates independently of party organizations and loyalties; see Lee, "America the Blue? Thoughts on Racial Divides, Immigration Reform and Electoral Alignments," presentation at the John Galbraith Conference on Immigration, October 11, 2013, Washington, D.C.

49. Paul Starobin, "The Daddy State," *National Journal*, March 28, 1998.

50. Stern, quoted in Jeff Zelony, "Punching Bag or President?," *International Herald Tribune*, September 8, 2011.

51. Phillip Rucker and Robert Costa, "Battle for the Senate: How the GOP Did It," *Washington Post*, November 5, 2014.

9 • The Democratic Fit
Party Reform and the Eugenics Tool
Nicole Mellow

Everywhere they looked, Progressives in the early twentieth century saw things askew.[1] The organization of nineteenth-century political parties no longer fit the twentieth-century nation. The existing parties mobilized citizens into empty campaigns that provided little sense of the great stakes at issue for the country. Like the Constitution, parties failed to address the problems of governing in a modern, urban, industrial age. Progressives' criticisms were harsh, but they did not give up in despair. Instead, they set out to realign relations between state and society in accord with their own sense of order.

If popular energies were to be channeled toward effective national action, America's parties would have to be reformed. The organs of nineteenth-century democracy had coordinated widely dispersed power to some degree, giving form and coherence to national life. In a country of great size and diversity, they served as "kindly oil upon the disordered waters of the sea."[2] Yet the traditional party system, with its patronage, corruption, and local orientation, was not up to the task of advancing the sort of muscular, programmatic national action that Progressives believed the country needed. Reforming the parties so that they more effectively united citizens around a democratically chosen national agenda became a Progressive imperative. Dislodging the existing machinery of party power, concentrated as it was in the hands of local party bosses, was one part of the project. But merely altering the institutional form of the parties or the processes of election would not be sufficient for the transformation that Progressives envisioned. If they did not cultivate the proper political ground for these new institutions, their hopes for party government would never materialize. Part and parcel of the project was to reconstruct the body politic, to break its fealty to the old party system and infuse it with the capacity for meaningful participation in the reorganized parties. Many Progressives advocated eugenics-based policies with these tasks in mind.

Faith in social scientific principles led Progressives to propose initiatives that they imagined would, on one hand, provide government with the expert administrative capacities to solve national problems and, on the other hand, equip voters to make rational decisions about the course of state action. Progressive reforms—civil service reform, the creation of independent commissions, direct primaries, the secret ballot—sought to marry more enlightened state action to a more meaningful sovereignty of the people. Parties were the connective tissue, instruments for linking a state infused with expertise with a democratically empowered national community. But if national political leaders were to transmit great principles to voters capable of acting on them, the existing mosaic of local party organizations would have to be replaced by nationally coherent bodies under the direction of true statesmen. Woodrow Wilson's dictum—"No leaders, no principles; no principles, no parties"— encapsulates both his dismissal of the boss-dominated party system that then existed as well as his vision for a reformed party structure.[3] While repudiating existing parties, Theodore Roosevelt's 1912 Progressive Party was constructed with a similar logic. Under the guidance of a "popular statesman," a successful party would articulate national needs and proffer a program of action to authorizing voters. Members of the same party elected across institutions would then work together to govern accordingly.[4]

The mismatch perceived between what existed and what was needed was profound, and the remedy was correspondingly sweeping. Machines with local power bases and extensive networks of patronage reinforced myopia in state-society relations. Voters' party identities, far from being expressions of thoughtful deliberation about the common good, were deeply entrenched through a highly participatory culture of political theater, evident in local clubs and marching companies, campaign spectacle, and partisan presses.[5] Voters' mental, moral, and physical capacities for citizenship also concerned Progressives, especially since the extension of the franchise and successive waves of immigration were making the electorate increasingly heterogeneous. In the existing political system, Progressives had neither the instruments of party nor the necessary public constituency that they desired for their ideas.

Reformers set out to groom a new public, one that was freed from old allegiances, national in orientation, and capable of the sort of liberal-democratic exercise that they envisioned. Progressives varied, however, in their conceptions of the democratic project. For example, advocacy of both more direct

democracy and more robust, centralized national power led Theodore Roosevelt to seek the inculcation of relatively specific character attributes in citizens. In contrast, Woodrow Wilson had a more restrained view of national
democratic action: "The freedom of the democratic nation consists . . . not in
governing itself: for that it cannot do; but in making undictated choices of the
things it will accept and of the men it will follow."[6] Wilson placed great emphasis on the interpretive skills of political leaders attuned to the general, or
commonsense, ideas of the public and on the roles of intermediary organizations and a decentralized administration in making national democracy functional. Distrustful of citizens' capacities, Walter Lippmann increasingly argued
for a constrained public role, while John Dewey had greater faith in the prospects for democratic action, given proper education and the unbiased provision of expert information.[7]

Just as they had different conceptions of the role of the public in the new
national democratic order, Progressives varied in their beliefs about the sort of
public they believed necessary for their ideas to take root. At one end, Progressives such as Roosevelt and Wilson insisted on the superiority of Anglo-
American cultural attributes and argued that newcomers, especially the
immigrants from southern and eastern Europe then arriving in the United
States in large numbers, should be welcomed into the polity only to the extent
that they repudiated their origins and fully adopted American ideas, habits,
and mores. As Roosevelt wrote in 1903, "Where immigrants, or sons of immigrants, do not heartily and in good faith throw in their lot with us, but cling
to the speech, the customs, the ways of life, and the habits of thought of the
Old World which they have left, they thereby harm both themselves and us."[8]
At the other end, the cultural pluralism expressed by John Dewey and others
registered a more expansive view of the American citizenry, one that celebrated the contributions and interactions of the country's many cultural
groups as integral to a thriving democratic polity.[9]

Despite differences in Progressives' views on the precise nature and requisite features of the new democratic order they sought, reformers nonetheless
agreed that the cultivation of certain attributes in the democratic community
was necessary to ensure mass receptivity to the Progressive agenda. Dewey
made it clear that citizens needed to share "aims, beliefs, aspirations, knowledge—a common understanding—like-mindedness" in order for a democratic society to function.[10] And as Wilson explained, "Let no one make the
mistake of supposing that the cultivated and thinking class in any community,
the class that squares its beliefs and its conduct by rational standards, is in any

practical sense the directing and determinant portion of the community, a commission to administer its mind and regulate the courses of its life. Political ideas do not become practicable until they become virtually universal."[11] The challenge for reformers was to cull from the existing hodgepodge of democratic life a national constituency with a sufficient uniformity of civic orientation and capacity for meaningful party governance.

The need to generate a citizenry receptive to their ideals led Progressives to support a wide variety of well-known policy tools, including economic justice, public health, and civic education initiatives. For many, especially those with a culturally pluralistic vision of America, education and welfare policies were sufficient and appropriate tools for developing public capacity. Yet others were concerned that such assistance alone would not create the necessary political community for Progressive Party governance, and thus also sought restrictions to effectively limit the citizenry. Jim Crow restrictions, which were enacted with the support of some Progressives and flourished at this time, represent perhaps the most thoroughgoing effort to limit the public. Eugenics-based enterprises including immigration restriction, coerced sterilization, and reproduction encouragement among the "right stock" of Americans also presented themselves as tools for this task, and Progressive ideas lent plausibility to eugenic efforts. Sometimes Progressivism was exploited by racial restrictionists committed to eugenics for other reasons. But for many Progressives, eugenic practices were a useful device for fashioning the right kind of civic consciousness. Considered in this light, eugenics cannot be dismissed as an expression of the scientific racism of the time (though it was that). Rather, it was a policy tool, to be deployed with many others, for building the Progressive political community, the electorate that reformers thought necessary for modern democratic governance.[12]

The Progressive Community and the Ideal Citizen

In a nation as large and diverse as the United States, there is always going to be a trade-off between mobilizing interests into national politics and supporting robust programs of national action. The party-based machines of the nineteenth century aggregated interests from the bottom up and achieved unprecedented levels of political participation, but as the Progressives well understood, these very strengths made governmental direction and concerted responses to social problems all the more difficult. The reverse was also the case: great programmatic parties were difficult to sustain in the face of increasing social heterogeneity. In their efforts to displace machine politics and to reconstruct American parties, Progressives grappled with this predicament. National programmatic parties required a keen sense of common interests and strong civic homogeneity. The ideal citizen, one fit for the great task of democratic governance, needed to possess a minimum degree of intelligence and reasoning capacity, a habit of independence and self-sufficiency, moral instincts in line with Judeo-Christian beliefs, and an appreciation for, and fealty to, democratic institutions. Reflecting middle-class, professional values, these attributes were also often racialized. With the solidification of Jim Crow and northern acceptance of the South's racial order, African Americans were, by and large, relegated to the realm of "unfit" citizens. But the growing numbers of "in between peoples," largely, immigrants from southern and eastern Europe yet to be established as *white* ethnics, clouded the easy racial distinction between fit and unfit.[13] Leading Progressives expressed concern that immigration would further degrade the presence of desirable civic qualities in the population. Policing citizenship, along with the individual rights and perceived macro-level sociopolitical costs that came with it, was thus a pressing concern for Progressives intent on nurturing a new national political community. This prompted many to support eugenic measures in an attempt to increase the proportion of citizens with desirable traits relative to those deemed incapable of acquiring such traits, and in so doing, to shape the citizenry to more closely approximate the (racialized) ideal.

The minimum requirement of fitness as a citizen was the capacity for independent thought and rational action. Only a citizen free of unthinking religious, familial, ethnic, or other pre-political commitments (including economic dependencies) had the requisite capacity to objectively evaluate his interests, national conditions, and leadership options. Compared to a party boss, a leader, in Teddy Roosevelt's estimation, got "his hold by open appeal to the reason and conscience of his followers."[14] Reforms such as primaries and the secret ballot were designed to make possible voters' reasoned decision making, but they were for naught if citizens squandered the opportunity out of blind tribal allegiance. Roosevelt worried that bosses were especially influential with those who maintained a "clan-loyalty" to the boss, of the sort that was "right and proper among primitive people still in the clan stage of moral development" but not fitting for Progressive democracy.[15] Similarly, in Wilson's formulation, citizens needed to be able to "think straight, maintain a consistent purpose, look before and after, and make their lives the image of their thoughts"—in short, to behave independently, rationally, and purposefully.[16]

The modern democratic citizen also needed to be educable. While citizens were not presumed to play an especially active role in politics, they had to have an interest in, and a capacity for, instruction about national problems and governing principles so that they could make reasonable democratic choices. Roosevelt opined, "No man can be a really good citizen unless he takes a lively interest in politics *from a high standpoint*."[17] And as Wilson explained, "The success of free democratic institutions demands of our people education, intelligence, patriotism."[18] For Wilson, successful reform leaders pulled society forward by appealing to the best version of the "common" sensibilities of the people and by staying in step with accepted principles but applying them to new circumstances.[19] Yet this sort of governing instruction required citizens (or a society, to more accurately capture Wilson's ideas) capable of modifying their opinions based on new information—in other words, citizens capable of learning.

The need for a baseline of reasoning intelligence in the citizenry was accompanied, in the Progressive mind, by the need for a sound moral foundation. In expressing his views on immigration, for example, Wilson stressed the country's need for citizens of "sound morals, sound mind, and sound body."[20] Perhaps unsurprisingly given the history of regional disputes over American slavery, Wilson was relatively circumspect about what constituted sound morals, but Roosevelt was prolific and often quite specific in his discussion of the need for a proper moral foundation among citizens. In an early attack on political machines, Roosevelt wrote, "In a society properly constituted for true democratic government—in a society such as that seen in many of our country towns, for example—machine rule is impossible. But in New York, as well as in most of our other great cities, the conditions favor the growth of ring or boss rule. The chief causes thus operating against good government are the moral and mental attitudes towards politics assumed by different sections of the voters."[21]

Roosevelt went on to identify the source of urbanites' moral and mental laxity in the greater proportion of "densely ignorant," "criminal class," and "laboring men, mostly of foreign birth or parentage," who are "very emotional" and make poor judgments as a result.[22] Once he began outlining his Progressive philosophy, Roosevelt called for government to cultivate moral probity in the citizenry through social and economic legislation. But he saw government action as an addition to, not a substitute for, the foundation of proper character in the citizenry, without which the entire enterprise of democratic governance would fail: "If he has not got [good character], then no law that the wit of man can devise, no administration of the law by the boldest and strongest executive, will avail to help him. We must have the right kind of character—character that makes a man, first of all, a good man in the home, a good father, a good husband—that makes a man a good neighbor."[23]

The demand for good character among citizens encompassed a requirement for economic independence. In his 1912 campaign comments on immigration policy and again in his veto of 1915 immigration legislation, Wilson made it clear that the capacity for self-sufficiency was a proper test of character or personal fitness for any immigration policy.[24] Roosevelt, characteristically, went further, underscoring the virility of independence: "The good citizen . . . must first of all be able to hold his own" economically (and militarily if necessary).[25] And while he saw a willingness to help deserving others as a virtue, he was adamant that aid to the "thriftless, the lazy, the vicious, the incapable" would bring dire consequences: "Let us try to level up, but let us beware of the evil of leveling down."[26] In Roosevelt's estimation, self-sufficiency among citizens was necessary so that they would not burden society, but also so that they would develop the self-respect and fortitude necessary for the nation as a whole to maintain its strength in pursuit of collective goals.

Just as self-sufficiency had practical and moral dimensions, so too did Progressives' concern for self-restraint among the citizenry. Fearful of unrest and foreign economic and political agitation, Progressive leaders stressed the need for self-control. At a minimum, this meant respecting the nation's laws and majority decisions.[27] Ideally, the emphasis on self-restraint spoke to a sense of civic duty and responsibility that transcended the base requirements of democratic liberalism. Describing the "law of liberty," Wilson urged, "It is not the law of doing what we please, but the law of *pleasing to do what is right*."[28] He saw democracy as a form of character, an inherited condition of a people possessing "the steadiness and self-control of political maturity," and not simply a form of government that anyone (or any society) could adopt without proper prior cultivation.[29] From a similar vantage on the polity, Roosevelt sought a community of citizens who privileged the interests of the whole of society over themselves as individuals or their particular group or class interests—this was the essence of responsibility and the duty of self-restraint.[30]

Given Progressives' emphasis on the primacy of community welfare over individual rights, and their belief in the malleability of human nature, ideal citizen attributes were more than a mere abstraction: they were necessary features of the political community if Progressive Party democracy was to flourish. Whereas later forms of liberalism might tolerate a greater diversity of individual action, Progressives leaned heavily toward a more constrained definition of acceptable behavior. As Wilson noted, "Society is not a crowd, but an organism; and, like every organism, it must grow as a whole or else be deformed. . . . It is an organism also in this, that it will die unless it be vital in every part. That is the only line of reasoning by which we can really establish the majority in legitimate authority."[31] Citizens were interdependent, on this view, and those who departed from the ideal were a societal problem in that they could infect the body politic and compromise the political community. The possibility that a portion could damage the whole of the national community was not to be underestimated. This type of reasoning justified state intervention to enforce adherence to the citizen ideal and to regulate those exhibiting deviant behavior. For Roosevelt, this was the call to duty for Progressives: "The prime problem of our nation is to get the right type of good citizenship, and, to get it, we must have progress, and our public men must be genuinely Progressive."[32] Progressive belief in different rates of social evolution among the races meant that this was an inherently racialized proposition.

Just as Progressives sought party and electoral-process reforms to advance Progressive democracy, so too did they trust social reforms to help advance the right citizenry for their project. Like their system reforms, social reforms reflected the Progressive faith in the capacities of purpose-driven social science and professional administration. The most generous of these were the social and economic justice reforms that Progressives sought in order to improve conditions for poor Americans, thus eliminating some of the grossest inequities and eliminating obstacles to successful civic participation. Americanization programs and initiatives, too, were advanced to "help" those new to the country assimilate existing habits, ideas, and practices. Yet in the same spirit of creating a more homogeneous political community, one suited to the demands of a Progressive democracy mediated by national, principled parties, Progressives turned to eugenics to improve the balance of "fit stock" citizens relative to the "unfit stock."

Eugenics and the Progressive Agenda

National democratic action required programmatic parties, and neither was possible without a community of citizens possessing common capacities and commitments. Cultivating a citizenry with the necessary attributes—at minimum, independence, rationality, moral behavior, and devotion to American institutions—out of the patchwork polity entrenched in the existing party system led Progressives to support eugenic initiatives.[33] Alternative policies and practices, including the array of Progressive social and economic justice reforms as well as Americanization programs, served to nurture the growth of "ideal citizen" characteristics, and in the face of ethnocultural change, these policies were tools to help new immigrants assimilate to "American" ways. Yet for those presumed to be politically unassimilable because of their heredity, no amount of education or other positive state intervention would help. While some prominent Progressives, including John Dewey and Walter Lippmann, challenged the claims of eugenic reasoning, others, putting stock in its scientific grounding and its compatibility with expert administrative solutions, found eugenics a reasonable means for culling those they believed to be genetically incapable of developing the characteristics presumed necessary for the Progressive political project.[34]

Against the backdrop of growing immigration and urban industrial poverty, the eugenics campaign, targeting the "socially inadequate," flourished as an effort to increase the proportion of citizens deemed fit to those identified as unfit.[35] Teddy Roosevelt, whose concerns about "race suicide" led him to speak and write often on the topic, was among the most high-profile advocates of eugenics, campaigning actively to encourage greater reproduction rates among those citizens possessing ideal citizen characteristics ("positive eugenics"). In a letter to Charles Davenport, the head of the Eugenics Record Office in Cold Spring Harbor, New York, Roosevelt mused: "Some day we will realize that the prime duty, the inescapable duty, of the *good* citizen of the right type is to leave his or her blood behind him in the world; and that we have no business to permit the perpetuation of citizens of the wrong type."[36] For Roosevelt and other Progressive promoters of eugenics, it was an imperative duty of good citizens—as he described them, "the average college graduates of either sex, the average sane and worthy philanthropists, the average men and women who lead in any branch of the higher life of our people"—to have large families and provide their children with instruction in the habits and mores of citizenship.[37] This would ensure that the necessary attributes for a well-functioning citizenry would become more widespread.

The concern for increasing the number of citizens of good character led Roosevelt to be especially concerned about the birth control movement, believing that those most attracted to birth control were precisely those who should, in his estimation, be reproducing in greater numbers. Citing a study on the declining birthrates of Yale and Harvard graduates, Roosevelt called for "birth encouragement" among "Americans of the old stock" and college graduates, especially because the foreign-born stock was replenishing at a significantly greater rate than the native-born stock; he worried that it was "fatal for a nation to import its babies."[38] This stance put him at odds with some other Progressive eugenicists, including Margaret Sanger, who, in reply to Roosevelt, argued: "The best thing that the modern American college does for the young men or women is to make of them highly sensitized individuals, keenly aware of their responsibility to society. They quickly perceive that they have other duties toward the State than procreation of the kind blindly practiced by the immigrant from Europe."[39] Revealed in this debate is not a difference in opinion among Progressives about the need to cultivate a constituency for their project, nor about which citizens were best suited to that task, but rather about how to most effectively maximize the resources of their desired constituency—increase their numbers in the electorate or cultivate their public participatory responsibilities.

Pursued through a broad campaign of exhortation and reward, positive eugenics signaled, and provided justification for, a racialized hierarchy among citizens, with Anglo-Saxon Protestants presumed to be the carriers of the most beneficial civic disposition. Promoters of positive eugenics sought to establish and reinforce particular physical characteristics, psychological attributes, and social norms (all of which were thought to be correlated) as superior because they connoted fitness as a citizen. In the "Better Baby" and "Fitter Family" contests held at state fairs around the country, family histories that included feeble-mindedness, migraines, or frequent nightmares, for example, were problematic, while the birthplaces of relatives and "special tastes" (including taste in music and literature) were likewise indicative of the quality of citizens' character.[40] By rewarding high eugenic scores in combination with high reproduction rates, Fitter Family contests sought to incentivize behavior (to literally expand the size of the desired constituency) and to provide a forum for popular education about traits, such as independence, intelligence, and moral fortitude, that Progressives believed needed to be inculcated in the citizenry, to the extent possible, for party democracy to work.

Positive eugenics did not have the same coercive edge as legally sanctioned "negative eugenics." Including national-level immigration restrictions and state laws mandating sterilization and restricting marriage, punitive eugenic laws and policies were championed by nativists and Progressives alarmed by the changing demographic makeup of the citizenry. Rather than symbolically elevating the status of some citizens (and encouraging their reproduction), negative eugenics laws aimed to change the political community through direct population control—restricting either current access to citizenship (immigration) or future access (sterilization and marriage laws).

Roosevelt and Wilson supported immigration laws intended to uphold the moral, physical, and character fitness of the citizenry. As president, Roosevelt proclaimed his openness to all immigrants "of the right kind," but he argued for a broad set of character restrictions in order to ensure "fitness for citizenship," including restrictions on "not merely the anarchist, but every man of anarchistic tendencies, all violent and disorderly people, all people of bad character, the incompetent, the lazy, the vicious, the physically unfit, defective, or degenerate" as well as "insane, idiotic, epileptic, and pauper immigrants."[41] Wilson outlined a similar set of characteristics that he believed immigration policy should guard against.[42] Once these basic character attributes had been screened for, Wilson expressed confidence that "civil capacity" could be imparted to "the best of those who come to us with other blood in their veins."[43]

For Roosevelt and Wilson, immigration policy was a tool for shaping the political community to ensure that only those with desirable civic habits, or the potential for such, would be admitted. Many Progressives at the time argued that not all immigrants were equally endowed with these civic capacities, a sentiment that found a wide audience, especially after World War I. Following the lead of the Dillingham Commission, which had concluded earlier in the century that southern and eastern European immigrants were racially inferior and less assimilable than older northern European immigrants, Progressive restrictionists sought to impose sharp country quotas or literacy tests. These latter were understood as targeting, in Henry Cabot Lodge's words, "the Italians, Russians, Poles, Hungarians, Greeks, and Asiatics" rather than "English-speaking emigrants and Germans, Scandinavians, and French."[44] With the passage of the Immigration Acts of 1921 and 1924, which were sponsored by Progressives and imposed severe national-origin restrictions, the capacities for productive citizenship were cast in explicitly racialized terms.[45]

The ability to regulate the flow of immigrants into major American cities made immigration policy a valuable tool for Progressives intent on both undermining the resources of the old party machines and developing the constituency for the new national, programmatic party. A concern about a rise in the defective characteristics of the existing citizenry, largely attributed to ongoing immigration, led many Progressives to support such eugenics-based state laws as marriage restrictions and sterilization laws for people in prisons and mental health institutions. Particularly worrisome was the problem of the "alien insane." As one scholar has written, "No conviction about insanity was more widely shared in late nineteenth- and early twentieth-century American than the belief [that] . . . immigrants were more likely to fall victim to insanity than the native born."[46] This belief was nurtured by eugenics experts who pointed to the high rates of incarceration and institutionalization (for the "socially inadequate") among the foreign-born as evidence (circular as that logic was), by nativist organizations such as the Immigration Restriction League, and by leading medical organizations, many of which supported immigration restriction on the grounds that the country's new immigrants were biologically and culturally more predisposed to insanity than native-stock Americans.[47]

Just as Progressives sought to increase reproduction among the citizens they believed most fit for party democracy, they similarly strove to limit reproduction among those whose "defective genes" prevented them, and their offspring, from developing the capacities for democratic citizenship. In addition to widespread antimiscegenation laws, by 1912 thirty-four states had outlawed marriage between "lunatics."[48] In addition, coercive sterilization laws that targeted prison inmates and residents in institutions for the insane or "feeble-minded" were passed in two-thirds of the states; sixteen states, including many where Progressivism flourished, passed their laws in the heyday of Progressive activity, 1907–17.[49] Given the link that eugenics experts effectively established between immigrants, insanity, and institutionalization, the effects of these laws were not racially or ethnically neutral.

State sterilization laws were constitutionally legitimated in 1927 with the Supreme Court's *Buck v. Bell* decision, which upheld the sterilization of a "feebleminded" Virginia woman. Likening sterilization to vaccination, Justice Oliver Wendell Holmes, writing for the majority, focused in the decision on the individual as well as the community impact of reproduction by the "socially inadequate." Holmes justified sterilization partly as a duty of citizenship: "We have seen more than once that the public welfare may call upon the best citizens for their lives. It would be strange if it could not call upon those who already sap the strength of the State for these lesser sacrifices, often not felt to be such by those concerned, in order to prevent our being swamped with incompetence. . . . Three generations of imbeciles are enough."[50] In this rendering, "unfit" citizens were made to approximate good citizens by relinquishing their reproductive capacities and thus helping improve society overall—much as when the child in a school choir who cannot sing well is asked to mouth the words instead of joining her classmates in the actual singing of songs.

Policies to limit reproduction were often linked to Progressives' efforts for social and economic justice. For example, Herbert Croly argued for "enforced celibacy of hereditary criminals and incipient lunatics," but suggested that the state should simultaneously attend to the social welfare of its citizens.[51] For Croly and others at the *New Republic*, the government's welfare commitments would generate support for a "policy of extinction of stocks incapable of profiting from their [state-provided] privileges."[52] The link between social welfare and population control, made here explicitly by Croly but also implicit in the support that individual Progressives offered for both types of policies, is revealing. It suggests the extent to which social welfare and eugenics functioned together as forms of social control deployed toward the end of building a new political community. More fundamentally, it gives the lie to the idea that Progressive thought can be neatly and normatively separated from the eugenic notions to which so many Progressives subscribed. On the contrary, these two sets of ideas were intertwined for many Progressives who believed that the success of the reform agenda depended, at least in part, on the success of the eugenic project.

A starker tension is evident in the contrasting underpinnings of Americanization education and eugenic policies. Progressive belief in the ability of the reform agenda to transform individuals and society led logically to the advocacy of economic-justice initiatives and Americanization education; while the former would liberate citizens for proper democratic action, the latter would provide the tools to enable such action. Although Progressives varied in their ideas about the content of civic education, there was nonetheless fairly broad support for the idea that some common curricular instruction would help forge the necessary democratic public out of the country's cultural and ethnic groups. Yet eugenics policies conceded a limit to the Progressive reform project and to the prospects of education, since some people, by virtue of their hereditary, could not change ("Three generations of imbeciles is enough"). And indeed, some Progressive proponents of eugenics were highly skeptical of what could be achieved with Americanization education. Ultimately, the inconsistency between the belief in education and the belief in hereditary limits led some Progressives, such as John Dewey, to a forceful critique of eugenics and a strong defense of the prospects of education, and it may have laid the foundation for the eventual repudiation of eugenics. Yet for many Progressives at the time who supported both eugenics and Americanization education, the incompatibility of the two ideas was likely subsumed by the perceived urgency of the problem of constructing a new public and by the expediency of having multiple policy tools at hand.

Conclusion

Uniting a heterogeneous democratic community to effect national action is an enduring challenge in liberal America. Anxious about majority tyranny and fearful of ideologically charged movements, the Founders produced a constitutional structure that would not just limit democracy but also disable great programmatic parties by amplifying the discordance of a diversity of interests. Progressives saw these problems and endorsed national programmatic parties that could overcome institutionally disaggregated power and the limitations of the nineteenth-century electoral system. Yet if Progressive ambition was to energize government through programmatic parties, it was not because Progressives were uniformly more sanguine about the prospects of majoritarian democracy. Democratization, along with economic and ethnocultural change, had increased electoral diversity. If not effectively harmonized around the Progressive agenda, the electorate would either abuse party governance or squander its potential. National party power could be made safe, in the Progressive imagination, only by fashioning a citizenry worthy enough to wield it. Thus, the ideas of programmatic action and democratic governance that Progressives promoted opened onto a narrow vision of the electorate—a vision they sought to realize through social reforms encompassing education, welfare, and eugenics, as well as through changes in the electoral process.

The Progressive legacy in this regard is mixed. In the pursuit of their political project, Progressives cleared the ground for—and legitimized the idea of—nationalized parties and programmatic government. Even today, elite partisans debate principles of national governance, framed as what is best for "the people," singularly conceived, and when elected, each party claims a mandate to enact programmatic reforms that have been democratically legitimated. Yet if Progressives succeeded in instilling in the country's politics some aspects of national party governance, they failed to create the national political community upon which they pegged the real success of their vision. Still stumbling on the fiction of a common civic consciousness, party elites today continue to struggle to marshal a heterogeneous electorate around national purposes.[53]

The problem of "fit," of how to align a diverse nation with strong national parties, endures. We may be repelled by the Progressives' solution, but it is hard, in view of the parties of our day, to simply dismiss the problem with which they grappled. The American people are more diverse than ever before, and that makes it even more difficult than before to enlist them in political programs of great national aspiration. One response has been to continue to seek civic homogeneity, often through reliance on exclusionary practices. To-day this strategy is most evident in the Republican ranks, where policies with an exclusionary twist are typically justified on narrowly conceived assertions about American national identity and necessary standards of citizenship. Arguments to restrict immigration and against multiculturalism reveal both a sense of threat associated with increasing diversity and the need to maintain a strict definition of "Americanness," all of which is reminiscent of the Progressive era.[54] The policy preferences of social and cultural conservatives, including school prayer and traditional definitions of the family, strain to articulate a "Judeo-Christian" conception of Americanness. The history of conservative Republican efforts to distinguish between governmental assistance to "deserving" and "undeserving" Americans is also implicitly racialized in a way that reflects Progressive conceptions of civic ideals.[55] And efforts to expunge voters from the rolls, whether through felony disenfranchisement, voter identification laws, or other means, suggest a continued belief in the legitimacy of restricting the electorate in ways that normatively, often racially, define citizenship. The success and power of the Republican Party bear witness to the appeal of a strong but narrow conception of the national community.

The racially exclusionary practices of the Democratic Party, found in its long history of refusing civil rights for African Americans and in the racial cast of its New Deal and World War II benefits, is well documented.[56] Since the 1960s, however, Democrats have adopted a different approach and embraced the growing racial and ethnic diversity of the nation. In their greater reliance on finding support across the board, Democrats have employed many familiar Progressive policies—welfare provision, access to education, labor protection. But for all this, contemporary Democrats grapple with the flip side of the Republicans' problem: the very diversity of their coalition undermines their pursuit of common ends. Democrats too repeatedly bump up against the Progressives' insight: concerted national action is difficult without a national community of engaged citizens, and building a community on difference is more difficult still. This raises a point broached earlier by Eldon Eisenach. The modern Democratic Party seems incapable of rising above naked pragmatism and interest-group liberalism and leading with its values. It has begun to avoid justice-oriented solutions in favor of "post-partisanship" or neoliberalism on issues such as health care, immigration, or budgetary policy. In other words, rather than giving their national principles a temporal and contextual specificity that would privilege some at the expense of others, the Democratic solution, more often than not, is to accommodate all interests in the name of rational management and social adjustment. This is neither a high aspiration nor a mobilizing formula.

We have yet to square this circle. The eugenics tool has been abandoned, but it stands as a telling reminder of the mismatch between programmatic government and national diversity. Our parties offer exclusion or inclusion, but they do not offer a compelling view of national citizenship. The unresolved legacy of the Progressive era is to be found here in the weakness of the civic ideals behind the strong state.

Notes

1. The author is grateful to Emily Hertz, at the University of California, Berkeley, for her tremendous research assistance and to the Sentinels of the Republic Research Fund at Williams College for financial support.

2. Woodrow Wilson, *Constitutional Government in the United States* (New York: Columbia University Press, 1908), 220.

3. Woodrow Wilson, "Cabinet Government in the United States," *International Review* 6 (August 1879), in *The Public Papers of Woodrow Wilson: College and State* (New York: Harper and Brothers, 1925), 1:37. Also see Woodrow Wilson, *Congressional Government: A Study in American Politics,* 9th ed. (Boston: Houghton Mifflin, 1892); and James Ceaser, *Presidential Selection: Theory and Development* (Princeton, N.J.: Princeton University Press, 1979).

4. Although leading Progressives agreed on how the deficiencies of the existing party system corroded the prospects for Progressive democracy, they differed in their ideas of how parties *should* function. Woodrow Wilson made the strongest case for reformed parties in the modern political system. For others, like Herbert Croly and Teddy Roosevelt, the promise of Progressivism was its ability to ultimately move beyond parties and unite people and government directly; nonetheless, their anti-party-system spirit was tempered by an acknowledgment of the democratizing and legislating success of parties in particular moments (including under President Wilson) and an acceptance of the practical need for parties "for a long time." See Herbert Croly, *Progressive Democracy* (New York: Macmillan, 1914), 337–48, quotation on 344; Theodore Roosevelt, *Thomas Hart Benton* (New York: Charles Scribner's Sons, 1926), in *The Works of Theodore Roosevelt,* national ed., ed. Hermann Hagedorn (New York: Charles Scribner's Sons, 1926), 7:53–54; Theodore Roosevelt, "Machine Politics in New York City," *Century,* November 1886, in *Works,* 13:76–77. On Roosevelt's criticism of the existing party system and his desire for more direct popular control, see Theodore Roosevelt, "A Charter of Democracy," address before the Ohio Constitutional Convention, Columbus, Ohio, February 21, 1912, *Works,* 17:119–48; Theodore Roosevelt, "How I Became a Progressive," *Outlook,* October 12, 1912, *Works,* 17:316; and Sidney M. Milkis, *Theodore*

Roosevelt, the Progressive Party, and the Transformation of American Democracy (Lawrence: University Press of Kansas, 2009), 238–39.

5. Michael McGerr, *The Decline of Popular Politics: The American North, 1865–1928* (New York: Oxford University Press, 1986).

6. Woodrow Wilson, "Democracy," December 5, 1891, in *The Papers of Woodrow Wilson*, ed. Arthur S. Link (Princeton, N.J.: Princeton University Press, 1977), 7:359.

7. On Roosevelt, see "The New Nationalism," speech at Osawatomie, Kansas, August 31, 1910, in *Works*, 17:5–22; also Milkis, *Roosevelt, the Progressive Party, and Democracy*. On Wilson's view of national power, see Woodrow Wilson, *The New Freedom: A Call for the Emancipation of the Generous Energies of a People* (New York: Doubleday, 1913); Stephen Skowronek, "The Reassociation of Ideas and Purposes: Racism, Liberalism, and the American Political Tradition," *American Political Science Review* 100, no. 3 (August 2006): 385–401. Also see Walter Lippmann, *Public Opinion* (New York: Free Press, 1997 [1922]) and *The Phantom Public* (New York: Harcourt, Brace, 1925); and John Dewey, *The Public and Its Problems* (New York: Holt, 1927).

8. The quotation is from Roosevelt's "True Americanism," as quoted in Jeffrey Mirel, *Patriotic Pluralism: Americanization, Education, and European Immigrants* (Cambridge, Mass.: Harvard University Press, 2010), 26.

9. Mirel, *Patriotic Pluralism*, 31–32.

10. Ibid., 32.

11. Woodrow Wilson, "Democracy," *Papers*, 7:366.

12. For a discussion of Progressivism's "policy paradox," which combined an expansion of the welfare state with a contraction of civil rights and liberties for marginalized groups, see Eileen McDonagh, "Race, Class, and Gender in the Progressive Era: Restructuring State and Society," in *Progressivism and the New Democracy*, ed. Sidney Milkis and Jerome Mileur (Amherst: University of Massachusetts Press, 1999). For a thoughtful discussion of the conceptions of civic identity advanced by different strains of Progressivism, including the variation in Progressive thought about African Americans' civic status, as well as a review of the broader efforts to construct the civic order, see Rogers Smith, *Civic Ideals: Conflicting Visions of Citizenship in U.S. History* (New Haven, Conn.: Yale University Press, 1997), esp. chap. 12. On the ambivalence within the Progressive Party, specifically, about the stance to be taken on African American civil rights, see Milkis, *Roosevelt, the Progressive Party, and Democracy*, 166–76. And for a broad review of the success of efforts to demobilize the mass electorate at this time, see Walter Dean Burnham, "The System of 1896," in *The Evolution of American Electoral Systems*, ed. Paul Kleppner (Westport, Conn.: Greenwood, 1981); and McGerr, *Decline of Popular Politics*.

13. The term "in between peoples" is from David Roediger, *Working toward Whiteness: How America's Immigrants Became White; The Strange Journey from Ellis Island to the Suburbs* (New York: Basic Books, 2005).

14. Theodore Roosevelt, "The New Nationalism and the Old Moralities," speech at Syracuse, New York, September 17, 1910, in Theodore Roosevelt, *The New Nationalism* (New York: Outlook, 1910), 242–43.

15. Theodore Roosevelt, *Theodore Roosevelt: An Autobiography* (New York: Charles Scribner's Sons, 1926), in *Works*, 20:155.

16. Woodrow Wilson, "What Is Constitutional Government?," in Wilson, *Constitutional Government*, 23. On the general transformation from a partisan "spectacle" politics to the rationalized electoral politics of the early twentieth century, see McGerr, *Decline of Popular Politics*.

17. Theodore Roosevelt, "Civic Helpfulness," *Century*, October 1900, in Theodore Roosevelt, *The Strenuous Life: Essays and Addresses* (New York: Century, 1902), 107 (emphasis added).

18. Woodrow Wilson to James Duval Phelan, telegram, May 3, 1912, published in the *New York Independent*, October 10, 1912, in Wilson, *Papers*, 24:383. On the ideal of the educated citizen more generally, also see Michael Schudson, *The Good Citizen: A History of American Civic Life* (Cambridge, Mass.: Harvard University Press, 1998).

19. Woodrow Wilson, "Leaders of Men," June 17, 1890, *Papers*, 6:659–60.

20. Woodrow Wilson to Cyrus Adler, October 21, 1912, *Papers*, 25:450.

21. Theodore Roosevelt, "Machine Politics in New York," 78.

22. Ibid., 78–79.

23. Theodore Roosevelt, "The New Nationalism," 22. Roosevelt was prolific in his comments and writing about character, calling it the "one indispensable requisite" for the individual and the nation; see Theodore Roosevelt, "Character and Success," *Outlook*, March 31, 1900, in Roosevelt, *Strenuous Life*, 121.

24. Woodrow Wilson to Anthony Geronimo, August 16, 1912, in Wilson, *Papers*, 25:40–41. Woodrow Wilson, veto message, January 28, 1915, full text at the American Presidency Project, www.presidency.ucsb.edu/ws/index.php?pid=65386&st=Veto+message&st1=. It is worth noting that Wilson's stance on immigration evolved, either through experience or for reasons of political expediency. In *A History of the American People*, a younger Wilson famously wrote, "Throughout the [19th] century men of the sturdy stocks of the north of Europe had made up the main strain of foreign blood which was every year added to the vital working force of the country, or else men of the Latin-Gallic stocks of France and northern Italy; but now there came multitudes of men of the lowest class from the south of Italy and men of the meaner sort out of Hungary and Poland, men out of the ranks where there was neither skill nor energy nor any initiative of quick intelligence . . . men whose standards of life and of work were such as American workmen had never dreamed of hitherto." See Wilson, *A History of the American People* (New York: Harper and Brothers, 1902), 5:212–13.

25. Theodore Roosevelt, "Citizenship in a Republic," speech delivered at the Sorbonne, Paris, France, April 23, 1910; available at http://design.caltech.edu/erik/Misc/Citizenship_in_a_Republic.pdf.

26. Ibid.

27. Wilson, "Democracy," in *Papers*, 7:347, 364; Theodore Roosevelt, "The Progressive Party," *Century Magazine*, October 1913, in *Works*, 17:409. In discussing immigration law as the new president, Roosevelt made reference to the need for law that kept out those lacking the capacity to act "sanely" and with respect for American institutions (a reference directed at anarchists) but also those whose "ignorance" feeds anarchism; see Roosevelt, First Annual Message, December 3, 1901, in *Works*, 15:96.

28. Wilson, "Democracy," 363 (emphasis in the original).

29. Woodrow Wilson, "United States in Constitutional Development," in *Constitutional Government*, 52–53.

30. Roosevelt, "Citizenship in a Republic"; Theodore Roosevelt, "Fellow-Feeling as a Political Factor," *Century*, January 1900, in Roosevelt, *Strenuous Life*, 77–79, 85–86; Theodore Roosevelt, "The Labor Question," speech delivered at the Chicago Labor Day Picnic, September 3, 1900, in *Strenuous Life*, 302–5, 317–18.

31. Wilson, "Leaders of Men," 659.

32. Roosevelt, "The New Nationalism," 22. Also see Wilson Carey McWilliams, "Standing at Armageddon: Morality and Religion in Progressive Thought," in Milkis and Mileur, *Progressivism and the New Democracy*.

33. An outgrowth of the era's scientific racism, eugenics was defined by Francis Galton as "the science which deals with all influences that improve the inborn qualities of a race; also with those that develop them to the utmost advantage"; see Francis Galton, "Eugenics: Its Definition, Scope, and Aims," *American Journal of Sociology* 10, no. 1 (July 1904): 1.

34. Progressive efforts to mold the citizenry to enhance a uniform set of civic virtues recall the republicanism of the founding. Whereas early restrictions of the franchise (and other citizenship privileges) provided a degree of civic homogeneity, increasing democratization and ethnocultural change throughout the nineteenth century led Progressives to turn to additional policy tools in order to achieve similar results. A highlighting of the republicanism of Progressive reformers can be found in Michael Sandel's *Democracy's Discontent*, though his discussion of Progressives' "formative ambition" elides the coercive, ethnocentric edge that I am stressing; see Sandel, *Democracy's Discontent: America in Search of a Public Philosophy* (Cambridge, Mass.: Belknap Press, 1996), chap. 7.

35. The eugenics campaign was broad, institutionally established, and well funded, and it counted among its supporters a host of prominent Progressives. The "epicenter" of the movement was the Eugenics Record Office (ERO) in Cold Spring Harbor, New York, led by Charles Davenport, a Harvard-trained biologist, and Harry Laughlin, a social reform Progressive and the "expert eugenics agent" of the House Committee on Immigration and Naturalization. With financial support from leading philanthropists, including Andrew Carnegie, John D. Rockefeller, and the railroad baroness Mrs. E. H. Harriman, and directed by prominent Progressives, including David Starr Jordan

(president of Stanford University), Irving Fisher (Yale economist), and the inventor Alexander Graham Bell, the ERO coordinated with other funding and scientific research institutes (for example, the American Breeders Association, the Race Betterment Foundation, the American Eugenics Society, the Human Betterment Foundation, and the Galton Society) to conduct research, lobby governments, and train caseworkers in eugenic practices.

36. Theodore Roosevelt to Charles Davenport, January 3, 1913, reprinted in Harry Bruinius, *Better for All the World: The Secret History of Forced Sterilization and America's Quest for Racial Purity* (New York: Vintage, 2007), 190–91. In his concern about declining birth rates among native-stock Americans, Roosevelt was especially scathing in his condemnation of the descendants of New England Puritans: "It is lamentable to see this Puritan conscience, this New England conscience, so atrophied, so diseased and warped, as not to recognize that the fundamental, the unpardonable crime against the race is the crime of race suicide"; see Theodore Roosevelt, "Twisted Eugenics," *Outlook*, January 3, 1914, in *Works*, 12:202.

37. Roosevelt, "Twisted Eugenics," 201–4. Also see his advocacy of positive eugenics (that is, more reproduction by "good" citizens) in his address "Christian Citizenship," to the Young Men's Christian Association, Carnegie Hall, New York, December 30, 1900, in Roosevelt, *Strenuous Life*, 330; see also Theodore Roosevelt, "Manhood and Statehood," address at the Quarter-Centennial Celebration of Statehood in Colorado, at Colorado Springs, August 2, 1901, in Roosevelt, *Strenuous Life*, 258; Roosevelt, "Citizenship in a Republic"; and Roosevelt, "Social Evolution," *North American Review*, July 1895, in Theodore Roosevelt, *American Ideals, and Other Essays Social and Political* (London: Putnam's Sons, 1897), 327–28.

38. Theodore Roosevelt, "Birth Control—From the Positive Side," *Metropolitan Magazine*, October 1917, reprinted in *The Pivot of Civilization in Historical Perspective: The Birth Control Classic by Margaret Sanger*, ed. Michael W. Perry (Seattle: Inkling Books, 2003), 237–41.

39. Margaret Sanger, "Birth Control: Margaret Sanger's Reply to Theodore Roosevelt," *Metropolitan Magazine*, December 1917, 66–67, retrieved at the Margaret Sanger Papers Project, www.nyu.edu/projects/sanger/webedition/app/documents/show.php ?sangerDoc=320325.xml.

40. Bruinius, *Better for All the World*, 235–38. Also see "Fitter Families Examination, Kansas State Fair, Topeka: Nervous and Mental History," circa 1924, Eugenics Archive, ID #191, retrieved at www.eugenicsarchive.org/html/eugenics/index2.html?tag=191; "'Large Family' Winner, Fitter Families Contest, Texas State Fair (1925): Individual Examinations," 1925, Eugenics Archive, ID #171, retrieved at www.eugenicsarchive.org/html/eugenics/index2.html?tag=171; "'Large Family' Winner, Fitter Families Contest, Eastern States Exposition, Springfield, MA (1925): Fitter Families Examination," 1925, Eugenics Archive, ID #148, retrieved at www.eugenicsarchive.org/html/eugenics/index2.html?tag=148.

41. Theodore Roosevelt, Fifth Annual Message, December 5, 1905, in *Works*, 15:319–20. Both Roosevelt and Wilson supported restrictions on Asian immigration.

42. Woodrow Wilson to Anthony Geronimo, in Wilson, *Papers*, 25:40–41.

43. Wilson, "Democracy," 358. Interestingly, President Wilson twice vetoed immigration bills that included literacy requirements, calling them "not tests of quality or of character or of personal fitness, but tests of opportunity"; see Wilson, veto message. This suggests the desire for citizens who are educable, but not necessarily already educated, especially if that education were received elsewhere, and it likely reflects his contempt for political radicalism, since opponents of the literacy test argued that the measure did nothing to prevent the entry of anarchists and socialists, who were "almost always well-educated"; see Hans Vought, "Division and Reunion: Woodrow Wilson, Immigration, and the Myth of American Unity," *Journal of American Ethnic History* 13, no. 3 (Spring 1994): 25, 39.

44. Quoted in Nancy Cott, *Public Vows: A History of Marriage and the Nation* (Cambridge, Mass.: Harvard University Press, 2000), 141.

45. For a thoughtful discussion of Progressives and immigration policy, see Daniel Tichenor, *Dividing Lines: The Politics of Immigration Control in America* (Princeton, N.J.: Princeton University Press, 2002); see also Robert Zeidel, *Immigrants, Progressives, and Exclusion Politics: The Dillingham Commission, 1900–1927* (DeKalb: Northern Illinois University Press, 2004).

46. Richard W. Fox, *So Far Disordered in Mind: Insanity in California, 1870–1930* (Berkeley: University of California Press, 1978), 105. There was debate, however, about how much of this problem was hereditary and how much environmental, because of poor living conditions and the experience of immigration.

47. See Harry H. Laughlin, "Biological Aspects of Immigration," testimony before the Committee on Immigration and Naturalization, House of Representatives, 66th Cong., 2nd sess., April 16–17, 1920; also, "New York Has Spent $25,000,000 on Alien Insane," *New York Times*, April 7, 1912; "Another Argument for Exclusion," *Los Angeles Times*, March 20, 1902; Fox, *So Far Disordered in Mind*, 105–6; Ian Robert Dowbiggen, *Keeping America Sane: Psychiatrists and Eugenics in the United States and Canada, 1880–1940* (Ithaca, N.Y.: Cornell University Press, 1997), 191–217.

48. McDonagh, "Race, Class, and Gender," 160.

49. See Harry Hamilton Laughlin, *Eugenical Sterilization in the United States* (Psychopathic Laboratory of the Municipal Court of Chicago, 1922). Dates of state laws are presented in map form in the document "Date on Which Each State Inaugurated Its Eugenical Sterilization Law" (circa 1935), Eugenics Archive, ID #959, www.eugenics archive.org/html/eugenics/index2.html?tag=959; also see Rudolph J. Vecoli, "Sterilization: A Progressive Measure?," *Wisconsin Magazine of History* 43, no. 3 (1960); Alexandra Minna Stern, "Sterilized in the Name of Public Health: Race, Immigration, and Reproductive Control in Modern California," *American Journal of Public Health* 95, no. 7 (2005).

50. *Buck v. Bell*, 274 U.S. 200 (1927).

51. Herbert Croly, *The Promise of American Life* (New York: Macmillan, 1909), 345–46.

52. Editorial Notes, *New Republic*, March 18, 1916, 166, retrieved at the *New Republic* Archive, http://search.ebscohost.com/login.aspx?direct=true&db=fjh&AN=15052217& site=ehost-live (subscription required).

53. James Morone, *The Democratic Wish: Popular Participation and the Limits of American Government* (New York: Basic Books, 1990).

54. Samuel Huntington, "One Nation Out of Many: Why 'Americanization' of Newcomers Is Still Important," *American Enterprise*, September 2004, 20–25; Nathan Glazer, "American Epic: Then and Now," *Public Interest* 130 (Winter 1998), 3–20.

55. Theda Skocpol and Vanessa Williamson, *The Tea Party and the Remaking of Republican Conservatism* (New York: Oxford University Press, 2013).

56. Ira Katznelson, *When Affirmative Action Was White: An Untold Story of Racial Inequality in Twentieth-Century America* (New York: Norton, 2006).

10 • Toward a More Inclusive Community

The Legacy of Female Reformers in the Progressive State

Carol Nackenoff

Many social welfare initiatives that have found their way into the administrative state can be traced to proposals advanced by the mobilized women of the Progressive era. These female reformers identified a range of new social problems and pressed government to address them with new policy initiatives.[1] Behind their efforts lay the vision of a new polity, a national community built from the bottom up and transformed by maternalist perspectives and sensibilities. These reformers sought to foster a new, interconnected citizenry by developing inclusive and dynamic democratic practices. They aimed to empower citizens to participate more fully in community life. They sought to cultivate civic knowledge through increased exposure to the different backgrounds and traditions of the American people. Maternalism was not just a strand of Progressivism, but also a holistic understanding of reform and of the Progressive program itself. It was the self-confident assertion of values missing from the public sphere; the ambition was to confer the qualities and values of women onto a reconstituted nation.

This vision of national community anticipated significant changes in how Americans would relate to one another and to the state. The key elements were association, collaboration, and mutual learning. The potential reach and broad compass of these values tend to be obscured in strongly critical assessments of the narrow and culturally defensive posture of Progressivism, and it is easy to see why. When theory was put into practice, a variety of tensions in the maternalist vision came to the fore. In retrospect, it appears that the project was undermined in headlong pursuit of its own ambitions, and that the conception of a holistic change in national life kept bumping up against the particular character of the agents promoting it. It was not that the vision was weak or narrowly conceived. It was in fact arrestingly new and strongly democratic. But this vision came from only a part of the Progressive movement and indeed from only a segment of American women. Disagreements with other Progressives and disagreements among women were accentuated in on-the-ground problem solving and policy implementation. The problem was not a narrow conception but a narrowing in the execution.

This chapter examines three particular tensions that emerged as the vision of a national community of newly empowered and aware citizens operating at local levels to solve newly uncovered social problems clashed with other values shared by the reformers. First, the inclusiveness of the project and the aspiration to build mutual respect among equals was in tension with the idea of maternalism, which employed sex differences and female sensibilities as the basis of social transformation. Second, and relatedly, there was a clash between the reform processes advocated and the substantive ends sought. Reformers recognized the civic and educative value of diversity, but they worked to achieve particular policy goals that often devalued the very alternatives that civic diversity brought to the fore. And third, the aim of empowering citizens to act locally on their own behalf proved incongruous with a simultaneous emphasis on expertise and a keen interest in the specialized knowledge needed to solve social and economic challenges of the day. Consequently, a vision meant to recast the community at large, to draw insight from diversity, and to empower the marginalized tended in practice to lock in traditional gender roles, traditional notions of proper family life, and reliance on expertise and administration to achieve political ends.

For many female reformers, creating new, interconnected citizens through more inclusive and dynamic practices of democracy was vital to the success of the Progressive project and to governing in modern America. They demanded not only access to the public sphere but also fundamental changes in its orientation and operation. And their determination to develop practices that might further open the public sphere to groups previously excluded unleashed enormous energy and political creativity. Nevertheless, these hopes were largely unfulfilled. The experience of Progressive women reformers is suggestive of problems likely to arise in the course of reform efforts more generally. This holistic vision of a new community had its origins in a part of the whole, and that proved self-limiting. Indeed, it seemed to channel reform toward antithetical ends.

The gap between aspirations and performance haunts all reform movements. The shortfalls are not to be denied, but neither are they an indictment of the effort itself. These female reformers accomplished much, and their experience offers some constructive lessons for our present moment. These reformers located politics in the borderlands between public and private, self and community. They opened relations of power and authority within those spaces to political scrutiny and political contestation. They brought problems not previously seen as state work into the public sphere.[2] Identifying their objectives can inspire new approaches to the political problems they perceived; identifying the obstacles they encountered can inform new reform strategies.

Building a Democracy Through Interaction with Difference

Female Progressive reformers, especially those influenced by the settlement movement and in particular by Jane Addams's practices of pragmatism,[3] contended that new democratic citizens had to be forged if twentieth-century social problems were to be addressed effectively. Industrialization, urbanization, and the shift toward the provision of many traditional household goods and services outside the home challenged older ideas of self-reliance and rugged individualism. Reformers argued that provisions for food safety, health, sanitation, water, light, and the protection of children and homes could be better arranged collectively. Just as many urban homes shared walls, the fortunes of Americans were increasingly interlinked.[4] For Addams, the forms of social action that women were promoting countered the male-dominated ethos of individual autonomy that had prevailed in the nineteenth century, and embraced the interdependent society that was fast emerging as a matter of fact.[5] In the words of one female Chicago reformer, "Individuals are so interrelated and dependent that each one depends on the rest for obtaining his own ends."[6] Even many philanthropic activities that had been the purview of late-nineteenth-century women were becoming matters of public concern, and women who clung (mistakenly, in Addams's view) to traditional notions of domesticity were left "in a household of constantly narrowing interests."[7] The world was opening to the concerns of women, and it was drawing women out of the confines in which they had pursued those concerns in the past. Just as clinging to outmoded notions of women's place in the domestic sphere was inappropriate, the expression of individual self-interest was no longer a viable expression of citizenship.[8] For Addams, such obsolete ideas perpetuated "a great deal of wrong."[9]

The female reformers linked to Addams and to the settlement movement were hardly alone in stressing the obsolescence of the individual as a force in modern democratic politics. Mass-membership organizations such as the General Federation of Women's Clubs and the National American Woman Suffrage Association were already networking across the nation, and theories linking associational activity to democracy were not far behind. Arthur Bentley's *The Process of Government* (1908) characterized the nation "as made up of groups of men [*sic*], each group cutting across many others, each individual man a component part of very many groups." Groups, not individuals, were perceived as the raw material of political life, and ideas and feelings were understood as social.[10] Collective solutions to social problems were increasingly viewed as more ethically advanced than individualistic ones, and the state itself was approached as an important association that could be usefully deployed to address social problems.[11]

Reformers' sense that new democratic citizens had to be forged along lines of association and collaboration was further shaped by the presence of immigrants from the many nations flooding into cities in the several decades before World War I. The development of urban ethnic neighborhoods in proximity to downtowns and to established bourgeois neighborhoods highlighted differences between them. In this changing environment, a number of turn-of-the-century middle-class female reformers, including those involved in the juvenile court movement, immigrant protection, child labor legislation, the unionization of female workers, and suffrage movements, worked alongside other women—and sometimes men—with very different experiences and backgrounds from their own.

For these reformers, wider experience "becomes the source and expression of social ethics." In sharp contrast to other Progressives on the national stage, such as Teddy Roosevelt, whose vision of national community embraced eugenics, female reformers associated with the settlement movement tended to value the experiential and educational potential of interacting with multiple and diverse groups. To build this experience required open-minded and social scientific inquiry; democratic practitioners needed to understand the lives of diverse people with diverse experiences, as Addams put it, "not only in order to believe in their integrity, which is after all but the first beginnings of social morality, but in order to attain to any mental or moral integrity for ourselves or any such hope for society."[12] In Dewey's formulation, "the extension in space of the number of individuals who participate in an interest so that each has to refer his own action to that of others, and to consider the action of others to give point and direction to his own, is equivalent to the breaking down of those barriers of class, race, and national territory which kept men from perceiving the full import of their activity." With "more numerous and more varied points of contact" there is "a greater diversity of stimuli to which an individual has to respond."[13] And, for Addams, appreciation for varied perspectives and experiences required contact, understanding, sympathy, humility, discussion, and deliberation—both outside and inside political institutions.[14] The writings and practices of some of these reformers demonstrate a nuanced approach to diversity that undermines contemporary critics' blunt charge that all Progressives were wholly racist or inattentive to the value of ethnic and cultural pluralism.

This urban vision of interaction within and among diverse ethnic communities went hand in hand with the Progressive emphasis on developing state-of-the-art methods of data collection. Importantly, such data was not only to be used to promote policy goals. Rather, the process of its collection would foster a democratic spirit in and of itself. Through data collection, reformers would acquire knowledge and wider experience of their neighbors. It would encourage the breakdown of economic and social barriers that defined urban spaces. Hull-House residents and affiliates had engaged in data gathering since 1893. In that year, U.S. Bureau of Labor staff members joined Florence Kelly to collect data on their local community door-to-door, and in 1895 they produced the *Hull-House Maps and Papers*.[15] Turn-of-the-century women's organizations embraced data collection and the dissemination of reports in newspapers, journals, and pamphlets as a means of acquainting themselves and their communities with social problems in their backyards. As they did, their projects filled out an emerging vision of a more activist democratic governance. Inclusion demanded information; it "emphasized social science ideas and methods, organization, and collective responsibility for social conditions."[16]

Data collection was envisioned neither as a one-way dynamic nor as a single instance; it was to be part of an educational, interactive, and iterative process of mutual discovery. The self-expressed needs and interests of the people with whom the reformers met were expected to shape the reformers' own perceptions of problems and policy options. For those inspired by Addams, Dewey, and William James, inquiry, continually applied, would yield good policy choices, but for this practice to be successful, ongoing community relationships had to be maintained. Knowledge acquisition was a dynamic process, involving ongoing adjustment on the basis of experimentation and experience.[17]

According to urban female reformers of the settlement movements, engaging with the experiences and standpoints of others was the very means by which men and women would transform themselves civically and politically.

Interaction and deliberation might not make differences in goals and values disappear, but the experience of face-to-face communication would better teach each citizen, dynamically and incrementally, consideration for others' preferences. Addams and her contemporaries pressed for a sort of "strong democracy"—"civic activity [that] educates individuals how to think publicly as citizens." Put another way, creating new democratic citizens depended on personal interactions at the neighborhood level, on building social capital and trust face to face, and on facilitating "coordination and cooperation for mutual benefit."[18] Creating a decidedly *social* ethic was central to the task of fostering the development of new democratic citizens. Inclusion, respect, cooperation, and a sense of community were vital for Addams and her colleagues.

Given how things turned out, it is notable that reformers explicitly warned against imposing their own view of what was desirable or healthy on the communities under study; they knew that imposition would backfire and tempt failure. Hull-House is illustrative: when specially trained settlement residents offered local neighbors foods prepared according to the latest nutritional science at Hull-House's cooperative Diet Kitchen, the intended beneficiaries, with "wide diversity in nationality and inherited tastes," did not like the fare; a far more successful coffeehouse was substituted.[19] It is likely, then, that the continued engagement of Hull-House-inspired reformers in some of the public programs they helped create was strategic—an outgrowth of the belief that ongoing relationships with those the programs were designed to serve was necessary for what we might today refer to as constructing positive "feedback loops": experience, experimentation, practice, and dynamic knowledge production were part of the process of policy design. Hybrid governing arrangements were implicit in this iterative process. The case of Chicago's juvenile court, in which reformers incrementally designed experimental programs that succeeded in developing and modifying the court after its formal establishment, illustrates the dynamic that reformers sought.[20]

For these female reformers, forging new democratic citizenship required work at multiple levels. It involved the state, large-scale organizations, and interactions in the neighborhood. The approach here again was pragmatic. Rather than envisioning stark choices between state or nonstate action, or top-down versus grassroots efforts, these urban Progressives understood their objective as requiring all these approaches. Consequently, these reformers were not, in any simple sense, nationalist Progressives.[21] For them, the appropriate level of government to be applied to an identified social problem depended on the nature of the problem itself and the constitutionally plausible warrants for involving the national government. Since solutions to industrial and social problems were better and more ethically advanced when they were collective and associational rather than individualistic or laissez-faire, the state was often considered a desirable location for addressing them. The Progressive-era state had important roles to play in the democratic project: enabling concerted action to address poverty and social welfare needs through new institutions, policies, and resources, and suppressing harmful behaviors and practices through legislation and regulation.

What Became of This Vision?

Even when they were successful in creating new institutions and new policies, the vision of these female reformers was challenged on a number of fronts. Many of the difficulties encountered were what one might expect for any movement advocating social change. The problems identified were often too complex for the solutions devised. Resistance from oppositional forces and established institutions was often intense. Unexpected developments in the economy shifted the ground from under once well-positioned activists.[22]

But beyond these generic problems, Progressive women were plagued by specific tensions internal to the women's movement and to reform in Progressive-era America. Their democratic vision was undermined in part from within. First, there was a clash between a maternalist project for empowering women, on the one hand, and a parallel desire to forge rich collaborative relationships among citizens considered equal. The project not only was inspired by an ethic of sex difference, but also tended to reinforce a white, middle-class gender norm. The contention that a woman's perspective harbored the makings of a new democracy unintentionally tended to lock many women into roles that limited their opportunities and discredited alternatives. Relatedly, the value these women ascribed to diversity, interaction, and learning was constantly challenged by their sense of what an advanced civilization should look like. In other words, these reformers were invested in a clear, substantive policy outcome even as they valued a radically new process of achieving that outcome. Ultimately, their preconceived substantive vision conflicted with the democratic and educational value that reformers placed on learning through interaction and data collection. Third, the project of empowering citizens stood in tension with other Progressive projects. While the maternalists adopted an instrumentalist view of the state, their ambitions were all too easily deflected and absorbed by other Progressive reformers whose goals more explicitly involved building and empowering the state.

The maternalist vision of democratic reform held no monopoly on Progressive ambitions. Different Progressive ideals were vying to shape the national political community and, with it, emerging political institutions and policy choices. While the pragmatist-inspired urban reformers emphasized local interaction as the route to social knowledge, other Progressives had a different understanding of good government and scientific management. Some proponents of Progressive democracy embraced a top-down approach, contending that concentrating power at the center was the most effective way to increase popular control over government.[23] Consequently, these urban reformers competed ideologically and politically not only with opponents but also with other Progressive forces. Agreement on the imperative to create a new democracy was far wider than agreement on exactly what it should look like and how it should be built.

Empowering Women with Maternalist Appeals Versus Forging Equal Citizenship

As they participated in identifying social problems and positioning themselves to become part of the solution, middle-class female reformers found new pathways to power. By developing specific expertise in particular policy domains through practice, research, and investigations, they created openings in local, state, and federal governments that they were uniquely suited to fill. For example, Julia Lathrop, one of the crusaders for the establishment of the Juvenile Court of Cook County, moved from local success to become, in 1912, the first head of the federal government's Children's Bureau. But women empowered to help shape social policy did not readily empower many women, especially those who were targets of social policies.

The maternalist approach has a complicated legacy. The reformers grounded their case in a claim that they brought different and vital perspectives and values to public life; their contribution to democratic governance was derived from their experiences, roles, and responsibilities within the family and the community.[24] By the last years of the nineteenth century, they had used new organizational models and employed home-extending metaphors to expand notions of public work and their own role in it.[25] Maternalists who read or knew about the work of Antoinette Brown Blackwell, Lester Ward, Patrick Geddes and J. Arthur Thomson, and William I. Thomas had been given reason to believe that among advanced civilizations, the female was not simply equal to the male but indeed the more highly evolved of the two sexes.

Evolution was supposedly tending toward "both social feeling and social organization"—functions in which women specialized.[26] Women needed at least to have an equal place in the public sphere because their skills were very much needed. Whether because of nature, experiences, or social roles, for many of these reformers, "it seemed perfectly clear that women were the only people in America capable of bringing about a new order in which democracy would find social as well as political expression."[27]

For Addams, men valued individualism and independence, while women gravitated toward social action and social consciousness. Women therefore stood in the vanguard of a more advanced democratic project. Women were associated with a more mature, social, and ethical democratic citizenship: "To attain individual morality in an age demanding social morality, to pride one's self on the results of personal effort when the time demands social adjustment, is utterly to fail to apprehend the situation."[28] In "If Men Were Seeking the Franchise," Addams argued, somewhat playfully, that women would want to consider carefully the male proclivity for destructive military ventures and expenditures and for celebrating individual competition and unbridled capitalism. Blame for the social and industrial ills of the city and for the failure to address the problems of immigrants and industrial workers could be laid at the feet of men. Women were community builders and nurturers, and were more committed than men to education, industrial safety, and social welfare.[29]

Addams's aspirations for developing collaborative and respectful processes for building a social ethic among equals did not mesh well, however, with maternalist imagery about care, nurture, and dependency, all of which conjured up asymmetrical relationships between unequals. Consequently, maternalism of this sort carried potential challenges for the goal of forging an inclusive community of equal democratic citizens. While arguments about what women could distinctively contribute to government and society played a role in their successes, such claims also erected barriers to inclusiveness for some women and helped inscribe dependency relations into social policy formation and implementation.

State recognition of the public contributions made by mothers and mothering, and more generally of the importance of family to the state, has been claimed as an important factor in the establishment of robust welfare states.[30] Yet some early-twentieth-century policies reinforced traditional gender roles and, with them, working-class women's economic dependence on men and on the state. Maternalism defined female recipients of governmental assistance as dependents. Mothers' pensions or family pensions, for example, administered through juvenile courts at least through the 1920s, were usually conditioned on female domesticity—providing the in-home service of raising the next generation of citizens—and were awarded or withheld according to how well women conformed to middle-class expectations of worthy behavior. Progressive reformers often touted these pensions as ushering in a new, enlightened era of family-centered policy and of recognition of the work that women performed for the state.[31] The policy was designed to enable women "to *care* for their families and not, by and large, to *provide* for them in the sense that is expected of a breadwinner." American social policy helped maintain these relations of dependency as well as women's "secondary role in financial provision."[32]

From mothers' pensions to social programs such as Aid to Dependent Children (later, Aid to Families with Dependent Children), maternalism has been charged with subjecting beneficiaries to degrees and forms of social control that those who are fully citizens do not, and should not, experience.[33] While some scholars do not find deliberate intent in the gender and race patterning of New Deal social programs, nevertheless, "public policies and institutional arrangements organize the citizenry and shape the meaning and character of citizenship."[34] Women who claimed that their special provenance derived from their identity and abilities as nurturers transposed the mother-child bond to other categories of vulnerable people (new immigrants, the poor) whose problems required public attention. Even if reformers viewed dependency as temporary, images and rhetoric of maternalism helped them impose middle-class, Victorian norms on other people in a manner inconsistent with empowering equal citizens.[35] Maternalism reinforced tiered citizenship and paved the way for more privileged women, by speaking authoritatively for the interests of others, to approximate the political prerogatives of white males.[36]

Treating the supposed beneficiaries of policies as children or dependents had material consequences. One stark example was found with female reformers involved in fieldwork to make Indians into "men." During the Dawes Act era (1887–1934), these reformers frequently spoke and thought of American Indians as their children or babies. Women such as Alice Fletcher were treated as authorities by friends of the American Indians back East because she had worked in the field, ostensibly on their behalf.[37] The consent of these native peoples was not essential to the policies imposed on men, women, and children alike because children did not understand what was in their best interest. Whether it was removal of the young to boarding schools, forced allotments, bans on certain tribal rituals, the undermining of tribal governance, or instruction in how to live in proper single-family homes, reformers had considerable capacity to punish or to provide benefits, depending on compliance. Policies that enforced compliance with notions of home and family imported from middle-class urban reform circles contributed to death, destitution, and decline among many American Indian communities in the Progressive era.[38]

Valuing Diversity Versus Embracing Certainty of Direction and Goals

It was an ironic twist. Progressive women, who believed they represented the ethical advance guard of civilization, were seeking to combat an outmoded individualism; autonomous selves were to become interdependent and social. In principle, association and collaboration were to inspire action. But the danger in attacking claims to individual autonomy was that it could easily open onto remedies that were socially coercive, and Progressive women were not well prepared to resist that alternative. Their rhetorical and, in some cases, actual commitment to becoming more informed about ethnic and cultural diversity clashed with their simultaneous acceptance of a defined civilized ideal of familial relations. And many female reformers therefore became part of a state-building project that would discipline the nation along "the model of sober, white, native-born, Protestants."[39] From this perspective, Progressive-era women's political projects that included reforming working-class behaviors and mores were directed more toward conformity with prevailing norms than toward developing empathy and understanding for the values, histories, and traditions of others.

Settlement-influenced female reformers valued diversity, but that value was romanticized, and when pursuing the substantive goals in which they had the most confidence, their actual respect for diversity was quite limited. To be sure, their maternalist arguments were grounded in a claim about the importance of incorporating different perspectives. And they routinely included newcomers and workingmen and workingwomen in their vision of a new democratic public. Addams, in particular, urged the preservation of newcomers' cultural arts and community networks of care; the latter represented primitive manifestations of the social ethic she expected the larger community—with the aid of women—to embrace. Older generations were encouraged to preserve and transmit traditions that younger members of immigrant communities were eager to forget in their drive to Americanize, and Hull-House reformers believed that maintenance of ethnic communal and familial ties could keep the young from running headlong into urban temptations and vices. When these reformers turned to the state to bring its resources to bear on problems of national scope, they sought ways to include the voices and perspectives of those with whom they interacted.

But these were self-assured women, and they had standards of their own. Their faith in progress was not only strongly gendered but also strongly racialized. Progress was largely a white affair.[40] In the prevailing view of the period, advanced peoples were Caucasian; progress was driven by those who had succeeded rather than by the more "barbaric races."[41] Having faith that their social ethic represented the highest stage of civilization, many Hull-House Progressives had a certainty of vision; they believed they were natural leaders forward. If exposure to diversity broadened sympathy and understanding for the experiences, problems, and perspectives of others and expanded the horizons of all (including reformers), gendered and racialized visions of citizenship too frequently led to positing, rather than hearing and comprehending, the interests of others.

For example, the Immigrants' Protective League, under the leadership of Grace Abbott, participated in a successful crusade to put immigrant banks and fringe banks out of business in Chicago in the name of protecting vulnerable immigrants. The reformers not only addressed the real abuses brought to their attention but also curtailed the provision of many financial services accessed by the poor at a time when established banks maintained inconvenient hours, lacked foreign-language employees, were located at a distance from immigrant communities, and often made immigrants feel unwelcome.[42] Postal savings banks, while safe places to deposit money, did not provide the same range of services as immigrant banks.

There was little pushback from other segments of the reform community. Other Progressives, as discussed in the chapter by Nicole Mellow, were even less interested in enriching the polity with diverse experiences. The case for diversity ran up against the more general view that progress hinged on creating a more knowledgeable and rational citizenry. There was "no safe or sound democracy which is not based upon an educated, intelligent electorate."[43] Continuing waves of immigration from southern and eastern Europe could pose a direct challenge to those working for progress. "Backward" newcomers who retained so-called Old World attitudes were perceived as a threat to reform's larger goals. Especially when possessed of the ballot, immigrant males could thwart reform projects.[44] Each new wave of immigrants required remedial work. A more enlightened democratic citizenship, then, might be possible only by excluding undesirables from American shores or the ballot. Addams's ideal position—that diversity was vital to democratic citizenship—was, by the second decade of the twentieth century, becoming a minority position within the larger Progressive movement.

Empowering Citizens Versus Empowering the State

Among the most important tensions for female Progressives inspired by Addams and Dewey was that between the turn toward the national state for solutions to many social and economic problems and the desire for vibrant, meaningful participation and interaction of diverse citizens at the grassroots. These reformers turned to the state while resisting bureaucratic claims to a kind of scientific expertise and efficiency divorced from the very people public officials were hired to serve.[45] For Dewey, "how we come to understand political problems and respond implied a kind of local knowledge and communal vision that is beyond the purview of experts."[46]

Learning through democratic experimentalism, monitoring results, and making incremental adjustments was part of the idealized process of governing. The local, state, and national policy initiatives that Addams and her associates spearheaded were experiments; they were observed, adjusted, and copied as appropriate across jurisdictions and across issue areas. Local reformers shared and borrowed one another's policy ideas. They also developed and field-tested several new institutions, funding and staffing prototypes for what would become the Juvenile Court of Cook County and the federal immigration station near the primary train station at which immigrants arrived in Chicago.[47] The Illinois Juvenile Court Act, enacted in 1899, was amended repeatedly on the basis of reformers' experience during the court's first decade.[48] Lines of responsibility were often elided as state and nonstate actors participated in building this institution. Long-term collaboration—in the community and with state authorities—was necessary to create deliberative, evolving, problem-solving institutions.[49]

But many Progressive reformers and intellectuals considered the engine of progress to be driven by professionalism, objectivity, and new social scientific knowledge unencumbered by lay input. The desire to insulate government, skilled experts, and bureaucrats from popular pressure grew out of a strain of thinking about what constituted knowledge acquisition, and how it related to democracy and progress, that was very different from Addams's vision for participatory democracy in the neighborhood and within government. The Progressives who put their faith in experts were potentially at odds with those who celebrated the rise of organized groups and looked to them for help in designing and administering social policy.

Rather than empower a democratic public, processes of knowledge acquisition developed by urban reformers could unwittingly bolster the control that bureaucrats or experts had over policy decisions. As Hull-House activists—often college-educated women with developing social scientific skills—collected data and wrote reports to broaden their understanding of the problems faced by their fellow citizens and neighbors, they sought to persuade others that public action to alleviate these public problems was necessary. But they also contributed to the modern state's capacity to see and control categories of people.[50] While the interactive process could foster relations on the ground in line with urban reformers' robust localist democratic vision, the data produced from these interactions could and would be used in efforts to expand bureaucratic control and regulation. In naming new public problems and working to frame them, these women were not just engaged in a project of expanding state activity into new arenas. The work they did helped emerging institutions and actors within them "see" like a state. They were part of a modern state-building project of making unruly and inconvenient subjects legible and manageable.[51]

These women expanded mechanisms of governance, too, by entering homes and tenements in the private sphere, where men could not readily go, to collect information about family members and their habits.[52] This move was facilitated by the efforts that Addams and her contemporaries had made to shift political discourse by telling new stories about the porous borders between public and private spaces and about the role of women's skills, traditional areas of expertise, and "brooms" in a shifting public space.[53] The reform movement that created the nation's first juvenile court, in Cook County, Illinois, affords a good example. Progressive reform women implemented (and for a while funded) a system of paid and volunteer probation officers (many of whom were women), who assisted the court by entering homes and tenements and collecting data. They recommended which children should be removed from homes, determined who was a fit parent, and attempted to regulate habits, behaviors, and living arrangements. Parents or guardians who allowed young people to frequent poolrooms, bars, dance halls, or to roam the streets could be legally deemed guilty of neglect, as could those too poor to provide for their young. Such a judgment brought them within the purview of the juvenile court system.[54] Although the juvenile court movement emphasized supervision and rehabilitation of the young and their separation from the adversarial criminal justice system, the reform agenda fit equally well into the effort to expand the reach of the law and the administrative state by extending legal supervision to older youth and even to parents and guardians.

Reformers were overly optimistic about the prospects of making institutions dynamic, flexible, and responsive. New public policies and programs created bureaucracies, constituencies, and stakeholders, further complicating the kind of experimentation and knowledge building that Addams and Dewey envisioned. Not only were participation, feedback loops, and iterative processes for adjustment to new evidence at odds with emerging bureaucratic rules and regulations, but the data gathered from these processes also produced opportunities for regulatory expansion. And the solutions chosen to address social problems established path-dependent trajectories that made change difficult. These policies became sticky over time, gathering entrenched interests, and chances for innovation waned.

Progressive Resonance: Ongoing Work and Promising Rediscoveries

The female reformers' vision succumbed to the limitations of its agents, and it was in many ways in advance of their actual practice, but it continues to inspire. Despite the tensions and shortfalls, the relevance and appeal of parts of this reform aspiration have never been completely extinguished. The reformers' focus on the interrelationships among gender, citizenship, and inclusion, and their interest in flexible institutions, can inform efforts at innovation today.

First, though maternalist rhetoric declined after women gained the franchise, the differences between men and women that Addams playfully tweaked did not disappear. Even before the gender gap emerged in voting behavior, many surveys picked up a persistent gender difference in public policy preferences. Regardless of whether these differences are essentialist or normatively constructed over time, women are consistently found to be somewhat more supportive than men of government spending for social welfare, education, health care, and regulation of unsafe practices; women are less inclined to support the death penalty, the unregulated accessibility of firearms, recent wars, and the use of force more generally.[55] More than their male counterparts, they continue to support key aspects of the social welfare state, much in the way Addams suggested they did a century ago. One reason advanced for why these gendered preferences are not reflected in political agendas in the contemporary era is the failure of women's organizations to mobilize around females' sentiments on these issues, alongside a decline of the kinds of nationally organized, participatory, mass-membership organizations that prevailed a century ago.[56] Women remain underrepresented in elective office, and many governmental policies better reflect men's than women's preferences, so gender continues to be linked to power and policy choices. There is still much that women, mobilized around gendered perspectives, can accomplish.

We are beginning to understand, however, just how much deeper the problem of inclusion reaches. The early-twentieth-century effort to shift public and private boundaries and include women's historic interests and concerns in the public sphere encountered formidable resistance. What recent feminist scholars have seen, and what perhaps Addams and her allies did not, is how much women's absence from the public sphere was due to the limits of liberalism and not simply to "the misogynist prejudices of early modern moral and political theory." Building a national political community entailed challenging public-private boundaries, but the sphere of discourse that Addams and her supporters embraced—one that associates the female with the realm of nature, the household, and the private sphere—maintains gendered notions of individual autonomy in ways that underpin modern liberalism. Individualism has remained more resilient than Progressives expected, and the sphere of care and child work still remains largely outside the realm of politics.[57] The inability of female reformers and fellow travelers to more fully displace these boundaries—despite their new narratives about public work—meant that the prospects of Progressive reform would likewise remain constrained.[58]

Moving to the institutional side, it is becoming increasingly clear that centralization generates challenges for building a vibrant democratic community of the sort envisioned by Progressive women. The dominant narrative about the transition from the nineteenth- to the twentieth-century state is of a shift in power from states to the national government and from private and voluntary activity to public and governmental responsibility. And yet the New Deal state hardly absorbed all private or voluntary initiatives, and may even be seen as another variant on a historical pattern of "intermingling of state and private means of extending public authority."[59] In other words, rediscovering the original Progressive commitment to public-private partnerships, one that was perhaps most fully embraced by female reformers, is crucial to revitalizing contemporary progressivism and challenging the persistent conservative critique of modern liberalism as being capable only of turning to the state. While political conservatives imagine themselves as the champions of current proposals for public-private partnerships, room remains for modern progressives to rethink possibilities for collaboration between state institutions and nonstate organizations. If the role of such collaborations during the Progressive era and other periods of American history is better understood, then their potential benefits and liabilities in state building and governance today may be more fully assessed.

Indeed, some of the ideas and approaches of the early Progressive female reformers are being rediscovered. A new generation of reformers, critical of unresponsive, inflexible public responses to large-scale problems such as the environment and the criminal justice system, has found much to appreciate in the kinds of reforms undertaken by Progressives a century ago.[60] The earlier reformers sought to foster opportunities for experimentation and knowledge building that included learning from programs' participants and beneficiaries, and from incorporating public-private partnerships in institution building. Their twenty-first-century heirs find evidence that these earlier reformers had some success in maintaining the accountability of local public officials and of community service providers, and that programs can respond effectively to local diversity.[61] In the face of recent efforts to defund and dismantle the social welfare state, experimental institutional innovations are being quietly initiated. Alternative courts for drug offenders, new community courts, human-trafficking courts, veterans' courts, teen courts with peer judges, and new problem-solving courts, all with expanded intervention options, have begun to flourish.[62] Participants consent to participate in alternative courts rather than courts that would normally have jurisdiction over the offense in question. These initiatives have begun both because traditional solutions to social problems were not working and because institutions themselves were seen to be incapable of innovation. Some argue that consumers of services should be included in coproducing such services, since consumers have unique understandings of particular and local circumstances that should be taken into account if those services are to be useful to them.[63] There is more we stand to learn by revisiting some of the social program efforts launched by the pragmatic women of the Progressive era—not just about designing effective policies but also in nourishing the growth of active citizen stakeholders.

Progressivism promised more than it could deliver,[64] and Addams's vision was no exception. She put great stock in the capacity of ordinary people, working with their neighbors, to forge a democratic citizenry that would work to build an enlightened polity. But the follow-through was disappointing.

Ultimately, shortfall is engrained in all reform projects. It is hardly surprising that the reform ideas of a century ago ran into difficulties, that their achievements were limited, or that their implementation failed to conform to our own more enlightened views. What is remarkable is the extent to which we are still grappling with the tensions and trade-offs that they encountered, and what is most astounding of all is just how vibrant and relevant their most advanced ideas remain. In our day, with progressivism under siege, it is more important than ever to recall the democratic aspirations of Progressive-era women, for many of their ideals are still very much worth pursuing.

Notes

Thanks to Stephen Skowronek, Bruce Ackerman, Stephen Engel, and participants in the Yale conference on the Progressives' century, November 1–2, 2013, and especially to Stephen Engel and Stephen Skowronek for invaluable comments on a draft of this paper.

1. On women's roles in creating modern social policy, see Theda Skocpol, *Protecting Soldiers and Mothers* (Cambridge, Mass.: Belknap Press, 1992); Theda Skocpol, Marjorie Abend-Wein, Christopher Howard, and Susan Goodrich Lehmann, "Women's Associations and the Enactment of Mothers' Pensions in the United States," *American Political Science Review* 87, no. 3 (September 1993): 686–701; contributions by Kathryn Kish Sklar and Sonya Michels in *Mothers of a New World: Maternalist Politics and the Origins of Welfare States*, ed. Seth Koven and Sonya Michel (New York: Routledge, 1993); Virginia Sapiro, "The Gender Basis of American Social Policy," *Political Science Quarterly* 101, no. 2 (1986): 221–38; Paula Baker, "The Domestication of Politics: Women in American Political Society, 1780–1920," *American Historical Review* 89, no. 3 (1984): 620–47.

2. On boundary construction as a social process, see Charles Tilly, *Stories, Identities, and Political Change* (Lanham, Md.: Rowman and Littlefield, 2002), 11.

3. I refer to Addams's practices rather than Dewey's writings. For Addams's influence on Dewey, see Louis Menand, *The Metaphysical Club: A Story of Ideas in America* (New York: Farrar, Straus and Giroux, 2001), 310–16; and Charlene Haddock Seigfried, *Pragmatism and Feminism* (Chicago: University of Chicago Press, 1996), 29–30, 45, 48–49, 58–66, 73–78.

4. Charlotte Perkins Gilman, *The Home: Its Work and Influence* (New York: Source Book, 1970 [1903]), 330–35.

5. Jane Addams, *Twenty Years at Hull House* (New York: Macmillan, 1923 [1910]), chap. 18; Addams, *Democracy and Social Ethics*, ed. Anne Firor Scott (Cambridge, Mass.: Belknap Press, 1964 [1902]), 86.

6. Jessie Taft, *The Woman Movement from the Point of View of Social Consciousness* (Chicago: University of Chicago Press, 1916), 49. Taft had earned a University of Chicago Ph.D. under the direction of George Herbert Mead.

7. Jane Addams, "Why Women Should Vote," *Ladies' Home Journal* 27, no. 1 (January 1910), 21 (reprinted in pamphlet form, New York: National American Woman Suffrage Association, 1912, 14); Addams, "Philanthropy and Politics," *Ladies' Home Journal* 30, no. 1 (January 1913), 25.

8. Carol Nackenoff, "New Politics for New Selves: Jane Addams's Legacy for Democratic Citizenship in the Twenty-First Century," in *Jane Addams and the Practice of Democracy*, ed. Marilyn Fischer, Carol Nackenoff, and Wendy Chmielewski (Chicago: University of Illinois Press, 2009), 119–42, quotation on 119.

9. Addams's Iowa College lectures on "ethical survivals," delivered in March 1898, quoted by Louise Knight, *Citizen: Jane Addams and the Struggle for Democracy* (Chicago: University of Chicago Press, 2005), 398.

10. Arthur Bentley, *The Process of Government* (Evanston: Principia Press of Illinois, 1949 [1908, 1935]), 204.

11. Brian Balogh, *A Government Out of Sight: The Mystery of National Authority in Nineteenth-Century America* (Cambridge: Cambridge University Press, 2009), chap. 9, especially 352–55; Arthur F. Bentley, *The Process of Government*, ed. Peter H. Odegard (Cambridge, Mass.: Belknap Press, 1967 [1908]), 199, 262. Bentley did not draw a sharp distinction between government and other forms of social activity.

12. Addams, *Democracy and Social Ethics*, 11, 176, quotation at 177.

13. John Dewey, *Democracy and Education* (New York: Macmillan, 1920 [1916]), 101.

14. On deliberation and participation inside bureaucratic institutions, see Camilla Stivers, *Bureau Men, Settlement Women: Constructing Public Administration in the Progressive Era* (Lawrence: University Press of Kansas, 2000).

15. *Hull-House Maps and Papers: A Presentation of Nationalities and Wages in a Congested District of Chicago* (Boston: Crowell, 1895) was the Chicago portion of a national study commissioned by Congress of the slums of four major cities.

16. Baker, "Domestication of Politics," 641.

17. Carol Nackenoff, "The Private Roots of American Political Development: The Immigrants' Protective League's 'Friendly and Sympathetic Touch,' 1908–1924," *Studies in American Political Development* 28, no. 2 (Fall 2014): 129–60; Erik Schneiderhan, "Pragmatism and Empirical Sociology: The Case of Jane Addams and Hull-House, 1889–1895," *Theory and Society* 40 (2011): 609.

18. Benjamin R. Barber, *Strong Democracy: Participatory Politics for a New Age* (Berkeley: University of California Press, 1984), 152–53; Robert D. Putnam, "The Prosperous Community: Social Capital and Public Life," *American Prospect* 13 (Spring 1993): 35, 40; Putnam, *Bowling Alone: The Collapse and Revival of American Community* (New York: Simon & Schuster, 2000).

19. Addams, *Twenty Years at Hull-House*, 131; Schneiderhan, "Pragmatism and Empirical Sociology," 608–9.

20. Nackenoff, "Roots of American Political Development"; Carol Nackenoff and Kathleen S. Sullivan, "The House that Julia (and Friends) Built: Networking Chicago's Juvenile Court," in *Statebuilding from the Margins: Between Reconstruction and the New Deal*, ed. Carol Nackenoff and Julie Novkov (Philadelphia: University of Pennsylvania Press, 2014), 171–202.

21. On nationalist Progressives, see Marc Stears, *Progressives, Pluralists, and the Problems of the State: Ideologies of Reform in the United States and Britain, 1909–1926* (Oxford: Oxford University Press, 2002). A number of chapters in Nackenoff and Novkov, *Statebuilding from the Margins*, focus on the development of institutions at the state level during the late nineteenth and early twentieth centuries.

22. Skocpol, *Protecting Soldiers and Mothers*, 527.

23. Walter E. Weyl, *The New Democracy* (New York: Macmillan, 1912), 159.

24. Alice Paul's crusade for equal rights starting in the 1910s stands as an exception; see Christine A. Lunardini, *From Equal Suffrage to Equal Rights: Alice Paul and the National Woman's Party, 1910–1928* (New York: New York University Press, 1986).

25. See Elisabeth S. Clemens, "Organizational Repertoires and Institutional Change: Women's Groups and the Transformation of U.S. Politics, 1890–1920," *Journal of Sociology* 98 (January 1993): 755–98; Robyn Muncy, *Creating a Female Dominion in American Reform, 1890–1935* (New York: Oxford University Press, 1991); Daphne Spain, *How Women Saved the City* (Minneapolis: University of Minnesota Press, 2001); Carol Nackenoff, "Gendered Citizenship: Alternative Narratives of Political Incorporation in the United States, 1875–1925," in *The Liberal Tradition in American Politics*, ed. David F. Ericson and Louisa Bertch Green (New York: Routledge, 1999), 137–69.

26. See Rosalind Rosenberg, "In Search of Woman's Nature," *Feminist Studies* 3 (Fall 1975): 141–54; Patrick Geddes and J. Arthur Thomson, *The Evolution of Sex* (London: Walter Scott, 1889).

27. Jill Ker Conway, "Women Reformers and American Culture, 1870–1930," *Journal of Social History* 5 (Winter 1971–72): 164–77.

28. Addams, *Democracy and Social Ethics*, 86, quotation at 2–3; Addams, *Twenty Years at Hull-House*, chap. 18.

29. Addams, "If Men Were Seeking the Franchise," *Ladies' Home Journal* 30, no. 6 (June 1913), 21.

30. Eileen McDonagh, "Ripples from the First Wave: The Monarchical Origins of the Welfare State," *Perspectives on Politics* 13 (2015): 992–1016; and McDonagh, *The Motherless State* (Chicago: University of Chicago Press, 2009).

31. Sapiro, "Gender Basis of American Social Policy," 221–38; Frederic C. Howe and Marie Jenney Howe, "Pensioning the Widow and the Fatherless," *Good Housekeeping*, September 1913, 282–91; Kathleen S. Sullivan and Carol Nackenoff, "Family

Matters as Public Work: Reformers' Dreams for the Progressive Era Juvenile Court," paper presented at the 2013 meeting of the American Political Science Association, Chicago.

32. Sapiro, "Gender Basis of American Social Policy," 224–25, 230–31, 235, quotations at 231 and 235. See also Susan M. Sterett, *Public Pensions: Gender and Civic Service in the States, 1850–1937* (Ithaca, N.Y.: Cornell University Press, 2003), 127; Sonya Michel, *Children's Interests, Mothers' Rights: The Shaping of America's Child Care Policy* (New Haven, Conn.: Yale University Press, 1999), 3.

33. Gwendolyn Mink, *The Wages of Motherhood: Inequality in the Welfare State, 1917–1942* (Ithaca, N.Y.: Cornell University Press, 1995), 8.

34. Suzanne Mettler, *Dividing Citizens: Gender and Federalism in New Deal Public Policy* (Ithaca, N.Y.: Cornell University Press, 1998).

35. Peggy Pascoe, *Relations of Rescue: The Search for Female Moral Authority in the American West, 1874–1939* (New York: Oxford University Press, 1990).

36. Nackenoff, "Gendered Citizenship," 165; Pascoe, *Relations of Rescue*.

37. Alice Fletcher was one prominent figure who used such language in the late 1800s; see Joan Mark, *A Stranger in Her Native Land* (Lincoln: University of Nebraska Press, 1988).

38. Carol Nackenoff, "Constitutionalizing Terms of Inclusion: Friends of the Indian and Citizenship for Native Americans, 1880s–1930s," in *The Supreme Court and American Political Development*, ed. Ronald Kahn and Ken I. Kersch (Lawrence: University Press of Kansas, 2006), 366–413.

39. Ken I. Kersch, *Constructing Civil Liberties: Discontinuities in the Development of American Constitutional Law* (Cambridge: Cambridge University Press, 2004), 28, quotation at 75.

40. In *Race, Hull-House, and the University of Chicago* (Westport, Conn.: Praeger, 2002), Mary Jo Deegan notes the persistence of a color line at Hull-House: the "Hull-House life and worldview" was "neither particularly comfortable nor welcoming to black Americans" (38). Gail Bederman emphasizes the role that Charlotte Perkins Gilman played in this discourse; she "magnified the importance of race to civilization and minimized the importance of gender"; Bederman, *Manliness and Civilization: A Cultural History of Race in the United States, 1880–1917* (Chicago: University of Chicago Press, 1995), 44.

41. Rosenberg, "In Search of Woman's Nature," 142–44.

42. Mehrsa Baradaran, "How the Poor Got Cut Out of Banking," *Emory Law Journal* 62 (2013): 483–548; Jared N. Day, "Credit, Capital and Community: Informal Banking in Immigrant Communities in the United States, 1880–1924," *Financial History Review* 9 (April 2002): 65–78; see also Grace Abbott, "Report of the Director," in *Sixth Annual Report of the Immigrants' Protective League: For the Year Ending January 1st, 1915* (Chicago: Immigrants' Protective League, 1915), available from the Internet Archive, http://archive.org/details/annualreportofim1919091917immi.

43. Carrie Chapman Catt, Presidential Address, International Woman Suffrage Alliance, Geneva, Switzerland, June 1920, quoted in Ida Husted Harper, *History of Woman Suffrage* (New York: National American Woman Suffrage Association, 1922), 6:861.

44. Even Addams was not above making the instrumental argument for women's suffrage in congressional testimony: enfranchising women would provide a counterweight to immigrant male voting, and immigrant women were unlikely to vote in large numbers; Addams, Testimony before the House Committee on the Judiciary, March 13, 1912, 77. She added that she was "not one of the people who believe that the immigrant vote is a vote to be feared."

45. Camilla Stivers, *Bureau Men, Settlement Women,* chap. 4; Stivers, "A Civic Machinery for Democratic Expression," in *Jane Addams and the Practice of Democracy,* ed. Marilyn Fisher, Carol Nackenoff, and Wendy Chmielewski (Urbana: University of Illinois Press, 2009), 87–97.

46. Melvin L. Rogers, "Introduction: Revisiting the Public and Its Problems," *Contemporary Pragmatism* 7 (June 2010).

47. On the juvenile court, see Nackenoff and Sullivan, "The House that Julia Built," 201–2; on the Immigrants' Protective League, see Nackenoff, "Roots of American Political Development."

48. David S. Tanenhaus, *Juvenile Justice in the Making* (New York: Oxford University Press, 2004); Michael Willrich, *City of Courts: Socializing Justice in Progressive Era Chicago* (Cambridge: Cambridge University Press, 2003).

49. Michael C. Dorf and Charles F. Sabel, "A Constitution of Democratic Experimentalism," *Columbia Law Review* 98, no. 2 (March, 1998): 322. The argument about reformers' sense of ownership and desire to remain involved in the juvenile court is made in Nackenoff and Sullivan, "The House that Julia Built."

50. James C. Scott, *Seeing Like a State: How Certain Schemes to Improve the Human Condition Have Failed* (New Haven, Conn.: Yale University Press, 1998).

51. Ibid.*;* Kersch, *Constructing Civil Liberties,* 30.

52. See Patricia Strach and Kathleen Sullivan, "The State's Relations: What the Institution of Family Tells Us about Governance," *Political Research Quarterly* 64 (March 2011): 94–106.

53. See Nackenoff, "Roots of American Political Development." On the role of stories in contesting political borders and boundaries, see Charles Tilly, *Stories, Identities, and Political Change* (Lanham, Md.: Rowman & Littlefield, 2002), 11–12.

54. See, for example, William H. DeLacy, "Functions of the Juvenile Court," *Annals of the American Academy of Political and Social Sciences* 36 (July 1910): 61–63; Grace Abbott, "Abstract of Juvenile Court Laws," appendix 3 in Sophonisba P. Breckinridge and Edith Abbott, *The Delinquent Child and the Home* (New York: Charities Publication Committee, Russell Sage Foundation, 1912), 255–56; appendix 6 in ibid., 334, 340.

55. See Kristin A. Goss and Theda Skocpol, "Changing Agendas: The Impact of Feminism on American Politics," in *Gender and Social Capital*, ed. Brenda O'Neill and Elisabeth Gidengil (New York: Routledge, 2006), 323–56. Robert Y. Shapiro and Harpreet Mahajan examined 267 repeat questions from a variety of surveys in "Gender Differences in Policy Preferences: A Summary of Trends from the 1960s to the 1980s," *Public Opinion Quarterly* 50, no. 1 (Spring 1986): 42–61.

56. Goss and Skocpol, "Changing Agendas," 324–25, 327, 341–46, 350–51. They claim that more recent women's groups have redefined women's issues narrowly, becoming more like single-issue advocacy groups with self-regarding agendas. The authors assert that women of the early twentieth century achieved suffrage and policy gains by speaking less self-interestedly (349).

57. See Seyla Benhabib, *Situating the Self: Gender, Community, and Postmodernism in Contemporary Ethics* (New York: Routledge, 1992), 157; Carole Pateman, *The Sexual Contract* (Stanford, Calif.: Stanford University Press, 1988); Christine DiStefano, *Configurations of Masculinity: A Feminist Perspective on Modern Political Theory* (Ithaca, N.Y.: Cornell University Press, 1991), chap. 3; Joan Tronto, *Moral Boundaries: A Political Argument for an Ethic of Care* (New York: Routledge, 1993); Nancy Hirschmann, "Freedom, Recognition, and Obligation: A Feminist Approach to Political Theory," *American Political Science Review* 83, no. 4 (1991): 1227–44.

58. See Eileen McDonagh and Carol Nackenoff, "Gender and the American State," in the *Oxford Handbook of American Political Development*, ed. Richard Valelly, Suzanne Mettler, and Robert Lieberman (Oxford University Press, 2016).

59. Balogh, *Government Out of Sight*, 354. An example of the argument that women developed social welfare programs and handed them off to the state is found in Baker, "Domestication of Politics." Elisabeth S. Clemens suggests that reasons for hybrid governing arrangements are inadequately captured by the argument that a weak state borrows capacity until it can take over programs ("Lineages of the Rube Goldberg State: Building and Blurring Public Programs, 1900–1940," in *Rethinking Political Institutions*, ed. Ian Shapiro, Stephen Skowronek, and Daniel Galvin [New York: New York University Press, 2006], 187–215).

60. Dorf and Sabel, "Constitution of Democratic Experimentalism," 267–473. Bureaucratic rationality tended to emphasize uniformity of policies and procedures. The kind of critique leveled against command-and-control environmental regulation of the "golden era" of the 1960s and 1970s is that rule-oriented regulatory policy is easier to administer and monitor but assumes that one size fits all, failing to take disparate situations and local knowledge into account; see Robert F. Durant, Daniel J. Fiorino, and Rosemary O'Leary, *Environmental Governance Reconsidered* (Cambridge, Mass.: MIT Press, 2004).

61. Dorf and Sabel, "Constitution of Democratic Experimentalism," 314.

62. On the drug courts, see Shelli B. Rossman, John K. Roman, Janine M. Zweig, Michael Rempel, and Christine H. Lindquist, *The Multi-Site Adult Drug Court*

Evaluation: Executive Summary (2011), available at the National Criminal Justice Reference Service website, https://www.ncjrs.gov/pdffiles1/nij/grants/237108.pdf. New juvenile justice alternatives attempt to move beyond several Supreme Court cases of the 1960s that triggered a procedural-due-process revolution for juveniles and generally made juvenile courts more formalistic.

63. Dorf and Sabel, "Constitution of Democratic Experimentalism," 317.

64. Michael McGerr makes this claim in *A Fierce Discontent: The Rise and Fall of the Progressive Movement in America, 1870–1920* (New York: Free Press, 2003), xiv.

11 • Progressivism, Liberalism, and the Rich
Michael McGerr

More than a century on, progressivism remains an intriguing mixture of conservatism and radicalism. At its core, the dynamic ideology that emerged out of the conditions of middle-class American life in the late nineteenth century strongly supported capitalism and an essentially Victorian culture. But to conserve those institutions and to promote a national community that embraced middle-class values, Progressives adopted an often radical reform agenda: a scathing assault on individualism, an eager pursuit of "association" across social dividing lines, a willingness to use governmental power aggressively in new ways, and a troubling determination to transform other Americans into middle-class beings by manipulating their physical and social environments. That agenda produced oft-celebrated campaigns to purify politics and control corporations. It also led to coercive crusades that many commentators have preferred to forget: campaigns against divorce, prostitution, alcohol, dancing, and on and on.[1] Twentieth-century liberalism, even as it adopted many Progressive goals and methods, mostly abandoned the intrusive desire to meddle in private life and make over social groups. Yet for decades, many liberals still clung to the Progressive belief in transforming the rich and thereby protecting the nation's identity.

This focus on the wealthiest Americans was crucial to Progressivism and liberalism alike: both effectively demonized the rich as alien beings who threatened the national community. More radical and more successful than we recognize, the campaign against great wealth produced a paradoxical denouement. By the 1940s, the liberals' crusade helped create the seemingly homogeneous, essentially middle-class national community they wanted. But by the end of the twentieth century, the liberals' very success undermined their vigilance against the threat of wealth, helped make the rich seem safely like other Americans, and, paradoxically, made a liberal governmental elite appear to be the true threat to national community. As a result, liberalism has, in recent years, proved too conservative and too ineffective against the continuing resurgence of great fortunes in the early twenty-first century.

The Assault on Hereditary Wealth

Progressivism rested on a sweeping indictment of the wealthiest Americans. As industrialization produced unprecedented fortunes after the Civil War, many people feared the rich not only for their economic and political power, but also for their cultural power and dynastic ambitions.

The example of one of the richest families conveys the multifaceted threat. By the mid-1870s, the willful, individualistic "Commodore" Cornelius Vanderbilt had become a railroad "king" by consolidating the New York Central and Hudson River Railroad and using it to put together a trunk line from New York City to Chicago. Vanderbilt's economic strength translated into substantial power over politicians and into the largest fortune—some $90 million—amassed in the United States up to that time. When he died in 1877, Americans discovered just how apt the title "king" really was. Like the monarchs of Europe, the Commodore wanted to pass on his "kingdom"—control of his railroads and almost all of his fortune—to his eldest son, William. This near primogeniture set off public controversy and a remarkable two-year court battle with some of William's siblings. But the legal system failed to stop the Commodore's dynastic plan; so did the State of New York and the federal government, which left his estate essentially untaxed.[2]

An astute businessman in his own right, William more than doubled his father's fortune, vastly expanded the Vanderbilts' railroad system, and extended the family's political operation, in part through his faithful servant Chauncey Depew, renowned orator, Republican warhorse, and fixer extraordinaire. Also dubbed a king, William inadvertently summed up the individualism of the rich with his off-the-cuff exclamation, "The public be damned!" Moreover, "William Vanderbilt Rex" established the Vanderbilts as a disturbing element in American culture by building a vast "triple palace" for himself and two daughters on Fifth Avenue, ostentatiously collecting art and prize horses, founding the Metropolitan Opera, and establishing the fashion for European vacations. King Vanderbilt made his family's dynastic pretentions unmistakably clear by adopting a coat of arms inspired by the Medici and installing each of two elder sons as "chairman of the board"—an alien position imported from Britain—of a major family railroad. "The Vanderbilt family have evidently come to the conclusion that the proper thing for them to do is to . . . become aristocrats on the English plan," the *St. Louis Globe-Democrat* observed in 1883. "The Vanderbilts are showing us how it is to be done."[3]

After William's death in 1885, his sons took up their grandfather's ambition; they also took up the family fortune, which was again essentially untaxed. Expanding the Vanderbilt system of railroads to more than fifteen thousand miles, Cornelius Vanderbilt II and William Kissam Vanderbilt kept the family fortune growing. Through their mouthpiece, Chauncey Depew, the president of the New York Central, who eventually became a senator from New York, they continued to exercise quietly effective political power. Along with their siblings, Cornelius II and William reveled in a lifestyle of aristocratic luxury and leisure. William was known for his very long vacations on board the *Valiant,* the largest private yacht in the world, which carried him to his residences in Scotland, London, Paris, and Normandy. A few of the Vanderbilt women wore crowns in public. The third generation of rich Vanderbilts was obsessed with copying the British nobility—a condition the press dubbed "Anglomania." The malady's chief expression was a series of magnificent country "seats" on the English plan, often including farms tilled by submissive workers: Cornelius II's Breakers in Newport, Rhode Island; William's Marble House in Newport and Idlehour on Long Island; younger brother Frederick's Hyde Park in Duchess County, New York; and youngest brother George III's fabulous Biltmore in Asheville, North Carolina. To make aristocratic ambition still more obvious, William's wife, Alva, married off their daughter Consuelo to the ninth Duke of Marlborough, master of the great Blenheim Palace, in a sensational Fifth Avenue wedding in 1895. That year, too, William and Alva divorced in a notorious front-page proceeding that scandalized the relatively divorce-free American public. "The social leprosy which lay at the foundation of the destruction of Greece and Rome and which has sapped the vitality of the nobility of France and England, is already discernible in this country," the *Atlanta Constitution* fumed after the Vanderbilt divorce. "It has made its appearance with the advent of the multi-millionaire."[4]

No matter: the Vanderbilts were well on their way to nobility. "The Vanderbilts are to all intents and purposes a feudal family," a society journal insisted. "Their control of railways and other corporations really amounts to that *imperium in imperio,* which feudal holding was. . . . The Vanderbilts have practically as much control over their vassals as had the Hapsburghs [sic] or Hohenzollerns in the middle age."[5]

That was what worried many Americans, including the emerging ranks of middle-class Progressives: the House of Vanderbilt, along with the Astors, the Goulds, the Whitneys, the Rockefellers, and the rest of the industrial super-rich, gave every sign of creating some sort of hereditary nobility in the heart of the United States. In 1904, *Everybody's Magazine* asked, "Is America Developing an Aristocracy?" It seemed so improbable; yet that was what rich people plainly intended. "America's resources and modern methods of wealth production shall build an aristocracy that shall outshine anything the world ever saw," one commentator foresaw. "Babylonian, Assyrian, Persian, Egyptian, Greek, Roman, Western European or Oriental aristocracy shall be fully compared with the American brand. . . . Such, at least, appear to be the fond hopes of the founders and heads of the modern 'houses.'" It was an appalling prospect. "The moral effect of all this is disastrous alike to rich and poor," moaned the *Chicago Journal* in 1907. "The division of young Americans into classes, and the upbuilding of social strata founded on wealth alone, is ruinous. The effect upon the real workers of this country, especially the underpaid, is discontent and radicalism. The effect upon the rich themselves is moral poverty, selfishness and arrogance." Along with the *Journal,* many Americans concluded, "The involuntary rich need to be saved from themselves."[6]

The question was how. In the first decade of the twentieth century, Progressives searched for weapons against the incipient industrial aristocracy. Unlike the poor, the rich made a difficult, privileged target. Progressive reformers could pass laws to improve working-class tenements in New York City, but they couldn't put limits on Cornelius Vanderbilt II's vast chateau, which took up one whole blockfront along Fifth Avenue. It was impossible to ban yachts, crowns, and so-called titled marriages. Some Progressives tried to stop divorce, but that campaign got nowhere, even as Vanderbilt marriages broke up so often that divorce became known as the "Vanderbilt curse." David Graham Phillips sensationally revealed Chauncey Depew's political service to the Vanderbilts—one of the Progressive writer's famous articles in the series "The Treason of the Senate"—but Depew kept his seat, along with his title as chairman of the board of the New York Central.[7]

In truth, there was only one device that struck simultaneously at the aristocratic ambition and the economic, political, and cultural power of the rich: taxation. A federal income tax, especially a graduated one that took a higher percentage of the largest incomes, had obvious attractions. But in 1895, the U.S. Supreme Court had struck down the relatively modest income tax enacted by Congress the year before. Not surprisingly, Progressives also looked to taxes on the estates of the rich and the inheritances of their legatees. For one thing, the Supreme Court hadn't ruled out such measures. In 1897, New York, home to more millionaires than any other state, enacted an estate tax; a year later, the federal government followed with a temporary transfer tax on estates to help pay for the Spanish-American War. But these two measures didn't take much from the rich. Authorities valued the estate of Cornelius Vanderbilt II, who died in 1899, at just under $73 million, but governments ended up taking less than $1 million.[8]

Undeterred, Progressives pushed for a federal inheritance or estate tax. Their most prominent convert was President Theodore Roosevelt. Like a number of mainstream politicians, Roosevelt was drawn to the Progressive agenda on practical and ideological grounds. There was a rather complicated personal dimension as well. Raised in the cradle of Anglomania on Fifth Avenue, Roosevelt came from the rich Knickerbocker elite who saw their fortunes surpassed by the landowning Astors and then the railroading Vanderbilts. Yet the newcomers weren't entirely alien beings. Cornelius Vanderbilt II, the Fifth Avenue neighbor whose interests spanned business, philanthropy, and the entertainments of fashionable society, was rather like Roosevelt's father, Theodore Sr. The future president was the renegade—a writer and politician. Although he loved the English sport of fox hunting and lived in an English-style country seat on Long Island, Roosevelt was, as early as the 1880s, a harsh critic of the "contemptible ... Anglomania at present prevailing in the higher circles." "Those who ape foreign customs, especially those of the European leisure class, can only excite our contempt," he declared in 1890.[9]

Roosevelt's critique of the culture and ambition of the Anglomaniacs, along with his worries about their economic and political power, led him to support income and inheritance taxes in conjunction with the regulation of railroads and the other economic legislation that made up his Square Deal. In his annual message to Congress in 1906, he called for a graduated inheritance tax aimed at "those swollen fortunes which it is certainly of no benefit to this country to perpetuate." A year later, Roosevelt elaborated on the case for keeping the rich from passing on much of their fortunes to their children. "No advantage," he declared, "comes either to the country as a whole or to the individuals inheriting the money by permitting the transmission in their entirety of the enormous fortunes which would be affected by such a tax; and ... such a tax would help to preserve a measurable equality of opportunity for the people of the generations growing to manhood." In his last message, in 1908, the president put the case against the inheritance of "great fortunes" more bluntly. "They rarely do good," he insisted, "and they often do harm to those who inherit them in their entirety."[10]

As Americans' fears about the power and ambition of the rich intensified, the Progressives' tax crusade won support from workers, farmers, and the middle class. In 1909, Roosevelt's successor, William Howard Taft, proposed the Sixteenth Amendment, legalizing the income tax. After its ratification in 1913, Congress followed immediately with the Revenue Act of 1913, which imposed a graduated income tax with a top rate of 7 percent on incomes above $500,000. The Revenue Act of 1916 raised the top rate to 15 percent on incomes above $2 million and implemented an estate tax with a top rate of 10 percent on estates valued at more than $5 million. Faced with paying for the nation's participation in World War I, Congress increased the estate tax's top rate to 25 percent the next year. By 1924, the top rate had reached a remarkable 40 percent on estates valued at more than $10 million.[11]

In all, the era of Progressive activism in the early twentieth century achieved a good deal. Although a conservative counterassault during the administration of Calvin Coolidge managed to reduce the rate to 20 percent, the estate tax became an enduring feature of public policy—and at a top rate far higher than the one imposed on the fortune of Cornelius Vanderbilt II. After the death of William K. Vanderbilt I in 1920, his estate paid about $12 million in taxes to the federal government and the states of New York and Pennsylvania on a fortune assessed at $54,530,000. Nevertheless, he had managed to shield much of his wealth by giving away tens of millions as "gifts" to his children in the years before his death. Thanks in part to this dodge, he was able to pass on diminished but effective control of the New York Central Railroad to his two sons, William K. Vanderbilt II and Harold Vanderbilt—the fourth generation of Vanderbilts to rule at Grand Central.[12]

From Progressivism to Liberalism

In critical respects, the New Deal liberalism of the 1930s and 1940s marked a basic shift from Progressivism. Progressives and their liberal successors shared a fundamental commitment to governmental involvement in the economy, to economic justice, and to political participation. But the liberalism that emerged in the Great Depression abandoned much of Progressivism, including the focus on regulating private behavior and transforming people. In 1933, the repeal of Prohibition, a quintessential Progressive measure, summed up the change. But there was a crucial exception: New Deal liberals renewed the Progressive campaign to transform the rich by taking as much of their money as possible. This adversarial toughness was not only a point of continuity between these two movements, but also a critical factor in their bid to define a national community. Committed to capitalism, liberals, like the Progressives, clarified their national political ambitions by confronting the disruptive power and ambition of the rich.

President Franklin Roosevelt, the leader of the New Deal, was rather like his cousin, the leader of the Square Deal. Here was another wealthy Knickerbocker who abandoned his forebears' interest in business, philanthropy, and high society for politics. And like Theodore, Franklin was contemptuous of the Anglomaniacal super-rich and their dynastic ambitions. Accepting the Democratic nomination for a second term in Philadelphia, in 1936, FDR scornfully linked the rich, would-be dynasts of the Industrial Revolution, to the traitorous Royalists who stayed loyal to the British Crown in the eighteenth century. "For out of this modern civilization economic royalists carved new dynasties," the president explained. "New kingdoms were built upon concentration of control over material things. Through new uses of corporations, banks and securities, new machinery of industry and agriculture, of labor and capital—all undreamed of by the fathers—the whole structure of modern life was impressed into this royal service." These new "royalists"—"the privileged princes of these new economic dynasties, thirsting for power"—controlled the government and denied equality and opportunity to the rest of the nation.[13]

Roosevelt's attack on the "economic royalists" resonated with the culture of Depression-era America. In his muckraking book *America's 60 Families*, the journalist Ferdinand Lundberg detailed the dynastic histories of the Vanderbilts, the Rockefellers, and the other super-rich. One Hollywood film after another—including *Love Among the Millionaires* (1930), *It Happened One Night* (1934), *Down to Their Last Yacht* (1934), *Soak the Rich* (1936), *My Man Godfrey* (1936), and *Easy Living* (1937)—catalogued the failings of the rich, including their ludicrous extravagances, their dysfunctional family lives, and their insensitivity to ordinary people. The real-life millionaires did their part, too: in addition to its usual procession of divorces, the Vanderbilt family offered the spectacle of Gertrude Vanderbilt Whitney, the daughter of Cornelius Vanderbilt II, going to court to win custody of her niece Gloria—the "poor little rich girl"—on the grounds that Gloria's widowed mother was unfit. Watching the bizarre family battle unfold, Eleanor Patterson, publisher of the *Washington Herald*, concluded, "With that amazing chameleon-like gift of the American snob, the Vanderbilt clan took unto themselves the distinguishing characteristics of old world aristocracy. They lost the sense of actuality."[14]

Against this backdrop, Americans seized the Progressives' twin weapons: income taxes and estate taxes. In 1932, the federal estate tax reached 45 percent on top incomes; two years later, the rate jumped to 60 percent. Meanwhile, Huey Long of Louisiana offered a punitive tax program under the banner "Share Our Wealth." Pushed from the left, Roosevelt offered his own tax program in 1935. In his message to Congress, the president flatly rejected the legitimacy of dynastic wealth. "The transmission from generation to generation of vast fortunes by will, inheritance, or gift is not," he insisted, "consistent with the ideals and sentiments of the American people." Going further, Roosevelt questioned the legitimacy of large fortunes themselves. "Great accumulations of wealth cannot be justified on the basis of personal and family security," he argued. "In the last analysis such accumulations amount to the perpetuation of great and undesirable concentration of control in a relatively few individuals over the employment and welfare of many, many others." Like the Progressives, Roosevelt rooted his case in a critique of individualism. "Wealth in the modern world does not come merely from individual effort," he observed; "it results from a combination of individual effort and of the manifold uses to which the community puts that effort. . . . Therefore, in spite of the great importance in our national life of the efforts and ingenuity of unusual individuals, the people in the mass have inevitably helped to make large fortunes possible." In other words, the rich didn't have a claim to their money. So, quoting his cousin's 1907 message at length, Roosevelt called for inheritance taxes. He also demanded a more steeply graduated income tax on individuals and a tax on corporate income. "Social unrest and a deepening sense of unfairness," the president maintained, "are dangers to our national life which we must minimize by rigorous methods."[15]

Roosevelt didn't get the inheritance tax; instead, Congress increased the estate tax to 70 percent in the Revenue Act of 1935. This "soak the rich" measure also boosted the corporate tax rate and increased the top individual income tax rate to 75 percent on annual income above $5 million. Two years later, Congress moved to close the sort of loopholes in the tax code that William K. Vanderbilt I had exploited. A series of measures further boosted taxes until the Revenue Act of 1942, passed during World War II, put the top estate tax rate at 77 percent and the top individual income tax rate at 88 percent.[16]

As critics have pointed out, New Deal tax policy didn't radically redistribute wealth from the rich to the poor.[17] But that wasn't the intention: Roosevelt and his liberal allies wanted the destruction of great, potentially dynastic fortunes. On that score, the New Deal was successful. In 1938, Frederick W. Vanderbilt,

Roosevelt's Duchess County neighbor, died after a long and quietly lucrative career as an investor. Despite the Depression and a luxurious lifestyle that included big yachts and stunning mansions, bashful "Uncle Fred" had turned his $10 million inheritance into an estate valued at almost $73 million. Between them, the federal government and the State of New York took much more than half—$42,836,278 in taxes. Franklin Roosevelt took Fred's Italian Renaissance–style country seat, Hyde Park, complete with Medici coat of arms and the late Louise Vanderbilt's Empress Josephine–inspired bedroom, as a kind of trophy; no one else wanted this costly relic of an era apparently gone forever. With Roosevelt's encouragement, the Park Service opened Hyde Park as a tourist attraction. "The National Park Service has designated the Vanderbilt Estate an historic site on the theory now popular in Washington that the last of the industrial barons have been deposed—and that the way they lived therefore becomes a matter of history interest," a newspaper announced in 1940. "Whether or not the theory holds water, your eyes will pop at the weighty magnificence of the mansion."[18]

The End of Adversarial Liberalism

By the end of World War II, the victory over hereditary wealth seemed to be more than a theory. "We little people don't have to fret about the millionaires," the writer Paul Gallico declared in 1946. "Uncle Sam takes care of them—but good! He has a way of doing it with the inheritance tax, which, by appropriate application, can wipe out a fortune of $50,000,000 in three generations." Just look at how the federal government and New York State combined to reduce the fortune of William K. Vanderbilt II, who died in 1944, from $35 million to a mere $5 million. "The roars of the outraged Commodore must be ringing down the corridors of Valhalla," Gallico imagined, " 'by gad, they can't do that to me!' " The writer happily concluded "that the day of the pyramiding fortune handed down and increased from generation to generation is over."[19]

Indeed, the postwar era became a golden age of relative economic equality. The rich were cut down to size. It wasn't just taxation, of course: economic and familial vicissitudes had taken a heavy toll, too. Allowing for inflation, no individual fortune of the 1950s came close to John D. Rockefeller's $1 billion or so in the 1910s. Hereditary dynasties ceded control of corporations. After four generations of family dominance, William K. Vanderbilt II's brilliant younger brother Harold—three-time winner of the America's Cup yacht races and the inventor of contract bridge—finally lost the New York Central Railroad in an epic proxy battle in 1954. The rich also gave up more of the palatial estates that had epitomized their Anglomaniacal aspirations to nobility. In Newport, Marble House, the famed villa of Harold's parents, joined The Breakers, the equally famed villa of his Uncle Cornelius II, as museum tourist attractions. Meanwhile, more and more ordinary Americans, thanks to higher incomes, could afford to enjoy a version of the lifestyle that had once made the rich so exotic and so frightening—home ownership, college educations, automobiles, boats, vacations, and divorces. The golden age of relative income equality was also a golden age of relative cultural equality.[20]

So Americans had the chance to tour Marble House, The Breakers, and Hyde Park and absorb the history of liberal triumph over the rich. "Nothing so perfectly illustrates the leveling influence of the income tax as the rise and fall of the stately homes of America's 400," a travel writer exclaimed in 1957. The tale was now pat: seemingly every development in recent American history had inexorably raised taxes and beaten down the haughty owners of those mansions. "Between the gay nineties and the prohibition era, what went up came down in the rapidly changing economic pattern of the United States," the writer noted. "First there was the income tax. Then World War I, the Big Depression, more and bigger taxes, World War II, even bigger taxes, the Korean War and now United States responsibility on a global scale and all that implies." It was a clear lesson in the liberal-enabled victory of democracy over nobility, meritocracy over heredity. The Vanderbilts and their Newport neighbors, the writer concluded, "represented an emerging American aristocracy of inherited wealth, now superseded by an American aristocracy of achievement."[21]

That simple conclusion was intoxicating. Was it any wonder, then, that liberals themselves succumbed to the triumphalism of the tour guides? As the historian John Morton Blum observes, the liberals' "pugnacity" had already begun to vanish during World War II. The apparently urgent necessity of collaborating with corporate leaders for the sake of war production had led liberals to ease up; so did their increasing faith that a prosperous economy would produce plenty for all without the need for tiresome battles with the rich. "In the hope for eternal prosperity, built on eternal consumer spending, the adversary toughness of the 1930's disappeared," Blum writes. "The distrust of big business that had so often marked American liberalism hardly survived the wartime accommodation between the service departments and the defense industries." Increasingly, liberals were ardent Keynesians: by managing fiscal policy, the blend of taxes and spending, the federal government could stimulate consumer demand and maintain prosperity. Why waste time fighting the remnants of the rich?[22]

Although some liberals kept the old faith, the country was more open to conservative ideas, including hostility to high taxes. Before the war ended, the Democratic-controlled Congress enacted the Revenue Act of 1945, which included major income-tax cuts. The next year, Republicans, pushing for a congressional majority, campaigned hard against high taxes. Rewarded with control of the 80th Congress, the Republicans passed a further tax cut, but President Harry Truman vetoed the bill in 1947. When the Republicans tried again the next year, Truman vetoed that measure, too—and saw Congress override him: the Revenue Act of 1948 notably weakened inheritance, estate, and gift taxes. Yet Truman was unbowed. In his famous rear-platform presidential campaign that year, he repeatedly slammed "economic royalists."[23]

Truman's startling election in 1948 had surprisingly little effect on mainstream liberal thought. Unlike the president, liberals had moved away from the traditional Rooseveltian focus on Anglomaniacs and "economic royalists." Increasingly concerned about African American civil rights, liberals lost interest in class conflict.

Arthur M. Schlesinger Jr., the leading liberal intellectual of the postwar period, typified the change. In his prize-winning history books, Schlesinger celebrated the Democratic presidents Franklin Roosevelt and Andrew Jackson for their assaults on entrenched privilege. In his seminal restatement of liberal ideology, *The Vital Center* (1949), Schlesinger kept class conflict at the core of the nation's history and his own political faith. "The fight on the part of the 'humble members of society' against business domination has been," he insisted, "the consistent motive of American liberalism." But the historian believed that the fight was over. Essentially endorsing the triumphalist postwar assessment of the rich, Schlesinger contemptuously dismissed the leaders of corporate America. "Not only does the business community lack the skill to govern society in its own interests," he declared. "It is increasingly lacking the will to do so." The rich really didn't matter anymore. The United States was, Schlesinger insisted, a "thoroughly middle-class country." In victory, Schlesinger found common ground with the rich. Now he saw ideological convergence between old antagonists. "The modern American capitalist ... has come," Schlesinger observed, "to share many values with the American liberal: beliefs in personal integrity, political freedom and equality of opportunity."[24]

Why such a benign view? Focusing on a new conflict, Schlesinger was ready to see the old one in a new light. The Cold War—the global competition with communism—made it crucial to bury past differences and find new unity at home. To that end, Schlesinger turned angrily on the small band of renegade liberals who had left the Democratic Party to support former vice president Henry Wallace in his Progressive Party campaign for the presidency in 1948. Too sympathetic to communism, the Progressives, Schlesinger believed, were like the nineteenth-century doughfaces of the North, who had tolerated Southern slavery. Not only that, these modern doughfaces were too hostile to America's capitalists, whom they denigrated as robber barons. "The robber baron, of course, used to sally forth from his castle and steal the goods of innocent travelers," Professor Schlesinger lectured. "Does even the most unregenerate Doughface consider this to be analogous to the achievements of Andrew Carnegie or John D. Rockefeller?" The rich, would-be aristocrats whom the Roosevelts had battled once upon a time weren't so bad after all. "The fact is, of course, that this nation paid a heavy price for industrialization—a price in political and moral decadence, in the wasteful use of economic resources, in the centralization of economic power," Schlesinger reasoned. "But the price we paid, though perhaps exorbitant, was infinitely less in human terms than the price paid by the people of Russia."[25]

The 1950s brought Schlesinger and other liberals little else to celebrate. Twice, the liberal hero Adlai Stevenson sallied forth to battle General Dwight Eisenhower; twice, the Democrat came back in defeat. The Eisenhower presidency—notable for its close ties to big business—didn't provoke Schlesinger into shouting the old liberal battle cry against the rich. Taking up his pen in 1960, the historian called for a return to the strong national leadership of the two Roosevelts. Yet Schlesinger drew a careful distinction between past and present. "The New Deal arose in response to economic breakdown," he noted. "It had to meet immediate problems of subsistence and survival. Its emphasis was essentially quantitative—an emphasis inevitable in an age of scarcity." In contrast, the "economy of abundance" meant that America could focus on "the quality of life" in the 1960s. "The new issues will be . . . those of education, health, equal opportunity, community planning," Schlesinger predicted. "A guiding aim, I believe, will be the insistence that every American boy and girl have access to the career proportionate to his or her talents and characters, regardless of birth, fortune, creed, or color."[26]

Schlesinger's distinction between quantitative and qualitative neatly summed up the change in liberalism from the 1930s to the 1960s. So, too, his reference to "color" indicated the increasing importance of race for modern liberalism. But his mention of "fortune" was only rhetorical. In the age of "qualitative" liberalism, the new Roosevelt, unlike his predecessors, wouldn't have to fight the Anglomaniacs and royalists all over again.

Schlesinger got his wish—more or less. Narrowly elected president in 1960, John F. Kennedy gave powerful voice to the new liberalism, even if he accomplished relatively few of its goals. He certainly did embody liberals' attitude toward the rich. Like Schlesinger, who became his special assistant, Kennedy didn't talk about millionaires or capitalists, let alone Anglomaniacs or royalists. Instead, the president used the blander and intentionally broader terms "business" and "businessmen." It wasn't so much that he was a rich man himself; the two Roosevelts hadn't let their wealth get in the way of their pursuit of the rich. Rather, Kennedy preferred the new liberalism's rather conflict-free approach to economic issues. His most notable economic policy initiative was a tax cut—not a tax increase—in order to stimulate economic growth. "A rising tide," he liked to say, "lifts all the boats." It didn't matter whether some of those craft were yachts. Fittingly, Kennedy's speechwriter, Ted Sorensen, had cribbed the line from the New England Council, a regional business lobbying group.[27]

Kennedy's formula didn't save him from friction with corporate leaders, most of whom would have preferred a Republican president. But he could tell them with plenty of justice, as he did in a speech in 1962, that there was no basic conflict in the relationship. "When you do well, the United States does well, and our policies abroad do well," Kennedy declared. "And while we may differ on the policies which may bring this country prosperity, there is no disagreement, I am sure, on either side, about the tremendous importance of you gentlemen moving ahead, and prospering, and contributing to the growth of this country."[28]

Kennedy's liberal successor, Lyndon Johnson, held essentially the same view. Presiding over prosperity and a steeply progressive tax system, the Texan could afford to back off the rhetoric that had defined Progressivism and liberalism in his youth. Despite his proud service to Franklin Roosevelt and the New Deal in the 1930s, Johnson explicitly distanced himself from his hero on the subject of the rich. "As a young man, I grew up hearing a lot of name-calling," the president recalled in 1968. "Some of it was applied to the economic royalists and the business community and the free enterprise system. I am glad that has gone out of fashion in this country." As he pushed for his Great Society, which was firmly grounded in Schlesinger's "qualitative" liberalism, Johnson offered an essentially Whiggish view of the harmonious interdependence of social classes. At a campaign rally in October 1964, he sounded like Calvin Coolidge or William McKinley. "If business puts everything that it has and all it can muster into the pot," he told the crowd, "and you put, as workers, everything you have into that pot, and then you take a spoon and scoop it up and make a big pie out of it, the bigger that pie is the more you will get and the more they get if we divide it reasonably equitably." Of course, Johnson, a true twentieth-century liberal, included the government as a partner along with business and workers. "I will tell you something else that is important," Johnson offered: "After business gets a return on their investment and their machinery and their management, and the worker gets a return on his sweat and what he did all day long, then Uncle Sam, the Government, I come in and I take my knife, and the bigger that pie is the more I get for the Government because I get 52 percent of all that is left." That was the comfortable new liberalism. "So it just seems to me that it is good sense for all of us to try to have peace at home and try to get along," Johnson concluded. "That is why you don't hear me talking about economic royalists, big business, big labor, racketeers, profit-makers, and things like that."[29]

The Lost Critique

Before Johnson's presidency ended, the liberals' world had started to collapse. The golden age of relative economic equality gradually gave way to a yawning divide reminiscent of the Gilded Age. As the incomes of many Americans essentially stagnated, individual fortunes rose again to astonishing heights. By the mid-1990s, the inflation-adjusted wealth of Microsoft founder Bill Gates became the first fortune to rival John D. Rockefeller's storied $1 billion eighty years before. In the first decade of the twenty-first century, billionaires were commonplace. Several factors, including deindustrialization, international competition, digitization, and recession, contributed to the decline of economic equality. So did the resurgence of political conservatism: the antiregulation, antiunion Ronald Reagan and George H. W. Bush administrations made liberals almost nostalgic for the Eisenhower age. Conservatism also brought an era of dramatic tax cutting. By the close of the second George W. Bush administration, in 2009, the top rate of the individual income tax had dwindled to 35 percent; the estate tax, which had dropped to 45 percent, was due to end altogether in 2010.[30]

For liberals, the times might have been ripe for a return to the old religion. But those who dusted off Rooseveltian sermons got nowhere. Accepting the Democratic nomination to run against President Reagan in 1984, Senator

Walter Mondale of Minnesota tried to stir up ancient resentments. "What we have today is a government of the rich, by the rich, and for the rich," the long-time liberal exclaimed. "First, there was Mr. Reagan's tax program. What happened was, he gave each of his rich friends enough tax relief to buy a Rolls Royce—and then he asked your family to pay for the hub caps." Mondale's crushing defeat meant the end of Rooseveltian rhetoric. Four years later, the Democratic nominee, Governor Michael Dukakis of Massachusetts, steered clear of taxes on the rich; instead of class conflict, he invoked the "idea of community," but without much attention to its boundaries or how it might be achieved. Bill Clinton offered the occasional riff on social class when he ran against President George H. W. Bush in 1992: "He has raised taxes on the people driving pickup trucks and lowered taxes on the people riding in limousines. We can do better." But the Clinton presidency was about tax cuts and credits, not higher taxes on those limousine owners. "At the end of the century, we seem to be returning to the Gilded Age," a liberal observer lamented. "Americans are hearing no meaningful debate on taxing vast fortunes, no voices of moral outrage, no passionate reminders of the American ideal of equality. Are there any politicians who can now honestly claim to follow the Roosevelt brand of leadership?"[31]

Even after the frightening economic meltdown of 2008 and its bleak aftermath, the answer was no. By then, many on the political left, abandoning the term "liberal," were calling themselves progressives. That self-description had oddly contradictory implications. For some cautious Democrats such as Hillary Clinton, the use of "progressive," at least at first, was a way to avoid unpopular notions, including high taxes, associated with liberalism. For others, the moniker "progressive" was a way to reclaim liberalism's quondam "adversary toughness" with the rich. The Occupy Wall Street movement also marked a renewed willingness to confront the wealthy, who were characterized as the "1 percent"—a term less pointed than "economic royalists."[32]

Despite the times, despite the pressure from neo-progressives and Occupy, President Barack Obama—"No Drama Obama"—avoided inflammatory rhetoric about the rich. Indeed, he spoke mostly about the middle class and rarely about the class presumably located above it. Unlike Kennedy and Johnson, this Democratic president didn't typically take refuge in the broad, bland word "business"; Obama did call the rich "the rich." He also referred to "millionaires," "billionaires," and occasionally even the "1 percent." But the president never questioned the legitimacy of these groups; he never suggested that great fortunes shouldn't exist. For Obama, taxation wasn't an instrument to destroy the rich or to curb their economic, political, and cultural power. Notably, this reflective man didn't lead a national discussion about the meaning of the estate tax. Instead, he presented estate and income taxes on the rich as a matter of fairness as well as a source of necessary revenue; the president wanted the rich, he said, to pay their "fair share." In 2011, he began advocating the so-called Buffett rule—the billionaire financier Warren Buffett's insistence that loopholes in the tax code shouldn't allow rich men like himself to pay taxes at a rate smaller than the one his secretary paid. So Obama proposed that an American earning $1 million or more should pay at least a 30 percent tax—chicken feed by New Deal standards.[33]

Obama didn't get the Buffett rule enacted. But he did get higher rates on the largest incomes and fortunes. In 2010, Congress restored the estate tax, which was due to expire that year, at a 35 percent top rate; in 2012, Congress raised the top estate tax rate to 40 percent—the highest pre–New Deal figure. Meanwhile, the Obama tax laws pushed the top marginal income tax rate to 39.6 percent. In this respect, as in others, the Obama administration hardly proved to be the second coming of the New Deal.[34]

"Adversary Toughness" and Community Identity

Liberalism's loss of "adversary toughness"—its gradual unwillingness to contest the legitimacy of great wealth and to tax it punitively—clearly reflected liberals' own caution, complacency, and creeping conservatism. The changing nature of the rich played a crucial role, too. The incomes and fortunes of today's postindustrial rich certainly rival those of the industrial rich of the Gilded Age and the early twentieth century. For sheer economic and political power, the billionaires of the twenty-first century may even rival the "kings" of the industrial era. But in two key respects, the contemporary rich are far smaller figures. Unlike the rich of the early twentieth century, the billionaires of today don't have the same cultural power to awe and repel; their lifestyles are not nearly as imposing and controversial as the palaces, yachts, vacations, crowns, and divorces of the Vanderbilts, Astors, Rockefellers, Whitneys, and Goulds. For all their lobbyists, political action committees, and friendly politicians, the rich of today don't visibly own elected officials the way the Vanderbilts owned Chauncey Depew. Even the willful individualism of the rich no longer offends as it once did. Moreover, the rich don't openly scheme to become some sort of national aristocracy. It is rare for one of the wealthiest Americans to plot a dynasty built openly on family corporate control, like the one contrived by

Commodore Vanderbilt. In short, the rich no longer pose the same cultural and dynastic threat as before.

Accordingly many Americans can find common ground with the rich, rather as Arthur Schlesinger Jr. managed to do after World War II. Now that taxation affects so many middle- and working-class Americans, they are more protective of the rights of property and more reluctant to use income and estate taxes to go after wealth. No wonder Republicans and conservatives accuse Democrats, liberals, and progressives of "class warfare" at the first mention of tax hikes: rightly or wrongly, blows against the rich can seem like blows against other classes as well.

Paradoxically, then, the rich are smaller figures, but therefore safer and perhaps more powerful ones, too. The paradox doesn't end there. It isn't just that the rich now find allies across class lines; it is also that liberals and progressives have seemingly switched places with the rich. Liberalism's very success in creating an intrusive, regulating, taxing federal government in the twentieth century has made it possible to demonize liberals and progressives, rather than the rich, as the alien threat to the national community. "Those of us who go about our lives earning a living and leaving others alone are the targets of an aggressive Progressive political class that is erecting a formidable mechanism of bureaucratic domination," declares a conservative blogger. "At this point in time, 'we the people' of the private, taxpaying sector are losing the war." Few liberals or progressives would agree with that assessment. Indeed, compared with the halcyon days of the New Deal, there is barely a war going on at all.[35]

Perhaps things will change. Perhaps the growing gap in wealth will prod the very rich into arrogant, would-be aristocracy again. Just as in the Gilded Age, the rich may fail to realize how good they have it compared with everyone else. Just as in the Gilded Age, a series of friendly decisions from a sympathetically conservative Supreme Court on campaign spending and corporate rights may encourage the rich to overplay their hand and grab too much for themselves. Or perhaps they will follow Tom Perkins in a self-pitying overreaction to the supposed "parallels" between "fascist Nazi Germany" and "its war on its 'one percent,' namely its Jews," on one hand, and "the Progressive war on the American one percent, namely the 'rich,'" on the other. America's wealthy would not be the first group in history to create the very circumstances they fear. Perhaps the rest of the nation will get angry enough, not to wage a new *Kristallnacht,* but to use liberal weapons to destroy great fortunes once again; perhaps then more politicians will start to emulate Senator Elizabeth Warren's fresh willingness to use the old adversarial language at the highest level of our politics. Perhaps. But it is telling that the scenario requires the rich to blunder. For now, liberalism remains critically weakened. No longer contesting the legitimacy of great wealth, liberals have a much harder time justifying their fundamentally conservative stance on capitalism. Progressives and New Deal liberals understood that national community depended in part on taming wealth; their successors have yielded that hard-won understanding.[36]

Notes

1. Michael McGerr, *A Fierce Discontent: The Rise and Fall of the Progressive Movement in America, 1870–1920* (New York: Free Press, 2003).

2. T. J. Stiles, *The First Tycoon: The Epic Life of Cornelius Vanderbilt* (New York: Knopf, 2009). For Vanderbilt as "king" and dynast, see "The Railroad King," *New York Evening Express,* May 18, 1867, and "Drew and Vanderbilt," Mar. 25, 1868; "Founding a Family," *New-York Daily Tribune,* Dec. 6, 1877. This paragraph and the following paragraphs on the Vanderbilts draw on research from my forthcoming book, *"The Public Be Damned": The Kingdom and the Dream of the Vanderbilts.*

3. Mrs. Frank Leslie, *California: A Pleasure Trip from Gotham to the Golden Gate, April, May, June, 1877* (New York, 1877), 18; untitled editorial, *New York Truth,* Feb. 18, 1881: 2; "The Vanderbilt Departure," *St. Louis Globe-Democrat,* May 7, 1883; "Blue-Blooded Citizens," *New York World,* Dec. 23, 1883.

4. "The First Tinge of Leprosy," *Atlanta Constitution,* Mar. 9, 1895.

5. Untitled, *New York Town Topics,* Oct. 4, 1894.

6. "Is America Developing an Aristocracy?" *Everybody's Magazine,* June 1904, 781; *Madison (Fla.) New Enterprise,* Dec. 17, 1903, 2; Olive M. Johnson, "'Blue Blood' Aristocracy," *New York Daily People,* Jan. 24, 1909; "Taxing the Dead," *New Orleans Item,* June 14, 1901; "For an Inheritance Tax as Check on Rich," *Wall Street Journal,* Oct. 26, 1907 (includes the quotation from the *Chicago Journal*); "Personal Taxes," Jan. 22, 1907, and "Are We a 'Patriciate'?," Aug. 7, 1907, *New York Times.*

7. "Divorce: The Vanderbilt Curse," *Chicago Daily Tribune,* Oct. 24, 1909; McGerr, *Fierce Discontent,* 90–92; David Graham Phillips, "The Treason of the Senate," *Cosmopolitan,* Mar. 1906, 487ff.

8. "Vanderbilt Millions Earn Less Than Four Per Cent," *New York Evening Telegram,* Dec. 11, 1900; "Vanderbilt Estate Worth $52,099,867," Jan. 24, 1901, "Vanderbilt War Tax Legal," Jan. 16, 1903, and "W. K. Vanderbilt Wins," Feb. 21, 1905, *New-York Daily Tribune;* W. Eliot Brownlee, *Federal Taxation in America: A Short History,* 2nd ed. (Cambridge: Cambridge University Press, 2004), 13–57.

9. Theodore Roosevelt, "Phases of State Legislation," *Century,* Apr. 1885, 830; "Roosevelt on M'Allister," *New York World,* Dec. 19, 1890; Theodore Roosevelt, "A Colonial Survival," *Cosmopolitan,* Dec. 1892, 229–36.

10. Theodore Roosevelt, Sixth Annual Message (Dec. 3, 1906), Seventh Annual Message (Dec. 3, 1907), and Eighth Annual Message (Dec. 8, 1908). All the quoted remarks of presidents and presidential candidates cited here and below are from Gerhard Peters and John T. Woolley, the American Presidency Project, www.presidency.ucsb.edu.

11. Sidney Ratner, *Taxation and Democracy in America* (New York: Wiley, 1967); Robert Stanley, *Dimensions of Law in the Service of Order: Origins of the Federal Income Tax, 1861–1913* (New York: Oxford University Press, 1993); Brownlee, *Federal Taxation*, 58–81.

12. "$50,222,842 Net Estate of W. Vanderbilt," *New-York Tribune*, Mar. 7, 1923; "Vanderbilt Gives Millions to Daughter?," *New York Times*, Aug. 23, 1919, and "Marlborough Got Vanderbilt Riches," Mar. 14, 1923.

13. Franklin D. Roosevelt, "Acceptance Speech for the Renomination for the Presidency, Philadelphia, Pa., June 27, 1936."

14. "Mrs. Patterson Raps Ruling in Gloria Case," *Brooklyn Daily Eagle*, Dec. 3, 1934; Ferdinand Lundberg, *America's 60 Families* (New York: Vanguard, 1937).

15. Brownlee, *Federal Taxation*, 81–84; Franklin D. Roosevelt, "Message to Congress on Tax Revision, June 19, 1935."

16. Mark H. Leff, *The Limits of Symbolic Reform: The New Deal and Taxation, 1933–1939* (Cambridge: Cambridge University Press, 1984); Brownlee, *Federal Taxation*, 84–112.

17. Leff, *Limits of Symbolic Reform*; Barton Bernstein, "The New Deal: The Conservative Achievements of Liberal Reform," in *Towards a New Past: Dissenting Essays in American History*, ed. Barton Bernstein (New York: Pantheon, 1968), 263–88.

18. "Disappearing Fortunes," *Portsmouth Herald*, Jan. 12, 1942; "An American Palace," *Albany Knickerbocker News*, Aug. 5, 1940.

19. Paul Gallico, "Tax Heat Melting Those Famous Fortunes," *San Antonio Light*, Feb. 10, 1946, magazine, 6–7.

20. Kevin Phillips, *Wealth and Democracy: A Political History of the American Rich* (New York: Broadway, 2002), 68–82; John Tebbel, *The Inheritors: A Study of America's Great Fortunes and What Happened to Them* (New York: Putnam, 1962).

21. Irene Korbally Kuhn, "Income Tax Is Great Leveler of Influence," *Syracuse Herald-Journal*, Oct. 19, 1957.

22. John Morton Blum, *V Was for Victory: Politics and American Culture During World War II* (New York: Harcourt Brace Jovanovich, 1976), 327.

23. "James Roosevelt Explains Defeat of Democrats," *Los Angeles Times*, Dec. 17, 1946; Brownlee, *Federal Taxation*, 121–25; Harry S. Truman, "Rear Platform Remarks in California, September 23, 1948," "Rear Platform and Other Informal Remarks in Texas and Oklahoma, September 28, 1948," and "Rear Platform and Other Informal Remarks in Illinois, Indiana, and Kentucky, September 30, 1948."

24. Arthur M. Schlesinger Jr., *The Vital Center: The Politics of Freedom* (New York: Da Capo, 1988 [1949]), 26, 29, 33, 172.

25. Ibid., 44.

26. Arthur M. Schlesinger Jr., *The Politics of Hope* (Boston: Houghton Mifflin, 1962), 84, 92.

27. John F. Kennedy, "Remarks in Pueblo, Colorado Following Approval of the Fryingpan-Arkansas Project, August 17, 1962" and "Remarks in Heber Springs, Arkansas, at the Dedication of Greers Ferry Dam, October 3, 1963"; Ted Sorensen, *Counselor: A Life at the Edge of History* (New York: Harper, 2008), 140.

28. Jim F. Heath, *John F. Kennedy and the Business Community* (Chicago: University of Chicago Press, 1969); Kennedy, "Address in New York City to the National Association of Manufacturers, December 6, 1961."

29. Lyndon B. Johnson, "Remarks at a Meeting of the National Alliance of Businessmen, March 16, 1968" and "Remarks at an Airport Rally in Wilmington, Delaware, October 31, 1964."

30. Phillips, *Wealth and Democracy*, 83–168; Brownlee, *Federal Taxation*, 147–248; Michael J. Graetz and Ian Shapiro, *Death by a Thousand Cuts: The Fight over Taxing Inherited Wealth* (Princeton, N.J.: Princeton University Press, 2005); James T. Patterson, "Transformative Economic Policies: Tax Cutting, Stimuli, and Bailouts," in *The Presidency of George W. Bush: A First Historical Assessment*, ed. Julian E. Zelizer (Princeton, N.J.: Princeton University Press, 2010), 114–39.

31. Walter F. Mondale, "Address Accepting the Presidential Nomination at the Democratic National Convention in San Francisco, July 19, 1984"; Michael S. Dukakis, " 'A New Era of Greatness for America': Address Accepting the Presidential Nomination at the Democratic National Convention in Atlanta, July 21, 1988"; William J. Clinton, "Address Accepting the Presidential Nomination at the Democratic National Convention in New York, July 16, 1992" and "Remarks Accepting the Presidential Nomination at the Democratic National Convention in Chicago, August 29, 1996"; Susan Dunn, "Teddy Roosevelt Betrayed," *New York Times*, Aug. 9, 1999.

32. "Why 'Liberal' Doesn't Quite Fit," *USA Today*, Aug 7, 2007; "Liberals Adopt Name for Progress," *Washington Times*, June 22, 2007; Paul Krugman, "We Are the 99.9 Percent," *New York Times*, Nov. 24, 2011.

33. Barack Obama, "Remarks to the AFL-CIO in Philadelphia, April 2, 2008," "Remarks on Tax Reform and the Extension of Unemployment Insurance Benefits, December 6, 2010," "The Budget Message of the President, February 14, 2011," "Remarks on Income Tax Reform, April 11, 2012," "Remarks at a Campaign Rally in Mansfield Ohio, August 1, 2012," "Remarks at a Campaign Rally in Bowling Green, Ohio, September 26, 2012," "Presidential Debate in Hempstead, New York, October 16, 2012," "Address Before a Joint Session of Congress on the State of the Union, February 12, 2013," and "Remarks at Knox College in Galesburg, Illinois, July 24, 2013."

34. Kenneth Gould, "The Roosevelts Would Be Appalled," *American Magazine*, Dec. 17, 2010, www.american.com/archive/2010/december/the-roosevelts-would-be-appalled; "Tentative Deal Is Reached to Raise Taxes on the Wealthy," *New York Times*, Dec. 31, 2012.

35. Mark Hendrickson, "The Real Class Warfare in America Today," *Forbes.com*, May 2, 2014, www.forbes.com/sites/markhendrickson/2014/05/02/the-real-class-warfare-in-america-today.

36. Tom Perkins, "Progressive Kristallnacht Coming?," *Wall Street Journal*, Jan. 24, 2014.

12 • The Progressive Seedbed
Claims of American Political Community in the Twentieth and Twenty-First Centuries
Rogers M. Smith

Building on but also profoundly revising their nation's intellectual and political heritage, Progressive-era thinkers and activists advanced a range of conceptions of America's political community. Three have proved especially significant in American political development: the white middle-class reformist nationalism of Herbert Croly and Theodore Roosevelt; the varied and more radical efforts to blend democracy with cultural pluralism advanced by John Dewey, Randolph Bourne, Horace Kallen, and W. E. B. Du Bois; and the visions of economic democracy urged by Walter Weyl, Florence Kelley, and the National Consumers League. Although all have since remained politically important, their relative political prominence and their places on the prevailing American political spectrum have shifted over time.

The mainstream Progressivism of Croly and TR gave way in the New Deal to views that stressed economic democracy largely as a means to assist American workers and those in need, often through the mobilization of consumers to address workers' burdens as well as their own. Then as post–World War II anticommunism contributed to a decline in the American labor movement, economic democracy became more purely "consumer democracy," a vision of the United States as a nation of, especially, middle-class consumers. This middle-class consumerism retained its appeal in the New Frontier and Great Society eras, even as the modern civil rights movement began to bring cultural-pluralist themes to the fore. Then, after severe economic and foreign policy difficulties and controversies over racial and social issues brought these latter-day progressive positions into disrepute in the 1970s, political actors—especially Ronald Reagan and Barack Obama—gained power by recombining some elements of progressivism with other themes to craft new, politically potent, but sharply opposed visions of America. The result by the second decade of the twenty-first century was stifling political polarization in which passionate differences over progressive commitments played major roles. Through all these shifts and thematic combinations, the challenge of achieving a broadly compelling view of American political community has remained central to the nation's politics.

Progressive-Era Visions of American Political Community

To grasp these developments, it is best first to sketch the range of views of American political community that Progressives built from their inheritances amid the changing economic, social, religious, and intellectual contexts of the late nineteenth and early twentieth centuries.[1] Progressivism was a diverse seedbed of ideas, but it displayed certain broadly shared roots and general reform trajectories. Most Progressive thinkers and activists were products of suburban or small-town, moderately prosperous, Protestant families, inspired by Abraham Lincoln and their faiths to believe in the nobility of moral initiatives in public life, but buffeted by the upheavals of the late nineteenth century. These included urbanization, immigration, and industrialization; African American emancipation; and shocking new theories of evolution. These developments worried many who became Progressives, but many also believed they provided opportunities for exciting reforms.

Progressives sought to comprehend, to purify, and to direct their rapidly transforming world. They built new institutions and professions, seeking especially to draw on the scientific managers of corporations and on new public administrative bodies to improve all collective endeavors. Toward that end, they deployed the ideas of the scientific lawyers, economists, political scientists, sociologists, social psychologists, and social workers, as well as the theologically liberal social gospel reformers, who joined Progressive causes and helped define their aims. Most Progressives had great faith in emerging forms of empirical scientific experimentation and in prospects for greater efficiency via rational organization. They gave intellectual allegiance to concepts of evolution, of democracy as a source of goals, of instrumental rationality as a guide to means of achieving those goals, and of the fundamental reality of human interdependence. They thought these beliefs supported ultimate democratic control of government, enhancement of public and private organizational competence via modern scientific expertise, and moral values of honesty, community service, and virtuous personal self-realization, in accordance with the precepts of Social Gospel theology.

Most now recognize that the Progressives' commitments to democracy, however sincere, had embedded within them profoundly undemocratic elements. First, many in the larger American public remained skeptical of scientific pragmatism, the wisdom of experts, Social Gospel reforms, and conceptions of interdependence—so Progressives often acted as elites imposing their beliefs on recalcitrant masses. Many mainstream Progressives, moreover, thought science and experience justified denials of the rationality and the claims to equal rights of nonwhites, non-Christians, and poor men, and most assigned women a distinct nature that limited their economic and political roles.

Yet these very limitations of the Progressives' vision reassured many who would otherwise have been threatened by it. And because numerous Gilded Age changes seemed to help only a wealthy few, so many Americans responded to the Progressives' call during the first two decades of the twentieth century that both major parties and the main third parties all came to be headed by Progressive leaders. The Progressive era also generated four constitutional amendments—providing for a national income tax, for direct election of senators, for extensive limits on alcohol sales, and for women's suffrage—expressing Progressive commitments to ensuring that the wealthy served the common good, that representative institutions and the franchise were made more democratic, and that government acted more forcefully in the service of morality.

These convergences did not mean an end to right, left, and center divisions in American politics. Some Progressives, like Croly, embraced large corporations and trusts, suitably regulated and countered by powerful unions, as valuable for national growth. Others, like Louis Brandeis, decried the "curse of bigness" and favored breaking up large enterprises or else more restrictive regulation of them, even public ownership. They wished both to protect workers, consumers, and the environment, and to permit meaningful, active participation in civic self-governance. Partly because of disagreements over how best to achieve effective self-governance, Progressives differed on where best to locate democratic power, looking everywhere from local neighborhoods to cities to states to national institutions and even transnational associations. Many favored heightened democratic participation and decision making, including for poorer workers and women, in virtually every sphere. Equally as many Progressives, and often many of the same Progressives, also favored politically insulated expert governance, along with special legislation for women and strict limits on racial and religious inclusiveness.

Though their views of American political community consequently displayed great diversity, three basic types have had the most enduring impact.

Many Progressives, including Herbert Croly and Theodore Roosevelt, wedded their conceptions of the American democratic community extensively to the racial, religious, gender, and class orderings preferred by predominantly white, Social Gospel Protestant, paternalist-minded middle-class Americans. Others, such as Horace Kallen and the young W. E. B. Du Bois, instead articulated culturally pluralist visions minimizing American nationality in favor of ethnocultural groups, and they were broadly reinforced by the views of John Dewey and Randolph Bourne, who stressed the importance of a range of group memberships that could vary in many respects, though all ought to be internally democratic and to contribute to democratic life in ways that transcended group and national boundaries. Finally, some Progressives, such as the economist Walter Weyl and the consumer activist Florence Kelley, advanced what proved a politically appealing middle way, favoring an economic vision of American democracy that sought to forge strong alliances between consumers and producers. Their vision was more inclusive than that of Croly and Roosevelt, though it placed far less stress on group pluralism than did Kallen, Dewey, Bourne, or Du Bois.

The Mainstream Progressive Visions of Herbert Croly

The journalist Herbert Croly urged Progressives to embrace Hamiltonian means for Jeffersonian ends. He understood those ends as "democracy devoted to the welfare of the whole people," which was to be achieved by "a conscious labor of individual and social improvement."[2] This meant that government should seek to build community and prosperity at the national level, especially by favoring large-scale, more efficient forms of economic organizations, both big business and big labor unions, as well as national governmental regulatory powers. Jacksonian Democratic notions of decentralized governance, laissez-faire, and governmental neutrality toward individual choices all struck Croly as expressions of "disintegrating" forms of individualism.[3] He thought national policies should treat inefficient small businesses and nonunion workers "ruthlessly," as weeds to be pulled from the national garden.[4] He believed individuals would flourish best in a national economy offering "innumerable special niches" in which they could realize their talents, even as national policies propelled them into the work they could do that was worth most to the community.[5]

Croly's vision provided a rationale for extensive economic regulation favoring enterprises and actors that were not only economically efficient but also socially valuable. Still, it expressed a sharply bounded conception of who could share fully in America's promise. Though Croly's rhetoric was often universalistic, its notions of the "welfare" of different groups were severely hierarchical, especially in regard to race, nationality, and religion, but also class and gender. In this, Croly was typical of mainstream Progressives and the sorts of "moral reform" they thought democracy should serve.[6] Croly's hero Theodore Roosevelt, for example, championed American imperialism as part of what Croly called "the march of Christian civilization," the "colonial expansion" of the "Christian community of nations" over the "majority of Asiatic and African communities" in order to provide the "preliminary process of tutelage" that those peoples needed in order to achieve any "genuine national advance."[7] Croly and TR also believed that African Americans, Native Americans, and working-class immigrants required "tutelage" before they would be ready to be full American citizens, regardless of what the Fourteenth Amendment said.[8]

But like many northern Progressives, Croly preferred to focus on America's economic inequalities, not its ethnocultural ones. The promise of American life (the title of his 1909 book) was, in his formulation, built on the nation's prospects for sustained prosperity. He said much about corporate power, labor unions, political economy, corrupt party bosses, public administration, and public education, but little about religion, and nothing about the domestic issues of racial and gender inequality the United States faced. He remarked only that while slavery was incompatible with democracy, southern slave owners had been "right" in believing "that the negroes were a race possessed of moral and intellectual qualities inferior to those of the white men."[9] Regarding the intersection of religion and politics, Croly said that the Catholic Church was fighting "a losing battle with political authority," for it was destined to be subordinated to national governing institutions, just as American Protestants wished.[10] And though Croly repeatedly endorsed the notion that democratic representatives should be "solicitous of the interests of the whole state," he did not address the disfranchisements of African Americans or women.[11] In so doing, Croly acted in alliance with the beliefs shared by most Progressives that the pursuit of American democratic principles should be conducted with recognition of the superiority of the values and abilities of white middle-class Christian (predominantly Protestant) Americans, especially benevolently paternalistic men. That, after all, was who most Progressives were.

It is likely that beyond what Croly presented as the Jeffersonian goal of realizing democratic principles, his embrace of the "march of Christian civilization" was central to the purpose that animated most parts of the diverse

Progressive reform coalitions—the aim to "remake the nation's feuding, poly-glot population in their own middle-class image."[12] Centrist Progressives sought to restrain the rich, uplift the poor, unify the North and the South, Americanize immigrants, civilize "more primitive" races, and reform the morality of all people along ascetic Protestant lines. The Progressives' acquiescence in, and often advocacy of, segregation laws and black disfranchisement was for many crucial to this mission. These policies promised simultaneously to make all whites feel themselves to be partners in one great nation, truly ending the Civil War, and to make whites feel secure against the threatening presence of aspiring nonwhites.

Potent as it was, this mainstream Progressive vision of American national community proved ill suited for long-term hegemony. Even many white Protestant Americans proved unable to abide by its moral asceticism, especially in regard to alcohol and sex. Prohibition simply made these pleasures into horns of plenty for organized crime. Over time, many other Americans resisted the Progressives' racial and religious ordering of the nation, and as the United States gained global prominence, its inequalities proved an albatross in international affairs. The mainstream Progressive vision of America as a leader of white Christian civilization has hardly disappeared; but it has been substantially eclipsed by different views, often rooted in liberal progressive thought. Today it appears largely on the right end of the modern American political spectrum, sustained by foes of contemporary progressivism.

Pluralist Visions

The philosopher John Dewey shared many political positions with Croly and Roosevelt, but he rejected their stress on the importance of American national community. Dewey's all-out commitment to democracy was accompanied by an insistence that in modern times, groups created "for promoting the diversity of goods that men share have become the real social units."[13] Those "groupings" or "associations" could be of many types—economic, religious, cultural, ethnic—but they all should become increasingly "voluntary . . . amenable to human choices and purposes—more directly changeable at will" by their members.[14]

During the Progressive years, Dewey contended that the modern democratic national state should be seen only as "an instrumentality for promoting and protecting other and more voluntary forms of association, rather than a supreme end in itself"[15]—though by the late 1920s he had accepted that the

conditions of modern industrialism demanded extensive "utilization of government as the genuine instrumentality of an inclusive and fraternally associated public."[16] Still, as Dewey's reference to inclusiveness indicates, even as he
embraced a larger role for national governance, he continued to decry narrow
forms of "nationalism," including conceptions of America as an "Anglo-
saxondom." After the horrors of World War I, Dewey stressed that "voluntary
associations" of "trans-national interests" could legitimately challenge the
"claim of independent sovereignty in behalf of the territorial national state."[17]
Most fundamentally, for Dewey all associations—"government, business, art,
religion, all social institutions"—had to have a democratic purpose: "to set free
and to develop the capacities of human individuals without respect to race,
sex, class or economic status," contributing to "the all-around growth of every
member of society."[18] The American national community at its best could
serve this goal, but so could many other groups, which therefore had equal
value. Many Progressives were deeply influenced by this grand vision, even as
most still presumed that educated white Christian Americans embodied the
pinnacle of civilization.[19]

Over time, the contentions of Dewey and other Progressives that repressive
institutions and practices, rather than inherent deficiencies, accounted for
most differences in how groups developed helped propel many to push to
make American institutions more democratic and inclusive. But by intent,
there was nothing in Dewey's view that made American nationality seem particularly special or inspiring, nor did his ideas provide any comfort to those
attached to the nation's prevailing ethnocultural and economic orderings. His
democratic philosophy was therefore not well suited to serve, and never did
serve, as a conception of American political community around which a broad
coalition of American voters could be built.

Ironically, the brilliant young journalist Randolph Bourne elaborated his
wartime criticisms of American militarism into a still-more radical account of
"trans-national" attachments, which he nonetheless presented, more than
Dewey, as a kind of "Americanism." Bourne urged his fellow citizens to see
themselves as proud members of the first "international nation," one devoted
to a "nationalism of internationalism," by embracing dual or even multiple
citizenships and building up "democratic and pacific" communities of sympathy and cooperation across existing national lines. Bourne proposed that
young people contribute to this endeavor as members of a new system of non-
military national service that would include international outreach—an idea
partly incorporated into John F. Kennedy's proposals for what became the

Peace Corps and VISTA.²⁰ But though Bourne's ideas inspired later innovations and have renewed saliency today, in the Progressive era they were too challenging to American self-conceptions to become widely embraced—in part because, to many, they presented national patriotism as something to be transcended.

In different ways, the philosopher Horace Kallen and the African American intellectual W. E. B. Du Bois offered more specifically cultural-pluralist visions of America than Dewey or Bourne endorsed, in forms that would more directly influence American struggles over immigration, race, and national identity. For Kallen, an émigré Jew, persons' cultural group identities were most fundamental to their personal fulfillment. Consequently, he, too, minimized American national identity as "no more than citizenship in any land with free institutions." He did, to be sure, value free institutions, but chiefly for their instrumental contributions. Kallen argued that America should be a "democracy of nationalities, cooperating voluntarily and autonomously through common institutions in the enterprise of self-realization through perfection of men according to their kind."²¹ He wrote largely to oppose the most severely assimilative forms of Americanization of immigrants and to challenge the growing support for a "national origins" quota system of immigration restriction. In his time Kallen's arguments helped win respect for the desires of white ethnic groups to sustain distinct cultural identities while becoming equal members of the American political community. But again, in the Progressive era most Americans were far from ready to embrace this strongly culturally pluralist conception of their national identity.

Many African Americans resisted this vision because Kallen at that time did not endorse *their* inclusion as equal members of the American "democracy of nationalities"—though he would later turn his arguments for cultural pluralism to support for the civil rights movement of the 1950s. In that later incarnation, Kallen's democratic cultural pluralism came to resemble what Du Bois had argued for in the first two decades of his career—an "Americanism" in which Americans of different races could share "political ideals," political institutions, and broadly equal opportunities while choosing to maintain a "social equilibrium" in which "men of different races" could simultaneously strive to advance their distinct "race ideals."²² David W. Southern argues that Du Bois was therefore "an early cultural pluralist" who "steered a middle course between integrationists like Frederick Douglass and black nationalists like Marcus Garvey."²³ He also stresses, however, that unlike Kallen, Du Bois quickly came to denounce Jim Crow segregation and new disfranchising laws as violations of the political and economic rights all Americans should share. The writings of both men, but especially Du Bois, therefore served to challenge the conceptions of racial and religious ordering that structured so many mainstream Progressive conceptions of American national community, in ways that activists later sought to combine with economically centered views of American democracy.

Economic Progressivism: Allying Consumers and Producers

Those activists did so because it was in fact economic and increasingly consumerist conceptions of American democracy that gained the greatest political prominence from the New Deal through the end of the Great Society era, and continue to have substantial influence today. That political trajectory makes it advisable to give greater attention to Walter Weyl, the economist who cofounded the *New Republic* with Croly and Walter Lippmann. As Lawrence Glickman has written, Progressives like Weyl believed that "in the assertion of consumer power, guided by knowledgeable experts," lay "the key to the most vexing question of their age: how could a robust practice of citizenship be reconciled with the massive economic changes" in America?[24]

Michael Sandel has noted that in the late nineteenth century, radical labor leaders sought to join America's producers and consumers into supporters of a "cooperative commonwealth" in which many economic institutions would be publicly owned.[25] But in the early twentieth century, middle-class Progressives began to minimize "producer-based issues, such as industrial democracy," in favor of "problems that confronted people as consumers and taxpayers," such as high streetcar fares, taxes, and industrial pollution.[26] Writing partly to contribute to Theodore Roosevelt's 1912 Progressive Party campaign and to push it further left, Weyl elaborated this consumer-centered vision in *The New Democracy,* though he still linked it firmly with the improvement of conditions for America's producers.[27] Like Croly, Weyl focused on economic inequalities and the promise of prosperity. He documented the harms of the new plutocracy and criticized the narrowness of America's individualism and undue reverence for the Constitution.[28] Weyl urged a sweeping reform agenda aimed at "the improvement, physical, intellectual, and moral, of the millions who make up the democracy."[29]

And in contrast to Croly, Weyl wrote favorably of "woman's suffrage" while expressing concern about the recent assaults on "Negro suffrage." He warned,

"If the democracy in America is to be a white democracy . . . let the white civilization beware."[30] Calling the "Negro problem" the "mortal spot of the new democracy," Weyl contended that in the end, whites' "self-protection, as much as our sense of justice, must impel us towards the increase in the Negro's ability, *morale,* and opportunity."[31] Just how that should be achieved, however, Weyl did not say. And though he urged that Americans "need not claim a superiority over the people who throng in at Ellis Island," Weyl contended that immigration restriction was "imperative" in order to protect "the congested districts of our cities" from "too near a contact with European poverty."[32] In the end, Weyl neither endorsed nor mounted strong challenges to Croly's view of America as a premier white Christian civilization.

Weyl did, however, propose a less ethnocultural, more purely economic conception of the American democratic community. Unlike many nineteenth-century predecessors, including Marxist theorizers of class struggle, Weyl argued that it was "the increasing wealth of America, not the growing poverty of any class, upon which the hope of a full democracy must be based."[33] This wealth made possible "a new ethics" based on "the dignity of human life, by which society, because of its greater wealth, becomes morally responsible . . . for the provision of facilities by which the highest physical, intellectual, moral, and social capacities of all citizens, born and to be born, may best be secured."[34] In particular, America's prosperity was increasingly accompanied, despite the new plutocracy, despite poverty and distress, by "enormous consumption . . . by the average American, by the comfortable, and especially by the poor, by the people who must work to live."[35]

For Weyl, this new role of the mass of the citizenry as consumers with "enormously increased spending power" meant the development of "overwhelming aggregate economic power" in "the great mass of the population."[36] He believed the new American consumer citizen had enough "material prosperity" not to need to sell his vote, and to fear "neither landlord nor employer."[37] Through their purchasing power, consumers could demand better media and education, generating a "growing intelligence of the American masses" that American democracy needed.[38] Weyl reasoned that if this "mass of citizens . . . can unite," they "should be able to secure control of government and of industry and to reconstitute America according to the wishes of democracy."[39]

And Weyl thought that unity was attainable because "the various democratic groups have two chief elements of solidarity: a common antagonism to the plutocracy, and a common interest in the social surplus," motives that might unite "factory workers, farmers, shopkeepers, professional men," and more.[40] All should want to attain "a common share . . . in the material and moral accumulations of a century," which had been aided by publicly granted franchises, lands, bounties, and more.[41] When plutocrats used their publicly subsidized wealth to charge high prices and pay low wages, the "great mass" of the populace was injured "in its capacity of wage earner, salary earner, tax-payer and consumer."

Of these capacities, Weyl maintained, "that of the consumer is the most universal, since even those who do not earn wages or pay direct taxes consume commodities."[42] And consumers were "undifferentiated"—all "who buy shoes" are "interested in cheap good shoes."[43] Because Weyl thought people were increasingly voting "as consumers" to "secure their rights as consumers," he believed they were beginning to "unite as citizens to obtain a sensitive pop-ular government."[44] So he concluded: "Out of the great inchoate democratic mass of the community, with enlistments from below and with defections to the class above, will come the motive force to revolutionize society, to displace our present duality of resplendent plutocracy and crude ineffective democracy with a single, broad, intelligent, socialized, and victorious democracy."[45]

As many scholars have noted, the National Consumers League (NCL) and its state affiliates, led by the settlement house veteran Florence Kelley in the Progressive years and by the labor advocate Lucy Mason during the early New Deal, exemplified the most activist version of Weyl's economic democratic vi-sion, similarly mobilizing Americans as consumers in opposition to plutoc-racy and the exploitation of workers and the general public.[46] Indeed, the state consumer groups that worked with University of Pennsylvania economists when Weyl was a student of the Penn economist Simon Patten may well have inspired his later arguments.[47]

In an 1899 statement of the "aims and principles" of the new National Consumers League, which was being built out of state predecessors, Kelley argued as Weyl would do that "every person is a consumer."[48] Therefore this identity was the best basis for political coalition building. But Kelley made clear that the league's main goal was to improve the conditions of *workers* by boycotting products made under substandard labor conditions and by campaigning for laws regulating work and wages.[49] Her consumer activism served producers' causes; and unlike Weyl, Kelley soon added racial activism, helping found the NAACP and organizing with it a boycott of the film *Birth of a Nation*.[50] But at the same time, Kelley and the NCL long opposed the pro-posed Equal Rights Amendment, believing women needed special protective labor laws.[51]

After Kelley's death in 1932, Lucy Mason, who had been inspired by the Social Gospel movement to become a labor advocate, became general secretary of the NCL. She served in that position until 1937, when she moved to the Congress of Industrial Organizations. Mason lobbied actively for better labor codes in the 1933 National Recovery Act and for the 1938 Fair Labor Standards Act; and she, too, championed the rights of southern black workers.[52] For both Weyl and the NCL, consumer democracy really meant an allied "workers and consumers" democracy that would be less racially restrictive than Croly's Progressivism, even if middle-class experts would still provide much of the leadership. But after the New Deal, as Lizabeth Cohen has argued, conceptions of America as a more purely "consumer's republic" began playing a greater role in American political rhetoric and policies.[53]

After the Progressive Era: New Deal, New Frontier, and Great Society Themes

As Stephen Skowronek has argued, when Franklin D. Roosevelt answered an inquiry about his ideology by saying, "I am a Christian and a Democrat—that's all," he said more than first meets the eye.[54] Roosevelt was not simply a Christian; he was a Christian allied with reformist Social Gospel Protestantism. And he was not just a Democrat; he was a Progressive Democrat who, in the context of the Depression, focused on "meeting the problem of under consumption, of adjusting production to consumption, of distributing wealth and products more equitably," as the Democratic presidential candidate put it in his Commonwealth Club address of 1932.[55] Roosevelt called also for "an economic declaration of rights, an economic constitutional order" aimed at ensuring that "purchasing power is well distributed throughout every group in the nation," with "wages restored and unemployment ended."[56] Those words paralleled the advocacy of Weyl and Kelley for an American democracy in which consumers and producers would unite to restrain the power of the wealthy, improve conditions for workers, and restructure the economy so that its productivity would be widely shared.

These economic themes remained central throughout FDR's many years in the White House. In his 1941 State of the Union address (the "Four Freedoms" speech), Roosevelt identified the "basic things expected by our people" as including besides "jobs for those who can work," and "security for those who need it," "the enjoyment of . . . a wider and constantly rising standard of living."[57] In his 1944 State of the Union address, FDR elaborated an "economic bill of rights" that included the "right to a useful and remunerative job . . . the right to earn enough to provide adequate food and clothing and recreation," along with rights to "a decent home," "a good education," "adequate medical care," "adequate protection from the economic fears of old age, sickness, accident, and unemployment."[58] This list suggested an array of governmental employment and social welfare programs and concerns for workers and the poor as well as for American consumers. Collectively, these recurrent themes of Roosevelt's speeches justify the assertion that his New Deal won support in large measure by presenting the value of America's national community chiefly in economic terms, depicting the "promise of American life" as one of sharing in the abundant productivity that American institutions and resources generated.

To be sure, FDR and the New Dealers developed other themes as well. Roosevelt's 1941 speech claimed broad bipartisan support for policies that sought to keep "war away from our Hemisphere," even as the United States also sought to ensure "that the democratic cause shall prevail" everywhere in the world.[59] Roosevelt's invocation of a strong America that would use its power to protect democracy globally was far from central to his appeal, but nonetheless, with the onset of war and the adoption of a more militant role, the U.S. government increasingly began to portray itself as the champion of democracy and human rights without racial restrictions. Philip Klinkner and I are among many who argue that this repositioning provided a context for civil rights reforms.[60]

Nevertheless, FDR's 1944 State of the Union address presents a vision of American community that continued to foreground economic themes, and the promise that all citizens would have meaningful shares in their nation's prosperity was unmistakable. It is not hard to see why this was so. The central fact of national life when Roosevelt was elected was the economic catastrophe of the Great Depression. The apogee of the Progressives' effort to remake American life in accord with their notions of morality, Prohibition, had proved disastrously counterproductive.[61] The appeal of strict Protestant moralism declined accordingly. At the same time, the influence of Franz Boas and other critics of inegalitarian racial theories was growing. Probably more importantly, the New Deal coalition included many Catholic and Jewish European immigrants who had arrived before the adoption of the national-origin quota system, as well as many African Americans who had moved north to work in factories during World War I. Northern Democrats like FDR therefore had reasons to retreat from the Protestant moralism and dominant racial positions of the Progressive era, even if their reform impulses were muted by their reliance on southern white Democrats. Given Roosevelt's clear need to address economic concerns, along with the greater liabilities associated with the Progressives' moral, racial, and religious themes, it is understandable that he advanced a "producers and consumers republic" vision of American political community.

When the United States emerged from World War II as the stronger of two global superpowers and as the world's largest economy, in competition with communists, who primarily attacked the U.S. economic system, leaders of both parties emphasized, as a primary reason for American allegiance, the nation's superior capacity to generate prosperity and peace for all. Many New Deal programs for the middle class expanded in the postwar era, including social security and medical programs, tax breaks for homebuyers and home-owners, and funding for higher education. But aid to the poor and support for organized labor came to be tainted in this period, seen as indications of social-ism or even communism. Conservatives passed the Taft-Hartley Act in 1947, reducing labor rights and triggering a decline in union membership, espe-cially in the private sector, that has continued.[62]

As the power of labor began to wane, organizations including the National Consumers League and even some unions increasingly stressed the interests of their members primarily as consumers. Lizabeth Cohen has noted how the NCL board in 1934 still insisted that it should focus on using purchasing power to express "the consumer's conscience" primarily about *production* practices. But within a few years, the organization began a transition that had led it by 1969 to identify its primary goal as simply "achieving effective repre-sentation of the consumer interest in both private and public decision-making."[63] The first post–New Deal Democratic president, John F. Kennedy, championed not FDR's broader "economic bill of rights" but a "Consumer's Bill of Rights" calling for rights "to safety, to be informed, to choose, and to be heard."[64] Like Kennedy's revival of Bourne's ideas for national service, this proposal retained some sense that consumer citizens should participate ac-tively in public life; but the emphasis now was far more on the rights of con-sumers than on their civic duties, or on the interests of labor. Even the efforts of Ralph Nader, whose energetic revival of the consumer movement in the late 1960s and 1970s was broadly supportive of many labor causes, nonetheless featured calls for a Consumer Protection Agency and safety and environmen-tal regulations more than pro-union labor laws.[65]

What were the consequences of these shifts from the Progressive era to the 1960s, from the Square Deal's conception of America as a leader in the march of white Christian civilization to New Frontier and Great Society portraits of America as a consumers' republic that was more racially inclusive but had less robust commitments to American workers and to civic duties more generally? Four bear emphasis.

First, as Weyl hoped, the vision of America as a consumer democracy proved suitable for building broad political coalitions and helping Progressives win elections, since most citizens could indeed see themselves as sharing consumer interests. And again, through the New Deal, those mobilizations aided workers as well as consumers. In addition, consumer-democracy themes in post–World War II narratives of America reinforced a simultaneous occurrence—the struggles of African Americans, women, and others against various forms of second-class citizenship.

To be sure, Deweyan ideas of equal democratic membership proved serviceable in those struggles; Social Gospel beliefs were inspirational; and though the emphases on racial differences expounded by cultural pluralists like Du Bois and Kallen were not broadly influential, their opposition to racial and ethnic hierarchies helped motivate battles against discrimination. But the contributions of consumer-democracy conceptions to civil rights struggles were real. Even in the Progressive era, urban white women and African American activists, especially in the Jim Crow South, relied on consumer boycotts as weapons to advance interests that they lacked the direct political power to defend.[66] Though conservatives during the Cold War sought to portray all reformers as closet Reds, they found it hard to disparage groups for exercising their purchasing power within America's market systems. Similarly, it was easier for white men to presume that African Americans, women, and others lacked the intellectual capacity for certain types of work, education, and political rights than it was to portray nonwhites and women as nonconsumers.

As a result, not only many middle-class Americans, but also many female workers and African Americans heightened their activism on the basis of their identities as consumers from the New Deal era on. They demanded equal terms in employment, retail sales and services, and housing transactions, and they resorted to consumer protests and boycotts when denied them.[67] As civil rights proponents, reinforced by international pressures, assaulted all rationales for second-class citizenship, the ascendancy of economically centered conceptions of American democracy made more equal treatment of all citizens, at least with respect to basic welfare, seem appropriate.

A second consequence of this increasing emphasis on consumer identities tempered and circumscribed the first: the accounts of American political community that heirs of Progressivism advanced focused more heavily over time on the material concerns of the middle class. That development was far from inevitable. It mattered tremendously that the increasingly anticommunist political and intellectual climate of the postwar years made advocacy of workers' interests seem increasingly antagonistic to, rather than an ally of, the well-being of American consumers. The resulting narrowing of economy-centered democratic visions meant that they proved over time less able either to assist or to be assisted by organized labor. Despite Lyndon Johnson's War on Poverty and Nader's citizen crusades for wide-ranging reforms, the agenda of proponents of American economic democracy gradually became less ambitious. FDR's hopes for legally institutionalized economic rights that would ensure access to jobs, homes, nutrition, health care, education, and retirement support for all became less central than policies that would regulate or, with the rise of neoliberal arguments in the 1970s, deregulate economic actors according to what appeared to best serve middle-class consumer interests.[68]

Third, if the notion that the political community should serve citizens as consumers came to seem like common sense, it rarely sparked the passionate devotion to America that the Progressives' vision of their community as the world's best exemplar of white Christian civilization had done. The slow shift away from the Weyl-Kelley view of consumers using their purchasing power to promote labor interests and other social goods, and toward one in which citizens of the consumers' republic chiefly championed their own rights and economic interests, embodied a retreat from Progressive hopes not just for workers' well-being but also for a broader politics of robust, civic-minded participation in the service of moral purposes.

Fourth and finally, consumer-democracy notions proved over time unable to answer many difficult questions raised by rejection of mainstream Progressives' hierarchical conceptions of race, religion, gender, and culture. The fact that Americans as consumers were undifferentiated did not clarify whether civic equality meant that they should be treated as undifferentiated in all other regards, as many NAACP and National Woman's Party leaders argued, or whether the Kallenesque advocates of pluralism were right to insist that distinctive cultural, ethnic, religious, and gender identities should be publicly accommodated and often celebrated. As the barriers of Jim Crow segregation and female legal restrictions began to fall, the questions whether new sorts of different treatment were appropriate, either to overcome historic disadvantages or to allow the pursuit of distinctive ways of life, became more central but also more contentious in American politics. Policies that focused only on achieving greater prosperity remained appealing, but did not provide guides to all these intense disputes.

Partly because of these limitations, consumer democracy was never the whole story of American Progressive conceptions of community in the post–World War II era; and in regard to civil rights struggles, it was not even predominant. Again, along with their claims as consumers, civil rights activists used Social Gospel appeals, constitutional claims that all citizens were equal, cultural-pluralist themes, and more to win judicial and legislative victories that over time became a new source of national pride for many Americans. These developments contributed to Lyndon Johnson's reformulation of consumer-democracy ideas into a view of America as the Great Society, which would both fight racial discrimination and wage the War on Poverty. This vision moved America much further toward fulfilling some of the most enduring aspirations of both mainstream and more radical Progressives.

It did so, however, without changing the basic message that America was great because it provided material benefits, now to all. So long as the economy continued to grow and most Americans felt themselves to be experiencing rising prosperity, this vision remained highly persuasive. But narratives of political community that inspire allegiance chiefly by promising economic and political benefits are vulnerable during economic bad times and periods of perceived community weakness.[69] The evolving consumer-democracy views that were increasingly central to the New Deal, the New Frontier, and the Great Society had precisely those vulnerabilities—compounded by their limited capacities to respond to the special needs of many groups in America, and their limited ways of explaining how these different groups shared a common national identity.

Beyond the Community of Consumers: Contemporary Mixtures

In the late 1960s, the increasing cost of the Vietnam War, urban violence from black Americans seeking more rapid change, and white resistance to efforts to reduce their still-entrenched advantages all left the proponents of Great Society programs vulnerable. Many struggled to decide how to deal with new claims from identity groups including black nationalists, Chicanos, women's liberation organizations, gay rights proponents, disability advocates, and more. Some thought the challenge was to integrate and assimilate these diverse groups into the values and ways of life of white middle-class Americans, with identical rights for all and special privileges for none. Others believed that the pursuit of true civic equality required honoring many of the demands for special treatment. As Great Society views of American community became embattled on the right and the left, alienated Americans elected Richard Nixon, and many voted for George Wallace.

The Arab oil embargo in the early 1970s, combined with the decline of American manufacturing, intensified contestation over liberal economic policies, and controversies over affirmative action, abortion, and a range of cultural issues made the decade one of general disillusionment. Nixon resigned because of scandal, and voters threw out the next two presidents, Gerald Ford (Republican) and Jimmy Carter (Democrat), as failures. The Progressives' vision of America as a model white Christian civilization had become politically incorrect, but many Americans nonetheless were unhappy about unfulfilled economic promises and the uncertain, intensely conflicted approaches to issues of ethnocultural diversity and national unity that seemed to flow from Progressive conceptions of America.

So Ronald Reagan was able to become the champion of a broad and enduring modern conservative coalition. This was in part—but only in part—because he used supply-side economics and other neoliberal arguments to promote the efficacy of a low-tax, low-spending, low-regulation state and to develop an optimistic story about the free-market path to prosperity. In part, it was because he attracted national-security conservatives through his long-standing Cold War militancy. But important as those themes were, they were not enough. Beginning in 1974 with his "City Upon a Hill" speech at the first Conservative Political Action Conference, Reagan started advancing providentialist interpretations of America that won him the support of the emerging Religious Right. Adherents opposed liberal Social Gospel views, yet their fervent endorsement of the idea that America represented the height of Christian civilization echoed sentiments expressed by Progressives like Croly, to which many Americans still responded. Reagan also began endorsing color-blind approaches to racial issues in ways that appealed to racial conservatives after doctrines of white supremacy came to be widely discredited and affirmative action policies advanced.[70]

In so doing, Reagan offered a somewhat less recognizably Protestant version of earlier religious conceptions of American nationality. He presented America as a country committed to civil rights for all, but in ways that did not threaten further governmental assaults on white advantages. In this way, he and his allies broadened his political vision to include themes of moral purpose that went beyond economic concerns and that drew on stirring tropes previously advanced by Progressives. Reagan linked his disparate economic, national security, providential, and racial messages together by narrating America as a nation that would, at its best, reward virtuous character and punish vicious character.[71]

This conservative "character democracy" view competed well against liberals' consumer democracy after the nation had experienced hardships, scandals, and policy failures that made Americans feel neither prosperous nor powerful, much less virtuous.

The Reagan coalition dominated national politics and shaped the policy positions of both parties, including those of the Clinton interregnum, up through Barack Obama's election in 2008. But from his electric Democratic Convention speech in 2004 onward, Obama, who was steeped in progressive democratic thought during his early years, recombined a range of earlier progressive themes into a broadly captivating new vision of American political community. Obama made central to his career an account of America as dedicated to the principle of "E pluribus unum." While celebrating, not denying, their diversity, he insisted that Americans could, through expert-aided deliberative democratic processes, find a common agenda. He imagined give-and-take compromises that would yield satisfactory solutions to their problems, problems that Obama most often defined in terms reminiscent of FDR's robust economic democracy: jobs, homes, health care, and education—accessible ladders of mobility.[72] As Obama stated at Cairo University in 2009, he saw Americans as "shaped by every culture, drawn from every end of the Earth, and dedicated to a simple concept: E pluribus unum: 'Out of many, one.'"[73] That united effort to help meet everyone's needs was to be achieved, Obama frequently argued, by recognizing that "what makes this country work" is not only a commitment to individualism and self-reliance but also the religious belief that "I am my brother's keeper, I am my sister's keeper."[74] This ethical sense of shared responsibility for all members' well-being, Obama contended, is what enables Americans at their best to reach the compromises that the nation's divided structure of governmental powers renders necessary for effective action.

In so arguing, Obama invoked a Social Gospel sense of moral purpose, especially as articulated in the black church's social justice traditions of the sort that first led him to embrace Christianity.[75] He also suggested a Du Boisian–Kallenesque embrace of the nation's racial and cultural diversity, blended with Dewey-like hopes that democratic processes could produce consensus on how to resolve common problems in order to facilitate progress. This vision of American community inspired extraordinary fervor and increased political involvement by many previously less engaged groups in 2008, and despite severe setbacks in 2010, it helped Obama win again in 2012.

Obama's record in office, however, showed that his revised progressive vision remained anathema to many Americans. The Tea Party uprisings that spurred GOP victories in 2010 explicitly attacked "progressivism" on many grounds.[76] Some opposed governmental economic interventions, some attacked multilateralism, some criticized liberal religiosity, and some were repelled by the racial and cultural diversity that Obama championed.[77]

But it is also true that as president, Obama minimized some of his progressive themes. He relied extensively on the hope that despite intense conservative opposition, good compromise solutions to most policy questions could be worked out through inclusive engagement in deliberative democratic processes. Perhaps to avoid controversy, he neither elaborated his Social Gospel–black church sense of moral purpose nor provided much guidance on whether differentiated treatment of America's racial, religious, cultural, class, and other groups should be pursued. Perhaps as a result, from the 2010 election on he proved unable to sustain broad confidence that his progressivism offered a unifying account of compelling common goals while appropriately recognizing diversity. In his embattled second term, he increasingly had to resort to constitutionally vulnerable, unilateral executive actions.

Obama's hopes of unity were also dampened, to be sure, because his views were too conservative for many other heirs of Progressive traditions. Despite his invocations of diversity, he chose to side with Christianity and most elements of traditional morality; with a patriotic faith in America's exceptional character and mission; and most of all, with reformist but not radical changes to America's economic and political structures. Today, many on the left believe that mounting economic inequalities, the accompanying shift to an economy dominated by the financial sector, increased governance by elites and experts, and the growth of multinational and transnational economic associations all mean that strongly left-progressive positions on the economy, on democracy, and on the declining value of national states—views like those of Bourne, Dewey, and Du Bois at their most radical—need to be revived, intellectually modified, and politically strengthened. That was never Obama's agenda.

Conclusion

What do these developments tell us about Progressive conceptions of American political community in the twentieth and twenty-first centuries? They suggest, on the one hand, that although Progressive views have always been politically powerful and often predominant since their inception, they have repeatedly needed to be revised in response to changing conditions and their own internal difficulties. The moral vision of early-twentieth-century Progressives was too tied to religious, racial, national, and class forms of inequality to be sustainable as a genuinely democratic position. The ensuing view of America as an inclusive economic democracy had broad appeal in the Depression and held its support through eras of prosperity. It faltered when its focus on workers' interests became tainted as a move toward socialism, when progressive economic policies did not produce greater and more widely shared wealth, and when progressives divided on how far many kinds of diversity should be recognized or promoted. And especially since the early New Deal, progressives have chiefly offered rather bland, uninspiring, consumerist accounts of what unites Americans into one community.

Obama's recent reformulation of these views into advocacy for an America that embraces racial, religious, and cultural pluralism and democratic processes in order to improve the well-being of all in accord with moral commitments to mutual assistance has real strengths, both as politics and as policy. Still, the alienation from it on both the right and the left is understandable. It does not offer what its opponents most desire—either a return to an America of small governments operating in the service of predominantly white, Christian, middle-class interests, on the one hand, or a more radically egalitarian transformation of American economic and democratic institutions, indeed the global nation-state system, on the other. And again, its answers to what kinds of recognition of diversity and what sorts of bases of unity Americans should adopt remain unclear.

Still, all political positions have problems. Positions that try to stake out a coherent view of a nation as diverse as America face especially heavy burdens. It is hard to maintain full ideological consistency without losing supporters. It does not seem likely that views sharply to the right or the left of Obama-style progressivism will be able to build coalitions broad enough to gain enduring American national power (much less transnational potency) in the foreseeable future. It is now a commonplace that the changing demographics of America are working against the prospects of conservatives and may well produce something like liberal predominance in the future, despite gerrymandering, voter suppression, and more—though because nonwhite Americans are highly concentrated in large cities and in only some states, limiting their potential to win control of state legislatures and Congress, most analysts believe progressive successes are likely to take time.

The developments reviewed here suggest that success will in fact require more than time. Favorable demographics alone cannot substitute for a clear sense of purpose. To depict a vision of American political community that can be broadly inspiring, and to provide some guidance on the difficult question of what forms of diversity should be encouraged and what sorts should be combated, modern progressives may well need to elaborate American social justice traditions more convincingly. They may have to explain more fully what sorts of political communities and what forms of civic equality are appropriate today. Those hurdles do not appear insuperable. It is entirely possible that if its social justice aims were better defined, defended, and articulated as a program of concrete policies that set clear goals for democratic processes, something like Obama's progressive vision of a harmoniously pluralistic, democratic America would succeed to a greater extent than occurred during his presidency. But there will be dangerous stretches on the road to any greater success, and there are many difficult choices that must be made to decide what kind of political community progressives can and should be seeking to reach.

Notes

1. This paragraph and the next two are based primarily on Rogers M. Smith, *Civic Ideals: Conflicting Visions of Citizenship in U.S. History* (New Haven, Conn.: Yale University Press, 1997), 410–24 (and some phrasing is derived from there), as well as on Michael McGerr, *A Fierce Discontent: The Rise and Fall of the Progressive Movement in America, 1870–1920* (New York: Free Press, 2003), esp. 64–74, and David W. Southern, *The Progressive Era and Race: Reaction and Reform, 1900–1917* (Wheeling, Ill.: Harlan Davidson, 2005), esp. 44–47,

2. Herbert Croly, *The Promise of American Life* (1909; repr., New York: Dutton, 1963), 153–54, 214.

3. Ibid., 185.

4. Ibid., 359, 387.

5. Ibid., 196–97, 414.

6. Southern, *Progressive Era and Race*, 45.

7. Croly, *Promise of American Life*, 259, 263.

8. McGerr, *Fierce Discontent*, 183, 192–94.

9. Croly, *Promise of American Life*, 81.

10. Ibid., 283.

11. Ibid., 328–29.

12. McGerr, *Fierce Discontent*, xiv.

13. John Dewey, *Reconstruction in Philosophy* (1920; repr., Boston: Beacon, 1957), 204.

14. Ibid., 203.

15. Ibid., 202–3.

16. John Dewey, *The Public and Its Problems* (New York: Henry Holt, 1927), 109.

17. Dewey, *Reconstruction in Philosophy*, 204–5.

18. Ibid., 186.

19. McGerr, *Fierce Discontent*, 102; Southern, *Progressive Era and Race*, 62–63.

20. Randolph Bourne, *War and the Intellectuals*, ed. Carl Resek (New York: Harper and Row, 1964), 124–31; Bourne, *The Radical Will: Selected Writings, 1911–1918*, ed. O. Hansen (New York: Urizen, 1977), 255–62.

21. Horace Kallen, *Culture and Democracy in the United States* (New York: Boni and Liveright, 1924), 59, 64, 116, 123–24.

22. W. E. B. Du Bois, *Dusk of Dawn* (1940; repr., New York: Schocken, 1968), 817–25, 842, 847–48.

23. Southern, *Progressive Era and Race*, 154.

24. Lawrence B. Glickman, *Buying Power: A History of Consumer Activism in America* (Chicago: University of Chicago Press, 2009), 156.

25. Michael J. Sandel, *Democracy's Discontent: America in Search of a Public Philosophy* (Cambridge, Mass.: Harvard University Press, 1996).

26. Ibid., 222.

27. I therefore think Sandel goes too far in attributing to Weyl an *antiproducerist* vision of consumer democracy that made him a "prophet of the procedural republic" that Sandel believes Americans embraced in the latter part of the twentieth century (ibid., 224–26).

28. Walter E. Weyl, *The New Democracy: An Essay on Certain Economic and Political Tendencies in the United States* (New York: Macmillan, 1912), 15, 33–35, 78–95.

29. Ibid., 319.

30. Ibid., 272, 302, 345.

31. Ibid., 342, 345.

32. Ibid., 346–47.

33. Ibid., 191.

34. Ibid., 197.

35. Ibid., 202, 218.

36. Ibid., 216–17, 219.

37. Ibid., 224.

38. Ibid., 224–26, 232.

39. Ibid., 233.

40. Ibid., 244.

41. Ibid., 249.

42. Ibid., 249–50.

43. Ibid., 250.

44. Ibid., 251, 253.

45. Ibid., 254.

46. Andrea Tone, *The Business of Benevolence: Industrial Paternalism in Progressive America* (Ithaca, N.Y.: Cornell University Press, 1997), 127–28; Glickman, *Buying Power,* 155.

47. Florence Kelley, "Aims and Principles of the Consumers' League," *American Journal of Sociology* 5, no. 3 (1899): 289–304; Weyl, *New Democracy,* 191n1; Louis L. Athey, "Florence Kelley and the Quest for Negro Equality," *Journal of Negro History* 56, no. 4 (1971): 249.

48. Kelley, "Principles of the Consumers' League," 289.

49. Ibid., 289, 303–4.

50. Athey, "Florence Kelley and Negro Equality," 250–54; Glickman, *Buying Power,* 179.

51. Landon R. Y. Storrs, *Civilizing Capitalism: The National Consumers League, Women's Activism, and Labor Standards in the New Deal Era* (Chapel Hill: University of North Carolina Press, 2000), 44–48.

52. Ibid., 22–24, 54, 67, 119–20, 187.

53. Lizabeth Cohen, *A Consumer's Republic: The Politics of Mass Consumption in Postwar America* (New York: Vintage, 2003), 18–31.

54. Stephen Skowronek, *The Politics Presidents Make: Leadership from John Adams to George Bush* (Cambridge, Mass.: Belknap Press, 1993), 297–302.

55. Franklin Roosevelt, speech to the Commonwealth Club, San Francisco, September 23, 1932; reprinted in Scott J. Hammond, Kevin R. Hardwick, and Howard L. Lubert, eds., *Classics of American Political and Constitutional Thought,* vol. 2, *Reconstruction to the Present* (Indianapolis: Hackett, 2007), 407.

56. Ibid.

57. Franklin Roosevelt, State of the Union address, January 6, 1941; reprinted in Hammond, Hardwick, and Lubert, *American Political and Constitutional Thought,* 2:416.

58. Franklin D. Roosevelt, "State of the Union Message to Congress," January 11, 1944, American Presidency Project, www.presidency.ucsb.edu/ws/?pid=16518.

59. Roosevelt, State of the Union address, 1941; in Hammond, Hardwick, and Lubert, *American Political and Constitutional Thought,* 2:413–14.

60. Philip A. Klinkner, *The Unsteady March: The Rise and Decline of Racial Equality in America,* with Rogers M. Smith (Chicago: University of Chicago Press, 1999), 161–201.

61. McGerr, *Fierce Discontent,* 248–78.

62. Storrs, *Civilizing Capitalism,* 10, 255–56; Cohen, *Consumer's Republic,* 153–64.

63. Storrs, *Civilizing Capitalism,* 250–51; Cohen, *Consumer's Republic,* 153, 418n35, 520n45.

64. John F. Kennedy, "Special Message to the Congress on Protecting the Consumer Interest," March 15, 1962, American Presidency Project, www.presidency.ucsb.edu/ws/?pid=9108; Glickman, *Buying Power,* 266, 282.

65. Ralph Nader, *The Ralph Nader Reader* (New York: Seven Stories, 2000), 209–74.

66. Glickman, *Buying Power*, 163–74.

67. Ibid., 263–68; Cohen, *Consumer's Republic*, 165–91.

68. Storrs, *Civilizing Capitalism*, 250–51.

69. Rogers M. Smith, *Stories of Peoplehood: The Politics and Morals of Political Membership* (Cambridge: Cambridge University Press, 2003), 102–21.

70. Rogers M. Smith, "Identity Politics and the End of the Reagan Era," *Politics, Groups, and Identities* 1, no. 1 (2013): 122–23.

71. Desmond S. King and Rogers M. Smith, *Still a House Divided: Race and Politics in Obama's America* (Princeton, N.J.: Princeton University Press, 2011), 122–23.

72. Barack Obama, "Democratic National Convention Keynote Address," July 27, 2004, American Rhetoric: Online Speech Bank, www.americanrhetoric.com/speeches/convention2004/barackobama2004dnc.htm (accessed September 28, 2014); Rogers M. Smith, "The Constitutional Philosophy of Barack Obama: Democratic Pragmatism and Religious Commitment," *Social Science Quarterly* 93 (2012): 1251–71.

73. Barack Obama, "Remarks by the President at Cairo University," June 4, 2009, www.whitehouse.gov/the-press-office/remarks-president-cairo-university-6-04-09.

74. Obama, "Democratic National Convention Keynote Address," 2004.

75. Barack Obama, *The Audacity of Hope: Thoughts on Reclaiming the American Dream* (New York: Three Rivers, 2006), 206–8.

76. Bill Flax, "The Tea Party and Progressives Speak Separate Languages in a Divided America," Forbes.com, August 16, 2012, www.forbes.com/sites/billflax/2012/08/16/the-tea-party-and-progressives-speak-separate-languages-in-a-divided-america; Richard A. Viguerie, *Takeover: The 100-Year War for the Soul of the GOP and How Conservatives Can Finally Win It* (Washington, D.C.: WND, 2014).

77. Christopher S. Parker and Matt A. Barreto, *Change They Can't Believe In: The Tea Party and Reactionary Politics in America* (Princeton, N.J.: Princeton University Press, 2013).

Part III
The New State: Management and Expertise

13 • Completing the Constitution

Progressive-Era Economic Regulation and the Political
Perfection of Article I, Section 8

Daniel Carpenter

> Let us see what will be the consequences of not authorizing the Federal
> Government to regulate the trade of these states. . . . Many branches of
> trade hurtful to the common interest would be continued for want of
> proper checks and discouragements.
> —Alexander Hamilton, *The Continentalist* 6, 1782

It is now fashionable to describe the Progressive era as a decisive rupture
with the institutions and traditions of the founding and the early American
republic. Among the most symbolic (and simplistic) of these claims comes in
the columnist George Will's reduction of contemporary American politics to
the tension between Madison and Wilson. Since Wilson's election in 1912,
Will argues, "American politics has been a struggle to determine which of
these two Princetonians best understood what American politics should be.
Should we practice the politics of Woodrow Wilson of Princeton's class of
1879, or the politics of the class of 1771?"[1] Whether with respect to the size and
scope of government, directly elected by the people, or to the role of religion in
the public and civil spheres, commentators on the left and the right ascribe
this transformation—from limited government to social democracy and expansive government—to the Progressive era or the New Deal.[2]

Although there were some discernible shifts from the republican vision of the
founding and early republic and the democratic-republican vision of the Progressive era—principally with the rise of plebiscitary institutions at the state and
local level, the emergence of executive and expert forms of administration in lieu
of judicial decision making, and in some areas the emergence of planning and
systematic budgeting in government—the arena of economic regulation saw as

much continuity as break in doctrine and in practice. New understandings of government emerged, accompanied by broad transformations of administrative machinery. Yet much of the machinery was reassembled from earlier parts. And Progressive-era politicians and intellectuals wrestled long and hard with the question of interstate commerce. In many ways, the Progressive era witnessed the slow, steady extension to the national level of the police powers consensually possessed and used by states and localities at the beginning of the republic, earlier in the colonial period, and later throughout the nineteenth century.

This remapping of regulatory space characterized the governance of transportation, food and drugs, utilities, and other arenas. While labor policy points to a more expansive notion of governmental power and national scope (especially in the New Deal), commercial regulation transported a rigorous pattern of state-level governance to the national level. In these fields, regulatory institutions were adapted and resized to deal with a more far-flung pattern of commercial activity. Not merely the commerce itself but also the organization of industry in economic regulation began to cross state boundaries, and some of the most powerful actors in the creation of Progressive-era economic regulation were those agents deeply familiar with the police power of regulation, namely, state government officials and politicians.

The construction of the national regulatory state—starting not in 1887 with passage of the Interstate Commerce Act but at least a decade earlier—built upon the Commerce Clause (Article I, Section 8, Clause 3) in two senses: first in the narrow sense that more and more commerce crossed state boundaries and that the physical and informational distance between consumers grew apace, and second in the sense that regulated economic agents increasingly spanned state boundaries in their organization, their operations, and their political behavior.[3] The late nineteenth and early twentieth centuries saw the application of police powers to interstate commerce and to interstate commercial agents in steamboat regulation, in meatpacking, in food and drug regulation, in railroad and utility regulation, in interstate trucking, and in corporate combinations and trusts. Police powers and the interstate character of trade and markets explain not only the incidence of much economic regulation in the Progressive era—which markets and industries were regulated, and when—but also the institutional forms taken in a range of agencies including the Bureau of Chemistry and the Federal Trade Commission.[4]

Perhaps most critical to this account is a thread largely missing from the institutional narratives of American political development: the political action of state government officials. Some of the most active participants in the expansion of federal regulatory power were state governments and their elected representatives and career administrators. In forming associations of regulators to coordinate solutions to common problems, state officials, state attorneys general, and state regulators often created model laws, experimental institutions, and templates for the creation, evolution, and adaptation of federal regulatory statutes.

To be sure, these changes marked profound institutional transformations. The idea of the executive department as a coordinating and planning mechanism for interstate regulation was emerging in the nineteenth-century imagination. Yet the elaboration of that notion became concrete and institutionalized in the Progressive period as bureau chiefs took the reins of comprehensive new programs.[5] While state administrative officials had been forging and occupying more active roles since the Gilded Age, their Progressive-era boundary-spanning work became vital material for regulatory coalitions that supported national-level institutions.

This essay is meant to be, in part, a counterpoint to the poorly researched and weakly supported myth of an alleged Madison-to-Wilson shift. These hallucinations not only get the early republic wrong but in fact were debunked a generation ago, by Oscar and Mary Handlin, Willard Hurst, and then Gordon Wood; in addition, William Novak's painstaking inquiries have shown that republican regulation continued through the nineteenth century. These fantasies construct an equally imaginary, radicalized Progressive era, one that underplays critical transformations before 1900 and ignores the role of state governments in the changes that occurred. Progressive-era commercial regulation would not have been possible without the institutional models provided by earlier state laws and agencies, and it would not have succeeded politically without the active participation of state government regulators and elected officials.

To be clear, however, the metaphor of perfection in this chapter's title derives not from any normative admiration of the Progressive era but from a general intent to describe its transformations as an elaboration of the previous constitutional and legal framework. Perfection means not a full attainment of objectives but, owing to its Latin roots, a form of elaboration and completion.

Salus populi suprema lex est—Police Power in Early American Regulation

Until recently, the practice of regulation in the early American republic and the nineteenth century remained outside the purview of empirical research. In his exhaustive look at nineteenth-century statutes, administrative practices, and court cases—*The People's Welfare: Law and Regulation in Nineteenth-Century America* (1997)—William Novak decisively raised the bar for comprehensive work. Novak demonstrated that state and local governments in the nineteenth century regulated public safety, economic exchange, property use, public health, moral dimensions of human behavior, and a range of other activities. Far beyond the doctrine of eminent domain and even nuisance law, states and cities could and did regulate any number of activities in support of what their legislatures considered the common good. And in public health, state and local governments created—most notably in New York's health agencies of 1793 and 1805—some of the first administrative agencies endowed with broad police and seizure powers.[6]

One of the most common forms of economic regulation in the antebellum period came in licensure, not only the licensing of occupations but also the more common "licenses to trade." Maryland outlawed virtually all forms of nonlicensed trade in 1832. The Tennessee Supreme Court in *French v. Baker* (1856) gave its sanction to these laws—other state legislatures and courts had done so, too, in Pennsylvania, Missouri, and California—and held that an individual's status as a merchant derived not from any natural right but instead was a privilege that could be granted only by the state.[7] The very notion of a marketplace, as Novak observes,[8] was created by state and municipal laws that stipulated the place of commerce as well as the public posting of prices, uniform or standard weights and measures, and prohibitions on a wide variety of what was considered "unfair" economic practice.[9]

It was rare and remarkable for courts at any level to challenge these regulations. In a range of critical cases—*Vanderbilt v. Adams* (1827), *Stuyvesant v. Mayor of New York* (1827), *Baker v. Boston* (1831), and *Village of Buffalo v. Webster* (1833)—state courts legitimated public safety regulations upon property.[10] Through the mid-1860s, courts occasionally held that regulations did not serve a public purpose or that they were unduly discriminatory in the context of state constitutions, but the existence of a plausible public purpose to be served by regulation was a virtual guarantee of judicial legitimacy.

The argument that persons (individuals or corporately established) had a natural right to engage in economic activity, dispose of or sell their property, or take up any form of labor was occasionally made, but continually rejected. Two cases from Massachusetts were exemplary. Attorneys for Massachusetts liquor sellers lamented that the state's licensing laws violated their rights in the marketplace. Chief Justice Lemuel Shaw agreed with Whigs who argued instead that fully "three fourths of our general laws" would be similarly offensive were the liquor interests' claims upheld, including those statutes governing or prohibiting gambling houses, brothels, lotteries, and quarantines. Whigs countered more generally that the state had the general liberty to use its police power to regulate those businesses that aim for "the destruction instead of the promotion of the common good."[11] The Massachusetts liquor-licensing debate showed that to jurists and contemporaries in the antebellum republic, the power of the government to regulate liquor was considered to be cut from the same cloth as the power to license and the power to restrict trade. Justice Shaw went further and legitimized licensing laws in two 1837 cases. When Robert Rantoul argued that licensing laws were unconstitutional because they legislated a form of inequality among citizens, Shaw replied that it was the liberty of the General Court to "judge what the welfare of the community may require." When Rantoul argued in the second case that state licensing laws wrongly regulated interstate commerce, Shaw argued that nothing in Article I, Section 8 prevented the states from creating statutes with a view to "the peace, safety, health, morals and general welfare of the community."

So thoroughgoing were these understandings of *salus populi suprema lex esto* (let the welfare of the people be the supreme law) that as staunch a Democrat (and states'-rights enthusiast) as Roger Taney could appear before the Supreme Court in 1827 and maintain, without any hint of discord in the chamber, that there is no vested right to sell in the Constitution (*Brown v. Maryland,* 25 U.S. 419).[12] The question about Maryland's license laws was not whether they unconstitutionally restricted liberty—all agreed that the restrictions were entirely constitutional in that sense—but whether they infringed upon properly interstate commerce (Marshall, writing for the Court in a 6–1 decision, held that they did not).

The consensual nature of state economic restrictions was, to be sure, restricted to legitimacy and constitutionality. There were clear political disagreements over these statutes and their enforcement, yet the political consensus on the limits of rights and the primacy of the *res publica* was clear.

The state-level consensus, moreover, illuminates the question of national-level powers and obligations. It is quite clear that some of the Founders regarded federal regulation as all the more important in the face of far-flung commercial patterns, some of which were emerging even as they wrote. Alexander Hamilton, as the chapter epigraph indicates, suggested as much. His justification for the Commerce Clause was, in other words, one that explicitly invoked *salus populi,* and his characterization of regulation as "checks and discouragements" reminds us of Montesquieu's well-regulated society.

It should come as little surprise, then, that among the set of national regulatory functions served by Hamiltonian designs was regulation of the states.

Begin with finance. It is now well understood that the Second Bank of the United States was not essentially an instrument of monetary policy but rather an agent of regulation, governing state banks' practices.[13] To some degree, these regulations were embodied less in the Commerce Clause than in the Constitution's charge that Congress should "coin money and regulate the value thereof" (Article 1, Section 8, Clause 5). Yet as Marshall noted in *McCulloch v. Maryland* (1819), much of the utility of the Second Bank came from its position among and above state banks. This hard lesson was learned during the interregnum of 1811 to 1816, when the "necessity of resorting to the instrumentality of the banks incorporated by the states" was observed.[14] Marshall's opinion conveyed not only the injunction against state taxation of federal institutions, and not only the permissibility of government corporations, but also the clear supposition that the national bank was understood in part as a regulatory tool tackling charges that state banks alone could not, in Congress's view, address sufficiently.[15] Madison's well-known argument that the Commerce Clause did not justify the creation of a bank merely pointed to the stakes of *McCulloch;* it was understood that the constitutionality of the bank was inseparable from its status as a (partly) regulatory institution.[16]

As in finance—where the regulatory issue came from the multiplicity of state banks—many of the early federal efforts at economic regulation concerned cases in which the interstate or cross-border dimension was clear. Chief among these were the national state's century-long efforts to regulate water travel by steamboat. These efforts began with the Steamboat Inspection Act of 1838 and matured greatly with the Steamboat Safety Act of 1852, which created a Board of Supervising Inspectors with broad discretionary power to enforce the act. As Jerry Mashaw shows, the board was a genuine administrative agency with licensing powers and rule-making authority. Congress drew deeply on steamboat precedents when constructing the Interstate Commerce Act of 1887, less because of the Commerce Clause than because of the nature of the regulated object: transportation.[17]

The Institutional Confrontation of an Interstate World: Constitutional Elaboration in Meat, Dairy, and Drugs

Understanding the development of national-level economic regulation requires, in part, grappling with a set of economic and political changes in the objects of regulation. Two critical developments in the late nineteenth and early twentieth centuries lay behind those transformations: the explosion of interstate and indeed intercontinental commerce (driven heavily by the emergence of transcontinental railroad networks) and the transformation of economic production. Intertwined with these developments were changes in the political status of the firm and a set of informational asymmetries prevailing between consumers and producers that eventuated in safety and quality problems in the marketplace. Importantly, although these indicators of modernization corresponded to and even necessitated regulatory change, examination of the regulation of meat, dairy, drugs, and trade demonstrates that the foundations of interstate regulation had been well understood and developed by key state actors before the Progressive era arrived.

One of the most important measures of postbellum economic regulation came with the establishment of the Bureau of Animal Industry in 1884, which replaced the Treasury Cattle Commission, created three years earlier. The BAI was empowered to inspect and seize export cattle infected with pleuropneumonia and to conduct research into infectious cattle diseases. More broadly, it was empowered to administer statutes and regulations to protect the public from infected or disease-bearing meat products, eradicate animal diseases, and improve livestock quality. The broader Meat Inspection Act of 1891 both drew upon and expanded capacities in the U.S. Department of Agriculture (a department of government that George Washington had proposed in his Farewell Address in 1796). It authorized the USDA to inspect meatpacking and production facilities and to seize goods found to be unsafe (the term "adulteration" was more specific to the Pure Food and Drugs Act of 1906 and Progressive-era moral discussion). And it created a large cadre of inspectors stationed at different posts around the country. In many respects, it authorized a far more intrusive form of regulation than had existed, creating standards of purity and grade and endowing federal inspectors stationed locally (in lieu of, but also in cooperation with, state agents).

Yet like so many of its antebellum counterparts, the Meat Inspection Act and the Bureau of Animal Industry remain largely neglected by scholars. My sense is that the bureau and the law suffer from neglect not only because contemporary students have found meat less alluring than railroads, but also because they do not fit within the previously tidy frameworks that governed our understanding of this era—regulation by independent commissions (the 1884 law establishing the Bureau of Animal Industry entrusted enforcement entirely to an executive department), a clear break in 1887 (the Interstate Commerce Act), and a focus on regulation as rate setting and price focused (the BAI statute and the Meat Inspection Act can be read as an elaboration of the police powers that had been exercised in the early national states and throughout the nineteenth century.[18]

Far from being a substitute for state economic regulation, federal food regulation functioned as an institutional complement. For throughout the late nineteenth and early twentieth centuries, state legislatures eagerly passed pure dairy and food laws. The most comprehensive research on these laws and their spread has been conducted by the economic historian Marc Law, whose inquiries demonstrate three patterns: the dominant explanation of the laws was not rent seeking, but asymmetric information; the laws were not associated with an increase in regulated commodity prices; and exactly as theories of asymmetric information would predict, the adoption of these laws was associated with a subsequent increase in consumer demand for the product (rent-seeking theories are powerless to explain such a result).

The fact that the Meat Inspection Act preceded the Interstate Commerce Act and the fact that it coincided with state efforts to regulate dairy and other food markets mean that the usual story of a Progressive-era break with the early republic must be jettisoned (table 1). What had changed concerned not an interpretation of the constitutional order but the complexity of products and the processes of bringing them to market, and the attendant information asymmetries between producers and consumers.[19] Enforceable dairy laws were enacted primarily at the state level because the markets remained much more locally situated; some of the best evidence for this relative "locality" of dairy markets comes from farmers' political organizations, which expressed a logic of geographically conditioned commodity-price variability. Those farmers who joined the Populist movement were, as Elizabeth Sanders has rightly emphasized, those whose commodity prices had been buffeted most heavily by international price swings and disturbances in the money supply—that is, grain, cotton, and tobacco farmers. Dairy farmers, whose prices were determined mainly in local markets, were less likely to join the movement. Unlike enforceable dairy laws, then, enforceable meat laws moved to the federal level because meat was becoming a dominant middle- and upper-class food product—a development driven as much by a change in tastes as by a change in production—and because its commerce was interstate and its production was characterized increasingly by the economies of scale that had eluded dairy agriculture.[20]

Recent research on the experience with meat and food inspection in other Progressive-era settings suggests a similar interpretation—namely, that the federal statutes served as extensions of the police power previously held by states over those markets where changes in production and transportation created

Table 1: Timing of State Pure Food Laws

State	Year when product or product group was regulated and the enforceability of regulation
Alabama	Butter (1895, NE), food (1896, NE)
California	Butter/cheese/milk (1897, E), food (1895, NE)
Colorado	Butter/cheese/milk (1895, E),[a] food (1887, 1893 NE)
Connecticut	Butter/cheese/milk (1895, E), food (1895, E)
Delaware	Butter (1895, NE)
District of Columbia	Butter/cheese/food (1898, E), milk (1895, E)
Georgia	Butter/cheese/milk/food (1895, NE)
Illinois	Butter/milk/cheese (1897, E),[b] food (1899, E)
Indiana	Butter/milk (1897, NE), food (1899, E)
Kansas	Milk (1897, NE), food (1897, NE)
Kentucky	Butter (1900, E), food (1900, E)
Louisiana	Butter (1886, E), food (1882, E)
Maine	Butter/cheese (1895, E), milk (1893, E), food (1895, NE)
Maryland	Butter/milk/cheese (1900, NE), food (1890, E)
Massachusetts	Butter/milk/cheese (1891, NE),[c] food (1882, E)
Michigan	Butter/milk (1899, E), cheese (1897, E), food (1893, E)
Minnesota	Butter/milk/cheese (1899, E), food (1899, E)[d]
Missouri	Butter (1896, E), cheese (1897, E), milk (1891, E), food (1899, NE)
New Hampshire	Butter (1891, E), butter/cheese (1895, E), food (1891, E)
New Jersey	Butter/cheese/milk (1886, E),[e] food (1886, E)
New York	Butter/cheese/milk (1900, E), food (1898, E)[f]
North Carolina	Butter (1895, NE), food (1899, E)
Ohio	Butter/cheese/milk (1896, E), food (1886, E)
Pennsylvania	Butter (1899, E), cheese/milk (1897, E), food (1893, E)
Rhode Island	Butter/milk (1896, E), food (1896, NE)
South Carolina	Butter/milk/cheese (1896, NE), food (1898, E)
Tennessee	Butter (1895, E), food (1897, E)
Texas	No regulations enacted.
Virginia	Butter/cheese/milk (1891, NE), food (1887, NE)
Washington	Butter/cheese/milk (1899, E), food (1899)
West Virginia	Butter/cheese (1891, NE), food (1891, NE)
Wisconsin	Butter/cheese/milk (1899, E),[g] food (1899, E)

Source: Data from U.S. Senate, *Adulteration of Food Products.* This table is reproduced from Marc T. Law, "The Origins of State Pure Food Regulation," *Journal of Economic History* 63, no. 4 (December 2003): 1111–12.

Notes: The year in parentheses refers to the year in which a law regulating a particular product was enacted. *E* and *NE* denote whether the law was enforceable or nonenforceable. Because separate laws regulating butter, cheese, and milk were frequently enacted, these products are listed individually. The category "Food" refers to the general pure food laws that were enacted by state governments and that regulated products including sugar, molasses, vinegar, and canned goods. This table contains information only for those states for which I was able to find city-level retail prices in the Bureau of Labor's retail price survey. The states included for each of the six food and dairy products I examine in this chapter are:

    Butter, molasses, and sugar: All states in the table.

    Cheese: All states in the table except Connecticut, Kentucky, and North Carolina.

    Milk: All states in the table except Connecticut, Indiana, Louisiana, North Carolina, and Rhode Island.

    Vinegar: All states in the table except Colorado, Delaware, Georgia, Indiana, Michigan, Minnesota, New Hampshire, New Jersey, Rhode Island, Texas, Virginia, Washington, and Wisconsin.

[a] Laws regulating dairy products were enacted in 1887 and 1893, but no enforcement authority was specified until 1895.

[b] Dairy products were regulated by earlier laws, but no enforcement authority was specified until 1897.

[c] Earlier laws were enacted in 1884 and 1887, but no enforcement authority was specified until 1891.

[d] Earlier laws regulating food were enacted, but no enforcement authority was specified until 1899.

[e] Laws regulating dairy products were enacted in 1882, 1883, and 1884, but no enforcement authority was specified until 1886.

[f] Laws regulating both food and dairy products were enacted in earlier years, but no enforcement authority was specified until 1898 and 1900, respectively.

[g] Laws were enacted in 1887, 1893, 1895, and 1897, but no enforcement agency was specified until 1899.

and amplified information asymmetries, and detection technologies, in the absence of regulation, worsened the asymmetry. The late nineteenth century saw an explosion of interstate commerce in meat and the slaughterhouses and abattoirs that characterized Chicago and New Orleans. Some of the local-level regulation that presaged the BAI statute of 1884 and the Meat Inspection Act of 1891 came in the development of municipal regulations for abattoirs and slaughter standards.[21] Yet for infectious diseases that could kill entire herds of cattle and potentially sicken consumers as well, these municipal laws ranged from weak to powerless in the capacity to combat the problem. (In these cases, information asymmetries combined with a pernicious form of externality, requiring enforceable uniform minima of production standards.) When bovine tuberculosis emerged, "relying on litigation and reputation mechanisms proved unequal to the task," as two economic historians have recently put it. Accordingly, enforcement of federal statutes alone was able to eradicate the problem.[22]

The history of meat and dairy regulation points to a different approach to both the Constitution's remarks on interstate commerce and some celebrated cases of constitutional jurisprudence. In the landmark case of *Gibbons v. Ogden* in 1824 (22 U.S. 1), Chief Justice Marshall ruled that navigation was a part of interstate commerce and was therefore subject to federal rather than state regulation. But he added that "inspection laws, quarantine laws, and health laws of every description" were among the "immense mass of legislation" that was "not surrendered to the general government" and that could "be most advantageously exercised by the states themselves."[23] This notion of inspection as a core police power of the state is found not only in the implied powers of Article I, Section 8 (what it means to "regulate"), but also in Article I, Section 10, which reads in part, "No state shall, without the consent of the Congress, lay any imposts or duties on imports or exports, except what may be absolutely necessary for executing it's [sic] inspection laws." Finally, this reading of police powers allows us—more properly, has enabled others—to interpret anew the celebrated *Slaughterhouse* cases (1873). Those decisions have been frequently understood as a pronouncement on the Fourteenth Amendment, one that, according to many contemporary scholars, misreads the Privileges and Immunities Clause. Yet it is more plausible and consistent with the historical evidence to read the case as the legitimation of state-based police-power regulation under common law principles and not as a constraint on the Privileges and Immunities Clause.[24]

The historical development of drug regulation has been discussed elsewhere,[25] but suffice it to say that the interstate nature of the drug trade was recognized very early in U.S. history. For those features of health services that were provided intrastate—pharmacists and pharmacies, physicians and nurses—the Progressive era left regulation in state hands.[26] Yet the inadequacy of state power over drugs was recognized early on by the Association of State Food and Drug Commissioners, who helped lobby for federal regulation. When the Pure Food and Drugs Act of 1906 was considered in the courts, the issue of the federal government's police powers over interstate trade in drugs was never a serious issue. In *U.S. v. Johnson* (1916), the Court held that the Food and Drugs Act did not prohibit false medical claims generally but only false and misleading statements about the ingredients or identity of a drug specifically. Congress then passed the Sherley Amendment in 1917 to clarify the matter, yet the police powers of the Bureau of Chemistry (and later the FDA) in interstate commerce were never in doubt.

Was it then the case that police powers of inspection and seizure in the name of health and safety resided only in the states? The understanding of Hamilton and the consensual constitutionality of both the Steamboat Inspection Act and the Meat Inspection Act suggest otherwise. Hamilton clearly understood that the federal government had police powers over those matters that flow in interstate commerce. What remains is to consider those issues raised and debated in *United States v. E. C. Knight*, 156 U.S. 1 (1895), and *Swift & Co. v. United States*, 196 U.S. 375 (1905)—namely, whether the production of goods that enter interstate commerce is subject to regulation under the Commerce Clause. That is a matter for statutory and constitutional interpretation. But it is clear that the actors of the time (including state governments) regarded the federal government's police powers as a solution to the ungovernability of exploding interstate commerce and amplifying information asymmetries.

It is, finally, worth considering that inspection and police powers over safety hazards also functioned as an important rationale for railroad safety regulation at the federal level. Here too the federal government's role followed numerous state-level measures and commenced well before 1900, with the Safety Appliance Act of 1893, which required that all freight trains carry safety couplers and air brakes. A 1901 statute compelled interstate freight carriers to report all accidents, each report constituting testimony under oath, and in the depths of the financial crisis of 1907–8, Congress passed legislation that regulated working hours for trainmen and telegraphers. After a second accident-reporting statute was passed in 1910, Congress passed the Locomotive Boiler Inspection Act of 1911, which established the Bureau of Locomotive Inspection in the ICC.[27]

The Institutional Confrontation of an Interstate World: Police Powers in a Federal Market Regulator and the Case of the Federal Trade Commission

An understanding of Progressive-era regulation as the extension of consensually defined state-level police powers to interstate commerce assists not only in interpreting the timing and incidence of regulation across markets but also in understanding the institutional forms taken by regulatory regimes. The Progressive-era origins of trade regulation, including fair trade regulation and, to a lesser degree, antitrust, owe much to the creation of a federal inter-state trade regulatory commission that was conceptualized by its proponents as a way to monitor newly emergent markets. Summarizing this perspective, Louis Brandeis contended that to confront the new realities of interstate eco-nomic interconnection, the well-understood republican doctrine of police powers needed to be expanded: "We need the inspector and the policeman, even more than we need the prosecuting attorney."[28]

The origins of the Federal Trade Commission lay in judicial, economic, and political debates over trade practices and trusts. The antitrust issues involved were occasioned by interpretations of the Sherman Antitrust Act, construed strictly from the *Trans-Missouri* case in 1897 and more leniently in the series of "rule of reason" decisions beginning in 1911. With the Supreme Court's re-writing of the Sherman Act, popular and academic dissatisfaction with national-level trade regulation and antitrust ranged widely.[29]

An important organizational force behind the Federal Trade Commission Act was the Bureau of Corporations, which made a consistent and persuasive case to Congress that neither statutes (which is to say, the power of congres-sional committees) nor courts (delegitimized in the wake of the "rule of rea-son" decisions) had proved capable of responding to changes in industrial organization. The infrastructure below the five-member commission was composed initially of the employees and records of the Bureau of Corpora-tions. Yet the final structure of the act differed materially from the licensing structure that some bureau members and some members of Congress had wanted. As Martin Sklar has noted:

> Absent from the regulatory legislation of 1914 were those proposed mea-sures that had been at the heart of the license-registration plans, and that would constitute, or lay the basis for, a government-directed market, namely: (1) registration of all large corporations; (2) submission of all their contracts, agreements, and combinations to the commission for approval or disapproval; (3) commission control over prices; (4) commis-sion control over corporations' capitalization, stock issue, or investment policy; (5) commission control over corporations' accounting, bookkeep-ing and records; (6) commission condemnation and seizure of monopo-listic corporations . . . ; finally, and most decisive, . . . (7) federal license, or incorporation, as the condition for engaging in commerce, and com-mission power to issue and revoke license, or corporate charter, and to bar from commerce any corporation without license or charter.

Indeed, one of the major obstacles to a licensing-based corporation came from the complaints of states'-rights votaries that a national licensure agency would interfere with the powers of state governments over corporate charter.[30]

Conceptualizing the FTC as a police agency is not a modern, revisionist reading; rather, it stems from the statute itself and the set of observable compromises that brought it to fruition and passage. As Scott James has demonstrated in his skillful analysis of the legislative history of the ICC and of federal utilities regulation in the New Deal, the Democrats were able to move the commission forward only by threading a middle path through their more corporate liberal wing and their more populist, antimonopoly agrarian wing.[31] The commission was charged with investigative powers, and its compulsory force lay in cease and desist orders that, like the enforcement powers of state agencies and fair trade statutes, were subject to judicial review. Alleged violations of antitrust laws were to be submitted to the attorney general.

In the vast conflicts over industrial combination that shot through the Gilded Age and the Progressive era, the FTC's police powers merely recognized the emergence of interstate production and commerce, with which earlier combatants had wrestled. The very basis of the disputes in *E. C. Knight* (1895) and *Swift* (1905) concerned whether the Sherman Act prohibitions on restraint of trade applied to manufacturing activity for goods that were *known* to later enter into interstate transport.[32] Put differently, whether commerce entailed the manufacture of goods intended for cross-border transport or simply the transfer of those goods across state boundaries was one of the central issues of early Sherman Act jurisprudence. Questions about the empirical composition of interstate commerce also led Congress to establish a department of statistics within the ICC to investigate the breadth and extent of interstate commerce. The existence of these debates and institutions demonstrates not that all parties were agreed on what constituted commerce, but that two branches of government were wrestling with the issue as they rarely if ever before had done.[33]

State Participation in the Building of National Regulation and Principles for the Twenty-First Century

If the rise of a far-flung dynamic of interstate commerce explains Progressive-era economic regulation, it might stand to reason that those actors most intimately familiar with the problem—state regulators exercising their lawful

police powers—not only would have been supportive of national-level regulation but also would have participated in its construction. The templates for the
Motor Carrier Act of 1935 and, earlier, for the Pure Food and Drugs Act of 1906
were both set in interstate cooperation of regulators who considered model
standards and model statutes.

The governance of transportation markets saw the slow but steady extension of state-level powers to federal-level governance. In the writing of the Interstate Commerce Act of 1887, Congress looked to the transportation model
of the Steamboat Act of 1852, which, as Mashaw argues, "anticipated the organizational form, the practical operation, and the congressional politics of
much modern health and safety regulation."[34] To be sure, in its rate regulation
the ICC departed from the earlier paradigms of steamboat governance. Yet it
did not radically transcend the powers that state governments and commissions had exercised in their governance of railroads. The Illinois Constitution
of 1870 and the regulatory arrangements created in 1873 had regulated rates
through commission rate setting or (in other states) litigation-based enforcement (with, for example, triple damages).[35]

Except for Stephen Skowronek's treatment of the Transportation Act of
1920 and Lawrence Rothenberg's study of interstate trucking, little attention
has been paid to a set of developments that were equally important to the
twentieth-century economic infrastructure of the United States: trucking and
highways.[36] The development of horseless carriages and small-scale freight
transportation on public roads introduced a competitive dynamic to the interstate freight market and posed important challenges to state governments. For
example, the expansion of individualized transportation was accompanied by
a rise in the number of accidents. In addition, the incentives for trucks to carry
heavy per-trip loads led to a commons problem in which roads and bridges
wore out faster than states could repair them (and without appropriate contributions from those imposing the costs of their freight upon others).

The primary organ through which these problems were tackled was not the
ICC—at least not at first—but a fascinating and little-understood network of
state commissioners who began meeting in the late 1880s: the National Association of Railway and Utility Commissioners (NARUC). ("Railway" was
changed to "Railroad" in 1923, and the same acronym now stands for National
Association of Regulatory Utility Commissioners.) NARUC sponsored annual
meetings at which cross-state coordination of standards could be feasibly
designed, and perhaps most notably it created model statutes to limit the
variability in diffusion of regulations across the states. As a result, state-level

regulation of transportation—and later, utilities, foods, drugs, and a range of other commodities—began to closely resemble one another. The laboratories of American democracy were, through pragmatic and cooperative federalism, increasingly correlated in their decisions and institutions.

The Nobel laureate in economics George Stigler missed this point as much as any other scholar did. In his rightly celebrated—not for its empirics, but for the elegance of his theory—article on regulation, Stigler examined a data array of state-level trucking weight limits and proceeded to regress these limits upon several variables designed to measure the power of special interests (table 2). Yet in ways that eluded Stigler, his data were characterized by a clumping of states upon the very limits outlined by model statutes. In his data, fully fourteen of the forty-seven observations on state trucking weight limits for four-axle carriers were identical (at 24,000 pounds), and another seven

Table 2: Clustering in State Trucking Weight Limits, 1932–33

Maximum weight (tons), by wheel count				
4-wheel / 12	4-wheel / 11	4-wheel / 10	6-wheel / 20	4-wheel / 12 6-wheel / 20
Idaho	Arizona	Alabama	Colorado	Idaho
Illinois	California	Florida	Connecticut	Illinois
Indiana	Georgia	New Hampshire	Idaho	Indiana
Iowa		North Carolina	Illinois	Iowa
Kansas		Oklahoma	Indiana	Nebraska
Missouri		South Carolina	Iowa	West Virginia
Montana		South Dakota	Maryland	
Nebraska		Tennessee	Nebraska	
North Dakota		Vermont	Nevada	
Ohio			New Jersey	
Washington			New Mexico	
West Virginia			New York	
Wisconsin			Oregon	
			Pennsylvania	
			Rhode Island	
			West Virginia	

Source: Data from George J. Stigler, "The Theory of Economic Regulation," *Bell Journal of Economics and Management Science* 2, no. 1 (Spring 1971): 19.

took a second-most common value (20,000 pounds). These clusterings did not occur by chance; they were the result of model statutes diffused through NARUC and its committee system.[37]

As states began to develop their standards, however, the need for further coordination became evident. A six-axle, legally compliant truck traveling from Michigan to Ohio would, in the 1920s, have been forced to drop over ten tons of freight in order to cross state boundaries. It is for this reason and to solve other coordination problems that NARUC began to suggest that only a national-level commission could provide a structure for coordinated solutions to regulatory governance. Many of these suggestions were taken up in the Motor Carrier Act of 1935, which both expressed and further established public-social cooperation between the ICC and NARUC.

In the area of food and drug regulation, the Association of Official Agricultural Chemists (AOAC) was a standard-setting group that involved federal officials and state-level regulators. The AOAC also offered model regulations and testing standards, and unlike NARUC, it predated the major federal regulatory law of the sphere. The AOAC held congresses in 1899 and 1900, and its model statute for a new, national-level regime became the operative template for the Pure Food and Drugs Act of 1906.[38] After the passage of the act, the AOAC continued to serve as a coordinating mechanism between the states and the federal government.

To be sure, state governments did not greet every Progressive-era regulatory reform with uniform approval. The National Association of State Dairy and Food Departments, for instance, often resisted the USDA's accretion of power. Yet state chemists and scientists employed at a range of institutions and universities provided an alternative voice. The more important point is that standardization across states was achieved both through interstate coordination and through federal-level regulation, and that one of the most powerful constituencies for the latter was the very organizations that executed the former.

Conclusion: Republican Regulation and the Future

Two metaphors have governed recent studies of the history of American commercial regulation. The changes wrought in the early twentieth century amount to either the primary rupture with the founding, an unprecedented and unintended expansion of state power, or the mere continuation of a tradition of economic regulation that emerged from the colonial period. The interpretation here leans more toward that of continuity, but it notes three essential transformations. The first was that developmentally, the Progressive era's reliance on republican "police power" meant that national regulation was more likely to be modeled on policing forms of regulation as opposed to nationalization of industries. In other words, the republican past of American commercial regulation bounded the possibilities of its Progressive future, not least in contrast to European and Japanese models that emerged in the same period. The principal exception to this approach, the national development and expansion of the postal system in the early twentieth century, further demonstrated the power of an interpretive framework that privileged republican models entrenched in the early nineteenth century.

A second transformation was that the necessary participation of the states resulted in new roles for state administrators in the national system. In ways that were not true of their nineteenth-century counterparts, state agencies and officials became active governing agents in markets that traversed their boundaries. Whether in participating on committees that drafted model legislation or in consulting with federal agencies, or in their later work in national regulation that drew heavily on state administrative experiences (for example, Harvey Wiley and the Pure Food and Drugs Act of 1906), state officials began to occupy multidimensional roles. The normative corollary is that in some ways, Progressive-era commercial regulation emerged in ways that not only preserved but also revitalized American federalism and its institutional laboratory for policy formation.

Third, a road that brought a previously decentralized police power to the national government permitted an applicable yet realistic national model of commercial governance. Regulation by police power may well be more desirable than either of the more fashionable alternatives that have arisen in the last thirty to forty years: the litigation state, in which torts at the state and federal level become stand-ins for republican government, and the behavioral paradigm now popular in Washington, in which regulation is either seized on or forgone in the name of "nudge"-like interventions that aim to preserve a fictionalized consumer freedom while correcting for plausible behavioral biases of citizens.[39] It is plausible that the litigation state has been effective where budget-emasculated and ideologically hamstrung agencies have not.[40] Yet as a substitute for regulation, it undermines the mixed-regime of republican government that, even after the Progressive era, has remained vital to American constitutionalism.[41] As for nudge-based solutions to policy dilemmas, which tend to regard the sovereign choices to regulate production, marketing, and consumption as "paternal" and thereby to delegitimize by assumption progressive regulatory institutions, I think they are potentially useful for a very small subset (2 percent to 5 percent) of the range of problems that republics face in regulating commerce. A review of some proposals coming from this school of thought suggests that libertarian paternalism has been proposed and tried in policy arenas and social contexts in which the historical stakes were remarkably low (slight changes to savings account options, for example). Consequently, it is difficult to see how a society can tackle food and drug safety, industrial monopoly, commercial fraud, price transparency, quality disclosure, environmental harm, pollution externalities, and a range of other problems by using nudge-based tools. While they constitute an addition to the tool kit of governance and merit further policy experimentation, they are marginal solutions to marginal problems, and have been undertaken in a context in which large areas of concern have already been tackled (and in many cases solved) by designs conceived and implemented through republican institutions.

It is not necessary to conclude that all police-power forms of regulation are necessarily desirable. Yet it is possible to maintain that in the presence of political competition and the republic of time—overlapping temporal intervals of service and, hence, of the consequences attendant on elections—democratic republics are as likely as any other regimes to learn from their mistakes. It is less clear that jury-based regulation possesses the learning and stability properties of republics, and much less clear that nudge-based regulation responds as much to the *salus populi* and its multiform expression in a mixed regime.

The Progressive era marked a fundamental break with many patterns of American institutions, but much Progressive policy in economic regulation reappropriated and refashioned a set of earlier republican traditions. The republican standpoint provides, to be sure, a range of plausible criticisms of the Progressive era, not least its substitution of plebiscitary majority democracy for mixed-regime republican government in which the people are represented variably yet stably in the republic of time. Yet an indispensable fact for understanding the history of economic regulation in the United States is that the regulation of interstate commerce became institutionally similar to either previous state-level regulation through police powers or to earlier notions of interstate commercial regulation (including steamboat inspection, meat and health inspection, and others that were created before 1887 and before 1914). I do not claim that *all* economic regulation in the Progressive era or other periods can be described this way. Yet the idea of police-power regulation functions as a basic account against which claims of institutional rupture must be examined empirically.

Regarding the relationship of these police powers to the Constitution, there is little doubt about the direct constitutionality of police powers, but genuine debate about how they should be constructed. No one plausibly claims that economic regulation falls outside the enumerated powers of Congress. More common today (but not common at the origins of the American republic) is the idea that the Bill of Rights provides some sort of precedent claim against economic regulation in protections of property rights and, more recently, commercial speech. This pattern of claims has arisen at two moments in American history: first, the jurisprudence that came about in the *Lochner* era, and second, more recent arguments entertained in the Roberts Court's jurisprudence.

The absence of any sustained consensus on the regulation-limiting powers of the Bill of Rights in the early republic seems critical here. If constitutional interpretation is to be guided—whether partially or fully—by original understanding and historical context, it would appear dispositive that a range of licensing laws, marketing restrictions, and restrictions on advertising have been presumptively within the consensually understood powers of the state. Even the recently fashionable commercial speech doctrine—or, put more moderately, some of the extreme uses that some of its advocates intend—must be called into question as plausibly inconsistent with an originalist reading of the Constitution and with republican traditions of government.[42]

In its extension of state-level police powers over interstate commerce, the architects of the Progressive era—not just Wilson and Roosevelt, but hundreds of state commissioners and regulators—advanced their understanding that markets need cops. Indeed, they understood what theoreticians from Montesquieu to Hamilton understood and what modern scholars often neglect: it is often through the police power of republican government that competitive marketplaces with credible prices and trustworthy commodities are forged.

Notes

Originally prepared for presentation at the Progressives' Century Conference, Yale University, November 2013. I thank Jaehyuk You for research assistance, and I wish to express my particular gratitude to Bruce Ackerman, Samuel DeCanio, Stephen Engel,

Richard Epstein, Karen Orren, and Stephen Skowronek for their frank and searching comments on an earlier version of this paper.

The chapter epigraph is from Alexander Hamilton, *Writings*, ed. Joanne Freeman (New York: Library of America, 2001), 112.

1. George Will, "Religion and the American Republic," *National Affairs* (Summer 2013), 120. Having graduated from Princeton himself, Will is, I think, inclined to attribute too much influence to these two individuals as opposed to a range of others. Will's binary, like most, fundamentally misleads.

2. See also Richard Epstein, *How Progressives Rewrote the Constitution* (Washington, D.C.: Cato Institute, 2006); Robert Levy and William Mellor, *The Dirty Dozen: How Twelve Supreme Court Cases Radically Expanded Government and Eroded Freedom* (Washington, D.C.: Cato Institute, 2009).

3. On the trans-state behavior of these corporations, see Richard White, *Railroaded: The Transcontinentals and the Making of Modern America* (New York: Norton, 2011).

4. My argument is thus similar to but fundamentally different from that of Edward Glaeser and Andrei Schleifer in "The Rise of the Regulatory State," *Journal of Economic Literature* 41 (June 2003): 401–25, who ask whether judges and bureaucrats have capacities that change in relevance when the size or complexity of the firm changes.

5. Daniel Carpenter, *The Forging of Bureaucratic Autonomy: Networks, Reputations, and Policy Innovation in Executive Agencies, 1862–1928* (Princeton, N.J.: Princeton University Press, 2001).

6. William Novak, *The People's Welfare: Law and Regulation in Nineteenth-Century America* (Chapel Hill: University of North Carolina Press, 1996), 201–2.

7. Ibid., 91–92.

8. Ibid., 95–105.

9. Ibid., 290–91.

10. Ibid., 70.

11. Johann Neem, *Creating a Nation of Joiners* (Cambridge, Mass.: Harvard University Press, 2008), 158–59 (discusses Whig response to Democrats and liberty-based claims against regulation); Leonard W. Levy, The *Law of the Commonwealth and Chief Justice Shaw* (Cambridge, Mass.: Harvard University Press, 1957), 229–65; Christopher Tomlins, *Law, Labor and Ideology in the Early American Republic* (New York: Cambridge University Press, 1993), 35–59.

12. Novak, *People's Welfare*, 111.

13. Eric Lomazoff, " 'Turning (Into) the Great Regulating Wheel': The Conversion of the Bank of the United States, 1791–1811," *Studies in American Political Development* 26, no. 1 (April 2012): 1–23.

14. *McCulloch v. Maryland*, 17 U.S. 316, 354 (1819).

15. *Id.* at 353.

16. Jefferson's argument so heavily invokes the regulatory logic of Article I, Section 8 that it bears a full rehearsal:

To 'regulate commerce with foreign nations, and among the States, and with the Indian tribes.' To erect a bank, and to regulate commerce, are very different acts. He who erects a bank, creates a subject of commerce in its bills, so does he who makes a bushel of wheat, or digs a dollar out of the mines; yet neither of these persons regulates commerce thereby. To make a thing which may be bought and sold, is not to prescribe regulations for buying and selling. Besides, if this was an exercise of the power of regulating commerce, it would be void, as extending as much to the internal commerce of every State, as to its external. For the power given to Congress by the Constitution does not extend to the internal regulation of the commerce of a State, (that is to say of the commerce between citizen and citizen,) which remain exclusively with its own legislature; but to its external commerce only, that is to say, its commerce with another State, or with foreign nations, or with the Indian tribes. Accordingly the bill does not propose the measure as a regulation of trade, but as 'productive of considerable advantages to trade.' Still less are these powers covered by any other of the special enumerations.

For this characterization of the regulatory powers of the Second Bank, I rely heavily on the painstaking research in Lomazoff, "'Great Regulating Wheel.'" See also Jerry Mashaw, *Creating the Administrative Constitution: The Lost One Hundred Years of American Administrative Law* (New Haven, Conn.: Yale University Press, 2011), chap. 9.

17. Mashaw, *Creating the Administrative Constitution*, 202–8.

18. See, for example, Oscar Handlin and Mary Flug Handlin, *Commonwealth: A Study of the Role of Government in the American Economy; Massachusetts, 1774–1861* (Cambridge, Mass.: Harvard University Press, 1947), 65.

19. In treating the Meat Inspection Act and the Interstate Commerce Act as Progressive-era creations, I am deliberately opening the question of when the Progressive era began; for purposes of a conference dedicated to the Progressives' century, however, it is worth gesturing to those features of late-nineteenth-century economic regulation that shaped twentieth-century governance. Just as my friend Ira Katznelson is fond of saying that the long nineteenth century ended in 1917, so it is possible to read the Progressive era as overlapping with what Mark Twain awkwardly termed the Gilded Age or, as in Daniel Rodgers's reading, in *Atlantic Crossings* (Cambridge, Mass.: Harvard University Press, 1993), as having extended into the New Deal.

20. Elizabeth Sanders, *Roots of Reform: Farmers, Workers, and the American State, 1877–1917* (Chicago: University of Chicago Press, 1990).

21. Christine Meisner Rosen, "The Role of Pollution Regulation and Litigation in the Development of the U.S. Meatpacking Industry, 1865–1880," *Enterprise and Society* 8, no. 2 (2007): 297–347. According to Rosen: "As the number of animals led to the slaughterhouse skyrocketed, traditional regulatory methods of dealing with these foul-smelling waste streams broke down. . . . Prior to the advent of good municipal sewerage

and sewage treatment, the use of water to clean the killing floors simply washed the ever-increasing quantities of putrefying organic material into open street drains and local waterways." Rosen's article covers the insufficiency of zoning ordinances and nuisance laws for dealing with slaughterhouse waste, and her fascinating and well-researched conclusion is that municipal regulations constituted new, more technologically advanced marketplaces in meat production: "Management response to pollution regulation, litigation, and public protest—not just market conditions—shaped the processes of technological innovation, spatial reorganization, and vertical integration, which led to the development of the modern packing industry."

22. Alan L. Olmstead and Paul W. Rohde, " 'The Tuberculosis Cattle Trust': Disease Contagion in an Era of Regulatory Uncertainty," *Journal of Economic History* 64, no. 3 (2004): 929–63.

23. Marshall of course did not, in this holding, rule out a federal role for inspection and health laws, and in the economic environment of the time the presumption that the dominant flows of commerce in these areas were intrastate as opposed to interstate was entirely reasonable.

24. See Novak, *People's Welfare*, 230–33, and Herbert Hovenkamp, "Technology, Politics, and Regulated Monopoly: An American Historical Perspective," *Texas Law Review* 62 (April 1984): 1295–96. In "Pollution Regulation and Litigation," Rosen argues, "It is only relatively recently that legal historians . . . rediscovered the role that public health reformers played in the creation of the abattoir and recognized that the majority Supreme Court decision was really about upholding the state's right to use its police powers to regulate business to protect the public health and welfare." Furthermore, the abattoir company was not a conventional monopoly but more in line with what we would today call a public-private partnership. The abattoir company "was the operator of a French-style abattoir, an enterprise that was carefully designed to meet the best sanitary standards of the day, in which all of New Orleans' butchers were entitled (as well as required) to carry on their businesses and pay a rent that was set by law—not the abattoir company—and where most of their slaughtering waste was converted into products on site, under the watchful eyes of state sanitary inspectors."

25. See Daniel Carpenter and Gisela Sin, "Crisis and the Emergence of Economic Regulation: The Food, Drug and Cosmetic Act of 1938," *Studies in American Political Development* (Fall 2007). On subsequent development, see also Daniel Carpenter, *Reputation and Power: Organizational Image and Pharmaceutical Regulation at the FDA* (Princeton, N.J.: Princeton University Press, 2010). On the 1906 statute, see the authoritative account of James Harvey Young, *Pure Food: Securing the Pure Food and Drugs Act of 1906* (Princeton, N.J.: Princeton University Press, 1996). I discuss the role of state officials in lobbying for the law in *Forging Bureaucratic Autonomy*, chap. 8.

26. A useful reminder of this state of affairs comes in the weakness of Massachusetts institutions in regulating compounding pharmacies during the meningitis outbreak of 2012. I pass here on whether the institutions are optimal or whether other

institutions are desirable and note only that to Progressive-era officials, there was no inherent conflict between regulating health services at the state level and food and drug commodities at the federal level.

27. Mark Aldrich, "Running Out of Steam: Federal Inspection and Locomotive Safety, 1912–1940," *Journal of Economic History* (2007). See also Barbara Welke, *Recasting American Liberty: Gender, Race, Law, and the Railroad Revolution, 1865–1920* (New York: Cambridge University Press, 2001).

28. In *Letters of Louis D. Brandeis*, vol. 2, *1907–1912*, ed. Melvin I. Urofsky and David W. Levy (Albany: State University of New York Press, 1972), 686–94; quoted in Scott James, *Presidents, Parties, and the State: A Party System Perspective on Democratic Regulatory Choice, 1884–1936* (New York: Cambridge University Press, 2000), 160.

29. On dissatisfaction with the Court's economic reasoning, see Martin J. Sklar, *The Corporate Reconstruction of American Capitalism, 1890–1916: The Market, the Law, and Politics* (Cambridge: Cambridge University Press, 1990), 203. Wilson understood that the antimonopoly radicalism of the agrarians was not tenable as economic policy. As he said in 1912, "I dare say we shall never return to the old order of individual competition, and that the organization of business upon a great scale of co-operation is, up to a certain point, itself normal and inevitable" (nomination acceptance speech, reprinted in the *Commoner*, August 16, 1912; quoted in James, *Presidents, Parties, and the State*, 157). He also remarked that even though "competition can not be created by statutory enactment, it can in large measure be revived by changing the laws and forbidding the practices that killed it, and by enacting laws that will give it heart and occasion again."

30. Sklar, *Corporate Reconstruction*, 195–203, quotation on 330; Jonathan Chausovsky, "From Bureau to Trade Commission: Agency Reputation in the Statebuilding Enterprise," *Journal of the Gilded Age and Progressive Era* 12, no. 3 (July 2013): 343–78.

31. James, *Presidents, Parties, and the State*.

32. See also Sklar, *Corporate Reconstruction*, 123–27.

33. On the Department of Statistics within the ICC, see the announcement in U.S. ICC, *Interstate Commerce Reports: Decisions and Proceedings of the Interstate Commerce Commission*, vol. 1 (May 1887 to June 1888), 354 (July 1887) (Rochester, N.Y.: Lawyer's Cooperative Publishing, 1887), and the circular of October 20, 1887, ibid., 601, which offers an exemplary case illustrating the department's inquiries.

34. Mashaw, *Creating the Administrative Constitution*, 208.

35. Mark Kanazawa and Roger Noll argue that "the federal law paralleled the Granger statutes in that it limited long-haul, short-haul rate differentials and established the ICC to control rates. Moreover, the Interstate Commerce Act became the blueprint for subsequent federal regulatory statutes"; Kanazawa and Noll, "The Origins of State Railroad Regulation: The Illinois Constitution of 1870," in *The Regulated Economy: A Historical Approach to Political Economy*, ed. Claudia Goldin and Edward Glaeser (Chicago: University of Chicago Press, 2008), 22.

36. Stephen Skowronek, *Building a New American State: The Expansion of National Administrative Capacities, 1877–1920* (New York: Cambridge University Press, 1982), chap. 8; Lawrence S. Rothenberg, *Regulation, Organizations, and Politics: Motor Freight Policy at the Interstate Commerce Commission* (Ann Arbor: University of Michigan Press, 1994).

37. There are other problems with Stigler's statistical estimations—not least the highly nonrandom assignment of his treatment variables (trucks per population, agricultural labor force, and road quality)—and some measurement problems. For a critique, see Daniel Carpenter, "Detecting and Measuring Capture," in *Preventing Regulatory Capture: Special Interest Influence and How to Limit It,* ed. Daniel Carpenter and David A. Moss (Cambridge: Cambridge University Press, 2013). For a mathematical proof of the invalidity of Stigler's principle of inference in his 1971 article and his later *The Citizen and the State: Essays on Regulation* (Chicago: University of Chicago Press, 1974), see Carpenter, "Protection Without Capture: Product Approval by a Politically Responsive, Learning Regulator," *American Political Science Review* (November 2004).

38. Carpenter, *Forging Bureaucratic Autonomy,* 262.

39. Richard Thaler and Cass Sunstein, *Nudge: Improving Decisions About Health, Wealth, and Happiness* (New Haven, Conn.: Yale University Press, 2008); Cass Sunstein, *Simpler: The Future of Government* (New York: Simon & Schuster, 2013).

40. Sean Farhang, *The Litigation State: Public Regulation and Private Lawsuits in the United States* (Princeton, N.J.: Princeton University Press, 2010).

41. The notion of a mixed-regime republic that I have in mind gestures to an older model of republican government wherein different officials and their organizations represent different orders and, perhaps as important, different time horizons. Hence, the separation of powers amounts to only a threadbare fact expressed in the mixed regime.

42. Put simply, no federal or state judge would have regarded (and no judge did regard) any of the commercial regulations—one thinks of the manifold strict restrictions on advertising and marketing, which include restrictions on claims made about products—as an infringement on speech as defined in the First Amendment. The police power of the American republic over product claims and other aspects of commerce was clear and, from a First Amendment "speech" standpoint, unassailable. See again Novak, *People's Welfare.*

14 • Rights Through Knowledge and Reason
Civil Rights Aspirations in the Progressive-Era
Department of Labor
Paul Frymer

It is now well established that the intellectual vitality and political achievements of the Progressive era coincided with extensive reversals in civil rights and racial equality. Although a time of critical political innovation, when reformers increasingly looked to administrative institutions operationalized through national and local governments to help solve a range of societal ills caused by increasing industrialism and economic inequality, the Progressive era also marked a period frequently referred to as the nadir of American race relations.[1] The racism of the period came not just from southern whites reasserting their dominance in the aftermath of Reconstruction by imposing Jim Crow and voter disenfranchisement, but from many northern Progressives who injected a range of eugenic, social Darwinist, and male-dominant heteronormative ideas to promote xenophobic, segregationist, nationalistic, and imperialistic political agendas.[2]

Progressive-era racism was of significant consequence, since the ideas of the period became institutionalized in New Deal policies that promoted economic and social regulation in racially bifurcated ways. New Deal legislation including the National Labor Relations Act, the Social Security Act, and the Fair Labor Standards Act exempted critical coverage for African Americans seeking respite from economic and racial inequality.[3] As a result, it was not until the "rights revolution" of the mid–twentieth century that democratic idealism became meaningfully inclusive. The rights revolution, in turn, relied on a set of tactics and instruments befitting a different political time and context, one in which both newly emergent organizations and older institutions found themselves importantly altered by ongoing changes in society and government. Political parties and administrators by no means disappeared, for instance, but

they were, importantly, joined and pushed by increasingly aggressive and organized civil rights activists and a sympathetic legal community of plaintiffs, lawyers, and judges who, in turn, institutionalized civil rights policies in a manner
that transformed and altered the New Deal regime.[4]

This history has led scholars on both the left and the right to juxtapose
Progressive-era regulation against the lack of commitment to racial equality
and to see the rights revolution as essential to eradicating the racism that was
always the subtext of early-twentieth-century reforms. In recent years, some
scholars have gone further, suggesting that Progressivism was a detour on the
road to equality. In its most extreme formulation, Progressivism was discredited by its racism, and it is argued that only a full-throated commitment
to individual rights in the contemporary period holds out the promise of redeeming the potential of the Gilded Age to join democracy with laissez-faire
economics.

Consider in this regard recent scholarly attempts to "rehabilitate" *Lochner v.
New York* (1905). This ruling has traditionally been understood as vindicating
an imagined vested right that was used to defend individual freedom to contract against an invasive Progressive agenda to regulate in the name of the
public good. *Lochner* was discredited when the Supreme Court declared that
no such fundamental right to contract existed and that government had the
authority to pursue reforms associated with the New Deal and, later, Great
Society programs. Those now seeking to rehabilitate *Lochner* argue that the
Progressives' critique of rights merely abetted a view of the public good that
was racially charged and discriminatory. They assert that the rights upheld in
Lochner would have—if defended—helped protect African Americans who
were entering into a racially stratified labor market in which white male domination of both corporate capital and the trade unions served to deny blacks
entry into many workplaces.[5] In short, the effort to rehabilitate the old order of
the *Lochner* era is part of a broader and sustained attack against the core principles of the Progressive order. More broadly, the racism of the era is being
used as evidence of the failure of a reform idea: the use of governmental regulation to address societal inequalities.

Perhaps the most vocal of these rehabilitators of *Lochner* is David Bernstein, who charges that Progressive legal scholars and judges enabled and defended segregation as part of the police power and did not treat it as a violation
of the Equal Protection Clause.[6] He defends the jurisprudence of the *Lochner*
decision as one that "pioneered the protection of the right of women to compete with men for employment free from sex-based regulations, the right of

African Americans to exercise liberty and property rights free from Jim Crow legislation, and civil liberties against the states ranging from freedom of expression to the right to choose a private school education for one's children."[7] Had the Old Court's defense of rights won out over Progressive-era efforts, Bernstein implies, African Americans would have benefitted from the free market. His attack, then, is part of a larger critique of both the Progressives' and the New Deal's reliance on governmental regulation of the economy as a tool used against inequality and on behalf of unions.

Both the traditional understanding of *Lochner*—as upholding an individual right to contract versus the governing authority to regulate for the public good—and the new scholarship—which reframes *Lochner* as maintaining individual rights against Progressive regulatory aims infused with racist intent—rely on false juxtapositions of concepts like regulatory administration and rights, and on dichotomies among governments, courts, and individuals. They also, in the course of drawing such dichotomies, ironically subordinate race to other considerations and deny its foundational status in any explanation of American political development. The scholarly debate is about rights versus regulation, and race, racism, and racial inequality in American society become reduced to mere exemplars. This debate presumes that rights and regulation can and do exist outside racial stratification, offering seemingly neutral, though contrasting, institutional responses.

Activists and scholars interested in racial power rarely make such distinctions, instead seeing different democratic approaches as offering historically specific opportunities in the ongoing battle to attack the long-standing bastions of racial inequality. Civil rights lawyers in both the *Lochner* and the New Deal eras looked creatively for *any* opportunity to challenge racial hierarchies.[8] From W. E. B. Du Bois to Ralph Bunche to A. Philip Randolph, they attacked Progressive ideals and policies that excluded and hurt African Americans.[9] But they did not then leap to the false juxtapositions and stark alternatives that characterize today's debate. In fact, their critiques tended to be largely consistent within the Progressive framework of the time. Many black leaders, especially those focused on economic reform, by and large endorsed the chief tenets of Progressivism, from the promotion of regulation to the aspirational emphasis on knowledge, science, and education. What distinguished them most from their white Progressive allies was that they demanded recognition of the race problem as something distinctive and central to the human condition, and they demanded enactment of specific measures to extend Progressive policies to the African American community.

To illuminate this distinction between, on the one hand, a trade-off between rights and regulation, and, on the other hand, the mutual entailments of rights and regulation, the rest of this chapter focuses on the work of African American activists in the Department of Labor (DOL) during the Progressive era, and on two men in particular: W. E. B. Du Bois and George E. Haynes. The labor problem was in many ways at the heart of the Progressive project, and the establishment of the Department of Labor and its forerunner, the Bureau of Labor, represented an early victory. Like many of these early institutional victories, the DOL was not a huge success. Its power was at the margins, and it rarely used such power for anything more than conciliation and tepid reformism. In the area of race, the Department of Labor did little to disturb a racially fragmented labor market dominated by white employers and by unions that discriminated against African Americans. But the department, following the Progressive spirit of believing in the power of knowledge, science, and expertise to expose societal problems and begin the process of solving them, participated in a quite wide-ranging examination of black labor in American life. Some of this was through issued reports. Du Bois wrote three of these reports for the Bureau of Labor in the years around 1900, compiling empirical data on African Americans that would help form the basis of his monumental book *The Philadelphia Negro*. In addition, the DOL created the Division of Negro Economics, headed by George Haynes. The division was consistently hampered by the broader constraints of the department and the times, but nonetheless represented one of the first civil rights employment agencies in American history.

My goal here is not to reclaim the Department of Labor as a force of Progressivism that sharply joined its agendas with understandings of racial power. At the end of the day, it did not. Instead, I want to explain why these two civil rights activists were drawn to the Progressive project. First, I show that they shared the Progressives' faith in the empirical findings of social scientists and other leading experts. They looked, in particular, for applications of Progressive techniques that might spur progress in race relations. Second, I retrace their discovery that science and expertise were not enough to focus the attention of the larger public on racial inequality and, through that discovery, that race and racial oppression were independent forces that could not be completely subsumed within the Progressive mantle of reform.[10] Neither of these men succeeded in making their visions mainstream, either in the nation or in the Progressive movement. But their vision was decidedly not rights versus regulation. It was instead that racial progress required that the two be joined.

Rights are as race-less as regulation. The primary figures discussed in this chapter were interested in neither rights nor regulation per se. Instead, they sought to address the problem of racial inequality and to mobilize whatever resources were available to that end. Federal labor regulators wanted to know more about the lived experience of African Americans, and they enlisted the likes of Du Bois and Haynes as experts in this endeavor. When Du Bois and Haynes reciprocated, they acted on the Progressive premise that an objective assessment of the facts on the ground would lead both to an understanding of social problems and to progress toward their solution. Their studies were exemplary of the Progressive intent to identify social trends and to prepare the ground for action. They became disillusioned when politicians construed their findings in a way that served their own prejudices and ultimately questioned the whole premise of research targeted at racial problems. The racism was not in the techniques employed, but in the mindset of those politicians who reviewed the findings. Indeed, those Progressive techniques remained invaluable to the cause of promoting equality even after racism was assaulted more directly by the demand for civil rights. It was only when the Progressive commitment to social knowledge was joined to a commitment to equality that a civil rights agenda was more fully realized.

W. E. B. Du Bois and the Bureau of Labor's Reports on African American Life

Responding to the "constant, pressing, and growing demand for authentic information upon the subject of labor," Congress established the Bureau of Labor in 1884 to respond to the more than ten million people in the United States engaged in manual labor.[11] The bureau reflected the ideas of the budding Progressive movement and followed the development of similar labor bureaus in numerous northern states dealing with industrial strife and alarming societal conditions. Massachusetts was first, creating its Bureau of Labor Statistics in 1869, with the mission of using social science and statistics to alert politicians and the broader public to workplace problems and to consider what might be done to promote greater peace and harmony. Legislators in Congress argued that a new federal bureau was needed to foster "a greater, profounder, and more extended knowledge of the general character, habits, manners, customs, and dispositions of the people, their social status, their progress in civilization and intelligence, their material and sanitary condition, their advancement in moral and mental culture"; its object would be "to promote a more general diffusion and better comprehension of social science . . . based upon statistics which collects, collates, arranges, and compares facts, from which the statesman ascertains, and without which he can not ascertain, those great principles in accordance with which the state must act if it would promote and foster the well-being and happiness of its citizens."[12] They selected Carroll D. Wright, the former head of the Massachusetts labor board, to be the first head of the bureau. Wright, following in the Progressive spirit of Mary Parker Follett and others, stressed the need to use the bureau's knowledge for mediation and conciliation in order to avoid the conflicts arising from labor unrest and unionization movements around the country.[13]

Although the creation of the bureau occurred during the last decades of the nineteenth century, when racial discrimination, legal exclusion, and segregation were widespread, it was not an object of controversy for southern white legislators in the same way that New Deal legislation would be a half century later. White southerners had reestablished their obstructionist role in Congress toward civil rights policy, but their views toward a potential labor bureau reflected a range of realities. First, southerners worried throughout the era of black migration to the North that their region would be left without a suitable labor force. A bureau or department of labor might prove helpful in this regard. Second, although opposed to labor activism, southerners saw the budding labor movement as a potential ally, seeing northern labor leaders' antagonism toward African Americans and Chinese immigrants as helpful to their own desires to keep black labor from migrating north and west.[14]

This is not to suggest that southerners were indifferent to the potential role the new bureau might play with regard to the racial hierarchies in the segregated South. Senator John Tyler Morgan of Alabama worried at the time of the bureau's establishment in 1884 that such a new agency might harm the southern economy by meddling in the region's agricultural affairs. Morgan responded with fear:

> This commissioner I suppose will send his emissaries, his agents, into my State among the people who live in the hill country, the white people who own the land and work it themselves, and who would not allow a negro to come within sight of a fence if they could help it. Not only are they not co-laborers, they are not associates with them; they are nothing more than the inhabitants of the same country upon terms of ordinary friendship between the races. Your commissioner's employee goes to one of these families and says to the head of it, "you are a laborer; you own this land, it is true; but you toil upon it, you raise crops from year to

year, you support and educate your children; I want to make an inquiry of you for the purpose of making a report to the Senate of the United States or to the commissioner of labor as to the social, intellectual, and moral prosperity of these laboring people upon your plantation."[15]

Morgan went on that these commissioners would be inquiring about racial conditions, and anticipated their questions:

I want to know whether you are in the habit of recognizing as equals the colored people that live in your neighborhood; I want to inquire whether it is in accordance with your views of social duty that you should associate with every person that you meet. What is the rule of social intercourse between you and your neighbor? What do you do if a colored man or colored woman wants to come and sit down at your table and the like? That is part of my duty to make this inquiry about you because you are a laboring man or a laboring woman, and I want to know your social condition.[16]

But other southerners supported creation of the bureau because it might help the South reverse rising migration patterns. Senator James George of Mississippi argued that the new bureau "would inquire and report as to the special employments of the colored people in this country, how many are employed in any particular class of manufacturers or in agriculture." George thought it "important that the people of this country shall know how the colored labor of this country is distributed and in what it is principally engaged," adding, "[I] believe that there are very few, if any, colored laborers in the factories of New England."[17] He wanted the bureau's purview to be limited to those people who were wage laborers. George, like other southerners in Congress, joined in supporting the establishment of the bureau because black labor was a big business for the South. The estimated value of black labor at the time was announced in Congress at more than $235 million: $138 million for the production of cotton, $100 million for the menial services of women and children, $50 million for mechanical work, $23 million for tobacco, $13 million for sugar and molasses, $8 million for transportation.[18] To prevent black workers from fleeing the South and leaving capital in the region without an adequate workforce, southern politicians campaigned for a federal agency that would make clear to the nation that black workers would fare no better anywhere else. Indeed, as a special report issued by a congressional committee with a majority of Democratic legislators declared in 1880, African Americans were leaving not because of "deprivation of their political rights or any hardship in their condition," but instead had "undoubtedly [been] induced in a great degree by Northern politicians, and by negro leaders in their employ."[19]

The desire of members of Congress, both northerners and southerners, for more information provided an opportunity for the new bureau to study African American life. As mentioned above, the bureau's first chief, Carroll D. Wright, was particularly interested in empirical studies. Among the many dozens of reports that he commissioned, he published nine at the end of the nineteenth century on the condition of black Americans. Wright argued that labor statistics promoted the "material, social, intellectual, and moral prosperity" of working Americans, and he found the perfect collaborator to provide information on African American workers—a young professor beginning work at Atlanta University, W. E. B. Du Bois. Du Bois shared Wright's sentiments, arguing at the time, "There is only one sure basis of social reform and that is Truth—a careful, detailed knowledge of the essential facts of each social problem. Without this there is no logical starting place for reform and uplift."[20] Du Bois likewise emphasized the importance of studying black workers: white academics at the time, he wrote, failed "to recognize the true significance of an attempt to study systematically the greatest social problem that has ever faced a great modern nation."[21] As he put it in an 1898 essay: "Though we ordinarily speak of the Negro problem as though it were one unchanged question, students must recognize the obvious facts that this problem, like others, has had a long historical development, has changed with the growth and evolution of the nation; moreover, that it is not *one* problem, but rather a plexus of social problems, some new, some old, some simple, some complex."[22] Du Bois argued strongly for the methods of social science: "Whenever any nation allows impulse, whim or hasty conjecture to usurp the place of conscious, normative, intelligent action, it is in grave danger. The sole aim of any society is to settle its problems in accordance with its highest ideals, and the only rational method of accomplishing this is to study those problems in the light of the best scientific research."[23] He thought social science would allow scholars to overcome long-standing biases and prejudices, compel people to realize the need for reform. Perhaps most importantly, he argued that scientific inquiry would force "all partisans and advocates" to "explicitly admit what all implicitly postulate—namely, that the Negro is a member of the human race, and as one who, in the light of history and experience, is capable to a degree of improvement and culture, is entitled to have his interests considered according to his numbers in all conclusions as to the common weal."[24]

Du Bois wrote three reports for the bureau, material that coincided with conferences he hosted at Atlanta University on the study of African American life. These studies were works of social science, relying on extensive statistical computations, beginning with a large-scale study of black socioeconomic conditions in 1897.[25] His bureau-sponsored studies reflected his methodological and ideological approach. At each turn, he emphasized variation and development, and in so doing, he transformed African Americans from a category to a group of individuals. He began his study of Farmville, Virginia, with the assertion that "there has been but the one object of ascertaining, with as near an approach to scientific accuracy as possible, the real condition of the Negro." Like all his writings for the bureau, this one relied extensively on census data, marching through the conditions of the black population in Farmville. For the most part, he made few additional comments, though he remarked that there was "considerable dissatisfaction over the state of domestic service" among his interviewees, and that "Negroes are coming to regard the work as a relic of slavery and as degrading, and only enter it from sheer necessity, and then as a temporary makeshift."[26] His research was intended to dispel binary notions of blacks' status: "The question then becomes, not whether the Negro is lazy and criminal, or industrious and ambitious, but rather what, in a given community, is the proportion of lazy to industrious Negroes, of paupers to property holders, and what is the tendency of development in these classes."[27]

Du Bois argued that computation was needed in the study of black people in order to humanize the race in the eyes of white majorities, and to emphasize empirical variation, which would show both the possibilities of black progress and the social scientific reasons for the exceptions. His study of African American land ownership in Georgia relied on meticulously collected census data on black landholding, and he found slow but surprising progress of black land ownership in Georgia after 1870: by 1890, 470,000 blacks had gained possession over a million acres of land.[28] The reports are as neutral as they are meticulous, reporting pages and pages of census statistics without editorializing. But an occasional comment reflects his broader goal of uncovering variation, development, and humanity. In documenting "an unfinished cycle of property accumulation," Du Bois wished to show the possibilities of black citizenship: "The fact that an increasingly large proportion of the total property of the State is in the hands of town Negroes shows that it is not merely the idle and vicious that are drifting to town."[29]

Of course, this evidence of the economic significance of the African American population did not satisfy Du Bois, and he remained skeptical of the potential efforts of the bureau and the Progressive spirit of reform. He fought with the bureau when it decided not to publish a fourth study, one on Lowndes County, Alabama.[30] Moreover, the mainstream media of the day distorted his findings and frequently turned them on their head. For instance, the *Atlanta Constitution* put an absurdly positive spin on one of Du Bois's reports: "As a rule, the negroes are doing fairly well all over the south. They enjoy with the whites in the enjoyment of public school advantages, and every incentive to thrift, economy and upright citizenship is held out to them. Between the two races in the south there exist the kindliest feelings, broken only by such occasional outbreaks of passion on the part of the negro race as call for vigorous treatment. But the foul brutes who suffer from the righteous, though illegally enforced penalties of lynch law, can hardly be said to represent the negro race."[31] The *New York Times* ignored the bulk of the lengthy empirics in his report on Farmville, focusing on two lines in his conclusion: "The industrious and property-accumulating class of the negro citizens best represents, on the whole, the general tendencies of the group. At the same time, the mass of sloth and immorality is still large and threatening."[32]

Moreover, Du Bois's writings for the bureau were just an early stage in his own intellectual evolution. He became increasingly radicalized by the violence of southern reaction and by racism across the nation generally: "One could not be a calm, cool, and detached scientist while Negroes were lynched, murdered and starved."[33] A few years after publishing his final report for the bureau, Du Bois titled a chapter of his book *The Souls of Black Folk* "On the Meaning of Progress." He used the chapter to express his disillusionment with the Progressive project and to lament the failed ideals of another Progressive reformer, Josie, a woman who tried valiantly to improve her community's condition, only to be thwarted and left destitute. Du Bois concluded the chapter with the question, "How shall man measure Progress there where the dark-faced Josie lies? How many heartfuls of sorrow shall balance a bushel of wheat? How hard a thing is life to the lowly, and yet how human and real! And all this life and love and strife and failure,—is it the twilight of nightfall or the flush of some faint-dawning day?" After "sadly musing," he left Josie and "rode to Nashville in the Jim Crow car."[34]

At the heart of Du Bois's ultimate disillusionment was his recognition of the fundamental incompatibility between his empirical findings and the extant power relations in the nation at large. Using social science to provide further insight into the problems facing African Americans could go only so far in convincing those in power. But Du Bois's disillusionment did not alter his goals for Progressive reform; it just redirected the focus of his primary efforts. The racism lay in institutions, and social investigation would not stimulate reform until the foundations of those institutions changed.

George Haynes and the Division of Negro Economics

Although the number of reports commissioned on black workers declined after 1900, the bureau and the Department of Labor (established 1913) continued to provide statistics and reports on the activities of the black worker. World War I spurred the department's efforts because of renewed interest in the control of labor patterns and the promotion of weapons manufacture. The department responded as well to the Great Migration of the war years, in which an estimated half a million African Americans left the South for what they believed were better job and life prospects in northern cities. An estimated 150,000 to 300,000 African Americans left their homes in the South in the summers of 1916 and 1917 alone.[35] Many civil rights activists, such as Du Bois and James Weldon Johnson of the NAACP, celebrated this movement, arguing that it would benefit blacks all over the nation by making their labor more competitive and resulting in an increase in wages and opportunities.[36] National news outlets, however, tended to broadcast voices that were far more alarmist.[37] Samuel Gompers believed migration was being fueled by antilabor activists intent on disrupting trade unionism in the North, and southern politicians believed it was being done for political purposes; believing that northerners and the Department of Labor were involved, many southern states passed laws forbidding the solicitation of laborers for work outside the state.[38] Some legislators perceived the migration as being responsible for riots in the North, alarming members of Congress further.[39] The *New York Times* wrote, "The negro problem has entered upon a new and dangerous phase," and feared that "bloodshed on a scale amounting to a local insurrection at least will be threatened in more than one section where large white and black populations face each other unless some program of conciliation is adopted."[40]

Fear of black migrants was pervasive, but it also provided an opportunity for the Department of Labor to do something novel in a policy arena—the state of black workers—that had previously been untouched by federal officials. In 1918, the department established the Division of Negro Economics, a unit that quickly developed into one of the nation's first economic employment agencies. Its establishment was in part motivated by the rates of black migration, since this movement led southern whites to rethink the value of black labor, but it was most directly driven by the need to mobilize black workers for the

war effort.[41] As labor secretary William B. Wilson stressed to Mississippi orga-
nizers of a "War Workers' Conference" in 1918: "It is especially important at
this crucial period, when we need to conserve all the resources of the Nation for
the conduct of the War, that these principles should be applied to all the people
of our Country, including the Negro people, who constitute about one-sixth of
the total laboring population."[42] The impact of the war was of special interest
because African Americans were "freely admitted to many of the occupations
formerly monopolized by white workers and from which Negroes were previously excluded. With the demand for labor so much greater than the supply,
the fear of white workmen that Negroes would be their competitors at a lower
wage was greatly lessened in many semi-skilled and skilled occupations."[43]

With the end of the war, the division moved on to play an important role in
the demobilization of thousands of black soldiers; it "is not an exaggeration to
say that the return of the Negro soldier to civil life is one of the most delicate
and difficult questions confronting the Nation, north and south."[44] The secretary of labor argued that "the question of living conditions of Negro wage-
earners must receive more attention during the period of peace that it could
receive during the war period," and he counseled the need for cooperation and
information to avoid further disturbances and tension.[45] For these reasons, a
surprising coalition of southern business owners and northern labor leaders
looked to the Labor Department to take the lead in stabilizing labor conditions
at the end of the war by reestablishing blacks in the South, for the benefit of
the southern economy and northern white labor unionists.[46] Black organizations were generally supportive; both the NAACP and the Urban League provided vocal support for the creation of a specific adviser within the department
to handle issues directly related to African American workers.[47]

George Edmund Haynes, a professor of sociology and a cofounder and first
executive director of the National Urban League, was picked to run the division. Since black workers constituted about one-seventh of the working population, Haynes wrote in explaining the need for the division, "it is reasonable
and right that they should have representation in council when their interests
are being considered and decided."[48] Haynes argued that three central facts
about race in America would direct the mission of the division:

> First, not only are negro workers employed by white employers, but they
> also work on jobs and in occupations with white workers; second, this
> racial difference is the occasion of many of the misunderstandings,
> fears, prejudices and suspicions. The labor problems growing out of
> such differences are in a real sense negro labor problems: third, such

racial labor problems must be worked out in local communities on a co-operative basis, for they arise between local employers and employees. Although they are local they have a national bearing on the welfare of all wage earners, white and colored, on the interests of all employers, and of the whole people.[49]

With these goals in mind, Haynes worked immediately at creating Negro Workers' Advisory Committees in eleven states. They were intended to foster cooperation between white employers, white workers, and black workers in order to "develop racial understanding and good will."[50] Because the "two races are thrown together in their daily work" there were inevitably "misunderstandings, prejudices, antagonisms, fears, and suspicions which must be removed by mutual understanding and cooperation."[51] Very much in keeping with the ideals of the era, the goal of these committees was to provide jobs and industrial opportunity; conciliation, deliberation, and knowledge were prioritized over ending segregation or promoting any kind of destabilization of race relations. Haynes and the division consistently emphasized that the goal of promoting cooperation was not intended to create conflict within existing societal relations among racial groups. Haynes's methods were exemplified by a conference in Florida that he promoted and that resulted in the governor of the state calling for the formation of a state Negro Workers' Advisory Committee to promote a better understanding of employment matters and to ease the "discontent of workers, in order that greater production of food and supplies might ensue."[52] The division attempted to increase the representation of African Americans on the workers' committees and to respond to the "misunderstandings, prejudices, antagonisms, fears and suspicions" that come from "the two races . . . thrown together in daily work."[53]

It is unclear whether these committees were successful. The Labor Department pointed to the creation of assistance organizations designed to help teenagers, women, and other groups in "all matters related to Negro labor," and it believed that these campaigns "gave stimulation" to "amicable relations between white and colored workers and white employers," which in turn promoted "stability and thrift among Negro wage earners" and "reduced the labor turnover and absenteeism in a number of plants."[54] Employers, the department noted, "gladly arranged hours" for talks on "race pride, promptness, regularity, full-time work and increased opportunities for large earnings."[55] The fact that the programs and conferences resulted in "only one case of a member of one committee whose relationship on the committee has caused friction or made necessary a request for his resignation," and that "there has been the heartiest response for this work from citizens of both races everywhere" might well suggest that the work of the committees was not terribly ambitious.[56] Nonetheless, the work of the division and the committees it helped spawn should not be dismissed out of hand. As the department pointed out, "In many of the localities by the holding of the conferences and the establishment of the Negro Workers' Advisory Committees, the principle of Negroes having representation in council when matters affecting their interest were being considered and decided was acted upon for the first time."[57]

Moreover, even the division's tentative efforts disturbed the existing racial order. In Florida, for instance, the new committee upset representatives of a lumber association, who blamed the division for "inflammatory propaganda" that created "unrest" among black workers.[58] As a chief assistant to Haynes reminded him, there was great potential for good work because both the department's and the division's mandates were quite amorphous. The division's establishment created a "means of exchange of information and cooperation between this Department and other departments of the government both state and Federal the scope of which and the jurisdiction of which are almost unlimited."[59] The field of action was wide open: "The scope of the jurisdiction and authority of the Secretary of Labor have in no sense reached the plane which Congress had in mind when it created the Department of Labor. It is obvious that a wide span was left vacant over which the Department of Labor may, and should, leap in fostering and promoting the welfare of wage earners."[60] He pushed Haynes to seize the opportunity: "The destinies of 10 million Negroes are at bar in a way never before seen. The shift of the economic status, loyalty and citizenship of 10 million Negroes is more noticeable than ever before. . . . Should not every resource be invoked to insure peace, good will and justice to Americans, white and black?"[61]

Southern politicians increasingly worried about exactly that. Efforts by the division were threatening racial hierarchies in the region, and since its mandate lacked a clear limit, southern legislators increasingly put pressure on the Labor Department to get rid of the division entirely.[62] With war's end, the protests of these legislators got louder, and governors from the region joined in the lobbying, arguing that the division was meddling in local affairs and promoting migration of blacks to the North.[63] Republicans cut the appropriation for the division in 1920 after southern legislators claimed that its funding was unconstitutional. The national elections of that year further weakened the division's hope for longevity. Wilson's presidency had ended, and Republicans significantly widened their congressional majorities. From that point forward, even studying social problems through the lens of race became illegitimate.

Shortly after the election, the new secretary of labor, James Davis, formally abolished the division on grounds that he opposed segregating workers on the basis of race: "Our laws do not distinguish between white men and Negroes or any other class or classes."[64]

Haynes, however, continued to fight consistently for the awareness of racial divisions. He wrote, "There is a deep concern and fear expressed among Negroes in various ways, when one gets at exactly how they are feeling, that many of the plans laid for their help, even when meant in a friendly way, may work so as to limit the scope of their activities and development so as really to work in the end to a new handicap for them."[65] In true Progressive fashion, he argued that the best way out of this conundrum was by educating the public and "by presenting objectively the facts and conditions relating to both sides." A year later, he wrote, "The very issue of whether or not there will soon be a warless world is involved because the problem of the twentieth century is the problem of the contacts of the white and colored races. With such interests involved, no student of American race relations can well dogmatize or scold."[66] Like many others in the Progressive era, and like Du Bois during his time with the bureau, Haynes believed that a combination of learning and participating in community life would create the dialogue and compromise necessary to lead to improvements in race relations: "There is now available a growing body of scientific and religious ideas and principles to guide the feeling, thinking, attitudes, and actions on such social questions."[67]

Haynes went before Congress to plead his case to have the division restored: "The colored people are now in a very restless condition because they gave a great deal during the war. . . . They have expected something from their Government."[68] Referring to a wave of racial violence in the year after the war, Haynes correctly predicted that such violence would precipitate a more aggressive and affirmative demand for rights by African Americans in the coming years. But Haynes was not in a position to be heard in a way that mattered. In a striking exchange between Haynes and members of Congress, the two sides battled intensely about the meaning of race in America. The bipartisan focus of the committee centered on the question whether race was an important category. The chairman of the House committee, James Good of Iowa, told Haynes, "It does occur to me that with a broad organization like that of the Department of Labor it would be unfortunate if it should ever be found necessary to have a separate division for Italian workers, for instance, a separate division for German workers, a separate division for persons coming from France, etc., and then a separate division for the white population of the United

States and a separate division for the Negro population of the United States. It seems to me that this would be bound to lead to duplication in that service." In the Senate, Chairman Francis Warren of Wyoming told Haynes something similar: "You are exactly equal under the law. You are exactly equal, of course, under those appropriations. But as far as we are concerned, there should not be a division between classes of workmen, one against the other. . . . We have to look at it with the idea of preserving equality. The same rule applies to both."[69]

Haynes was no radical, and he frequently promoted conservative views of culture and economics.[70] Nonetheless, as he told Congress, "there is a general feeling among all classes of Negroes that the Federal Government should do something to remedy their condition." The government needed to respond to the black community's fears of mobs and lynching, and it needed to do something affirmative. The "feeling of the Negroes (was) that something should be done for them through the Federal Government." The counter by Republicans, however, did not address whether governmental intervention was right or wrong, but whether race mattered at all. In particular, Haynes went back and forth with New York representative Walter Magee, who contended that there were no race problems in America. Haynes countered this absurdity: pointing to an array of northern cities, he argued, "The Negro population is segregated from the white population in this country as no other group is. . . . Experience shows that there is a need of some special help for the Negroes. Help is required to adjust the Negroes and in giving them an opportunity to find adjustment in the ordinary every-day occupations."[71] After Magee responded that people of all nationalities "must be treated alike," Haynes countered: "But as a matter of fact all of them have not been treated alike. The Negro has been the one group that has not been treated like other groups."

Conclusion

Both Du Bois and Haynes were products of and contributors to the intellectual spirit of the Progressive era and its political activism. They promoted a worldview of social justice that emphasized the value of knowledge, the possibilities of the human condition, and the important role played by the government as a primary weapon in engineering such progress. The contours of their own political developments were still very much in formation when they worked in the Labor Department and its predecessor; both moved over the years, for instance, from believing that capitalism could incorporate civil rights to contending that capitalism was a central part of the problem. But what remained constant, and what they would continually fight both fellow Progressives and conservatives over, was the centrality of race to American power relations. The problem, as they saw it, was neither just about the promotion of regulation over rights, or of rights over regulation; it was critically about race. Race was the central organizing principle that governed how inequality was experienced and maintained. The concept of race mattered, and it mattered independently of any universal idea of human progress, whether such an idea was premised on Progressive regulation or individual rights. Whether the agendas emphasized self-promotion, capitalist gains, educational attainment, voting rights, or social policy and socialism, these activists were acutely aware of how easily race could be squeezed out of mainstream agendas.

One lesson from these brief case studies is that the debate over whether rights or regulation better promotes racial equality ultimately distracts from the central importance that race played in American society at the time, and more specifically, how race was and remains wrapped into questions of power. Another lesson is that regulation and rights might be compatible, and that their connection might well be essential to progress toward racial equality. Progressive faith in expertise was not enough, but that finding doesn't make Progressivism, by definition, the problem. All this is lost in both the conventional readings of the *Lochner* era that applaud Progressive aims and in the new scholarship that rehabilitates *Lochner* as standing firm against Progressive racism.

Rather than continuing to view Progressive reform as fundamentally at odds with the rights revolution, my retelling makes clear some basic connections. The rights revolution of the mid–twentieth century was necessary to attack the deeply entrenched nature of racism and its consequences in American society, but not to attack Progressivism in particular. And the breakthrough for rights, when it finally occurred, did not speak for itself either. The rights gained were essentially open-ended and forward looking and quite compatible with long-standing Progressive goals. This fact was recognized by an unprecedented burst of new interest in social inquiry and governmental policy aimed at making racial equality a reality. In the end, then, the assault on Progressive racism, warranted as it is, should not take on a life of its own and justify rights without other commitments that are fundamentally progressive.

Notes

Thanks to Heather Hicks for her excellent research assistance in finding documents at the National Archives. Thanks as well to Stephen Engel, Megan Francis, Desmond Jagmohan, Daniel LaChance, Stephen Skowronek, and Sarah Staszak for their helpful suggestions.

1. See Rayford Logan, *The Negro in American Life and Thought: The Nadir, 1877–1901* (New York: Dial, 1954).

2. See, for example, Gail Bederman, *Manliness and Civilization: A Cultural History of Gender and Race in the United States, 1880–1917* (Chicago: University of Chicago Press, 1996); Gary Gerstle, *American Crucible: Race and Nation in the Twentieth Century* (Princeton, N.J.: Princeton University Press, 2001); Glenda Elizabeth Gilmore, *Gender and Jim Crow: Women and the Politics of White Supremacy in North Carolina, 1896–1920* (Chapel Hill: University of North Carolina Press, 1996); Matthew Frye Jacobson, *Barbarian Virtues: The United States Encounters Foreign Peoples at Home and Abroad, 1876–1917* (New York: Hill and Wang, 2000); Robin D. G. Kelley, "We Are Not What We Seem: Rethinking Black Working-Class Opposition in the Jim Crow South," *Journal of American History* 80, no. 1 (June): 75–112; Eileen McDonagh, "Race, Class, and Gender in the Progressive Era: Restructuring State and Society," in *Progressivism and the New Democracy*, ed. Sidney Milkis and Jerome Mileur (Amherst: University of Massachusetts Press, 1999); Nell Irvin Painter, *Standing at Armageddon: A Grassroots History of the Progressive Era* (New York: Norton, 2008); Aziz Rana, *The Two Faces of Freedom* (Cambridge, Mass.: Harvard University Press, 2010), 236–65; Daniel T. Rogers, "In Search of Progressivism," *Reviews in American History* 10 (1982); Rogers M. Smith, *Civic Ideals: Conflicting Visions of Citizenship in U.S. History* (New Haven, Conn.: Yale University Press, 1997); David W. Southern, *The Progressive Era and Race: Reaction and Reform* (Wheeling, Ill.: Wiley-Blackwell, 2005).

3. See, for example, Ira Katznelson, *When Affirmative Action Was White: An Untold History of Racial Inequality in Twentieth-Century America* (New York: Norton, 2004); Robert C. Lieberman, *Shifting the Color Line: Race and the American Welfare State* (Cambridge, Mass.: Harvard University Press, 1998).

4. This is a claim that I have made elsewhere, but it remains a point of contestation, with much important work arguing that the civil rights era *was* a completion of the New Deal and not a sharp turning point. For different opinions on this point, see Bruce Ackerman, *We the People*, vol. 3: *The Civil Rights Revolution* (Cambridge, Mass.: Belknap Press, 2014); Paul Frymer, *Black and Blue: African Americans, the Labor Movement, and the Decline of the Democratic Party* (Princeton, N.J.: Princeton University Press, 2008); Ken I. Kersch, *Constituting Civil Liberties: Discontinuities in the Development of American Constitutional Law* (New York: Cambridge University Press, 2004); Karen Orren, *Belated Feudalism: Labor, the Law, and Liberal Development in the United States* (New York: Cambridge University Press, 1992); Jill Quadagno,

The Color of Welfare: How Racism Undermined the War on Poverty (New York: Oxford University Press, 1996); Stephen Skowronek, *The Politics Presidents Make: Leadership from John Adams to Bill Clinton* (Cambridge, Mass.: Belknap Press, 1993), chap. 7.

5. David E. Bernstein, *Rehabilitating "Lochner": Defending Individual Rights Against Progressive Reform* (Chicago: University of Chicago Press, 2011); David E. Bernstein, *Only One Place of Redress: African Americans, Labor Regulations, and the Courts from Reconstruction to the New Deal* (Durham, N.C.: Duke University Press, 2001); Paul D. Moreno, *Black Americans and Organized Labor: A New History* (Baton Rouge: Louisiana State University Press, 2007). Regarding the consequences of a racially stratified workforce, see Quadagno, *Color of Welfare;* William Julius Wilson, *When Work Disappears: The World of the New Urban Poor* (New York: Vintage, 1997).

6. Bernstein, *Rehabilitating "Lochner,"* 82.

7. Ibid., 5.

8. For important work making these claims, see, for example, Susan D. Carle, "Race, Class, and Legal Ethics in the Early NAACP (1910–1920)," *Law and History Review* 20 (Spring 2002): 97–146; Megan Francis, *Civil Rights and the Making of the Modern American State* (New York: Cambridge University Press, 2013); Risa Goluboff, "The Thirteenth Amendment and the Lost Origins of Civil Rights," *Duke Law Journal* 50 (2001): 1609–95; William B. Gould, *Black Workers in White Unions: Job Discrimination in the United States* (Ithaca, N.Y.: Cornell University Press, 1977); Evelyn Brooks Higginbotham, *Righteous Discontent: The Women's Movement in the Black Baptist Church, 1880–1920* (Cambridge, Mass.: Harvard University Press, 1993); Kenneth W. Mack, "Rethinking Civil Rights Lawyering and Politics in the Era Before *Brown*," *Yale Law Journal* 115 (2005); Roger L. Rice, "Residential Segregation by Law, 1910–1917," *Journal of Southern History* 34 (1968): 191–94.

9. See, for example, Eric Arnesen, "A. Philip Randolph: Labor and the New Black Politics," in *The Human Tradition in American Labor History,* ed. Eric Arnesen (Wilmington, Del.: Scholarly Resources, 2004); Cornelius L. Bynum, *A. Philip Randolph and the Struggle for Civil Rights* (Champagne-Urbana: University of Illinois Press, 2010); Ralph J. Bunche, "A Critique of New Deal Social Planning as It Affects Negroes," *Journal of Negro Education* 5 (1936): 59–65; W. E. B. Du Bois, "Of the Meaning of Progress," in Du Bois, *Souls of Black Folk* (New York: Vintage, 1990 [1903]).

10. Regarding the importance of these themes among middle-class reformers in the Progressive era, see Kevin Mattson, *Creating a Democratic Public: The Struggle for Urban Participatory Democracy During the Progressive Era* (University Park: Pennsylvania State University Press, 1998); John Louis Recchiuti, *Civic Engagement: Social Science and Progressive-Era Reform in New York City* (2007); Daniel T. Rodgers, *Atlantic Crossings: Social Politics in a Progressive Age* (Cambridge, Mass.: Harvard University Press, 1998); Theda Skocpol, *Protecting Soldiers and Mothers: The Political Origins of Social Policy in the United States* (Cambridge, Mass.: Harvard University Press, 1992); Jonathan Zimmerman,

Distilling Democracy: Alcohol Education in America's Public Schools, 1880–1925 (Lawrence: University Press of Kansas, 1999).

11. "Creating Bureau of Labor Statistics," 2254 HR Report 342 (February 12, 1884).

12. *Congressional Record,* April 19, 1884, 3146, quoting Congressman Foran.

13. See Sarah Staszak, *No Day in Court: Access to Justice and the Politics of Judicial Retrenchment* (New York: Oxford University Press, 2015), chap. 3.

14. Gwendolyn Mink, *Old Labor and New Immigrants in American Political Development* (Ithaca, N.Y.: Cornell University Press, 1986).

15. *Congressional Record,* May 14, 1884, 4156.

16. Ibid.

17. Ibid., 4149–54.

18. Ibid., part 2, 248.

19. Select Committee to Investigate the Causes of the Removal of the Negroes from the Southern States to the Northern States, 46th Congress, S. Rep. No. 693 (June 1, 1880). The committee members were D. W. Voorhees (D-Ind.), Zebulon B. Vance (D-N.C.), and George H. Pendleton (D-Ohio); William Windom (R-Minn.) and Henry W. Blair (R-N.H.) submitted a dissenting report.

20. Both are quoted in Jonathan Grossman, "Black Studies in the Department of Labor, 1897–1907," *Monthly Labor Review* 97 (June 1974): 19.

21. W. E. B. Du Bois, "The Relations of the Negroes to the Whites in the South," (1904), in *W. E. B. Du Bois on Sociology and the Black Community,* ed. Dan S. Green and Edwin D. Driver (Chicago: University of Chicago Press, 1978), 59.

22. W. E. B. Du Bois, "The Study of the Negro Problems," *Annals of the American Academy of Political and Social Science* (January 1898; reprinted, March 2000), 14.

23. Ibid., 19.

24. Ibid., 24.

25. W. E. B. Du Bois, "Conditions of the Negro in Various Cities," *Bulletin of the Department of Labor* 10 (May 1897): 257–369.

26. W. E. B. Du Bois, "The Negroes of Farmville, Virginia: A Social Study," *Bulletin of the Department of Labor* 14 (January 1898), 55th Cong., 2nd sess., HR Doc. no. 206, 21.

27. Ibid., 38.

28. W. E. B. Du Bois, "The Negro Landholder of Georgia," *Bulletin of the Department of Labor* 32 (January 1901), 56th Cong., 2nd sess., HR Doc. no. 315, 647–777.

29. Ibid., 777, 676.

30. Grossman, "Black Studies," 24–25.

31. "A Study of Negro Life in the South," *Atlanta Constitution,* January 30, 1898.

32. "A Study of Negro Life," *New York Times,* January 30, 1898.

33. W. E. B. Du Bois, *Dusk of Dawn: An Essay Toward an Autobiography of a Race Concept* (New York: Oxford University Press, 2014 [1940]), 34. See also Adolph L. Reed Jr., *W. E. B. Du Bois and American Political Thought: Fabianism and the Color Line* (New York: Oxford University Press, 1997).

34. Du Bois, *Souls of Black Folk*, 58.

35. U.S. Department of Labor, Division of Negro Economics, "Negro Migration in 1916–17" (1919), Record Group 174.4.7, Records of the Division of Negro Economics. This was not the first migration of blacks, nor was it the first to be noticed by Congress. In the 1870s, Congress investigated a migration, or "exodus," of roughly 30,000 blacks from southern to northern states, chiefly to Kansas (the black population of Kansas increased by 26,000 between 1870 and 1880) and Indiana in the "Exodus of 1879." In a nearly 1,700-page report filled with testimony, Democrats in the Senate argued that northern politicians, black leaders, and railroads had induced the exodus. Republicans in the North, who wanted black voters in order to turn their states toward their party, argued that the migration was due to bad conditions in the South; see the report by the Select Committee to Investigate the Causes of the Removal of the Negroes from the Southern States to the Northern States (June 1, 1880).

36. "Negro Exodus from South Laid to Oppression," *New York Tribune*, July 8, 1917.

37. "An Alarming Migration of Negro Labor," *New York Tribune*, October 22, 1916; Ralph W. Tyler, "Negroes Are Moving Northward: 326,000 of Native Blacks Cross Mason and Dixon Line in Last Two Years—What of Result?," *Indianapolis Star*, October 15, 1916.

38. "An Alarming Migration of Negro Labor," *New York Tribune*, October 22, 1916; J. A. Hallomon, "Will Negro Supply Labor Exodus North?," *Atlanta Constitution*, June 19, 1919.

39. "East St. Louis Riot Investigation," Select House Committee to Investigate the Race Riots in East St. Louis, 1917 (November 8, 1917).

40. "For Action on Race Riot Peril: Radical Propaganda Among Negroes Growing," *New York Times*, October 5, 1919.

41. George Edmund Haynes, "Effect of War Conditions on Negro Labor," *Proceedings of the Academy of Political Science in the City of New York* 8 (February 1919): 165–78.

42. W. B. Wilson to Dr. J. E. McCulloch, July 9, 1918, Record Group 174.4.7, Records of the Division of Negro Economics.

43. Haynes, "Effect of War Conditions on Negro Labor," 168.

44. Office of the Secretary of Labor, "Function and Work of the Division of Negro Economics," March 15, 1919, Record Group 174.4.7, Records of the Division of Negro Economics.

45. Ibid., 2.

46. Henry P. Guzda, "Social Experiment of the Labor Department: The Division of Negro Economics," *Public Historian* 4 (Autumn 1982): 11.

47. Though some saw it as another Jim Crow creation designed to promote black economic opportunities within the segregated South; see Guzda, "Social Experiment of the Labor Department," 17.

48. George E. Haynes, "To Avert Friction with Negro Labor," *New York Times*, June 15, 1919.

49. Ibid.

50. See Department of Labor, Office of the Secretary, "Matters of Record," Record Group 174.4.7, Records of the Division of Negro Economics; George Edmund Haynes, *The Trend of the Races* (New York: Council of Women for Home Missions and Missionary Education Movement of the U.S. and Canada, 1922), 118.

51. "Annual Report of the Secretary of Labor," 7734 H.Doc. 422 (November 10, 1919), 133.

52. Department of Labor, "Matters of Record," 2.

53. Ibid., 3.

54. "Annual Report of the Secretary of Labor," 134–35.

55. Ibid., 134.

56. Department of Labor, "Matters of Record," 3. As the report itself stated, "It has been readily recognized that Washington could not settle problems between an employer in Mississippi and his Negro worker in Mississippi" (11).

57. Ibid., 7.

58. "Negro Economics in Florida," Record Group 174.4.7, Records of the Division of Negro Economics.

59. His assistant (Karl Phillips) to the director of Negro Economics, "Confidential Memorandum: Advisory Departmental Relationship Regarding Negro Matters," June 17, 1919, Record Group 174.4.7, Records of the Division of Negro Economics.

60. Ibid., 2.

61. Ibid., 3.

62. Senator James Vardaman to Secretary Wilson, May 16, 1918 (defending segregation in the South). Wilson both doubted and accepted the Mississippi senator's claim (Wilson to Vardaman, June 1918, file 129/14, Record Group 174).

63. Governor Sidney Catts to Secretary Wilson, April 7 and 22, 1919, file 8/102, Record Group 174; "Negroes Are Migrating from Southern States," *Atlanta Constitution*, October 24, 1916, 3; "Government Watching Migration of Negroes," *Atlanta Constitution*, October 28, 1916; "The South Aroused over Secretary Wilson's Labor Policies," *New York Tribune*, April 21, 1919.

64. "Sec'y of Labor Stops Separation of Workers," *Chicago Defender*, May 7, 1921.

65. Director of Negro Economics to Mr. R. H. Leavell, January 13, 1921, Record Group 174.4.7, Records of the Division of Negro Economics.

66. Haynes, *Trend of the Races*, xi.

67. Ibid.

68. "Division of Negro Economics, Statements of George E. Haynes and Karl F. Phillips," in Sundry Civil Appropriation Bill, 1921, pt. 2, subcommittee of House Committee on Appropriations, 66th Cong., 2nd sess. (March 20, 1920), 2157.

69. Ibid., 2160–64.

70. George E. Haynes, "Grasping the Hands of Economic Opportunity" (n.d.), U.S. Department of Labor, Division of Negro Economics, "Negro Migration in 1916–17" (1919), Record Group 174.4.7, Records of the Division of Negro Economics.

71. "Division of Negro Economics, Statements of George E. Haynes and Karl F. Phillips," 2165.

15 • The Progressives' Deadly Embrace of Cartels

A Close Look at Labor and Agricultural Markets, 1890–1940

Richard A. Epstein

The many facets of the Progressive movement, which played such a powerful role in United States politics from about 1900 to 1940, are difficult to encapsulate in any single, overall evaluation. But amid that diversity one constant and powerful theme demands more attention than it commonly receives. That theme involves the systematic Progressive embrace of cartelization over both competition and monopoly. I address this fundamental choice of industrial organization from a neoclassical point of view that ranks these three broad types of arrangement in this order: competition first, monopoly second, and cartelization third. The Progressive movement, with its deep suspicion of market institutions, chose a different order: cartels first, competition second, monopoly third.

These two disparate rankings depend on a complex set of economic and political factors that were imperfectly understood at the time and that are still imperfectly understood today. This chapter traces the comparative logic of the traditional classical liberal and the Progressive approaches to problems of industry concentration, with special reference to agriculture and labor. The dominant Supreme Court view at the time took a strong stance against the protection of cartels under the antitrust law, whether of businesses or unions, while at the same time working to protect regulated industries against the risk of confiscation through direct regulation. The Progressive response exempted unions and agriculture from the antitrust laws and worked assiduously to promote their monopoly power through direct forms of regulation. By resorting to democratic policies of cartel members, Progressives generated substantial social losses, which were not justified by any collateral end.

Of necessity, this analysis starts by looking at business cartels before the Clayton Act of 1914, passed in Woodrow Wilson's first term, which hived labor and agricultural markets from the rest of the antitrust law.[1] The contrast could not be more dramatic. Section 6 of the Clayton Act exempts both labor and agriculture organizations from the strictures of the antitrust law.[2] Simultaneously, Section 7 extends the antitrust prohibitions of the Sherman Act of 1890 to cover cases where "the effect of such acquisition may be substantially to lessen competition . . . or to tend to create a monopoly."[3] The approach found in the Clayton Act carried through to the end of the New Deal and thus frames the discussion of much that follows. The antitrust laws form one essential portion of the inquiry. The second part consists of the transformation of labor law, both in the courts and the legislature, with the National Labor Relations Act of 1935[4] and the Fair Labor Standards Act of 1938.[5] The third part consists of the various Agricultural Adjustment Acts of the 1930s.[6] This inquiry covers not only the substantive economic issues but also two key constitutional dimensions, relating first to the protection of economic liberties and second to the expansion of federal power under the Commerce Clause.

Part 1 addresses the question of how the Old Court conservatives—the targets of the Progressive movement—addressed the unified treatment of industrial and labor combinations that acted in restraint of trade, and it defends their analytical approach. Part 2 switches focus to address the institutional challenges and resource misallocations that took place once the Clayton Act irretrievably split the regulation of business from the regulation of labor and agriculture. It covers the economic effects of cartel arrangements as well as evaluates why the electoral systems set up in labor and agricultural markets sparked political success of Progressive politicians. These politicians used those devices to consolidate political support, especially in the 1930s, by the active promotion, organization, and support of these cartel arrangements.

Competition, Cartels, and Monopoly: The Neoclassical View

One of the most common misconceptions about the Old Court, whose views, roughly speaking, prevailed until the constitutional revolution of 1937, was that it had an uncritical fascination with the principle of freedom of contract, one that it extended to allegedly unacceptable ends by adopting a hands-off attitude toward big business. This misconception is often based on a single-minded obsession with the 1905 decision in *Lochner v. New York*,[7] which all too often has been said to loom so large as to define an entire "*Lochner* Era."[8] That case did, to be sure, limit the ability of the states and the federal government to pass maximum hour and minimum wage legislation, but *Lochner* was situated in a complex line of cases, many of which *upheld* labor statutes, including a minimum wage law for women in 1908.[9]

The *Lochner* line of cases on health and safety played little role in the Old Court's approach to the monopolization issues of the late nineteenth century. The rapid industrialization of those decades gave birth to the new fields of antitrust and public utility regulation, which represented complementary responses to the problem of monopoly. The rate regulation cases sought to set fair, reasonable, and nondiscriminatory rates of return for those natural monopolies that could not be broken up without some loss of efficiency. The antitrust law regulated the business arrangements among separate firms from which the path to monopoly profits lay through combinations and mergers among competitive rivals that enjoyed none of the efficiencies of natural monopolies. Many modern champions of Chicago-style economics treat these early cases as exemplars of sensible economic regulation.[10]

The rate regulation cases arose first under the unpromising banner of industries "affected with the public interest."[11] That doctrine was first announced by Sir Matthew Hale (1609–1676) in his treatise *De Portis Maribus* (On the gates of the sea), and was incorporated into English law in *Allnutt v. Inglis*[12] in 1810. It worked its way into American law in *Munn v. Illinois*[13] in 1876, which upheld return regulation for real or "virtual monopolies"—the latter term coming straight out of *Allnutt*. That regulation exposed any large public utility with huge front-end costs to the risks of expropriation by setting rates so low that the regulated firm could recover only a bit more than its variable costs, and thus could not recoup total costs over the lifetime of the project. The early rate-making cases sought to negotiate safe passage between two extremes, one of which results in confiscation of invested capital and the second in the capture of monopoly profits by a public utility facing no direct competition in its geographic or product market. In general, these decisions were sophisticated, good-faith efforts to steer that middle course by moving to the intellectual gold standard of a competitive rate of return.[14]

The same attitude carried over to the antitrust law. In dealing with this issue, there were two initial prohibitions. Section 1 of the Sherman Act of 1890 provided that "every contract, combination in the form of trust or otherwise, or conspiracy, in restraint of trade or commerce among the several States, or with foreign nations, is hereby declared to be illegal."[15] Section 2 further provided that "every person who shall monopolize, or attempt to monopolize, or combine or conspire with any other person or persons, to monopolize any part of the trade or commerce among the several States, or with foreign nations, shall be deemed guilty of a misdemeanor."[16] After the Supreme Court expressed initial doubts about the scope of federal power under the Commerce Clause in *United States v. E. C. Knight*,[17] it reversed field in *Addyston Pipe & Steel Co. v. United States*, turning the legal debate to substantive antitrust issues.[18] The Court took a hard-line approach to cartelization in the 1897 case of *United States v. Trans-Missouri Freight Association*,[19] in which Justice Rufus Peckham (who later wrote *Lochner*) gave the Sherman Act a broad reading that attacked cartel formation.[20] At the same time, he understood that a single solution did not fit all potential antitrust problems. He therefore rightly applied the more flexible rule of reason (whereby efficiency benefits were traded off against any tendency to restrict competition) to the kinds of covenants not to compete commonly found in agreements for the sale of a business or for the termination of an employment relationship.[21] The trade-off arises because the covenant eliminates one potential competitor, which is restrictive. But it also facilitates the sale of the business or the hiring of the employee, which is precompetitive. Peckham also well understood the difficulties associated with running a business with high fixed costs, but refused to turn the antitrust law into a form of the direct rate regulation that propped up railroad rates. That point was, moreover, driven home by Peckham's opinion a year later in *United States v. Joint Traffic Association*,[22] in which he explicitly rejected the constitutional challenge claiming that the Sherman Act, as construed, necessarily violated the defendants' constitutional protections of property under the Due Process and Takings Clauses of the Fifth Amendment.[23] The Old Court did not show any dogmatic defense of freedom of contract on matters of industrial concentration, and it resisted the pleas of "ruinous competition" that quickly led to cartelization during the New Deal. *Trans-Missouri Freight* set the right course for the further development of the antitrust law, using traditional neoclassical economic principles as its guide.

A second notable feature of the early antitrust law was its unwillingness to discriminate between horizontal arrangements by business and those by labor. Both arrangements constrained price and reduced supply. This point was vividly illustrated by the 1908 decision in *Loewe v. Lawlor*,[24] which dealt with the secondary boycott in the *Danbury Hatters* case against a union that sought through collective action to induce third parties not to deal with the plaintiffs. A unanimous Court, speaking through Justice Melville Fuller, imposed liability under Section 7 of the Sherman Act, which authorized treble-damage actions by any person "injured in his business or property" by the acts made illegal under Sections 1 and 2.[25]

In *Loewe*, Justice Fuller first invoked *Trans-Missouri* and its progeny to conclude that any collective refusal to deal was per se illegal.[26] This carryover from industrial monopoly to labor monopoly had been defended as consistent with the language and structure of the Sherman Act in the 1893 decision in *United States v. Workingmen's Amalgamated Council*[27] and was then carried over to the famous Pullman strike in *In re Debs*.[28]

More concretely, the Court found that the Commerce Clause applied to actions that intended to block the shipment of goods in interstate commerce, that is, union activities by the 9,000 members and 1,400,000 affiliates of the American Federation of Labor. In the 1915 sequel, *Loewe v. Lawlor,* Justice Holmes, speaking for a unanimous Court, affirmed the judgment against individual union members because of the cumulative "evidence that made it almost inconceivable that the defendants, all living in the neighborhood of the plaintiffs, did not know what was done in the specific case."[29] This resulted in a judgment of $252,130, which threatened to exhaust the union's treasury.[30] None of the justices hesitated in applying the standard antitrust principles to labor organizations, and so the stage was set for the political transformation.

The Progressive Response to the Neoclassical Model

The political response to the 1908 decision in *Loewe* was in marked contrast to the Supreme Court decision. By the efforts of organized labor, *Loewe* "became a major political issue in the 1912 national election"[31] and later resulted in the enactment of Section 6 of the Clayton Act in 1914. The supporters of Section 6 never confronted the basic intellectual framework of *Trans-Missouri* and *Loewe*, but instead relied on two major arguments. First, *Loewe* was wrong textually because the drafters of the Sherman Act intended to confine it to industrial operations. Second, it was inappropriate that "the man who sells his labor—his God-given right—should be classed as conspiring against trade or in unlawful combination against the anti-trust laws." That argument was then extended to cover farmers' unions. Congressman David J. Lewis hammered home this point by insisting "there is this distinction between labor and a barrel of oil, a commodity: labor is never in truth a commodity."[32] At no point did the defenders of Section 6 confront the more functional critique of concerted action. They did not explain why, if labor is not a commodity, it could be sold collectively, or why the antitrust laws could not apply to monopolies of both goods and services.

Similarly, the defenders of Section 6 never proposed any intermediate position on labor unions. The point here is important because labor unions can serve all sorts of mediating functions between employers and workers unrelated to their exercise of monopoly power.[33] But those functions can be fully performed by unions within the traditional framework of the antitrust law, which adopts a rule of reason for practices whose efficiency justifications offset their restrictive impact. The Clayton Act exemption becomes critical whenever unions seek by collective action to raise wages by excluding rivals. The categorical scope of the antitrust exclusion was intended to, and largely did, protect unions in that key function.

The Progressive movement criticized the empty formalisms of the Old Court justices in order to show that they were bereft of modern social understanding.[34] But that critique does not explain why labor combinations were less lethal than industrial ones. Indeed from a functional perspective, labor cartels are likely to prove more dangerous. Industrial monopolies and cartels do not profit from the disruption of services; they do not gain by the use of threat or force against third parties, as by putting protestors on picket lines to disrupt ordinary business transactions. Unions, especially in service industries such as transportation, have disruptive third-party effects beyond those achieved by monopoly pricing. In this regard, their control over labor is more dangerous than that of a business cartel setting the price of oil. Indeed, the antitrust laws are not directed to products as such, but to the firms that conspire to reduce output and raise prices. No one finds a "God-given" right for these cooperative activities. Why then do so for the cartelization of labor markets? Any serious natural-law proponent in the tradition of Aristotle, Aquinas, or Blackstone would quake in his boots at this grandiose union claim.

What is ironic about the situation, moreover, is that this major exemption from antitrust laws did *not* give labor a sufficient platform from which to mount its organization campaign. In part, the difficulty arose from the Court's interpretation of Section 6 in *Duplex Printing Co. v. Deering*,[35] which limited the labor exemption to situations analogous to those in *Loewe*, that is, in which workers and their unions coordinated solely their own activities. But the text itself does not easily settle the question whether the exemption should also apply when unions join forces with nonunion forms in order to browbeat holdout firms into compliance. *Duplex* involved a formidable combination between unions and three printing companies that sought to force a fourth, nonunion shop to recognize the union, by focusing attention on its suppliers, transport forms, repair shops, and customers. Wholly apart from the close statutory-construction question, the case undermined the claim that unionized firms have an efficiency advantage over their nonunion rivals. Were that indeed the case, then the three unionized firms should have wished for the fourth firm to remain nonunion, which they decidedly did not. To be sure, unionization need not have the same impact on all unionized firms. Cooperative unions often maintain cordial relations with management (as at Southwest Airlines). But in other cases, confrontation and disruption are the order of the day (as at Northwest Airlines). But notwithstanding the variations in union styles, the cases are few and far between in which a union that does not have the support of management can improve a firm's internal operations.

This simple observation generates a powerful implication. We cannot expect firms that lose from unionization to bargain voluntarily with unions, with or without an antitrust exemption. Hence, employers consistently exercised their exit option at common law by refusing to bargain. Unions stymied on this front sought to impose mandatory collective bargaining obligations on employers. Early efforts toward this aim were rebuffed by the Court, first in 1908 at the federal level in *Adair v. United States*[36] and then, a year after the Clayton Act, in *Coppage v. Kansas*,[37] decided in 1915. I regard the economic logic of these two opinions as unimpeachable, but they did not long remain good law. The Railway Labor Act of 1926[38] introduced a mandatory bargaining system for the railroads in line with union aims, and was sustained in *Texas & New Orleans R.R. Co. v. Bhd. of Ry. & S.S. Clerks*[39]—a disingenuous opinion by Justice Charles Evans Hughes.[40] Progressive legislation tightened the screws by killing off the opt-out option for employers in what became an essential feature of the National Labor Relations Act.

The second line of defense available to employers after Section 6 of the Clayton Act was the so-called Yellow Dog contract, whereby employers contractually secured a promise from individual workers not to join a union so long as they remained in the firm's employ. These contracts were common in the coalfields, since no mining company could move its coal to a new location when a union came calling. Individual suits against workmen for quitting improperly were useless, but an injunction against the union from seeking to have them leave their jobs on cue was a remedy with real bite. It also helped to preserve competition in labor markets. The 1917 decision in *Hitchman Coal & Coke v. Mitchell*[41] essentially preserved that employer option, and thus became an instant target of the labor movement. Labor achieved its objective with the passage of the Norris-LaGuardia Act,[42] which restricted in federal court the use of injunctions in labor cases to situations that imposed an imminent threat of violence, effectively undercutting *Hitchman*.

Norris-LaGuardia did not require the employer to bargain in good faith with the union, but the National Industrial Recovery Act of 1933 did.[43] Its full title speaks volumes of the Progressive mindset: "An Act to encourage national industrial recovery, to foster fair competition, and to provide for the construction of certain useful public works, and for other purposes."[44] The NIRA agenda, as reported in an official government summary, shows a complete inversion of the neoclassical view:

> The passage of NIRA ushered in a unique experiment in U.S. economic history—the NIRA sanctioned, supported, and in some cases, enforced an alliance of industries. Antitrust laws were suspended, and companies were required to write industry-wide "codes of fair competition" that effectively fixed prices and wages, established production quotas, and imposed restrictions on entry of other companies into the alliances. The act further called for industrial self-regulation and declared that codes of fair competition—for the protection of consumers, competitors, and employers—were to be drafted for the various industries of the country and were to be subject to public hearings. Employees were given the right to organize and bargain collectively and could not be required, as a condition of employment, to join or refrain from joining a labor organization.[45]

It would not be possible to give a better description of how the NIRA substituted government-run cartels for market mechanisms. The previous defense of competitive forces was explicitly rejected, and collective bargaining for labor unions explicitly authorized. The key term "fair competition" in the NIRA bore no relation to its common-law definition. Indeed, as Chief Justice Hughes noted in *Schechter Poultry Corp. v. United States*,[46] fair competition "is a limited concept. Primarily, and strictly, it relates to the palming off of one's goods as those of a rival trader."[47] This account fits neatly into the libertarian prohibition against misrepresentation. In contrast, the NIRA uses the term "fairness" to maintain minimum price levels, which are necessarily higher than the competitive rate. The government backstop thus makes it harder for individual cartel members to chisel against other cartel members.

The NIRA also provided the president with power to approve "codes of fair competition" only if he found "that such code or codes [we]re not designed to promote monopolies or to eliminate or oppress small enterprises."[48] Under its broad authorization, the Roosevelt administration went to town: "In the course of its short life from August, 1933, to February, 1935, the Administration formulated and approved 546 codes and 185 supplemental codes . . . [and] issued over 11,000 administrative orders. . . . Most of [these codes] had *minimum wage* and *maximum hour* provisions. One or another of them had provisions for *minimum price* or prohibitions against minimum price or prohibitions against *sales below 'cost'*; . . . provisions *prohibiting exceptional* discounts, rebates, and other devices of *price competition*" (emphasis in the original).[49]

The magnitude of this shift cannot be gainsaid. Business practices that were per se illegal under standard antitrust law now became per se legal under the new Progressive regime—a 180-degree turn in policy that was put in place with no justification other than the bland assertion that the older system had failed. Once the NIRA was struck down in *Schechter* on the ground of excessive delegation (which I regard as an incorrect outcome, given the close coordination between the president and Congress),[50] its labor piece was reconstituted separately as the National Labor Relations Act of 1935 (NLRA).

The NLRA made the union the exclusive bargaining agent for all workers if it prevailed in its organizing campaign, usually by secret ballot. Three years later, the Fair Labor Standards Act, in the name of worker protection, introduced wages and hours legislation that reduced the ability of nonunion firms and workers to compete by lowering wages. These two statutory outgrowths of the original NIRA in effect authorized unions to cartelize by two devices in tandem. First, the law allows a union to control internal governance of the bargaining unit. Second, the FLSA shields the union from nonunion competition.[51] This one-two punch has had profound implications for firms and the nation.

The first relevant measure goes to resource allocation. On that score, a cartelized firm is always inferior to its competitive and monopolistic rivals. The comparison between competition and cartelization is clear enough. Cartels reduce output, raise prices, and diminish social welfare. The comparison between monopolization and cartelization is more nuanced. Typically, the monopolist will outperform the cartel by realizing the efficiencies of a unified operation, which a fragmented cartel cannot achieve.

Note how a well-lubricated cartel like OPEC, which is able to operate aboveboard, decides who produces how much oil. Oil is not of uniform quality; nor is the cost of its extraction constant across all sources. A single firm with multiple sources will direct its production to that oil source that, on net, generates the greatest profit. So a single firm would pump all its light Saudi Arabian crude before extracting any Venezuelan heavy crude. The former is cheaper to extract and cheaper to refine. Put the two sources of crude oil under separate ownership, and any decision to shut down the Venezuelan crude now requires some side payments to keep those wells idle. But no one knows how to calibrate this amount. So the cartel sidesteps this valuation problem by resorting to quotas that set aside some portion of the market for high-cost, low-value output. That inefficient allocation represents an added social loss beyond that of monopoly pricing.

A similar issue faces the unionized firm, which has to preserve its membership base when its member workers have many different skill levels.[52] This issue is serious for traditional AFL craft unions, which are characterized by high levels of homogeneity. The problem of apportioning monopoly rents is even more acute in plants with many workers in different classes. These plant-wide unions were commonly represented by the Congress of Industrial Organizations (CIO), which gained strength in late 1935, shortly after the passage of the NLRA. Designating the proper bargaining unit became a point of bitter contention because the NLRA did not address statutorily the choice whether any given facility should be home to one plant or multiple craft unions under section 9(b), which only calls for union elections "in a unit appropriate for such purposes." The loose command forced the National Labor Relations Board to trade off complex factors, dealing with history, common interest, and business structure.[53] These tensions became more acute in connection with the so-called *Globe* doctrine, which tipped the balance in favor of the craft workers in the AFL whenever the NLRA's general formula was thought to be in equipoise.[54] There was no neutral technocratic solution to the many disputes—sometimes between unions and sometimes between unions and employers—that played out along these lines. The implicit wealth transfers in wage scales under collective bargaining also made it more difficult for employers to hire the right mix of workers. Collective bargaining has also created an intergenerational conflict between workers with seniority and those without it. These internal struggles could, and did, turn ugly when these job allocations were done on racial lines, as with the events that led to *Steele v. Louisville & Nashville R.R. Co.*,[55] which arose under the Railway Labor Act of 1926.[56] Finally, the entire NLRA bargaining practice works in jumps and starts, blocking constant but small wage adjustments in response to changes in supply and demand. The case for unions was often said to rest on their ability to maintain industrial peace, but the strike wave that followed the enforced peace during

World War II showed the basic instability of this state-mandated structure. The hit to overall production from unionization exceeds that from any firm's exercise of monopoly power.

A complete analysis of unionization must also take into account the key political element, which made (and makes) cartelization the more attractive institutional arrangement. The original NIRA used two strategies to soften the public-interest objection to these mandatory bargaining arrangements. First, it announced emphatically that the defense of these joint worker activities was in service of "the general welfare" as part of Congress's overall effort to remove "obstructions to the free flow of interstate and foreign commerce."[57] To support that point, the legislation explicitly denied any efforts to "promote monopolies" by throwing its full support behind the protection of "small enterprises." The best way to suppress competition is to denounce monopolies in order to allow cartels to flourish. This quasi-libertarian and welfarist theme was then backed up by the use of statutory elections for union representation, which lends a patina of democratic legitimacy to these union organizations, even if union democracy in practice has worked fitfully at best.[58] Franklin D. Roosevelt got much-needed political cover by attacking the few monopolists as enemies of the people while courting the political support of unionized workers.

His strategy worked in the short run, as union membership shot up to about 35 percent of the labor force in 1954. But in the long run, the economic inefficiencies of a collective bargaining system led to its eventual breakdown; by 2013, unions were down to 6.3 percent of the private labor market. As markets became more global and competitive, monopoly rents shrank. New businesses found they could migrate to jurisdictions, for example, right-to-work states, less sympathetic to union power. The strike ceased to be a credible threat, given the want of monopoly rents to extract from the firm. Today's union power often stems from its activities outside the bargaining table, often through antidumping actions and local zoning laws that seek to create space for monopoly profits. Modern progressives reverse this trend by still more coercive regulation, such as that contained in the Employee Free Choice Act, which will not cure the basic structural weaknesses of a union cartel. In other words, the classical liberal path to labor market reform requires repealing the federal labor statutes and, of course, the minimum wage and overtime regulations that are part and parcel of the grand progressive scheme. Today's labor market instability is a product of vigorous enforcement of labor policies of a bygone era.

Agricultural Markets

Statutory innovation after the Clayton Act bracketed agricultural operations with labor unions in their exemptions from the antitrust laws. Agricultural regulation follows a path parallel to that taken by cartelization, one that has, on average, proved more durable than Progressive efforts to regulate labor markets. There is no point here in going through all the complex technical details of programs whose central purpose was to restrict output by using either elaborate tax schemes,[59] or direct quota allocations to restrict total output.[60] But the ambition of the scheme, and the massive destruction of agricultural output in a time of hunger and dire need, must be stressed. As Lawrence W. Reed writes: "Roosevelt secured passage of the Agricultural Adjustment Act (AAA), which levied a new tax on agricultural processors and used the revenue to supervise the wholesale destruction of valuable crops and cattle. Federal agents oversaw the ugly spectacle of perfectly good fields of cotton, wheat, and corn being plowed under. Healthy cattle, sheep, and pigs by the millions were slaughtered and buried in mass graves."[61]

On the political economy side, the logic used to justify agricultural cartels followed that used for the unions. *Wickard v. Filburn*[62] is generally studied for its expansive reading of the Commerce Clause, which shielded the Agricultural Adjustment Acts of 1938[63] and 1941[64] from constitutional attack. In *Wickard,* the proposed aggregate allocation was approved by some 81 percent of the farmers who participated in the election, organized by the Department of Agriculture, after which the department set marketing quotas to allocate fractions of that total output first by state, then by county, and then by farm. Indeed, the first portion of *Wickard,* commonly ignored, rejected the claim that the election had to be set aside because of improper governmental statements during the referendum. The point was no coincidence, because the AAA used the same voting mechanism found under the NLRA. Roscoe Filburn was fined for producing more than his quota.

This agricultural system backstops a well-functioning cartel. The simple quota allocation functions here much as it does under OPEC, only more efficiently. Because cost differences are smaller than those are found for oil reserves of different nations, the quota allocations come at lower cost than they do with oil. Finally, the increase in production and the reduction in costs help conceal the role of monopoly power. So the system of agricultural cartels operates without the risk of strikes or the other kinds of high-visibility disruptions found in labor relations. More concretely, no agricultural cartel faces opposition from recalcitrant employers. Overall, the agricultural system operates with visibility and efficiency. It also enjoys the advantage of bipartisan support from farm-state senators, who have disproportionate influence in Congress. The durability of these agricultural cartels is a source of social loss, not of social gain.

The strong cartel features of the Progressive agricultural program are revealed in Supreme Court case law that address both rate regulation and antitrust, most notably in *Nebbia v. New York*[65] and *Parker v. Brown*.[66] *Nebbia,* the critical 1934 decision by Justice Owen Roberts, spelled the end of the traditional doctrine of "affected with the public interest," which permitted the government to regulate the rates that monopolists could charge their customers. In those cases, the challenge was to set rates high enough to allow cost recovery and a reasonable rate of return on capital that would allow the utility to become stable.[67]

The situation in *Nebbia* was the converse. It was widely understood that the dairy industry in New York offered "no suggestion of any monopoly or monopolistic practice."[68] The case for deviation from the competitive solution therefore necessarily depended on other arguments, which were offered in abundance. The government's basic claim was that the sharp decline in milk prices in the New York market brought on by the Depression had left many families in desperate straits.[69] Through extensive public hearings, New York assembled extensive evidence on the operation of the milk industry. The state then concluded that higher rates within the industry were necessary in part to prevent spoilage and contamination in milk—a classic police-power justification based on health and safety. In addition, price stabilization was treated as an essential ingredient of a sound policy.[70] The legislature thus let governmental officials set both the maximum and minimum milk prices because the evils in industry "could not be expected to right themselves through the ordinary play of the forces of supply and demand, owing to the peculiar and uncontrollable factors affecting the industry." The newly created Milk Control Board (MCB) required the defendant retailer to pay dealers five cents per pint, or eight cents per quart, and to resell to his consumers at no less than six cents per pint and nine cents per quart. Nebbia sold two quarts and one loaf of bread for eighteen cents combined, for which he was criminally prosecuted under the statute.

By setting minimum milk prices in a competitive industry, the MCB engaged in classic cartel coordination for which neither of its two stated justifications applied. First, the risks of contamination and spoilage were always subject to government regulation under the state's police power, explicitly recognized in *Lochner*, over all matters of health and safety. That regulation did not, and should not, vary according to the profitability of the industry. Second, this market self-corrected because government regulation propped up inefficient firms. The better approach is always to handle the glut of production by allowing inefficient firms to exit the market or cut down production, at which point the excess capacity should be eliminated. State price controls block that orderly option and lead to chronic overcapacity, which often results in the deliberate destruction of crops at no inconsiderable cost to poor people in need of the nutrients that milk provides.[71]

Justice Roberts assayed none of these alternatives, but he did review the extensive history of rate regulation, and was correct to note that historically rate regulation was not practiced exclusively as a counterweight to monopoly power.[72] But in his willingness to extend rate regulation to ordinary competitive transactions, he never articulated a limiting principle on how far state regulation could go, a point that generated much unease among the more classically liberal justices.[73] Nor did Roberts ever explain why the usual rule—namely, that "the use of property and the making of contracts are normally matters of private and not of public concern"[74]—should have been displaced in these chaotic conditions. Nor did he ask whether this state intervention would have negative consequences on outsiders, including the individuals who had to bear the brunt of the increased cost of milk. In the New York Court of Appeals, the legislation was justified as a legitimate public response to a "temporary emergency,"[75] a justification that rings as hollow here as it does in cases of rent stabilization[76] or mortgage moratoria.[77] Temporary emergencies often, as in the case of rent control, tend to last forever. The difference between this approach and the one in *Trans-Missouri* is palpable.

The second of these decisions, *Parker,* involved a challenge to the California marketing scheme under the state's Prorate Act in Raisin Proration Zone No. 1, where about 90 percent to 95 percent of the world's raisin crop was produced, nearly all of it destined for consumption outside the state. This particular case had a unique lineup, in which the federal government filed a brief against the State of California (with Earl Warren, its attorney general, on the state's brief), claiming that the California arrangement was invalid both as a violation of the Sherman Act and as an undue burden on interstate commerce. Chief Justice Stone saw matters otherwise and sustained the local cartel on the ground that it did not offend the dormant Commerce Clause because there was no explicit discrimination in the prices to in-state and out-state consumers,[78] and, further, that no explicit provision of the Sherman Act banned the operation of state-sanctioned cartel arrangements. In this case the purpose of the state law was clear: "The California Agricultural Prorate Act authorizes the establishment, through action of state officials, of programs for the marketing of agricultural commodities produced in the state, so as to restrict competition among the growers and maintain prices in the distribution of their commodities to packers."[79]

Parker produces a rare double. First, the cartel arrangement in this instance was *more* dangerous than any private cartel because state enforcement blocked the private "cheating" that tends to drive prices down to competitive levels. Second, the benefits of the cartel operate within the state, while virtually all its burdens are felt either elsewhere in the United States or in foreign nations. The in-state political process therefore was peculiarly calculated to support this arrangement, since all its negative effects were out of state. Nonetheless, Chief Justice Stone thought that the principle of cooperative federalism let states cartelize unless the federal government imposed some explicit ban on that practice.[80] The acceptance of cartelization had become engrained into the social fabric by 1943.

Conclusion

Progressives offered a variety of rationales to justify their approach. They thought their principles promoted democratic politics, but they never explained why majority rule was better than the unanimous agreement that could be obtained through standard contracting devices. They thought that stabilization of markets was a legitimate social goal, but they never explained why the stabilization of prices and wages for their protected classes justified throwing the measure of uncertainty on other actors in the economy. Instead, their basic positions turned out to be a display of partisan politics that ignored the negative consequences on groups in society that had to pay the freight.

This chapter traces these developments chiefly through labor and agriculture markets, but these dangerous Progressive tendencies were not limited to these areas. During the Progressive era and afterward, they have also exhibited themselves in rent control, zoning, mortgage moratoria, ground and air transportation, and just about any other form of economic activity that one cares to mention. The Progressives found rhetorical devices to place a favorable hue over these economic activities. They relied on expertise; they celebrated extensive public participation and specialized elections in the service of democratic practices. But behind the patina of deliberative democracy, nothing in the Progressive worldview stopped these forms of government cartelization.

This critique of Progressive thought is not meant to pretend that there are no difficult issues in the area of governmental regulation. To the contrary, it is hard to develop effective schemes for environmental protection, for health and safety regulation, and for land use regulation. In all these cases, it is often difficult to disentangle the legitimate efforts of government to control behaviors that pose serious threats to other individuals. But the correct analysis of these complex systems requires a willingness to take steps to ensure that these schemes of regulation are not converted into covert efforts to prevent beneficial economic competition under the guise of health and safety laws.

To their credit, progressives in our day have joined forces with classical liberals on matters dealing with the dormant Commerce Clause[81] by taking a hard look at burdensome state regulations that interfere with interstate competition. In general, the current law permits these regulations only when they address bona fide health and safety issues. The world has not come to an end because of this form of judicial intervention; rioting and discord have not damaged American streets; the democratic processes within the states have not been degraded. Instead the overall rise of open competition in national markets has been an unalloyed good.

So why not build on good foundations and use that same conceptual framework to deal with the extensive forms of federal regulation that frustrate markets by creating cartels through national policy? To do so requires a rejection of the progressive mindset that starts from the premise that ruinous competition merits the level of governmental intervention used in the control of pollution and toxic wastes. The only way that government actions can be properly focused in these complex areas is to be alert to the risk that legitimate forms of regulation do not become co-opted for improper ends. The ongoing saga of labor and agricultural regulation is especially instructive in this regard because it shows how badly the Progressive approach has worked in areas where competitive solutions are indeed viable. Gaining support for this worldview seems to be a tall order in the face of the current resurgence of progressive ideals. But perhaps for that reason, this task in a declining America is more important today than ever before.

Notes

Thanks to Brian Mendick and Mallory Suede, NYU Law School Class of 2016, for their research assistance.

1. Pub. L. 63-212, 387 Stat. 730, codified in 15 U.S.C. §§ 12–27.

2. Codified in 15 U.S.C. § 17 (§ 6): "The labor of a human being is not a commodity or article of commerce. Nothing contained in the antitrust laws shall be construed to forbid the existence and operation of labor, agricultural, or horticultural organizations, instituted for the purposes of mutual help, and not having capital stock or conducted for profit, or to forbid or restrain individual members of such organizations from lawfully carrying out the legitimate objects thereof; nor shall such organizations, or the members thereof, be held or construed to be illegal combinations or conspiracies in restraint of trade, under the antitrust laws."

3. Codified in 15 U.S.C. § 18 (§ 7).

4. National Labor Relations Act of 1935, Pub. L. No. 74-198, 49 Stat. 449 (codified as amended at 29 U.S.C. §§ 151–69 [2016]).

5. Fair Labor Standards Act of 1938, Pub. L. No. 75-718, 52 Stat. 1060 (codified as amended at 29 U.S.C. §§ 201–19 [2016]).

6. Agricultural Adjustment Act of 1933 (Emergency Agricultural Relief Act), ch. 25, Pub. L. No. 73-10, 48 Stat. 31; Agricultural Adjustment Act of 1935 (Potato Control Act), §§ 1–62, Pub. L. No. 74-320, 49 Stat. 750; Agricultural Adjustment Act of 1937, ch. 296, Pub. L. No. 75-137, 50 Stat. 246; Agricultural Adjustment Act of 1938 (Cooley Tobacco Act), ch. 30, Pub. L. No. 75-430, 52 Stat. 31 (codified as amended at 7 U.S.C. §§ 1281 et seq. [2016]).

7. 198 U.S. 45 (1905).

8. For a response to that charge, see David Bernstein, *Rehabilitating "Lochner": Defending Individual Rights Against Progressive Reform* (Chicago: University of Chicago Press, 2011), 1: "*Lochner* has since become shorthand for all manner of constitutional evils, and has even had an entire discredited era of Supreme Court jurisprudence named after it."

9. *Muller v. Oregon*, 208 U.S. 412 (1908), written by the conservative justice David Brewer. For the damage from the decision, see Bernstein, *Rehabilitating "Lochner*," chap. 4.

10. See, for example, Ward S. Bowman Jr., "Toward Less Monopoly," *University of Pennsylvania Law Review* 101 (1953); Robert H. Bork and Ward S. Bowman Jr., "The Crisis in Antitrust," *Columbia Law Review* 65 (1965).

11. See generally, Richard A. Epstein, *Principles for a Free Society* (New York: Basic, 1998), 279–318.

12. 12 East 527, 104 Eng. Rep. 206 (K.B. 1810).

13. 94 U.S. 113, 127–28 (1877) (quoting *Allnutt*, 12 East at 539) (misspelling *Allnutt* as *Aldnutt*).

14. See Richard A. Epstein, "The History of Public Utility Rate Regulation in the United States Supreme Court: Of Reasonable and Nondiscriminatory Rates," *Journal of Supreme Court History* 38 (2013).

15. 26 Stat. 209, codified in 15 U.S.C. § 1 (2016).

16. Codified in 15 U.S.C. § 2.

17. 156 U.S. 1, 13–17 (1895).

18. *Addyston Pipe*, 175 U.S. 211 (1899).

19. 166 U.S. 290 (1897). For further discussion, see Richard A. Epstein, "The Proper Scope of the Commerce Power," *Virginia Law Review* 73 (1987).

20. *Trans-Missouri*, 166 U.S. at 327.

21. *Id.* at 347, relying on [1894] AC 535.

22. 171 U.S. 505 (1898).

23. *Id.* at 572–73.

24. 208 U.S. 274 (1908).

25. *Id.* at 297 (finding liability); *id.* at 286–88 (quoting sections 1 and 2 of the Sherman Act) (codified in 15 U.S.C. § 7).

26. *Loewe*, 208 U.S. at 297. Other cases adopting this argument include *United States v. Joint Traffic Association*, 171 U.S. 505 (1898); *Addyston Pipe & Steel Co. v. United States*, 175 U.S. 211 (1899); *Northern Securities Company v. United States*, 193 U.S. 197, 360 (1904) (striking down the merger of the Great Northern and Northern Pacific Railway Corporations); *Swift v. United States*, 196 U.S. 375, 391, 402 (1905) (finding illegal agreements of firms not to bid against each other, "except perfunctorily and without good faith").

27. 54 F. 994 (E.D. La. 1893), aff'd 57 F. 85 (5th Cir 1893), discussed in *Loewe*, 208 U.S. 301–2. The dispute was between warehousemen and their employers.

28. 158 U.S. 564 (1895), decided before *Trans-Missouri*, which upheld the statute against a Commerce Clause challenge.

29. 235 U.S. 522, 536 (1915).

30. See Joseph Kovner, "The Legislative History of Section 6 of the Clayton Act," *Columbia Law Review* 47 (1947), 752.

31. Ibid., 749.

32. Ibid., 754 (quoting 51 Cong. Rec. 9565 [1914]).

33. See Richard Freeman and James Madoff, *What Do Unions Do?* (New York: Basic, 1984) (describing how unions have two faces: a monopoly face that creates a cartel of labor services, and a "voice" face that helps improve labor-management relationships).

34. See also Louis Brandeis's sociological brief in *Muller v. Oregon*, 208 U.S. 412 (1908), available at http://louisville.edu/law/library/special-collections/the-louis-d.-brandeis-collection/the-brandeis-brief-in-its-entirety.

35. 254 U.S. 443, 466–71 (1921). For a fuller discussion, see Richard A. Epstein, *How Progressives Rewrote the Constitution* (Washington, D.C.: Cato Institute, 2006), 87–89.

36. 208 U.S. 161 (1908). *Adair* appears in the same volume of the Supreme Court reports as both *Muller* and *Loewe*.

37. 236 U.S. 1 (1915).

38. Pub. L. No. 69-257, 44 Stat. 577 (codified as amended at 45 U.S.C. §§ 151–88 [2006]).

39. 281 U.S. 548, 570–71 (1930).

40. For discussion, see Richard A. Epstein, "Labor Unions: Savior or Scourge?," *Capital University Law Review* 41 (2013): 23–25.

41. 245 U.S. 229 (1917).

42. 47 Stat. 70, 29 U.S.C. §§ 101 et seq. (2016).

43. P.L. 73-67, 48 Stat. 195.

44. *Id.* at 195.

45. U.S. National Archives and Records Administration, National Industrial Recovery Act, Our Documents, www.ourdocuments.gov/print_friendly.php?page=&doc=66 &title=National+Industrial+Recovery+Act+%281933%29.

46. 295 U.S. 495 (1935).

47. *Id.* at 531.

48. National Industrial Recovery Act § 3(a).

49. Louis L. Jaffe and Nathaniel L. Nathanson, *Administrative Law: Cases and Materials*, 4th ed. (Boston: Little, Brown, 1976), 52.

50. See generally Richard A. Epstein, *The Classical Liberal Constitution: The Uncertain Quest for Limited Government* (Cambridge, Mass.: Harvard University Press, 2014), 270–72.

51. For discussion, see Richard A. Epstein, *Free Markets Under Siege: Cartels, Politics, and Social Welfare* (Stanford, Calif.: Hoover Institution, 2005).

52. For a discussion of many of these issues, see Deborah Malamud, "The National Labor Relations Board and the White-Collar Worker in the Early New Deal" (unpublished manuscript on file with author).

53. "The considerations generally entering into the designation of a unit are: (1) The history of labor relations in the industry and between a particular employer and his employees as relates to collective bargaining units; (2) the community of interest or lack of such interest among employees in the matter of qualifications for work, experience, duties, wages, hours, and other working conditions; (3) the organization of the business of the employer from a functional, physical, and geographical viewpoint; and (4) the form which efforts at self-organization among the employees has taken, including the prerequisites for membership in the projected or established labor organization or organizations" (NLRB, First Annual Report, 113).

54. Globe Machine and Stamping Co., 3 NLRB 294 (1937).

55. 323 U.S. 192, 203 (1944).

56. For my analysis, see Richard A. Epstein, *Forbidden Grounds: The Case Against Employment Discrimination Laws* (Cambridge, Mass.: Harvard University Press, 1992), 122–24.

57. National Industry Recovery Act § 1.

58. Seymour Martin Lipset, Martin Trow, and James Coleman, *Union Democracy: The Internal Politics of the International Typographical Union* (New York: Free Press, 1957). Note that Congress passed the Landrum-Griffith Act in 1959 to reinforce democratic practices in unions.

59. See, for example, *United States v. Butler*, 297 U.S. 1 (1936) (noting process fees that were not refundable to farmers did not restrict output). This decision was effectively limited in *Helvering v. Davis*, 301 U.S. 619 (1937).

60. *Mulford v. Smith*, 307 U.S. 38 (1939) (sustaining quotas prescribed by local committees of farmers according to the statute and regulations); *U.S. v. Rock Royal Co-op.*, 307 U.S. 533 (1939) (sustaining milk-marketing order for the New York metropolitan area).

61. Lawrence W. Reed, "Great Myths of the Great Depression: Popular Accounts of the Depression Belong in a Book of Fairy Tales," August 1, 1998, Foundation for Economic Education, www.fee.org/the_freeman/detail/great-myths-of-the-great-depression. These policies continue in force today; see, for example, *Horne v. Dep't of Agric.*, 750 F.3d 1128, 1141–44 (9th Cir. 2014) (sustaining a marketing order requiring growers to divert a portion of their crop to a reserve to "stabilize market conditions for raisin producers"). For criticism, see Alden Abbott, "The Ninth Circuit Rescues the Government Raisin Cartel," Truth on the Market, May 15, 2014, available at http://truthonthemarket.com/2014/05/15/the-ninth-circuit-rescues-the-government-raisin-cartel, and James Bovard, "Why the California Raisins Have Stopped Singing," *Wall Street Journal*, May 27, 2014, available at http://online.wsj.com/news/articles/SB10001424052702304479704579579831038906554?mg=reno64-wsj (subscription required).

62. 317 U.S. 111 (1942).

63. 52 Stat. 31.

64. Pub. L. 77-74, 55 Stat. 203 (codified as amended in 7 U.S.C. [Supp. No. I] § 1340 [2006]).

65. 291 U.S. 502 (1934).

66. 317 U.S. 341 (1943).

67. For a description of the programs, see Kevin McNew, "Milking the Sacred Cow: A Case for Eliminating the Federal Dairy Program," Cato Policy Analysis 362, Dec. 1, 1999, available at www.cato.org/pubs/pas/pa–362es.html.

68. *Nebbia*, 291 U.S. at 531.

69. *Id.* at 515.

70. *Id.* at 517.

71. See Dale Heien and Cathy Roheim Wessells, "The Nutritional Impact of the Dairy Price Support Program," *Journal of Consumer Affairs* 22 (1988): 216 (calculating that removing government price supports would increase nutrient intake for all families, but especially for the poorest households). See also John Adrian and Raymond Daniel, "Impact of Socioeconomic Factors on Consumption of Selected Food Nutrients in the United States," *American Journal of Agricultural Economics* 59 (February 1976). I review this evidence in Richard A. Epstein, "In Defense of the 'Old Public Health': The Legal Framework for the Regulation of Public Health," *Brooklyn Law Review* 69 (2004).

72. *Nebbia*, 291 U.S. at 535 (citing inter alia, *German Alliance Insurance Co. v. Lewis*, 233 U.S. 389 [1915]).

73. *Budd v. New York*, 143 U.S. 517, 551 (1892) (Brewer, J., dissenting) ("If [the government] may regulate the price of one service, which is not a public service, or the compensation for the use of one kind of property which is not devoted to a public use, why may it not with equal reason regulate the price of all service, and the compensation to be paid for the use of all property?").

74. *Nebbia*, 291 U.S. at 523.

75. *Id.* at 541 (quoting *New York v. Nebbia*, 186 N.E. 694, 695 [N.Y. 694, 695]).

76. See, for example, *Block v. Hirsh*, 256 U.S. 135 (1921). The category of temporary emergency is easily manipulated when it is defined by a low vacancy rate, which low rents induce. New York has had emergencies every three years since 1969 under its current Rent Stabilization Act. For the history, see Richard A. Epstein, "The Takings Clause and Partial Interests in Land: On Sharp Boundaries and Continuous Distributions," *Brooklyn Law Review* 78 (2013).

77. *Home Building & Loan Assoc. v. Blaisdell*, 290 U.S. 398 (1934).

78. *Parker v. Brown*, 317 U.S. 341, 359–60 (1943).

79. *Id.* at 346.

80. *Id.* at 350–51.

81. For Progressive endorsements of the open natural market, see *Southern Pacific RR v. Arizona*, 325 U.S. 761 (1945) (Stone, C.J.); *H. P. Hood & Sons Inc. v. Du Mond*, 336 U.S. 525 (1949) (Jackson, J.); *Dean Milk Co. v. City of Madison, Wisconsin*, 340 U.S. 349 (1951) (Clark, J.)

16 • The (Long) Administrative Century
Progressive Models of Governance
Joanna Grisinger

Management of the national economy through administrative regulation owes its existence and its shape to the Progressive movement. Progressives were confident (perhaps overconfident) about their ability to diagnose and solve society's problems. Chief among the problems they perceived was that the newly industrialized economy was increasingly tilted to the benefit of the few rather than the many. If the market did not protect the broader interests of the public, Progressives reasoned, something else would have to. Their solution: federal institutions strong, efficient, and capable enough to redress the imbalance among interests and to realize broad public purposes. Standing in their way were the extant arrangements of American government—federalism and the separation of legislative, executive, and judicial authority—which thwarted such concerted action.

Progressives did not invent economic regulation or even federal economic regulation, but by thinking comprehensively about how regulatory authority should be structured, they laid the groundwork for an entirely new "branch" of the federal government. These reformers created an enduring model for federal management of the marketplace: independent commissions and relatively independent executive agencies given quasi-legislative, quasi-executive, *and* quasi-judicial authority (that is, all the powers that the Constitution intentionally kept separate).[1] This model was inherently optimistic. Reformers trusted that experts within these institutions would be free from the corruption of politics and the inefficiencies of separated powers, and would thus be able to locate and serve the interest of the public as a whole. Through a variety of such institutions—beginning with the Interstate Commerce Commission (ICC) in 1887, the first federal institution to combine legislative, executive, and judicial authority outside the three constitutional branches of government—Progressives moved decisively toward governance by federal bureaucrats.[2] As the political scientist Robert Cushman argued in 1940: "[The ICC] was more than a new bud on an old branch. It was a new limb of such major importance that it pointed the whole tree in a new direction."[3]

Scholars who label the twentieth century the "New Deal state" or who distinguish among the "regulatory regimes" of the Progressive era, the New Deal, and the public interest era too easily pass over the fact that these agencies all drew on similar assumptions about governance and were burdened with similarly expansive hopes and responsibilities.[4] The regulatory agency—which the historian Richard McCormick, looking at states, called "progressivism's most distinctive governmental achievement"—was almost infinitely customizable to new problems.[5] From the late nineteenth century onward, in fact, reformers more often than not created new agencies to "solve" economic problems as they arose. Enthusiastically embracing this model in its response to the Great Depression, the Roosevelt White House and the New Deal Congresses established an "alphabet soup" of agencies to handle economic sectors and problems including agriculture, labor, radio, and aviation. And this pattern continued: the civil rights and environmental movements a few decades later stimulated another burst of agency creation to manage employment discrimination, air and water pollution, and workplace and consumer safety—all problems that the marketplace had failed to resolve.

This enthusiasm for agencies (and particularly for new agencies) persisted even as, over several decades, politicians increasingly criticized what they saw as the numerous limitations of the Progressives' model. Progressives imagined governance in America without the problems they diagnosed as endemic to the constitutional design—that is, they sought to tap all the benefits of legislative, executive, and judicial powers without the inefficiencies of Congress, the intrusions of the White House, or the formality of the courts. But the idea of accommodating agency independence within a constitutional system of separation of powers was fraught from the beginning. The issue was not constitutional theory (courts proved relatively accepting of combining powers in the agencies) but practical concerns. The agencies always fit awkwardly into the existing landscape of federal power, and they were never simply left to their own devices. Congressional control of appropriations, White House control of appointments, and judicial control of procedure meant that the historical patterns and perceived pathologies of the constitutional branches of government were transferred to and quickly embedded in these purportedly independent or quasi-independent institutions. The ideal of administrative self-sufficiency thus competed with the realities of constitutional authority. Determined to protect their decision-making prerogatives, Congress, the White House, and the courts pulled against the Progressive model even as they sanctioned its broader reach.

In the face of substantive critiques of regulatory governance (critiques that became louder over the years), reformers steeped in the Progressive ethos and inspired by its social science orientation have refused to conclude that agencies created athwart the structure of the federal government cannot be successful within it. Instead, they have tried to improve the administration of the older agencies while tweaking the framework of new ones. The abiding theme in the story of economic management over the course of the Progressive century is this elusive quest to tap the benefits of concentrated power, concerted action, and neutral expertise within a system designed to divide power, disperse responsibilities, and represent interests. We can trace the Progressive legacy, then, not just to the growth of the administrative state but also to this ongoing determination to prove that agency governance can be reconciled with constitutionally separated powers. Without any firm resolution of this tension, twentieth-century governance was marked by these two systems of governance often working at cross-purposes, each compromising the integrity of the other.

Progressivism and the Drive to Concentrate Authority

Defining Progressivism is a challenge. The reform agenda included a wide variety of efforts to respond to the political, economic, and social dislocations caused by industrialization, urbanization, and immigration in the late nineteenth century. At its core, however, Progressivism appealed to the authority of experts and drew on the findings of a burgeoning social science to transform government into a problem-solving machine.[6] Progressives turned to the federal government, in particular, in response to the development of large-scale national businesses, including railroads, steel, oil, and sugar. These newly dominant trusts and corporations squeezed competitors out of the market, hiked rates, and broke unions. Shareholders often benefited, but market forces seemed unable to protect the larger public. Seeking a way to compel businesses to act in the interests of the public as a whole, Progressive reformers pushed for federal regulation to achieve the effects, even if not the actual conditions, of a competitive marketplace.[7]

Progressives were wary of placing new regulatory authority in Congress, the White House, or the federal courts. Government through the constitutional separation of powers was likely to prove slow, incoherent, and inefficient. Democratically elected officials were easily corrupted, and courts were passive and hidebound. All three branches were reactive, and lacked both the capability and the jurisdiction to stay on top of constantly changing economic conditions. Drawing on the work of Woodrow Wilson, Frank Goodnow, and others who argued that politics could be separated from administration, Progressive reformers envisioned a new model of government—the regulatory agency—that would be free to promulgate and administer policies by its own lights.[8] This model included everything Progressives liked (expertise and concentrated authority) and minimized everything they did not (political pressure and separation of powers).

Although there is ample evidence of state building via regulation long before the late nineteenth century, the powerful federal regulatory agency as imagined by the Progressives was a distinctively new form of governance.[9] The ideal agency featured a strictly defined jurisdiction, clear lines of authority, and impersonal and apolitical decision making by meritocratically appointed expert administrators.[10] Agencies including the ICC, the Federal Trade Commission, and bureaus in the Department of Agriculture were designed on this model; within a single agency, those with knowledge of the problem at hand could make rules about discriminatory rates and unfair competition and order violators to change their behavior. Expert administrators insulated from political influence and unhampered by checks and balances would, Progressives expected, carry out policy faster, better, and more cheaply than the existing branches when left to their own devices. Progressives also expected that these administrators, once freed from political influence, would do a better job of protecting the public interest than the older branches. Thus, they could be trusted with significant discretion in the administration of broadly cast mandates. Congress put the ICC in charge of complaints about "unjust and unreasonable" transportation charges,[11] and the FTC was directed to administer the ban on "unfair methods of competition in commerce."[12] Progressives assumed that expert administrators trained in the field could figure out what those policy guidelines meant in context and could apply this policy continually to new business practices without further input from the White House or Congress. As one senator argued in 1914 in defense of the FTC, "Such work must be done by a board or commission of dignity, permanence, and ability, independent of executive authority except in its selection, and independent in character."[13]

But questions of "how much" soon haunted these first great experiments in concentrated managerial authority.[14] The design of these new agencies revealed hesitancy over empowering administrators.[15] Congress intentionally limited the enforcement powers of the ICC and FTC, and there was no getting around congressional appropriations committees, even for so-called independent commissions. Skeptical courts restricted the ICC's statutory authority to set railroad rates and established broad administrative-law doctrines that emphasized procedural due process over efficient decision making. And while clear jurisdiction over industrial problems was central to the model, the constitutional branches still seemed to prefer to spread authority around. Authority over unfair market competition, for example, was shared among the FTC, the ICC, the Department of Agriculture, the Justice Department, and the Federal Alcohol Administration. No agency commanded the whole ground over which it acted, coordination proved difficult, and management remained site specific.

New Deal Elaborations and the Accommodation of the Constitutional Branches

The Progressive administrative model of economic regulation (adopted for agencies including the Maritime Commission, the Packers and Stockyards Administration, and the War Industries Board) might have been experimental in 1920 or 1930, but by 1940 it was clearly here to stay. Congress and the White House responded to the economic cataclysm of the Great Depression by grasping the Progressives' remedy and expanding the federal government's power to manage the economy in the public's interest. Between 1933 and 1936, Congress passed, and President Franklin D. Roosevelt signed, a wide range of statutes aimed at managing different segments of the economy. The result was not just more regulatory power but also new independent commissions and quasi-independent executive agencies (including the National Recovery Administration, the National Bituminous Coal Commission, the National Labor Relations Board, the Federal Communications Commission, and the Securities and Exchange Commission) with discretionary authority over a wider array of industries (for example, broadcasting and agriculture) and wider range of industrial problems (for example, securities and labor). As a Brookings Institution study in 1937 reported, the agencies and commissions "are handling large questions of social and economic policy which are too complicated, detailed, and changing in nature for Congress to deal with except in broad outline."[16] Some of the dozens of New Deal agencies were short-lived, but with America's entry into World War II, the federal government was prompted to extend its reach even further into the market through agencies such as the Office of Price Administration and the War Production Board. Energy for new regulatory commitments slowed following the wartime crisis, but by 1945 the bulk of federal economic management was being conducted by agencies and commissions that had been created during and since the New Deal.

These agencies generally had more enforcement power, and faced less hostile courts, than had earlier ones (in part because Congress and the White House had learned some lessons about what agencies needed and what courts wanted). But while this state was strong in some ways, it was weak in others. The historian Ellis Hawley describes it as a "hollow-core" administrative state without the power to manage or plan comprehensively.[17] Indeed, the Progressive habit of developing agencies to meet specific problems as they arose (an approach compelled in part by the experimental nature of the regulatory form and in part by the reluctance of the constitutional branches to give up their own powers) exacerbated this problem. Thus, the extension of the Progressive model both elevated managerial ideals and aggravated coordination problems.

The extension of the Progressive remedy also failed in practice to arrest charges of corruption and inefficiency. When agencies and commissions tried to operate independently of the constitutional branches, new problems emerged. Regulated businesses routinely pressured agencies to decide in their favor, both directly and through the other branches of government. Some influence was intentional; Congress required the NRA to solicit the participation of businesses and labor when drafting codes of fair competition, and other agencies were lauded for establishing good relationships with the parties before them. Some influence was less welcome, however, especially when regulated parties pressed members of Congress to act on their behalf. A 1940 study of the FCC reported that "attempts by Congressmen to utilize their official positions as an excuse for special pleading (under the guise of explaining 'peculiarities of local situations') are made with some degree of frequency from the time an application is filed until the Commission has rendered its final order."[18]

Curiously, though there was ample evidence throughout of political and institutional intrusions on agency autonomy, controversy surrounding New Deal extensions of the Progressive model focused on fears that the agencies were too independent. Arguing that power had been shorn from democratically responsible institutions and placed in autonomous ones, critics challenged the idea of government by administration.[19] Many questioned whether the public interest was actually being served by overly aggressive administrators abusing their already expansive discretion. Those resistant to administrative power wanted a larger role for the courts (which, by 1940, had made their peace with the administrative process). One result of this criticism was the Administrative Procedure Act of 1946, which established minimum standards for administrative hearings, formally distinguished between rule making and adjudication, and explicitly stated a uniform standard of judicial review. According to Senator Pat McCarran (D-Nevada), the act served as "a bill of rights for the hundreds of thousands of Americans whose affairs are controlled or regulated in one way or another by agencies of the Federal Government."[20] Although the act generally codified existing procedures, the spirited debates surrounding it invoked concerns about administrators regulating too enthusiastically.[21]

White House efforts to extend executive control over the independent commissions and executive agencies pulled against agency independence as well. These attempts were complicated, however, by the breadth of the administrative state in the post–New Deal era. In a 1937 fireside chat calling for more presidential power, Roosevelt argued that the White House's existing capacities were taxed by the "higgledy-piggledy patchwork of duplicate responsibilities and overlapping powers."[22] But this messiness was hardly accidental; Congress and the White House had intentionally established new agencies to run many New Deal programs rather than placing the programs in existing ones. New agencies, they hoped, could start their regulatory project from scratch instead of shoehorning new commitments alongside older ones. In one example, the Motor Carrier Act of 1935 placed regulatory authority for motor vehicles in the ICC, a seemingly natural fit with the commission's experience in regulating transportation. But the commission found regulating many small motor carriers to be a very different task from regulating a small number of railroads.[23] A few years later, when Congress turned to the regulation of aviation, authority was intentionally placed in a new independent agency—the Civil Aeronautics Board (CAB)—for fear that the ICC might prefer railroads to airlines in devising regulatory strategies.[24] New agencies were free to develop their own relationships with the regulated parties and free to staff new agencies with officers committed to the regulatory mission at hand. Accordingly, although the FTC was in charge of maintaining a competitive marketplace, a conservative southern commissioner's probusiness policies made it a poor choice for ambitious securities regulation, and thus the Securities and

Exchange Commission was established in 1934 to regulate financial securities.[25] Putting regulatory powers into new independent commissions was a way to secure the intentions of Congress, but it also meant that regulation would be resistant to central direction and coordination. As the Brookings Institution study acknowledged in 1937, "Vast and extremely important fields of Government activity [are] almost removed from the President's direct administrative control."[26] The president's inability to simply fire that intransigent FTC commissioner demonstrated as much.

The proliferation of agencies testified both to the appeal and to the limitations of the Progressive ideal, for even as the model was generalized, it created new problems of economic management. The sheer number of federal agencies, commissions, departments, and bureaus meant that agencies often worked at cross-purposes and often failed to coordinate their policies. Policy at the CAB, for example, bore directly or indirectly on activities at agencies including the Civil Aeronautics Administration, the State Department, the Maritime Commission, and the U.S. Post Office. This segmented approach weakened economic management and undermined efforts to define, much less protect, the public interest. Efficiency ideals opened onto an increasingly unwieldy state.

Roosevelt's Committee on Administrative Management was formed to address these problems. This panel of blue-ribbon Progressives concluded in 1937 that the president was ill equipped to supervise the dozens of agencies that reported to him; he had even less ability to control the independent commissions, which operated as "a headless 'fourth branch' of the Government, a haphazard deposit of irresponsible agencies and uncoordinated powers."[27] Adding a new twist to the Progressives' faith in concentrated authority, the committee proposed that all the agencies and commissions should be combined into twelve hierarchically organized executive departments in order to make them more amenable to presidential management. The committee also sought to strengthen the White House's own capacities. Famously stating that "the President needs help," the committee proposed improving and expanding presidential control over personnel, budgets, and planning.[28] Though Congress was not willing to cede so much control over administration to the president, and refused to eliminate the independent commissions, the Reorganization Act of 1939 did allow Roosevelt to create a management bureaucracy within the Executive Office of the President.

Congress too was worried by the proliferation of administrative agencies. It was concerned not only about the enormous expansion of executive power but also about the president's determination to control it. And although the Brookings Institution study argued that the independent regulatory commissions were "agents of Congress" and "in no sense agents of the President," Congress knew that it lacked the administrative capacity to supervise them effectively.[29] The legislative branch, members of Congress argued, needed to play a larger role in making sure that the agencies were correctly administering Congress's policy judgments.[30] If, as Representative Mike Monroney (D-Oklahoma) argued, Congress was "the board of directors of the world's largest enterprise," it was time to start acting like it.[31] Representative Jerry Voorhis (D-California) in 1945 admitted, "We do a lazy sort of job, we just say 'Here is a big problem,' and, therefore, we empower so-and-so to solve the problem, and appropriate so much money to enable him to do it."[32] Congress did, of course, investigate agencies, but these investigations tended to be sporadic, reactive, and often punitive. Regulated parties turned to Congress (often with some success) to get the agencies to do their bidding. Staffers at the FCC, for example, faced off against radio and television interests, supported by members of Congress, who had no desire to antagonize local media. Investigations were also often duplicative. When the FCC adopted a more aggressive regulatory posture in the late 1930s and early 1940s, it was investigated by the House and Senate Appropriations Committees, the House and Senate Committees on Interstate and Foreign Commerce, the House Un-American Activities Committee, *and* the House Committee to Investigate the Federal Communications Commission.[33]

Following much self-examination, Congress passed the Legislative Reorganization Act in 1946 to make itself a more effective participant in the new bureaucratic state. The act streamlined the committee structure in each house to reduce duplication, and existing committees were combined into a smaller number of standing committees based on the jurisdiction of the agencies and commissions. Multiple committees in each house would no longer have responsibility over the same parts of the administrative state. The new standing committees were directed to engage in "continuous watchfulness" of administrative behavior (echoing the agencies' own responsibility for continual management of economic problems), and they were authorized to hire their own expert staffers (like those at the agencies) to help.[34]

For those who sought to subordinate the administrative state to the constitutional branches, the Administrative Procedure Act, the Executive Reorganization Act, and the Legislative Reorganization Act were all disappointing compromises. Faith in the Progressive model still ran strong. It was reflected in judicial deference to the agencies, in the Progressive pedigree of the President's

Committee on Administrative Management, and in Congress's and the White House's decision to mimic agency specialization, staff expertise, and independent jurisdictions in their own reorganizations. But competition and jealousy among the branches worked against any one of them yielding too much control. Roosevelt successfully vetoed an earlier administrative code for passing too much supervisory power to the courts, and Congress defeated the original version of the Executive Reorganization Act for passing too much supervisory power to the president. The three constitutional branches were fortified to intervene here and there, but these fortifications implicitly conceded that the work of government largely would be entrusted to administrative managers in the agencies. The constitutional authorities were adjusting to this new reality by protecting their own interests within it and providing for some systematic housekeeping.

Subsequent proposals for executive reorganization illustrate this pattern. Although the two Commissions on Organization of the Executive Branch of Government (called the Hoover Commissions, after their chairman, Herbert Hoover) in the late 1940s and early 1950s originated in conservatives' desire to gut the federal government's economic-management responsibilities, political realities led to recommendations that were similar to those of Roosevelt's Committee on Administrative Management. Steering clear of a frontal assault, the Hoover Commissions identified organizational reasons for agencies' failures—diffuse power meant that agency heads and commissioners could not manage their own agencies. Contrary to the ideal of independence, the Hoover Commissions recommended, and the White House ultimately implemented, more political supervision by more powerful agency heads, and more supervision of agency heads by the executive branch. Based on these recommendations, more authority was given to several executive department heads, and the president gained the power to appoint chairmen at a number of the independent commissions.

The middling nature of these accommodations and the failure to settle on any single model of control was evident.[35] The organization of Congress had changed, but the motives of congressmen had not. Individual members continued to reach out to the agencies only as needed, and the new standing committees tended to ignore the day-to-day operations of the administrative process, preferring to intervene with publicity-seeking investigations when and if it suited their interests. As a Hoover Commission study of the FCC suggested in 1948, "The threat of a comprehensive investigation has thus become another sword which members of Congress can dangle over the heads of the

Commissioners."[36] The result was an awkward combination of administrative independence and agency uncertainty. Moreover, agencies often failed to gain support from the courts, the White House, or Congress when they most needed it. When it suited their purposes, the constitutional branches used the ideal of administrative independence to assume a posture of aloof indifference. A Hoover Commission researcher reported in 1948: "Many members and officials of the Maritime Commission have been struck by the disadvantages of 'independence' far more than by its advantages."[37]

Variously pummeled and left adrift by the constitutional branches, the administrative agencies found themselves charged with the very vices they had been created to remedy. Hoover Commission staff studies from 1948 found that agencies and commissions established to develop policies proactively and concertedly had failed to do so. FCC efforts at regulation "have been spasmodic or have involved the enunciation of high-sounding policies which have not been followed in practice."[38] Rather than staying on top of economic conditions, the agencies and commissions had become almost entirely reactive. The CAB was singled out for this failing: "[It] has seldom anticipated its problems or planned ahead to meet them. Generally, it has lagged behind the industry in recognizing emerging problems and has started to take effective action only when they could no longer be ignored."[39]

Limited financial resources and perverse political incentives pushed agencies away from wide-ranging investigations of industry problems. Administrators received criticism from Congress and from regulated parties when their agencies articulated broad policies, but not when they failed to do so. As the political scientist Fritz Morstein Marx observed, "Getting along with Congress is a motto so plainly inscribed above administrative portals that being 'good' in the eyes of the most immediately influential lawmakers becomes almost second nature."[40] In the face of this criticism, agencies and commissions were skittish about taking positive action and instead relied on policy making through reactive case-by-case adjudication. This approach seemed to mock the Progressives' promise of efficiency. As a Hoover Commission study of the FTC noted, "Delays which would not be tolerated in the ordinary court are the customary order of the day."[41] Agencies might be even *worse* than courts; a commission can, "in its absorption with specialized problems, lose the common touch which ordinary courts—faced daily with a vast miscellany of different problems—cannot easily do."[42]

In the face of ongoing criticism from Congress and the White House, agencies and commissions became more dependent on the parties they regulated for support, thereby further exposing themselves to accusations of corruption. Administrators were often extremely friendly with the parties they regulated, in ways that seemed contrary to the public interest. Some agencies—like the CAB and the Maritime Commission—had the seemingly contradictory task of both promoting and regulating their industries. Hoover Commission researchers found that the CAB was "frequently criticized for being saturated with the aviation industry's point of view," and that some called the Maritime Commission "the 'kept woman of the shipping industry.' "[43] Even the agencies more exclusively regulatory in their mandate had long been encouraged to work informally and cooperatively with businessmen. As the political scientist Marver Bernstein explained in 1955, a commission "discovers that its administrative career can be more convenient, less hazardous, and less exhilarating when its activities do not interfere with managerial freedom except as affirmative governmental action is requested by regulated groups."[44] An investigation by a subcommittee of the House Interstate and Foreign Commerce Committee in 1957 revealed that commissioners at a number of agencies had accepted gifts from and done favors for those they regulated. Three years later, James Landis, a former commissioner at the SEC and the CAB, issued his critical report on the regulatory agencies to president-elect John Kennedy. Long delays, high costs, and biased administrators were "threatening to thwart hopes so bravely held some two decades ago by those who believed that the administrative agency, particularly the 'independent' agency, held within it the seeds for the wise and efficient solution of the many new problems posed by a growingly complex society and a growingly benevolent government."[45]

But through all this critique of the regulatory agency's failings as a model for governance, no one seriously entertained an alternative that would jettison Progressive ideals altogether. Criticism was harsh, even fundamental, but the pragmatic disposition on all sides was to make the system work better. The evidence was mounting that there were two different systems of management in play, that their operating principles were antithetical to each other, and that their simultaneous operation compromised both. The Progressive faith in administrative management survived, fittingly enough, on hopes of improvement.

The Public Interest Era: Expansion and Disembodiment of the Agency Form

During the 1960s and early 1970s, even as many were lamenting the moribund state of American administration, Congress vastly expanded the federal government's responsibility over alleviating poverty, racial discrimination, and environmental harm, and ensuring workplace and consumer safety. Although the problem had changed from maintaining an economically competitive marketplace to correcting for the market's failures, much of this was done by using traditional forms of federal authority. The Civil Rights Act of 1964 established the Equal Employment Opportunity Commission to manage employment discrimination by private businesses, and Lyndon B. Johnson's Great Society programs established a host of agencies to administer new benefit programs. The EEOC was originally modeled on the NLRB, although congressional resistance to a strong civil rights agency meant that the commission's authority to issue cease-and-desist orders and bring its own cases was stripped out of the bill before passage.[46] Soon thereafter, from the late 1960s through the mid-1970s, Congress passed a number of environmental and safety laws to be administered by new agencies, including the Environmental Protection Agency (EPA), the National Highway Traffic Safety Administration, the Occupational Safety and Health Administration, and the Consumer Product Safety Commission. Factory owners already accustomed to complying with the NLRB and the Department of Labor regarding labor laws, and with the FTC and Justice Department regarding antitrust laws, faced new regulatory burdens under the Civil Rights Act (1964), the Clean Air Act Amendments (1970), the Occupational Safety and Health Act (1970), and the Federal Water Pollution Control Act (1972), to name just a few.

These new agencies owed much to the Progressive model of independent or quasi-independent agencies with expert administrators exercising combined legislative, executive, and judicial authority. New agencies received broad authority over distinct social problems that straddled multiple industries, similar to the broad and overarching authority of the NLRB over labor and the FTC over competitive practices. The EPA was given jurisdiction over environmental concerns writ large (which came to include air and water pollution, pesticides, and radiation). At the same time, political compromises and constitutional limits meant that these agencies were created both from and alongside other agencies with similar tasks. The EPA, created by moving agencies from within the Departments of Health, Education and Welfare (HEW), Agriculture, and Interior into a single independent agency within the executive branch, was burdened with the administrative difficulties resulting from combining so many different organizations.

In crafting these laws, Congress tried to limit executive branch interference by making its own preferences clear.[47] Efforts to ensure beforehand that regulators considered social harms regardless of cost joined later efforts at oversight. Drawing on a move already under way to encourage agencies to make clear policies, statutory language required new agencies to live up to their planning potential by articulating broad rules (rather than relying on case-by-case adjudication) with specified outcomes.[48] The Clean Air Act of 1970, for example, gave the EPA deadlines for establishing national standards for ambient air quality and for setting emissions levels to achieve specified reductions.[49] Plenty of discretion remained for expert administrators. The Clean Water Act of 1972, which called for limits on industrial waste in water, required the EPA to determine how much waste more than two hundred thousand individual permit holders were each allowed to discharge.[50] And whereas regulated parties' ties to Congress meant that parties' access to administrators was already protected formally or informally at most existing agencies, Congress now encouraged similar access by public interest groups. Explicit statutory language allowed groups such as the Sierra Club and the Natural Resources Defense Council—which had increasingly strong ties to congressional committees—to protect Congress's new noneconomic definitions of the public interest during administrative proceedings and to go to court to challenge administrative orders to the contrary.[51]

Acting at times to support and at times to check this significant expansion of congressional activity, the federal courts became much more active in scrutinizing the work of the administrative state. While the administrative process traditionally welcomed the participation of "interested parties," courts broadened this definition to allow the alleged beneficiaries of regulation to share their views with agencies. Courts also inserted themselves into public interest determinations, demanding that agencies take noneconomic factors (such as civil rights, health, safety, and the environment) into consideration. For example, the FCC, which was required to ensure that broadcasting licenses served the "public convenience, interest, or necessity," was sharply rebuked by the D.C. Circuit for sticking to an economic and technological definition of the public interest in light of civil rights activists' claims that a prosegregation Mississippi television station was failing the interests of its own public.[52] As the law professor Richard Stewart observed in 1975, administrative law was providing "a surrogate political process to ensure the fair representation of a wide range of affected interests in the process of administrative decision."[53] Courts no longer deferred to administrators as the voice of the public interest, especially as "public interest" groups made their own claims clear.

In addition, courts expanded the doctrine of standing to allow new parties to challenge administrative orders after the fact. In expanding "legal liberalism" to the administrative state, reviewing courts took the opportunity they had provided themselves to probe further into administrative decision making and, in a change from their deferential stance in previous decades, question the substantive basis of administrative orders.[54] In some cases, presumably in response to problems with the administrative state that they had observed firsthand, courts pushed the agencies to regulate more vigorously. Rejecting the EPA's efforts to balance the interests involved, reviewing courts in the 1970s demanded that the agency go beyond specific statutory requirements and issue increasingly stringent standards, in keeping with the act's general ethos.[55] At the same time, courts moved toward demanding procedural protections for administrative rule making that went beyond what the Administrative Procedure Act required. Although the Supreme Court in 1978 struck down "hybrid" informal rule-making procedures that combined adjudication and rule-making procedures, it continued to endorse stricter substantive review of administrative policies.[56]

Responding strongly to this expansion of federal power and the resulting costs of administrative rule making (especially regarding environmental protection) on businesses, the White House redoubled its efforts to manage old and new agencies through traditional methods. Presidents during the 1960s and 1970s continued to suggest (without much success) that merging executive departments (into a small number of "superdepartments") and combining independent commissions would make the president's job of supervising them easier. Presidents were more successful in reorganizing the White House to better handle the task of supervision. In 1970, President Richard Nixon transformed the Bureau of the Budget in the Executive Office of the President into the Office of Management and Budget (OMB), which gained expanded management powers. Given the costs of administrative rule making (especially in the environmental area) and the recessionary context, the OMB increasingly tried to establish some presidential control over the administrative state. Nixon also used the federal budget to more directly contravene Congress, impounding funds for programs he opposed.

Congress increasingly pushed back against these presidential efforts to control the administrative state, particularly in the post-Watergate period. The Congressional Budget and Impoundment Control Act of 1974 limited presidential impoundment and allowed Congress to actively participate in setting budget priorities, rather than ceding leadership to the OMB. Congress also further stressed transparency in the operations of the executive branch and the independent commissions. The Freedom of Information Act in 1966 gave the public access to additional information about the inner workings of agencies and commissions, and the Government in the Sunshine Act of 1976 allowed the public to attend administrative hearings and have access to administrative records. Similar rule changes in Congress opened up hearings and voting records to the public. The Government in the Sunshine Act also required public disclosure of certain ex parte contacts between the regulators and the regulated, and the Ethics in Government Act (1978) tried to root out conflicts of interest by requiring public financial disclosures by government officials in all branches.

Concerns about the economic basis of regulation arose not just in the new and costly areas of oversight. Economists, lawyers, and politicians during the 1970s became aware that many agencies were failing at their traditional task of competitive regulation. Regulators trying to manage too much competition (in the case of the airlines) or too little (in the case of the railroads) were not succeeding, and although the public desired low prices and decent service, it instead was subjected to high prices and poor service. The CAB, for example, was in charge of both promoting the airlines and mimicking competitive conditions, but the former goal seemed to trump the latter. By refusing to allow new carriers to enter the market, the CAB kept airline prices high and plenty of airplane seats empty. Echoing the claims of many, the economist George Stigler concluded in an influential essay in 1971, "As a rule, regulation is acquired by the industry and is designed and operated primarily for its benefit."[57] Through White House and congressional action in the 1970s, deregulation went from an academic critique to a policy cause, and price and entry regulation (and the commissions in charge of it) were abolished in the airline industry and the railroad and trucking industries.[58]

The Reagan White House, hostile to both the Progressive ideal of government management and to the policies administered by agencies in the Progressive model, aggressively moved to take control of the administrative state. Using many of the executive branch prerogatives (established both by the Constitution and by previous reorganization efforts), the White House was able to stymie much social and environmental regulation. Reagan used his appointment power to install agency heads (such as James Watt at Interior and Anne Gorsuch at the EPA) who were hostile to the agencies they supervised, and his efforts to politicize the civil service process and cut staffing through budget reductions led many experienced mid- and lower-level staffers to leave government service.[59] In addition, Reagan used the OMB more strongly than previous presidents, and in the early weeks of his administration, he issued Executive Order 12291, requiring agencies to engage in a cost-benefit analysis of new rules. The year before Reagan took office, Congress established the Office of Information and Regulatory Affairs (OIRA) within the OMB to supervise agency rule making and evaluate agencies' cost-benefit analyses. As one scholar has noted, the OIRA "is not only useful in stymieing the regulatory process, but it is also an effective device for torturing the bureaucrats with a healthy taste of their own medicine"—that is, "the frustration of dealing with an obdurate, recalcitrant, and stubborn federal bureaucracy, OMB."[60]

Reagan administration efforts to substantively roll back environmental, health, and safety regulation failed, however. Congress was unwilling to undo legislative initiatives it had only recently passed, and the legislature resented the White House's ability to wrest control of the administrative state. In addition, these deregulation attempts were politically unpopular and often lacked clear evidence that the costs of such regulation outweighed the benefits.

Conclusion

Progressives' vision of governmental institutions operating beyond the competitive divisions ingrained in the Constitution was a revolution in statecraft. Americans ever since have met new economic (and noneconomic) problems with the tool of combined powers shielded from much political control. But concentrating power in a divided system has put governance at cross-purposes. Agencies conceived of as independent and reliant on apolitical expertise were embedded within a system built on compromise, divided powers, and constituents' input. The constitutional branches expanded the administrative state and then tried to disembowel their own handiwork. The new agencies were to manage the economy by best practices but also to be more responsive to the courts, Congress, the White House, and the regulated parties. Little wonder, then, that they began to manifest all the problems that the Progressive model had sought to avoid.[61] Reformers' response has been to try to make the model work better. Reformers in each branch turned to judicial review, to expertise, to executive and legislative supervision, to public participation, and then again to judicial review, all with the hope that organizational and procedural tools could improve the operation of the regulatory state. Such solutions—all focused on expanding one branch's control over administrative decision making—instead exacerbated interbranch tensions over control.

For all their problems, the agencies endure. Each branch's stake in the administrative state pushes and pulls at the integrity of the agencies and commissions; however, that same stake perpetuates them. Congress and the White House fight to prevent the other from dominating the administrative state, and judicial interest in control ebbs and flows. Remarkably few nonemergency agencies and commissions have fully disappeared from the federal landscape. The dominant trend then has been the exact opposite of what Progressives intended, namely, the compromise of independence and the exacerbation of constitutional conflict.

The Progressive legacy retains its hold on the organization chart of modern government. Progressives would likely recognize the regulatory agencies that exist today, but would lament how the independent ideal of combined powers has given way to interference from Congress, the White House, and the courts. Progressives today might want to consider moving away from the Progressive model of administration, now more than a century old. Instead, they might fruitfully take inspiration from the Progressive imagination and try to conjure for themselves a fundamentally new way of governing.

Notes

1. Although independent commissions and executive agencies lived in different places on organization charts, they had much in common: they were given control of a problem or an industry, were oriented toward efficiency, had combined powers, suffered from congressional interference, and were largely subject to the same administrative law doctrines.

2. Focusing on this shift places the Progressive era squarely in the late nineteenth century (what the historian Rebecca Edwards calls the "Long Progressive Era") rather than the more common early-twentieth-century periodization; see Rebecca Edwards, "Politics, Social Movements, and the Periodization of U.S. History," *Journal of the Gilded Age and Progressive Era* 8, no. 4 (2009): 463–73, 472–73.

3. Robert E. Cushman, *The Independent Regulatory Commissions* (New York: Oxford University Press, 1941), 19.

4. See Michael W. McCann, *Taking Reform Seriously: Perspectives on Public Interest Liberalism* (Ithaca, N.Y.: Cornell University Press, 1986); Ira Katznelson and Bruce Pietrykowski, "Rebuilding the American State: Evidence from the 1940s," *Studies in American Political Development* 5, no. 2 (1991): 301–39; Richard A. Harris and Sidney M. Milkis, *The Politics of Regulatory Change: A Tale of Two Agencies*, 2nd ed. (New York: Oxford University Press, 1996).

5. Richard L. McCormick, "The Discovery That Business Corrupts Politics: A Reappraisal of the Origins of Progressivism," *American Historical Review* 86, no. 2 (1981): 247–74, 268.

6. Robert H. Wiebe, *The Search for Order, 1877–1920* (New York: Hill and Wang, 1967); Daniel T. Rodgers, "In Search of Progressivism," *Reviews in American History* 10, no. 4 (1982): 113–32; Morton Keller, *Regulating a New Society: Public Policy and Social Change in America, 1900–1933* (Cambridge, Mass.: Harvard University Press, 1994).

7. For their part, businessmen were often willing, even eager, to comply with (and help make) national regulatory policy; see Gabriel Kolko, *Railroads and Regulation, 1877–1916* (Princeton, N.J.: Princeton University Press, 1965); James Weinstein, *The Corporate Ideal in the Liberal State, 1900–1918* (Boston: Beacon, 1968).

8. See John A. Rohr, *To Run a Constitution: The Legitimacy of the Administrative State* (Lawrence: University Press of Kansas, 1986); Matthew Holden, *Continuity and Disruption: Essays in Public Administration* (Pittsburgh: University of Pittsburgh Press, 1996).

9. See Matthew A. Crenson, *The Federal Machine: Beginnings of Bureaucracy in Jacksonian America* (Baltimore: Johns Hopkins University Press, 1975); Michael Nelson, "A Short, Ironic History of American National Bureaucracy," *Journal of Politics* 44, no. 3 (1982): 747–78; William E. Nelson, *The Roots of American Bureaucracy, 1830–1900* (Cambridge, Mass.: Harvard University Press, 1982); William J. Novak, *The People's Welfare: Law and Regulation in Nineteenth-Century America* (Chapel Hill: University of North Carolina Press, 1996); Brian Balogh, *A Government Out of Sight: The Mystery of National Authority in Nineteenth-Century America* (Cambridge: Cambridge University Press, 2009); Jerry L. Mashaw, *Creating the Administrative Constitution: The Lost One Hundred Years of American Administrative Law* (New Haven, Conn.: Yale University Press, 2012).

10. Max Weber, "Bureaucracy," in *Economy and Society*, vol. 2 (Berkeley: University of California Press, 1978).

11. Interstate Commerce Act, 24 Stat. 379 § 1 (1887).

12. Federal Trade Commission Act, 38 Stat. 717 § 5 (1914).

13. Sen. Francis Newlands (D-Nevada), quoted in Cushman, *Independent Regulatory Commissions*, 190.

14. See Stephen Skowronek, *Building a New American State: The Expansion of National Administrative Capacities, 1877–1920* (Cambridge: Cambridge University Press, 1982).

15. Morton Keller, "The Pluralist State: American Economic Regulation in Comparative Perspective, 1900–1930," in *Regulation in Perspective: Historical Essays*, ed. Thomas K. McCraw (Cambridge, Mass.: Harvard University Press, 1981), 56–94; Barry D. Karl, *The Uneasy State: The United States from 1915 to 1945* (Chicago: University of Chicago Press, 1983); Morton Keller, *Regulating a New Economy: Public Policy and Economic Change in America, 1900–1933* (Cambridge, Mass.: Harvard University Press, 1990).

16. Brookings Institution, *Investigation of Executive Agencies of the Government: Report on the Government Activities in the Regulation of Private Business Enterprises*, U.S. Senate Select Committee on Investigation of Executive Agencies of the Government, 75th Cong., 1st sess., 1937, Committee Print, 65.

17. Ellis W. Hawley, "The New Deal State and the Anti-Bureaucratic Tradition," in *The New Deal and Its Legacy: Critique and Reappraisal*, ed. Robert Eden (New York: Greenwood, 1989), 77–92, 87.

18. Attorney General's Committee on Administrative Procedure, *Federal Communications Commission*, Monograph no. 3 (Washington, D.C.: Government Printing Office, 1940), 59.

19. Hawley, "New Deal State"; Barry D. Karl, "Constitution and Central Planning: The Third New Deal Revisited," *Supreme Court Review* 1988 (1988): 163–201; Joanna L. Grisinger, *The Unwieldy American State: Administrative Politics Since the New Deal* (Cambridge: Cambridge University Press, 2012).

20. U.S. Senate Proceedings (Mar. 12, 1946), reprinted in U.S. Senate, *Administrative Procedure Act: Legislative History, 79th Cong., 1944–46*, S. Doc. 248 (Washington, D.C.: Government Printing Office, 1946), 298.

21. See Grisinger, *Unwieldy American State*.

22. Fireside Chat, Oct. 12, 1937, in *Public Papers and Addresses of Franklin D. Roosevelt*, vol. 1937, ed. Samuel I. Rosenman (New York: Macmillan, 1941), 435.

23. Ernest W. Williams, *Staff Report on the Interstate Commerce Commission* (Commission on Organization of the Executive Branch of the Government, 1948), I-22.

24. Edward C. Sweeney, *Staff Report on the Civil Aeronautics Board* (Commission on Organization of the Executive Branch of the Government, 1948), IV-10.

25. William E. Leuchtenberg, "The Case of the Contentious Commissioner," in *The Supreme Court Reborn: The Constitutional Revolution in the Age of Roosevelt* (New York: Oxford University Press, 1995), 52–81.

26. Brookings Institution, *Investigation of Executive Agencies*, 85.

27. President's Committee on Administrative Management, *Report of the President's Committee: Administrative Management in the Government of the United States* (Washington, D.C.: Government Printing Office, 1937), 40.

28. Ibid., 5. As the political scientist and former Budget Bureau staffer Harold Seidman argued, "No development in the past quarter century has been more significant than the transformation of the White House from a personal office to a bureaucratic organization"; Seidman, *Politics, Position, and Power: The Dynamics of Federal Organization*, 5th ed. (New York: Oxford University Press, 1998), 58.

29. Brookings Institution, *Investigation of Executive Agencies*, 87.

30. See Grisinger, *Unwieldy American State*.

31. 92 *Congressional Record*, 10039, July 25, 1946.

32. U.S. Joint Committee on the Organization of Congress, *Organization of Congress: Hearings*, 79th Cong., 1st sess., 1945, pt. 1, 39.

33. Susan L. Brinson, *The Red Scare, Politics, and the Federal Communications Commission, 1941–1960* (Westport, Conn.: Praeger, 2004).

34. Legislative Reorganization Act, 60 Stat. 812 § 136 (1946).

35. See Grisinger, *Unwieldy American State*.

36. William W. Golub, *Staff Report on the Federal Communications Commission* (Commission on Organization of the Executive Branch of the Government, 1948), III-43. See Erwin G. Krasnow and Lawrence D. Longley, *The Politics of Broadcast Regulation*, 2nd ed. (New York: St. Martin's, 1978).

37. James MacGregor Burns, *Staff Report on the United States Maritime Commission* (Commission on Organization of the Executive Branch of the Government, 1948), IV-7.

38. Golub, *Staff Report on the Federal Communications Commission*, II-35.

39. Sweeney, *Staff Report on the Civil Aeronautics Board*, II-23.

40. Fritz Morstein Marx, "Congressional Investigations: Significance for the Administrative Process," *University of Chicago Law Review* 18, no. 3 (1951): 503–20, 508.

41. Irene Till, *Staff Report on the Federal Trade Commission* (Commission on Organization of the Executive Branch of Government, 1948), II-22.

42. Ibid., IV-2.

43. Sweeney, *Staff Report on the Civil Aeronautics Board*, III-45; Burns, *Staff Report on the United States Maritime Commission*, III-28.

44. Marver Bernstein, *Regulating Business by Independent Commission* (Princeton, N.J.: Princeton University Press, 1955), 99.

45. James M. Landis, *Report on Regulatory Agencies to the President-Elect*, U.S. Senate Committee on the Judiciary, 86th Cong., 2nd sess., 1960, Committee Print, 5.

46. Richard K. Berg, "Equal Employment Opportunity under the Civil Rights Act of 1964," *Brooklyn Law Review* 31, no. 1 (1964): 62–97. The EEOC's authority was strengthened somewhat in the Equal Employment Opportunity Act of 1972, which empowered the EEOC to sue on behalf of parties.

47. See David Vogel, "The 'New' Social Regulation," in McCraw, *Regulation in Perspective*, 155–86; R. Shep Melnick, *Regulation and the Courts: The Case of the Clean Air Act* (Washington, D.C.: Brookings Institution, 1983).

48. Reuel E. Schiller, "Rulemaking's Promise: Administrative Law and Legal Culture in the 1960s and 1970s," *Administrative Law Review* 53, no. 4 (2001): 1139–88.

49. Melnick, *Regulation and the Courts;* Marc K. Landy, Marc J. Roberts, and Stephen R. Thomas, *The Environmental Protection Agency: Asking the Wrong Questions from Nixon to Clinton*, rev. ed. (New York: Oxford University Press, 1994).

50. Alfred Marcus, "Environmental Protection Agency," in *The Politics of Regulation*, ed. James Q. Wilson (New York: Basic, 1980), 267–303.

51. McCann, *Taking Reform Seriously;* Harris and Milkis, *Politics of Regulatory Change;* Sidney M. Milkis, "Remaking Government Institutions in the 1970s: Participatory

Democracy and the Triumph of Administrative Politics," *Journal of Policy History* 10, no. 1 (1998): 51–74; Vogel, "'New' Social Regulation"; Melnick, *Regulation and the Courts.*

52. Communications Act, 48 Stat. 1064 § 303 (1934); *Office of Communications of the United Church of Christ v. FCC,* 359 F.2d 994 (D.C. Cir. 1966); *Office of Communications of the United Church of Christ v. FCC,* 425 F.2d 543 (D.C. Cir. 1969); see Kay Mills, *Changing Channels: The Civil Rights Case That Transformed Television* (Jackson: University Press of Mississippi, 2004); Steven D. Classen, *Watching Jim Crow: The Struggles over Mississippi TV, 1955–1969* (Durham, N.C.: Duke University Press, 2004).

53. Richard B. Stewart, "The Reformation of American Administrative Law," *Harvard Law Review* 88, no. 8 (1975): 1667–813, 1670.

54. Reuel E. Schiller, "Enlarging the Administrative Polity: Administrative Law and the Changing Definition of Pluralism, 1945–1970," *Vanderbilt Law Review* 53, no. 5 (2000): 1389–1453.

55. Melnick, *Regulation and the Courts.*

56. Schiller, "Rulemaking's Promise."

57. George J. Stigler, "The Theory of Economic Regulation," *Bell Journal of Economics and Management Science* 2, no. 1 (1971): 3–21, 3.

58. Stephen Breyer, *Regulation and Its Reform* (Cambridge, Mass.: Harvard University Press, 1982); Martha Derthick and Paul Quirk, *The Politics of Deregulation* (Washington, D.C.: Brookings Institution, 1985).

59. Michael E. Kraft and Norman J. Vig, "Environmental Policy in the Reagan Presidency," *Political Science Quarterly* 99, no. 3 (1984): 415–39.

60. Marianne K. Smythe, "An Irreverent Look at Regulatory Reform," *Administrative Law Review* 38, no. 4 (1986): 451–70, 465.

61. As Matthew Holden explains, "The models that emphasize the hypothesis of agency 'captivity' to client interests, or the model of decaying energy and effectiveness due to 'aging,' implicitly or explicitly treated these alleged characteristics as difficulties to be overcome. They were not treated as indicators of the inherent deficiency of government when compared to the marketplace" (*Continuity and Disruption,* 111).

17 • A Century of Reason

Experts and Citizens in the Administrative State

Sheila Jasanoff

Expertise as a Public Problem

The long echoes of Progressivism, the reform movement that rose and fell in roughly one generation centered on 1900, have resounded through a century of policy making. Some of Progressivism's basic tenets are so deeply embedded in contemporary policy practices that they have lost any claim to freshness, let alone radicalism. Most basic is the assumption that policy should be rational, grounded in expert knowledge and judgment. What government today would embark on projects in education, health care, environmental protection, economic policy, crime prevention, or urban development without calling on advice from trained specialists? Dedicated academic disciplines, and "interdisciplines," have risen around each of these policy domains, and their findings must be taken seriously by anyone hoping to make reasoned decisions. Increasingly, too, policy makers depend on complementary knowledge of how to adapt disciplinary and professional skills to real-world problems. That translational expertise is cultivated nationally, and also internationally, by a growing array of public policy schools.[1] Indeed, Progressivism's most lasting legacy may well be a new kind of delegation: from elected politicians to the technicians who advise them;[2] from government of, by, and for the people to the rule of experts.

Tensions associated with the movement from politics at the polls to policy based on expertise have occupied theorists of democracy for decades. One set of concerns focuses on inappropriate influence by, and insufficient accountability of, experts—in short, the problem of technocracy. As long ago as 1931, Harold Laski, then a professor of political science at the London

School of Economics, worried that the unexamined values contained in expert judgments might reconstitute themselves as ruling values: "Above all, perhaps, and this most urgently where human problems are concerned, the expert fails to see that every judgment he makes not purely factual in nature brings with it a scheme of values which has no special validity about it."[3] A generation later, in 1965, the American political scientist Don K. Price, first dean of Harvard's school of government, noted that science has the power to distort democratic politics by usurping from elected officials the right to set the goals and priorities of public policy. Even more urgent than fixing organizational deficits in government, Price suggested, was the need for a "theory of the politics of science."[4]

As the urgency of two world wars faded, concerns that scientists might seize the reins of state power also receded, although one might see in the early twenty-first century angst over a too close alliance between economists and bankers a similar fear of capture.[5] Accountability, by contrast, remains a pervasive worry, encompassing today not only the enduring question of how experts, with their specialist knowledge, can be held accountable to public values, but also, in reverse, how politicians and policy makers can be held accountable to expert judgments. Scholarly attention has focused on both facets of the expert-public relationship, generating an extensive literature on the appropriate design of scientific advisory processes,[6] public participation in technical decisions,[7] the communication of science to the public,[8] and the illegitimate politicization of science.[9]

Much of this work recognizes that the boundaries between science and politics—and thus between experts, politicians, and publics—are constructed and maintained through politically inflected "boundary work."[10] Put differently, the balance between reliance on science and reliance on politics is itself a product of social accommodation and power plays. Price, for example, acknowledged the fuzzy border between truth and power long before the so-called demarcation problem crystallized as a topic in science and technology studies (STS). His book on the scientific estate can be read as an inquiry into how the boundary between facts and values should be patrolled. Price's solution was expertise of a third kind. He advocated for a cadre of trained mediators who would bridge "the spectrum from truth to power." Today, public policy schools such as Harvard's are in the business of turning out just such professional experts in science and technology policy, a new order of technocrats trained to see their role as simply that of applying rational rules to solve predetermined social problems.

In many complex policy domains, who counts as a legitimate expert and by what criteria of legitimacy remain hugely contested questions.[11] Yet the fiction persists that science and politics are separable: how one settles questions of knowledge should have little bearing on how one settles questions of politics, and vice versa. Widely shared, this belief has risen to the status of cultural common sense. President George H. W. Bush, for example, made a bow to the supposed autonomy of science in a 1990 speech to the National Academy of Sciences. He acknowledged the necessity of delegation to experts: "And as the frontiers of knowledge are increasingly distant from the understanding of the many, it is ever more important that we can turn to the few for sound, straight-forward advice."[12] At the same time, he hailed the academy, an elite scientific body, for its ability to guarantee science's objectivity and impartiality.[13]

Bush's endorsement of a rationally governed democracy, grounded in in-dependent expertise and sound technical advice, accords well with the Pro-gressive vision. But such statements of faith do little to explain the continued polarization of opinion in the United States on such issues as agricultural biotechnology, climate change, stem cell research, and public funding of sci-entific and technological innovation. In all these domains, despite high levels of expert consensus, there is considerable disagreement about whether to be-lieve what the experts say. This is not the result of growing scientific illiteracy, as scientists often proclaim, nor the corruption of good science by biased stud-ies funded by special interests. Rather, as I argue in this chapter, it reflects a retreat from the Progressives' commitment to an educable and knowledgeable citizen who can be trusted to see reason. In delegating increasing responsibil-ity for governance to experts, the public has gradually been distanced from the processes of expert assessment, to the point where in elite policy-making cir-cles the very idea of a reasoning public is once again in doubt.

To be sure, worries about the rationality of the demos are not new to political theory. Famously captured in the debate between Walter Lippmann and John Dewey in the 1920s,[14] the elusiveness of the public was at the heart of Progres-sive thought. Was the public a "phantom," inattentive, heedless, easily swayed by the media, and not capable of meaningful self-government, as Lippmann asserted? Or was it, as Dewey contended, a reasoning and educable collective that could, with due opportunities for debate and deliberation, ensure (among other things) that technical judgments would remain in line with broad social values? That long-ago debate, however, did not take on board the connections we see today between representing reality, on the one hand (classically, the stuff of science), and representing the polity, on the other (classically, the stuff

of politics). One way to chart the history of Progressivism across the past century is to ask how the questions that occupied Lippmann and Dewey have been
framed and reframed as political actors are forced to grapple with the interpenetration of those two forms of representation.

My approach to this inquiry rejects any a priori division between finding facts
and determining values. My point of departure is the basic STS proposition
that, in the policy domain, resolving matters of fact inevitably entails resolving
questions that are part of politics. Epistemic and normative order are, in this
respect, coproduced.[15] From this standpoint, delegation to experts—authorizing
the few to know for the many—is not simply a question of deciding who knows
best about the factual matter at hand. It involves as well a characterization of the
public's intellectual capacity, in particular its ability to understand and critique
exercises of expert judgment. In other words, the demarcation of a domain of
autonomy for experts (such as the National Academy of Sciences) demands a
simultaneous construction of the governable, and governing, political subject—
the citizen on whose behalf the expert produces specialized knowledge, but
who, in a democracy, must remain the ultimate custodian of the public good.

During the hundred or so years since the end of the Progressive era, two
broad movements have sought to balance the demands of scientific and political representation in the United States. One is a wide-ranging effort to create
administrative forums and processes through which laypeople can access and
question technical information, and thus enjoy greater parity with experts.
These moves presuppose, in effect, a Deweyan, knowledge-*able* public, capable of self-government when properly informed. The second is a characterization of the political subject as hampered by built-in cognitive biases and unable
to recognize its own interests, let alone to further them through rational action. The accompanying policy response is not information provision but
rather a "choice architecture" that imperceptibly steers, or nudges, people
toward making the right choices in spite of themselves.[16] This construction of
the public as nudge-able rather than knowledge-able is one that Laski might
have appreciated more keenly than Price, as a predictable overextension of expertise. In a secularizing world, it is equivalent to letting experts define not
only epistemic but also normative virtue.

Expertise and Judgment: The Original Position

Before Progressivism took root as a philosophy of government, understanding facts and exercising value judgments were not regarded as intellectually

incompatible. Reliance on experts had been growing since well before the mid-nineteenth century, but the feasibility of integrating factual knowledge with political choice was not in question. That capability, seen as a virtue in itself, was thought to lie within the traditional institutions of government. In the United States, for example, Oliver Wendell Holmes's essay "The Path of the Law," from 1897, claimed just such a role for the law.[17] Vigorously denying that the logic of the law derives from frozen precedents, Holmes championed a vision of law as actively attuned to social consequences and mindful of its effects on the human condition. From its first sentence ("When we study law, we are not studying a mystery but a well-known profession") to its rousing conclusion, he sought to lead law students away from arcane doctrinal hair-splitting toward pragmatic, consequentialist, and evidence-based modes of reasoning: "I look forward to a time when the part played by history in the explanation of dogma shall be very small, and instead of ingenious research we shall spend our energy on a study of the ends sought to be attained and the reasons for desiring them. As a step toward that ideal it seems to me that every lawyer ought to seek an understanding of economics."[18] What Holmes advocated was not the sacrifice of law and morality on the altar of objective facts but the cultivation of a modern legal sensibility, favoring enlightenment over mystery while remaining true to the higher purposes of the law. His text ended with a soaring appeal to law students to transcend technocratic and acquisitive motives: "The remoter and more general aspects of the law are those which give it universal interest. It is through them that you not only become a great master in your calling, but connect your subject with the universe and catch an echo of the infinite, a glimpse of its unfathomable process, a hint of the universal law."[19]

Another landmark moment, less lofty in aspiration but more immediate in its implications for social order, came with the transition from *Lochner v. New York*[20] in 1905 to *Muller v. Oregon*[21] in 1908. *Lochner* struck down a New York state law imposing limits on working hours for bakers, on the ground that it violated the liberty of contract. It took the "Brandeis brief," a 113-page compendium of expert opinion from a wide variety of national and international governmental reports, to persuade the Supreme Court to change its thinking. Without repudiating *Lochner*, the Court concluded in *Muller* that limiting working hours for women was constitutional: the potential for harm to women's health and morals justified abridging to some degree the contractual freedom the earlier decision protected. The path of the law between the two decisions was entirely consistent with Holmes's vision. Not doctrinal dictates but attention to consequences—economic, physical, and moral—drove the *Muller* judgment. The brief was compiled by a lawyer and evaluated by justices who expressed no self-doubt about their capacity to find or act upon the facts relevant to the application of law. Law functioned as a site and an instrument for integrating knowledge, expertise, and norms as the Court ratified through principle the coproduced world that legislatures, medical professionals, the market, and workers themselves were already converging upon.

On the other side of the Atlantic, Max Weber famously wrestled with the meshing of facts and norms, or reality and aspiration—only Weber, possibly reflecting differences between German and American political cultures, saw politics rather than law as the site of integration. In his 1919 essay "The Vocation of Politics," he painted the ideal politician as someone who could offer the mix of expertise and judgment needed for good government.[22] Weber was intensely involved in political activity while also lecturing as an academic sociologist in Munich in the brief two years between the end of World War I and his untimely death in 1920. From that engaged yet detached vantage point, he argued that three characteristics were essential for someone with a true calling for politics: passion for a cause; responsibility for carrying out that cause; and a sense of proportion, or *Augenmass*. This mix of properties gave the politician the right to lead. As if anticipating the horrific future he did not live to see, Weber placed his rhetorical weight on the last quality, proportion tempering passion and producing a politics of reason. He prized the carpenterly eye of the master builder, whose patience guides the "strong, slow boring through hard boards," thereby allowing a cause to be achieved and a structure to be built. Politics and policy were thus seamlessly integrated in the Weberian scheme of things. There was no hint that a good politician needed exogenous expertise to supply the intellectual foundations on which he could construct his dreams.

In the decades after World War II, the harmony between knowledge and judgment contemplated in these essays by Holmes and Weber began to fall apart. Neither law nor politics could any longer presume to rule on its own. Rather, this period saw the rise of specialist agencies, offspring in the United States of the New Deal, but becoming more numerous and wielding more power with the expansion of social regulation in the 1970s. Regulatory politics during this period became an embattled arena in which the mechanics of integrating technical knowledge with normative agenda setting emerged as a big problem for democratic governance. In a period characterized by growing human domination of the nonhuman world, those conflicts arose from different presumptions about how to link good representations of nature with legitimate representations of the polity.

A Separation of Powers

The proper division of power between experts and laypeople is a recurrent theme in the politics of regulation. Relegating some issues to expert authority necessarily raises questions about which issues should remain with the public and its legitimate representatives. Who, for instance, is responsible for deciding when an issue is ripe for expert assessment, and how much autonomy should experts enjoy in defining the limits of their own jurisdiction?[23] As policy domains evolve and more knowledge accumulates, whose business is it to make sure that the questions asked are still the right questions?[24] And if experts need to account publicly for their judgments, who should get the last word on the adequacy of that accounting?

The spate of regulatory statutes enacted during America's environmental decade, from the passage of the National Environmental Policy Act (NEPA) in 1969 through the 1970s, offers some answers. This was the decade of transparency, open information, and citizen access. Wide-ranging disclosure provisions built into law implicitly endorsed the Deweyan, and Jeffersonian, ideal of the citizen as a capable consumer in the marketplace of ideas—in brief, as knowledge-able. However informed or uninformed to start with, the ideal citizen was believed to be endowed with the capacity to absorb, evaluate, and act upon information, and to make rational choices based on what she knew. That burst of legislation created an entire bundle of informational rights:

- Right to know
  Of exposure to risks (freedom of information laws)
  For informed consumption (consumer protection laws)
  For fairness in litigation (discovery rules for litigants)
- Right to give informed consent (rules for protecting medical patients and human subjects in research)
- Right to demand reasons (administrative procedure laws)
- Right to participate and offer expertise (rules for consultation and participation)
- Right to challenge irrational decisions (environmental, health, and safety laws)
- Right to appeal adverse decisions (laws granting access to courts).[25]

Rights, however, are not self-executing, even when conferred by law, and laws need interpretation in the light of new situations, knowledges, and understandings. The task of aligning legislative prescriptions with the demands of a changing world falls to regulatory agencies, long regarded as the "fourth branch" of government. Situated in the executive arm, yet functioning at the nexus of rule making and adjudication, regulatory agencies are often in the uncomfortable position of triangulating between science, politics, and law. In the United States, their relationship with Congress has never been easy. Indeed, as recently as 2001, the Clean Air Act of 1970 survived a challenge for unlawfully delegating to the Environmental Protection Agency (EPA) the power to make what petitioners claimed was a legislative decision: how much public health protection is enough in setting national ambient air quality standards for pollutants such as ozone and particulate matter.[26]

While such fundamental challenges occasionally surface in the courts, a less visible struggle over representation goes on largely behind the scenes, in persistent attacks on the technical assessments that support regulatory standard setting.[27] These on their face can be regarded as contests over the nature and extent of a rule-making body's epistemic discretion. What does an agency know with reasonable certainty and how does it know it? But the effort to answer those questions brings with it more foundational inquiries into the agency's responsibility toward both science and democracy. Regulators sit, in effect, in the crosshairs of modern governmental accountability—they are required to get the facts right but also to serve the people's will. Three regulatory controversies between 1970 and 1990 illustrate how the effort to strike a balance between those two kinds of representation—of nature and of politics—entails a struggle over how to construct the "public": first, about procedural choices in administrative decision making; second, about the proper institutional locus of risk assessment; and third, about the conduct of regulatory peer review. In each debate, we observe the coproduction of policy-relevant knowledge along with ideas about the rightful place of the demos in American democracy.

THE OBLIGATION TO CONSULT

The Administrative Procedure Act of 1946 (APA),[28] a cornerstone of American law, established the proposition that policy reasoning, however technical or arcane, should be open to public critique. The APA provides that agencies must at a minimum give notice of their proposed actions and solicit public comment. The act also specifies that decisions must be grounded in an adequate evidentiary record and that agencies must give reasons if they do not factor important countervailing arguments into their final decisions. Who decides, however, whether the public has been sufficiently consulted? Should that judgment belong to the same agency that evaluated the evidence and made the challenged policy; or should some third-party watchdog, such as a court, determine whether concerned citizens were adequately informed and their input properly solicited?

Back in the 1970s this was an extraordinarily lively issue. Two highly respected judges on the D.C. Circuit Court of Appeals, Harold Leventhal and David Bazelon, staked out competing positions on how to assess whether agency procedures had given technical issues the airing needed for reasoned, democratic decision making.[29] Leventhal favored the "hard look" doctrine, whereby courts would determine whether the agency had looked closely enough at the issues in the record and would remand decisions if the scrutiny was found to be insufficient. Bazelon maintained that judges were not competent to steep themselves so thoroughly in the technical minutiae of administrative decisions. Instead of taking a second look at the evidence, he proposed, judges should simply demand additional procedures if they felt the agency had acted without adequate consultation. Which view would prevail?

Matters came to a head in a series of lawsuits over the licensing of nuclear power plants in the 1960s and 1970s. Environmental groups such as the Natural Resources Defense Council (NRDC) were just beginning to flex their muscles, mirroring in their mix of scientific and legal expertise the hybridity of the government's own regulatory agencies. Homing in on the licensing of the Vermont Yankee power plant, the NRDC argued that the Atomic Energy Commission (AEC) had failed to properly assess the hazardous consequences of high-level radioactive waste disposal, as required by the National Environmental Policy Act of 1969, or to consider alternatives.[30] At stake for the NRDC was the adequacy of the AEC's public reasoning, and the D.C. circuit agreed. Indeed, Chief Judge Bazelon made it clear that, for him, too, the issue was "the manner and extent to which information concerning the environmental effects of radioactive wastes must be considered on the public record in decisions to license nuclear reactors."[31]

Especially damning for Bazelon was the AEC's cursory treatment of waste disposal, based on a vague but optimistic twenty-page report by one of the agency's own officials, Dr. Frank K. Pittman. That record, the court concluded, was terminally deficient. The AEC could not reasonably have made a finding of safety on the strength of Pittman's assessment. Given the agency's shortcomings, only the court could ensure that public expectations of sound and transparent reasoning were properly met: "Our duty is to insure that the reasoning on which such judgments depend, and the data supporting them, are spread out in detail on the public record. Society must depend largely on oversight by the technically-trained members of the agency and the scientific community at large to monitor technical decisions. The problem with the conclusory quality of Dr. Pittman's statement—and the complete absence of any probing of its underlying basis—is that it frustrates oversight by anyone: Commission, intervenors, court, legislature or public."[32] The court did not dictate the procedures the AEC should follow, but it did indicate that more was needed to generate an information base that would, in turn, allow the public to meaningfully monitor the agency's expert claims.

The standoff between court and commission eventually made its way to the Supreme Court. In *Vermont Yankee Nuclear Power Corporation v. Natural Resources Defense Council,*[33] the Court insisted—in a sharply worded, unanimous opinion—that only Congress could specify the minimal procedures that agencies should adopt, although agencies could go further if they felt that more extensive fact-finding was warranted. It was not the judiciary's prerogative to mandate more elaborate procedures than those the legislature had deemed sufficient.

The Supreme Court's opinion in *Vermont Yankee,* as well as much subsequent commentary, turned on the question of administrative regularity rather than democratic principle. Over and over, Justice William H. Rehnquist, writing for the Court, emphasized the confusion that would grip the administrative process if the judiciary set itself up to second-guess an agency's procedural choices. Nonetheless, the opinion provides glimpses into the Court's theory of deliberation on technical matters, which deviated markedly from that of the lower court. The clearest indications emerge from Justice Rehnquist's treatment of the AEC's obligation to expose its thinking to public criticism, particularly with regard to its reliance on its Advisory Committee on Reactor Safeguards (ACRS).

The court of appeals had faulted the ACRS for failing to lay out a detailed basis for its findings in terms "understandable to a layman."[34] The AEC, in the D.C. circuit's view, should have returned the defective report to the ACRS for further clarification—a reasonable holding if Congress's intent was to ensure adequate deliberative opportunities for knowledgeable citizens. In the Supreme Court's opinion, the law demanded no such direct accountability to the public. The mere fact that the ACRS was required to publish its report did not mean that it had to address every facet of nuclear power that members of the public saw fit to question. Rather, the ACRS's "main function [was] that of providing technical advice from a body of experts uniquely qualified to provide assistance."[35] The fault line between the two courts ran along different conceptions of how to represent the public interest on an issue as grave as nuclear safety. For the D.C. circuit, the administrative agency remained the conduit through which publics could and should gain access to expert opinion. Judge Bazelon, possibly reflecting his early training as a United States attorney, sought to evaluate for himself whether the AEC had satisfied deliberative norms by ensuring that "a real give and take was fostered on the key issues."[36] The Supreme Court, by contrast, saw the agency more as a bulwark between experts and the people, entrusted by Congress with receiving and processing technical information on the public's behalf, but with only limited obligation to share every detail of its knowledge with citizens.

The Supreme Court's theory of delegation, allowing agency discretion to trump public doubt so long as the legislature's procedural mandates were met, gained force in later jurisprudence. Five years after rejecting the lawfulness of judicially mandated procedures in *Vermont Yankee*, the Court upheld the Nuclear Regulatory Commission's on-its-face-implausible finding that the storage of nuclear wastes causes no significant adverse environmental effects.[37] The principle of judicial deference to executive agencies received even stronger support the following year in *Chevron U.S.A., Inc. v. Natural Resources Defense Council, Inc.*[38] Here the Court held that when an agency is faced with silence or ambiguity about a particular provision in its governing statute, the agency's interpretation of the statute must be allowed to stand. Even in *Massachusetts v. EPA*,[39] the case from 2007 in which the Court overturned the EPA's decision not to regulate motor vehicle emissions of greenhouse gases under the Clean Air Act, the majority stressed that it was overruling not the agency's policy determinations but only its failure to give reasons in accordance with the law. It was not that the EPA had failed to involve the public in an exercise of democratic deliberation; rather, the agency had failed to obey its own statutory mandate.

THE "SCIENCE" OF RISK ASSESSMENT

The Supreme Court's positioning of regulatory agencies as ultimate arbiters of the adequacy of public participation—constrained only by directives from Congress—did not sit well with regulated industries. True, the judiciary had effectively barred the agency doors against populist demands for open entry, but in the private sector's eyes this still left mission-conscious regulators with far too much leeway to interpret indeterminate science in ways that damaged industry interests. Struggles over the practices of regulatory risk assessment in the early years of the Reagan administration showed how battle lines between government and industry were redrawn in the theater of executive action.

Risk assessment entered the tool kit of regulation in the early days of the New Deal. The Federal Navigation Act (1936), for example, asked the U.S. Army Corps of Engineers to justify its projects by weighing construction costs against benefits such as avoidance of losses from flooding.[40] Calculation, however, became a lot more political in the 1970s, when new health, safety, and environmental laws began calling for standards based on risk-benefit balancing. It took the better part of a decade for agencies to develop systematic approaches to analyzing risks and benefits, and for those practices in turn to achieve some degree of harmonization across regulatory domains.[41] The mere fact that several agencies regulated the same hazardous product or activity did not mean that all would calculate risks and benefits in the same way.[42] Disparities arose from multiple sources: differences in the governing statutory language, the nature of the harm to be avoided, the kinds of expertise drawn upon, and divergent agency traditions for dealing with uncertain knowledge.

Inconsistent assessments provided fertile ground for questioning the scientific competence of regulatory agencies. The EPA emerged as a favorite whipping boy, but other agencies, such as the Occupational Safety and Health Administration and the Consumer Product Safety Commission, were also frequent targets. Risk assessment, industry representatives argued, had become altogether too political, taking its cues from the agencies' clamoring clients rather than from objective knowledge. The most effective way to counter capture by activists was to circumscribe the epistemic authority of regulatory agencies, especially those seen as particularly vulnerable to public interest lobbying, like the EPA. The chemical, transportation, and energy industries dreamed of an institutional solution that would create a one-stop shop for risk analysis, staffed by allegedly neutral experts unaffected by any sense of mission toward particular regulatory goals. In short, this was an effort to mobilize the familiar discourses of scientific independence and objectivity to undercut the government's epistemic and policy discretion, which had been upheld by decisions such as *Vermont Yankee* and *Chevron*.

Rising private-sector pressure caused Congress to turn to the National Research Council (NRC) for a resolution. The NRC was asked to conduct a three-pronged study:

- To assess the merits of separating the analytic functions of developing risk assessments from the regulatory functions of making policy decisions
- To consider the feasibility of designating a single organization to do risk assessments for all regulatory agencies
- To consider the feasibility of developing uniform risk-assessment guidelines for use by all regulatory agencies.[43]

Behind this bland wording are thinly veiled assumptions that run counter to most STS analysis:[44] that facts can be isolated from values, and that policy-relevant knowledge can be generated independently of any consideration of what purposes it serves or how it will be put to use.

As a formal matter, the demand for fundamentally reorganizing the practices of regulatory risk assessment failed to carry the day. The NRC report, known as the *Red Book* because of its cover color, concluded that risk analysis did not need to be moved to a new institutional setting. Unsatisfactory outcomes were due more to inadequacies in the knowledge base than to deficiencies in the agencies themselves. Going further, the report concluded it would be a mistake to construe risk assessment as "a strictly scientific undertaking."[45] In spite of its careful caveats, however, the *Red Book* handed a substantial rhetorical victory to opponents of the Supreme Court's interpretation of agency discretion. Instead of combining science and judgment, the *Red Book* proposed that the agencies should try as hard as possible to separate knowledge from values. The first and best known of the NRC's ten recommendations reads as follows: "Regulatory agencies should take steps to establish and maintain a clear conceptual distinction between assessment of risks and the consideration of risk management alternatives; that is, the scientific findings and policy judgments embodied in risk assessments should be explicitly distinguished from the political, economic, and technical considerations that influence the design and choice of regulatory strategies."[46] Though the authors acknowledged that a stringent separation of science and judgment could not be achieved in practice, this recommendation was quickly taken up as an operational injunction that regulatory agencies should find the facts first and bring normative concerns on board only after scientific analysis had run its course.

Since the publication of the *Red Book* in 1983, regulatory agencies around the world have taken up the mantra that risk assessment must be separate from risk management. For our purposes, however, it is more important to see what this separatist ideology implies for democratic processes and understandings of the public. To the extent that risk assessment is regarded as an exercise that precedes and must be kept insulated from value questions, it also requires little in the way of direct public accountability. This formula precludes the very sorts of vigilance that Judges Leventhal and Bazelon (and Laski before them) thought necessary in order to keep technical practices in line with public understandings of the ends to be attained.

PEER REVIEW OF REGULATORY SCIENCE

A still more direct attack on the expertise of federal health, safety, and environmental agencies took issue with their methods of peer-reviewing their findings, claiming that they did not measure up to the standards of rigor and impartiality that are the norm in research science.[47] Debate ensued on who counts as a satisfactory "peer" for purposes of regulatory review,[48] with each side backing its claims by more or less subtle forms of boundary work distinguishing good (or "sound") from bad (or "unsound") science.[49] There is in practice no exogenous "pure science" position from which a neutral "peer" can evaluate the quality of policy-relevant expertise. Nonetheless, the rhetorical insistence that such a standpoint exists, but is being corrupted in regulatory peer review, served for decades to justify attacks on scientific assessments that did not serve the interests of regulated industries.

The persistent and uniquely American debates around peer review shed light on the peculiar position of science as a source of authority in U.S. politics. As the Administrative Procedure Act and the subsequent history of administrative law illustrate, assertions of expertise are not alone enough to keep interest groups from questioning regulators' technical determinations. To escape second-guessing, expertise has to seek refuge in an inner sanctum from which it can claim to speak as the voice of science, providing incontrovertible truth rather than educated opinion. Science, in short, serves in a quasi-constitutional role as a backstop to the representations of reality provided by experts. But in a litigious environment that continually deconstructs scientific claims, how can publics know which representations to accept as authentic pronouncements of science? This is where peer review comes into play as a powerful surrogate marker, resting on the widespread consensus that peer-reviewed science is per se good science. This was the argument that petitioners made to the Supreme Court in the early 1990s in demanding that all offers of novel scientific evidence in civil litigation should be peer-reviewed and published. Though the Court rejected that rigid test in *Daubert v. Merrell Dow Pharmaceuticals*[50] (citing, as it happens, my work on peer review),[51] it did affirm that, from the standpoint of the law, peer review is a critically important, indeed indispensable, component of the practice of good science.

If the political function of peer review—as a valve for regulating power between public and private interests—needed proving, that demonstration came in 2003 in an initiative by the Office of Information and Regulatory Affairs (OIRA), an arm of the Office of Management and Budget. In brief, the business-friendly OIRA sought to take over the control of peer review across the entire regulatory system. Its *Proposed Bulletin on Peer Review and Information Quality*[52] was couched in the modest language of ensuring objectivity and sound scientific methods: "A 'peer review,' as used in this document for scientific and technical information relevant to regulatory policies, is a scientifically rigorous review and critique of a study's methods, results, and findings by others in the field with requisite training and expertise. Independent, objective peer review has long been regarded as a critical element in ensuring the reliability of scientific analyses. For decades, the American academic and scientific communities have withheld acknowledgment of scientific studies that have not been subject to rigorous independent peer review."[53] The OIRA's institutional body language, however, was anything but modest. It alone would serve as peer review czar for the government. Widely seen as an imperious move to subordinate regulatory science to White House economic policy, the *Bulletin* drew floods of protest from an unlikely coalition of the nation's leading scientists, Democratic members of Congress, and academic social scientists interested in the accountable production of regulatory science.[54] The OIRA, under heat, retreated from this unexpectedly contentious front line, issuing a much toned-down guideline in 2004. In the remaining years of the George W. Bush administration, politics influenced science a good deal more crudely, through selective editing of important reports and even outright suppression of agency assessments on issues ranging from contraceptive safety to climate change.[55]

As teachable moments go, the OIRA peer review initiative was hardly a moment of triumph for progressivism. Public reason suffered as the heavy hand of politics reinscribed the texts of regulatory science to make them more palatable to clients of the state. But reason suffered more serious harm through a failure, on the left as well as the right, to make a space for expert judgment inside contemporary democratic theory. The tactics of the right, cleverly reflected in OIRA's proposed peer review bulletin, appeared to recognize the constructedness of scientific claims, a view that in this respect aligned well with insights from science and technology studies. But the OIRA played fast and loose with the norm of public accountability by trying to seize and control an all-important passage point in the process of knowledge production: peer review. Under the banner of scientific rigor, the *Bulletin* tried to contain the selection of regulatory reviewers inside one of the most opaque and nonaccountable corners of the federal machinery. The liberal left successfully resisted this maneuver, but it did so through appeals to a purist view of good science that denies the hybridity of regulatory science. It was easy, and efficacious, for liberals to charge the OIRA with politicizing science. It would have been more difficult, but more productive for deliberative democracy, to recognize that regulatory peer review always contains elements of politics, and then to consider how to make that politics more accountable.

Nudge and Neoliberalism

The job of expert agencies in the postwar administrative state included the production of a scientific record on the basis of which capable citizens could evaluate regulatory decisions and demand better reasons if needed. How far the agencies were obliged to draw citizens into the processes of generating and reviewing the science was, as we have seen, unsettled and contested. In particular, the Supreme Court rebuffed the D.C. circuit's efforts to allow judges to stand in for the public through post hoc assessments of the adequacy of rule-making procedures. Nonetheless, the state's obligation to serve up information for public consumption, and to maintain some degree of transparency, was never in question.

Beginning in 1980, with Ronald Reagan's electoral victory on a fiercely antiregulatory agenda, that version of the state's role began to yield to a new construction of government's primary responsibility toward private enterprise and the free market. Effective roadblocks against the production of policy-relevant science had already been erected in some areas. Thus, repeated legal challenges to the Toxic Substances Control Act of 1976 more or less dismantled that statute's knowledge-forcing design within a few years after its enactment. By 2000, it had become almost an article of faith in U.S. policy that markets do the job of regulating better than states. Economic instruments, in other words, were thought to work more efficiently across the board than traditional practices of command and control based on the government's expert knowledge. So complete was this neoliberal turn that it hardly needs exhaustive discussion or documentation here for our purposes. One sees it, for example, in the embrace of cap and trade as the only feasible option for reducing greenhouse gases, in the popularity of public-private partnerships for governance, and in the rise of direct-to-consumer marketing for once tightly regulated products such as pharmaceuticals.

Governance—a term that tellingly shies away from the old-fashioned associations of government as overly top-down, burdensome, and inefficient—draws justification from skepticism toward regulatory authority. Even the most respected of federal regulatory agencies, the Food and Drug Administration (FDA), had to rebuild its reputation on different foundations from those that supported it midcentury, when it presciently (and expertly) kept thalidomide and the birth defects it induced out of the American market.[56] The EPA, ever vulnerable to charges of scientific ineptitude and overregulation, saw its power steadily decay. A specially damaging blow was the Obama administration's decision in 2011, on the eve of a presidential campaign, to abandon a proposed EPA rule reducing the ground-level ozone standard from 75 to 60–70 parts per billion.[57] Bolstered by the OMB's oversight authority over the economic impact of regulations, the administration questioned whether a costly policy change would see more people dying from ozone exposure or from unemployment. In a tug-of-war over which form of expertise was most relevant to public health protection—scientific or economic—cost-based arguments, unlawfully in the view of prominent legal analysts,[58] won presidential approval.

The old order of rule by experts, but under vigorous public supervision, changed beyond recognition between 1970 and 2000 toward a regime of letting markets enjoy much freer play. But states are protean entities, and by century's end a rebirth of sorts was in the works for state power. The American federal state was still determined to govern, even if it meant performing an almost complete turnaround from its earlier self-understanding as promoter of democracy and codifier of the public good. In this new era of market thinking and market talk, the state too sought to reconstitute itself as an agent of the invisible hand, and the key practice of governance that emerged out of this transition was "nudge." As articulated by the behavioral economist Richard Thaler and the legal scholar Cass Sunstein,[59] nudging is an instrument of "libertarian paternalism." It depends on the expertise of a new genre of policy practitioners, "choice architects," who shape the overall framework within which citizens are entitled to express their preferences. Citizens, innocent victims of habit and faulty memory, remain unaware of the benevolent paternalism that has, through background architectural design, set rational limits on their freedom to choose. A canonical example of choice architecture places employees in opt-out versus opt-in programs for savings, knowing that inertia—a demonstrated feature of psychosocial behavior—will keep them enrolled in the plan and keep them saving adequately, provided that economic experts have properly calibrated the right levels of savings in advance.

Based on the Nobel Prize–winning research of the psychologist Daniel Kahneman and colleagues, nudge theory offers an appealing justification for the state's continued relevance in an era of market ascendancy. Only, in this vision, it is no longer social injustice or rights violations that stand at the center of the state's fix-it imagination, but rather the figure of the mentally disabled citizen, chronically incapable of making rational decisions even in his or her own best interests. Nudging and its accompanying physiological construct, the biased brain, have caught on as the fashion of the moment in policy circles. An example from a well-known instructor at the Harvard Kennedy School is more colorful than average, but quite mainstream in its assessment of the problem:

> Through millions of years of evolution, lust, gluttony, greed, sloth, wrath, envy, and pride were "evils" necessary for man's ability to reproduce and find sustenance, [Dutch] Leonard [a professor of public management] explained at the Kennedy School's Bell Hall Thursday afternoon (Dec. 14). "The seven deadly sins may be built into us from an evolutionary perspective."
>
> Research has also revealed, said Leonard, anomalies in the ways in which people use information and respond to situations. Decision-making is often based on people's direct experience—and that of others close to them—rather than on reason. Short-term pleasure often overrides potential long-term drawbacks.
>
> "The ability to reason [Leonard said] is a relatively new arrival to which humans have not yet adapted."[60]

Invoking evolutionary biology to support his construction of the irrational human subject, Leonard does a complete about-face from earlier presumptions of citizens as both knowing and knowledgeable.

Back to the Future: Expertise and Redemption

Way back in the nineteenth century, expertise emerged as a counterweight to religion. The eminent historian of medicine Charles Rosenberg details that emergence in his influential study of the rise of public health as a professional and institutional presence in the United States during the "cholera years" of the mid–1800s.[61] Tracing the history of three cholera epidemics, in 1832, 1849, and 1866, Rosenberg tells in effect a story of secularization, precursor to the Progressivism that flowered a generation on. In the beginning, nothing much was known of what caused the disease, but people noticed its co-occurrence with dirt, filth, and poverty. Clearly, the loose personal morality and fecklessness of those afflicted were largely to blame. While physicians concocted bizarre and ineffectual remedies, clergymen proclaimed that cholera was a scourge sent by God to punish vice and sin, and, as if by way of proof, the poor died in the thousands. As Rosenberg summarizes a widely held view of that time: "The pestilence was an inevitable result of man's failure to observe the laws of nature. Man has free will, and when he fails to observe these laws brings inescapable punishment upon himself."[62] Unsurprisingly, great discomfort set in when, occasionally, cholera took away a patient from the well-off classes, whose social virtues were supposed to keep them safe from harm.

By the time of the third epidemic year, the world had changed. Armed with new scientific findings from Europe that traced the disease to germs, not vice, public authorities could imagine and execute preventive measures with considerable hope of success. As Rosenberg tells it, 1866 became remarkable in the annals of public health as the year the epidemic was mostly averted, at least in New York, through the efforts of a newly empowered Metropolitan Board of Health. Inspection, sanitation, and quarantine became the instruments of prevention, wielded by an expert agency with a mandate to do what it took to keep cholera at bay.

Though Progressivism was no more than a pale gleam on the horizon, as America after the Civil War emerged into full-fledged modernity, the rise of the professional classes, along with changes in university education and public administration, was part of that evolution. In the process, the American citizen, too, gained emancipation, not only those enslaved as property but also those enslaved by religion and superstition. It was not possible in the United States of 1866 to imagine the bitter debates about the constitutional merits of a national day of prayer, fasting, and humiliation that had roiled the nation in June 1832, setting pro- and anti-Jacksonian forces against each other.[63] The last of the three cholera years ushered in a paternalistic state, but it also liberated people from bearing individual moral responsibility for collective ills. Besides, through expanded opportunities for public education, many more could hope to rise from the masses of the poor and ignorant to the ranks of experts and ruling elites.

One hundred and fifty years later, the wheel has come full circle. The state is in retreat on many fronts except as a creator and fixer of markets, and by extension as a repairman for the deficient citizen who has not yet learned to reason well as a consumer and an economic agent, and thereby to function effectively in a market. Once again, responsibility falls back upon the individual, who must be nudged out of lethargy and the propensity to see reality through biologically distorted lenses of the mind. A sad state for democracy! The publics constructed by opinion surveys, focus groups, and deliberative polling—not to mention the minds "revealed" through behavioral economics, trolley problems, brain imaging, and neuroeconomics—seem so much less teachable and energetic than the citizens of a mere forty years ago. But history suggests that today's publics, along with today's scientific expertise, are just as much constructs of particular times and particular traditions as those of a generation or a century ago. As new conversations start, such as those represented in this volume, perhaps we can project forward to newly progressive ways of imagining citizens—as complex in their thinking, adaptive in their receptivity to new knowledge, and active in their own self-rule.

Notes

1. The oldest public policy training program in the United States, a precursor to the Gerald R. Ford School of Public Policy, was established in 1914 at the University of Michigan. Harvard University's John F. Kennedy School of Government celebrated its seventy-fifth anniversary in 2012. Public policy programs have recently been established at leading international universities such as Oxford and Cambridge. On the need to train policy experts in how to use technical evidence, see National Research Council, *Using Science as Evidence in Public Policy* (Washington, D.C.: National Academies Press, 2012).

2. Sheila Jasanoff, *The Fifth Branch: Science Advisers as Policymakers* (Cambridge, Mass.: Harvard University Press, 1990).

3. Harold J. Laski, *The Limitations of the Expert,* Fabian Tract 235 (London: Fabian Society, 1931), 4.

4. Don K. Price, *The Scientific Estate* (Cambridge, Mass.: Harvard University Press, 1965), 5.

5. See, in this connection, the director Charles Ferguson's 2010 Academy Award–winning documentary *Inside Job.*

6. See, for example, Stephen Hilgartner, *Science on Stage: Expert Advice as Public Drama* (Stanford, Calif.: Stanford University Press, 2000); Alexander Bogner and Helger Torgersen, eds., *Wozu Experten? Ambivalenzen der Beziehung von Wissenschaft und*

Politik (Wiesbaden: Verlag für Sozialwissenschaften, 2005); Angela Guimarães Pereira and Silvio Funtowicz, eds., *Science for Policy: Ecological Economics and Human Well-Being* (New Delhi: Oxford University Press, 2009); Justus Lentsch and Peter Weingart, eds., *The Politics of Science Advice* (Cambridge: Cambridge University Press, 2011). Also see Jasanoff, *Fifth Branch.*

7. Melissa Leach, Ian Scoones, and Brian Wynne, eds., *Science and Citizens* (London: Zed, 2005).

8. Massimiano Bucchi and Brian Trench, eds., *Handbook of Public Communication of Science and Technology* (London: Routledge, 2008).

9. Thomas O. McGarity and Wendy Wagner, *Bending Science: How Special Interests Corrupt Public Health Research* (Cambridge, Mass.: Harvard University Press, 2008); David Michaels, *Doubt Is Their Product: How Industry's Assault on Science Threatens Your Health* (New York: Oxford University Press, 2008).

10. Thomas F. Gieryn, *Cultural Boundaries of Science: Credibility on the Line* (Chicago: University of Chicago Press, 1999); see also Jasanoff, *Fifth Branch.*

11. Harry Collins and Robert Evans, *Rethinking Expertise* (Chicago: University of Chicago Press, 2007).

12. George H. W. Bush, Remarks to the National Academy of Sciences, Washington, D.C., April 23, 1990, American Presidency Project, www.presidency.ucsb.edu/ws/?pid=18393.

13. For a sociological account of how the academy's claim to objectivity is constructed, see Hilgartner, *Science on Stage.*

14. See especially Walter Lippmann, *The Phantom Public* (New York: Macmillan, 1927); John Dewey, *The Public and Its Problems* (New York: Holt, 1927).

15. Sheila Jasanoff, "Ordering Knowledge, Ordering Society," in *States of Knowledge: The Co-production of Science and Social Order,* ed. Jasanoff (London: Routledge, 2004), 13–43.

16. Richard Thaler and Cass Sunstein, *Nudge: Improving Decisions About Health, Wealth, and Happiness* (New Haven, Conn.: Yale University Press, 2008).

17. Oliver Wendell Holmes, "The Path of the Law," *Harvard Law Review* 10 (1897): 457.

18. Ibid., 474. It is ironic that in his push for consequentialism in law, Holmes recommended an embrace by lawyers of a discipline (economics) that assiduously denies any involvement in defining human ends or the reasons for desiring them.

19. Ibid., 478.

20. *Lochner v. New York,* 198 U.S. 45 (1905).

21. *Muller v. Oregon,* 208 U.S. 412 (1908).

22. Max Weber, "The Vocation of Politics" ["Politik als Beruf"], in *Weber: Political Writings,* ed. Peter Lassman and Ronald Spears (Cambridge: Cambridge University Press, 1994), 352–69.

23. This question is elided in classic works on political agenda setting such as John Kingdon, *Agenda, Alternatives, and Public Policies* (Boston: Little, Brown, 1984).

24. Paul Stern and Harvey Fineberg, eds., *Understanding Risk: Informing Decisions in a Democratic Society* (Washington, D.C.: National Academy Press, 1996).

25. Sheila Jasanoff, "The Politics of Public Reason," in *The Politics of Knowledge*, ed. Patrick Baert and Fernando Dominguez Rubio (Abingdon, U.K.: Routledge, 2011), 11–32.

26. *Whitman, Administrator of Environmental Protection Agency v. American Trucking Association*, 531 U.S. 457 (2001).

27. Sheila Jasanoff, "Contested Boundaries in Policy-Relevant Science," *Social Studies of Science* 17, no. 2 (1987): 195–230.

28. 5 U.S.C. Chapter 5, Subchapter II, § 551–59.

29. Sheila Jasanoff, *Science at the Bar: Law, Science, and Technology in America* (Cambridge, Mass.: Harvard University Press, 1995), 75–78.

30. 42 U.S.C. Chapter 55.

31. *Natural Resources Defense Council v. U.S. Nuclear Regulatory Commission*, 547 F. 2d 633, at 637 (CADC 1976).

32. *Id.* at 651.

33. *Vermont Yankee Nuclear Power Corporation v. Natural Resources Defense Council*, 435 U.S. 519 (1978).

34. *Id.* at 556.

35. *Id.*

36. *Natural Resources Defense Council*, 547 F. 2d at 645.

37. *Baltimore Gas & Electric Co. v. Natural Resources Defense Council, Inc.*, 462 U.S. 87 (1983).

38. *Chevron U.S.A., Inc. v. Natural Resources Defense Council, Inc.*, 467 U.S. 837 (1984).

39. *Massachusetts v. EPA*, 549 U.S. 497 (2007).

40. Theodore Porter, *Trust in Numbers: The Pursuit of Objectivity in Science and Public Life* (Princeton, N.J.: Princeton University Press, 1995).

41. The EPA issued its first formal risk-assessment guidelines, the Interim Procedures and Guidelines for Health Risk and Economic Impact Assessments of Suspected Carcinogens, in 1976.

42. Ronald Brickman, Sheila Jasanoff, and Thomas Ilgen, *Controlling Chemicals: The Politics of Regulation in Europe and the United States* (Ithaca, N.Y.: Cornell University Press, 1985).

43. National Research Council, *Risk Assessment in the Federal Government: Managing the Process* (Washington, D.C.: National Academies Press, 1983), 2; this work is commonly referred to as the *Red Book*.

44. For a review of these arguments, see Jasanoff, *Fifth Branch*.

45. *Red Book*, 150.

46. Ibid., 151.

47. Robert K. Merton, "The Normative Structure of Science," in *The Sociology of Science: Theoretical and Empirical Investigations*, ed. R. K. Merton and Norman W. Storer (Chicago: University of Chicago Press, 1973), 267–78.

48. Jasanoff, "Contested Boundaries in Policy-Relevant Science."

49. Jasanoff, *Fifth Branch*.

50. *Daubert v. Merrell Dow Pharmaceuticals*, 509 U.S. 579 (1993).

51. "Another pertinent consideration is whether the theory or technique has been subjected to peer review and publication. Publication (which is but one element of peer review) is not a *sine qua non* of admissibility; it does not necessarily correlate with reliability, see S. Jasanoff, The Fifth Branch: Science Advisors as Policymakers 61–76 (1990)" (*Id.* at 593).

52. OIRA, *Proposed Bulletin on Peer Review and Information Quality*, August 29, 2003.

53. *Bulletin*, Supplementary Information, 68 *Fed. Reg.* 54024.

54. See, for example, a letter dated May 26, 2004, to Joshua Bolten, director of the Office of Management and Budget, from twelve prominent Democratic members of Congress, www.whitehouse.gov/sites/default/files/omb/inforeg/peer2004/25.pdf.

55. Chris Mooney, *The Republican War on Science* (New York: Basic, 2005).

56. Daniel Carpenter, *Reputation and Power: Organizational Image and Pharmaceutical Regulation at the FDA* (Princeton, N.J.: Princeton University Press, 2010).

57. John M. Broder, "Obama Administration Abandons Stricter Air-Quality Rules," *New York Times*, September 2, 2011.

58. Lisa Heinzerling, "Ozone Madness," *Grist*, September 4, 2011, http://grist.org/article/2011-09-03-ozone-madness ("The reason the president gave for asking EPA to withdraw its standard is an unlawful reason").

59. Thaler and Sunstein, *Nudge*.

60. Sarah Abrams, "Seven Deadly Sins on Collision Course with Market Forces," *Harvard Gazette*, February 1, 2007, http://news.harvard.edu/gazette/story/2007/02/seven-deadly-sins-on-collision-course-with-market-forces.

61. Charles E. Rosenberg, *The Cholera Years: The United States in 1832, 1849, and 1866* (Chicago: University of Chicago Press, 1962, 1987).

62. Ibid., 45.

63. President Andrew Jackson maintained that it was beyond his constitutional powers to recommend a national fast day, though individual denominations were free to recommend one for their congregations if they chose (ibid., 48).

18 • From Science to Alchemy

The Progressives' Deployment of Expertise and the Contemporary
Faith in Science to Grow the Economy and Create Jobs

John D. Skrentny and Natalie Novick

The Progressives were well known for their rational deployment of expertise in government and for advocating the federal government's use of science
to solve pressing national problems. But do federal policy makers promote
expertise rationally today? Has a faith in science become a blind faith—an
unscientific hope to have science and engineering magically rescue us from
our ills?

Consider the American politics of science in the 2000s. Political leaders,
especially presidents but others as well, are very public subscribers to a seemingly simple causal theory. Their statements suggest that natural science, and
thus scientists, produces technological innovation, and that innovation leads
to jobs, economic growth, national competitiveness, and national security. The
argument seems obviously true—one can easily name a new technology that
fostered job and wealth creation (for example, consider how Apple's iPhone
created a whole new economy in "app" development). Presidents, including
Barack Obama and George W. Bush before him, have thus argued for increased spending on basic scientific research in universities, increased domestic production of scientists and engineers, and increased immigration of
scientists and engineers to universities and tech companies. If science and
scientists produce innovation, and innovation produces so many wonderful
things, then the more we have, the better off we will be.

Yet we know surprisingly little about how this causal theory works. There is,
to be sure, a large and vibrant literature, especially in economics, management,
and history, regarding technological innovation.[1] This work, however, does not
provide a clear foundation for the causal theory common in contemporary policy discourse. Critics are alert to the problem. They recognize that we are almost

completely in the dark when it comes to assertions about how greater investment in scientists and engineers works to foster more national growth.[2] This
critique has reached into the highest offices of state. John Marburger III, George
W. Bush's director of the Office of Science and Technology Policy and a former
director of the Brookhaven National Laboratory, argued that the whole science
policy enterprise was severely limited by a lack of data or evidence to support its
basic conclusions. In one essay, he argued that even comparing the numbers of
engineers in the United States with those in other countries—a practice that
had driven policy here for half a century—made little sense because of difficulties in cross-national comparisons.[3] Marburger ultimately called for a "science
of science policy" because of the evident failure to set policy in rational ways. As
he later wrote, "My policy speeches from 2005 and thereafter expressed my
frustration over the inadequacy of data and analytical tools commensurate with
science policymaking in a rapidly changing environment."[4]

The absence of a science of science policy is no small irony. A causal connection between science and technology on one hand and job and wealth creation on the other is clear in presidential speeches, policy guidelines, and
legislation. It drives much of the contemporary enthusiasm for immigration
reform. But in the face of critiques pointing to the holes in the argument,
policy makers' call for more science does appear to have become a matter of
blind faith, a faith that resembles alchemy more than it resembles the Progressives' rational deployment of scientific expertise.

Specifically, there are three problems with faith in this causal connection.
First, we do not know which branch of science should be receiving the most
political attention and governmental investment. Which scientific fields are
most likely to produce job-creating innovation? Policy makers have not even
asked this question, let alone answered it.

Second, we do not know who is most likely to produce this innovation.
While there are calls for increased immigration of scientists and engineers,
does that mean more electrical engineers or mechanical engineers, more bi-
ologists or botanists? Which kind of science and engineering professional is
most likely to innovate and produce jobs? What is the optimal ratio of scientists to engineers? Even more basically, policy makers are fond of using the
acronym STEM, which refers to science, technology, engineering, and math,
and to call for more STEM workers. This sounds clear enough until we try to
define exactly what is included in these terms or even to specify the needed
level of degree (Ph.D., M.S., B.S.—or even something less rigorous?)—which
is almost never even attempted.

Third, we do not know when a causal connection actually exists. Does technological innovation always produce (good) jobs in America, and if not, under what conditions does it produce good jobs in America? How does the number of new science and technology positions affect the amount of innovation? Economists have long argued that technological innovation produces jobs, and better jobs than previously existed. Yet there are some who argue that this connection is breaking down, primarily because of advances in robotics and artificial intelligence.[5] It is not even clear what counts as "innovation," and whether the most valuable innovations really produce the most jobs.[6] The argument for recruiting more technical talent has, however, long since taken on a life of its own.

This chapter does not provide the missing link, a nuanced causal theory of the relationship between scientists and national performance. Instead, it details the historical developments that have gradually obviated any perceived need for such a theory. Contemporary political rhetoric expressing a faith in a hypothesized (yet little understood) causal connection between scientific expertise and jobs and wealth creation—part of what Daniel Sarewitz has astutely called "the myth of infinite benefit" of science[7]—has roots in Progressivism. It also marks a significant transformation of the Progressive vision of how the federal government should use the natural sciences. Even as Progressives embraced vague and sometimes contradictory impulses and beliefs,[8] Progressive governance sought social betterment primarily through the use of *existing* scientific expertise to achieve specific, identified goals.[9] The Progressives' typical use of science was to develop standards and measures (for example, to ensure safe food). What constituted success for the Progressives might have been a reduction in illnesses due to impure food, or the number of specific experts housed in a bureau with a defined mission. Recent decades, however, have seen the rise of vaguer measures of success—the *overall* number of scientists and engineers, working in *any* field, or the overall number of federal dollars allocated to research.

The movement from the Progressive approach and toward an unmoored enthusiasm advanced in stages, each characterized by competitive pressures. In the first stage, the federal government significantly ramped up its investments in science as part of the effort to win World War II. In the second stage, corresponding to the 1950s and the Cold War, policy makers focused on the number of scientists and engineers as an indicator of national security preparedness against the Soviet Union. In the third stage, occurring mostly in the 1980s, policy makers shifted the rationale from security to economic growth and to concerns over Japan's economic might, which was built on science and engineering. In the fourth stage, from the 1990s to the present, a clear competitor is no longer on the horizon, but a pervasive sense of threat remains, and so policy makers have begun to focus on importing foreign science and engineering workers through immigration. Over time, the original impulse to use scientific expertise to solve some specific problem at hand has spun out visions ever more general and abstract. In the absence of a foreign competitor or any single benchmark, the dominant argument now is that the more scientists and engineers there are, the greater their economic magic: more innovation, more economic growth, and more job creation. The key to all good things, science has shed its progressive realism to become the government's fantasy elixir.

Politics, not measured scientific analysis, drove these transitions. Political elites who really believed in the powers of science—or who simply sought votes and power—used their positions to pursue opportunities created by perceptions of threat (specifically, threats created by wars—hot, cold, and trade).[10] They pushed the Progressives' limited and specific use of scientific expertise into greatly expanded and mostly unjustified directions. Once established in the culture, faith in the power of science proved useful for a variety of political elites. Science administrators have used it to seek more resources and more discretion to use those resources. Members of Congress have used it to sell hope to the voters and gain the support of key constituents. And scientific and tech industry leaders have used it to gain more resources and to promote specific regulatory changes, including in the area of immigration policy.

The Progressive Approach to Government and Science

Federal support for science and engineering's cornucopia is a staple of presidential speeches today, and one can find a faith in science for progress, and a stress on training for scientific competence, in writings going back to Jefferson, Franklin, and others who worked to found the nation.[11] The Constitution recognizes the benefits of scientific progress and authorizes Congress to create incentives for inventions by establishing copyright and patent protection. But it did not explicitly authorize Congress to do science or make scientists.[12] It was by no means a smooth path to the perspective adopted today, the urgent, open-ended, and unexamined push for more scientists and engineers.

The Progressive vision of government is perhaps best known for its focus on rational management. The "search for order" that Robert Wiebe described referred to a state of continual management by experts.[13] "Efficiency" became a goal and even a virtue in countless contexts, and Progressives used science and engineering as part of this pursuit of rational management, focusing on the ability of scientists to solve specific problems that drew on existing expertise. The Progressives' desire to use natural science, as well as the growing social sciences, to create standards and improve efficiency was often misguided.[14] It was perhaps at its worst and most destructive on matters of race and ethnicity.[15] Consider the rise of eugenics during the period,[16] or firms' use of the rational management of ethnic stereotypes ("racial adaptability") to promote efficiency and profits.[17] In the area of immigration, Progressives employed rational management to improve America by building on traditions of excluding unwanted races, ethnicities, and religions, as well as refining exclusions of those with mental and physical disabilities.[18] The Progressive approach of using immigration policy to *exclude* the undesired, rather than to *attract* the desired, contrasts starkly with the current era (see below).

But the Progressives' faith was directed at clearly articulated problems. The late 1800s also saw the federal government's growing faith in and reliance on existing expertise in agricultural, chemical, and other natural sciences. Experts, often housed in new bureaus, typically deployed routinized skills to test and apply standards to ensure safety and uniformity.[19] Their purpose was to assist ongoing commercial enterprises, often in rural areas, rather than to generate new industries. For example, the Hatch Act (1887) established experiment stations to test and develop fertilizer.[20] The Bureau of Mines facilitated extractive industries and sought to make mines less dangerous; the Bureau of Entomology helped farmers control pests; and the Bureau of Animal Industry worked to control diseases affecting livestock.[21] Progressives also brought the federal government's facilitating role in science to mass consumers and industrialization. In the early twentieth century, the Bureau of Chemistry began a rapid expansion of its duties concerning testing the safety of food.[22] By 1916, the Bureau of Standards, in the words of the historian A. Hunter Dupree, had become "a direct link between government and industry," though "usually staying in the background."[23]

The federal government rarely conducted original research (which was occurring in the nation's growing research universities), nor was it involved in the creation of scientists and engineers.[24] World War I did foster new direct research by the federal government in specific projects designed to win the war.[25] When the war ended, however, there was a return to a hands-off approach. America's scientists preferred a decentralized structure in order to preserve their autonomy. They resisted an effort to make the National Research Council a permanent scientific coordinating agency; accordingly, it simply advised the government and became a distributor of funds from the Rockefeller and Carnegie Foundations for postdoctoral fellowships and various projects.[26]

The Progressive approach, then, was an abiding though limited faith in the government's use of science to solve existing problems, combined with a decentralized organizational structure that left basic science research to universities and private foundations. A rapidly growing number of corporate laboratories took on the task of applied research (corporate labs grew from 300 in 1920 to 1,624 by 1930, when they employed about 34,000 workers).[27]

In retrospect, however, the rhetoric of Progressivism may have been as important as the reality, for the reform movement did affirm the power of science to provide amazing, unimagined public benefits.[28] W. J. McGee, a prominent Progressive-era geologist and conservationist, put it this way: "America has become a nation of science. There is no industry, from agriculture to architecture, that is not shaped by research and its results; there is not one of our fifteen millions of families that does not enjoy the benefits of scientific advancement; there is no law on our statutes, no motive in our conduct, that has not been made juster by the straightforward and unselfish habit of thought fostered by scientific methods."[29] In the 1920s, Herbert Hoover, the secretary of commerce under presidents Harding and Coolidge and a former mining engineer, began to promote investment in basic science. He argued that both "pure and applied scientific research" were "the foundation of genuine labor-saving devices, better processes and sounder methods,"[30] and complained in 1925 that $200 million was spent on applied science, but only $10 million on basic science, though "the raw material for these [applied science] laboratories comes alone from the ranks of pure science."[31] McGee's and Hoover's faith in science would find more advocates as the twentieth century advanced.

Stage 1: World War II and the Permanent Federal Role in Science

Although the Progressive era brought new roles and renewed faith in science and engineering to the federal government, it was (in the words of the historian Brian Balogh) the "triple crises" of the Depression, World War II, and then the Cold War that fully institutionalized the federal role in scientific research and the formation of the science and engineering workforce.[32] Scientists and engineers would help set the science agenda, which would direct federal resources, and the federal administrative apparatus would aid in implementation. A symbiotic relationship developed between professional experts and public bureaucracies.

World War II was perhaps the most important proving ground for the role of science—when directed by the federal government—to serve the national interest. The war was a key impetus in the creation of a system of national laboratories, which did basic science but concentrated on national security and weapons research.[33] It was also a spur to the creation of the National Science Foundation (NSF).[34]

A major force shaping the NSF was Vannevar Bush, an electrical engineer and inventor. From 1938, Bush was a member of one of the few federal science agencies, the National Advisory Committee for Aeronautics. From this position, he was able to convince President Roosevelt to establish the National Defense Research Committee to coordinate research on war technologies in 1940 (with Bush in charge), and in 1941, Roosevelt appointed Bush head of a larger organization: the Office of Scientific and Research Development. The focus remained on war technologies, including the Manhattan Project, but the name denoted a broader mission.

As the war drew to a close, Bush penned an influential report, *Science: The Endless Frontier,* in which he advocated for the creation of the NSF, or what he then called the National Research Foundation. Roosevelt had asked Bush to explore how the federal government could "profitably" use the wartime research infrastructure in times of peace.[35] Bush maintained that the federal government had key roles to play in the support of basic science research in nonprofit institutions; industry could not be counted upon to make these investments in a timely matter, because of their noncommercial nature. The federal government also needed to support the development of a scientific workforce (through the provision of fellowships) and—of course—continued military research. Bush eloquently stated the causal connections between science and engineering, the associated workforce, and innovation and job creation. In a section of the report entitled "Science and Jobs," Bush wrote:

> We will not get ahead in international trade unless we offer new and more attractive and cheaper products.
>
> Where will these new products come from? How will we find ways to make better products at lower cost? The answer is clear. There must be a stream of new scientific knowledge to turn the wheels of private and

public enterprise. There must be plenty of men and women trained in science and technology for upon them depend both the creation of new knowledge and its application to practical purposes.

More and better scientific research is essential to the achievement of our goal of full employment.[36]

Here was a clear break with the Progressive use of government and science. Rather than deploy existing expertise to solve specific and limited problems, Bush advised the government to *create* expertise, and the expertise to be created was to be used in *unknown* ways to develop *unknown* products.

Stage 2: Keeping the Science and Engineering Score During the Cold War

In 1906, President Theodore Roosevelt said to the nation: "Our federal form of government, so fruitful of advantage to our people in certain ways, in other ways undoubtedly limits our national effectiveness. It is not possible, for instance, for the National Government to take the lead in technical industrial education, to see that the public school system of this country develops on all its technical, industrial, scientific, and commercial sides."[37] In the 1950s, the obstacles to a federal role in creating a science and engineering workforce that concerned Roosevelt, as well as Vannevar Bush, were swept away.

The vitality of scientific research and the size of the science and engineering workforce became national crises during the Cold War struggle with the Soviet Union. In the absence of direct confrontations on the battlefield, policy elites as well as journalists looked to other measures to see who was winning. In doing so, they contributed to the simplistic causal theory that science and scientists in some magical way led to innovation and the good things that innovation produced—and in these years, those good things were related to national security. Simple science-oriented scorecards became a way to assess America's prospects in the Cold War.

One scorecard was funding for research and development (R&D). The Department of Defense started to measure research investments in 1953, finding that 1952's total included $3.75 billion, or 1 percent of the gross national product, and that the federal government footed the bill for 60 percent of it. The NSF then began to regularly score the United States on R&D, though this was understood as part of the overall innovation system rather than as only a measure of defense and preparedness.[38]

Though experts such as Lee DuBridge, then president of the California Institute of Technology, argued against it, the *number* of scientists and engineers also became part of the scorecard and a measure of innovative capacity.[39] Multiple studies, from sources with close ties to the federal government, sounded the alarm that the Soviet Union was creating many more science and engineering workers than the United States. By 1955, it appeared that the USSR was graduating about 95,000 engineers and applied scientists per year, while the United States lagged far behind at about 57,000 per year. In 1954, even before these figures were published, the *New York Times* learned of the deficit and put on its front page a story announcing, "Russia Is Overtaking U.S. in Training of Technicians."[40] Secret CIA testimony confirmed the threat of the "manpower gap."[41]

Into this context emerged *Sputnik*, the first man-made satellite, launched by the Soviet Union in 1957. *Sputnik* shocked the world—especially U.S. science and engineering policy makers. To American policy elites keeping score in the science and engineering race, *Sputnik* looked like a walk-off home run in the World Series. The climate of urgency and crisis ratcheted up, and it changed the politics of education and science forever.

A federal role in education had been thwarted for decades. There were three major forces against a federal role in education: critics who argued that education was properly a matter of local control; conflicts regarding the issues of how to manage the southern states' de jure segregated schools; and concerns related to governmental funding of parochial schools.[42] But an urgency born of the need for national security ended all that.[43]

The National Defense Education Act of 1958 stated in its preamble: "The security of the Nation requires the fullest development of the mental resources and technical skills of its young men and women. . . . The national interest requires . . . that the federal government give assistance to education and programs which are important to our national defense."[44] The law provided loans to college students, funds to improve science and engineering education, and National Defense Fellowships. Although the law was not limited to science and engineering, that area was a major focus, and another statute, the National Aeronautics and Space Act of 1958, contained provisions to recruit new science and engineering talent to serve the national interest.[45]

By 1959, the federal government's leading role in the advance of science was unquestioned, and scorecard thinking of "the more, the better" was unexceptional, even by Republicans. When signing an executive order creating the Federal Council for Science and Technology, President Dwight D. Eisenhower approvingly cited growing funding for R&D, stating, "It is the responsibility of the Federal Government to encourage in every appropriate way the scientific activities of non-Government institutions."[46]

The Cold War competition with the Soviet Union also spawned the deployment of scientists to create a new kind of expertise: the ability to travel to the moon. While this involved a specific goal, the "space race" empowered science-funding advocates, who began to voice a faith in science to produce unknown wonders. For example, Hugh Dryden, the deputy director of the new National Aeronautics and Space Administration, told the Senate Committee on Appropriations that space technology would benefit all Americans in unknown ways through "a great variety of new consumer foods and industrial processes that will raise our standard of living and return tremendous benefits to us in practically every profession and activity."[47]

Stage 3: Numbers of Science and Engineering Workers, the Japan Threat, and the "Pipeline Problem"

By the 1970s, national competitiveness joined national security as justifications for large but ill-defined investments in R&D and the science and engineering workforce. President Nixon announced this shift in a special message to Congress on science and technology, promising the formation of federal policy to foster "innovation" and its resulting cornucopia of goods.[48] The discourse of economic competition became more prominent in the 1980s as Japan became a technological and economic powerhouse.[49] Responding to Japan proved to be good politics. Congress moved into action, and bills were submitted in the House with names like "National Engineering and Science Manpower Act of 1982" and "Emergency Mathematics and Science Education Act of 1983."[50]

These efforts emphasized engineering and technology (more than basic science research), and were meant to compete with Japan's perceived strength in these fields. A new focus on higher education aimed to facilitate innovation in the nation's research universities by making it easier for universities to patent innovations (the Bayh-Dole Act of 1980).[51] The NSF created sites where universities and firms could collaborate on research, such as the 1985 program for Engineering Research Centers.[52]

The conviction that science could set things right continued to substitute for precise policy and verifiable outcomes. One failed bill aimed to establish a National Technology Foundation to spur innovation and the human resources to create it. In 1980 hearings for the bill, advocates emphasized that innovation fostered job creation, among other benefits: "The development of new technologies promises fuller national employment . . . new goods or services for the national welfare . . . [and] existing goods and services at lower costs." With a focus on technology and engineers, the NTF would be an important counterpoint to the NSF, which, advocates claimed, had neglected both.[53]

Although the bill failed, its impact was felt. Lewis Branscomb, the chair of the National Science Board, which oversaw the NSF, and also a vice president and the chief scientist at IBM, was sympathetic to the goals of the proposed NTF. Branscomb added his voice to groups such as American Association of Engineering Societies and the American Society of Engineering Education to call for more engineers while emphasizing their power to boost national competitiveness.[54] Branscomb's National Science Board reoriented the NSF to deal with the perceived crisis, issuing an unnerving statement: "The United States is at a critical juncture in its industrial leadership. Not since Sputnik in 1957 has there been so much cause for concern about the adequacy of our science and technology base and our ability to capitalize on our scientific strengths to sustain industrial leadership. We face foreign competitors who have growing skills, lower costs, and higher productivity growth. These factors affect the security of our Nation, the standard of living of our people, and our legacy for future generations."[55]

In 1982, Douglas Pewitt, the assistant director for science policy at the Office of Science and Technology Policy, requested that the NSF study its data collection on science and engineering in order to identify possible shortages, and the NSF responded with a report in 1984 on the science and engineering labor market, reinforcing the notion of such workers' role in innovation.[56] An even bigger boost was the highly publicized report of the National Commission on Excellence in Education, ominously titled *A Nation at Risk*. It warned that American preeminence in science and technological innovation (among other things) was being lost because of mediocre education.[57]

Although Democrats and Republicans differed on the means, they seemed to agree that more science and engineering workers were needed to ensure the nation's competitiveness. The simplistic assessment of America's capacity for innovation—counting the number of science and engineering workers—that had marked the run-up to the National Defense Education Act found new life, but now the comparisons were with Japan rather than the Soviet Union. In a Senate hearing in 1982 on authorizing the NSF, Senator Edward Kennedy (D-Massachusetts) stated:

The Japanese now have doubled the number of engineering graduates in the last 10 years. We have held about level. . . . We see the movement of R&D in the military area that is again going to draw [engineers] from the civilian area. I think that what we need are some flow charts and flow lines of what the implications of this are going to be in terms of our economy, in terms of jobs, where we are going to be internationally over a period of time. [. . .] There is a flow line that is taking place in our society, and I think there is an agency that has to awaken this country as to what our needs are going to be.[58]

Similarly, the moderate Republican Margaret Heckler of Massachusetts stated at a House hearing:

I feel we are frightfully behind. . . . Now we know that on the one hand we have the technology problems, the personnel problems, the academic training needs, the productivity lag between the U.S. and Japan, all these enormous difficulties facing the industry and jobs affected by it, and here we have an enormous resource in the population of women and minorities and we do not really seem to be making the right linkages.[59]

President Ronald Reagan, when proposing to double the budget of the NSF, did not express fright, but he did share the lead-into-gold alchemical vision: "Science and technology are fundamental to U.S. competitiveness. . . . But, we must recognize that our trading partners, in their desire to improve their standards of living and market share, are catching up. We must ensure that adequate incentives are in place that will not only maintain our preeminence in initiating ideas and know-how, but also our lead in setting the pace at which these are translated into new products and processes."[60]

Other respected voices in national science policy contributed similar arguments. The National Research Council formed its Committee on the Education and Utilization of the Engineer (with the NSF director, Erich Bloch, an electrical engineer who had worked under Branscomb at IBM as vice president for technical personnel development,[61] as a member). In 1985 and 1986, this committee issued reports continuing the drumbeat of support for more bodies in the engineering pipeline, and attempting elaborate and (ostensibly) scientific modeling of the engineering supply infrastructure.[62] At this point, the metaphor of a pipeline became more common in the discourse. The perceived problem was limited and undirected flow; creating a pipeline would deliver more bodies to perform more (unspecified) scientific work to achieve American goals of economic competitiveness.

Bloch worked to reorient the NSF to pursue the problem of the science and engineering pipeline. Part of this effort involved issuing more reports on the problem. He directed the NSF's Policy Research and Analysis Division (PRA) to educate the public about the need for large numbers of new scientists and engineers in order to maintain American competitiveness. The premise of this enterprise also focused on the pipeline flow of students moving through the educational system toward science and engineering careers. The policy challenge was to encourage more of them to enter the pipeline (especially those from underrepresented groups, which primarily meant women and minorities), and then to encourage more to stay rather than to leak out in high school, in college, or in graduate degree programs.[63]

Congress kept up the pressure to bring more women and minorities into the science and engineering pipeline. In 1986, it passed legislation creating the Task Force on Women, Minorities and the Handicapped in Science and Technology.[64] Its report, published three years later, sounded the decade's usual tones of alarm and threat: "It is time for action. Our Interim Report and many other studies have detailed the looming crisis in the science and engineering workforce. America faces a shortfall of scientists and engineers by the year 2000. We can meet these shortfalls only by utilizing all our talent, especially those traditionally underrepresented in science and engineering—women, minorities and people with disabilities. Without this kind of world-class science and technical excellence, America's competitive prospects dim."[65]

During the 1980s, then, American political elites expressed what one observer called "an almost religious belief" in the power of science and technology to produce wonders.[66] Experts paid little or no attention to which fields were most important for innovation, nor was there any serious attempt to understand how numbers translate to innovation rates, or how salaries might affect the pipeline flow. Moreover, a 1992 congressional investigation found the PRA's analysis claiming a shortage of science and engineering workers to be badly flawed methodologically and incorrect in its conclusions.[67]

Stage 4: Immigration as the Source of Innovation, Growth, and Jobs

In the latest stage, the 1990s to the present day, the movement away from the Progressive vision has reached a high point. Advocates for science and engineering today need not have in mind specific, existing expertise to deploy (which was the Progressive vision). They need not align the creation of new experts with specific problems that need to be solved (which had been the prominent World War II approach). And they need not have specific security or economic threats to serve as prods (as in the Cold War and during the competition with Japan). Moreover, unlike the Progressives, who sought to foster national development by excluding certain immigrants, advocates in government and in industry now seek to improve America by attracting immigrants with science and engineering skills.

Congress had used immigration policy to attract skilled immigrants in the Immigration and Nationality Act of 1952, which set aside visas for immigrants with "urgently needed" skills, including those with technical training.[68] Yet there is little evidence that policy makers saw immigration policy as a major source of science and engineering workers in the 1950s, and the Hart-Cellar Act of 1965, which profoundly remade immigration policy, gave far more priority to immigrants reunifying their families than to those with job skills of any kind.[69]

Congress began to rectify this situation with the Immigration Act of 1990. This legislation created the H-1B visa for skilled workers and offered means for making skilled workers permanent residents by offering green cards.[70] Urged on by industry lobbyists, the law had bipartisan support and was made possible in part by Senator Edward Kennedy's continued interest in the issue.[71]

This mobilization of immigration policy as part of the struggle to increase the numbers of science and engineering workers was a new stage in a decades-long process. By the 1990s, concerns about the Soviet Union were gone; with the collapse of the communist regime, Russians figured into the debates about American science policy less as a competitor and more as a source of talent. Russia was hemorrhaging scientists, and foreign countries and universities sought to acquire Russia's best and brightest.[72] The Japanese threat was also fading. But the momentum was not arrested. By this time, a group of industry lobbyists within the National Association of Manufacturers (later known as Compete America) joined with the American Immigration Lawyers Association and information technology companies to agitate inside the Beltway for more H-1B visas.[73]

The politics of expertise, by this stage, and especially in the 2000s, ran on free-floating anxiety. Arguments for increasing the number of science and engineering workers became more abstract. Although China emerged as a new threat, in most of the discourse of the period the United States was competing against no one in particular, but everyone in general. There were no firm standards for success, and no clear goals for policy. The old equation of "science produces innovation, which produces jobs" held strong, but at least as it regarded science and engineering workers, the only rationale was the more, the better.

The buzzword of official reports in the 2000s was "innovation." The word took center stage in the economic rhetoric and policy proposals of presidents George W. Bush and Barack Obama. Innovation would keep America ahead of the pack and dispel fears of national decline. In 2005, a bipartisan group of senators asked the National Academies of Science, Engineering, and Medicine for a report and list of recommendations "to enhance the science and technology enterprise so that the United States can successfully compete, prosper, and be secure in the global community of the 21st century."[74] The report, titled ominously yet hopefully *Rising Above the Gathering Storm,* (not surprisingly) called for more science and engineering workers and also for immigration reform to attract them. Congress responded in 2007 with the America COMPETES Act, which authorized more investments in science and engineering, though funds did not flow until 2009.[75] Nevertheless, a follow-up report, *Rising Above the Gathering Storm, Revisited,* had an even more ominous subtitle: *Rapidly Approaching Category Five.*[76]

In 2013, the Senate passed a comprehensive immigration reform bill that grouped several immigration issues together. Most prominent in the public debate was a legalization package for approximately eleven million undocumented immigrants, combined with increased security at the border and the imposition of new requirements on employers to ensure they were not hiring undocumented immigrants. But to secure the support of business, especially in the tech sector, the reform package included an expansion in the number of H-1B visas. Another sweetener for businesses was a provision mirroring a bill that had floated around Congress for years, the so-called STAPLE Act. This bill was so named because it would metaphorically staple a green card to the diploma of any foreign student at an American university who was earning an advanced degree in science, technology, engineering, or math, and who had a job offer. Since the 1990s, these fields were increasingly grouped together, first with the acronym SMET, and then referred to as STEM. Despite offering the very valuable green card to foreigners with STEM degrees and the potentially large impact on graduate schools and labor markets, the Senate bill not only did not identify which degrees were most valuable to innovation and economic growth, but did not even define STEM.[77]

Advocates for increasing the science and engineering workforce have used the mass media to promote immigration of the highly skilled. The op-ed pages have been filled with arguments such as that of Steve Case, the former CEO of AOL and a major force behind the "Startup Act," which, much like the STAPLE Act, sought to give permanent residency to fifty thousand noncitizens who earned master's or doctorate degrees in a STEM field. Case equated the number of science and engineering immigrants with innovation. He brought back the old international comparisons and numerical benchmarks, arguing that the United States was falling behind, in various ways, Germany, China, Canada, and Australia (for example, "Australia—despite having an economy 14 times smaller than America's—will, as of Sept. 1, offer as many employment-based green cards as the U.S."). Case made dire warnings of imminent peril, linking skilled immigrants with jobs: "Will we win this global battle for talent—successfully recruiting and retaining the men and women who start American companies that create jobs, who drive innovation forward with creativity and expertise, who power these economic engines with their drive and passion?"[78]

Business interests have become involved in various ways, making similar arguments. A group of tech businesses formed a group to lobby for the science and engineering workers that the immigration reform bill would provide, calling itself the March for Innovation.[79] The American Association of Universities and the Association of Public and Land-Grant Universities sought to promote a problem they called the "innovation deficit," which could be measured by relatively low figures for R&D investment and the number of science and engineering students. Another part of the problem was declining numbers of foreign students in science and engineering: "Even though the number of international students attending U.S. universities increased between 2000 and 2011, the U.S. share of total international students declined by more than 25%. Meanwhile, nations like Germany, New Zealand, and the UK have seen significant increases both in numbers and in total share of international students during this time."[80] Compete America launched a "jobs lost calculator" that purported to show not just the jobs created by more science and engineering workers, but also the jobs lost by Congress's failure to expand the number of H-1B visas. It increased by 1 every sixty-three seconds, and reached 500,000 on April 1, 2014.[81]

Conclusion

The Progressive era's faith in expertise has moved far—very far—from its modest beginnings. Although faith in science to produce benefits through innovation has existed in the United States since the nation's founding, the contemporary period's approach of promoting innovation through unspecified numbers of vaguely defined science and engineering workers developed in four distinct stages, each of which moved policy aims further from the limited and applied Progressive vision. World War II marked the institutionalization of the federal government's role in developing science and engineering, even as this development was limited to solving specific war-related problems. The Cold War began the trend of equating the numbers of science and engineering workers with innovation capacity, and this continued when Japan became the major threat and the goal moved from national security to economic competitiveness. The 1990s and especially the 2000s have marked the latest stage, in which policy makers have sought to increase the numbers of science and engineering workers without any clear benchmark or goal—other than their mysterious ability to (somehow) produce innovation, which in turn produces jobs. Policy as problem solving has become policy as conviction.

There is little reason to doubt that science and engineering—and workers in those fields—*do* produce national security, economic growth, and jobs. But trying to tap this potential without knowing how exactly it delivers benefits has turned science into alchemy. Policy makers push a vision, in effect selling hope to voters, without knowing, much less explaining, how the process works.[82] U.S. science policy has sought to mix a variety of ingredients, including increased R&D funds and outreach to those with an expansive variety of science and engineering skills, in order to produce what Americans want. Although few in the Progressive era would have recognized this approach, and although it took decades and multiple global conflicts to elaborate it, the Progressives' efforts provided a foundation for what has become a policy of faith.

Notes

For helpful comments on earlier drafts of this chapter, the authors wish to thank the editors of this volume, participants in the conference on which it is based, and anonymous reviewers for the Press, as well as Gareth Davies, Jason Owen-Smith, and Tom Sugrue.

1. See, for example, David C. Mowery and Nathan Rosenberg, *Technology and the Pursuit of Economic Growth* (New York: Cambridge University Press, 1989); Richard R. Nelson, *Technology, Institutions, and Economic Growth* (Cambridge, Mass.: Harvard University Press, 2005); and Mary Lindenstein Walshok and Abraham J. Shragge, *Invention and Reinvention: The Evolution of San Diego's Innovation Economy* (Stanford, Calif.: Stanford University Press, 2014).

2. Donald Kennedy, Crispin Taylor, Kirstie Urquhart, and Jim Austin, "Supply Without Demand," *Science*, February 19, 2004, http://sciencecareers.sciencemag.org/career_magazine/previous_issues/articles/2004_02_19/nodoi.9424811656219924021. For an analysis of these debates, see Michael S. Teitelbaum, *Falling Behind? Boom, Bust, and the Global Race for Scientific Talent* (Princeton, N.J.: Princeton University Press, 2014).

3. John Marburger III, "Wanted: Better Benchmarks," *Science*, May 20, 2005, 1087.

4. John H. Marburger III, "Why Policy Implementation Needs a Science of Science Policy," in *The Science of Science Policy: A Handbook*, ed. Kaye Husbands Fealing, Julia I. Lane, John H. Marburger III, and Stephanie S. Shipp (Stanford, Calif.: Stanford Business, 2011), 9–29, 14–15. Marburger's tenure in the Bush administration was not without controversy, since he defended an administration that many scientists saw as antiscience, but his calls for a science of science policy have been influential; see Jeffrey Mervis, "John Marburger's Impact on U.S. Science Policy," *Science*, August 1, 2011, available at http://news.sciencemag.org/2011/08/john-marburgers-impact-u.s.-science-policy.

5. See, for example, Eric Brynjolfsson and Andrew McAfee, *Race Against the Machine: How the Digital Revolution Is Accelerating Innovation, Driving Productivity, and Irreversibly Transforming Employment and the Economy* (Digital Frontier Press, 2012); Eric Brynjolfsson and Andrew McAfee, *The Second Machine Age: Work, Progress, and Prosperity in a Time of Brilliant Technologies* (New York: Norton, 2014); Martin Ford, *The Lights in the Tunnel: Automation, Accelerating Technology, and the Economy of the Future* (Acculant Publishing, 2009).

6. Facebook, for example, was lauded as an innovative technology company, and was worth more than $100 billion when it employed fewer than 3,500 people. Facebook purchased the photo-sharing app company Instagram for $1 billion when that company employed 13 people; see Evelyn M. Rusli, "Facebook Buys Instagram for $1 Billion," *New York Times*, April 9, 2012, http://dealbook.nytimes.com/2012/04/09/facebook-buys-instagram-for-1-billion/?_php=true&_type=blogs&_r=0.

7. Daniel Sarewitz, *Frontiers of Illusion: Science, Technology, and the Politics of Progress* (Philadelphia: Temple University Press, 1996), 17.

8. See, for example, Daniel T. Rodgers, "In Search of Progressivism," *Reviews in American History* 10 (1982): 113–32, and Peter G. Filene, "An Obituary for 'The Progressive Movement,'" *American Quarterly* 22 (1970): 20–34.

9. In this chapter, we focus only on the natural sciences, and avoid for now the Progressives' enthusiasm for using social science to improve government. On the Progressives and social science, see, for example, Thomas C. Leonard, "Retrospectives: Eugenics and Economics in the Progressive Era," *Journal of Economic Perspectives* 19, no. 4 (2003): 207–24.

10. On the role of war in American state building and policy making, see Ira Katznelson and Martin Shefter, eds., *Shaped by War and Trade: International Influences*

on *American Political Development* (Princeton, N.J.: Princeton University Press, 2002); John D. Skrentny, *The Minority Rights Revolution* (Cambridge: Belknap Press, 2002).

11. Scott L. Montgomery, "Science, Education, and Republican Values: Trends of Faith in America: 1750–1830," *Journal of Science Education and Technology* 4, no. 2 (1993): 521–40.

12. Article I, Section 8 states that Congress has the power "to promote the Progress of Science and useful Arts, by securing for limited Times to Authors and Inventors the exclusive Right to their respective Writings and Discoveries."

13. Robert H. Wiebe, *The Search for Order, 1870–1920* (New York: Hill and Wang, 1967).

14. Jennifer Alexander, "Efficiencies of Balance: Technical Efficiency, Popular Efficiency, and Arbitrary Standards in the Late Progressive Era USA," *Social Studies of Science* 38, no. 3 (2008): 323–49. Also see Samuel Haber, *Efficiency and Uplift: Scientific Management in the Progressive Era, 1890–1920* (Chicago: University of Chicago Press, 1964). On enthusiasm for the training of engineers, see Christophe Lécuyer, "MIT, Progressive Reform, and 'Industrial Service,' 1890–1920," *Historical Studies in the Physical and Biological Sciences* 26, no. 1 (1995): 35–88.

15. Morton Keller, *Regulating a New Society* (Cambridge, Mass.: Harvard University Press, 1994).

16. Leonard, "Eugenics and Economics."

17. James R. Barrett and David Roediger, "Inbetween Peoples: Race, Nationality and the 'New Immigrant' Working Class," *Journal of American Ethnic History* 16 (1997): 3–44.

18. On racist exclusions, see David FitzGerald and David Cook-Martin, *Culling the Masses: The Democratic Origins of Racist Immigration Policy in the Americas* (Cambridge, Mass.: Harvard University Press, 2014). On other exclusions, see Keller, *Regulating a New Society*.

19. Brian Balogh, *Chain Reaction: Expert Debate and Public Participation in American Nuclear Power, 1945–1975* (New York: Cambridge University Press, 1991); A. Hunter Dupree, *Science in the Federal Government: A History of Policy and Activities to 1940* (Cambridge, Mass.: Belknap Press, 1957).

20. John Hillison, "The Origins of Agriscience, or Where Did All That Scientific Agriculture Come From?," *Journal of Agricultural Education* 37 (1996): 8–13.

21. Dupree, *Science in the Federal Government*, 160–64.

22. Ibid., 176.

23. Ibid., 266–67. On this period, also see David M. Hart, *Forged Consensus: Science, Technology, and Economic Policy in the United States, 1921–1953* (Princeton, N.J.: Princeton University Press, 1998).

24. One historian claimed that the government was only a "reluctant patron of science" until the 1940s; see Harvey M. Sapolsky, "Science Policy in American State

Government," *Minerva* 9, no. 3 (1971): 322. The creation of the science and engineering workforce was left to universities; see Lécuyer, "MIT, Progressive Reform."

25. Roy MacLeod, "Science and Democracy: Historical Reflections on Present Discontents," *Minerva* 35, no. 4 (1997): 369–84.

26. Dupree, *Science in the Federal Government*, 327–29.

27. Ibid., 337.

28. David K. van Keuren, "Science, Progressivism, and Military Preparedness: The Case of the Naval Research Laboratory, 1915–1923," *Technology and Culture* 33, no. 4 (1992): 710–36.

29. Quoted in Dupree, *Science in the Federal Government*, 301.

30. Ibid., 338.

31. Ibid., 341. As president, Hoover would continue to extol the promise of basic science research, stating, "Research both in pure science and in its application to the arts is one of the most potent impulses to progress," and "Our scientists and inventors are amongst our most priceless national possessions"; see Herbert Hoover: "Address on the 50th Anniversary of Thomas Edison's Invention of the Incandescent Electric Lamp," October 21, 1929, at the American Presidency Project, www.presidency.ucsb.edu/ws/?pid=21967.

32. Balogh, *Chain Reaction*, 12.

33. Peter J. Westwick, *The National Labs: Science in an American System, 1947–1974* (Cambridge, Mass.: Harvard University Press, 2003).

34. On the origins of the NSF, see, among others, Daniel Lee Kleinman, *Politics on the Endless Frontier: Postwar Research Policy in the United States* (Durham, N.C.: Duke University Press, 1995).

35. John F. Sargent Jr. and Dana A. Shea, *The President's Office of Science and Technology Policy (OSTP): Issues for Congress* (Washington, D.C.: Congressional Research Service, November 26, 2012), 2.

36. Vannevar Bush (director of the Office of Scientific Research and Development), *Science: The Endless Frontier; A Report to the President* (Washington, D.C.: Government Printing Office, 1945), available at http://www.nsf.gov/about/history/nsf50/vbush1945_content.jsp.

37. Theodore Roosevelt: "Sixth Annual Message," December 3, 1906, at the American Presidency Project, www.presidency.ucsb.edu/ws/?pid=29547.

38. Benoît Godin, "National Innovation System: The System Approach in Historical Perspective," *Science, Technology, and Human Values* 34, no. 4 (2009): 476–501.

39. Teitelbaum, *Falling Behind?*, 34.

40. David Kaiser, "The Physics of Spin: Sputnik Politics and American Physicists in the 1950s," *Social Research* 73 (2006): 1225–52, quotation on 1231.

41. Ibid., 1233.

42. Norman C. Thomas, *Education in National Politics* (New York: McKay, 1975).

43. Barbara Barksdale Clowse, *Brainpower for the Cold War: The Sputnik Crisis and the National Defense Education Act of 1958* (Westport, Conn.: Greenwood, 1981), 9, 59, 63.

44. James L. Sundquist, *Politics and Policy: The Eisenhower, Kennedy, and Johnson Years* (Washington, D.C.: Brookings Institution, 1968), 179; David B. Tyack, *The One Best System: A History of American Urban Education* (Cambridge, Mass.: Harvard University Press, 1974), 275–76; Sidney W. Tiedt, *The Role of the Federal Government in Education* (New York: Oxford University Press, 1966), 30.

45. Pamela Ebert Flattau (project leader), with Jerome Bracken, Richard Van Atta, Ayeh Bandeh-Ahmadi, Rodolfo de la Cruz, and Kay Sullivan, *The National Defense Education Act of 1958: Selected Outcomes* (Washington, D.C.: Institute for Defense Analyses/ Technology Policy Institute, 2007).

46. Dwight D. Eisenhower: "Presidential Statement upon Signing Order Establishing Federal Council for Science and Technology," March 13, 1959, at the American Presidency Project, www.presidency.ucsb.edu/ws/?pid=11681.

47. Walter A. McDougall, . . . *The Heavens and the Earth: A Political History of the Space Age* (New York: Basic, 1985), 383.

48. Richard Nixon, "Special Message to the Congress on Science and Technology," March 16, 1972, at the American Presidency Project. www.presidency.ucsb.edu/ ws/?pid=3773.

49. On the threat of Japan, see Michael J. Heale, "Anatomy of a Scare: Yellow Peril Politics in America, 1980–1993," *Journal of American Studies* 43 (2009): 19–47.

50. Juan C. Lucena, *Defending the Nation: U.S. Policymaking to Create Scientists and Engineers from Sputnik to the "War Against Terrorism"* (Lanham, Md.: University Press of America, 2005), 84–87; on the House bills, see 122n1.

51. Bhaven N. Sampat, "Patenting and U.S. Academic Research in the 20th Century: The World Before and After Bayh-Dole," *Research Policy* 35, no. 6 (2006): 772–89.

52. Roger L. Geiger and Creso M. Sá, *Tapping the Riches of Science: Universities and the Promise of Economic Growth* (Cambridge, Mass.: Harvard University Press, 2008), 72–74.

53. House Committee on Science and Technology, *H.R. 6910 National Technology Foundation Act of 1980*, 96th Cong., 2nd sess., 1980; Lucena, *Defending the Nation*, 88–89.

54. House Committee on Science and Technology, *Engineering Manpower Concerns*, 97th Cong., 1st sess., 1981, 70; Lucena, *Defending the Nation*, 93.

55. "Statement on the Engineering Mission of the NSF over the Next Decade as Adopted by the National Science Board at Its 246th Meeting on August 18–19, 1983," quoted in Panel on Engineering Graduate Education and Research, Subcommittee on Engineering Educational Systems, Committee on the Education and Utilization of the Engineer, National Research Council, *Engineering Graduate Education and Research* (Washington, D.C.: National Academy Press, 1985), 4.

56. Lucena, *Defending the Nation*, 99; National Science Foundation, *Projected Response of the Science, Engineering, and Technical Labor Market to Defense and Nondefense Needs, 1982–84* (Washington, D.C.: National Science Foundation, 1984).

57. National Commission on Excellence in Education, *A Nation at Risk: The Imperative for Educational Reform; A Report to the Nation and the Secretary of Education, United States Department of Education* (Washington, D.C.: National Commission on Excellence in Education, 1983). Another influential report came out of a think tank called the Hudson Institute, which argued (with support from the Department of Labor) that America was not prepared for the future. In *Workforce 2000*, the focus expanded from high-end innovation provided by science and engineering workers to include more basic competencies: the spread of technology was changing the nature of work, creating a demand for skilled workers throughout the economy. In this view, American workers lacked the appropriate skills in appropriate numbers, and the problem was particularly acute among minorities, creating a skill mismatch that would limit economic growth and competitiveness; see William B. Johnston and Arnold E. Packer, *Workforce 2000: Work and Workers for the Twenty-First Century* (Indianapolis: Hudson Institute, 1987).

58. Quoted in Lucena, *Defending the Nation*, 102; bracketed ellipsis points added, other ellipsis points in the original.

59. House Committee on Science and Technology, *Science and Engineering Education and Manpower*, 97th Congress, 2nd sess., 1982, 534.

60. Ronald Reagan, Message to the Congress on "A Quest for Excellence," January 27, 1987, at the American Presidency Project. www.presidency.ucsb.edu/ws/?pid=34441.

61. Lucena, *Defending the Nation*, 90.

62. Ibid.; Panel on Engineering Graduate Education and Research, Subcommittee on Engineering Educational Systems, Committee on the Education and Utilization of the Engineer, National Research Council, *Engineering Infrastructure Diagramming and Modeling* (Washington, D.C.: National Academy Press, 1986). .

63. Lucena, *Defending the Nation*, 108–12.

64. Pub. L. 99-383, §8, Aug. 21, 1986, 100 Stat. 815.

65. Task Force on Women, Minorities and the Handicapped in Science and Technology, *Changing America: The New Face of Science and Engineering; Final Report* (Washington, D.C.: Task Force on Women, Minorities and the Handicapped in Science and Technology, 1989).

66. David Dickson, *The New Politics of Science* (Chicago: University of Chicago Press, 1988 [1984]), 3.

67. Teitelbaum, *Falling Behind?*, 53; Thomas J. Espenshade, "High-End Immigrants and the Shortage of Skilled Labor," Office of Population Research, Working Paper No. 99-5, June 1999, available at http://westoff.princeton.edu/papers/opr9905.pdf.

68. Immigration and Nationality Act (1952), a.k.a. the McCarran-Walter Act (An act to revise the laws relating to immigration, naturalization, and nationality; and for other purposes), H.R. 13342; Pub.L. 414; 182 Stat. 66; Section 203.

69. Skrentny, *Minority Rights Revolution,* chap. 2; FitzGerald and Cook-Martín, *Culling the Masses.*

70. Espenshade, "High-End Immigrants."

71. Daniel J. Tichenor, "The Politics of Immigration Reform in the United States, 1981–1990," *Polity* 26 (1994): 333–62; Peter H. Schuck, "The Emerging Political Consensus on Immigration Law," *Georgetown Immigration Law Journal* 5 (1991): 1–33; Teitelbaum, *Falling Behind?,* 57.

72. See, for example, the 1990 congressional testimony of William E. Kirwan, president of the University of Maryland, at http://users.nber.org/~peat/ReadingsFolder/PrimarySources/Kirwan.1990.html.

73. Teitelbaum, *Falling Behind?,* 57–58.

74. Committee on Prospering in the Global Economy of the 21st Century, *Rising Above the Gathering Storm: Energizing and Employing America for a Brighter Economic Future* (Washington, D.C.: National Academies Press, 2007), xi.

75. Teitelbaum, *Falling Behind?,* 68.

76. Members of the 2005 "Rising Above the Gathering Storm" Committee, *Rising Above the Gathering Storm, Revisited: Rapidly Approaching Category Five* (Washington, D.C.: National Academies Press, 2010).

77. Another immigration-related program does define STEM. The "Optional Practical Training" program allows foreigners on student visas to work for twelve months after earning their degrees, but those with STEM degrees can earn a seventeen-month extension. The list of eligible degrees includes urban forestry, air conditioning technician, and animal health; list available on the Immigration and Customs Enforcement website, www.ice.gov/doclib/sevis/pdf/stem-list.pdf.

78. Steve Case, "As Congress Dawdles, the World Steals Our Talent," *Wall Street Journal,* September 9, 2013, http://online.wsj.com/news/articles/SB10001424127887324577304579054824075952330 (subscription required).

79. The March for Innovation, www.marchforinnovation.com.

80. See the Information Deficit website: http://www.innovationdeficit.org/facts.

81. Gabrielle Karol, "Immigration Reform Group Launches 'Job Loss' Clock," FoxBusiness.com, http://smallbusiness.foxbusiness.com/legal-hr/2014/03/19/immigration-reform-group-launches-job-loss-clock.

82. For an insightful critique of this approach, see Sarewitz, *Frontiers of Illusion,* chap. 2.

Part IV
An Unsettled Legacy

19 • Barack Obama and the Traditions
of Progressive Reform

James T. Kloppenberg

A self-proclaimed progressive, Barack Obama has inherited the aspirations, the methods, and many of the limitations of the American reformers who preceded him by a century. The obstacles that have prevented him from achieving his most ambitious goals are familiar as well and speak to some of the most enduring aspects of American culture. More than most in this line of reformers, Obama has pondered the problems and prospects of progressivism, and it seems appropriate that his leadership prompts us to do the same.

Obama's progressivism is broadly based. First, he aspired to the ideals of the Social Gospel and invoked the idea of a shared national purpose, a common good that transcended the particular interests of the separate classes, ethnic groups, and regions that have shaped American political struggles. Aiming to realize the Kingdom of God on Earth, Progressives, many of whom were the children of Protestant ministers, infused their reformist crusade with moral and religious fervor. In addition to the standard American references to freedom and rights, they, like Obama, spoke a language of responsibility, obligation, and justice.

Second, Obama resurrected the Progressives' emphasis on political and economic reforms. The Progressives aimed to identify and advance the public interest by seizing control of the political process from urban bosses and political machines, and they sought to empower experts to tackle social and economic problems with the latest skills and knowledge. Informed regulation seemed to them to offer the best way to identify, advance, and protect the shared interests of all Americans. In contrast to Ronald Reagan and centrist Democrats like Bill Clinton, Obama has not shied away from this faith in government. As Obama sees it, the work of bodies such as the Environmental

Protection Agency and the Consumer Financial Protection Bureau are part of the solution; the problem is, as Progressives foretold, a "do-nothing Congress" dominated by fierce partisans who answer to the narrowest (and wealthiest) fringes of their parties. Even though scholars have shown the danger of such agencies being captured by those they are designed to control, the Progressives' faith in executive stewardship action and extralegislative bodies persists.[1]

Third, Obama inherited the Progressives' pragmatism, their uneasiness with dogma, their commitment to achieving moderate, incremental progress through trial and error, and their confidence in the application of the scientific method to politics. Many Progressives renounced what Walter Lippmann termed the "panacea habit of mind" and embraced instead the ideas of pragmatist philosophers, notably Lippmann's teacher William James and his fellow champion of democratic experimentation, John Dewey. At a time when conservatives defended laissez-faire and many Americans on the left embraced more radical alternatives—including anarchism, communism, Edward Bellamy's state socialism, Henry George's single tax, and the incompatible strategies advanced by the Knights of Labor and the American Federation of Labor—many middle-class Progressives proposed piecemeal reforms designed not to replace capitalism but only to rein in its excesses.[2]

The obstacles to Obama's progressivism run deep as well. He has had to wrestle with four stubborn features of American culture that have hamstrung reformers since the nation's founding: persistent localism, distrust of the federal government, a deep ambivalence about engaging in world affairs, and a racism that appears nearly as entrenched in the twenty-first century as it was in the eighteenth, nineteenth, and twentieth. From the debates between Federalists and Anti-Federalists over the Constitution through the battles between the Whigs and the Jacksonians to today's widespread animosity toward the federal government, Americans have always disagreed about the proper roles of local and national authority. Many Progressives supported Woodrow Wilson's League of Nations, but early-twentieth-century battles over whether to wage war and how to ensure peace constituted just one skirmish in the persistent struggle between Americans who considered it their national destiny to redeem the world and those who believed that imperial adventures corrupted the republic. Conflicts over race are likewise as old—and as intractable—as the nation itself. Although the Constitution provided for the eventual end of the African slave trade, the refusal of the founding generation to confront the age-old practice of slavery itself merely put off the reckoning that would

come with the Civil War. The failure of Reconstruction again deferred fulfillment of the promise of racial equality, and neither Progressives nor New
Dealers effectively challenged the doctrine of white supremacy. The vicious
attacks on the first president of the United States with an African parent suggest that the bitter legacy of racial animosity continues to poison twenty-first-
century American politics. Many of Obama's domestic and foreign-policy
initiatives have echoed Progressives' ideas, and the problems he has faced
likewise recall the dynamics of the early twentieth century.

Obama's Progressivism

Historians generally agree that we should think of Progressivism as a constellation of distinct yet allied forms of social action. They remind us that these
reformers, though often grouped together by convention, were a mixed bag,
often inconsistent in their ideas and purposes. Nevertheless, connections are
not difficult to discern. The Progressive idea of the common good and the
Progressive aversion to political partisanship, for example, were connected to
the Social Gospel, the reorientation of mainstream Protestant religious denominations away from salvation in the next life and toward varieties of social
and economic reform. The Social Gospel manifested itself in multiple forms.
It inspired the seminars of the economist Richard T. Ely at the University of
Wisconsin, the incubator for the "Wisconsin idea" of regulation in the public
interest and a graduated income tax. Strikingly, not only was Ely the first
secretary of the American Economic Association, but his books were also
assigned reading in seminaries as well as departments of economics.

The Social Gospel made its mark on Progressivism at the local and the
national level. Washington Gladden instructed upper-middle-class congregations wary of unionization that Christ's law of love extended even to striking
coal miners. Walter Rauschenbusch's widely read books made him the most
visible Protestant minister to champion Progressive reforms, and the popularity as well as the persuasiveness of his work helped make him a valued adviser
to Progressive presidents Theodore Roosevelt and Woodrow Wilson. The Social Gospel also helped inspire Jane Addams, Robert Woods, Mary Simkho-
vitch, and other pioneers of the social settlement movement, which brought
middle-class American women and men into immigrant neighborhoods to
address problems of poverty, alcoholism, and prostitution and to provide services such as nursery schools, public baths, and English-language instruction
for those who needed them most. In the wake of a generation of scholars who

denigrated settlement workers for their paternalism, younger historians are reevaluating their commitments. Perched precariously between condescension and compassion, struggling over how best to serve without knowing how to bridge the chasm between middle-class reformers and recent immigrants, settlement workers sought to help recent arrivals to urban America cope with the economic and cultural challenges they faced and to construct institutions of civil society that might offer alternatives to urban machines.

Obama's progressivism is, like Progressivism itself, the product of several crisscrossing patterns of thought and practice. Obama has written that he became committed to American politics, and to seeking elective office, because he believes that something lies beyond the partisanship that prompts so much unpalatable political maneuvering in contemporary America. That faith, so characteristic of Progressives, has been tested again and again. Obama's effort to get beyond partisanship has been the defining feature of his political career. Even the intransigence of his Republican opponents, a stubbornness that shut down the government, evidently did not change his mind. He first became accustomed to the roadblocks of democratic politics when he worked as a community organizer in the far South Side of Chicago. He wrestled with the challenge of forging alliances in the Illinois State Senate and then the U.S. Senate. In *The Audacity of Hope,* a book written after his inspiring speech at the Democratic nominating convention in 2004 catapulted him to national prominence, Obama conceded that it had become more difficult to sustain commitments to conciliation and compromise amid what he called the "industry of insult" that was drowning out more moderate voices. But before and since his election as president, again and again, he has explained his continuing allegiance to civility by invoking a tradition that he says stretches from the nation's founding to the civil rights movement, in his words "a tradition based on the simple idea that we have a stake in one another, and that what binds us together is greater than what drives us apart."[3]

Appropriately enough for someone who lived and worked in Chicago's South Side, in neighborhoods not that far from Jane Addams's Hull House, Obama's reference to "what binds us together" echoes the almost identical words that Addams used to explain herself in *Twenty Years at Hull House* (1910). Repeating a phrase she attributed to the founder of the English settlement house movement, Addams professed her belief "that the things which make men alike are finer and better than the things that keep them apart, and that these basic likenesses, if they are properly accentuated, easily transcend the less essential differences of race, language, creed, and tradition." Addams derived her cultural cosmopolitanism from the democratic ideal she shared with John Dewey. In her words, "Hull-House was soberly opened on the theory that the dependence of classes on each other is reciprocal. [Because] the social relation is essentially a reciprocal relation, it gives a form of expression that has peculiar value, the value added by expanding the appreciation of individuals for those unlike themselves."[4]

Obama's fondness for this formulation deepened over the course of his presidency. He used it in his Cairo address to the Islamic world, in his Nobel acceptance speech in Oslo, in his speech in Tucson after the shooting of Arizona congresswoman Gabrielle Giffords and those around her, and on many other occasions. It has been a staple of his weekly radio addresses and of the messages he has taken to meetings around the United States. He used versions of it at the ceremony marking the fiftieth anniversary of the March on Washington, in his speech at the end of the government shutdown two months later, and in his speech commemorating the march from Selma to Montgomery, Alabama. For him, it captures the heart of democracy.

That commitment derives from two sources that many Americans find inconsistent or at least paradoxical. One source, the tradition of pragmatism, to which I will return, is philosophical; the other source, the Social Gospel, is religious. Among the most vivid passages in Obama's memoir *Dreams from My Father* is his account of his religious conversion in Jeremiah Wright's Trinity United Church of Christ. Although Obama's mother, a cultural anthropologist, raised him to appreciate the sacred texts of several cultures, he did not embrace any particular tradition until he found, in Wright's congregation, a spiritual home. Even when he distanced himself from Wright during the 2008 presidential campaign, he went out of his way to say that he could no more renounce Wright than he could renounce his maternal grandmother. Although a stupefying number of Americans persist in believing that Obama is a Muslim, he remains a practicing Christian who has hosted an Easter breakfast and a Passover Seder in the White House.

Obama calls himself "a Christian and a skeptic," a formulation that puzzles or repels many Americans who likewise call themselves Christians, either because they are unaware of how old that tradition of Christian skepticism is or because they are unwilling to accept it as a legitimate form of religious faith. Reflecting on his conversion, Obama writes that joining Wright's church "helped me shed some of my skepticism and embrace the Christian faith." He also observes, however, that faith "doesn't mean that you don't have doubts, or that you relinquish your hold on this world." His conversion occurred "as a choice and not an epiphany; the questions I had did not magically disappear." Although his doubts remained, he said he "felt God's spirit beckoning me," and he responded accordingly: "I submitted myself to His will, and dedicated myself to discovering His truth." Conceiving of Christianity as a quest, a continuing journey rather than a set of firmly held beliefs, strikes many Americans—both religious and atheist—as peculiar. Its lineage, though, can be traced back to the earliest communities of Christians, and it has surfaced periodically ever since. It is a tradition that Obama inherited directly from the Social Gospel, which inspired so many Progressive reformers and later black preachers, including Martin Luther King Jr. as well as Jeremiah Wright.[5]

Obama only indirectly refers to the ideas and example of Ely, Rauschen-busch, and Addams in *The Audacity of Hope,* but in his general approach to reform and, more specifically, in his reform agenda, the connections to their conception of "good works" is unmistakable. Many Progressives, disgusted with the tactics employed by urban bosses and convinced that democracy was being poisoned rather than practiced by corrupt political machines, preferred either appointed city managers or reconfigured citywide elections designed to break the parties' grip. Obama's frequent criticism of the fierce partisanship that so often prevents any compromise and paralyzes government, criticism that first catapulted him to prominence after his speech at the 2004 Democratic Party Convention in Boston, harks back to the Progressives' recurrent invocations of the "common good" and their preference for commissions, boards of arbitration, and other methods of resolving conflict by evading partisan politics. Progressives wanted calm, rational arguments to replace vote buying by party regulars, who rounded up voters and delivered them, by whatever means (and as often as) necessary. They wanted to persuade voters to elect reformist candidates committed to the common good. Those techniques of persuasion are precisely the techniques that Obama himself prefers, techniques that, at least until he was elected president, he had shown a rare ability to deploy successfully. From the Chicago church basements where he worked as a community organizer through his election as the first black president of the *Harvard Law Review,* from his first forays into electoral politics to his unexpected success in the 2008 presidential primaries, it was his persuasive power that kept drawing people to him and propelling him forward. Whether that predilection for nonpartisanship and compromise is high-minded idealism or an escapist fantasy is a perennial question posed by scholars of American politics, one that almost every U.S. citizen has probably asked about a president repeatedly stymied by Republican intransigence. Again and again Obama has proposed legislation in the name of the public interest—legislation that opinion polls indicate often has the support of a substantial majority of voters—only to see it characterized, and rejected, as a narrow, partisan challenge to the "American way of life."

Two other ideas repeatedly endorsed by Obama, the use of a graduated, or "progressive," income tax and government regulation of the economy, were also mainstays of the Progressive commitment to social improvement. Drawing on a long history of practice in local and state government, these reforms were introduced at the national level in the late nineteenth century and elaborated most aggressively by Democrats from the presidency of Woodrow Wilson in 1912 through the presidency of Lyndon B. Johnson. Wilson began to be drawn toward such ideas while serving as governor of New Jersey. His complete conversion to that strategy as president is now thought to be largely the result of the persuasive powers of his friend Louis Brandeis and the erstwhile champions of Theodore Roosevelt who edited the *New Republic*. As a result, Wilson ended up bringing to fruition much of the Progressive reform agenda, surprising many observers by enacting much of the platform of Roosevelt's 1912 Progressive Party.[6]

Since 1980, Republicans and many centrist Democrats have repudiated such ideas. In recent decades, a bipartisan consensus has formed about the desirability of lowering taxes and has hardened around the theory, which the catastrophic recession that began in 2008 appears not yet to have shaken entirely, that government regulation of the economy is less efficient than reliance on free markets. The imperviousness of many political convictions to disproof by experience suggests one of the many difficulties involved in applying the scientific method to politics. In addition to problems of path dependency and feedback loops that complicate the dispassionate assessment of results in public affairs, many people refuse even to consider the possibility that their political views are based on false information or inaccurate perceptions of reality. To illustrate that point, there is widespread and growing agreement among economists, regardless of whether they applaud or deprecate the fact, concerning one of the consequences of deregulating the economy and reducing taxes on the wealthy: the gap separating the richest from the poorest Americans has grown dramatically in recent decades. Obama first made that point in *The Audacity of Hope*, and he has emphasized it repeatedly as president. Even though many Americans continue to deny it, the evidence is now clear that the gap separating the wealthiest Americans not only from those at the bottom but also from those in the middle of the range of income distribution shrank from the New Deal until roughly the time of the oil crisis of 1973. It shrank not by accident or through simple economic growth but because of four deliberate strategies, all of which date from the Progressive era: graduated (or progressive) taxation, economic regulation, support for unionization, and investment in higher education. In the aftermath of Ronald Reagan's election to the presidency, Republicans have challenged all four of those progressive strategies, less because the evidence demands it than because such measures are said to be inconsistent with free enterprise. At least partly as a consequence, inequality has soared to levels unseen at least since the late nineteenth century and perhaps unprecedented in American history.[7]

Like the Progressives and New Dealers before him, and like John Adams and Thomas Jefferson before them, Obama has written that such increasing economic inequality is inimical to democracy. Although his sharp critique of inequality in *The Audacity of Hope,* where he first endorsed what has come to be called the Buffett rule, might seem to place him at the edge of twenty-first-century American political debate, it descends from a long-standing commitment to the importance of social and economic equality for democracy. The connection was identified by Alexis de Tocqueville in the 1830s as the defining feature of American democracy, and it mobilized reformers between the 1890s and the 1920s. The Progressive Party platform of 1912 advanced an array of ambitious social policies aimed at narrowing disparities, and Wilson's achievements to that end as president persuaded many of Theodore Roosevelt's supporters to endorse him for reelection in 1916. Franklin D. Roosevelt, after initially resisting the Progressives' approach, resurrected it in at least some parts of the New Deal. In Obama's words, the Social Security Act of 1935 was "the centerpiece of the new welfare state, a safety net that would lift almost half of all senior citizens out of poverty, provide unemployment insurance for those who had lost their jobs, and provide modest welfare payments to the disabled and the elderly poor." Although it was full of holes, the Social Security Act represented a beginning, and as it expanded, it provided much wider coverage, particularly for senior citizens. Some of Obama's supporters hope that a similar process of gradual expansion and consolidation might provide a model for the future of the Affordable Care Act, a plan originally conceived by the conservative Heritage Foundation and first enacted in Massachusetts under Governor Mitt Romney, in the decades to come.[8]

Despite their many limitations, New Deal programs established a precedent for the legitimacy of social provision, which enabled later generations to extend those principles and expand the range of Americans covered by those programs. Obama explained in *The Audacity of Hope* that he carried similar aspirations with him as he entered the U.S. Senate. Obama continued to high-light the Progressives' campaigns against inequality and for economic regula-tion throughout his first term as president, and when he decided to launch his 2012 campaign for reelection in Osawatomie, Kansas, he did so precisely be-cause he wanted to emphasize his debts to Theodore Roosevelt and the Pro-gressive Party. Not only did Obama invoke the Kansas roots of his mother's family, and not only did he restate his conviction that "we are greater together than we are on our own," he reminded his audience of Republican president Theodore Roosevelt's Progressive principles and his embrace of governmental regulation on behalf of the public interest.[9]

The cultural and political resonance between Obama's political persona and the Progressivism of a century ago has a philosophical dimension as well. This aspect of his thought and practice is reflected most clearly in his tena-cious commitment to conciliation, moderation, and experimentation. Against the prevailing orthodoxies of right and left, a generation of early-twentieth-century philosophers and political reformers carved out a via media between laissez-faire liberalism and revolutionary socialism, and some of the most in-fluential of those thinkers grounded their politics on the philosophical prag-matism of William James and John Dewey. Reformers as diverse as Herbert Croly and W. E. B. Du Bois, Walter Lippmann and Jane Addams, saw in the pragmatists' denials of dogma and embrace of uncertainty a fruitful orienta-tion toward social action, and their ideas helped fuel not only much Progres-sive reform but also many of the later initiatives of Franklin D. Roosevelt's New Deal. Although the pragmatism of James and Dewey fell out of favor with many academic philosophers during the four decades following the onset of World War II in 1939, it continued to inspire many American scholars, reformers, writers, and artists. Thanks to the work of philosophers such as Richard Rorty, Hilary Putnam, and Richard J. Bernstein, the 1980s and 1990s saw a resurgence of pragmatism that spread across the American academic landscape.[10]

Just as late-nineteenth-century pragmatism was an American variant of the antifoundationalism that found expression across the Atlantic in the writings of thinkers such as Friedrich Nietzsche and Max Weber, so the revival of prag-matism did not occur in a vacuum. Instead it followed in the wake of, and added increased momentum to, multiple intellectual challenges to the reign of Anglo-American linguistic analysis and ostensibly value-free empirical so-cial science. Spearheading these challenges was a diverse group of thinkers including not only Rorty but also the philosopher of science Thomas S. Kuhn and the cultural anthropologist Clifford Geertz. Together these thinkers—and many others often grouped together (somewhat unhelpfully) as poststructuralists or postmodernists—denied even the possibility of discovering stable, certain truth in both the natural sciences and the human sciences. Although of course such challenges met resistance—and in many disciplines, notably mainstream economics, they barely registered—they nevertheless exerted a transformative influence in much of American academic life.[11]

It was during these years, when renegade thinkers waving the banners of antifoundationalism, historicism, and pragmatism were at the peak of their influence, that Barack Obama came of age intellectually. In his two years at Occidental College in California, his most influential teacher, Roger Boesche, introduced him not only to Tocqueville and Marx, James and Nietzsche, but also to the republican interpretation of the American founding and recent historical scholarship on the Progressive era and the New Deal. At Columbia he majored in political science and international relations, and after his time as a community organizer in Chicago he arrived at Harvard Law School at the height of the theory wars racking the legal academy. Debates over the merits of legal pragmatism, critical race theory, feminist jurisprudence, law and economics, legal realism, originalism, and thinkers such as Rorty, Kuhn, and Geertz not only enlivened law students' conversations, but also showed up in the normally sedate (and sedating) pages of the *Harvard Law Review*. Before he served on the editorial board of that journal and then as its president (as the elected editor in chief is called), Obama served as Laurence Tribe's research assistant for an article titled "The Curvature of Constitutional Space: What Lawyers Can Learn from Modern Physics," published in the review in 1989. That article, which Tribe acknowledged he could not have written without Obama's help, deployed the ideas of Rorty, Kuhn, Geertz, and many other radical theorists to advance an argument concerning the instability and inevitable historicity of the law. Countering the claims of Reaganites concerning judicial restraint and originalism, Tribe insisted that law always reflects social pressures and always shapes the culture, just as physicists had shown that a star curves gravity in the space that surrounds it. At Harvard Law School, Obama learned about the impermanence of ideas, the contingency of principles, the variability and mutability of cultures, and the inescapability of history and interpretation. At the midpoint of his legal studies, all these ideas came together in a major conference on legal pragmatism held at Harvard Law School in 1990.[12]

Not surprisingly, those ideas helped shape Obama's own approach to the law. When he taught his own courses at the University of Chicago Law School in the early 1990s, he went out of his way to present all sides of every issue, and he required his students to do the same in the papers they wrote for him. When he served in the Illinois legislature and then in the U.S. Senate, he drove his staffers crazy by refusing to take a position until he was sure he had all the evidence and understood every perspective. It was his pragmatic skepticism about the supposed truths of African as well as American culture that made *Dreams from My Father* an exceptional meditation on identity. There Obama described the universalism of the middle decades of the twentieth century as an "illusion" or a "fiction." He admitted his impatience with his mother and her parents because of their uncritical acceptance of ideas such as the brotherhood of man and the ideals proclaimed by the U.N. Universal Declaration of Human Rights. He made clear that he had learned to see all points of view as partial, and all ideals as particular rather than universal, historical rather than timeless, contingent rather than grounded on bedrock. That book made clear, in short, that much of what conservatives dislike about Obama is accurate: he really does think differently from those of his contemporaries, mostly but not exclusively conservatives, who profess to believe in unchanging truths. He disagrees with them not only about politics and policy, but also about basic issues such as what can be known with certainty. Like many— although by no means all—of those who attended top-flight universities in the 1980s and 1990s, Obama learned to think historically, to accept the instability of perspectivalism and antifoundationalism.

Obama's resistance to simplistic nostrums, his refusal to toe the party line, make *The Audacity of Hope* an unusually bracing analysis of American history and politics. Unfortunately, it is precisely his insistence of the complexity of issues, his refusal to offer neat formulas to solve messy problems, and his unwillingness to grant that one side or the other has a monopoly on good judgment or goodwill that have made it hard for him to succeed as chief executive. Those tendencies, assets until he ascended to the presidency, have made him vulnerable to critics on the left who misunderstood his cultural radicalism for political and economic radicalism and now believe he has betrayed them. It has also outraged his critics on the right who think he has betrayed the nation.

The qualities of mind and character that earned Obama the respect of his teachers and his associates—his equanimity, his analytical acuity, his incisiveness, his inoculation against dogma, his broad-mindedness, what some observers describe as his "cool"—derive not only from his personality, his family background, his status as an outsider, and his canny strategic judgment, important as all those are. They manifest as well the particular habits of mind, the ways of thinking, that entered American culture during the Progressive era, through the pragmatism of James and Dewey, and persist into our own day. For many Americans, particularly but not exclusively in the academic world, those qualities signal an admirable critical sensibility. From the perspective of many other Americans, however, they indicate instead a fatal lack of principle, a failure of conviction, a lack of backbone. They mark Obama as different, alien, other. In the words of Newt Gingrich, who spoke for many of his fellow conservatives, those characteristics place Obama "so outside our comprehension" that many of his fellow Americans cannot understand how he thinks. As the stubborn persistence of the myths about Obama's birth outside the United States, his alleged adherence to Islam, and his supposedly communist, socialist, and anticolonial sympathies attest, the second half of his self-description as "Christian and skeptic" upsets many Americans as much as does his understanding of the meaning of the first half of it.[13]

Impediments Old and New

The obstacles that have thwarted Obama in meeting his objectives and, more broadly, in infusing American politics with his particular sensibilities, are many. The most profound have historical roots as deep as Obama's progressivism, but others of more recent vintage deserve at last passing attention. The proliferation of new and old media outlets, for one, is intensifying partisanship by providing echo chambers where activists' convictions are intensified and their hatreds deepened. Another, the reapportionment of congressional districts by state legislatures, has led to the creation of safer and safer districts, particularly although not exclusively for the most conservative Republicans in Congress. Big money coming from committed billionaires is now deployed effectively at the state as well as national level, and that development too has changed the calculus of electoral politics. Finally, there have been changes in the presidential tool set, the resources on which leaders can draw.

Not only did the most successful reformist presidents, from Abraham Lincoln, Theodore Roosevelt, and Woodrow Wilson through Franklin D. Roosevelt and Lyndon B. Johnson, enjoy solid majorities in both houses of Congress when they achieved their legislative triumphs—as Obama never did—they had at their disposal a combination of carrots and sticks to persuade reluctant congressmen to vote for the measures they proposed. For a variety of reasons, none of those strategies has worked for the Obama administration. On one hand, effective presidents wielded enticements such as jobs, pork barrel projects, and other kinds of rewards—think of the carrots offered by the unsavory operative portrayed by James Spader in Stephen Spielberg's film *Lincoln*. On the other hand, presidents could threaten to withdraw the support of the national party, pull funds, otherwise obstruct elected officials' favored projects, or by various means weaken the standing of uncooperative congressmen in their own party. As Obama has discovered since he proposed the $800 billion stimulus package early in his first term, however, such stratagems no longer work. Many Republicans reject such carrots, either because they are more worried about challenges from right-wing insurgents or because their ideological animus against government is so deep that they refuse to accept funding for projects such as infrastructure improvements and other initiatives thought to benefit their districts, which congressmen have long welcomed. Many Democrats, either ensconced in equally safe seats or able to raise sufficient funds to secure reelection without depending on the national party apparatus, are likewise insulated from presidential pressure. According to Michael Grunwald's detailed study *The New New Deal*, this development was the biggest surprise of the first years of Obama's presidency. Obama's aides assumed they could go back to Congress later and secure authorization to spend more than the $800 billion if it became necessary. They were wrong. Neither the lure of dollars nor threats from party leaders now work the magic they once did. Because the sources of funding have changed, the national parties no longer always control the purse strings of congressional campaigns. Neither Tea Party Republicans nor a considerable number of Democrats count much on the support of their national parties; many openly defy party leaders because they are more worried about threats from their flanks than about the sticks wielded by mainstream party leaders.[14]

But if our time is marked by important historical discontinuities in the means available to reach progressive ends, the most formidable obstacles are the most long-standing. Many Americans, not only conservatives but also many on the left, distrust the federal government and much prefer local initiatives. This anxiety dates from the debate over ratifying the Constitution, and it has extended from the Anti-Federalists and the Jacksonians to Deweyan radicals and FDR haters, the Occupy movement and the Tea Party. It has fueled many forms of resistance to programs perceived as a threat to community.

Coupled with that anxiety has been an abiding distrust of government itself, a concern that anything worth doing can be done better by volunteers operating in the realm of civil society than by governmental officials. That confidence, which spawned the vibrant associational life praised by Tocqueville and by communitarians left and right ever since, intermittently nurtures progressive agendas, as it did from the 1890s through World War I, but it can also manifest itself in opposition to innovations of any kind. Obama's signature legislative proposals, the Affordable Care Act and the bill creating the Consumer Financial Protection Bureau, squeaked through Congress; if they survive, they might become the most important legacies of his presidency. But almost every other initiative—increases in the minimum wage, environmental protection, immigration reform, gun control, and expanded early childhood education—has been defeated by the same coalition of conservative populists and big business interests that allied to oppose Progressives a century ago.

Another recurring feature of American politics is public ambivalence about the nation's role on the world stage. Although Obama inherited the wars in Iraq and Afghanistan and seems likely to make good on his promise to end both before he leaves the White House, he has been assailed by critics across the political spectrum for failing to act more decisively in the realm of foreign affairs. Of course the nature of the decisive action called for has varied wildly: he should have been "tougher" with China, or Cuba, or Russia. He should have been "stronger" as the Arab Spring turned to chaos, or more aggressively moved to check violence or unrest in the Middle East, Latin America, or Africa. Exactly how that toughness or strength was to manifest itself was never quite clear, particularly since the American people have grown increasingly impatient with the failures of U.S. military action. But critics insisted that the president should have done *something*. Leftists too have rebuked the president for not withdrawing all American troops from Iraq and Afghanistan immediately and for failing to support a variety of insurgent groups that appeared, initially at least, to represent the forces of "democracy" against those of "autocracy."

The promise of Obama's early speeches in Oslo and Cairo now seems only a fading memory: the world, as it has always done, keeps spinning away from the course set for it by an American president with a vision of peaceful, self-governing nations. First proclaimed by Woodrow Wilson and reiterated by Franklin Roosevelt and some of his successors, that ideal has been repeatedly frustrated by inevitable upheavals in unexpected places. Although Americans are now joined by people everywhere in proclaiming fidelity to the ideals of democracy, disagreements continue to erupt about just what self-government means in particular circumstances. Some critics have clamored for the president to proclaim a coherent "Obama Doctrine." Not only would such a fixed agenda be inconsistent with his awareness of the contingencies and particularities of history and culture, but it also seems safe to predict that people everywhere, as they have done ever since Wilson embraced the ideal of self-determination, would doubtless refuse to stick to our script.

The last of the continuities between the Progressive era and the Obama presidency is the disquieting persistence of racism. The early twentieth century was the heyday of Jim Crow in the South and de facto segregation throughout the nation. These years were also when scientific racism, supposedly underwritten by Darwin's theory of natural selection, justified not only white supremacy but also widespread discrimination against recent arrivals from the unfamiliar cultures of eastern Europe, southern Europe, and Asia. Gussied up with the fancy name "eugenics," this mania for "100% Americanism" culminated in demands for immigration restriction, a policy implemented in 1924 over the protests of some Progressives but with the enthusiastic support of others. Although subsequent changes in immigration policy have transformed the composition of the American population, and judicial decisions and civil rights legislation have brought to an end the most egregious forms of racial segregation, discrimination persists against all people of color, and it remains particularly pronounced against African Americans.

Many white Americans, particularly but not exclusively those located in the former Confederacy and its cultural dependencies, have resisted most of the cultural changes of the past fifty years. Challenges dating from the civil rights movement and broadening to the campaigns for women's equality, legal abortion, gun control, and, more recently, same-sex marriage have antagonized many of those Americans who cherish older traditions threatened by such proposals. Many Americans perceive the elites on both coasts as self-righteous zealots committed to goals they do not share. To the surprise of many on the left, the anger and resentment felt by such Americans as a result of recent cultural changes trump whatever uneasiness they may feel about their own declining economic status. When left-leaning elites accuse them of false consciousness for continuing to vote for conservative Republicans instead of the progressive Democrats who claim to have their best interests at heart, they respond with furious denunciations of those who pretend to know what's good for them.

In the twenty-first century, as members of all groups—left as well as right, academics who read the *Huffington Post* as well as people who listen to right-wing talk radio—cluster in increasingly insulated communities and exchange ideas only with those who agree with them, the Progressives' goal of coming to common understandings seems to recede on the horizon. Accelerating changes in print, television, and online media only heighten the partisanship and the anger that Progressives thought Americans could transcend. Although Obama repeatedly invokes the ideas of shared purpose and a common good, he nevertheless exacerbates all these problems because he embodies everything such Americans fear. He is black. He is overeducated. He is not one of "us." He is either a Muslim or an atheist, a dyed-in-the-wool anticolonial communist, born in Kenya, who grew up hating America and embracing the cause of America's enemies. Moreover, he relies on a tiny cadre of equally overeducated advisers who refuse to listen to anybody else, who treat regular people with contempt, and who are committed to forcing their agenda down Americans' throats.

The Current Impasse

Barack Obama serves as a magnet for the hatreds of those Americans alienated by progressivism and what they consider its threat to eternal verities. He grew up internalizing critiques of unchanging values that originated in the Progressive era but became central to American academic life just when he came of age, in the 1980s and 1990s. He learned to think about American history and politics in the way most scholars now see it: instead of envisioning Americans as a chosen people with a unique history, a people dedicated above all to securing freedom for rights-bearing individuals, he learned to think critically about American history and to embrace historicism, fallibilism, and antifoundationalism. Those ideas, originating a century earlier with philosophers such as Nietzsche and the early American pragmatists, also shaped the thinking of critical race theorists, radical feminists, those involved with critical legal studies, and the historians and political theorists who turned away from Louis Hartz's notion of a unitary liberal tradition and toward the republican synthesis and communitarian critiques of Americans' so-called rugged individualism. Those are the ideas Obama encountered at Occidental, at Columbia, and at Harvard Law School; those are the ideas he taught in his own courses at the University of Chicago Law School. That is the sensibility that manifests itself in his writings and his speeches.

When Obama rejected his mother's and his maternal grandparents' commitments to World War II–era universalism as an "illusion" or a "fiction" that "haunted" him, and when he embraced instead the ideas of cultural anthropologists, historians of science, and other radical thinkers, he stood in a long tradition of progressive thinking. But the blend of progressive ideas that Obama imbibed in the post-civil-rights era was much less stable, and far more volatile, than were those of early-twentieth-century Progressives. Obama did not only endorse the social and cultural changes that had occurred since the 1960s and 1970s, he embodied them. His election signaled that voters had repudiated the presidency of George W. Bush and what his party stood for, and Obama's critics feared that he would consolidate a culture of dependency, abortion, and gun control at home and multilateralism abroad. Bad as Bill Clinton might have been, he was at least a southern "good ol' boy." His unruly appetites as much as his accent marked him as a son of Arkansas, not of Georgetown or Yale Law School. Obama, by contrast, lacked such redeeming qualities. He was deeply, radically other in a way that neither Theodore Roosevelt nor Woodrow Wilson, and neither Franklin D. Roosevelt nor Lyndon B. Johnson, had been.

As I have noted, the Progressive era was the age of Jim Crow, when white supremacy not only underwrote the segregation of Wilson's White House and America's armed forces but also authorized the rewriting of American history. Most early-twentieth-century historians portrayed the antebellum South as a paradise of politeness, the Civil War as the work of a bungling generation, a terrible error that never should have happened, and Reconstruction as a tragedy ended only by the restoration of white rule. One of the most incisive writers of the Progressive era, James's student W. E. B. Du Bois, denied that it could have been otherwise. So complete was the misunderstanding, so deep the hatred, between blacks and whites, Du Bois wrote in *The Souls of Black Folk*, that expecting a happy ending after the Civil War was naive, a cruel trick played on former slaves who lacked the resources to defend themselves from the southern whites who called themselves redeemers. Progressive reformers never directly tackled the regime of Jim Crow, and their legacy shackled the New Deal to its distinctly limited agenda. As Ira Katznelson has shown so convincingly in *Fear Itself,* from first to last the legislation of the New Deal was circumscribed by southern Democrats who successfully resisted all challenges, no matter how remote the threat, to the persistence of white supremacy. Every measure had to be shown to be compatible with Jim Crow.[15]

Obama has made clear that he holds no illusions about the mid-twentieth-century Democratic Party. He understands that it harbored and humored vicious southern racists who weighed every initiative against their overriding commitment to preserving white supremacy. He knows that the Democratic Party coalition was held together by inspiring ideals, what he called in *The Audacity of Hope* "a vision of fair wages and benefits," and by hard-nosed calculations—in his words, "patronage and public works." The question his presidency has raised is whether the Democratic Party of the post-civil-rights era is capable of delivering that same combination of progressive idealism and pragmatism, whether the common ground is still broad enough, and the commitment to compromise still strong enough. Or to put it more bluntly, was the racism of earlier times really the meeting ground of possibility? Ironically, Obama's astounding advance against Progressivism's most egregious sin seems to have placed in jeopardy all that he admires in the movement's past achievements. Theodore Roosevelt claimed that Progressives were standing at Armageddon and battling for the Lord, but today it is the opponents of Obama's progressive party who consider themselves the last defenders of the American way of life as they understand it. Recent studies of the Tea Party by party pollsters and by political scientists such as Theda Skocpol and Alan Abramowitz have shown that "racial resentment" is among the most striking characteristics of today's most obdurate conservatives. Many of them have not accepted the results of Appomattox, the Thirteenth, Fourteenth, and Fifteenth Amendments of the 1860s, or the Civil Rights Act and Voting Rights Act of the 1960s, let alone the results of the presidential elections of 2008 and 2012.[16]

Both the depth and the nature of that resistance trouble me. In a forthcoming study of democracy in Europe and America since the ancient world, I argue that civil war is a deathblow to democracy. The sixteenth-century wars of religion, the English Civil War of the 1640s, and the French Revolution, which also became a civil war, show how difficult it is for democracy to recover from the deep wounds inflicted when civil war destroys the ethic of reciprocity on which democracy depends. Unless one is willing to lose to one's worst enemies, majority rule is impossible. The stalemate that we are witnessing in contemporary American politics suggests that for some Americans at least, the stakes in the political contest over our culture are now too great to permit compromise. They deny that those issues can properly be decided by voting, which Henry David Thoreau dismissed scornfully as a kind of gambling. That way of thinking, shared in parts of the North as well as much of the South, brought on our own Civil War, a conflict that was tragic not because it could have been avoided but because it was absolutely necessary in order to bring slavery to an end. There was no alternative.[17]

What will it now take to establish, once and for all, that America's Civil War is over, that the Union won, and that the institutionalized racism that has long characterized American culture must come to an end? Are the resources of the progressive tradition—grounded in the ideals of the Social Gospel, suspicious of dogma and comfortable with uncertainty, and committed to finding a common good and using government to achieve it—adequate to enable us to cope with determined and persistent challenges to the basic principles of American democracy as well as deeply rooted suspicions of central government authority? The jury is still out.

Notes

1. On the theory and potential of regulatory capture, see Jean-Jacques Laffont and Jean Tirole, "The Politics of Government Decision-Making: A Theory of Regulatory Capture," *Quarterly Journal of Economics* 106 (November 1991): 1089–127, and Ernesto Dal Bo, "Regulatory Capture: A Review," *Oxford Review of Economic Policy* 22 (Summer 2006): 203–25. William Novak, *The People's Welfare: Law and Regulation in Nineteenth-Century America* (Chapel Hill: University of North Carolina Press, 1996), launched a wave of studies demonstrating that the pervasiveness of local, state, and federal government regulation of the economy was as old as American history. For a sample of recent work, see Steven Conn, ed., *To Promote the General Welfare: The Case for Big Government* (New York: Oxford University Press, 2012), and the chapter by Dan Carpenter in this volume.

2. Walter Lippmann, *Drift and Mastery* (New York: Mitchell Kennerley, 1914), 182–90. On the relation between the pragmatism of William James and John Dewey and the ideas and programs of Progressive reformers on both sides of the Atlantic, see James T. Kloppenberg, *Uncertain Victory: Progressivism and Social Democracy in European and American Thought, 1870–1920* (New York: Oxford University Press, 1986), and Kloppenberg, *The Virtues of Liberalism* (New York: Oxford University Press, 1998), chaps. 6, 7, and 8. See also Kevin Mattson, *Creating a Democratic Public: The Struggle for Urban Participatory Democracy During the Progressive Era* (University Park: Pennsylvania State University Press, 1998); Sidney M. Milkis and Jerome M. Mileur, eds., *Progressivism and the New Democracy* (Amherst: University of Massachusetts Press, 1999); Sarah Deutsch, *Women and the City: Gender, Space, and Power in Boston, 1870–1940* (New York: Oxford University Press, 2000); Louise W. Knight, *Citizen: Jane Addams and the Struggle for Democracy* (Chicago: University of Chicago Press, 2005); John Recchiuti, *Civic Engagement: Social Science and Progressive-Era Reform in New York City* (Philadelphia: University of Pennsylvania Press, 2007); Ariane Liazos, "The Movement for Good City Government: Municipal Leagues, Political Science, and the Contested Meaning of Progressive Democracy, 1880–1930," Ph.D. diss., Harvard University,

2007; Lauren Brandt, "Social Intercession: The Religious Nature of Public Activism Among American Women Reformers, 1892–1930," Ph.D. diss., Harvard University, 2009; and James J. Connolly, *An Elusive Unity: Urban Democracy and Machine Politics in Industrializing America* (Ithaca, N.Y.: Cornell University Press, 2010).

3. Barack Obama, *The Audacity of Hope: Thoughts on Reclaiming the American Dream* (New York: Random House, 2006), 21, 4. According to Obama's biographer David Remnick, one of Obama's Senate staffers reported that he poured "his whole soul" into this book (Remnick, *The Bridge: The Life and Rise of Barack Obama* [New York: Random House, 2010], 444–45). For detailed analysis of its arguments about American history and politics, see James T. Kloppenberg, *Reading Obama: Dreams, Hope, and the American Political Tradition,* 2nd ed. (Princeton, N.J.: Princeton University Press, 2012).

4. Jane Addams, *Twenty Years at Hull House* (New York: Signet, 1961 [1910]), 89.

5. Obama, *Audacity,* 245. For analysis of Obama's religious faith in the context of the two-thousand-year tradition of Christian skepticism, see James T. Kloppenberg, "Barack Obama and the Paradoxes of Progressive Christianity," in *Beyond the Culture Wars: Recasting Religion and Politics in the Twentieth Century,* ed. Darren Dochuk and Marie Griffith (forthcoming).

6. See Sidney Milkis, *Theodore Roosevelt, the Progressive Party, and the Transformation of American Democracy* (Lawrence: University Press of Kansas, 2009); Trygve Throntveit, *Power Without Victory: Woodrow Wilson and the American Internationalist Experiment* (Chicago: University of Chicago Press, forthcoming); *Reconsidering Woodrow Wilson: Progressivism, Internationalism, War, and Peace,* ed. John Milton Cooper Jr. (Baltimore: Johns Hopkins University Press for the Woodrow Wilson Center Press, 2008), esp. the following chapters: Trygve Throntveit, "Common Counsel: Woodrow Wilson's Pragmatic Progressivism, 1885–1913," 25–56, and W. Elliot Brownlee, "Wilson's Reform of Economic Structure: Progressive Liberalism and the Corporation," 57–89. See also "A Comparison of the Platforms of the Progressive Party and of the Social Scientists as to Social and Industrial Justice," 1912, reprinted in Recchiuti, *Civic Engagement,* 237–40.

7. For several years Thomas Piketty and Emmanuel Saez have maintained a website with data demonstrating this growing inequality: http://elsa.berkeley.edu/#at. See Piketty's recent book, *Capital in the Twenty-First Century,* trans. Arthur Goldhammer (Cambridge, Mass.: Belknap Press, 2014), for the most comprehensive collection of evidence concerning inequality in the United States, France, and Britain currently available. During World War II, the European and American conservatives who clustered around Friedrich Hayek in the Mont Pelerin Society agreed on the idea of graduated taxation and the necessity of a social safety net. On the striking transformation of American conservatism since World War II, see Angus Burgin, *The Great Persuasion: Reinventing Free Markets Since the Depression* (Cambridge, Mass.: Harvard University Press, 2012).

8. Obama, *Audacity,* 182. On the surprisingly social-democratic Progressive Party platform of 1912, and on the conversion of Roosevelt's supporters to Wilson, see Milkis, *Roosevelt, the Progressive Party, and Democracy,* 147–64, 335–36n54.

9. For Obama's speech in Osawatomie, Kansas, on December 6, 2011, see https://www.whitehouse.gov/the-press-office/2011/12/06/remarks-president-economy-osawatomie-kansas. On the significance of the 1912 presidential campaign, see Milkis, *Roosevelt, the Progressive Party, and Democracy*, and his chapter in this volume.

10. See James T. Kloppenberg, "Pragmatism: An Old Name for Some New Ways of Thinking?," *Journal of American History* 83, no. 1 (June 1996): 100–138, reprinted in *The Revival of Pragmatism*, ed. Morris Dickstein (Durham, N.C.: Duke University Press, 1998), 83–127; James T. Kloppenberg, "Pragmatism and the Practice of History: From Turner and Du Bois to Today," in *Pragmatism and the Limits of Philosophy*, ed. Richard Shusterman (Oxford: Blackwell, 2004), 197–220; and James T. Kloppenberg, "James's *Pragmatism* and American Culture, 1907–2007," in *100 Years of Pragmatism: William James's Revolutionary Philosophy*, ed. John Stuhr (Bloomington: Indiana University Press, 2010), 7–40.

11. For a more detailed discussion of these issues, see Kloppenberg, *Reading Obama*, 1–149; David A. Hollinger, "How Wide the Circle of the We? American Intellectuals and the Problem of the Ethnos Since World War II," *American Historical Review* 98, no. 2 (April 1993): 317–33, incorporated into chap. 3 of David A. Hollinger, *Postethnic America*, rev. ed. (New York: Basic, 2006); and Daniel T. Rodgers, *Age of Fracture* (Cambridge, Mass.: Harvard University Press, 2012).

12. See Laurence H. Tribe, "The Curvature of Constitutional Space," *Harvard Law Review* (November 1989); and Laurence H. Tribe and Michael C. Dorf, *On Reading the Constitution* (Cambridge, Mass.: Harvard University Press, 1991); Tribe and Dorf thank Obama, who "influenced our thinking on virtually every subject discussed in these pages," for likening constitutional interpretation to a "conversation," the image that governs their analysis. On Harvard Law School during Obama's time there, see the article by his fellow student Kenneth Mack, "Barack Obama Before He Was a Rising Political Star," *Journal of Blacks in Higher Education* 45 (2004): 98–101; and for more detailed analysis of the legal academy in the early 1990s, see Laura Kalman, *The Strange Career of Legal Liberalism* (New Haven, Conn.: Yale University Press, 1996).

13. Newt Gingrich quoted by Robert Costa, "Gingrich: Obama's 'Kenyan, Anti-colonial' Worldview," *National Review Online*, September 11, 2010, www.nationalreview.com/corner/246302/gingrich-obamas-kenyan-anti-colonial-worldview-robert-costa.

14. Michael Grunwald, *The New New Deal: The Hidden Story of Change in the Obama Era* (New York: Simon and Schuster, 2012); and on the myriad challenges facing Obama's presidency in the new landscape of American politics, see also Theda Skocpol, *Obama and America's Political Future*, with commentaries by Larry M. Bartels, Mickey Edwards, and Suzanne Mettler (Cambridge, Mass.: Harvard University Press, 2012).

15. See W. E. B. Du Bois, *Souls of Black Folk*, ed. David Blight and Robert Gooding Williams (Boston: Bedford/St. Martin's, 1997 [1903]), esp. chaps. 2 and 9; and Ira Katznelson, *Fear Itself: The New Deal and the Origins of Our Time* (New York: Liveright, 2014).

16. Theda Skocpol and Vanessa Williamson, *The Tea Party and the Remaking of Republican Conservatism* (New York: Oxford University Press, 2012); and Alan Abramowitz, *The Polarized Public? Why American Government Is So Dysfunctional* (New York: Pearson, 2013).

17. James T. Kloppenberg, *Toward Democracy: The Struggle for Self-Rule in European and American Thought* (New York: Oxford University Press, 2016).

20 • How the Progressives Became the Tea Party's Mortal Enemy

Networks, Movements, and the Political Currency of Ideas

Steven M. Teles

In the wake of the Democrats' sweeping victory in 2008, and faced with the threat of legislation that sought to restructure the health care and financial sectors, reform the nation's immigration laws, increase taxes on high earners, and price carbon emissions, conservatives sought to understand how things could have gone so wrong. Many decided that this onslaught was not actually so new, but was just the latest guise of an old foe—Progressivism.

Conservatives see in Obama's leadership many of the same qualities described by James Kloppenberg in the previous chapter. The most popular proponent on the right of the idea that Obama was channeling Herbert Croly was the talk show host Glenn Beck. But whereas Kloppenberg contends that Obama's liberalism was an indigenous American tradition, Beck introduced into the bloodstream of popular conservatism the idea that liberalism was part of a century-long conspiracy against American values and the Constitution, carried out by a cadre of experts seeking to undermine popular governance. In one of his many widely disseminated history lessons, Beck attacked Cass Sunstein, who was then running the Office of Information and Regulatory Affairs in the Office of Management and Budget, for his part in this elite conspiracy.

> I told you before that Cass Sunstein is the most dangerous man in America. And even congressmen and senators look at me like I'm a mad man, and I hope I'm wrong. But he is the head of the Office of Information and Regulatory Affairs in the White House. . . . Sunstein is taking a page right from [Woodrow] Wilson's playbook. And by the end of this episode, you are going to know why you do not want to even look at that playbook. The idea is simple, that the governing elite knows best. That's why they have all these czars and everything else, because they know

best. They don't need to go to Congress. They don't need to listen to the people, because the people are uninformed and incapable of choosing what's best for them in society or for society on the whole.

Further, Beck advanced a frightening idea: "Progressives also look to use war or the moral equivalent of war, an economic crisis, a human rights issue to push through their progressive agenda, which always includes the suspension of basic rights. You can never waste a good crisis and the ends justify the means. That is Woodrow Wilson and that is Saul Alinsky." In the wake of the financial crisis, Beck sensitized his viewers to the possibility that this was the opportunity that liberals had been looking for to strip the nation of its basic rights and constitutional forms: "They also view the Constitution as an organic document, outdated in its original form. It's open to modern interpretation. Wilson I think hated it. . . . I hate this SOB [Wilson] and the more you learn about this guy, the more you will, too. This is—this is the most evil guy I think we've ever had in office."[1] Beck taught his followers that liberalism sprang from a poisoned root, and that its influence spread into every nook and cranny of American society: "Back to what I taught you on the 1915 Progressives. They figured it out. They knew they couldn't do everything they wanted to do in 1915, because we were too tied to the Constitution. We were too tied to the Founders. And we were too tied to our churches. And so they changed history. They went in, and all these progressives in the universities, they started to change the history books. They went into our faith with something called social justice. That is from the Progressive movement."[2] Liberalism was not, therefore, a decent adversary holding a different interpretation of a shared political culture. It was an insidious, unscrupulous, alien force with which there could be no compromise. The mission of the opposition was to expose the heretics and purge their influence root and branch—including their influence on conservatives themselves.

Beck's discovery quickly became a touchstone for the Tea Party movement, fuel for its effort to push back against the Obama administration and, more broadly, against the liberal accomplishments of the previous century. In their study of the Tea Party, Theda Skocpol and Vanessa Williamson found that Beck's argument took hold in the fertile soil of the movement's grass roots:

> One Virginia Tea Partier told us that the "problems" the United States is now facing "go back to Roosevelt" and the New Deal. Looking back even further, many who watched Fox News anchor Glenn Beck echoed his criticisms of Woodrow Wilson. Indeed, the Minnesota Tea Partiers

affiliated with the large and vibrant Southwest Metro Tea Party see themselves as part of a long tradition battling American liberalism. As their
"Principles" explain, the Tea Party's goal is to reverse the work of "Woodrow Wilson's Progressivism, FDR's New Deal, LBJ's Great Society and
President Obama's 'fundamentally transforming America.'"[3]

Through Beck, the Tea Party learned that its battle against Obama was a
historic crusade to recover America's authentic values, values that a century of
reform had mocked and squandered. The enemy had changed its masks over
the years, but its heresy was all of a piece.

The idea that progressivism was the hidden source of big government
might have been a revelation for many in the movement at large, but the basic
argument had been gestating for some time. A small group of conservative
intellectuals, mainly in the academy, had long been at work on a comprehensive critique of the early-twentieth-century Progressives. They had documented the reformers' break with the founding and traced their influence
forward on contemporary liberalism. In the traumatic events of 2008, movement activists latched onto this critique. They translated it and popularized it.
A core part of orthodox conservative mythology was thus forged in this connection between intellectuals and movement popularizers.

All fundamentalisms are rooted in an account of history that begins with
an authoritative founding, followed by a fall from right ordering, and succeeded by a battle to return to the founding orthodoxy. The Tea Party, with its
public call for a return to the Constitution and reverence for the Framers as
secular saints, was nothing if not a kind of fundamentalism. But what the Tea
Party initially lacked was a coherent account of the fall. The intellectual critique of early-twentieth-century Progressives provided that account. It identified Progressivism as a belief system that was as comprehensive as it was
foreign and threatening. For a Tea Party movement already convinced that
conservatives were at a pivotal moment in the nation's development, the
Progressives' apostasy served as the demonic menace. The nation stood at a
precipice: turn back the corruption of Progressivism or watch the country
finally succumb. In this narrative construction, President Obama was not dismissed as a moderate liberal reformer. He was something much more sinister,
a representative of ideas wholly alien to America's constitutional and cultural
traditions. These beliefs provided a framework within which complete,
uncompromising conservative opposition to the president, and unrelenting
pressure on their Republican allies to refuse to compromise or collaborate in
any way, made sense.

In an earlier essay in this volume, Ken Kersh traced an intellectual shift in the object of conservative criticism from the New Deal back to the Progressive era, and from a narrow dispute over the reach of the Commerce Clause to a root-and-branch rejection of the Progressives' critique of the Constitution. In this chapter, I focus on the network of intellectuals and media elites that was knit together around those ideas and that has given contemporary conservatism a common historical narrative. The first section traces the roots of the stylized history of Progressivism's role in American liberalism found in the pronouncements of Glenn Beck and the Tea Party to a small cadre of conservatives grouped around the Claremont Institute, with the political philosopher Charles Kesler at its center. It explains how the ideas of these political thinkers spread through the conservative movement, with particular attention to the Heritage Foundation as a central node of the network, and how it came to be available when the opportunity for wider dissemination opened. The second section examines how this critique exploded into broader circulation within the conservative movement. The third section investigates why the attack on Progressivism was so avidly embraced by Tea Party conservatives at this precise time, how it provided a coherent story of America and, with that, the emotional energy needed to mobilize an already historically inflected movement. These three sections ground the analysis in a set of interviews with prominent thinkers connected with the Claremont Institute, who offered insight into the ideational networks they formed, maintained, and extended via popular media outlets. The fourth section moves from detached analysis, beginning with the observation that this fundamentalist perspective on the nation's history, and on President Obama's place in it, has more than its share of outright lunacy. It is easy for outsiders to dismiss, and that makes it harder to confront the real problems of governance that the Progressives bequeathed to us. I argue that the wilder versions of antiprogressivism advanced by Beck and the less cautious scholars who influenced him have obscured and overtaken a more nuanced critique within conservatism, one that liberals would do well to take seriously. The wrong response to Tea Party fundamentalism is to respond in kind and simply hunker down in an alternative belief system.

Where Did the Tea Party Critique of Progressivism Come From?

The critique of Progressivism that became a prominent part of the Tea Party reaction to the Obama administration did not, as it may have seemed, come fully blown from the imaginations of Glenn Beck and Jonah Goldberg.

Its roots can be traced to the 1970s, concentrated in one very specific corner of the conservative intellectual movement: the "West Coast" Straussianism associated with the Claremont Institute and, even more specifically, with the institute's founder, Charles Kesler. This critique had been germinating for years, through students trained by Kesler at the Claremont Graduate School, fellows supported by the Claremont Institute, and authors published in the *Claremont Review of Books*. Patient scholarly work marched on decade after decade, without much of a popular audience, until it suddenly found a set of media entrepreneurs in 2008 capable of matching it with a popular movement hungry for a usable history that explained the contemporary moment. Before unpacking the content of these ideas, it is essential to explain where they came from and why they became a part of the Tea Party's imagined history of the American republic.

Much of Glenn Beck's widely disseminated tirades against the Progressives were drawn directly from two sources: Ronald Pestritto's *Woodrow Wilson and the Roots of Modern Liberalism* and Jonah Goldberg's *Liberal Fascism*, both of which became touchstones for the Tea Party. To understand how Progressives became the bête noire of the reaction against Obama and liberalism more generally, the origins of the arguments in these books needs to be traced. And both point directly to the Claremont Institute and the pivotal role of Kesler.

Pestritto and Goldberg were deeply influenced by Kesler. According to Pestritto: "For me, Charles Kesler was hugely influential—he pointed out the relevance of Wilson to those of us studying American political thought. And then of course I had [the University of Virginia political scientist James] Ceaser for a couple of years in grad school, when he came out to Claremont."[4] It was in Kesler's classes that Pestritto "first read Wilson seriously." He studied other political thinkers with Kesler as well: "I also took his class on Hegel, and that really helped me to see the influence that the German thinkers had on American Progressives." Kesler exposed Pestritto to the earlier work of Paul Eidelberg, James Ceaser, and Jeffrey Tulis, all of whom had criticized particular aspects of the Progressive project. Kesler taught in his classes that the Progressives were the deepest source for the "disregard for constitutional government." That realization had important consequences: "It leads one to ask the question, quite naturally: where in the American tradition did this start in a serious way? And then you read the Progressives, and it's clear as day."[5]

What Pestritto got from Kesler and others in the orbit of West Coast Straussianism was also a way of thinking about the sources of historical change:

Remember, we're talking not just theorists, but Straussians—that's where this whole criticism of progressivism comes from. We look at the ideas of Progressives directly—what, exactly, did they have to say about the American constitutional order? . . . What liberalism today gets from the Progressives is that it is programmatic—it is always on the move, always responding to new problems history throws at us. This is very different from the take of most Straussians (certainly "western" Straussians, who are influenced by Jaffa), who emphasize the permanent accounts of human nature that underlie works like the *Federalist*. It is those teachings that Progressives find most problematic.[6]

Methodologically, the approach that Pestritto took from Kesler, and that eventually filtered down to Beck and other popular conservatives, was to analyze Progressives' thought largely independent of the political conflicts in which they were engaged—regulating railroads, reforming urban police departments, fighting big-city political machines. Such abstraction, perhaps inherently, has a tendency to accentuate the movement's more radical pretensions and to deflect from the nature of the opposition that Progressives faced.

I look very carefully at what TR and Wilson actually say. And they both feel it necessary to go after the fundamental principles of the founding. In other words, they don't say that the principles were okay but have become corrupted. They take square aim at the ideas of the founding. They say they are wrong. They go right at the basic assumptions about human nature that are at the heart of American constitutionalism. And these guys aren't dumb. They know that what they are proposing is not just a reaction in the present—they know that they are laying out wholly new principles. Hence the overt drawing from foreign sources.[7]

Despite other differences, this general approach to understanding Progressive aims was shared by all the scholars upon whom Beck drew. As Pestritto put it: "Others in Western Straussian circles were on the show too—Brad Watson, Matt Spalding, Brian Kennedy. All affiliated with Kesler."

"Charles is the key," Pestritto recalled, "Many of us wrote the books that he should have written." In this network, Kesler was "key" not just as a source of intellectual inspiration, but also as an organizational entrepreneur. Kesler observed that the Claremont Institute, in which he has played a leading role since arriving at Claremont McKenna College in the early 1980s, has been central in moving the critique of Progressivism to the center of conservatism.

[For] 30 years or whatever it is, the institute has had summer classes, first the Publius program, then in addition the Lincoln program, and now yet another one in addition to those, the Marshall Fellows program. Some of the brightest young conservatives were brought to Claremont every year for the summer. We . . . did a miniature course whose curriculum was the political thought of the American founding, of Lincoln, and then of modern liberals and conservatives. We've been teaching generations of young, bright conservatives who have gone on, many of them, to do very interesting and important things in the conservative movement. There's a direct effect that all of these now several hundred, 400 or more, fellows have had in spreading the Claremont critique within the movement. Then you had Matt Spalding, [who] becomes vice president of Heritage. We've always known a lot of people at AEI. We have been teaching or persuading other institutions and . . . analysts and so forth in the conservative movement for a long time. Gradually it spread. The critical mass has grown.[8]

On top of the Claremont Institute's work with young conservatives, the *Claremont Review of Books,* which Kesler has edited since its founding in 2000, has advanced the West Coast Straussian critique of the Progressives. The *Review* is now one of the most widely read conservative publications. At least twenty-one articles in the publication have addressed the Progressives, and the overall critique has appeared in many more. Through all these mechanisms, what Jonah Goldberg humorously refers to as the "Claremonster" has made the critique of the Progressive roots of liberalism an understood, respectable part of the standard conservative package of beliefs—even before that critique exploded into popular consciousness in the wake of the Tea Party's mobilization.

The *Review* provides a means to uncover the substantive content of the Claremont critique of Progressivism before it gained wider traction. In its pages, all the essential elements of the critique are laid bare. First, these thinkers question liberalism's supposed pragmatism and its roots in simple problem solving, arguing that when liberals allow their mask to slip, they reveal that contemporary liberalism has a much more comprehensive, disturbing set of objectives. For example, in a discussion of a recent book by Hillary Clinton, Steven Hayward discovered disturbing aspirations:

Perhaps the most revealing moment of Rodham-Clinton's time in the White House was her famous 1993 speech on "the politics of meaning."

In this speech she argued that we must "remold society by redefining what it means to be a human being in the 20th century," which will require "remaking the American way of politics, government, indeed life." This goes far beyond garden-variety liberal progressivism. The idea of "redefining who we are in this post-modern age" implies that there is no human nature, or that whatever human nature there is defines itself through sheer self-assertion. In other words, the human soul can be transformed at will. For Rodham-Clinton to say that we need to remake the American way of politics, government, and life is to imply that government has the right, even the duty, to change man into something he is not.[9]

Charles Kesler, in the immediate aftermath of Obama's election, detected a similar heresy in the words of the new president and identified its roots in the thought and practice of Woodrow Wilson:

> Now, "leadership" as the way to overcome the American government's (purported) chronic gridlock is one of the oldest of old liberal tropes, classically treated by Woodrow Wilson. Obama's prescription for American problems would come as no surprise to JFK and FDR, who in this respect are Wilson's students. Perhaps Obama pays more court to a politically engaged citizenry than did FDR or Wilson. ("Men are as clay in the hands of the consummate leader," wrote Wilson in a confident moment.) Yet all of these figures were eager in some degree to rouse the public from its cynical slumbers. And Obama admits that though the times must be right, it's up to the leader to recognize and exploit the favorable moment, to open the public's eyes to the possibility, indeed the imminence, of a political leap forward.[10]

Contemporary liberals, in this narrative, had learned from the Progressives to reject a stable grounding for politics, either in human nature or in a fixed Constitution. Doing so emancipated them from the shackles of "natural right" and opened the way for a large, ever-expanding government.

Second, from Wilson and others, subsequent liberals learned that the ends of politics could instead be found in history, and thus constitutional standards had to be mutable as well—hence the idea of a "living Constitution" rather than one with a fixed meaning. As John Marini argued: "Established on the foundation of natural rights, constitutionalism has been steadily undermined by the acceptance of the new doctrine of History. The Progressive movement, which is the political instrument of that theoretical revolution, had as its fundamental purpose the destruction of the political and moral authority of the U.S. Constitution. Because of the success of the Progressive movement, contemporary American politics is animated by a political theory denying permanent principles of right derived from nature and reason." In the place of a Constitution with a fixed meaning, Marini argued, liberals operating under the spell of the Progressives substituted the modern administrative state, governed by "unaccountable knowledge elites in the bureaucracy shielded from the popular control that might be exercised through elections."[11] This switch from constitutionalism to the administrative state was one that, in James Ceaser's words, was accomplished without the consent of the American people: "The Progressives favored a 'living constitution,' which in their account was said to be wholly at odds with the actual Constitution. This open attack on the Constitution failed to win the support of the American people. Grasping this error, the liberal heirs of the Progressives changed tactics, replacing frankness with stealth."[12] Modern liberalism thus attempts to conceal what the Progressives were really in favor of, pretending that they were simply good-government reformers when in fact their goals were to undermine the Constitution entirely. Rather than accepting failure, subsequent liberals "decided to bring the living constitution, like a Trojan Horse, inside the Constitution."[13] The revolution in American governance, the turn away from the Founders, was, in this telling, illegitimate, a kind of silent coup advanced through unscrupulous means by Progressive-liberals who then were able to write the histories that covered their tracks. Taken seriously, this is an argument for legitimate counterrevolution, for undoing the detour that American history took and returning the nation to its constitutional roots.

Third, and perhaps most frightening of all, contemporary liberals took from the Progressives the bacillus that they contracted from Europe, a "leadership" principle advocated by Nietzsche that was fitted to a conception of history taken from Hegel. As Kesler observed,

> When combined with liberalism's lust for strong leaders, this openness to Nietzschean creativity looms dangerously over the liberal future. If we are lucky, if liberalism is lucky, no one will ever apply for the position of liberal superman, and the role will remain vacant. But as Lincoln asked in the Lyceum speech, "Is it unreasonable then to expect, that some man possessed of the loftiest genius, coupled with ambition sufficient to push it to its utmost stretch, will at some time, spring up among us? And when such a one does, it will require the people to be united with each other, attached to the government and laws, and generally intelligent, to

successfully frustrate his designs . . ." More worrisome even than the danger of an *Übermensch* able to promise that everything desirable will soon be possible is a people unattached to its constitution and laws; and for that, liberalism has much to answer.[14]

It is but a short jump from such a stance to the accusation that liberalism is, literally, a form of fascism—a jump that many Tea Party conservatives, schooled by Jonah Goldberg, were quite willing to take. A frightening prospect, made worse by the fact that, as Harry Jaffa argued, "Modern conservatism suffers from the same nihilism and postmodernism that dominate liberalism and that suppress dissent on our campuses. If conservatism is not to become a mirror-image of decadent liberalism, we have to return the movement to its roots in the political thought and actions of the American Founders and Abraham Lincoln. Nothing is at stake but the soul of the American Revolution, and the salvation of Western civilization."[15] The battle to undo the legacy of Progressives starts, therefore, by purifying conservatism—a lesson that the Tea Party was all too ready to hear.

Why the Critique Went Mainstream

All intellectual ideas undergo a certain simplification by the time they are used by mass movements of any stripe. It is exceptionally rare that an idea—especially a historical account of actors a century old—is presented as ideological gospel in a nearly unmodified form. But this is what Glenn Beck did in the early years of the Obama administration. Whereas the first section explained how this conservative critique of liberals' poisoned Progressive roots became available before 2009, this section explains why it diffused completely, rapidly, and with such a profound political effect after 2009.

The intersection of Kesler's intellectual work with his organizational entrepreneurship at the Claremont Institute is especially vital to account for how Goldberg's controversial book *Liberal Fascism* put a muscular version of the Straussian critique of Progressivism in the hands of most ordinary conservatives. *Liberal Fascism,* which was for a time the best-selling book in the country, hit the shelves early in 2008, making it available as a part of a popular explanation for the otherwise infuriating and perplexing (to many conservatives) events that would occur later in the year (discussed in the next section). Importantly for our purposes, Goldberg acknowledged the vital role that Claremont connections had in shaping the character of his argument:

Well, I've been a fan of the *CRB* for a very long time, so I got a spotty sense of it from there. Oddly *National Review* never bought into it basically until I came along. But it was only when I was working on *Liberal Fascism* that my wife advised me to do a deep dive on the Claremont stuff on Wilson. She had been a Lincoln fellow [a Claremont summer program]. . . . The timing was propitious because Pestritto was getting on a roll right when I needed him. Kesler recommended to me I read all his stuff. . . . It absolutely helped me make the connection. . . . So I basically came at this backwards, looking at what was happening in Europe. I had read a lot of the "Old Right" . . . about the New Deal being fascist. But I realized that I was coming into the movie halfway in. I needed to look at America in the late teens, early twenties not in the late thirties. I started discovering crazy stuff about Wilson, and my wife was, like, "Oh, you really gotta talk to Kesler about all this."[16]

Conservative networks likewise helped Beck access the conservative critique of the Progressives, as Pestritto attested:

[The Princeton University politics professor] Robbie George was on Glenn Beck's show. And Beck, whatever one may think of him, is no dummy. He's the only media guy I've ever encountered who actually read the material of those he interviewed in any depth. And Beck mentioned that Robbie was at Wilson's school. Robbie told him that if he wanted to know about Wilson, to read Pestritto's book. That's when things went nuts. I heard from people that my name was being mentioned on TV and radio all the time, and book sales were going through the roof for reasons I couldn't explain.[17]

Claremont networks gave this set of ideas currency among elite conservatives, and the presence of Beck's program on Fox provided a pathway for the larger conservative movement to learn about them. There was no central meeting where it was decided that conservatives needed to take this tack. The outcome stemmed from a combination of steady investment in these seemingly obscure ideas, the networks between conservatives at several levels, and the creation of a broad platform (along with the fact that Jonah Goldberg had already softened the ground)—all of which together made it possible for chance conversations between scholars like Robert George and popularizers like Glenn Beck to generate a powerful movement theme.

The scholars around the Claremont Institute were able to draw upon a very powerful set of institutions in addition to Fox News to spread their understanding of the historical juncture to grassroots conservatives. For example, Matthew Spalding, who received his Ph.D. under Kesler, used his perch as head of the B. Kenneth Simon Center for Principles and Politics at the Heritage Foundation to inject the Claremont critique into mainstream conservative thought. In his recollection: "We did a lot of programs for congressional staff and members to make this argument to them, really trying to make it into a very public argument. Public debates turn on the narrative. What's the story? The argument to the left has always been that modern liberalism grows out of the founding in many ways, and is a natural outgrowth flowing out of that. FDR builds the Jefferson Memorial, after all. What we wanted to do was give a counterargument, to show there was a break."[18] Even before the Tea Party erupted into American politics, the Heritage Foundation provided a high-profile platform for the Claremont narrative of history. In 2007, just before the financial crisis and the election of Obama, the think tank sponsored talks by the Claremont scholars Thomas West and R. J. Pestritto, who discussed how contemporary America's governing ills were rooted in the Progressive era. Pestritto emphasized the role of the Progressives in bringing into being the modern administrative state. Thus, when the administrative state seemed to take a quantum leap in the early years of the Obama administration, the Claremont critique of its origins in the Progressive era was already in wide circulation among conservatives.

Heritage was joined in disseminating the ideas of the Claremont scholars by Hillsdale College, which has been led by the former Claremont Institute leader Larry Arnn. Hillsdale may be little known to people outside conservative circles, but the college has had a considerable role in spreading conservative ideas to a broader audience. For example, Hillsdale's monthly publication *Imprimis* claims a genuinely stunning circulation of 2.7 million. As a recent article about it in *Salon* argued, "To judge by its presence on the national media radar, *Imprimis* is an unknown entity. But in the conservative grass roots, among the people who populate Tea Party rallies and line up for Sarah Palin appearances, *Imprimis* is very well known, and is often passed from person to person like a Grateful Dead bootleg."[19]

Imprimis brought Claremont ideas to this mass audience. In March 2008— again, just before the Tea Party came onto the American scene—Charles Kesler reminded *Imprimis*'s readers that the enemy they faced in the 2008 election was a very old one, quoting Woodrow Wilson to the effect that "living constitutions must be Darwinian in structure and in practice," and thus "it is not the limited Constitution of the Founders, but the living Constitution, which is the ideal of Progressives and of modern liberal theory and practice."[20] In essence, Kesler was saying that the differences between liberals and conservatives were so deep that they each operated under entirely different Constitutions—that what conservatives understood as tyranny liberals took to be business as usual.

In addition, Hillsdale has placed the Claremont critique of Progressivism in a central place in its widely viewed online course, Constitution 101, in which two of the ten sessions feature lectures by R. J. Pestritto on the Progressives.[21] Through Heritage and Hillsdale, therefore, the ideas of Kesler and his followers were already widely available before the economic crisis and its political aftermath. While it seemed mildly bizarre to liberals that Glenn Beck would devote so much energy to darkly tracing Obama's policies back to the Progressives, even before Jonah Goldberg published *Liberal Fascism* these ideas were circulating widely within conservative institutional networks—and not just the narrow group of right-leaning academics.

What the Claremont Critique of Progressivism Provided the Tea Party

While this level of explanation helps account for the supply of the ideas, it doesn't explain why there was also movement demand for them. What function did the Claremont critique of Progressivism perform for the Tea Party movement, and what about it captivated conservatives across the country at this particular time? It is probably fairest to say that for an idea like this to take off in such a powerful way, a number of factors needed to converge simultaneously—which was exactly what happened in 2008 and 2009.

On the one hand, the Obama election and subsequent policy breakthroughs led American conservatives to believe that America really was changing, in a durable way, for reasons that seemed obscure and for which many conservatives were unprepared. Kesler believes that the key explanation for the explosion of interest in Progressivism could be found in "the phenomenon of Obama and his agenda."

> Liberalism seemed to have been tamed to some extent. It didn't look likely in the eighties or the nineties that . . . or even in the 2000s that such an aggressive liberalism was possible again. It looked like the age of Reagan was here. The era of big government was over. . . . Where Hillary

Clinton's health care bill had died ignominiously a decade before or two decades before . . . something like Obamacare could pass here as well as . . . Dodd-Frank and the stimulus and all the other things that he was able to accomplish in the first two years of his first term. Suddenly, something like a new New Deal seemed possible, and with rapidity and a long front engaging many different issues, it seemed like liberal shock and awe was back. Far from Reagan having tamed the beast that we were getting back to the sixties or the thirties in the sense of measuring the ambition and the successes of liberalism. A lot of people thought that this was a moment of crisis. You had to look again at American liberalism and find out . . . where its strength came from and what its basic arguments were that had suddenly appeared so successful and engaging at least to a large number of Americans once more after seeming to have been pacified for several decades.[22]

Pestritto adds, "Tea Party folks feel like something good in America has been lost, and that both parties are culprits. Our stuff on the Progressives helps to explain how and why it was lost."[23] The mood of conservatism had rapidly shifted from Reaganesque optimism and belief that the future would be better than the past to a much darker mood in which many valuable things—perhaps the country itself—were slipping from the grips of "normal Americans." To reverse the course of history, which had taken a turn toward decline, conservatives needed to recover their grounding in the founding and to identify where the turn from its principles had occurred. Progressivism offered a pivot point, a wrong turn now so deeply engrained that only radical reaction could arrest the false trajectory.

A significant part of this effort required a more thorough reconstruction of conservatism. The conservative establishment had just embraced George W. Bush's "compassionate conservatism," blurring its differences with liberalism.[24] Conservatism, Kesler recalled, "had grown stale and annoying and needed to become something more like Reagan, and flying bold colors, not pale pastels, seems urgently necessary."[25] Goldberg recalled that the sudden eruption of conservative anger and calls for internal purification were driven by suppressed frustration built up over the Bush years:

The Tea Party phenomenon needs to be understood as a delayed Bush backlash. There was a real sense among conservatives that we had lost our way . . . there was the spending, the compassionate conservatism, the fights over immigration etc. But conservatives stuck with Bush because they thought the attacks on the commander in chief during a war were so unfair. . . . And then they were asked to vote for John McCain, after a primary with no one they could love. Then we get Obama promising a "fundamental transformation of America" and all that. . . . And then we got TARP, stimulus, Obamacare and the disaffected Right was, like, "Enough! I hated this crap under Bush. I'll be damned if I'm going to put up with it under *this* guy." That's one reason we saw such a crazy-huge spike in Reagan nostalgia. It's why we keep hearing about the need for purity on the right and giving no quarter, etc. The do-over mentality is of a piece with the anger toward the "establishment" because, it's believed . . . they were all collaborators, as it were.[26]

The tone of conservatism had shifted from an emphasis on trying to "beat the liberals at their own game" to a last-ditch effort to delegitimize liberalism itself. And part of that was to purify conservatism of what it had, unwittingly, absorbed from liberalism—an effort that primed conservatives for a historical account of how everything had gone off the rails.

It was that mood of "no compromise" that also explains the runaway success of Jonah Goldberg's *Liberal Fascism.* "I think a big part of *LF*'s success and influence," Goldberg stated, "stems from a burning desire, fueled in no small part with disaffection for Bush's compassionate conservatism and then really ignited by Obama, to 'punch back.' "[27] That deep, gut-level motivation merged with the suspicion that liberals were succeeding in American life—of which the Obama election was the most striking example—because, fundamentally, they cheated. In the context of our subject, the example of cheating was the increasingly widespread belief that liberals had used their power in the academy to rewrite history, blotting out their sins and highlighting those of conservatives. This created a built-in constituency for alternative histories. Goldberg contends:

> All of the stuff about Wilson has been completely erased from the popular histories. I'm a fairly well-read guy. No academic, but historically literate by American standards. I had no idea about some of that stuff. So it was compelling on the merits. But it was also seen as evidence in a larger indictment that liberals have been "hiding" a lot of stuff from us. I don't mean that in the paranoid sense. But when *Liberal Fascism* came out there was a boom in history books purporting to tell the history liberals don't want you to know, yada yada yada. And this was stuff a lot of smart, book-reading people simply didn't know.[28]

Pestritto, Goldberg, Kesler, and, from a different angle, Amity Shlaes all provided the supply that met the conservative movement's demand for a re-written account of American history. In that revisionist history, liberals were the malefactors—importing un-American foreign ideas, undermining liberty, destroying the capacity for self-governance, and establishing crony capitalism. That explained the rapturous conservative consumption of Shlaes's account of the New Deal as authoritarian and Calvin Coolidge as a hero, the West Coast Straussians' descriptions of Woodrow Wilson as a wily destroyer of constitu-tional government, and, ultimately, Jonah Goldberg's final accusation that lib-erals carried in their Progressive bloodstream the infection of fascism.[29]

The Claremont critique of Progressivism caught fire among Tea Partiers because the elite advisers to the Tea Party put it in front of the movement's activists. Matthew Spalding recalls:

> My book came out in 2009, and at Heritage we very consciously mar-keted it to all the Tea Party groups. I spoke at all the Tea Party conven-tions and traveled a lot. . . . [Heritage was a cosponsor of] several of the Tea Party conventions around the country. . . . We were offering to send somebody up there to speak to them, to be a keynote speaker, that kind of thing. It just naturally came together. I would go out, and I would make the argument about the founding, the Progressives, and the situa-tion we're in. It fit naturally.[30]

The argument that he placed before Tea Party conservatives provided the missing piece in the historical narrative of the movement's activists, hence its appeal: "When a lot of these groups started doing things and having get-togethers and eventually conventions and what not, they were themselves naturally going back to and wanting to revive a sense of constitutional limits of the founding. We didn't have to tell them all that. What we did do is actively encouraged our work, our papers, our books, and I expanded on that to add the Progressive critique." Tea Partiers already knew that authority rested in the past, in the founding. But what they lacked was a coherent account of how the decline had occurred, and how that tied in to the particular problems that they were reacting to. Spalding and his allies provided what was missing: "People picked up on it pretty easily, largely because, you have to remember, what is the thing they're mostly objecting to right at that time when you have the Tea Party? It was these things about finances and bailing people out and cronyism, as we call it nowadays, a general bureaucratic rule. The Progressive argument really helped explain that."[31]

In the aftermath of the seeming betrayal of Bush and the onslaught of Obama, conservatives were no longer content simply to stand athwart history, like William F. Buckley, and yell, "Stop." In a classic moment of fundamentalist reaction, they saw their urgent mission as turning history back. As Kesler observed in a Heritage report that drew on his book, "For all his openness to change, there is one to which Obama consistently answers, 'No, we can't.' Any change that would move the country backward, in his view, is anathema. . . . He may not be exactly sure where history is going, but somehow he knows it's not going *there*."[32] The Claremont critique made clear the vital necessity of "going there," returning back to founding principles and scraping off all the accumulated barnacles that decades of Progressivism had stuck to the ship of state. To justify that degree of reaction, they needed to revise the history that liberals had written. And that is why—in addition to the fact that the ideas were actively placed before them—the Tea Party so avidly consumed the Claremont revisionist history, in which Wilson was the pivotal figure and Progressivism the moment when America turned away from its founding heritage.

The Conservative Critique That the Tea Party Submerged

The line of argument that ends with Goldberg accusing liberalism of being a cousin of fascism frames the Progressives for discarding America's authentic Constitution and political morality. Stripped of an account of why Progressives took the positions they did—the actual political conflicts they were presented with, the governing challenges they sought to overcome— Progressivism becomes an abstracted diabolical force, a caricature that is easy to dismiss. But there is another tradition, also beginning with Strauss, that more acutely and even sympathetically understood the Progressives, one that criticized their less savory innovations as tragic, mistaken, and unfortunate. This critique was not aimed at the destruction of the activist state but at its reconstruction on different and more defensible terms. Ken Kersh has recovered some of this critique in his contribution to this volume. I do not repeat here what he wrote, but point instead to a few aspects of this submerged conservative tradition, which liberals should take more seriously.

While Strauss did not devote more than a small percentage of his written work to the study of America, his students did. What they learned from Strauss was the necessity of reconstructing political science so that it could serve its genuine purpose in a liberal democratic regime, namely, to be a sympathetic critic of liberalism and democracy and to head off the dangers embedded in both those principles. By contrast, the political science born in the Progressive era undermined the moral case for liberal democracy while—perversely—simultaneously removing the possibility of sympathetic critique. Strauss's thoughts on this position are worth quoting at some length.

> While the new political science becomes ever less able to see democracy or to hold a mirror to democracy, it ever more reflects the most dangerous proclivities of democracy. It even strengthens those proclivities. . . . By teaching the equality of all values, by denying that there are things which are intrinsically high and others which are intrinsically low, as well as by denying that there is an essential difference between men and brutes, it unwittingly contributes to the victory of the gutter.
>
> Yet this same new political science came into being through the revolt against what one may call the democratic orthodoxy of the immediate past. It had learned certain lessons which were hard for that orthodoxy to swallow regarding the irrationality of the masses and the necessity of elites; if it had been wise, it would have learned those lessons from the galaxy of antidemocratic thinkers of the remote past. It believed, in other words, it had learned that contrary to the belief of the orthodox democrats, no compelling case can be made for liberalism (for example, for the unqualified freedom of such speech as does not constitute a clear and present danger) nor for democracy (free elections based on universal suffrage). But it succeeded in reconciling those doubts with the unfaltering commitment to liberal democracy by the simple device of declaring that no value judgments, including those supporting liberal democracy, are rational, and hence that an iron-clad argument in favor of liberal democracy ought in reason not even to be expected. The very complex pros and cons regarding liberal democracy have thus become entirely obliterated by the poorest formalism.[33]

The purpose of a Straussian study of American politics, therefore, would be to attend to, in Thomas Pangle's terms, "the ennobling of democracy"[34]—to pointing to those elements in the regime that could keep it from heading into Strauss's gutter.

Strauss's students retained a consistent interest in reassessing the political science initiated in the Progressive era as well as a concern for reevaluating what they took to be a critical turning point in American governance. But before getting to the substance of their critique of Progressivism, it is necessary to observe how different it is in tone from the works that most directly influenced

Glenn Beck and, through him, the Tea Party. First and foremost, one finds in these earlier Straussian works a recognition of the dilemmas of governance that the Progressives faced. They had a clear grasp of the fact that Progressives were not dealing with a purely theoretical problem but with real challenges thrown up in the course of history by the pragmatics of governance. The Straussian Jeffrey Tulis, for instance, in explaining the choices made by Teddy Roosevelt in the debate over the regulation of railroads, observed:

> The belief that railroad companies formed the center of a vast conspiracy on the part of huge corporations was supported not only by the fact that it was often true, but also by the physical representation of the railroad system itself—a vast network of arteries connecting the nation's parts to each other. Business interconnections with railroad companies resembled the routes of the railways where complicated switching was visible to all who ventured to the next town. . . . As railroads extended their routes, they often encountered private property owners who were not inclined to sell their land. . . . In situations like these, the railroads asserted their rights of eminent domain and took over the land for modest compensation. The question of the "public interest" was thus made concrete and symbolically real as law equated the interests of these vast corporations with the good of the public.[35]

The problems that Progressive-era politicians dealt with created genuine dilemmas for governance and legitimate questions of the adequacy of the Founders' institutional arrangements. Tulis argued:

> Woodrow Wilson's critique of the original Constitution contains a number of insights that cannot be dismissed. The pursuit of "extensive and arduous enterprises" that the founders noted as a great benefit to derive from a unitary, energetic, executive may not have been possible for some projects in the twentieth century without popular leadership. The rhetorical presidency appears to be a reasonable extension of executive power to the extent that it is necessary to effect such constitutionally legitimate enterprises as the New Deal. Energy, the possibility of social change, and democratic legitimacy were insufficiently fulfilled promises of the original Constitution.[36]

Unlike those later conservative theorists who treated the Progressives as a kind of monolith, wholly opposed to the thought of the Founders, Tulis noted, "His [Teddy Roosevelt's] attempt to exercise extraordinary power moderately, and with constant warnings about its possible abuse, was his attempt to re-solve the perennial problem that faces any statesman or institutional theorist who wishes to provide for emergency power on the one hand, yet make it safe on the other."[37] The Progressives, in other words, were not a monolithic evil. The problems that they dealt with were "perennial," inherent in old problems and tensions of governance and brought into sharp relief by the industrializa-tion of the country.

These earlier Straussians recognized that Progressive-era politicians and theorists wrestled with very disturbing and disorienting challenges to Ameri-ca's political economy and inherited governing structures, and that they were compelled to pursue often dramatic innovations in order to cope with them. They understood, better than their successors, why the Progressives turned so strongly against reigning constitutional orthodoxies, even as they pointed to the serious problems the Progressive responses generated and to the patholo-gies that their theoretical innovations would produce.

The early Straussian analysts of American politics were especially eager to raise questions about the Progressive critique of the Constitution as an essen-tially "conservative" document inspired by class interests. As Kersch suggests, the best known of these analysts was Martin Diamond. While sharply critical of many Progressive ideas, Diamond also was sympathetic to the political con-ditions that gave rise to them: "Understandably outraged by late nineteenth-century scholarship and statesmanship that tended to convert the Constitution into a fixed and immutable code enshrining liberty of contract, reformers began to search about for feet of clay, to show that the framers were not disinterested demigods but men rigging a government to protect their own interests. Debunking the Founding Fathers would emancipate the present from the moral claim of the past and open the way for drastic reform."[38] Diamond accepted that the Progressives had very real motivations for their actions, but unnecessarily cast the Founders as enemies of reform. Diamond observed that the Federalists "sought free government, they sought competent government—not minimum government safely chained down, but govern-ment broadly empowered and competent to a broad range of tasks."[39] Reason-able, moderate reform was consistent with constitutional principles. To be sure, he detected in the Progressives a spirit that sought to reach beyond such reformism by dissolving constitutional obstacles to change and, with them, the historical character of the American people. But it did not follow from Progressive overreach that the Constitution blocked a responsive, problem-solving approach to government.[40]

Perhaps the most profound student of American politics produced by Strauss was Herbert Storing, who devoted much of his considerable intelligence to a sympathetic understanding of how to reconcile a modern welfare-regulatory state with constitutional norms. Like Diamond, Storing gave Progressives their due, noting, for instance, of Woodrow Wilson: "[His] project of administrative science and [the] practice that followed from it were indeed extensions of the founders' own project. In the most crucial sense, it can be said that, for the founders, the problem of government is a matter of administration."[41] Also like Diamond's critique of Progressivism, Storing's rested on a characterization of it as immoderate, not as altogether misled or nefarious: "Just as the popular principle became radicalized, so did the 'science' of government or administration become radicalized. The founders' maxims of administrative statesmanship became Woodrow Wilson's 'one rule of good administration for all governments alike,' which in turn became Frederick Taylor's 'one best method,' and that in turn became the 'maximizing' model (and all of its various elaborations and qualifications) of contemporary decision-making science."[42]

By trying to make administration into a science, and one somehow entirely consistent with a purely democratic populism, Progressives undercut what Storing thought could be bureaucracy's leavening impact on liberal democracy: "A properly schooled bureaucracy might, however, be a solidly based source of the intelligence, stability, equity, and public-spiritedness that a democracy needs."[43] Storing—like the more radical Straussian critics of Progressivism and modern liberalism today—tied some of the problems of liberal principles and governance to their roots in Progressive-era thinking. But he was fundamentally sympathetic to the actual challenges of contemporary governance and administration. Indeed, in a wonderful essay entitled "The Problem of Big Government," Storing reached a conclusion that contemporary Tea Party thought would never countenance. He contended that the bureaucracy needed to be empowered—not constrained—to counter the defects of democratic government: "The central government is much less 'out of reach,' but the bureaucracy does to a very considerable extent (and might to a much greater extent) exercise a steady pressure upon our political leaders to transcend passing desires and prejudices. . . . That it has not performed its 'senatorial' functions as well as it might is due in no small part to the thoughtless, irresponsible, and sometimes violent attacks to which it is so often subjected, even by those groups whose natural ally it is."[44]

Building on Diamond's and Storing's insights, Jeffrey Tulis pointed out that even as advocates of the "rhetorical presidency" (Wilson first and foremost) had strong arguments for their innovations, they also generated durable problems of constitutional governance: "Yet these systemic benefits have brought with them systemic costs, among them an increasing lack of 'fit' between institution and occupant, a greater mutability of policy, an erosion of the processes of deliberation, and a decay in political discourse."[45] In particular, Progressive innovations in theory and practice created a durable "crisis politics" that made the presidency simultaneously stronger and weaker: "The long-term consequence of the rhetorical presidency may be to make presidents less capable of leadership at any time. If crisis politics are now routine, we may be losing the ability as a people to distinguish genuine from spurious crises. Intended to ameliorate crises, the rhetorical presidency is now the creator of crises, or pseudo-crises."[46] This emphasis on crisis politics is a theme that was taken up by the later Straussian-influenced conservative thinkers, but without the appreciation for the very real crises that gave rise to it over the course of the twentieth century.

These earlier generations of Straussians were concerned with the problematic conclusions to which the Progressives had been driven by the regime crises they confronted. Faced with opponents who defended their privileges under the mask of the Constitution, Progressives wrongly sought to find an alternative to it rather than a return to its true principles—principles that could undergird a properly conservative, institutionalized welfare state. The early Straussians, sought, in a way, to refound the welfare state on different grounds. This is an altogether different position from that taken by contemporary Tea Party activists, who simply view the welfare state begun by the Progressives as without foundation and wholly contrary to the nation's principles.

In short, it is possible, from a conservative point of view, to appreciate why Progressives sought the break they did, while finding it tragic that they were pushed by the forces they faced to do so. Such recognition that the welfare-regulatory state was necessary but also ill founded is not a contention unique to conservatives or Straussians. It is voiced within liberalism itself. Left-leaning scholars like Ted Lowi articulated it as far back as the 1960s.[47] Instead of instinctively standing up for the Progressives against their more wild-eyed critics, contemporary liberals should, like Lowi, be open to rethinking some of the Progressive legacy rather than claiming it as heartily and simplistically as Tea Party activists oppose it. In a time when American governance is so vexed, when so much of our apparatus of activist government seems to be creaking, contradictory, and incapable of vindicating our goals of social justice, it may be time to return to this earlier criticism of Progressivism for insight on how to reconstitutionalize the welfare state, rather than defend or oppose it in the abstract.

Notes

1. "Glenn Beck: Progressives' Fight for American Hearts and Minds," Fox News, May 27, 2010, FoxNews.com, www.foxnews.com/story/2010/05/27/glenn-beck-progressives-fight-for-american-hearts-and-minds.

2. "Progressives Have 'Almost-Complete Plan' to 'Destroy Our Faith,'" *The Glenn Beck Program,* Premiere Radio Network, May 24, 2010.

3. Theda Skocpol and Vanessa Williamson, *The Tea Party and the Remaking of Republican Conservatism* (Oxford: Oxford University Press, 2012), 81.

4. Ronald J. Pestritto, interview by the author, October 11, 2013.

5. Ibid.

6. Ibid.

7. Ibid.

8. Charles Kesler, interview by the author, October 24, 2013.

9. Steven F. Hayward, "Hillary's Makeover: A Review of *Living History* by Hillary Rodham Clinton," *Claremont Review of Books* 3, no. 4 (Fall 2003), www.claremont.org/article/hillarys-makeover/#.VXXUOOfduDg.

10. Charles Kesler, "The Audacity of Barack Obama," *Wall Street Journal,* October 21, 2008.

11. John Marini, "Abandoning the Constitution," *Claremont Review of Books* 12, no. 2 (Spring 2012), www.claremont.org/article/abandoning-the-constitution/#.VXXRZufduDg.

12. James W. Ceaser, "Restoring the Constitution," *Claremont Review of Books* 12, no. 2 (Spring 2012), www.claremont.org/article/restoring-the-constitution/#.VXXTV-fduDg.

13. Ibid.

14. Charles R. Kesler, "The Crisis of Liberalism," *Claremont Review of Books* 12, no. 3 (Summer 2012), www.claremont.org/article/the-crisis-of-liberalism/#.VXXVi-fduDg.

15. Harry Jaffa, "American Conservatism and the Present Crisis," *Claremont Review of Books* 3, no. 2 (Spring 2003), www.claremont.org/article/american-conservatism-and-the-present-crisis/#.VXYK_mBYXww.

16. Jonah Goldberg, interview by the author, October 17, 2013.

17. Ronald J. Pestritto, interview by the author, October 13, 2013.

18. Matthew Spalding, interview by the author, July 2, 2014.

19. Jordan Smith, "The Most Influential Conservative Publication You've Never Heard Of," *Salon*, May 13, 2010, www.salon.com/2010/05/13/imprimis_influential_conservative_publication.

20. Charles R. Kesler, "Limited Government: Are the Good Times Really Over?," *Imprimis* 37, no. 3 (March 2008), 5, http://imprimisarchives.hillsdale.edu/file/archives/pdf/2008_03_Imprimis.pdf.

21. "Constitution 101: The Meaning of History and the Constitution," Hillsdale College, http://online.hillsdale.edu/course/con101/schedule.

22. Charles Kesler, interview by the author, October 21, 2013.

23. Pestritto interview, October 13, 2013.

24. On compassionate conservatism, see Steven Teles, "The Eternal Return of Compassionate Conservatism," *National Affairs* 1 (Fall 2009), www.nationalaffairs.com/publications/detail/the-eternal-return-of-compassionate-conservatism.

25. Kesler interview, October 21, 2013.

26. Goldberg interview.

27. Ibid.

28. Ibid.

29. Amity Shlaes, *The Forgotten Man: A New History of the Great Depression* (New York: Harper Perennial, 2008); Amity Shlaes, *Coolidge* (New York, Harper, 2013).

30. Spalding interview.

31. Ibid.

32. Charles R. Kesler, "Barack Obama and the Crisis of Liberalism," *First Principles* no. 45 (October 15, 2012), http://thf_media.s3.amazonaws.com/2012/pdf/fp45.pdf.

33. Leo Strauss, *Liberalism Ancient and Modern* (Chicago: University of Chicago Press, 1968), 222–23.

34. Thomas Pangle, *The Ennobling of Democracy: The Challenge of the Postmodern Age* (Baltimore: Johns Hopkins University Press, 1993).

35. Jeffrey Tulis, *The Rhetorical Presidency* (Princeton, N.J.: Princeton University Press, 1988), 103.

36. Ibid., 175.

37. Ibid., 114–15.

38. Martin Diamond, "Conservatives, Liberals, and the Constitution," in *As Far as Republican Principles Will Admit: Essays by Martin Diamond*, ed. William Schambra (Washington, D.C.: AEI, 1992), 70.

39. Ibid., 74.

40. A similar argument that liberals and socialists have antipolitical tendencies can be found in Bernard Crick, *In Defense of Politics* (Chicago: University of Chicago, 1992).

41. Herbert Storing, "American Statesmanship: Old and New," in *Toward a More Perfect Union: Writings of Herbert Storing*, ed. Joseph Bessette (Washington, D.C.: AEI, 1995), 412.

42. Ibid., 414.

43. Ibid.

44. Herbert Storing, "The Problem of Big Government," in Bessette, *More Perfect Union,* 302–3.

45. Tulis, *Rhetorical Presidency,* 176.

46. Ibid., 181.

47. Theodore Lowi, *The End of Liberalism* (New York: Norton, 2009).

21 • What Is to Be Done?

A New Progressivism for a New Century

Bruce Ackerman

As Hegel and Skowronek teach us, you should never underestimate the power of No. Over the course of world history, movements and leaders have repeatedly gained authority by successfully repudiating the status quo.

But getting to Yes is a different story—full of half measures and historical ironies. This is, at least, the fate of progressivism. Its greatest triumphs have served only to reveal grave weaknesses in its program to enable American citizens to reclaim control of their government. If the progressive project is to regain momentum, the movement must rethink its old formulae and come up with a new program for realizing the promise of democratic government in the twenty-first century.

It is true, of course, that contemporary progressives already have a lot on their plates right now. My call for a new progressive agenda might seem an intellectual luxury at a time when the great achievements of the twentieth century are under all-out attack by Tea Party activists throughout the country and by Supreme Court "originalists" in their Marble Palace. But it is not enough to say no to the likes of Antonin Scalia and Ted Cruz. We must confront the fundamental inadequacies of the old Progressive agenda and say yes to a new reform program that will permit a realistic response to the pathologies of the Second Gilded Age.

Progressive Aspirations

Begin from the beginning. The Democratic Party of Andrew Jackson said no to the system of elite rule inherited from the Founding—generating a party system that poured new life into the project of popular self-rule for generations. By the close of the nineteenth century, however, Jacksonian democracy had degenerated into a system of boss rule, breeding massive cynicism about the very idea of government by the People.

This was, at least, how the Progressives saw it. They called for the root-and-branch destruction of the old regime, clearing the ground for a revitalized citizenry to take the public interest seriously.

This big no motivated some big yeses. The Progressives sought to make the ballot box safe for democracy by adopting the Australian ballot and by purging ignorant blacks and immigrants from the registration lists. They then tried to provide those whom they considered serious citizens with the tools they needed to keep the bosses in line—or even better, to replace bosses with reform leaders—by substituting party primaries for nominating conventions.

Even if party bosses managed to deflect challenges in the primaries, the Progressives would deny them a free hand to make shady deals with powerful economic interests. Campaign finance laws would ban corporate payoffs and control big-money contributions. No less importantly, citizens would be given direct powers to intervene in government through devices like the initiative, referendum, and recall.

Progressives also contended that politicos should share power with a burgeoning class of experts, who could set out fact-based solutions to real-world problems. These civil servants would displace patronage appointments at the operational core of government—providing a long-term view of the problems confronting the state and the nation.

Putting all these institutional mechanisms to one side, the larger challenge was to develop a new breed of politicians who would set their sights beyond party patronage and elaborate a politics of principle worthy of a democratic citizenry.

The ongoing communications revolution was to serve as critical catalyst for this larger transformation. Throughout the nineteenth century, the party press was a dominant force—Democratic and Republican newspapers engaged in unending partisan battle. But the rise of advertising broke the parties' stranglehold on newspapers—enabling muckraking journalists to expose the scandalous ways in which both Democratic and Republican bosses had joined with big business to undermine the public good. Moving beyond critique, reform candidates could use the newly independent press as a platform for calling on voters to join their campaigns against the political machine.

Looking beyond particular pathologies, the Progressives took aim at the Founders' vision. They went to Washington, D.C., with a new constitutional program.

Let's face it: for all their talk of the evils of "faction," Madison & Company didn't anticipate the pervasive way that boss rule would transform the House and Senate into representatives of local machines; nor could they have guessed how the Supreme Court could be readily captured by corporate interests. As the Progressives saw it, America's best hope was to revitalize the presidency. The White House should be transformed into a platform for the spokesman for the people, calling upon Congress and the Court to heed the "popular mandate" for Progressive change.

This wouldn't be easy, given Andrew Johnson's success in discrediting presidential leadership during Reconstruction. To be sure, Grover Cleveland and his fellow Democrats managed to repeal the Tenure of Offices Act and other unhappy reminders of Republican domination. But this ground-clearing operation was not nearly enough to revolutionize the system of congressional government described by the budding political scientist Woodrow Wilson. Indeed, the path to a Progressive presidency seemed blocked—until Leon Czolgosz's assassination of William McKinley opened the White House to Teddy Roosevelt, a political trouble-maker banished by New York Republicans to the powerless vice presidency in 1900.

Without Czolgosz's bullet, the chances of TR's becoming president were slim. If he had merely arrived at the 1904 convention as a sitting vice president, he would have had a tough time beating a more establishment figure—say, Elihu Root. And if he hadn't gotten the chance to win the 1904 election in his own right, he would have been in no position to lead a third-party movement in 1912—which split the Republican coalition and enabled Woodrow Wilson to win the presidency with 42 percent of the national vote.[1]

But facts are facts: with McKinley out of the way, TR's macho performance rid the presidency of the ghost of Andrew Johnson, and Woodrow Wilson followed up by putting his academic convictions into political practice. Defying the founding precedent set by Jefferson, Wilson personally delivered the State of the Union address to Congress, providing newspapers with a dramatic announcement of his reform vision; and building on TR's experiments, he established regular press conferences to rally voters to provide him with a popular mandate that would override congressional resistance to the public good.

To be sure, the bravura performances of the Progressive presidents culminated in the shattering defeat of Wilson's leadership when the Senate refused to ratify his Versailles Treaty. Nevertheless, their very real achievements set the stage for FDR's consolidation of the Progressive vision of the presidency—which continues to dominate modern political life.

There were many more triumphs to come. The Progressive ideal of professional journalism gained headway in the aftermath of the New Deal as local newspaper magnates used some of their monopoly profits to sponsor investigative reporting. While performance fell short of reality, the local and national news bureaus gave fact-based reporting sufficient credibility to serve as the reigning model for the next new great challenge. As television news came of age at midcentury, both the FCC and the three major networks embraced the ideal of "professional journalism," insisting on "fairness" as TV news came to dominate the general public's understanding of current events. Once again, there is no need to glorify the Age of Cronkite or the evolving system of presidential debates in order to recognize that the media revolution gave renewed support to a view of the presidency as engaged in a principled conversation with the American people over the nation's future.

The presidency's claim to have a "popular mandate" was further enhanced by the transformation of the nominating system after the fiasco of the 1968 Democratic Convention in Mayor Daley's Chicago. Until then, Progressive primary contests had played a secondary role in candidate selection—when push came to shove, it was up to local and state potentates to make the final decisions about their party's presidential choices in the proverbial "smoke-filled rooms." In this final gutting of the convention system, Progressivism all but cleared the field.

Emerging Pathologies and Prospects

An inspiring history—but based on a false premise: a century onward, it has become perfectly clear the Progressives were wrong in supposing that once liberated from boss rule and machine politics, ordinary Americans would overwhelmingly commit themselves to a serious engagement with national citizenship.

This hasn't happened. While political junkies may account for 10 percent of the population, knowledgeable engagement trails off dramatically after that, and overwhelming apathy and ignorance prevails in the bottom (and poorer) half. Worse yet, the Progressives' old nemesis, the Supreme Court, has destroyed the campaign finance restrictions that tried to keep big money from exploiting the situation.

As a consequence, the primary system often makes a mockery of progressive ideals. Long before voters make their choices, candidates compete in the money primary to establish their credibility—if they can't raise big bucks, they never get to the starting line. When the primary season starts, big money candidates, aided by cynical pollsters, use their dollars to bombard a passive public with hot-button issues that might jolt them out of their apathy enough to join the ridiculously small proportion of Americans who vote on primary day.

The result is a parody of Progressive hopes: instead of a mighty army of informed citizens taking on the machine in the primaries, we may see a scattering of poorly informed voters turning out in response to big-money propaganda operations.

To counter this grim prospect, citizen-activists might launch grassroots campaigns, which, with the help of ideological-driven plutocrats on the right or the left, use social media to mobilize their followers to defeat well-organized corporate interests. This looks more progressive, but the low turnout can make the old dream into a modern nightmare—enabling a relatively small percentage of activists to select major-party candidates while most Americans sleep through the primaries.

When the broader electorate awakes from its slumber in the fall, it could be confronted with two extremists running for the presidency. This dilemma could force voters to make a polarizing choice leading to right or left lurches that might be even less attractive than the plutocratic rent seeking that prevails when the money primary is the ruling force.

Progressive hopes for direct democracy have met a similar fate. Citizenship ignorance and apathy are, once again, at the root of the problem, though even ideal progressive citizens would have trouble mastering the multiplicity of referendum issues they confront in California or Oregon. Once again, the void is too often filled by big-money media blitzes that mislead the passive public about the true meaning of the initiatives placed on the ballot.

The larger process of misinformation is exacerbated by the decline of serious journalism that takes objectivity as a worthy ideal (however much it might be compromised in practice). The flood of fact-free opinionating on the Internet only adds to the confusion of the average American, who has better things to do with his time than piece together sensible opinions from the ongoing cacophony. In this setting, "citizen initiatives" to put a "reform" on the ballot may serve only to consolidate the hold of the well-organized interests that the Progressives hoped to dislodge.

And then there is the presidency. Beginning in 1972, the convention became a rubber stamp for the candidates who came out ahead in state primaries and caucuses—which increasingly became the intense object of manipulation by complex combinations of big money and ideological interest groups.

Even in today's degraded environment, the Progressive vision of the presidency has provided Americans with a certain focus for their political concerns. However distorted the nomination process, however noncognitive the media blitz, most Americans gain a vague sense of the stakes raised by the major-party candidates and make a bigger effort to get to the polls when the presidency is up for grabs. Their increased involvement sets the stage for the triumphant candidate to use the White House as a platform for claiming a "mandate from the People" for his political program.

Yet this progressive victory has come at a heavy price. Now that presidents have transformed themselves into voices of the People, they have increasingly used this authority to act unilaterally to execute the national will—especially when the House or Senate is controlled by the opposing party.

From Roosevelt's mass incarceration of Japanese Americans to Bush's abuses at Guantanamo, the most notorious cases have arisen during wartime emergencies. These (in)famous power grabs introduce a more pervasive, larger problem. As I explain in *The Decline and Fall of the American Republic*,[2] the past generation has seen the rise of an elite corps of presidential lawyers determined to expand the unilateral powers of the presidency by latitudinarian "interpretations" of existing law. Once the White House counsel or Office of Legal Counsel provides the president with a fig leaf of legality for his unilateral initiatives, it is tough for Congress to strike back.

Particular acts of presidential self-aggrandizement may seem problematic or egregious to the small group of lawyers and academics who follow such matters. But these power grabs rarely generate enough heated political controversy to make it plausible for opponents to threaten impeachment or massive funding cutoffs. When congressional barons attempt more modest legislative countermeasures, the president's legal establishment can often generate enough fog to permit his defenders to block effective legislative response at one veto point or another. Once a particular presidential initiative withstands congressional counterattack, the next group of executive-branch lawyers will use it as a precedent in their next round of "interpretations" that further expand the scope of unilateral presidential authority.

This ongoing dynamic governs not only fields like foreign policy and national security, which have long been arenas of privileged presidential action. It has also served as the principal engine for increasing White House domination of domestic policy making over the last generation. Through a series of executive orders beginning during the Carter and Reagan years, a highly politicized group of White House lawyers and economists have successfully wrested ultimate control over agency rule making from the Cabinet departments. This centralization of power has never gained express statutory approval—but it is now a central reality of the modern regulatory state.

And what is wrong with that? Isn't direct control by the White House much better than the old system in which congressional barons, special interests, and executive agencies formed "iron triangles" that shielded their parochial policy making and lawmaking from outside challenge? At least technocrats appointed by the president take the national (and international) interest much more seriously in determining the shape of policy and legal development. What is more, they are in a far better position to sustain their influence now that presidents have increasingly colonized the higher reaches of each department with political loyalists who defend White House priorities.

Sure, the evolving system falls far short of perfection, but that is generally true of life. The key question is whether it represents an advance over the iron triangle, and its pathologies, which Woodrow Wilson described with such prescience 125 years ago in *Congressional Government*. Whatever presidentialism's failures, the answer is an easy yes.

This is, at least, the worldly reassurance provided by the voice of Progressivism past—and it may well prove sound over the course of the next century. There are caveats, of course. As we look ahead, it is obvious that the ongoing shift in regulatory authority won't eliminate the role of big money. It will simply lead Beltway lobbyists to lavish greater attention on the burgeoning White House technocracy. Similarly, future presidents will be intensely concerned with short-term partisan advantage as well as the long-term public interest. Nevertheless, the transformation may look like a plus: over the long haul, won't the White House take the broader national and international interest more seriously than the iron triangles centered in Congress?

But future prospects darken once the implications of another Progressive reform are factored into the equation. As we have seen, the rise of the primary system makes it far easier for extremist groups to commandeer the presidential nomination process. When the party conventions were controlled by state bosses, they were relatively immune from ideology, but very alive to the need to pick a candidate who would successfully appeal to the median voter on Election Day. If state politicos made a bad choice, they would lose all that juicy federal patronage, and they might also get hurt in state and city elections, which were their central concern.

In contrast, while the current Progressive primary system may have abolished the smoke-filled room, it no longer guarantees a centrist choice.

Movement activists may well succeed in getting the party to nominate a presidential candidate who will present a "choice, not an echo" to the American people—even if their ideological choice loses in the short run, the nationwide campaign may strongly advance their great cause by giving it greater respectability over the longer run.

Moreover, an extremist candidate may not even lose in the short run—election results depend on economics no less than ideology, and the super-ideologue may get a boost from the latest blip in the gross domestic product. Or ideological dynamics might sweep both parties at the same time—generating a choice between a strong righty and a strong lefty in November, with centrists failing to come up with a credible third-party option.

It is only a matter of time before an extremist gets into the White House—and this essay is trying to take the long view. In this scenario, the increasing centralization of domestic regulation as well as foreign and national security policy takes on a sinister aspect. The danger escalates further once the highly politicized legal staffs at the White House counsel and Office of Legal Counsel come into view. As their president leads the nation into an inspiring adventure, they will be under intense pressure to intensify their legal rubber-stamping activities on behalf of the nation's greatest president since George Washington/Abraham Lincoln/Franklin Roosevelt/Ronald Reagan—who is leading the nation onward and upward.

As the rule of law dissolves in the executive branch, and congressional veto points prevent a coherent response, it is unlikely that the Supreme Court will serve as the last bastion of checks and balances. Most obviously, it may take a good deal of time before a case can get on the justices' docket—during which the plebiscitarian presidency can take aggressive action to change the facts on the ground in ways that the Court will find it tough to undo. No less important, the modern system of appointment generates jurists inclined to defer to presidential power.

During most of American history, Supreme Court nominees were legal notables with deep roots in one or another of the judicial circuits into which the federal courts have been divided since the Founding. When a sitting justice, say, from the Fourth Circuit retired from the bench, he was typically replaced by a notable lawyer or judge who gained the support of the region's senators. But over the course of the twentieth century, and especially since the Reagan years, a more nation-centered pattern has emerged: recent Supreme Court justices first stake their claim by taking a leadership position in the Justice Department or the White House in one or another administration; they are then rewarded with an appointment to the federal courts of appeal, where they retain sufficient links with the dominant legal network to win the president's approval when a Supreme Court vacancy opens up. Since their executive-branch service played a key role in their ultimate rise to preeminence, they will tend to bring to the Court a vivid sense of the importance of presidential prerogative within the constitutional order—even when they disagree profoundly on many other matters.

It is possible, of course, that five justices will rise to the occasion if confronted with a sufficiently egregious act of presidential unilateralism. But even if so inclined, they will then be obliged to confront the formidable powers and propaganda machine deployed by a runaway presidency. Will they really be in a position to sustain their judicial authority in a head-on conflict?

Many courts in countries that have adopted the American model have already confronted this question—and the results haven't been pretty. Reflecting on the past two centuries, Juan Linz famously urged future constitutional designers to build their systems along parliamentary, not presidential, lines. But given the presidency's grip on the American political imagination, such a sweeping reappraisal isn't going to happen any time soon. At the very least, my dark scenario should haunt the Progressive imagination: we are talking about a dynamic that would make George W. Bush's abusive responses to September 11th seem tame by comparison. Recall that Bush ran as a "compassionate conservative" in 2000, competing with his fellow centrist Al Gore for the support of the median voter. My scenario, in contrast, supposes that an unapologetic ideologue wins the White House and from day one exploits and creates "emergencies" as he vindicates his "mandate from the people" with sweeping unilateral initiatives endowed with the appearance of legality by elaborate memoranda supplied by White House lawyers.

With Congress at an impasse, and the Court on the sidelines, the civilian and military bureaucracies impose the president's vision of a brave new world on a confused citizenry.

This isn't quite what Woodrow Wilson had in mind.

Mismatch

Enough crystal-ball gazing.

I am no prophet: America has been lucky before; it may get lucky again and avoid falling off the presidentialist precipice. In any event, my nightmare scenario has the merit of emphasizing a key point: the mismatch between the

Progressive hopes for citizenship and the Progressive program for institutional reform. At earlier moments in American history, their experiments in grassroots democracy and presidential leadership might well have seemed promising vehicles for a renewal of popular sovereignty. But as we confront the Progressive constitutional legacy in today's America, its real-world operation threatens to betray these great promises: some reforms have become increasingly counterproductive—as in the case of initiative, referendum, and recall; others seem downright dangerous—as in the case of the plebiscitarian presidency. As we look forward, early-twentieth-century Progressives seem to have been naive in supposing that a mobilized citizenry would spontaneously emerge from the ashes of Jacksonian democracy.

The challenge is to confront this mismatch and to redesign the institutions of progressive democracy to harmonize with the capacities and interests of real-world citizens. My new reform agenda addresses this mismatch point by point in an effort to redeem Progressivism's promise for the twenty-first century.

Progressive Citizenship for the Twenty-First Century

Begin on an optimistic note: Americans of the twenty-first century are much better equipped for citizenship than their counterparts were at the dawning of the Progressive era. About 10 percent of young Americans graduated high school in 1910; it was almost 80 percent a century later.[3] The length of the workweek has also declined (except for the workaholics at the top), as has the proportion of people engaged in backbreaking labor. Life in the twenty-first century is no picnic; but large numbers of Americans have the time and training needed to increase their practical commitment to citizenship if they are offered suitable opportunities for constructive contribution.

Start with the problem of big money. To reform the system, we need something new: give every voter a special credit account containing $50 that they can spend only on federal election campaigns. Armed with their cards, voters could go to a secure Fair Election website and send their "patriot dollars" to favored candidates and political organizations. About 130 million Americans went to the polls in 2012. If they also had a chance to vote with their dollars, they would have injected about $6.5 billion federally funded patriot dollars into the campaign—greatly diluting the power of the private $5+ billion spent by all federal candidates and their nominally "independent" campaign supporters during the last electoral cycle.[4]

My colleague Ian Ayres and I work out the details at book length in *Voting with Dollars* (2004).[5] Over the past decade, Supreme Court decisions on campaign finance have enhanced the case for our initiative. In contrast to traditional Progressive efforts to suppress big money, patriot dollars increase the overall funding available for speech; big donors could keep on giving, but the statute would increase the $50 citizen grants over time to guarantee that two-thirds of all funding came from patriotic sources. Since the program relies entirely on each patriotic citizen's decisions, it also avoids standard First Amendment challenges that have led the Court to sweep away top-down forms of command-and-control regulation.

Even more important, such patriotic finance would invigorate the practice of ordinary citizenship. Once voters have fifty patriot dollars in their pockets, candidates will have a powerful incentive to reach out to them as they launch their campaigns. Fund-raising would become a community-building affair—a box lunch for two hundred could gross $10,000!

These outreach efforts will provoke ordinary Americans to take their citizenship seriously as they engage one another in hundreds of millions of day-to-day conversations: Who should get the money? Who is a charlatan, and who is really concerned about the country?

Patriot dollars have many merits, but one great limitation. Once citizens go to a secure website to beam their patriot money onward, the candidates will continue to spend most of the cash on sound-bite appeals for hot-button issues. Patriotic finance will redistribute the sound bites, emphasizing themes with greater resonance for ordinary citizens. But we will still be living in a sound-bite democracy, and this isn't good enough.

The next challenge is to provide citizens with the tools they need to engage in thoughtful political discussion. An exemplary model is the American jury. Twelve people begin in total ignorance, but they learn a great deal during the course of the trial. After hearing competing arguments, and reasoning together, they regularly—though not invariably—come up with sensible conclusions.

The task is to design a similar format for politics. My friend Jim Fishkin and I have come up with a practical proposal based on a new technique, deliberative polling, which Fishkin has field-tested in seventy-five settings throughout the world—from Australia to Bulgaria, China to the E.U., Athens to Philadelphia.

Each poll invites a few hundred citizens to spend a weekend deliberating on a major public policy issue. Before they arrive, participants respond to a standard questionnaire that explores their knowledge about, and positions on, the problem. They then answer the same questionnaire after completing their deliberations.

Comparing these before-and-after responses, Fishkin and his fellow social scientists have rigorously established that participants greatly increase their understanding of the issues and often change their minds concerning the best course of action. Ten-percentage-point swings are common. No less important, participants leave with a more confident sense of their capacities as citizens.

These experiments suggest a new way of thinking about democratic reform. In our book *Deliberation Day*,[6] Fishkin and I urge the creation of a new national holiday to be held two weeks before critical national elections. Ordinary business would come to a halt, and citizens would gather at neighborhood centers to discuss the central issues raised by the leading candidates. Nobody would be forced to attend, but as with jury service, participants should be paid a stipend for their day's work of citizenship. Deliberation Day (DDay) would begin with a televised debate between the candidates, but citizens would then continue the discussion in small groups of fifteen, and later in larger plenary assemblies.

The small groups begin where the televised debate leaves off. Participants engage in an hour's conversation that tries to define questions that the candidates left unanswered. Everybody then proceeds to a 500-citizen assembly to hear their questions answered by local representatives of the major candidates. After lunch, participants repeat the morning procedure. By the end of the day, citizens will have moved beyond the top-down television debate that kicked off the proceedings. They will achieve a bottom-up understanding of the choices confronting the nation. Discussions begun on DDay will continue during the run-up to Election Day. While many Americans may have skipped DDay, their casual conversations with DDay participants will draw them into the escalating national dialogue.

If Deliberation Day succeeds, sound-bite democracy will play a much-reduced role in campaigns. Candidates would have powerful incentives to create longer and more substantive infomercials. Newscasts would be full of exit polls determining the extent to which DDay discussions had changed voting preferences—framing the intensifying debate that culminates on Election Day.

Our book works out the proposal for DDay in detail. But it is more important to see how, together with patriotic finance, it begins to add up to a new progressive agenda for engaged citizenship. From the very beginning of the campaign, candidates will reach out to ordinary Americans with great vigor— if only to pick their pockets and get at patriot dollars. As citizens begin "to vote with their dollars," Deliberation Day will loom on the horizon. Candidates will no longer spend most of their money on thirty-second sound bites. They will beam longer infomercials to enable partisans to state their case intelligently on DDay. By the time Election Day arrives, voters will go to the polls with a far better sense of the choices confronting the nation, as well as the nature of the competing solutions proposed by the candidates.

The progressive promise of DDay can be further enhanced by an ongoing effort to shape the Internet as a force for citizenship deliberation. The blogo-sphere is destroying professional journalism. The speed of this transforma-tion is extraordinary. In the United States, the overall number of newspaper reporters and broadcast news analysts dropped from 66,000 in 2000 to 52,000 in 2009, including devastating cuts in the Washington press corps.[7] This is only the beginning. The very existence of journalism is at stake.

Blogging cannot be expected to take up the slack. First-class reporting isn't for amateurs. It requires extensive training, and plenty of contacts, and large expenses. It also requires reporters to have a well-honed capacity to write for a broad audience—something that eludes the overwhelming majority of think-tank policy wonks, not to mention academic specialists. And it requires edi-tors who recognize the need to maintain their organization's long-term credibility when presenting the hot-button news of the day. The modern news-paper created the right incentives for high-quality reporting, but without a comparable business model for the Net, blogging will degenerate into a postmodern nightmare—with millions spouting off without any concern for the facts.

Enter the Internet news voucher. Under my proposal, Internet users click a box whenever they read a news article that they think helps them understand their political choices. These reader "votes" are then transmitted to a National Endowment for Journalism, which would compensate the news organization originating the article, according to a strict mathematical formula: the more clicks, the bigger the check from the endowment.

As a safeguard against fraud, each reader would have to convince the en-dowment that she is a real person, not merely a computer program designed to inflate an article's popularity. Before she can click in support, she will have to spend a few seconds typing in some random words or syllables. Though the time spent typing may seem trivial, it will help discriminate between the cynics and the citizens. After all, the reader won't receive any private reward for "wasting" her time, day after day, clicking her approval of articles deserving public support. She will participate only if, as a good citizen, she is willing to devote a few moments to the larger project of creating a vibrant public dialogue.[8]

The resulting system will bear a family resemblance to voting with dollars and Deliberation Day. The National Endowment would set up a voucher system that, like patriot dollars, permits the decentralized show of support by concerned citizens. Like Deliberation Day, it engineers a credible microcontext for the responsible exercise of citizenship—but this time on a day-to-day basis.

No need to exaggerate. I am not asking modern Americans to don their togas and prance about some mythic version of Periclean Athens. I am asking them simply to spend a minute or two clicking in support of newspapers and candidates, and take a biannual holiday trip to their local community center to talk with their neighbors about the choices facing the country. These small but repeated acts of citizenship won't prevent Americans from building a fulfilling personal life—which is the key, so far as they are concerned, to the pursuit of happiness. But it will permit them to move beyond Progressive dreams and build, step-by-step, a practice of citizen engagement worthy of a democratic republic.

Institutional Remedies

But this is only the first step in our reassessment of the Progressive legacy, which also bequeathed a distinctive set of institutions for channeling citizenship into final outcomes.

Begin with the primary system—which, as we have seen, has gravely disappointed Progressives' hopes. To some extent, the new citizenship agenda will temper existing pathologies: as Americans get in the habit of voting with their dollars, supporting Internet journalism, and participating in Deliberation Days, they will increasingly spend the half hour it takes to cast a ballot in a party primary and thereby help block the existing path to extremist or plutocratic presidencies, which depend on low turnouts by ordinary voters.

But what if an increase in citizenship engagement serves only to convince many ordinary Americans to endorse one or another extremist message—leading tens of millions to join the campaign to destroy big government or save the environment or establish economic justice or . . . If this happened, wouldn't my institutional "cures" only exacerbate the populist "disease"—propelling presidencies forward in extremist directions?

This objection misunderstands my progressive anxieties. My argument does *not* oppose any and all efforts at presidential leadership aimed at sweeping transformations of the status quo. It focuses instead on a potential abuse of the Progressive vision in which a *relatively small* left- or right-wing group manages to exploit the primary system to gain control of the presidency *without* a broad-based showing of support. If, in contrast, a popular movement for small government or economic justice uses its enhanced citizenship tools to persuade an engaged majority of their fellow Republicans or Democrats to endorse its vision of a good society, they have *earned* the right to nominate a candidate who would offer the general electorate a "choice, not an echo" in November. This is what government "of the people, by the people, and for the people" is all about.

Nevertheless, even if such a movement-party-presidency emerges victorious at the polls, our constitutional separation of powers establishes limits, at least in principle, on the president's powers to act unilaterally and impose his vision on the rest of us. As I argue in my *We the People* trilogy, only if a president and his party manage to sustain their initial victory over a series of elections does our constitutional system award their rising political coalition the legitimate authority to transform fundamental commitments in the name of We the People.[9]

From this perspective, the increasing tendency of the presidency to engage in sweeping unilateral action is a very serious source of concern—allowing the chief executive to short-circuit the separation of powers and impose a new constitutional vision without allowing his opponents to urge the electorate to reject his initiatives by voting against them in the following congressional and presidential contests.

To counter this danger, constitutional reformers should supplement the traditional separation-of-powers system by creating a new checks-and-balances system within the executive branch. I provide the details in my *Decline and Fall of the American Republic*,[10] so only the briefest sketch is necessary here. Under my reform, presidents could no longer expect their White House lawyers to rubber-stamp their unilateral initiatives without serious and independent judicial scrutiny. Instead, whenever lawyers representing the House or the Senate believe that the president has exceeded his legal authority, they could mount a challenge before a newly created panel of independent judges established within the executive branch.

The Independent Executive Tribunal would be required by statute to reach a prompt judgment on these complaints after hearing White House lawyers' considered response to the congressional challenge. If the tribunal upheld Congress's view, it could not absolutely forbid the president from continuing his initiative—but it could suspend its operation unless and until the White House publicly declared that it was imperative to repudiate the tribunal's defense of the rule of law. But sitting presidents would take such a drastic action under only the most extraordinary circumstances—and even then, the tribunal's declaration of illegality would put Congress, and the larger public, on notice. Would they really be willing to give a green light to the president's claim that some grave national "emergency" justified his break from ordinary legal restraint?

The Independent Executive Tribunal, Deliberation Day, Internet vouchers, patriot dollars—I could add more to this list,[11] but it is better for you to join the effort and add or subtract on your own. The key point: it is time for progressives to move beyond the innovations that their predecessors have successfully entrenched in the living Constitution. Without renewed critique and reconstruction, it is all too likely that these earlier achievements will degenerate into farce or tragedy. Like it or not, we face the very same issue posed by Alexander Hamilton in *Federalist* 1: "It seems to have been reserved to the people of this country, by their conduct and example, to decide the important question, whether societies of men are really capable or not of establishing good government from reflection and choice, or whether they are forever destined to depend for their political constitutions on accident and force."

Will we prove equal to the challenge?

Notes

1. For further reflections on the role of the assassin's bullet in American constitutional development, see Bruce Ackerman, *We the People: The Civil Rights Revolution* (Cambridge, Mass.: Harvard University Press, 2014), 57–62, 79–80.

2. See Bruce Ackerman, *The Decline and Fall of the American Republic* (Cambridge, Mass.: Harvard University Press, 2010), 87–116.

3. Compare Larry Cuban, "Back to the Future," National Education Policy Center, February 18, 2013, http://nepc.colorado.edu/blog/back-future-high-school-graduation-rates, with *Education Week*, "The Nation's Long and Winding Path to Graduation" (chart), www.edweek.org/media/34gradrate-c1.pdf.

4. Blair Bowie and Adam Lioz, *Billion-Dollar Democracy* (Washington D.C.: Demos / U.S. PIRG, 2012), 3.

5. Bruce Ackerman and Ian Ayres, *Voting with Dollars* (New Haven, Conn.: Yale University Press, 2002). Larry Lessig has done a great job of popularizing a similar proposal in his *Republic, Lost: How Money Corrupts Congress—and a Plan to Stop It* (New York: Twelve, 2011).

6. Bruce Ackerman and James Fishkin, *Deliberation Day* (New Haven, Conn.: Yale University Press, 2004).

7. Compare Bureau of Labor Statistics data for 2000 ("2000 National Occupational Employment and Wage Estimates"), www.bls.gov/oes/2000/oes273020.htm, with data for 2009 ("Occupational Employment and Wages, May 2009"), www.bls .gov/oes/2009/may/oes273021.htm, and 2014 ("Occupational Employment and Wages, May 2014"), www.bls.gov/oes/current/oes273022.htm.

8. The initial idea for this proposal emerged from a particularly engaging lunch with Ian Ayres; see Bruce Ackerman and Ian Ayres, "A National Endowment for Journalism," *Guardian*, February 13, 2009, www.theguardian.com/commentisfree/ cifamerica/2009/feb/12/newspapers-investigative-journalism-endowments. I elaborate further at Ackerman, *Decline and Fall*, 131–35, and Ackerman, "One Click Away: The Case for the Internet News Voucher," in *Will the Last Reporter Please Turn Out the Lights: The Collapse of Journalism and What Can Be Done to Fix It,* ed. Robert McChesney and Victor Pickard (New York: New Press, 2011), 299–306.

9. See generally my *We the People* series, particularly *We the People: Foundations* (Cambridge, Mass.: Harvard University Press, 1991), 266–322.

10. See Ackerman, *Decline and Fall*, 143–52.

11. See my proposed adaptation of the referendum for purposes of revising the Constitution, in Ackerman, *We the People: Transformations*, 410–16; and the plan that Anne Alstott and I presented to provide an inheritance of $80,000 as a birthright of every American citizen; Ackerman and Alstott, *The Stakeholder Society* (New Haven, Conn.: Yale University Press, 1998).

Contributors

Bruce Ackerman is Sterling Professor of Law and Political Science at Yale University, and the author of eighteen books that have had a broad influence in political philosophy, constitutional law, and public policy, including his multivolume constitutional history, *We the People* (Harvard, 1991, 1998, 2014). His scholarship examines the theory and practice of political liberalism, both at home and abroad, and their implications for constitutional development.

Sonu Bedi is associate professor of government at Dartmouth College. He is the author of *Rejecting Rights* (Cambridge, 2009) and *Beyond Race, Sex, and Sexual Orientation: Legal Equality Without Identity* (Cambridge, 2013). His research interests are contemporary political theory, constitutional law and theory, and race, law, and identity.

Daniel Carpenter is Allie S. Freed Professor of Government and director of social sciences at the Radcliffe Institute for Advanced Study at Harvard University. His scholarship mixes theoretical, historical, statistical, and mathematical analyses in order to examine the development of political institutions, particularly public bureaucracies and the regulation of health and financial products in the United States. He is author of *The Forging of Bureaucratic Autonomy: Regulations, Networks, and Policy Innovation in Executive Agencies, 1862–1928* (Princeton, 2001) and *Reputation and Power: Organizational Image and Pharmaceutical Regulation at the FDA* (Princeton, 2010).

John Milton Cooper is the E. Gordon Fox Professor of American Institutions, emeritus, at the University of Wisconsin–Madison. His scholarship focuses on late-nineteenth- and early-twentieth-century U.S. political history, with emphasis on the South. In particular, his work has offered new understandings of the Progressive era and insight into the presidencies of Theodore Roosevelt and Woodrow Wilson. He is author of, among other books, *The Warrior and the Priest: Woodrow Wilson and Theodore Roosevelt* (Harvard, 1983), *Breaking the Heart of the World: Woodrow Wilson* *and the Fight for the League of Nations* (Cambridge, 2001), and *Woodrow Wilson: A Biography* (Knopf, 2009).

Eldon Eisenach is professor emeritus of political science at the University of Tulsa. He studies American political development and political thought, and has written extensively on Progressive political thought and American liberalism. He is author of *The Lost Promise of Progressivism* (Kansas, 1994), which explores how constitutional law, courts, and political parties resisted the Progressive political ideas that became dominant in nearly every other American political and cultural venue, and he is editor of the collection *The Social and Political Thought of American Progressivism* (Hackett, 2006), which illustrates the origins, ambition, and legacy of a movement he dates as beginning as early as the mid–nineteenth century.

Stephen M. Engel is associate professor and chair of politics at Bates College and an affiliated scholar of the American Bar Foundation. His research is in the areas of American constitutional law, American political development, and LGBTQ political mobilization. He is author of *The Unfinished Revolution: Social Movement Theory and the Gay and Lesbian Movement* (Cambridge, 2001), *American Politicians Confront the Court* (Cambridge, 2011), and, most recently, *Fragmented Citizens: The Changing Landscape of Gay and Lesbian Lives* (NYU, 2016).

Richard A. Epstein is Laurence A. Tisch Professor of Law at New York University School of Law, the Peter and Kirsten Bedford Senior Fellow at the Hoover Institution, and the James Parker Hall Distinguished Service Professor of Law Emeritus and senior lecturer at the University of Chicago. His research focuses on elaborating libertarian minimalism in constitutional interpretation, and it has evaluated the pitfalls of governmental regulation. He is author of numerous books connecting public policy with legal design and constitutional interpretation, including *Design for Liberty: Private Property, Public Administration, and the Rule of Law* (Harvard, 2011) and *How Progressives Rewrote the Constitution* (Cato, 2007).

Paul Frymer is professor of politics and the director of the Program in Law and Public Affairs at Princeton University. He is author of *Uneasy Alliances: Race and Party Competition* (2nd ed., Princeton, 2010), *Black and Blue: African Americans, the Labor Movement, and the Decline of the Democratic Party* (Princeton, 2008), and the forthcoming *Building an American Empire: Territorial Expansion in the Antebellum Era* (Princeton).

Joanna Grisinger is an associate professor of instruction in the Legal Studies Program at Northwestern University. Her research is on twentieth-century U.S. legal and political history, with a substantive focus on the administrative state. She is the author of *The Unwieldy American State: Administrative Politics Since the New Deal* (Cambridge, 2012), and she is currently working on a project that examines the relationship between administrative agencies and the civil rights movement.

Sheila Jasanoff is Pforzheimer Professor of Science and Technology Studies at the Harvard Kennedy School. Her work explores the role of science and technology in the law, politics, and policy of modern democracies, with particular attention to the nature of public reason. She has authored more than 100 articles and chapters and is author or editor of a dozen books, including *Designs on Nature* (Princeton, 2005) and an essay collection, *Science and Public Reason* (Routledge, 2012).

Ken I. Kersch is professor of political science at Boston College. His primary interests are American political and constitutional development, American political thought, and the politics of courts. He is the author of *Constructing Civil Liberties: Discontinuities in the Development of American Constitutional Law* (Cambridge, 2004), *The Supreme Court and American Political Development* (Kansas, 2006, with Ronald Kahn), and many articles, chapters, and reviews. He is currently completing a book on modern political conservatism and constitutional development.

James T. Kloppenberg, Charles Warren Professor of American History at Harvard, has been elected to the American Academy of Arts and Sciences and the executive board of the Organization of American Historians. He has served as the Pitt Professor at the University of Cambridge, as a visiting professor at the École des Hautes Études en Sciences Sociales, and has held NEH, ACLS, Guggenheim, Danforth, and Whiting fellowships. His books include *Uncertain Victory: Social Democracy and Progressivism in European and American Thought, 1870–1920* (Oxford, 1986), *The Virtues of Liberalism* (Oxford, 1998), *Reading Obama: Dreams, Hope, and the American Political Tradition* (Princeton, 2010), *Toward Democracy: The Struggle for Self-Rule in European and American Thought* (Oxford, 2016), and two coedited volumes: *A Companion to American Thought* (Blackwell, 1995, with Richard Wightman Fox), and *The Worlds of American Intellectual History* (Oxford, 2016, with Joel Isaac, Michael O'Brien, and Jennifer Ratner-Rosenhagen).

Michael McGerr, the Paul V. McNutt Professor of History at Indiana University, studies the modern United States, with a particular interest in power, ideology, culture, and the relationship of public and private life. His most recent book, *A Fierce Discontent: The Rise and Fall of the Progressive Movement in America, 1870–1920* (Oxford, 2005), traces the origin of modern liberalism to the transformation of the intimate, daily lives of the different social classes in the industrial United States. He is completing *"The Public Be Damned": The Kingdom and the Dream of the Vanderbilts*, a history of the once-richest American family.

Nicole Mellow is a professor of political science at Williams College. Her research focuses on American political development and partisanship. Her first book, *State of Disunion: Regional Sources of Modern American Partisanship* (Johns Hopkins, 2008), explores changes in the post–World War II party system and oscillations in the level of partisanship. She is currently finishing a book, with Jeffrey Tulis, on political loss and American political development, and is at work on a new project that examines the connection between American national identity and state building in the early twentieth century.

Sidney M. Milkis is the White Burkett Miller Professor of Politics and research associate at the Miller Center at the University of Virginia. His research focuses on the American presidency, political parties and elections, social movements, and American political development. He coedited a three-volume examination of twentieth-century political reform that evaluates the Progressive movement, the New Deal, and the Great Society. His books include *Theodore Roosevelt, the Progressive Party, and the Transformation of Democracy* (Kansas, 2011) and *The President and the Parties: The Transformation of the American Party System Since the New Deal* (Oxford, 1993). He is currently working on a project that examines the relationship between presidents and social movements.

Carol Nackenoff is the Richter Professor of Political Science at Swarthmore College. Her early work explored the relationship between economic transformations affecting working Americans and their beliefs about the American Dream. She is the author of *The Fictional Republic: Horatio Alger and American Political Discourse* (Oxford, 1994), coeditor of *Jane Addams and the Practice of Democracy* (Illinois, 2009, with Marilyn Fischer and Wendy Chmielewski), and coeditor of *Statebuilding from the Margins* (Pennsylvania, 2014, with Julie Novkov). Her current work examines conflicts over the extent and terms of incorporation of women, African Americans, Native Americans, workers, and immigrants into the polity between 1875 and 1925, and within these contexts, the role that organized women played in pressing new tasks and new definitions of public work on the American state.

Natalie Novick is a Ph.D. student in sociology at the University of California, San Diego, and a graduate student researcher at the Center for Comparative Immigration Studies. Her research examines how globalization and technological change affect demands and preferences for skilled-labor migration in North America and Europe. Her work explores how these forces impact self-selection among skilled migrants, and how demands for specific skills change policy preferences over time.

Karen Orren is distinguished professor of political science at the University of California, Los Angeles. Her research concentrates on American political institutions, social movements, and constitutional law, analyzed in historical perspective. With Stephen Skowronek, she founded the journal *Studies in American Political Development* and wrote *The Search for American Political Development* (Cambridge, 2004).

Aziz Rana is a professor of law at Cornell University Law School. His writing and research centers on American constitutional law and political development, with a particular interest in the intersection of citizenship with topics in national security and immigration. He is author of *The Two Faces of American Freedom* (Harvard, 2010). His current work explores how practices of constitutional veneration became dominant in the mid–twentieth century—especially against the backdrop of growing American global authority—and how such veneration shaped the boundaries of popular politics.

Stephen Skowronek is the Pelatiah Perit Professor of Political and Social Science at Yale University. His research concerns American national institutions and American political history, with a particular focus on executive institutions and the presidency. His publications include *Building a New American State: The Expansion of National Administrative Capacities, 1877–1920* (Cambridge, 1982), *The Politics Presidents Make: Leadership from John Adams to Bill Clinton* (Harvard, 1993), and *The Search for American Political Development* (Cambridge, 2004, with Karen Orren). He cofounded the journal *Studies in American Political Development,* which he edited between 1986 and 2007. He is currently working on another book with Karen Orren, which takes a developmental approach to the study of public policy.

John D. Skrentny is professor of sociology and codirector of the Center for Comparative Immigration Studies at the University of California, San Diego. His research has focused on the historical development of laws and public policies regarding inequality and opportunity in the United States, as well as the development and impact of science and technology policy. He has received grants from several foundations, including Sloan, Guggenheim, and Spencer. His most recent book is *After Civil Rights: Racial Realism in the New American Workplace* (Princeton, 2014).

Rogers M. Smith is Christopher H. Browne Distinguished Professor of Political Science at the University of Pennsylvania. His research is in constitutional law, American political thought, and modern legal and political theory, with special interests in questions of citizenship, race, ethnicity, and gender. His books include *Political Peoplehood: The Roles of Values, Interests, and Identities* (Chicago, 2015), *Still a House Divided: Race and Politics in Obama's America* (Princeton, 2011, with Desmond King), and *Civic Ideals: Conflicting Visions of Citizenship in U.S. History* (Yale, 1997).

Brian Z. Tamanaha is the William Gardiner Hammond Professor of Law at the Washington University School of Law. He is a legal theorist and law and society scholar. His recent books include *Beyond the Formalist-Realist Divide: The Role of Politics in Judging* (Princeton, 2010), *Law as a Means to an End: Threat to the Rule of Law* (Cambridge, 2006), *On the Rule of Law: History, Politics, Theory* (Cambridge, 2004), and *A General Jurisprudence of Law and Society* (Oxford, 2001).

Steven M. Teles is associate professor of political science at Johns Hopkins University and a fellow at the New America Foundation. His research examines the intersection of law, policy, and political development. He is the author most recently of *The*

Rise of the Conservative Legal Movement: The Battle for Control of the Law (Princeton, 2008), which explores how contemporary conservative mobilization was shaped by the legal profession, the legacy of the liberal movement, and the difficulties in matching strategic opportunities with effective organizational responses. He is currently writing a book on the role of private philanthropies and foundations in formulating public policies.

INDEX

FDR = Franklin D. Roosevelt; JFK = John F. Kennedy; LBJ = Lyndon B. Johnson; TR = Theodore Roosevelt; WW = Woodrow Wilson